D0515166

Summary of Contents

Build Your Own ASP.NET 2.0 Web Site Using C# & VB

by Cristian Darie

and Zak Ruvalcaba

Build Your Own ASP.NET 2.0 Web Site Using C# & VB

by Cristian Darie and Zak Ruvalcaba

Copyright © 2006 SitePoint Pty. Ltd.

Expert Reviewer: Wyatt Barnett
Expert Reviewer: Sara Smith
Managing Editor: Simon Mackie
Technical Editor: Craig Anderson
Technical Director: Kevin Yank
Printing History:
   First Edition: April 2004
   Second Edition: October 2006

Editor: Georgina Laidlaw
Index Editor: Max McMaster
Cover Design: Jess Mason
Cover Layout: Alex Walker

Published by SitePoint Pty. Ltd.

424 Smith Street Collingwood
VIC Australia 3066.
Web: www.sitepoint.com
Email: business@sitepoint.com

ISBN 0-9752402-8-5
Printed and bound in the United States of America

About the Authors

Zak Ruvalcaba has been designing, developing, and researching for the Web since 1995. He holds a Bachelor's Degree from San Diego State University and a Master of Science in Instructional Technology from National University in San Diego.

In the course of his career, Zak has developed web applications for such companies as Gateway, HP, Toshiba, and IBM. More recently, he's worked as a wireless software engineer developing .NET solutions for Goldman Sachs, TV Guide, The Gartner Group, Microsoft, and Qualcomm. Currently, Zak holds a programming position with ADCS Inc. in San Diego supporting internal .NET applications.

Previous books by Zak Ruvalcaba include *The 10 Minute Guide to Dreamweaver 4* (Que Publishing) and *Dreamweaver MX Unleashed* (Sams Publishing). He also lectures on various technologies and tools, including Dreamweaver and ASP.NET, for the San Diego Community College District.

Cristian Darie is a software engineer with experience in a wide range of modern technologies, and the author of numerous technical books, including the popular *Beginning E-Commerce* series. Having worked with computers since he was old enough to use a keyboard, he initially tasted programming success with a prize in his first programming contest at the age of 12. From there, Cristian moved on to many other similar achievements, and is now studying distributed application architectures for his PhD.

He always loves hearing feedback about his books, so don't hesitate to drop him a "hello" message when you have a spare moment. Cristian can be contacted through his personal web site at http://www.cristiandarie.ro.

About the Expert Reviewers

Wyatt Barnett leads the in-house development team for a major industry trade association in Washington DC. He also writes for SitePoint's .NET Blog, *The Daily Catch*.[1]

Sara Smith is an ASP.NET contractor for the US Army and is also a partner in a web development business, brainyminds. She has been working with the .NET framework since its early days. Sara just relocated to Belgium from the US with her family.

About the Technical Editor

Before joining SitePoint, Craig Anderson studied Computer Science at RMIT University, then worked as a web developer for five years. He spent much of this time trying to convince Visual Basic developers that one of these days they would have to learn object oriented programming.

---

[1] http://www.sitepoint.com/blogs/category/net/

Craig plays bass guitar in Melbourne rock band Look Who's Toxic,[2] and indulges in all the extracurricular activities you'd expect of a computer nerd/musician approaching 30 (other than role playing—somehow he never got into that).

About the Technical Director

As Technical Director for SitePoint, Kevin Yank oversees all of its technical publications—books, articles, newsletters, and blogs. He has written over 50 articles for SitePoint, but is best known for his book, *Build Your Own Database Driven Website Using PHP & MySQL*. Kevin lives in Melbourne, Australia, and enjoys performing improvised comedy theatre and flying light aircraft.

About SitePoint

SitePoint specializes in publishing fun, practical, and easy-to-understand content for web professionals. Visit http://www.sitepoint.com/ to access our books, newsletters, articles, and community forums.

---

[2] http://www.lookwhostoxic.com/

For my wife Jessica.

—Zak Ruvalcaba

To my family and friends.

—Cristian Darie

Table of Contents

Preface

Web development is very exciting. There's nothing like the feeling you have after you place your first dynamic web site online, and see your little toy in action while other people are actually using it!

Web development with ASP.NET is particularly exciting. If you've never created a dynamic web site before, I'm sure you'll fall in love with this area of web development. If you've worked with other server-side technologies, I expect you'll be a little shocked by the differences.

ASP.NET really is a unique technology, and it provides new and extremely efficient ways to create web applications using the programming language with which you feel most comfortable. Though it can take some time to learn, ASP.NET is simple to use. Whether you want to create simple web forms, or feature-rich shopping carts, or even complex enterprise applications, ASP.NET can help you do it. All the tools you'll need to get up and running are immediately available and easy to install, and require very little initial configuration.

This book will be your gentle introduction to the wonderful world of ASP.NET, teaching you the foundations step by step. First, you'll learn the theory; then, you'll put it in practice as we work through practical exercises together. To demonstrate some of the more complex functionality, and to put the theory into a cohesive, realistic context, we'll develop a project through the course of this book. The project—an intranet site for a company named Dorknozzle—will allow us to see the many components of .NET in action, and to understand through practice exactly how .NET works in the real world.

We hope you'll find reading this book an enjoyable experience that will significantly help you with your future web development projects!

Who Should Read this Book?

This book is aimed at beginner, intermediate, and advanced web designers looking to make the leap into server-side programming with ASP.NET. We expect that you'll already feel comfortable with HTML and a little CSS, as very little explanation of these topics is provided here.

By the end of this book, you should be able to successfully download and install ASP.NET and the .NET Framework, configure and start your web server, create and work with basic ASP.NET pages, install and run SQL Server 2005, create database tables, and work with advanced, dynamic ASP.NET pages that query, insert, update, and delete information within a database.

All examples provided in the book are written in both Visual Basic and C#, the two most popular languages for creating ASP.NET web sites. The examples start at beginners' level and proceed to more advanced levels. As such, no prior knowledge of either language is required in order to read, understand, learn from, and apply the knowledge provided in this book. Experience with other programming or scripting languages (such as JavaScript) will certainly grease the wheels, though, and should enable you to grasp fundamental programming concepts more quickly.

What's in this Book?

This book comprises the following chapters. Read them from beginning to end to gain a complete understanding of the subject, or skip around if you feel you need a refresher on a particular topic.

Chapter 1: Introducing ASP.NET
Before you can start building your database-driven web presence, you must ensure that you have the right tools for the job. In this first chapter, you'll learn how to find, download, and configure the .NET Framework. You'll learn where the web server is located, and how to install and configure it. Next, we'll walk through the installation of the Microsoft database solution: SQL Server 2005. Finally, we'll create a simple ASP.NET page to make sure that everything's running and properly configured.

Chapter 2: ASP.NET Basics
In this chapter, you'll create your first useful ASP.NET page. We'll explore all of the components that make up a typical ASP.NET page, including directives, controls, and code. Then, we'll walk through the process of deployment, focusing specifically on allowing the user to view the processing of a simple ASP.NET page through a web browser.

Chapter 3: VB and C# Programming Basics
In this chapter, we'll look at two of the programming languages that are used to create ASP.NET pages: VB and C#. You'll learn about the syntax of the two languages as we explore the concepts of variables, data types, conditionals, loops, arrays, functions, and more. Finally, we'll see how the two languages accommodate Object Oriented Programming principles by allowing you to work with classes, methods, properties, inheritance, and so on.

Chapter 4: Constructing ASP.NET Web Forms

Web forms are the ASP.NET equivalent of web pages but, as we'll see, the process of building ASP.NET web forms is a lot like composing a castle with Lego bricks! ASP.NET is bundled with hundreds of controls—including HTML controls, web controls, and so on—that are designed for easy deployment within your applications. This chapter will introduce you to these building blocks, and show how to lock them together. You'll also learn about master pages, which are a very exciting new feature of ASP.NET 2.0.

Chapter 5: Building Web Applications

A web application is basically a group of web forms, controls, and other elements that work together to achieve complex functionality. So it's no surprise that when we build web applications, we must consider more aspects than when we build individual web forms. This chapter touches on those aspects, beginning with a hands-on tour of the free IDE from Microsoft, called Visual Web Developer 2005 Express Edition. Next, we configure your web application, learn how to use the application state, user sessions, and cookies, explore the process for debugging errors in your project, and more.

Chapter 6: Using the Validation Controls

This chapter introduces validation controls. With validation controls, Microsoft basically eliminated the headache of fumbling through, and configuring, tired, reused client-side validation scripts. First, we'll learn how to implement user input validation on both the client and server sides of your application using Microsoft's ready-made validation controls. Then, we'll learn how to perform more advanced validation using regular expressions and custom validators.

Chapter 7: Database Design and Development

Undoubtedly one of the most important chapters in the book, Chapter 7 will prepare you to work with databases in ASP.NET. We'll cover the essentials you'll need to know in order to create a database using SQL Server Express Edition. Also in this chapter, we'll begin to build the database for the Dorknozzle intranet project.

Chapter 8: Speaking SQL

This chapter will teach you to speak the language of the database: Structured Query Language, or SQL. After a gentle introduction to the basic concepts of SQL, which will teach you how to write `SELECT`, `INSERT`, `UPDATE`, and `DELETE` queries, we'll move on to more advanced topics such as expressions, conditions, and joins. Finally, we'll take a look at how we can reuse queries quickly and easily by writing stored procedures.

Chapter 9: ADO.NET

The next logical step in building database-driven web applications is to roll up our sleeves and dirty our hands with a little ADO.NET—the technology that facilitates communication between your web application and the database server. This chapter explores the essentials of the technology, and will have you reading database data directly from your web applications in just a few short steps. We'll then help you begin the transition from working with static applications to those that are database-driven.

Chapter 10: Displaying Content Using Data Lists

Taking ADO.NET further, this chapter shows you how to utilize the `DataList` control provided within the .NET Framework. `DataLists` play a crucial role in simplifying the presentation of information with ASP.NET. In learning how to present database data within your applications in a cleaner and more legible format, you'll gain an understanding of the concepts of data binding at a high level.

Chapter 11: Managing Content Using GridView and DetailsView

This chapter explores two of the most powerful data presentation controls of ASP.NET: `GridView` and `DetailsView`. `GridView` supersedes ASP.NET 1.x's `DataGrid`, and is a very powerful control that automates almost all tasks that involve displaying grids of data. `DetailsView` completes the picture by offering us the functionality needed to display the details of a single grid item.

Chapter 12: Advanced Data Access

This chapter explores a few of the more advanced details involved in data access, retrieval, and manipulation. We'll start by looking at direct data access using ADO.NET's data source controls. We'll then compare this approach with that of using data sets to access data in a disconnected fashion. In this section, you'll also learn to implement features such as paging, filtering, and sorting using custom code.

Chapter 13: Security and User Authentication

This chapter will show you how to secure your web applications with ASP.NET. We'll discuss the various security models available, including IIS, Forms, Windows, and Passport, and explore the roles that the Web.config and XML files can play. This chapter will also introduce you to the new ASP.NET 2.0 membership model, and the new ASP.NET 2.0 login controls.

Chapter 14: Working with Files and Email

In this chapter, we'll look at the task of accessing your server's file system, including drives, files, and the network. Next, the chapter will show you how to work with file streams to create text files, write to text files, and read from text files stored on your web server. Finally, you'll get first-hand experience in sending emails using ASP.NET.

Appendix

Included in this book is a handy web control reference, which lists the most common properties and methods of the most frequently used controls in ASP.NET.

The Book's Web Site

Located at http://www.sitepoint.com/books/aspnet2/, the web site that supports this book will give you access to the following facilities.

The Code Archive

As you progress through this book, you'll note a number of references to the code archive. This is a downloadable ZIP archive that contains complete code for all the examples presented in the book. You can get it from the book's web site.[1]

The archive contains one folder for each chapter of this book. Each folder contains CS and VB subfolders, which contain the C# and VB versions of all the examples for that chapter, respectively. In later chapters, these files are further divided into two more subfolders: Lessons for standalone examples presented for a single chapter, and Project for files associated with the Dorknozzle Intranet Application, the project that we'll work on throughout the book.

Updates and Errata

No book is perfect, and we expect that watchful readers will be able to spot at least one or two mistakes before the end of this one. The Errata page on the book's web site will always have the latest information about known typographical and code errors, and necessary updates for new releases of ASP.NET and the various web standards that apply.

---

[1] http://www.sitepoint.com/books/aspnet2/code.php

The SitePoint Forums

If you'd like to communicate with us or anyone else on the SitePoint publishing team about this book, you should join SitePoint's online community.[2] The .NET forum, in particular, can offer an abundance of information above and beyond the solutions in this book.[3]

In fact, you should join that community even if you don't want to talk to us, because a lot of fun and experienced web designers and developers hang out there. It's a good way to learn new stuff, get questions answered in a hurry, and just have fun.

The SitePoint Newsletters

In addition to books like this one, SitePoint publishes free email newsletters including *The SitePoint Tribune* and *The SitePoint Tech Times*. In them, you'll read about the latest news, product releases, trends, tips, and techniques for all aspects of web development. If nothing else, you'll get useful ASP.NET articles and tips, but if you're interested in learning other technologies, you'll find them especially valuable. Sign up to one or more SitePoint newsletters at http://www.sitepoint.com/newsletter/.

Your Feedback

If you can't find your answer through the forums, or if you wish to contact us for any other reason, the best place to write is `books@sitepoint.com`. We have a well-manned email support system set up to track your inquiries, and if our support staff members are unable to answer your question, they will send it straight to us. Suggestions for improvements, as well as notices of any mistakes you may find, are especially welcome.

Acknowledgements

First and foremost, I'd like to thank the SitePoint team for doing such a great job in making this book possible, for being understanding as deadlines inevitably slipped past, and for the team's personal touch, which made it a pleasure to work on this project.

---

[2] http://www.sitepoint.com/forums/
[3] http://www.sitepoint.com/forums/forumdisplay.php?f=141

Particular thanks go to Simon Mackie, whose valuable insight and close cooperation throughout the process has tied up many loose ends and helped make this book both readable and accessible. Thanks again Simon for allowing me to write this book—I appreciate the patience and dedication you've shown.

Finally, returning home, I'd like to thank my wife Jessica, whose patience, love, and understanding throughout continue to amaze me.

—Zak Ruvalcaba

I'd like to thank Simon Mackie, the Managing Editor at SitePoint, for being extremely supportive during the process of writing this book. Warm thanks and gratitude go to my parents, my girlfriend, and my close friends for constantly being there for me.

—Cristian Darie

1

Introducing ASP.NET and the .NET Platform

ASP.NET is one of the most exciting web development technologies on offer today. When Microsoft released the first version a few years ago, many web developers thought all their dreams had come true. Here was a powerful platform with lots of built-in functionality, astonishing performance levels, and one of the best IDEs (Integrated Development Environments) around: Visual Studio. What more could anyone want? Indeed, ASP.NET showed the way for the faster, easier, and more disciplined development of dynamic web sites, and the results were impressive.

Time has passed, and ASP.NET has grown. ASP.NET 2.0 comes with extraordinary new features as well as an expanded and more powerful underlying framework. Not only that, but the basic versions of all development tools, including Visual Web Developer 2005 Express Edition and SQL Server 2005 Express Edition, are free!

This book shows you how to use all these technologies together in order to produce fantastic results. We'll take you step by step through each task, showing you how to get the most out of each technology and tool. Developers who have already worked with earlier versions of ASP.NET will find that the latest version has changed so much that entire chapters of this book are devoted to ASP.NET 2.0-specific features.

Let's begin!

What is ASP.NET?

For years, the Active Server Pages (ASP) technology was arguably the leading choice for web developers building dynamic web sites on Windows web servers, as it offered flexible yet powerful scripting capabilities. Early in 2002, Microsoft released a new technology for Internet development called ASP.NET. ASP.NET represents a leap forward from ASP both in its sophistication and the productivity gains it achieves for developers. It continues to offer flexibility in terms of language support, but rather than a range of simple scripting languages, several fully-fledged programming languages are now at the fingertips of ASP.NET developers. Development in ASP.NET requires not only an understanding of HTML and web design, but also a firm grasp of the concepts of object oriented programming and development.

In the next few sections, we'll introduce you to the basics of ASP.NET. We'll walk through the process of installing it on your web server, and step through a simple example that demonstrates how ASP.NET pages are constructed. But first, let's define what ASP.NET actually is.

ASP.NET is a server-side technology for developing web applications based on the Microsoft .NET Framework. Let's break that jargon-filled sentence down.

ASP.NET is a server-side technology; that is, it runs on the web server. Most web designers start their careers learning client-side technologies like HTML, JavaScript, and Cascading Style Sheets (CSS). When a web browser requests a web page created with only client-side technologies, the web server simply grabs the files that the browser (or client) requests and sends them down the line. The client is entirely responsible for reading the markup in those files and interpreting that markup to display the page on the screen.

Server-side technologies, like ASP.NET, are different. Instead of being interpreted by the client, server-side code (for example, the code in an ASP.NET page) is interpreted by the web server. In the case of ASP.NET, the code in the page is read by the server and used to generate HTML, JavaScript, and CSS that is then sent to the browser. Since the processing of the ASP.NET code occurs on the server, it's called a server-side technology. As Figure 1.1 shows, the client only sees the HTML, JavaScript, and CSS. The server is entirely responsible for processing the server-side code.

Figure 1.1. A user interacting with a web application

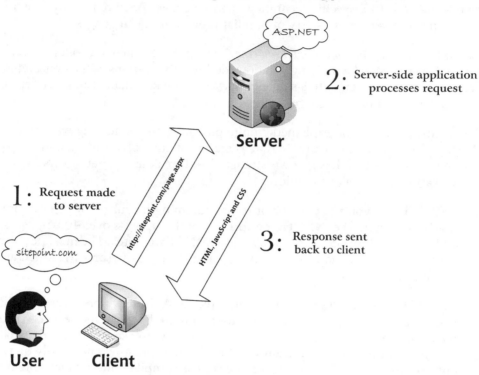

Note the three roles involved in such a transaction:

user
Never forget that there's a real person at the end (or beginning) of the line.

web client
This is the software program that the person uses to interact to the web application. The client is usually a web browser, such as Internet Explorer or Firefox.

web server
This is the software program located on the server. It processes requests made by the web client.

ASP.NET is a technology for developing web applications. A web application is just a fancy name for a dynamic web site. Web applications usually (but not always) store information in a database, and allow visitors to the site to access and change that information. Many different programming technologies and supported languages have been developed to create web applications; PHP, JSP, Ruby on Rails,

CGI, and ColdFusion are just a few of the more popular ones. However, rather than tying you to a specific technology and language, ASP.NET lets you write web applications using a variety of familiar programming languages.

ASP.NET uses the Microsoft .NET Framework. The .NET Framework collects all the technologies needed for building Windows desktop applications, web applications, web services, and so on, into a single package, and makes them available to more than 40 programming languages.

Even with all the jargon explained, you're probably still wondering what makes ASP.NET so good. The truth is that there are many server-side technologies around, each of which has its own strengths and weaknesses. Yet ASP.NET has a few features that really are unique:

❑ ASP.NET lets you use your favorite programming language, or at least one that's close to it. The .NET Framework currently supports over 40 languages, and many of these may be used to build ASP.NET web sites. The most popular choices are C# (pronounced "C sharp") and Visual Basic (or VB), which are the ones we'll cover in this book.

❑ ASP.NET pages are *compiled*, not interpreted. In ASP.NET's predecessor, ASP, pages were interpreted: every time a user requested a page, the server would read the page's code into memory, figure out how to execute the code (that is, interpret the code), and execute it. In ASP.NET, the server need only figure out how to execute the code once. The code is compiled into efficient binary files, which can be run very quickly, again and again, without the overhead involved in re-reading the page each time. This represents a big jump in performance from the old days of ASP.

❑ ASP.NET has full access to the functionality of the .NET Framework. Support for XML, web services, database interaction, email, regular expressions, and many other technologies are built right into .NET, which saves you from having to reinvent the wheel.

❑ ASP.NET allows you to separate the server-side code in your pages from the HTML layout. When you're working with a team composed of programmers and design specialists, this separation is a great help, as it lets programmers modify the server-side code without stepping on the designers' carefully crafted HTML—and vice versa.

❑ ASP.NET makes it easy to reuse common User Interface elements in many web forms, as it allows us to save those components as independent web user controls. During the course of this book, you'll learn how to add powerful features to your web site, and to reuse them in many places with a minimum of effort.

❑ You can get excellent tools that assist in developing ASP.NET web applications. Visual Web Developer 2005 is a free, powerful visual editor that includes features such as code autocompletion, code formatting, database integration functionality, a visual HTML editor, debugging, and more. In the course of this book, you'll learn how to use this tool to build the examples we discuss.

❑ The .NET Framework was first available only to the Windows platform, but thanks to projects such as Mono,[1] it's since been ported to other operating systems.

Still with me? Great! It's time to gather our tools and start building!

Installing the Required Software

If you're going to learn ASP.NET, you first need to make sure you have all the necessary software components installed and working on your system. Let's take care of this before we move on.

Internet Information Services (IIS) or Cassini

IIS is the web server of choice for running ASP.NET web applications. You'll need your copy of the Windows CD to install and configure it. Unfortunately, some versions of Windows (such as Windows XP Home Edition) don't support IIS. If you're one of those users, there's **Cassini**. Cassini is a small web server designed for hobbyists who are looking to build ASP.NET web sites. It isn't as robust, powerful, or user-friendly as IIS, but it will be sufficient for our purposes. When we come to use Visual Web Developer in Chapter 5, we'll be making use of that product's built-in development web server, so not having access to IIS on your system won't be a problem.

a modern web browser

Throughout this book, we'll be using Internet Explorer 6, but you can use other browsers during development if you wish. Any modern browser will do.

.NET Framework 2.0

As we've already discussed, the .NET Framework drives ASP.NET. When you install the .NET Framework, you'll automatically install the files necessary

---

[1] http://www.mono-project.com/

to run ASP.NET. You're likely to have the .NET Framework already, as it installs automatically through the Windows Update service.

.NET Framework Software Development Kit (SDK)
The .NET Framework 2.0 Software Development Kit (SDK) is a free download that contains the necessary Web Application development tools, a debugger for error correcting, and a suite of samples and documentation.

We're also going to need a database. In this book, we'll use the following:

Microsoft SQL Server 2005 Express Edition
This is the free, but still fully functional, version of SQL Server 2005. If you worked with previous versions of these technologies, you should know that SQL Server 2005 Express is a replacement for the previous Microsoft SQL Data Engine (MSDE). You can read more on the differences between various SQL Server 2005 editions at the Microsoft site.[2]

SQL Server Management Studio Express
Because the Express Edition of SQL Server doesn't ship with any visual management tools, you can use this free tool, also developed by Microsoft, to access your SQL Server 2005 databases.

Installing the Web Server

Installing Internet Information Services (IIS)

IIS comes with most versions of server-capable Windows operating systems—including Windows 2000 Professional, Server, and Advanced Server; Windows XP Professional; Windows XP Media Center Edition; and Windows Server 2003—but it's not installed automatically in all versions, which is why it may not be present on your computer. IIS isn't available for Home editions of these operating systems, such as Windows XP Home Edition. If you run this, you'll need to rely on Cassini, which we discuss below.

To see whether you have IIS installed and running, simply locate your Administrative Tools folder (sometimes it's a menu option; sometimes it's a folder in the Control Panel[3]) and check whether or not it contains a shortcut to Internet Information Services. If the shortcut isn't visible, then it's not installed. To install IIS, simply follow these steps:

---

[2] http://www.microsoft.com/sql/2005/productinfo/sql2005features.asp
[3] To see this folder, you'll need to view the Control Panel in "classic view."

1. In the Control Panel, select Add or Remove Programs.

2. Choose Add/Remove Windows Components. The list of components will become visible within a few seconds.

3. In the list of components, check Internet Information Services (IIS), as shown in Figure 1.2. The default installation options are enough for ASP.NET development, but you may want to click Details... to view the extra options you could add.

Figure 1.2. Installing IIS

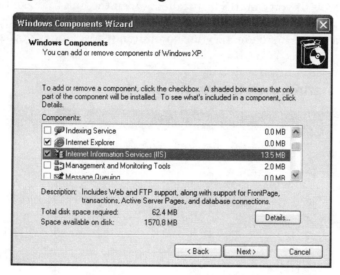

4. Click Next. Windows may prompt you to insert the Windows CD.

Tip

Add Administrative Tools to the Start Menu

Here's how to add Administrative Tools to the Windows XP Start menu:

1. Right-click on the Start button and select Properties to bring up the Taskbar and Start Menu Properties dialog.

2. Click the Customize... button to bring up the Customize Start Menu dialog.

3. If you're using the classic Start menu, check Display Administrative Tools, then click OK.

4. If you're using the Windows XP-style Start menu, click the Advanced tab, scroll through the Start menu items list until you get to System Administrative Tools, and select from Display on the All Programs menu or Display in the All Programs menu and the Start menu.

Once IIS is installed, close the Add or Remove Programs dialog. To check that IIS has installed correctly, see if you can find the Internet Information Services short cut in Administrative Tools. If you can, IIS is installed. Open the link to make first contact with the IIS management console, which is shown in Figure 1.3. In the left pane, you'll initially see the name of your computer, whose nodes you can expand.

Figure 1.3. The IIS administration tool

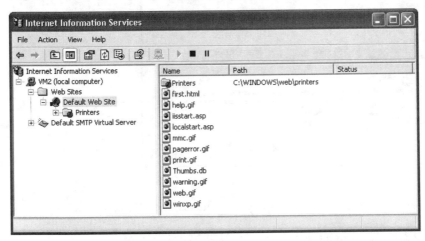

You can close this tool for now; you'll meet it again later.

You are now ready to host web applications. Although we won't cover the configuration of IIS for external use, we will show you how to configure IIS to support local development of ASP.NET applications in order that they may be uploaded to your external web hosting provider later.

Installing Cassini

If you're unable to install IIS, you'll need to download and install Cassini:

1. Go to the Cassini download page.[4]

2. Download the Cassini installer executable (`cassini.exe`).

3. Run `cassini.exe` and follow the steps presented by the installer, accepting the default options.

If the process went to plan, everything you need to run Cassini can be found in the folder `C:\Cassini`. Double-click `CassiniWebServer.exe` in that folder to start its management console, which is shown in Figure 1.4.

Figure 1.4. The Cassini management console

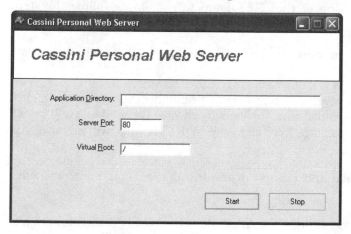

We'll need to do some more work to get Cassini up and running properly, but we'll need to install the .NET Framework and the Software Development Kit first.

Installing the .NET Framework and the SDK

To begin creating ASP.NET applications, you'll need to install the .NET Framework and the Software Development Kit (SDK). The .NET Framework includes

---

[4] http://www.asp.net/Projects/Cassini/Download/

the files necessary to run and view ASP.NET pages, while the SDK includes samples, documentation, and a variety of free tools.

Installing the .NET Framework

The best method of acquiring the .NET Framework is to download and install it directly from the Web. Note that it is also delivered through Windows Update, so you may already have it installed on your system. To check, open the folder `C:\WINDOWS\Microsoft.NET\Framework` (if your copy of Windows is installed somewhere other than `C:\WINDOWS`, change this path accordingly). If this folder doesn't exist, you definitely don't have the .NET Framework installed. If it does exist, you should find inside it at least one folder with a name like `v1.1.4322`. Each of these kinds of folders holds a different version of the .NET Framework you have installed. If at least one of these folders' names doesn't start with `v2` or higher, you'll need to install the latest version of the .NET Framework.

To install the latest version of the .NET Framework, simply follow the steps outlined below:

1. Go to the ASP.NET support site[5] and click the Download the .NET Framework link.

2. Under the .NET Framework Version 2.0 Redistributable Package heading, click the appropriate download link for your hardware. Remember, we'll install the redistributable package first, then the SDK. The link will advance you to a download page.

3. Choose the language and version of the installation you want, and click Download.

4. Save the file to a local directory. After the download is complete, double-click the executable to begin the installation.

5. Follow the steps presented by the wizard until installation completes.

Installing the SDK

Now that you've installed the redistributable package, you need to install the Software Development Kit (SDK):

---

[5] http://www.asp.net/

1. Go back to the ASP.NET support site and follow the Download the .NET Framework link again.

2. This time, click the appropriate download link under the .NET Framework Version 2.0 Software Development Kit heading. The link will advance you to a download page.

3. Choose the language version of the installation you want to use and click **Download**, as you did to download the redistributable package.

4. When prompted to do so, save the file to a local directory.

5. After the download is complete, double-click the executable to begin the installation. Before you do so, I strongly recommend that you close all other programs to ensure the install proceeds smoothly.

6. Follow the steps outlined by the .NET Setup Wizard until installation completes. When asked for setup options, it's safe to use the default values.

The SDK will take slightly longer to install than the framework.

A Big Download!

The .NET Framework SDK weighs in at about 350MB, so it will probably take a while to download.

Configuring the Web Server

Configuring IIS

After installing the .NET Framework and the SDK manually, you will need to configure IIS to make it aware of ASP.NET. To do this, you need to follow a few simple steps:

1. Open the command prompt by selecting Start > All Programs > Microsoft .NET Frameworks SDK v2.0 > SDK Command Prompt.

2. Type the following command to install ASP.NET:

```
C:\Program Files\...\SDK\v2.0>aspnet_regiis.exe -i
Start installing ASP.NET (2.0.50727).
........
Finished installing ASP.NET (2.0.50727).
```

3. Once ASP.NET is installed, close the command prompt and check again to confirm that ASP.NET installed correctly.

Running `aspnet_regiis.exe`

Depending on the circumstances, ASP.NET may already have been installed for you, but running `aspnet_regiis.exe` can't hurt. Also, remember that you need to run this utility again in case you reinstall IIS.

Configuring Cassini

If you've installed Cassini, you'll need to get under the hood of the .NET Framework to coerce Cassini into working as it should.

1. Open the command prompt by selecting Start > All Programs > Microsoft .NET Frameworks SDK v2.0 > SDK Command Prompt.

2. Enter the following command at the prompt:

```
C:\Program Files\...\SDK\v2.0>gacutil /i C:\Cassini\Cassini.dll
Microsoft (R) .NET Global Assembly Cache Utility. Version 2.0...
Copyright (c) Microsoft Corporation.  All rights reserved.

Assembly successfully added to the cache
```

Cassini is now ready to go.

Where do I Put my Files?

IIS Recommended

From here on in, the instructions we provide will be centered around IIS, as Cassini isn't suitable for production environments. Many of the concepts we'll discuss do not apply to Cassini, as it's much simpler and lacks many of IIS's features. Where needed, Cassini instructions will be given, but IIS will receive the bulk of the discussion.

Now that you have ASP.NET up and running, let's find out where the files for your web applications are kept on the computer. You can readily set IIS to look for web applications in any folder, including the My Documents folder, or even a network share. By default, IIS maps the C:\Inetpub\wwwroot folder of your disk to your web site's root directory, which is generally considered a good repository for storing and managing your web applications.

If you open this wwwroot folder in Windows Explorer, and compare its contents with the files that appear in the Default Web Site in the IIS administration tool, as shown in Figure 1.5, you'll notice that the files and folders are the same (some extra items will be listed in IIS; we'll look at these shortly). You need to use the IIS administration tool to set up the behavior of these files and folders under IIS. We'll see more on this soon.

Figure 1.5. Folders inside wwwroot also appear inside IIS

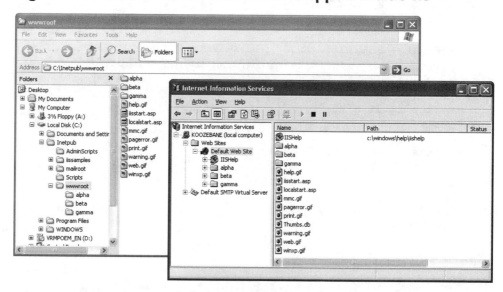

Using localhost

By putting your files within C:\Inetpub\wwwroot, you give your web server access to them. If you've been developing web pages for a long time, habit may drive you to open files directly in your browser by double-clicking on the HTML files. However, because ASP.NET is a server-side language, your web server needs to have a crack at the file before it's sent to your browser for display. If the server doesn't get this opportunity, the ASP.NET code won't be converted into HTML that your browser can understand. For this reason, ASP.NET files can't be opened directly from the disk using Windows Explorer.

Your local web server can be accessed through a special web address that indicates the current computer: http://localhost/. If you try this now, IIS will open up a default help page (although this behavior will vary depending on the settings of your Windows installation; for example, if you get an error instead of the default help page, don't worry).

What you need to keep in mind, though, is that the address you'll use to access local web applications will always start with http://localhost/, and that, by default, this root address points to the folder on your disk.

To see this in practice, create a new file named index.htm inside C:\Inetpub\www-root, with the following contents[6]:

File: **index.htm**

```
<!DOCTYPE html PUBLIC "-//W3C//DTD XHTML 1.0 Strict//EN"
    "http://www.w3.org/TR/xhtml1/DTD/xhtml1-strict.dtd">
<html>
  <head>
    <title>Simple HTML Page</title>
  </head>
  <body>
    <P>This is a simple HTML page.
  </body>
</html>
```

Now, load this page through http://localhost/index.htm, as shown in Figure 1.6.

Figure 1.6. Testing IIS

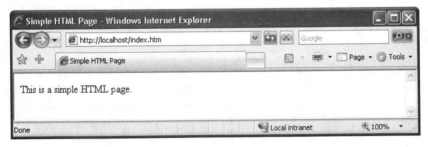

Experiencing an Error?

If the page doesn't load as illustrated in Figure 1.6, your IIS installation has problems. You might want to double-check that you correctly followed the steps for installing it, and re-check the IIS configuration procedure.

---

[6] All of the code and images used in this book are available for download from sitepoint.com. See the Preface for more information.

This localhost name is equivalent to the so-called loopback IP address, 127.0.0.1, so you can get the same results by entering **http://127.0.0.1/index.htm** into your browser. If you know them, you can also use the name or IP address of your machine to the same end.

Note that if you do try any of these equivalents, a dialog will appear before the page is opened, to ask you for your network credentials. This occurs because you're no longer using your local authentication, which is implicit with localhost.

Stopping and Starting IIS

Now that we have IIS up and running, and ASP.NET installed, let's look at how you can start, stop, and restart IIS if the need arises. For the most part, you'll always want to have IIS running; however, if you want to shut it down temporarily for any reason (such as security concerns), you can. Also, some external programs may stop IIS upon launch because of potential security vulnerabilities, so you'll need to start it again yourself. If you want to stop IIS when it's not being used, simply open the Internet Information Services management console, right-click on Default Web Site and select Stop. Alternatively, after selecting Default Web Site, you can use the Stop, Pause, and Play icons from the toolbar.

Virtual Directories

As we saw in the section called "Where do I Put my Files?", physical sub-folders of C:\Inetpub\wwwroot also become subdirectories of the web site. For instance, imagine your company has a web server that serves documents from C:\Inetpub\wwwroot. Your users can access these documents through http://www.example.com/. If you create a subfolder of wwwroot, named about, files in that directory can be accessed via http://www.example.com/about/.

You could also set up another subdirectory in your web site, but serve files from a different location on the disk. If, for instance, you were developing another web application, you could store the files for it in C:\dev\OrderSystem. You could then create within IIS a new virtual directory called, say, order, which mapped to this location. This new site would then be accessible through the URL http://www.example.com/order/. As this application is in development, you would probably want to set IIS to hide this virtual directory from the public until the project is complete; your existing web site would still be visible.

By default, a virtual directory, called IISHelp, is preconfigured in IIS; it maps to c:\windows\help\iishelp. You can see in Figure 1.7 that IISHelp contains subdirectories called `common` and `iis`—these are physical folders inside `c:\windows\help\iishelp`.

Figure 1.7. The `IISHelp` virtual directory

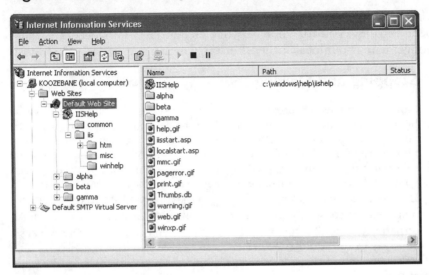

Let's create a virtual directory on your server, and test it with a simple page:

1. First, you need to create on your disk a folder to which your virtual directory will be mapped. Create a folder called `WebDocs` in an easily accessible location on your disk, such as `C:\`, and create a folder named `Learning` inside that folder. We'll use this folder, `C:\WebDocs\Learning`, for various exercises in this book.

2. Copy the `index.htm` file you created earlier into your newly created `Learning` folder.

3. In the Internet Information Services management console, right-click Default Web Site and select New > Virtual Directory. The Virtual Directory Creation Wizard will appear. Click Next.

4. You need to choose an alias for your virtual directory: enter **Learning**, then click Next.

5. Browse and select the `Learning` folder you created at step 1, or enter its full path (**C:\WebDocs\Learning**). Click Next.

6. In the next screen, you can select permissions settings for your directory. Typically, you'll want to leave the default options (Read and Run scripts) checked. Click Next.

7. Click Finish. You'll see your new virtual directory as a child of Default Web Site, as Figure 1.8 illustrates.

Figure 1.8. Creating a new virtual directory

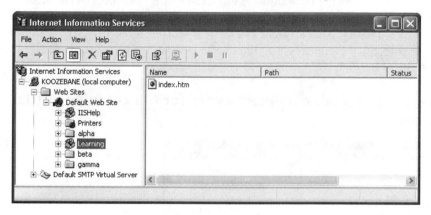

8. Load this link by entering **http://localhost/Learning/index.htm** into the address bar of your browser. If everything went well, you should see your little HTML page load, as has the one in Figure 1.9.

Figure 1.9. Testing your new virtual directory

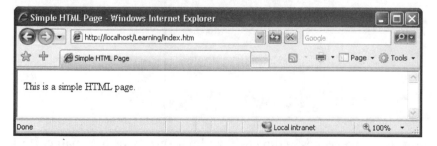

Note that by loading the page through the HTTP protocol, your request goes through IIS. Since index.htm is a simple HTML page that doesn't need any server-side processing, you can also load it directly from the disk. However, this won't be the case with the ASP.NET scripts you'll see through the rest of this book.

Once your new virtual directory has been created, you can see and configure it through the Internet Information Services management console shown in Figure 1.8. You can see the folder's contents in the right-hand panel.

As `index.htm` is one of the default document names, you can access that page just by entering **http://localhost/Learning/** into your browser's address bar. To see and edit the default document names for a virtual directory (or any directory, for that matter), you can right-click the directory's name in the IIS management console, click Properties, and select the Documents tab. You'll see the dialog displayed in Figure 1.10.

Figure 1.10. Default document types for the Learning virtual directory

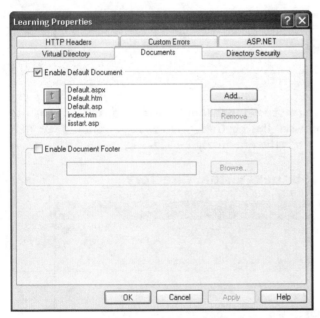

By default, when we request a directory without specifying a filename, IIS looks for a page with the name of one of the default documents, such as `index.htm` or `default.htm`. If there is no index page, IIS assumes we want to see the contents of the requested location. This operation is allowed only if the Directory Browsing option is selected for the directory in question. You'll find that option in the Directory tab of the Properties window.

Directory Browsing

Tip

Enabling directory browsing is not something you'd usually want to do. Allowing visitors to freely see and access all the files and directories that make up your web page is not only a little messy and unprofessional, but also increases the potential for security issues (you don't want any hackers to stick their nose into your code, do you?). So, by default, IIS won't allow directory browsing when a directory is requested: if a default file such as `index.htm` isn't there, ready to be served to the visitor, a message reading "Directory Listing Denied" will be served instead.

To change your virtual directory's options, you have to right-click the virtual directory (`Learning`, in our case) in the IIS console, and choose Properties. The Properties dialog that we've just used lets us configure various useful properties, including:

Virtual Directory

This option allows you to configure directory-level properties, including path information, the virtual directory name, access permissions, etc. Everything that was set up through the wizard is modifiable through this tab.

Documents

This option allows you to configure a default page that displays when the user types in a full URL. For instance, because `default.aspx` is listed as a default page, the user need only enter `http://www.mysite.com/`, rather than `http://www.mysite.com/default.aspx`, into the browser's address bar. You can easily change and remove these default pages by selecting the appropriate button to the right of the menu.

Directory Security

This option provides you with security configuration settings for the virtual directory.

HTTP Headers

This option gives you the ability to forcefully control page caching on the server, add custom HTTP Headers, Edit Ratings (this helps identify the content your site provides to users), and create MIME types. Don't worry about this for now.

Custom Errors This option allows you to define your own custom error pages. Rather than presenting the standard error messages that appear within Internet Explorer, you can customize error messages with your company's logo and messages of your choice.

ASP.NET This tab allows you to configure the options for the ASP.NET applications stored in that folder.

One thing to note at this point is that we can set properties for the Default Web Site node, and choose to have them "propagate" down to all the virtual directories we've created.

Using Cassini

If you're stuck using a version of Windows that doesn't support IIS, you'll need to make use of Cassini to get your simple ASP.NET web applications up and running. Cassini doesn't support virtual directories, security settings, or any of IIS's other fancy features; it's just a very simple web server that gives you the basics you need to get up and running.

To get started using Cassini:

1. Create a directory called `C:\WebDocs\Learning`, just like the one we created in the section called "Virtual Directories".

2. Copy `index.htm` into this folder. We first saw `index.htm` in the section called "Using localhost".

3. Start Cassini by opening `C:\Cassini` (or, if you chose to install Cassini somewhere else, open that folder), then double-click on the file `CassiniWebServer.exe`.

4. Cassini has just three configuration options:

    Application Directory
    It's here that your application's files are stored. Enter `C:\WebDocs\Learning` into this field.

    Server Port
    Web servers almost always operate on port 80, so we won't touch this setting.

Virtual Root
> This is similar to IIS's virtual directories feature, though it's nowhere near as flexible. By default, it's set to /, meaning that you can access the file `C:\WebDocs\Learning\index.htm` by entering the address **http://localhost/index.htm**. However, to match our IIS virtual directory configuration, we want to make this file's address `http://localhost/Learning/index.htm`. To create this effect, enter **/Learning/** into this field.

5. Once you have filled in the Application Directory and Virtual Root fields, click the Start button to start the web server.

6. After clicking Start, a link to the web site that's being served will appear toward the bottom of the window, as shown in Figure 1.11.

Figure 1.11. Cassini serving a web site

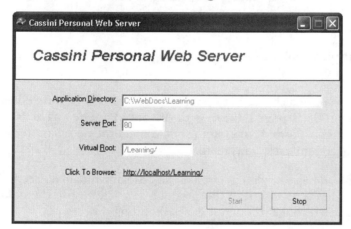

When you browse open this site in Cassini, you won't see `index.htm` straight away—you'll be presented with a list of files instead. Cassini only recognizes files named `default.htm` or `default.aspx` as default documents, and it doesn't allow you to configure this feature as IIS does.

Installing SQL Server 2005 Express Edition

After making sure IIS, the .NET Framework, and the SDK are installed correctly, it's time to move forward and install the next piece of software that you'll be using as we work through this book: SQL Server 2005 Express Edition.

SQL Server 2005 is Microsoft's database solution for medium to large companies and enterprises. SQL Server 2005 can be quite expensive, it generally requires its own dedicated database server machine, and, at times, it necessitates that a certified database administrator (DBA) be employed to ensure its maintenance; yet it does offer a robust and scalable solution for larger web applications.

For the examples in this book, we'll use SQL Server 2005 Express Edition, which is free and sufficiently powerful for our needs. Unlike the expensive versions, SQL Server 2005 Express Edition doesn't ship with visual management utilities, but you can use another free tool from Microsoft—SQL Server Management Studio Express, which we'll install next)—for these purposes.

You can install SQL Server 2005 Express Edition as follows:

1. Navigate to http://msdn.microsoft.com/vstudio/express/sql/, and click the Download Now link.

2. In the next page, you can choose between SQL Server 2005 Express Edition, and SQL Server 2005 Express Edition with Advanced Services. The former will be fine for our purposes. Your system should meet the necessary requirements, so go ahead and click Download.

3. Once the download has completed, double-click the downloaded executable file, and follow the steps to install the product. It's safe to use the default options all the way through, though it is a rather long process.

Provided that everything goes well, SQL Server 2005 Express Edition will be up and running at the end of the process. Like IIS, SQL Server runs as a service in the background, accepting connections to databases instead of web pages. The SQL Server is accessible at the address `(local)\SqlExpress`.

Installing SQL Server Management Studio Express

In order to use your SQL Server 2005 install effectively, you'll need some sort of administration tool that will allow you to work with your databases. SQL

Server Management Studio Express is a free tool provided by Microsoft to allow you to manage your installation of SQL Server 2005.

To install SQL Server Management Studio Express, follow these steps:

1. Navigate again to http://msdn.microsoft.com/vstudio/express/sql/, and click the Download Now link.

2. This time, download the SQL Server Management Studio Express edition that corresponds to the SQL Server 2005 version that you installed previously.

3. After the download completes, execute the file and follow the steps to install the product.

Once it's installed, SQL Server Manager Express can be accessed from Start > All Programs > Microsoft SQL Server 2005 > SQL Server Management Studio Express. When executed, it will first ask for your credentials, as Figure 1.12 illustrates.

Figure 1.12. Connecting to SQL Server

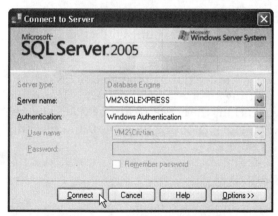

By default, when installed, SQL Server 2005 Express Edition will only accept connections that use Windows Authentication, which means that you'll use your Windows user account to log in to the SQL Server. Because you're the user that installed SQL Server 2005, you'll already have full privileges to the SQL Server. Click Connect to connect to your SQL Server 2005 instance.

Figure 1.13. Managing your database server

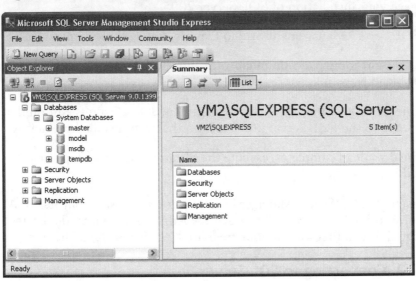

After you're authenticated, you'll be shown the interface in Figure 1.13, which gives you many ways to interact with, and manage, your SQL Server 2005 instance.

SQL Server Management Studio lets you browse through the objects inside your SQL Server, and even modify their settings. For example, you can change the security settings of your server by right-clicking the *COMPUTER\SQLEXPRESS* (where *COMPUTER* is the name of your computer), choosing Properties, and selecting Security from the panel, as shown in Figure 1.14.

SQL Server and Instances

You can run multiple SQL Servers on the one computer simultaneously—each SQL Server is called an **instance** of SQL Server. How is this useful? Imagine you have a production server that runs two applications with two separate databases on the same instance of SQL Server. If, for some reason, we need to restart SQL Server for the first application, the second application's database will become unavailable while the restart is taking place. If the second application's database was operating on a second instance of SQL Server, we wouldn't have such a problem—the second application would continue working without missing a beat.

Each instance of SQL Server requires a name. The default instance name for SQL Server 2005 Express Edition is **SQLEXPRESS**. When connecting to your

Figure 1.14. Changing server settings with SQL Server Management Studio

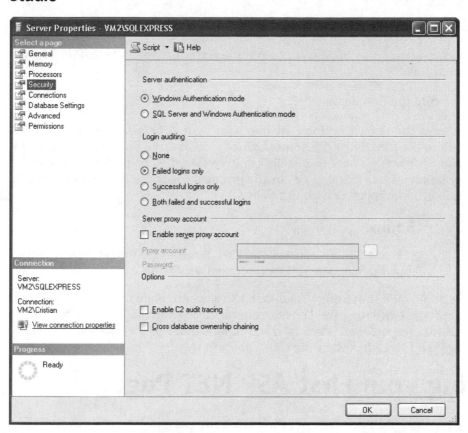

database server, you must specify both the name of the computer and the name of the SQL Server instance in the form *ComputerName/Instance-Name*. You can see this specification back in Figure 1.12 and Figure 1.13, where we're connecting to an instance called SQLEXPRESS on a computer called VM2.

Installing Visual Web Developer 2005

Visual Web Developer automates many of the tasks that you'd need to complete yourself in other environments, and includes many powerful features. For the first exercises in this book, we'll recommend you use a simple text editor such as

Notepad, but you'll gradually learn how to use Visual Web Developer to ease some of the tasks we'll tackle.

So let's install this tool to make sure we'll have it ready when we need it.

1. Go to http://msdn.microsoft.com/vstudio/express/vwd/ and click the **Download** link.

2. Execute the downloaded file.

3. Accept the default options. At one point, you'll be asked about installing Microsoft MSDN 2005 Express Edition, which is the product's documentation. It wouldn't hurt to install it, but you need to be patient, because it's quite big. (Note that you've already installed the .NET Framework 2.0 documentation, together with the SDK.)

Bonus!

If you've already installed the .NET Framework 2.0 SDK, you've already installed Microsoft MSDN 2005 Express Edition.

In this book, we'll start using Visual Web Developer to build real web applications in Chapter 5. Until then, we'll create examples using Notepad (or another simple text editor) so you're prepared to take full advantage of the features offered by Visual Web Developer when the time comes to use it.

Writing your First ASP.NET Page

For your first ASP.NET exercise, we'll create the simple example shown in Figure 1.15.

Figure 1.15. Your first ASP.NET page

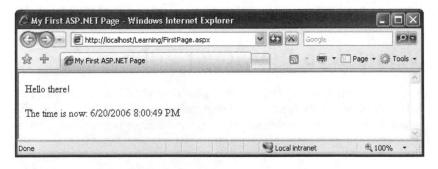

Let's get started! Open your text editor (Notepad is fine). If you have software that creates ASP.NET pages automatically, such as Visual Studio .NET or Visual Web Developer 2005 Express Edition, please don't use it yet—while these are great tools that allow you to get up and running quickly, they do assume that you already understand how ASP.NET works.

So, open your text editor, and create a new file named `FirstPage.aspx` in the `Learning` folder you created earlier. Start editing `FirstPage.aspx` by entering the HTML for our page, shown below:

File: **FirstPage.aspx (excerpt)**

```
<!DOCTYPE html PUBLIC "-//W3C//DTD XHTML 1.0 Strict//EN"
    "http://www.w3.org/TR/xhtml1/DTD/xhtml1-strict.dtd">
<html>
  <head>
    <title>My First ASP.NET 2.0 Page</title>
  </head>
  <body>
    <p>Hello there!</p>
    <p>The time is now: </p>
  </body>
</html>
```

So far, so good, right? Now, let's add some ASP.NET code that will create the dynamic elements of the page, starting with the time.

File: **FirstPage.aspx (excerpt)**

```
<!DOCTYPE html PUBLIC "-//W3C//DTD XHTML 1.0 Strict//EN"
    "http://www.w3.org/TR/xhtml1/DTD/xhtml1-strict.dtd">
<html>
  <head>
    <title>My First ASP.NET 2.0 Page</title>
  </head>
  <body>
    <p>Hello there!</p>
    <p>The time is now:
        <asp:Label runat="server" id="timeLabel" /></p>
  </body>
</html>
```

We've added an `<asp:Label/>` tag to the document. This is a special tag that lets us insert dynamic content into the page. The `asp:` part of the tag name identifies it as a built-in ASP.NET tag. ASP.NET comes with numerous built-in tags; `<asp:Label/>` is one of the simplest.

The `runat="server"` attribute identifies the tag as something that needs to be handled on the server. In other words, the web browser will never see the `<asp:Label/>` tag; when the page is requested by the client, ASP.NET sees it and converts it to regular HTML tags before the page is sent to the browser. It's up to us to write the code that will tell ASP.NET to replace this particular tag with the current time.

To do this, we must add some script to our page. ASP.NET gives you the choice of a number of different languages to use in your scripts. The two most common languages are VB and C#. Let's take a look at examples using both. Here's a version of the page in VB:

Visual Basic   File: **FirstPage.aspx (excerpt)**

```
<!DOCTYPE html PUBLIC "-//W3C//DTD XHTML 1.0 Strict//EN"
    "http://www.w3.org/TR/xhtml1/DTD/xhtml1-strict.dtd">
<html>
  <head>
    <title>My First ASP.NET Page</title>
    <script runat="server" language="VB">
      Sub Page_Load(sender As Object, e As EventArgs)
        timeLabel.Text = DateTime.Now.ToString()
      End Sub
    </script>
  </head>
  <body>
    <p>Hello there!</p>
    <p>The time is now:
        <asp:Label runat="server" id="timeLabel" /></p>
  </body>
</html>
```

Here's the same page written in C#:

C#   File: **FirstPage.aspx (excerpt)**

```
<!DOCTYPE html PUBLIC "-//W3C//DTD XHTML 1.0 Strict//EN"
    "http://www.w3.org/TR/xhtml1/DTD/xhtml1-strict.dtd">
<html>
  <head>
    <title>My First ASP.NET Page</title>
    <script runat="server" language="C#">
      protected void Page_Load(object sender, EventArgs e)
      {
        timeLabel.Text = DateTime.Now.ToString();
      }
    </script>
```

```
    </head>
    <body>
      <p>Hello there!</p>
      <p>The time is now:
          <asp:Label runat="server" id="timeLabel" /></p>
    </body>
</html>
```

Clues for Case Sensitivity

Note that C#, unlike VB, is case-sensitive. If you type the case of a letter incorrectly, the page won't load. If these languages look complicated, don't worry: you'll learn more about them in Chapter 3.

Both versions of the page achieve exactly the same thing. You can even save them both, giving each a different filename, and test them separately. If you've never done any server-side programming before, the code may look a little scary. But before we analyze it in detail, let's load the page and test that it works. Using your web browser, load `http://localhost/Learning/FirstPage.aspx`. Whether you load the C# version or the VB version, the output should look like Figure 1.15.

No Time?

If the time isn't displayed in the page, chances are that you opened the file directly in your browser instead of loading it through your web server. Because ASP.NET is a server-side language, your web server needs to process the file before it's sent to your browser for display. If it doesn't get access to the file, the ASP.NET code is never converted into HTML that your browser can understand, so make sure you load the page by entering an actual HTTP URL (such as `http://localhost/Learning/FirstPage.aspx`), not a local path and filename (such as `C:\WebDocs\Learning\FirstPage.aspx`).

What happens there? Let's break down the new elements of this page.

File: **FirstPage.aspx (excerpt)**

```
<script runat="server">
```

This tag marks the start of server-side code, or the **code declaration block**. Like the `<asp:Label/>` tag, this `<script>` tag uses the `runat="server"` attribute to let ASP.NET know that the tag should be processed before sending the page to the browser.

Visual Basic   File: **FirstPage.aspx (excerpt)**

```
Sub Page_Load(sender As Object, e As EventArgs)
```

C#   File: **FirstPage.aspx (excerpt)**

```
protected void Page_Load(object sender, EventArgs e)
{
```

I won't go into too much detail here. For now, all you need to know is that you can write script fragments that are run in response to different events, such as a button being clicked or an item being selected from a drop-down list. What the first line of code basically says is, "execute the following script whenever the page is loaded." Note that C# groups code into blocks with curly braces ({ and }), while Visual Basic uses statements such as End Sub to mark the end of a particular sequence. So, the curly brace in the C# code above ({) marks the start of the script that will be executed when the page loads for the first time.

Finally, here's the line that actually displays the time on the page:

Visual Basic   File: **FirstPage.aspx (excerpt)**

```
timeLabel.Text = DateTime.Now.ToString()
```

C#   File: **FirstPage.aspx (excerpt)**

```
timeLabel.Text = DateTime.Now.ToString();
```

As you can see, these .NET languages have much in common, because they're both built on the .NET Framework. In fact, the only difference between the ways the two languages handle the above line is that C# ends lines of code with a semicolon (;). In plain English, here's what this line says:

> Set the Text of timeLabel to the current date and time, expressed as text.

Note that timeLabel is the value we gave for the id attribute of the <asp:Label/> tag where we want to show the time. So, timeLabel.Text, or the Text property of timeLabel, refers to the text that will be displayed by the tag. DateTime is a **class** that's built into the .NET Framework; it lets you perform all sorts of useful functions with dates and times. The .NET Framework has thousands of these classes, which do countless handy things. The classes are collectively known as the **.NET Framework Class Library**.

The DateTime class has a **property** called Now, which returns the current date and time. This Now property has a **method** called ToString, which expresses that date and time as text (a segment of text is called a **string** in programming circles).

Classes, properties, and methods: these are all important words in the vocabulary of any programmer, and we'll discuss them in more detail a little later in the book. For now, all you need to take away from this discussion is that `Date-Time.Now.ToString()` will give you the current date and time as a text string, which you can then tell your `<asp:Label/>` tag to display. The rest of the script block simply ties up loose ends:

Visual Basic	File: **FirstPage.aspx** (excerpt)

```
End Sub
</script>
```

C#	File: **FirstPage.aspx** (excerpt)

```
}
</script>
```

The `End Sub` in the VB code, and the `}` in the C# code, mark the end of the script that's to be run when the page is loaded, and the `</script>` tag marks the end of the script block.

One final thing that's worth investigating is the code that ASP.NET generated for you. It's clear by now that your web browser receives only HTML (no server-side code!), so what kind of HTML was generated for that label? The answer is easy to find! With the page displayed in your browser, you can use the browser's View Source feature to view the page's HTML code. Here's what you'll see:

```
<!DOCTYPE html PUBLIC "-//W3C//DTD XHTML 1.0 Strict//EN"
    "http://www.w3.org/TR/xhtml1/DTD/xhtml1-strict.dtd">
<html>
  <head>
    <title>My First ASP.NET Page</title>
  </head>
  <body>
    <p>Hello there!</p>
    <p>The time is now:
      <span id="timeLabel">6/20/2006 8:00:49 PM</span></p>
  </body>
</html>
```

Notice that all the ASP.NET code has gone! Even the script block has been completely removed, and the `<asp:Label/>` tag has been replaced by a `<span>` tag (which has the same `id` attribute as the `<asp:Label/>` tag we used) that contains the date and time.

That's how ASP.NET works. From the web browser's point of view, there's nothing special about an ASP.NET page; it's just plain HTML like any other. All the ASP.NET code is run by your web server and converted to plain HTML that's sent to the browser. So far, so good: the example above was fairly simple. The next chapter will get a bit more challenging as we investigate some valuable programming concepts.

Getting Help

As you develop ASP.NET web applications, you will undoubtedly have questions that need answers, and problems that need to be solved. The ASP.NET support web site[7] was developed by Microsoft as a portal for the ASP.NET community to answer the questions and solve the problems that developers encounter while using ASP.NET. The support web site provides useful information, such as news, downloads, articles, and discussion forums. You can also ask questions of the experienced community members in the SitePoint Forums.[8]

Summary

In this chapter, you learned about .NET. You also learned of the benefits of ASP.NET and that it's a part of the .NET Framework.

First, you learned about the components of ASP.NET and how to locate and install the .NET Framework. Then, we explored the software that's required not only to use this book, but also in order for you or your company to progress with ASP.NET development.

You've gained a solid foundation in the world of ASP.NET! The next chapter will build on this knowledge as we begin to introduce you to ASP.NET in more detail, covering page structure, the languages that you can use, various programming concepts, and the finer points of form processing.

---

[7] http://www.asp.net/
[8] http://www.sitepoint.com/forums/

2

ASP.NET Basics

So far, you've learned what ASP.NET is, and what it can do. You've installed the software you need to get going, and, having been introduced to some very simple form processing techniques, you even know how to create a simple ASP.NET page. Don't worry if it all seems a little bewildering right now, because, as this book progresses, you'll learn how to use ASP.NET at more advanced levels.

As the next few chapters unfold, we'll explore some more advanced topics, including the use of controls, and various programming techniques. But before you can begin to develop applications with ASP.NET, you'll need to understand the inner workings of a typical ASP.NET page—with this knowledge, you'll be able to identify the parts of the ASP.NET page referenced in the examples we'll discuss throughout this book. So, in this chapter, we'll talk about some key mechanisms of an ASP.NET page, specifically:

❑ page structure

❑ view state

❑ namespaces

❑ directives

We'll also cover two of the "built-in" languages supported by the .NET Framework: VB and C#. As this section progresses, we'll explore the differences and similarities between these two languages, and get a clear idea of the power that they provide to those creating ASP.NET applications.

So, what exactly makes up an ASP.NET page? The next few sections will give you an in-depth understanding of the constructs of a typical ASP.NET page.

ASP.NET Page Structure

ASP.NET pages are simply text files that have the `.aspx` file name extension, and can be placed on any web server equipped with ASP.NET.

When a client requests an ASP.NET page, the web server passes the page to the **ASP.NET runtime**, a program that runs on the web server that's responsible for reading the page and compiling it into a .NET class. This class is then used to produce the HTML that's sent back to the user. Each subsequent request for this page avoids the compilation process: the .NET class can respond directly to the request, producing the page's HTML and sending it to the client, until such time as the `.aspx` file changes. This process is illustrated in Figure 2.1.

An ASP.NET page consists of the following elements:

❏ directives

❏ code declaration blocks

❏ code render blocks

❏ ASP.NET server controls

❏ server-side comments

❏ literal text and HTML tags

Figure 2.2 illustrates the various parts of a simple ASP.NET page.

Figure 2.1. The life cycle of the ASP.NET page

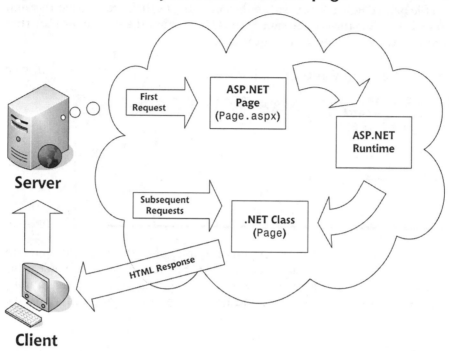

Figure 2.2. The parts of an ASP.NET page

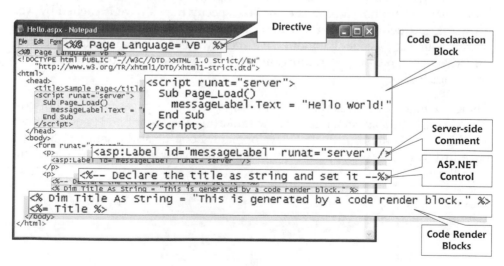

To make sure we're on the same page and that the code works, save this piece of code in a file named `Hello.aspx` within the `Learning` virtual directory you created in Chapter 1. Loading the file through `http://localhost/Learning/Hello.aspx` should render the result shown in Figure 2.3.

Figure 2.3. Sample Page in action

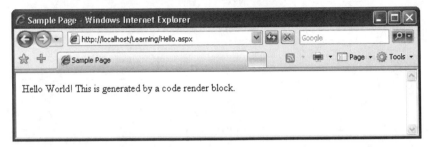

As you can see, this ASP.NET page contains examples of all the above components (except server-side includes) that make up an ASP.NET page. You won't often use every single element in a given page, but it's important that you are familiar with these elements, their purposes, and how and when it's appropriate to use them.

Directives

The directives section is one of the most important parts of an ASP.NET page. Directives control how a page is compiled, specify how a page is cached by web browsers, aid debugging (error-fixing), and allow you to import classes to use within your page's code. Each directive starts with `<%@`. This is followed by the directive name, plus any attributes and their corresponding values. The directive then ends with `%>`.

There are many directives that you can use within your pages, and we'll discuss them in greater detail later, but, for now, know that the `Import` and `Page` directives are the most useful for ASP.NET development. Looking at the sample ASP.NET page in Figure 2.2, we can see that a `Page` directive was used at the top of the page like so:

Visual Basic   File: **Hello.aspx (excerpt)**

```
<%@ Page Language="VB" %>
```

```
<%@ Page Language="C#" %>
```

In this case, the Page directive specifies the language that's to be used for the application logic by setting the Language attribute. The value provided for this attribute, which appears in quotes, specifies that we're using either VB or C#. A whole range of different directives is available; we'll see a few more later in this chapter.

Unlike ASP, ASP.NET directives can appear anywhere on a page, but they're commonly included at its very beginning.

Code Declaration Blocks

In Chapter 3, we'll talk about code-behind pages and how they let us separate our application logic from an ASP.NET page's HTML. However, if you're not working with code-behind pages, you must use code declaration blocks to contain all the application logic of your ASP.NET page. This application logic defines variables, subroutines, functions, and more. In our page, we've placed the code inside <script> tags, like so:

Visual Basic

```
<script runat="server">
  Sub mySub()
    ' Code here
  End Sub
</script>
```

Here, the tags enclose VB code, but it could just as easily be C#:

C#

```
<script runat="server">
  void mySub()
  {
    // Code here
  }
</script>
```

Comments in VB and C# Code

Both of these code snippets contain comments—explanatory text that will be ignored by ASP.NET, but which serves to describe to us how the code works.

In VB code, a single quote or apostrophe (') indicates that the remainder of the line is to be ignored as a comment.

In C# code, two slashes (//) achieve the same end. C# code also lets us span a comment over multiple lines if we begin it with /* and end it with */, as in this example:

C#

```
<script runat="server">
  void mySub()
  {
    /* Multi-line
       comment     */
  }
</script>
```

Before .NET emerged, ASP also supported such script tags using a runat="server" attribute. However, they could only ever contain VBScript and, for a variety of reasons, they failed to find favor among developers.

Code declaration blocks are generally placed inside the head of your ASP.NET page. The sample ASP.NET page shown in Figure 2.2, for instance, contains the following code declaration block:

Visual Basic   File: **Hello.aspx (excerpt)**

```
<script runat="server">
  Sub Page_Load()
    messageLabel.Text = "Hello World"
  End Sub
</script>
```

Perhaps you can work out what the equivalent C# code would be:

C#   File: **Hello.aspx (excerpt)**

```
<script runat="server">
  void Page_Load()
  {
    messageLabel.Text = "Hello World";
  }
</script>
```

The <script runat="server"> tag also accepts two other attributes. We can set the language that's used in this code declaration block via the language attribute:

Visual Basic
```
<script runat="server" language="VB">
```

C#
```
<script runat="server" language="C#">
```

If you don't specify a language within the code declaration block, the ASP.NET page will use the language provided by the `language` attribute of the `Page` directive. Each page's code must be written in a single language; for instance, it's not possible to mix VB and C# in the same page.

The second attribute that's available to us is `src`; this lets us specify an external code file for use within the ASP.NET page:

Visual Basic
```
<script runat="server" language="VB" src="mycodefile.vb">
```

C#
```
<script runat="server" language="C#" src="mycodefile.cs">
```

Code Render Blocks

If you've had experience with traditional ASP, you might recognize these blocks. You can use code render blocks to define inline code or expressions that will execute when a page is rendered. Code within a code render block is executed immediately when it is encountered—usually when the page is loaded or rendered. On the other hand, code within a code *declaration* block (within `<script>` tags) is executed only when it is called or triggered by user or page interactions. There are two types of code render blocks—inline code, and inline expressions—both of which are typically written within the body of the ASP.NET page.

Inline code render blocks execute one or more statements, and are placed directly inside a page's HTML between `<%` and `%>` delimiters. In our example, the following is a code render block:

Visual Basic   File: **Hello.aspx (excerpt)**
```
<% Dim Title As String = "This is generated by a code render " & _
    "block." %>
```

C#   File: **Hello.aspx (excerpt)**
```
<% string Title = "This is generated by a code render block."; %>
```

These code blocks simply declare a String variable called `Title`, and assign it the value `This is generated by a code render block`.

Inline expression render blocks can be compared to `Response.Write` in classic ASP. They start with `<%=` and end with `%>`, and are used to display the values of variables and methods on a page. In our example, an inline expression appears immediately after our inline code block:

File: **Hello.aspx (excerpt)**

```
<%= Title %>
```

If you're familiar with classic ASP, you'll know what this code does: it simply outputs the value of the variable `Title` that we declared in the previous inline code block.

ASP.NET Server Controls

At the heart of any ASP.NET page lie server controls, which represent dynamic elements with which your users can interact. There are three basic types of server control: ASP.NET controls, HTML controls, and web user controls.

Usually, an ASP.NET control must reside within a `<form runat="server">` tag in order to function correctly. Controls offer the following advantages to ASP.NET developers:

❑ They give us the ability to access HTML elements easily from within our code: we can change these elements' characteristics, check their values, or even update them dynamically from our server-side programming language of choice.

❑ ASP.NET controls retain their properties thanks to a mechanism called **view state**. We'll be covering view state later in this chapter. For now, you need to know that view state prevents users from losing the data they've entered into a form once that form has been sent to the server for processing. When the response comes back to the client, text box entries, drop-down list selections, and so on, are all retained through view state.

❑ With ASP.NET controls, developers are able to separate a page's presentational elements (everything the user sees) from its application logic (the dynamic portions of the ASP.NET page), so that each can be considered separately.

❑ Many ASP.NET controls can be "bound" to the data sources from which they will extract data for display with minimal (if any) coding effort.

ASP.NET is all about controls, so we'll be discussing them in greater detail as we move through this book. In particular, Chapter 4 explains many of the controls that ship with ASP.NET. For now, though, let's continue with our dissection of an ASP.NET page.

Server-side Comments

Server-side comments allow you to include within the page comments or notes that will not be processed by ASP.NET. Traditional HTML uses the <!-- and --> character sequences to delimit comments; any information included between these tags will not be displayed to the user. ASP.NET comments look very similar, but use the sequences <%-- and --%>.

Our ASP.NET example contains the following server-side comment block:

File: **Hello.aspx (excerpt)**
```
<%-- Declare the title as string and set it --%>
```

The difference between ASP.NET comments and HTML comments is that ASP.NET comments are not sent to the client at all; HTML comments are, so they're not suited to commenting out ASP.NET code. Consider the following example:

C#
```
<!--
<% string Title = "This is generated by a code render block."; %>
<%= Title %>
-->
```

Here, it looks as if a developer has attempted to use an HTML comment to stop a code render block from being executed. Unfortunately, HTML comments will only hide information from the browser, not the ASP.NET runtime. So, in this case, while we won't see anything in the browser that represents these two lines, they will be processed by ASP.NET, and the value of the variable `Title` will be sent to the browser inside an HTML comment, as shown here:

```
<!--

This code generated by a code render block.
-->
```

The code could be modified to use server-side comments very simply:

```
C#
<%--
<% string Title = "This is generated by a code render block."; %>
<%= Title %>
--%>
```

The ASP.NET runtime will ignore the contents of this comment, and the value of the `Title` variable will not be output.

Literal Text and HTML Tags

The final elements of an ASP.NET page are plain old text and HTML. Generally, you can't do without these elements—after all, HTML allows the display of the information in your ASP.NET controls and code in a way that's suitable for users. Let's take a look at the literal text and HTML tags that were used to produce the display in Figure 2.2:

Visual Basic   File: **Hello.aspx (excerpt)**

```
<%@ Page Language="VB" %>
<!DOCTYPE html PUBLIC "-//W3C//DTD XHTML 1.0 Strict//EN"
    "http://www.w3.org/TR/xhtml1/DTD/xhtml1-strict.dtd">
<html>
  <head>
    <title>Sample Page</title>
    <script runat="server">
      Sub Page_Load()
        messageLabel.Text = "Hello World!"
      End Sub
    </script>
  </head>
  <body>
    <form runat="server">
      <p>
        <asp:Label id="messageLabel" runat="server" />
      </p>
      <p>
        <%-- Declare the title as string and set it --%>
        <% Dim Title As String = "This is generated by a " & _
            "code render block." %>
        <%= Title %>
      </p>
    </form>
  </body>
</html>
```

```
C#                                                    File: Hello.aspx (excerpt)
<%@ Page Language="C#" %>
<!DOCTYPE html PUBLIC "-//W3C//DTD XHTML 1.O Strict//EN"
    "http://www.w3.org/TR/xhtml1/DTD/xhtml1-strict.dtd">
<html>
  <head>
    <title>Sample Page</title>
    <script runat="server">
      void Page_Load()
      {
        messageLabel.Text = "Hello World";
      }
    </script>
  </head>
  <body>
    <form runat="server">
      <p>
        <asp:Label id="messageLabel" runat="server" />
      </p>
      <p>
        <%-- Declare the title as string and set it --%>
        <% string Title = "This is generated by a code render " +
            "block."; %>
        <%= Title %>
      </p>
    </form>
  </body>
</html>
```

The bold code above highlights the fact that literal text and HTML tags provide
the structure for presenting our dynamic data. Without these elements, this page
would have no format, and the browser would be unable to understand it.

You now have a clearer understanding of the structure of an ASP.NET page. As
you work through the examples in this book, you'll begin to realize that, in many
cases, you won't need to use all of these elements. For the most part, your development will be modularized within code declaration blocks, and all of the dynamic
portions of your pages will be contained within code render blocks or controls
located inside a `<form runat="server">>` tag.

In the following sections, we'll explore view state, discuss working with directives,
and shine a little light on the languages that can be used within ASP.NET.

View State

As we saw briefly in the previous section, ASP.NET controls automatically retain their data when a page is sent to the server in response to an event (such as a user clicking a button). Microsoft calls this persistence of data "view state." In the past, developers would have had to use hacks to remember the item a user had selected in a drop-down menu, or store the content entered into a text box; typically, these hacks would have relied on hidden form fields.

This is no longer the case: once they're submitted to the server for processing, ASP.NET pages automatically retain all the information contained in text boxes and drop-down lists, as well as radio button and checkbox selections. They even keep track of dynamically generated tags, controls, and text. Consider the following ASP (not ASP.NET!) page, called `Sample.asp`:

File: **Sample.asp**

```
<!DOCTYPE html PUBLIC "-//W3C//DTD XHTML 1.0 Strict//EN"
    "http://www.w3.org/TR/xhtml1/DTD/xhtml1-strict.dtd">
<html>
  <head>
    <title>Sample Page using VBScript</title>
  </head>
  <body>
    <form method="post" action="sample.asp">
      <input type="text" name="nameTextBox"/>
      <input type="submit" name="submitButton"
          value="Click Me" />
      <%
      If Request.Form("nameTextBox") <> "" Then
        Response.Write(Request.Form("nameTextBox"))
      End If
      %>
    </form>
  </body>
</html>
```

Cassini and ASP

Cassini is an ASP.NET-only web server and will not execute pages written in ASP, such as `Sample.asp` above. Fortunately, this won't be a problem as you work your way through this book, as the above `Sample.asp` file is the only ASP code in this book.

If you save this as `Sample.asp` in the `Learning` virtual directory you created in Chapter 1, and open it in your browser by entering **http://localhost/Learning/Sample.asp**, you'll see that view state is not automatically preserved. When the user submits the form, the information that was typed into the text box is cleared, although it's still available in `Request.Form("nameTextBox")`. The equivalent page in ASP.NET, `ViewState.aspx`, demonstrates this data persistence using view state:

Visual Basic   File: **ViewState.aspx**
```
<!DOCTYPE html PUBLIC "-//W3C//DTD XHTML 1.0 Strict//EN"
    "http://www.w3.org/TR/xhtml1/DTD/xhtml1-strict.dtd">
<html>
  <head>
    <title>View State Example</title>
    <script runat="server" language="VB">
      Sub Click(s As Object, e As EventArgs)
        messageLabel.Text = nameTextBox.Text
      End Sub
    </script>
  </head>
  <body>
    <form runat="server">
      <asp:TextBox id="nameTextBox" runat="server" />
      <asp:Button id="submitButton" runat="server"
          Text="Click Me" OnClick="Click" />
      <asp:Label id="messageLabel" runat="server" />
    </form>
  </body>
</html>
```

C#   File: **ViewState.aspx**
```
<!DOCTYPE html PUBLIC "-//W3C//DTD XHTML 1.0 Strict//EN"
    "http://www.w3.org/TR/xhtml1/DTD/xhtml1-strict.dtd">
<html>
  <head>
    <title>View State Example</title>
    <script runat="server" language="C#">
      void Click(Object s, EventArgs e)
      {
        messageLabel.Text = nameTextBox.Text;
      }
    </script>
  </head>
  <body>
    <form runat="server">
```

```
      <asp:TextBox id="nameTextBox" runat="server" />
      <asp:Button id="submitButton" runat="server"
          Text="Click Me" OnClick="Click" />
      <asp:Label id="messageLabel" runat="server" />
    </form>
  </body>
</html>
```

In this case, the code uses ASP.NET controls with the runat="server" attribute. As you can see in Figure 2.4, the text from the box appears on the page when the button is clicked, but also notice that the data remains in the text box! The data in this example is preserved by view state.

Figure 2.4. ASP.NET maintaining the state of the controls

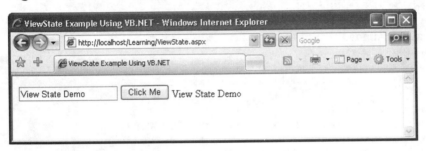

You can see the benefits of view state already. But where's all that information stored? ASP.NET pages maintain view state by encrypting the data within a hidden form field. View the source of the page after you've submitted the form, and look for the following code:

```
<input type="hidden" name="__VIEWSTATE" id="__VIEWSTATE"
    value="/wEPDwUKLTEwNDY1NzgOMQ9...0fMCR+FN5P6v5pkTQwNEl5xhBk" />
```

This is a standard HTML hidden form field. All information that's relevant to the view state of the page is stored within this hidden form field as an encrypted string.

View state is enabled for every page by default. If you do not intend to use view state, you can turn it off, which will result in a slight performance gain in your pages. To do this, set the EnableViewState property of the Page directive to false:

```
<%@ Page EnableViewState="False" %>
```

Disabling View State, Control by Control

View state can also be disabled for particular controls in a page: simply set their `EnableViewState` property to `false`. We'll see working examples of this in the following chapters.

Speaking of directives, it's time to take a closer look at these curious beasts!

Working with Directives

For the most part, ASP.NET pages resemble traditional HTML pages with a few additions. In essence, just using the `.aspx` extension for an HTML file will ensure that IIS passes the page to the .NET Framework for processing. However, before you can work with certain, more advanced features, you'll need to know how to use directives.

We talked a little about directives and what they can do earlier in this chapter. You learned that directives control how a page is created, how a page is cached, help with bug-fixing, and allow us to import advanced functionality for use within our code. Three of the most commonly used directives are:

Page
> This directive defines page-specific attributes for the ASP.NET page, such as the language used for server-side code. We've already seen this directive in use.

Import
> The `Import` directive makes functionality that's been defined elsewhere available in a given page. The following example, for instance, imports functionality from the `System.Web.Mail` namespace, which you could use to send email from a page. Namespaces are simply .NET's way of keeping all its functionality neatly organized—we'll see how they work in Chapter 3.

```
<%@ Import Namespace="System.Web.Mail" %>
```

> You'll become very familiar with this directive as you work through this book.

Register
> This directive allows you to register a user control for use on your page. We'll cover `Register` in detail in Chapter 4, but the directive looks something like this:

```
<%@ Register TagPrefix="uc" TagName="footer"
    Src="footer.ascx" %>
```

ASP.NET Languages

As we saw in the previous chapter, .NET supports many different languages; in fact, there's no limit to the number of languages that could be supported. If you're used to writing ASP, you may think the choice of VBScript or JScript would be an obvious one. But, with ASP.NET, Microsoft did away with VBScript, merging it with Visual Basic. ASP.NET's support for C# is likely to find favor with developers from other backgrounds. This section will introduce you to both these new languages, which will be covered in more depth in the next chapter. By the end of this section, you will, I hope, agree that the similarities between the two are astonishing—any differences are minor and, in most cases, easy to figure out.

Traditional server technologies are much more constrained in terms of the development languages they offer. For instance, old-style CGI scripts were typically written with Perl or C/C++, JSP uses Java, Coldfusion uses CFML, and PHP is a technology and a language rolled into one. .NET's support for many different languages lets developers choose the ones they prefer. To keep things simple, this book will consider the two most popular: VB and C#. You can choose the language that feels more comfortable to you, or stick with your current favorite if you have one.

Visual Basic

The latest version of Visual Basic is the result of a dramatic overhaul of Microsoft's hugely popular Visual Basic language. With the inception of Rapid Application Development (RAD) in the 1990s, Visual Basic became extremely popular, allowing in-house teams and software development shops to bang out applications two-to-the-dozen. The latest version of VB has many advantages over older versions, most notably the fact that it has now became a fully object oriented language. At last, it can call itself a true programming language that's on a par with the likes of Java and C++. Despite the changes, VB generally stays close to the structured, legible syntax that has always made it so easy to read, use, and maintain.

C#

The official line is that Microsoft created C# in an attempt to produce a programming language that coupled the simplicity of Visual Basic with the power and flexibility of C++. However, there's little doubt that its development was at least hurried along by Microsoft's legal disputes with Sun. After Microsoft's treatment (some would say abuse) of Sun's Java programming language, Microsoft was forced to stop developing its own version of Java, and instead developed C# and another language, which it calls J#. We're not going to worry about J# here, as C# is preferable. It's easy to read, use, and maintain, because it does away with much of the confusing syntax for which C++ became infamous.

Summary

In this chapter, we started out by introducing key aspects of an ASP.NET page including directives, code declaration blocks, code render blocks, includes, comments, and controls. As the chapter progressed, we took a closer look at the two most popular languages that ASP.NET supports, and which we'll use throughout this book.

In the next chapter, we'll create a few more ASP.NET pages to demonstrate form processing techniques and programming basics, before we turn our attention to the topic of object oriented programming for the Web.

3

VB and C# Programming Basics

As you learned at the end of the last chapter, one of the great things about using ASP.NET is that we can pick and choose which of the various .NET languages we like. In this chapter, we'll look at the key programming principles that will underpin our use of Visual Basic and C#. We'll start by discussing some basic concepts of programming ASP.NET web applications using these two languages. We'll explore programming fundamentals such as variables, arrays, functions, operators, conditionals, loops, and events, and work through a quick introduction to object oriented programming (OOP). Next, we'll dive into namespaces and address the topic of classes—seeing how they're exposed through namespaces, and which ones you'll use most often.

The final sections of the chapter cover some of the ideas underlying modern, effective ASP.NET design, including code-behind and the value it provides by helping us separate code from presentation. We finish with an examination of how object oriented programming techniques impact the ASP.NET developer.

Programming Basics

One of the building blocks of an ASP.NET page is the application logic: the actual programming code that allows the page to function. To get anywhere with ASP.NET, you need to grasp the concept of **events**. All ASP.NET pages will contain controls such as text boxes, checkboxes, and lists. Each of these controls allows the user to interact with the application in some way: checking checkboxes, scrolling through lists, selecting list items, and so on. Whenever one of these actions is performed, the control will raise an event. It is by handling these events within our code that we get ASP.NET pages to do what we want.

For instance, imagine that a user clicks a button on an ASP.NET page. That button (or, more specifically, the ASP.NET `Button` control) raises an event (in this case, it will be the `Click` event). A method called an **event handler** executes automatically when an event is raised—in this case, the event handler code performs a specific action for that button. For instance, the `Click` event handler could save form data to a file, or retrieve requested information from a database. Events really are the key to ASP.NET programming, which is why we'll start this chapter by taking a closer look at them.

It wouldn't be practical, or even necessary, to cover *all* aspects of VB and C# in this book, so we're going to discuss enough to get you started, and complete this chapter's projects and samples using both languages. Moreover, we'd say that the programming concepts you'll learn here will be more than adequate to complete the great majority of day-to-day web development tasks using ASP.NET.

Control Events and Subroutines

As I just mentioned, an event (sometimes more than one) is raised, and handler code is called, in response to a specific action on a particular control. For instance, the code below creates a server-side button and label. Note the use of the `OnClick` attribute on the `Button` control. If you want to test the code, save the file in the `Learning` virtual directory you've been using for the other examples.

File: **ClickEvent.aspx (excerpt)**

```
<!DOCTYPE html PUBLIC "-//W3C//DTD XHTML 1.0 Strict//EN"
    "http://www.w3.org/TR/xhtml1/DTD/xhtml1-strict.dtd">
<html>
  <head>
    <title>Click the Button</title>
  </head>
  <body>
    <form runat="server">
      <asp:Button id="button" runat="server"
          OnClick="button_Click" Text="Click Me" />
      <asp:Label id="messageLabel" runat="server" />
    </form>
  </body>
</html>
```

When the button's clicked, it raises the Click event, and ASP.NET checks the button's OnClick attribute to find the name of the handler subroutine for that event. In the code above, we told ASP.NET to call the button_Click routine, so perhaps we'd better write this subroutine! We'd normally place it within a code declaration block inside the <head> tag, like this:

Visual Basic   File: **ClickEvent.aspx (excerpt)**

```
<head>
  <title>Click the Button</title>
  <script runat="server" language="VB">
    Public Sub button_Click(s As Object, e As EventArgs)
      messageLabel.Text = "Hello World"
    End Sub
  </script>
</head>
```

C#   File: **ClickEvent.aspx (excerpt)**

```
<head>
  <title>Click the Button</title>
  <script runat="server" language="C#">
    public void button_Click(Object s, EventArgs e)
    {
      messageLabel.Text = "Hello World";
    }
  </script>
</head>
```

This code simply sets a message to display on the label that we declared with the button. So, when this page is run, and users click the button, they'll see the message "Hello World" appear next to it.

Figure 3.1. Handling the Click event

Hopefully, you're starting to come to grips with the idea of control events, and the ways in which they're used to call particular subroutines. In fact, there are many events that your controls can use, though some of them are found only on certain controls. Here's the complete set of attributes that the Button control supports for handling events:

OnClick

As we've seen, the subroutine indicated by this attribute is called for the Click event, which occurs when the user clicks the button.

OnCommand

As with OnClick, the subroutine indicated by this attribute is called when the button is clicked.

OnLoad

The subroutine indicated by this attribute is called when the button is loaded for the first time—usually when the page first loads.

OnInit

When the button is initialized, any subroutine given in this attribute will be called.

OnPreRender

We can use this attribute to run code just before the button is rendered.

OnUnload

This subroutine will run when the control is unloaded from memory—basically, when the user goes to a different page or closes the browser entirely.

OnDisposed

The subroutine specified by this attribute is executed when the button is released from memory.

OnDataBinding

This attribute fires when the button is bound to a data source.

Don't worry too much about the intricacies of all these events and when they occur; I just want you to understand that a single control can produce a number of different events. In the case of the Button control, you'll almost always be interested in the Click event; the others are only useful in rather obscure circumstances.

When a control raises an event, the specified subroutine (if one is specified) is executed. Let's take a look at the structure of a typical subroutine that interacts with a web control:

```
Visual Basic
Public Sub mySubName(s As Object, e As EventArgs)
  ' Write your code here
End Sub
```

```
C#
public void mySubName(Object s, EventArgs e)
{
  // Write your code here
}
```

Let's take a moment to break down all the components that make up a typical subroutine.

Public (Visual Basic)
public (C#)

This command defines the scope of the subroutine. There are a few different options to choose from, the most frequently used being Public (for a global subroutine that can be used anywhere within the entire page) and Private (for subroutines that are available for the specific class only).[1] We'll analyze these options in more detail a bit later in the chapter.

Sub (Visual Basic)
void (C#)

This command defines the chunk of code as a subroutine. A subroutine is a named block of code that doesn't return a result; thus, in C#, we use the void keyword, which means exactly what the name says. We don't need this in VB, though, because the Sub keyword implies that no value is returned.

mySubName(…)

This part gives the name we've chosen for the subroutine. The parameters and their data types are mentioned in the parentheses.

s As Object (Visual Basic)
Object s (C#)

When we write a subroutine that will function as an event handler, it must accept two parameters. The first is a reference to the control that fired the event. Each control has a particular type, such as Label or TextBox, but Object is a generic type that can be used to reference any kind of object in .NET—even basic types, such as numbers or strings. Here, we're putting that Object in a variable named s (again, we'll talk more about variables later in

---

[1] The C# equivalents of Public and Private are, perhaps predictably, public and private.

this chapter). We can then use that variable to access features and settings of the specific control from our subroutine.

e As EventArgs (Visual Basic)
EventArgs e (C#)
This, the second parameter, contains certain information that's specific to the event that was raised. Note that, in many cases, you won't need to use either of these two parameters, so you don't need to worry about them too much at this stage.

As this chapter progresses, you'll see how subroutines that are associated with particular events by the appropriate attributes on controls can revolutionize the way your user interacts with your application.

Page Events

Until now, we've considered only events that are raised by controls. However, there is another type of event: the page event. Technically, a page is simply another type of control, so page events are a particular kind of control event.

The idea is the same as for control events, except that here, it is the page as a whole that generates the events.[2] You've already used one of these events: the Page_Load event, which is fired when the page loads for the first time. Note that we don't need to associate handlers for page events as we did for control events; instead, we just place our handler code inside a subroutine with a preset name.

The following list outlines the most frequently used page event subroutines:

Page_Init
called when the page is about to be initialized with its basic settings

Page_Load
called once the browser request has been processed, and all of the controls in the page have their updated values

Page_PreRender
called once all objects have reacted to the browser request and any resulting events, but before any response has been sent to the browser

---

[2] Strictly speaking, a page is simply another type of control, so page events *are* actually control events. But when you're first learning ASP.NET, it can be helpful to think of page events as being different, especially since you don't usually use On*EventName* attributes to assign subroutines to handle them.

Page_UnLoad

called when the page is no longer needed by the server, and is ready to be discarded

The order in which the events are listed above is also the order in which they're executed. In other words, the `Page_Init` event is the first event raised by the page, followed by `Page_Load`, `Page_PreRender`, and finally `Page_UnLoad`.

The best way to illustrate how these events work is through an example. Create the following `PageEvents.aspx` file in the `Learning` virtual directory:

Visual Basic   File: **PageEvents.aspx (excerpt)**

```
<!DOCTYPE html PUBLIC "-//W3C//DTD XHTML 1.0 Strict//EN"
    "http://www.w3.org/TR/xhtml1/DTD/xhtml1-strict.dtd">
<html>
  <head>
    <title>Page Events</title>
    <script runat="server" language="VB">
      Sub Page_Init(s As Object, e As EventArgs)
        messageLabel.Text = "1. Page_Init <br/>"
      End Sub
      Sub Page_Load(s As Object, e As EventArgs)
        messageLabel.Text += "2. Page_Load <br/>"
      End Sub
      Sub Page_PreRender(s As Object, e As EventArgs)
        messageLabel.Text += "3. Page_PreRender <br/>"
      End Sub
      Sub Page_UnLoad(s As Object, e As EventArgs)
        messageLabel.Text += "4. Page_UnLoad <br/>"
      End Sub
    </script>
  </head>
  <body>
    <form runat="server">
      <asp:Label id="messageLabel" runat="server" />
    </form>
  </body>
</html>
```

C#   File: **PageEvents.aspx (excerpt)**

```
<!DOCTYPE html PUBLIC "-//W3C//DTD XHTML 1.0 Strict//EN"
    "http://www.w3.org/TR/xhtml1/DTD/xhtml1-strict.dtd">
<html>
  <head>
    <title>Page Events</title>
```

```
<script runat="server" language="C#">
  void Page_Init(Object s, EventArgs e)
  {
    messageLabel.Text = "1. Page_Init <br/>";
  }
  void Page_Load(Object s, EventArgs e)
  {
    messageLabel.Text += "2. Page_Load <br/>";
  }
  void Page_PreRender(Object s, EventArgs e)
  {
    messageLabel.Text += "3. Page_PreRender <br/>";
  }
  void Page_UnLoad(Object s, EventArgs e)
  {
    messageLabel.Text += "4. Page_UnLoad <br/>";
  }
</script>
</head>
<body>
  <form runat="server">
    <asp:Label id="messageLabel" runat="server" />
  </form>
</body>
</html>
```

You can see that the event handlers (the functions that are executed to handle the events) aren't specifically defined anywhere. There's no need to define them, because these events are generated by default by the ASP.NET page, and their handlers have the default names that we've used in the code (`Page_Init`, `Page_Load`, etc). As the page loads, it will generate a number of events. Within each event's event handler, we've added a message to the `Label` control; this will give us visual proof that the events actually fire in order. No matter which version of the code you execute (C# or VB), the output should look like Figure 3.2.

As you can see, `Page_UnLoad` doesn't generate any output. This is because, at that point, the HTML output has already been generated and sent to the browser.

Tip

Popular Page_Load

The event you'll make the most use of in your code is `Page_Load`. However, in certain situations the other events will be helpful as well. It's also worth noting that ASP.NET supports other events, which we haven't covered here. You'll only need those in certain, complex applications that aren't in the scope of this book.

Figure 3.2. Handling ASP.NET events

Variables and Variable Declaration

Variables are fundamental to programming, and you're almost certain to have come across the term before. Basically, variables let you give a name, or identifier, to a specific piece of data; we can then use that identifier to store, modify, and retrieve the data in question.

VB and C# have access to the same basic data types, which are defined as foundation classes of the .NET Framework. However, they can be named differently, as each language defines its own aliases. There are many different kinds of data types, including strings, integers (whole numbers), and floating point numbers (fractions or decimals). Before you can use a variable in VB or C#, you must specify the types of data it can contain, using keywords such as `String`, `Integer`, and `Decimal`, like this:

Visual Basic
```
Dim name As String
Dim age As Integer
```

C#
```
string name;
int age;
```

These lines declare the type of data we want our variables to store, and are therefore known as "variable declarations." In VB, we use the keyword `Dim`, which stands for "dimension," while in C#, we simply precede the variable name with the appropriate data type.

Sometimes, we want to set an initial value for variables that we declare; we can do this using a process known as initialization:

Visual Basic
```
Dim carType As String = "BMW"
```

C#
```
string carType = "BMW";
```

We can also declare and/or initialize a group of variables of the same type simultaneously. This practice isn't recommended, though, as it makes the code more difficult to read.

Visual Basic
```
Dim carType As String, carColor As String = "blue"
```

C#
```
string carType, carColor = "blue";
```

Table 3.1 lists the most useful data types available in VB and C#.

Table 3.1. A list of commonly used data types

VB	C#	Description
Integer	int	whole numbers in the range -2,147,483,648 to 2,147,483,647
Decimal	decimal	numbers up to 28 decimal places; this command is used most often when dealing with costs of items
String	string	any text value
Char	char	a single character (letter, number, or symbol)
Boolean	bool	true or false
Object	object	a generic type that can be used to refer to objects of any type

You'll encounter many other data types as you progress, but this list provides an overview of the ones you'll use most often.

Many Aliases are Available

These data types are the VB- and C#-specific aliases for types of the .NET Framework. For example, instead of Integer or int, you could use `System.Int32` in any .NET language; likewise, instead of Boolean or bool, you could use `System.Boolean`, and so on.

To sum up, once you've declared a variable as a given type, it can only hold data of that type: you can't put a string into an integer variable, for instance. However, there are frequently times when you'll need to convert one data type to another. Have a look at this code:

Visual Basic

```
Dim intX As Integer
Dim strY As String = "35"
intX = strY + 6
```

C#

```
int intX;
string strY = "35";
intX = strY + 6;
```

Now, you or I might think that this could make sense—after all, the string `strY` contains a number, so we might wish to add it to another number. Well, this isn't so simple for a computer!

VB performs some conversions for us. The VB version of the code will execute without a hitch, because the string will be converted to a number before the mathematical operation is applied. C#, on the other hand, will throw an error, as it's more strict than VB about conversions.

As a rule of thumb, it's better to stay on the safe side and avoid mixing types wherever possible.

Tip VB and C#—Strongly Typed Languages

Even though their behavior is a little bit different, both VB and C# are **strongly typed** languages. Strongly typed languages are those that are very strict about data types. Many other languages—mostly scripting languages such as JavaScript—are loosely typed, which means that they're more flexible when it comes to dealing with data types. For example, if you try to sum a number with a string, as we did in the previous code snippet, the JavaScript interpreter would make the conversion for you automatically. At times, despite being a strongly typed language at heart, VB does a bit of background work for you, which makes it slightly easier to work with.

In .NET, you can (and sometimes need to) explicitly convert, or **cast**, the string into an integer before you're able to sum them up:

Visual Basic

```
Dim intX As Integer
Dim strY As String = "35"
intX = Int32.Parse(strY) + 6
```

C#

```
int intX;
string strY = "35";
intX = Convert.ToInt32(strY) + 6;
```

Now, the computer will accept even with the C# code, because it ends up adding two numbers, rather than a number and a string, as we tried initially. This principle holds true whenever we're mixing types in a single expression.

Arrays

Arrays are a special variety of variable that's tailored for storing related items of the same data type. Any one item in an array can be accessed using the array's name, followed by that item's position in the array (its offset). Let's create a sample page to see how it's done. The results of this code are shown in Figure 3.3:

Visual Basic   File: **Arrays.aspx**

```
<!DOCTYPE html PUBLIC "-//W3C//DTD XHTML 1.0 Strict//EN"
    "http://www.w3.org/TR/xhtml1/DTD/xhtml1-strict.dtd">
<html>
  <head>
    <title>Arrays</title>
    <script runat="server" language="VB">
      Sub Page_Load()
        ' Declare an array
        Dim drinkList(4) As String
        ' Place some items in it
        drinkList(0) = "Water"
        drinkList(1) = "Juice"
        drinkList(2) = "Soda"
        drinkList(3) = "Milk"
        ' Access an item in the array by its position
        drinkLabel.Text = drinkList(1)
      End Sub
    </script>
  </head>
  <body>
    <form runat="server">
      <asp:Label id="drinkLabel" runat="server" />
```

```
    </form>
  </body>
</html>
```

C#   File: **Arrays.aspx**

```
<!DOCTYPE html PUBLIC "-//W3C//DTD XHTML 1.0 Strict//EN"
    "http://www.w3.org/TR/xhtml1/DTD/xhtml1-strict.dtd">
<html>
  <head>
    <title>Arrays</title>
    <script runat="server" language="C#">
      void Page_Load()
      {
        // Declare an array
        string[] drinkList = new string[4];
        // Place some items in it
        drinkList[0] = "Water";
        drinkList[1] = "Juice";
        drinkList[2] = "Soda";
        drinkList[3] = "Milk";
        // Access an item in the array by its position
        drinkLabel.Text = drinkList[1];
      }
    </script>
  </head>
  <body>
    <form runat="server">
      <asp:Label id="drinkLabel" runat="server" />
    </form>
  </body>
</html>
```

Figure 3.3. Reading an element from an array

There are some important points to pick up from this code. First, notice how we declare an array. In VB, it looks like a regular declaration for a string, except that the number of items we want the array to contain is provided in parentheses after the name:

Visual Basic	File: **Arrays.aspx (excerpt)**

```
Dim drinkList(4) As String
```

In C#, it's a little different. First, we declare that `drinkList` is an array by following the data type with two empty square brackets. We then specify that this is an array of four items, using the `new` keyword:

C#	File: **Arrays.aspx (excerpt)**

```
string[] drinkList = new string[4];
```

A crucial point to realize here is that, in both C# and VB, these arrays are known as **zero-based** arrays. In a zero-based array, the first item has position 0, the second has position 1, and so on through to the last item, which has a position that's one less than the size of the array (3, in this case). So, we specify each item in our array like this:

Visual Basic	File: **Arrays.aspx (excerpt)**

```
drinkList(0) = "Water"
drinkList(1) = "Juice"
drinkList(2) = "Soda"
drinkList(3) = "Milk"
```

C#	File: **Arrays.aspx (excerpt)**

```
drinkList[0] = "Water";
drinkList[1] = "Juice";
drinkList[2] = "Soda";
drinkList[3] = "Milk";
```

Note that C# uses square brackets for arrays, while VB uses standard parentheses. We have to remember that arrays are zero-based when we set the label text to the second item, as shown here:

Visual Basic	File: **Arrays.aspx (excerpt)**

```
drinkLabel.Text = drinkList(1)
```

C#	File: **Arrays.aspx (excerpt)**

```
drinkLabel.Text = drinkList[1];
```

To help this fact sink in, you might like to try changing this code to show the third item in the list, instead of the second. Can you work out what change you'd need to make? That's right—you need only to change the number in the brackets to reflect the new item's position in the array (don't forget to start at zero). In fact, it's this ability to select one item from a list using only its numerical location that makes arrays so useful in programming—we'll experience this first-hand as we get further into the book.

Functions

Functions are exactly the same as subroutines, but for one key difference: they return a value. In VB, we declare a function using the Function keyword in place of Sub, while in C#, we simply have to specify the return type in place of void. The following code shows a simple example:

Visual Basic   File: **Functions.aspx (excerpt)**

```
<!DOCTYPE html PUBLIC "-//W3C//DTD XHTML 1.0 Strict//EN"
    "http://www.w3.org/TR/xhtml1/DTD/xhtml1-strict.dtd">
<html>
  <head>
    <title>ASP.NET Functions</title>
    <script runat="server" language="VB">
      ' Here's our function
      Function getName() As String
        Return "Zak Ruvalcaba"
      End Function
      ' And now we'll use it in the Page_Load handler
      Sub Page_Load(s As Object, e As EventArgs)
        messageLabel.Text = getName()
      End Sub
    </script>
  </head>
  <body>
    <form runat="server">
      <asp:Label id="messageLabel" runat="server" />
    </form>
  </body>
</html>
```

C#   File: **Functions.aspx (excerpt)**

```
<!DOCTYPE html PUBLIC "-//W3C//DTD XHTML 1.0 Strict//EN"
    "http://www.w3.org/TR/xhtml1/DTD/xhtml1-strict.dtd">
<html>
  <head>
    <title>ASP.NET Functions</title>
    <script runat="server" language="C#">
      // Here's our function
```

```
    string getName()
    {
      return "Zak Ruvalcaba";
    }
    // And now we'll use it in the Page_Load handler
    void Page_Load()
    {
      messageLabel.Text = getName();
    }
  </script>
 </head>
 <body>
  <form runat="server">
    <asp:Label id="messageLabel" runat="server" />
  </form>
 </body>
</html>
```

When the page above is loaded in the browser, the Load event will be raised which will cause the Page_Load event handler to be called, which in turn will call the getName function. Figure 3.4 shows the result in the browser.

Figure 3.4. Executing an ASP.NET function

Here's what's happening: the line in our Page_Load subroutine calls our function, which returns a simple string that we can assign to our label. In this simple example, we're merely returning a fixed string, but the function could just as easily retrieve the name from a database (or somewhere else). The point is that, regardless of how the function gets its data, we call it in just the same way.

When we're declaring our function, we must remember to specify the correct return type. Take a look at the following code:

Visual Basic

```
' Here's our function
Function addUp(x As Integer, y As Integer) As Integer
  Return x + y
```

```
End Function
' And now we use it in Page_Load
Sub Page_Load(s As Object, e As EventArgs)
  messageLabel.Text = addUp(5, 2).ToString()
End Sub
```

C#

```
// Here's our function
int addUp(int x, int y)
{
  return x + y;
}
// And now we use it in Page_Load
void Page_Load()
{
  messageLabel.Text = addUp(5, 2).ToString();
}
```

You can easily adapt the previous example to use this new code so that you can see the results in your browser—just replace the code inside the <script> tags in Functions.aspx with the code above.

The first thing to notice in comparing this new code to the original version of Functions.aspx is that our function now accepts parameters. Any function or subroutine can take any number of parameters, of any type (there's no need for parameter types to match the return type—that's just coincidental in this example).

We can readily use the parameters inside the function or subroutine just by using the names we gave them in the function declaration (here, we've chosen x and y, but we could have chosen any names).

The other difference between this and the function declaration we had before is that we now declare our function with a return type of Integer or int, rather than String, because we want it to return a whole number.

When we call the new function, we simply have to specify the required number of parameters, and remember that the function will return a value with the type we specify. In this case, we have to convert the integer value that the function returns to a string, so that we can assign it to the label.

The simplest way to convert an integer to a string is to append .ToString() to the end of the variable name. In this case, we appended ToString on the function call which will return an integer during execution. Converting numbers to strings is a very common task in ASP.NET, so it's good to get a handle on it early.

Converting Numbers to Strings

There are more ways to convert numbers to strings in .NET, as the following lines of VB code illustrate:

```
messageLabel.Text = addUp(5, 2).ToString()
messageLabel.Text = Convert.ToString(addUp(5, 2))
```

If you prefer C#, these lines of code perform the same operations as the VB code above:

```
messageLabel.Text = addUp(5, 2).ToString();
messageLabel.Text = Convert.ToString(addUp(5, 2));
```

Don't be concerned if you're a little confused by how these conversions work, though—the syntax will become clear once we discuss object oriented concepts later in this chapter.

Operators

Throwing around values with variables and functions isn't of much use unless you can use them in some meaningful way, and to do so, we need operators. An **operator** is a symbol that has a certain meaning when it's applied to a value. Don't worry—operators are nowhere near as scary as they sound! In fact, in the last example, where our function added two numbers, we were using an operator: the addition operator, or + symbol. Most of the other operators are just as well known, although there are one or two that will probably be new to you. Table 3.2 outlines the operators that you'll use most often in your ASP.NET development.

Operators Abound!

The list of operators in Table 3.2 is far from complete. You can find detailed (though poorly written) lists of the differences between VB and C# operators on the Code Project web site.[3]

---

[3] http://www.codeproject.com/dotnet/vbnet_c__difference.asp

Table 3.2. Common ASP.NET operators

VB	C#	Description
>	>	greater than
>=	>=	greater than or equal to
<	<	less than
<=	<=	less than or equal to
<>	!=	not equal to
==	=	equals
=	=	assigns a value to a variable
OrElse	||	or
AndAlso	&&	and
&	+	concatenate strings
New	new	create object or array
*	*	multiply
/	/	divide
+	+	add
-	-	subtract

The following code uses some of these operators:

Visual Basic

```
If (user = "Zak" AndAlso itemsBought  <>  0) Then
  messageLabel.Text = "Hello Zak! Do you want to proceed to " & _
      "checkout?"
End If
```

C#

```
if (user  ==  "Zak" && itemsBought  != 0)
{
  messageLabel.Text = "Hello Zak! Do you want to proceed to " +
      "checkout?";
}
```

Here, we use the equality, inequality (not equal to), and logical "and" operators in an If statement to print a tailored message for a given user when he has put a product in his electronic shopping cart. Of particular note is the C# equality operator, ==, which is used to compare two values to see if they're equal. Don't use a single equals sign in C# unless you're assigning a value to a variable; otherwise your code will have a very different meaning than you expect!

Breaking Long Lines of Code

Since the message string in the above example was too long to fit on one line in this book, we used the string concatenation operator to combine two shorter strings on separate lines to form the complete message. In VB, we also had to break one line of code into two using the line continuation symbol (_, an underscore at the end of the line to be continued). Since C# marks the end of each command with a semicolon (;), you can split a single command over two lines in this language without having to do anything special.

We'll use these techniques throughout this book to present long lines of code within a limited page width. Feel free to recombine the lines in your own code if you like—there's no length limit on lines of VB and C# code.

Conditional Logic

As you develop ASP.NET applications, there will be many instances in which you'll need to perform an action only if a certain condition is met, for instance, if the user has checked a certain checkbox, selected a certain item from a DropDownList control, or typed a certain string into a TextBox control. We check for such occurrences using conditionals, the simplest of which is probably the If statement. This statement is often used in conjunction with an Else statement, which specifies what should happen if the condition is not met. So, for instance, we may wish to check whether or not the name entered in a text box is Zak, redirecting the user to a welcome page if it is, or to an error page if it's not:

Visual Basic
```
If (userName.Text = "Zak") Then
  Response.Redirect("ZaksPage.aspx")
Else
  Response.Redirect("ErrorPage.aspx")
End If
```

C#
```
if (userName.Text == "Zak")
{
  Response.Redirect("ZaksPage.aspx");
}
else
{
```

```
    Response.Redirect("ErrorPage.aspx");
}
```

Take Care with Case Sensitivity

Instructions are case-sensitive in both C# and VB, so be sure to use `if` in C# code, and `If` in VB code. On the other hand, variable and function names are case-sensitive only in C#. As such, in C# you could have two variables called `x` and `X`, which would be considered to be different; in VB, they would be considered to be the same variable.

Often, we want to check for many possibilities, and specify our application to perform a particular action in each case. To achieve this, we use the `Select Case` (VB) or `switch` (C#) construct:

Visual Basic

```
Select Case userName
  Case "Zak"
    Response.Redirect("ZaksPage.aspx")
  Case "Mark"
    Response.Redirect("MarksPage.aspx")
  Case "Fred"
    Response.Redirect("FredsPage.aspx")
  Case Else
    Response.Redirect("ErrorPage.aspx")
End Select
```

C#

```
switch (userName)
{
  case "Zak":
    Response.Redirect("ZaksPage.aspx");
    break;
  case "Mark":
    Response.Redirect("MarksPage.aspx");
    break;
  case "Fred":
    Response.Redirect("FredsPage.aspx");
    break;
  default:
    Response.Redirect("ErrorPage.aspx");
    break;
}
```

Loops

As you've just seen, an If statement causes a code block to execute once if the value of its test expression is true. Loops, on the other hand, cause a code block to execute repeatedly for as long as the test expression remains true. There are two basic kinds of loop:

❑ While loops, also called Do loops (which sounds like something Betty Boop might say!)

❑ For loops, including For Next and For Each

A While loop is the simplest form of loop; it makes a block of code repeat for as long as a particular condition is true. Here's an example:

Visual Basic   File: **Loops.aspx**

```vb
<!DOCTYPE html PUBLIC "-//W3C//DTD XHTML 1.0 Strict//EN"
    "http://www.w3.org/TR/xhtml1/DTD/xhtml1-strict.dtd">
<html>
  <head>
    <title>Loops</title>
    <script runat="server" language="VB">
      Sub Page_Load(s As Object, e As EventArgs)
        ' Initialize counter
        Dim counter As Integer = 0
        ' Loop
        Do While counter <= 10
          ' Update the label
          messageLabel.Text = counter.ToString()
          ' We use the += operator to increase our variable by 1
          counter += 1
        Loop
      End Sub
    </script>
  </head>
  <body>
    <form runat="server">
      <asp:Label id="messageLabel" runat="server" />
    </form>
  </body>
</html>
```

C#   File: **Loops.aspx**

```
<!DOCTYPE html PUBLIC "-//W3C//DTD XHTML 1.0 Strict//EN"
    "http://www.w3.org/TR/xhtml1/DTD/xhtml1-strict.dtd">
<html>
  <head>
    <title>Loops</title>
    <script runat="server" language="C#">
      void Page_Load()
      {
        // initialize counter
        int counter = 0;
        // loop
        while (counter <= 10)
        {
          // Update the label
          messageLabel.Text = counter.ToString();
          // C# has the ++ operator to increase a variable by 1
          counter++;
        }
      }
    </script>
  </head>
  <body>
    <form runat="server">
      <asp:Label id="messageLabel" runat="server"/>
    </form>
  </body>
</html>
```

If you load this page, you'll get the result illustrated in Figure 3.5.

Figure 3.5. Results of a While loop

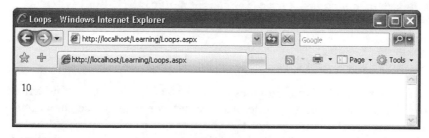

When you open the page, the label will be set to show the number 0, then 1, then 2, all the way to 10. Of course, since all this happens in Page_Load (i.e. before any output is sent to the browser), you'll only see the last value assigned: 10.

This demonstrates that the loop repeats until the condition is no longer met. Try changing the code so that the counter variable is initialized to 20 instead of 0. When you open the page now, you won't see anything on the screen, because the loop condition was never met.

The other form of the `While` loop, called a `Do While` loop, checks whether or not the condition has been met at the end of the code block, rather than at the beginning:

Visual Basic   File: **Loops.aspx (excerpt)**

```vb
Sub Page_Load(s As Object, e As EventArgs)
  ' Initialize counter
  Dim counter As Integer = 0
  ' Loop
  Do
    ' Update the label
    messageLabel.Text = counter.ToString()
    ' We use the += operator to increase our variable by 1
    counter += 1
  Loop While counter <= 10
End Sub
```

C#   File: **Loops.aspx (excerpt)**

```csharp
void Page_Load()
{
  // initialize counter
  int counter = 0;
  // loop
  do
  {
    // Update the label
    messageLabel.Text = counter.ToString();
    // C# has the operator ++ to increase a variable by 1
    counter++;
  }
  while (counter <= 10);
}
```

If you run this code, you'll see it provides the exact same output we saw when we tested the condition before the code block. However, we can see the crucial difference if we change the code so that the counter variable is initialized to 20. In this case, we will, in fact, see 20 displayed, because the loop code is executed once before the condition is even checked! There are some instances when this is just what we want, so being able to place the condition at the end of the loop can be very handy.

A `For` loop is similar to a `While` loop, but we typically use it when we know beforehand how many times we need it to execute. The following example displays the count of items within a `DropDownList` control called `productList`:

Visual Basic

```
Dim i As Integer
For i = 1 To productList.Items.Count
  messageLabel.Text = i.ToString()
Next
```

C#

```
int i;
for (i = 1; i <= productList.Items.Count; i++)
{
  messageLabel.Text = i.ToString();
}
```

In VB, the loop syntax specifies the starting and ending values for our counter variable within the `For` statement itself.

In C#, we assign a starting value (`i = 1`) along with a condition that will be tested each time we move through the loop (`i <= productList.Items.Count`), and identify how the counter variable should be incremented after each loop (`i++`). While this allows for some powerful variations on the theme in our C# code, it can be confusing at first. In VB, the syntax is considerably simpler, but it can be a bit limiting in exceptional cases.

The other type of `For` loop is `For Each`, which loops through every item within a collection. The following example loops through an array called `arrayName`:

Visual Basic

```
For Each item In arrayName
  messageLabel.Text = item
Next
```

C#

```
foreach (string item in arrayName)
{
  messageLabel.Text = item;
}
```

You may also come across instances in which you need to exit a loop prematurely. In these cases, you would use either `Exit`, if your code is in VB, or the equivalent (`break`) statement in C#, to terminate the loop:

Visual Basic

```
Dim i As Integer
For i = 0 To 10
  If (i = 5) Then
    Response.Write("Oh no! Not the number 5!!")
    Exit For
  End If
Next
```

C#

```
int i;
for (i = 0; i <= 10; i++)
{
  if (i == 5)
  {
    Response.Write("Oh no! Not the number 5!!");
    break;
  }
}
```

In this case, as soon as our `For` loop hits the condition `i = 5`, it displays a warning message using the `Response.Write` method (which will be familiar to those with past ASP experience), and exits the loop so that no further passes through the loop will be made.

Although we've only scratched the surface, VB and C# provide a great deal of power and flexibility to web developers, and time spent learning the basics now will more than pay off in the future.

Object Oriented Programming Concepts

VB and C# are modern programming languages that give you the tools to write structured, extensible, and maintainable code. The code can be separated into modules, each of which defines classes that can be imported and used in other modules. Both languages are relatively simple to get started with, yet they offer sophisticated features for writing complex, large-scale enterprise applications.

One of the reasons why these languages are so powerful is that they facilitate **object oriented programming** (OOP). In this section, we'll explain the fundamentals of OOP and learn how adopting good OOP style now can help you to develop better, more versatile web applications down the road. This section will provide a basic OOP foundation angled towards the web developer. In particular, we'll cover the following concepts:

❑ objects

❑ properties

❑ methods

❑ classes

❑ scope

❑ events

❑ inheritance

In the pages that follow, we'll discuss these concepts briefly, and from Chapter 4 onwards, you'll see some practical examples of OOP in action.

Objects and Classes

So what does the term "object oriented programming" mean? Basically, as the name suggests, it's an approach to development that puts objects at the center of the programming model. The object is probably the most important concept in the world of OOP; an **object** is a self-contained entity that has *state* and *behavior*, just like a real-world object.

In programming, an object's state is described by its **fields** and **properties**, while its behavior is defined by its **methods** and **events**. An important part of OOP's strength comes from the natural way it allows programmers to conceive and design their applications.

We often use objects in our programs to describe real-world objects—we can have objects that represent a car, a customer, a document, or a person. Each object has its own state and behavior.

It's very important to have a clear understanding of the difference between a class and an object. A class acts like a blueprint for the object, while an object represents an instance of the class. I just said that you could have objects of type

Car, for example. If you did, Car would be the class, or the type, and we could create as many Car objects as we wanted, calling them myCar, johnsCar, davesCar, and so on.

The class defines the behavior of all objects of that type. So all objects of type Car will have the same *behavior*—for example, the ability to change gear. However, each individual Car object may be in a different gear at any particular time; thus, each object has its own particular *state*.

Let's take another example: think of Integer (or int) as a class, and age and height as objects of type Integer. The class defines the behavior of the objects—they're numeric, and we can perform mathematical operations on them—and the instances of objects (age and height) have their behavior defined by the class to which they belong, but they also hold state (so age could be 20).

Take a look at the following code:

Visual Basic
```
Dim age As Integer
Dim name As String
Dim myCar as Car
Dim myOtherCar as Car
```

C#
```
int age;
string name;
Car myCar;
Car myOtherCar;
```

As you can see, the syntax for declaring an object is the same as that for declaring a simple integer or string variable. In C#, we first mention the type of the object, then we name that particular instance. In VB, we use the Dim keyword.

Object oriented programming sounds like an advanced topic, but getting started with it is actually very easy, because OOP offers us a natural way to conceive and design programs. Instead of writing long functions of code to perform specific tasks, OOP allows us to group pieces of related functionality into classes that we can reuse over and over, or even extend to incorporate new features. In OOP, one thinks of programming problems in terms of objects, properties, and methods. And, as we've seen, the best way to get a handle on these terms is to consider a real-world object and imagine how it might be represented in an OOP program. For the examples that follow, we'll use as our example my dog, an Australian Shepherd named Rayne.

Rayne is your average great big, friendly, loving, playful mutt. You might describe him in terms of his physical properties: he's gray, white, brown, and black, stands roughly one-and-a-half feet high, and is about three feet long. You might also describe some methods to make him do things: he sits when he hears the command "Sit," lies down when he hears the command "Lie down," and comes when his name is called.

So, if we were to represent Rayne in an OOP program, we'd probably start by creating a class called `Dog`. A class describes how certain types of objects look from a programming point of view. When we define a class, we must define the following two items:

Properties   Properties hold specific information relevant to that class of object. You can think of properties as characteristics of the objects that they represent. Our `Dog` class might have properties such as `Color`, `Height`, and `Length`.

Methods   Methods are actions that objects of the class can be told to perform. Methods are subroutines (if they don't return a value) or functions (if they do) that are specific to a given class. So the `Dog` class could have methods such as `Sit`, and `LieDown`.

Once we've defined a class, we can write code that creates objects of that class, using the class a little like a template. This means that objects of a particular class expose (or make available) the methods and properties defined by that class. So, we might create an instance of our `Dog` class called `rayne`, set its properties accordingly, and use the methods defined by the class to interact with Rayne, as shown in Figure 3.6.

Figure 3.6. An instance of Dog

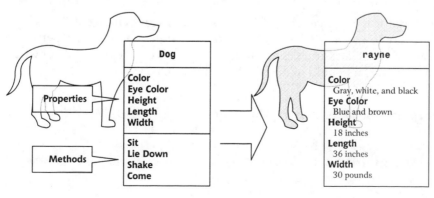

This is just a simple example to help you visualize what OOP is all about. In the next few sections, we'll cover properties and methods in greater detail, and talk about classes and class instances, scope, events, and inheritance.

Properties

As we've seen, properties are characteristics shared by all objects of a particular class. In the case of our example, the following properties might be used to describe any given dog:

❏ color

❏ height

❏ length

In the same way, the more useful ASP.NET `Button` class exposes properties including:

❏ `Width`

❏ `Height`

❏ `ID`

❏ `Text`

❏ `ForeColor`

❏ `BackColor`

Unfortunately for me, if I get sick of Rayne's color, I can't change it in real life. However, if Rayne was a .NET object, we could change any of his properties in the same way that we set variables (although a property can be read-only or write-only). For instance, we could make him brown very easily:

Visual Basic
```
rayne.Color = "Brown"
```

C#
```
rayne.Color = "Brown";
```

In this example, we're using an instance of our `Dog` class called `rayne`. We use the dot operator (`.`) to access the property `Color` that the object exposes and set it to the string `"Brown."`

Methods

With our dog example, we can make a particular dog do things by calling commands. If I want Rayne to sit, I tell him to sit. If I want Rayne to lie down, I tell him to lie down. In object oriented terms, I tell him what I want him to do by calling a predefined command or method, and an action results. For example, to make Rayne sit, we would use the following code to call his `Sit` method:

Visual Basic
```
rayne.Sit()
```

C#
```
rayne.Sit();
```

Given that `rayne` is an instance of our `Dog` class, we say that the `Sit` method is exposed by the `Dog` class.

Classes

You can think of a class as a template for building as many objects of a particular type as you like. When you create an instance of a class, you are creating an object of that class, and the new object has all the characteristics and behaviors (properties and methods) defined by the class.

In our dog example, `rayne` was an instance of the `Dog` class, as Figure 3.6 illustrated. In our code, we'd create a new instance of the `Dog` class called `rayne`, as shown below:

Visual Basic
```
Dim rayne As New Dog()
```

C#
```
Dog rayne = new Dog();
```

Constructors

Constructors are special kinds of method are that used to initialize the object. In OOP, when we create new instances of a class, we say we're **instantiating** that class. The constructor is a method of a class that's executed automatically when a class is instantiated.

At least one constructor will be defined for most of the classes you will write (though we can define more than one constructor for a class, as we'll see shortly), since it's likely that some data will need to be initialized for each class at creation time.

In C# and VB, the constructor is defined as a method that has the same name as the class, and has no return type.

Scope

You should now understand programming objects to be entities that exist in a program and are manipulated through the methods and properties they expose. However, in some cases, we want to create for use inside our class methods that are not available to code outside that class.

Imagine we're writing the `Sit` method inside this class, and we realize that before the dog can sit, it has to shuffle its back paws forward a little (bear with me on this one!). We could create a method called `ShufflePaws`, then call that method from inside the `Sit` method. However, we don't want code in an ASP.NET page or in some other class to call this method—it'd just be silly. We can prevent it by controlling the scope of the `ShufflePaws` method.

Carefully controlling which members of a class are accessible from outside that class is fundamental to the success of object oriented programming. You can control the visibility of a class member using a special set of keywords called **access modifiers**:

Public   Defining a property or method of a class as public allows that property or method to be called from outside the class itself. In other words, if an instance of this class is created inside another object (remember, too, that ASP.NET pages themselves are objects), public methods and properties are freely available to the code that created that instance of the class. This is the default scope for VB and C# classes.

Private   If a property or method of a class is private, it cannot be used from outside the class itself. So, if an instance of this class is created inside an object of a different class, the creating object has no access to private methods or properties of the created object.

Protected   A protected property or method sits somewhere between public and private. A protected member is accessible from the code within its class, or to the classes derived from it. We'll learn more about derived classes a bit later.

Deciding which access modifier to use for a given class member can be a very difficult decision—it affects not only your class, but also the other classes and programs that use your class. Of special importance are the class's public members, which together form the class's **public interface**. The public interface acts like a contract between your class and the users of your class, and if it's designed properly, it shouldn't change over time. If, for example, you mark the Sit method as public, and later decide to make it private, all the other classes that use this method will have to change accordingly, which is not good. For an extreme scenario, imagine that in a year, Microsoft decided to remove the ToString method from its classes—obviously, this would wreak havoc with your code.

Tip

Keep Everything Private until you Need It

As a simple guideline for designing your classes, remember that it's often easier just to make all the members private, and make public only those that really need to be public. It's much easier to add to a public interface than it is to remove from it.

Events

We've covered events in some depth already. To sum up, events occur when a control object sends a message as a result of some change that has been made to it. Generally, these changes occur as the result of user interaction with the control via the browser. For instance, when a button is clicked, a Click event is raised, and we can handle that event to perform some action. The object that triggers the event is referred to as the **event sender**, while the object that receives the event is referred to as the **event receiver**. You'll learn more about these objects in Chapter 4.

Understanding Inheritance

The term **inheritance** refers to the ability of a specialized class to refine the properties and methods exposed by another, more generalized class.

In our dog example, we created a class called Dog, then created instances of that class to represent individual dogs such as Rayne. However, dogs are types of animals, and many characteristics of dogs are shared by all (or most) animals. For instance, Rayne has four legs, two ears, one nose, two eyes, etc. It might be better, then, for us to create a base class called `Animal`. When we then defined the `Dog` class, it would inherit from the `Animal` class, and all public properties and methods of `Animal` would be available to instances of the `Dog` class.

Similarly, we could create a new class based on the `Dog` class. In programming circles, this is called **deriving a subclass** from `Dog`. For instance, we might create a class called `AustralianShepherd`, and one for my other dog, Amigo, called `Chihuahua`, both of which would inherit the properties and methods of the `Dog` base class, and define new classes specific to each breed.

Don't worry too much if this is still a little unclear. The best way to appreciate inheritance is to see it used in a real program. The most obvious use of inheritance in ASP.NET is in the technique called code-behind, and we'll build plenty of examples using inheritance and code-behind in Chapter 4.

Objects In .NET

If this is the first book in which you've read about object oriented programming, you've probably started to dream about objects! Don't worry, the effect of first exposure to objects doesn't usually last for more than a week. Even though this is yet another discussion about objects, I promise it won't be boring. Moreover, in the course of this section, we'll cover some important concepts that every serious .NET programmer must know.

So far, we've explored various concepts that apply in one form or the other to almost any truly object oriented language. Every language has its peculiarities, but the general concepts are the same in all of these languages.

You may already have heard the common mantra of object oriented programmers: "everything is an object." This has two meanings. First of all, in C#, every program consists of a class. In all stages of application development, from design to implementation, decisions must be made in regard to the way we design and relate objects and classes to each other. Yes, objects are everywhere.

.NET extends this to yet another level, giving the phrase "everything is an object" extra meaning. In the world of .NET, every class ultimately derives from a base class named `Object`, so "everything is an object" becomes "everything is an `Object`."

If you look at the documentation for the ASP.NET `Page` class, you can see the list of classes from which this class inherits, as shown in Figure 3.7.

Figure 3.7. The Page class's documentation

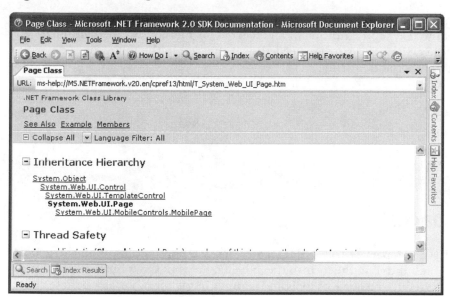

You'll remember from the last section that we said our hypothetical `AustralianShepherd` class would inherit from the more general `Dog` class, which, in turn, would inherit from the even more general `Animal` class. This is exactly the kind of relationship that's being shown in Figure 3.7—`Page` inherits methods and properties from the `TemplateControl` class, which in turn inherits from a more general class called `Control`. In the same way that we say that an Australian Shepherd is an Animal, we say that a `Page` is a `Control`. `Control`, like all .NET classes, inherits from `Object`.

Since `Object` is so important that every other class derives from it, either directly or indirectly, it deserves a closer look. `Object` contains the basic functionality that the designers of .NET felt should be available in any object. The `Object` class contains these public members:

❑ `Equals`

❑ `ReferenceEquals`

❑ `GetHashCode`

❑ `GetType`

❏ `ToString`

The only member we're really interested in at this moment is `ToString`, which returns the text representation of an object. This method is called automatically when conversions to string are needed, as is the case in the following code, which joins a number and a string:

Visual Basic
```
Dim age As Integer = 5
Dim message As String = "Current Age: " & age
```

C#
```
int age = 5;
string message = "Current Age: " + age;
```

Namespaces

As ASP.NET is part of the .NET Framework, we have access to all the goodies that are built into it in the form of the .NET Framework Class Library. This library represents a huge resource of tools and features in the form of classes; these classes are organized in a hierarchy of namespaces. When we want to use certain features that .NET provides, we have only to find the namespace that contains the desired functionality, and import that namespace into our ASP.NET page. Once we've done that, we can make use of the .NET classes in that namespace to achieve our own ends.

For instance, if we wanted to access a database from a page, we would import the namespace that contains classes for this purpose, which could be `System.Data.SqlClient`. You can view the namespace of a class when visiting its page in the .NET documentation. For example, the `Button` control's class can be found in `System.Web.UI.WebControls`.

To use a class that's part of a namespace that isn't available to you by default, you either need to import the namespace, or reference the class using its **fully qualified name**, such as `System.Web.UI.WebControls`. To import a namespace page, we use the `Imports` directive in VB, and `using` in C#:

Visual Basic
```
Imports System.Data.SqlClient
```

C#
```
using System.Data.SqlClient;
```

As we've imported that namespace, we have access to all the classes that it contains.

Using Code-behind Files

Most companies that employ web development teams usually split projects into two groups—visual design and functional development—because software engineers are usually poor designers, and designers are often poor engineers. Until now, our ASP.NET pages have contained code render blocks that place VB or C# code directly into the ASP.NET page. The problem with this approach is that there's no separation between the presentational elements of the page and the application logic. Traditional ASP was infamous for creating "spaghetti" code, which was scattered and intertwined throughout the presentation elements. This made it very tricky to manage the code between development teams, as you'll know if you've ever tried to pick apart someone else's ASP code. In response to these problems, ASP.NET introduced a new development approach that allows code developers to work separately from the presentation designers who lay out individual pages.

This new method, called **code-behind**, keeps all of your presentational elements (controls) inside the `.aspx` file, but moves all of your code to a separate class in a `.vb` or `.cs` code-behind file. Consider the following ASP.NET page, which displays a simple button and label:

Visual Basic   File: **Hello.aspx (excerpt)**

```
<!DOCTYPE html PUBLIC "-//W3C//DTD XHTML 1.0 Strict//EN"
    "http://www.w3.org/TR/xhtml1/DTD/xhtml1-strict.dtd">
<html>
  <head>
    <title>Sample Page using VB</title>
    <script runat="server" language="VB">
      Sub Click(s As Object, e As EventArgs)
        messageLabel.Text = "Hello World"
      End Sub
    </script>
  </head>
  <body>
    <form runat="server">
      <asp:Button id="submitButton" Text="Click Me"
          runat="server" OnClick="Click" />
      <asp:Label id="messageLabel" runat="server" />
    </form>
```

```
    </body>
</html>
```

```
<!DOCTYPE html PUBLIC "-//W3C//DTD XHTML 1.0 Strict//EN"
    "http://www.w3.org/TR/xhtml1/DTD/xhtml1-strict.dtd">
<html>
  <head>
    <title>Sample Page using C#</title>
    <script runat="server" language="C#">
      void Click(Object s, EventArgs e)
      {
        messageLabel.Text = "Hello World";
      }
    </script>
  </head>
  <body>
    <form runat="server">
      <asp:Button id="submitButton" Text="Click Me"
          runat="server" OnClick="Click" />
      <asp:Label id="messageLabel" runat="server" />
    </form>
  </body>
</html>
```

Let's see how this example could be separated into the following distinct files:

HelloCodeBehind.aspx
   layout, presentation, and static content

HelloCodeBehind.vb or **HelloCodeBehind.cs**
   code-behind files containing a custom page class

First, we take all the code and place it in the code-behind file (HelloCode-Behind.vb or HelloCodeBehind.cs). This file is a pure code file, and contains no HTML or other markup tags. Nevertheless, we can still access presentation elements from this file, using their IDs (such as messageLabel) as shown below:

```
' First off we import some useful namespaces
Imports System
Imports System.Web.UI
Imports System.Web.UI.WebControls
' The partial class
Public Partial Class HelloCodeBehind
```

```
  Inherits System.Web.UI.Page
  ' Here's the Click handler just as it appeared before
  Sub Click(s As Object, e As EventArgs)
    messageLabel.Text = "Hello World"
  End Sub
End Class
```

C#   File: **HelloCodeBehind.cs**

```csharp
// First off we import some useful namespaces
using System;
using System.Web.UI;
using System.Web.UI.WebControls;
// The partial class
public partial class HelloCodeBehind: System.Web.UI.Page
{
  // Here's the Click handler just as it appeared before
  public void Click(Object s, EventArgs e)
  {
    messageLabel.Text = "Hello World";
  }
}
```

Without code, the main ASP.NET page becomes a bit simpler:

Visual Basic   File: **HelloCodeBehind.aspx**

```html
<%@ Page Language="VB" CodeFile="HelloCodeBehind.vb"
    Inherits="HelloCodeBehind"%>
<!DOCTYPE html PUBLIC "-//W3C//DTD XHTML 1.0 Strict//EN"
    "http://www.w3.org/TR/xhtml1/DTD/xhtml1-strict.dtd">
<html>
  <head>
    <title>Sample Page Code Behind Demo using VB</title>
  </head>
  <body>
    <form runat="server">
      <asp:Button id="submitButton" Text="Click Me"
          runat="server" OnClick="Click" />
      <asp:Label id="messageLabel" runat="server" />
    </form>
  </body>
</html>
```

C#   File: **HelloCodeBehind.aspx**

```html
<%@ Page Language="C#" CodeFile="HelloCodeBehind.cs"
    Inherits="HelloCodeBehind"%>
<!DOCTYPE html PUBLIC "-//W3C//DTD XHTML 1.0 Strict//EN"
```

```
    "http://www.w3.org/TR/xhtml1/DTD/xhtml1-strict.dtd">
<html>
  <head>
    <title>Sample Page Code Behind Demo using C#</title>
  </head>
  <body>
    <form runat="server">
      <asp:Button id="submitButton" Text="Click Me"
          runat="server" OnClick="Click" />
      <asp:Label id="messageLabel" runat="server" />
    </form>
  </body>
</html>
```

As you can see, the only line that differs between these `.aspx` pages is the `Page` directive. Since the `.aspx` pages now contain only HTML layout, the contents are identical no matter what language you use for the code.

Partial Classes

Tip

If you have programmed with ASP.NET 1.1, you may already have noticed the changes in the code-behind model. In ASP.NET 2.0, the code-behind file is cleaner and smaller—a feat it achieves by using a new feature of VB and C# called **partial classes**. Read on for the details!

The code-behind file is written differently from what you've seen so far. While we no longer need `<script>` tags, we find a class definition in their place. As the VB example shows, we start with three lines that import namespaces for use within the code:

Visual Basic   File: **HelloCodeBehind.vb (excerpt)**

```vb
Imports System
Imports System.Web.UI
Imports System.Web.UI.WebControls
```

The next lines create a new class, named `HelloCodeBehind`. Since our code-behind page contains code for an ASP.NET page, our class inherits from the `Page` class:

Visual Basic   File: **HelloCodeBehind.vb (excerpt)**

```vb
Public Partial Class HelloCodeBehindSample
  Inherits System.Web.UI.Page
```

This is the practical application of inheritance that we mentioned earlier. The `HelloCodeBehind` class inherits from `Page`, borrowing all its functionality, and extending it according to the particular needs of the page.

But what does `Partial` mean? A new feature in .NET 2.0, partial classes allow a class to be spread over multiple files. ASP.NET 2.0 uses this feature to make programmers' lives easier. We write one part of the class in the code-behind file, and ASP.NET generates the other part of the class for us, adding the object declarations for all the user interface elements.

Take a look at the `Click` subroutine, though which we access the `messageLabel` object without defining it anywhere in the code:

Visual Basic   File: **HelloCodeBehind.vb (excerpt)**

```vb
Sub Click(s As Object, e As EventArgs)
  messageLabel.Text = "Hello World"
End Sub
```

That's pretty handy! However, don't be fooled into thinking that you can use objects that haven't been declared—the `messageLabel` object has been declared in another partial class file that the ASP.NET runtime generates for us. The file contains declarations for all the controls referenced in `HelloCodeBehind.aspx`.

As I hope you can see, code-behind files are easy to work with, and they can make managing and using our pages much more straightforward than keeping your code in code declaration blocks. You'll find yourself using code-behind files in most of the real-world projects that you build, but for simplicity's sake, we'll stick with code declaration blocks for one more chapter.

Summary

Phew! We've covered quite a few concepts over the course of this chapter. Don't worry—with a little practice, these concepts will become second nature to you. I hope you leave this chapter with a basic understanding of programming concepts as they relate to the ASP.NET web developer.

The next chapter will begin to put all the concepts that we've covered so far into practice. We'll begin by working with HTML Controls, Web Forms, and Web Controls, before launching into our first hands-on project!

4

Constructing ASP.NET Web Pages

If you've ever built a model from Lego bricks, you're well prepared to start building real ASP.NET web pages. ASP.NET offers many techniques that allow web developers to build parts of web pages independently, then put them together later to build complete pages.

The content we're organizing through our work with ASP.NET is almost never static. At design time, we tend to think in terms of templates that contain placeholders for the content that will be generated dynamically at runtime. And to fill those placeholders, we can either use one of the many controls ASP.NET provides, or build our own.

In this chapter, we'll discuss many of the objects and techniques that give life and color to ASP.NET web pages, including:

❏ web forms

❏ HTML server controls

❏ web server controls

❏ web user controls

❏ master pages

❑ handling page navigation

❑ styling pages and controls with CSS

If the list looks intimidating, don't worry—all of this is far easier to understand than it might first appear.

Web Forms

As you know, there's always new terminology to master when you're learning new technologies. But with ASP.NET, even the simplest terms that are used to describe the basics of web pages change to reflect the processes that occur within them.

The term used to describe an ASP.NET web page is **web form**, and this is the central object in ASP.NET development. You've already met web forms—they're the .aspx files you've worked with so far in this book. At first glance, web forms look much like HTML pages, but in addition to static HTML content they also contain ASP.NET presentational elements, and code that executes on the server side to generate dynamic content and perform the desired server-side functionality.

Every web form includes a <form runat="server"> tag, which contains the ASP.NET-specific elements that make up the page. Multiple forms aren't supported. The basic structure of a web form is shown here:

```
<html>
  <head>
    <script runat="server" language="language">
      …code here…
    </script>
  </head>
  <body>
    <form runat="server">
      …user interface elements here…
    </form>
  </body>
</html>
```

To access and manipulate a web form programatically, we use the System.Web.UI.Page class. You might recognize this class from the code-behind example we saw in Chapter 3. We must mention the class explicitly in the code-behind file. In situations in which we're not using code-behind files (i.e. we write all the code inside the `.aspx` file instead), the `Page` class is still used—we just don't see it.

We can use a range of user interface elements inside the form—including typical, static HTML code—but we can also use elements whose values or properties can be generated or manipulated on the server either when the page first loads, or when the form is submitted. These elements—which, in ASP.NET parlance, are called controls—allow us to reuse common functionality, such as the page header, a calendar, a shopping cart summary, or a "Today's Quote" box, for example, across multiple web forms. There are several types of controls in ASP.NET:

❏ HTML server controls

❏ web server controls

❏ web user controls

❏ master pages

There are significant technical differences between these types of controls, but what makes them similar is the ease with which we can integrate and reuse them in our web sites. Let's take a look at them one by one.

HTML Server Controls

HTML server controls are outwardly identical to plain old HTML tags, but include a `runat="server"` attribute. This gives the ASP.NET runtime control over the HTML server controls, allowing us to access them programatically. For example, if we have an `<a>` tag in a page and we want to be able to change the address to which it links dynamically, using VB or C# code, we use the `runat="server"` attribute.

A server-side HTML server control exists for each of HTML's most common elements. Creating HTML server controls is easy: we simply stick a `runat="server"` attribute on the end of a normal HTML tag to create the HTML control version of that tag. The complete list of current HTML control classes and their associated tags is given in Table 4.1.

Table 4.1. HTML control classes

Class	Associated Tags
HtmlAnchor	`<a runat="server">`
HtmlButton	`<button runat="server">`
HtmlForm	`<form runat="server">`
HtmlImage	`<img runat="server">`
HtmlInputButton	`<input type="submit" runat="server">`
	`<input type="reset" runat="server">`
	`<input type="button" runat="server">`
HtmlInputCheckBox	`<input type="checkbox" runat="server">`
HtmlInputFile	`<input type="file" runat="server">`
HtmlInputHidden	`<input type="hidden" runat="server">`
HtmlInputImage	`<input type="image" runat="server">`
HtmlInputRadioButton	`<input type="radio" runat="server">`
HtmlInputText	`<input type="text" runat="server">`
	`<input type="password" runat="server">`
HtmlSelect	`<select runat="server">`
HtmlTable	`<table runat="server">`
HtmlTableRow	`<tr runat="server">`
HtmlTableCell	`<td runat="server">`
	`<th runat="server">`
HtmlTextArea	`<textarea runat="server">`
HtmlGenericControl	`<span runat="server">`
	`<div runat="server">`
	All other HTML tags

For more details on these classes, see Appendix A.

All the HTML server control classes are contained within the `System.Web.UI.Htm-lControls` namespace. As they're processed on the server side by the ASP.NET runtime, we can access their properties through code elsewhere in the page. If you're familiar with JavaScript, HTML, and CSS, then you'll know that manipulating text within HTML tags, or even manipulating inline styles within an HTML tag, can be cumbersome and error-prone. HTML server controls aim to solve these problems by allowing you to manipulate the page easily with your choice of .NET language—for instance, using VB or C#.

Using the HTML Server Controls

Nothing explains the theory better than a simple, working example. Let's create a simple survey form that uses the following HTML server controls:

- ❑ HtmlForm

- ❑ HtmlButton

- ❑ HtmlInputText

- ❑ HtmlSelect

We'll begin by creating a new file named Survey.aspx. Create the file in the Learning folder you created in Chapter 1. The following code creates the visual interface for the survey:

File: **Survey.aspx (excerpt)**

```
<!DOCTYPE html PUBLIC "-//W3C//DTD XHTML 1.0 Transitional//EN"
    "http://www.w3.org/TR/xhtml1/DTD/xhtml1-transitional.dtd">
<html>
  <head>
    <title>Using ASP.NET HTML Server Controls</title>
    <!-- code will go here -->
  </head>
  <body>
    <form runat="server">
      <h2>Take the Survey!</h2>
      <!-- Display user name -->
      <p>
        Name:<br />
        <input type="text" id="name" runat="server" />
      </p>
      <!-- Display email -->
      <p>
        Email:<br />
        <input type="text" id="email" runat="server" />
      </p>
      <!-- Display technology options -->
      <p>
```

```
      Which server technologies do you use?<br />
      <select id="serverModel" runat="server" multiple="true">
        <option>ASP.NET</option>
        <option>PHP</option>
        <option>JSP</option>
        <option>CGI</option>
        <option>ColdFusion</option>
      </select>
  </p>
  <!-- Display .NET preference options -->
  <p>
    Do you like .NET so far?<br />
    <select id="likeDotNet" runat="server">
      <option>Yes</option>
      <option>No</option>
    </select>
  </p>
  <!-- Display confirmation button -->
  <p>
    <button id="confirmButton" OnServerClick="Click"
        runat="server">Confirm</button>
  </p>
  <!-- Confirmation label -->
  <p>
    <asp:Label id="feedbackLabel" runat="server" />
  </p>
  </form>
  </body>
</html>
```

From what we've already seen of HTML controls, you should have a good idea of the classes we'll be working with in this page. All we've done is place some `HtmlInputText` controls, an `HtmlButton` control, and an `HtmlSelect` control inside the obligatory `HtmlForm` control. We've also added a `Label` control, which we'll use to give feedback to the user.

Tip

HTML Server Controls in Action

Remember, HTML server controls are essentially HTML tags with the `run-at="server"` attribute. In most cases, you'll also need to assign them IDs, which will enable you to use the controls in your code.

When it's complete, the `Survey.aspx` web form will resemble Figure 4.1.

Figure 4.1. A simple form that uses HTML server controls

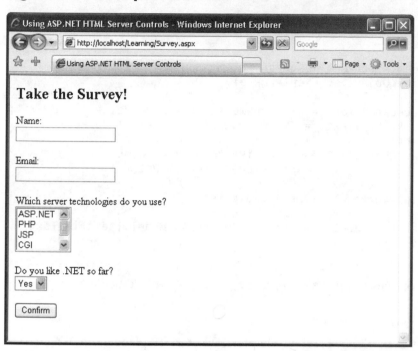

When a user clicks on the button, we'll display the submitted responses in the browser. In a real application, we'd probably be more likely to save this information to a database and perhaps show the results as a chart. Whatever the case, we'd access the properties of the HTML controls as shown below:

Visual Basic   File: **Survey.aspx (excerpt)**

```vb
<script runat="server" language="VB">
  Sub Click(ByVal s As Object, ByVal e As EventArgs)
    Dim i As Integer
    feedbackLabel.Text = "Your name is: " & name.Value & "<br />"
    feedbackLabel.Text += "Your email is: " & email.Value & _
        "<br />"
    feedbackLabel.Text += "You like to work with:<br />"
    For i = 0 To serverModel.Items.Count - 1
      If serverModel.Items(i).Selected Then
        feedbackLabel.Text += " - " & _
            serverModel.Items(i).Text & "<br />"
      End If
    Next i
```

```
      feedbackLabel.Text += "You like .NET: " & likeDotNet.Value
  End Sub
</script>
```

C#   File: **Survey.aspx (excerpt)**

```
<script runat="server" language="C#">
  void Click(Object s, EventArgs e)
  {
    feedbackLabel.Text = "Your name is: " + name.Value + "<br />";
    feedbackLabel.Text += "Your email is: " + email.Value +
        "<br />";
    feedbackLabel.Text += "You like to work with:<br />";
    for (int i = 0; i <= serverModel.Items.Count - 1; i++)
    {
      if (serverModel.Items[i].Selected)
      {
        feedbackLabel.Text += " - " + serverModel.Items[i].Text +
            "<br />";
      }
    }
    feedbackLabel.Text += "You like .NET: " + likeDotNet.Value;
  }
</script>
```

As with the examples in previous chapters, we start by placing our VB and C#
code inside a server-side script block within the <head> part of the page. Next,
we create a new Click event handler that takes the two usual parameters. Finally,
we use the Label control to display the user's responses within the page.

Figure 4.2. Viewing the survey results

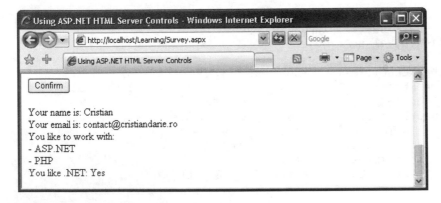

Once you've written the code, save your work and test the results in your browser. Enter some information and click the button. To select multiple options in the `serverModel` option box, hold down **Ctrl** as you click on your preferences. The information you enter should appear at the bottom of the page when the Confirm button is clicked, as shown in Figure 4.2.

In conclusion, working with HTML server controls is really simple. All you need to do is assign each control an ID, and add the `runat="server"` attribute. Then, you can simply access and manipulate them using VB or C# code on the server side.

Web Server Controls

Web server controls can be seen as more advanced versions of HTML server controls. Web server controls are those that generate content for you—you're no longer in control of the HTML being used. While having good knowledge of HTML is useful, it's not a necessity for those working with web server controls.

Let's look at an example. We can use the `Label` web server control to place simple text inside a web form. To change the `Label`'s text from within our C# or VB code, we simply set its `Text` property like so:

Visual Basic
```
myLabel.Text = "Mickey Mouse"
```

Similarly, to add a text box to our form, we use the `TextBox` web server control. Again, we can read or set its text using the `Text` property:

C#
```
username = usernameTextBox.Text;
```

Though we're applying the `TextBox` control, ASP.NET still uses an `input` element behind the scenes; however, we no longer have to worry about this detail. With web server controls, Microsoft has basically reinvented HTML from scratch.

Unlike HTML server controls, web server controls don't have a direct, one-to-one correspondence with the HTML elements they generate. For example, we can use either of two web server controls—the `DropDownList` control, or the `ListBox` control—to generate a `select` element.

Web server controls follow the same basic pattern as HTML tags, but the tag name is preceded by `asp:`, and is capitalized using Pascal Casing. Pascal Casing is a form that capitalizes the first character of each word (e.g. `TextBox`). The object IDs are usually named using Camel Casing, where the first letter of each word except the first is capitalized (e.g. usernameTextBox).

Consider the following HTML input element, which creates an input text box:

```
<input type="text" name="usernameTextBox" size="30" />
```

The equivalent web server control is the TextBox control, and it looks like this:

```
<asp:TextBox id="usernameTextBox" runat="server" Columns="30">
</asp:TextBox>
```

Remember that, unlike any normal HTML that you might use in your web forms, web server controls are first processed by the ASP.NET engine, where they're transformed to HTML. A side effect of this approach is that you must be very careful to always include closing tags (the </asp:TextBox> part above). The HTML parsers of most web browsers are forgiving about badly formatted HTML code, but ASP.NET is not. Remember that you can use the shorthand /> syntax if nothing appears between your web server control's opening and closing tags. So, you could also write this TextBox like so:

```
<asp:TextBox id="usernameTextBox" runat="server" Columns="30" />
```

To sum up, the key points to remember when working with web server controls are:

❑ Web server controls must be placed within a <form runat="server"> tag to function properly.

❑ Web server controls require the runat="server" attribute to function properly.

❑ We include web server controls in a form using the asp: prefix.

There are more web server controls than HTML controls, some offer advanced features that simply aren't available using HTML alone, and some generate quite complex HTML code for you. We'll meet many of the web server controls as we work through this and future chapters.

For more information on web server controls, including the properties, methods, and events for each, have a look at Appendix B.

Standard Web Server Controls

The standard set of web server controls that comes with ASP.NET mirrors the HTML server controls in many ways. However, web server controls offer some new refinements and enhancements, such as support for events and view state, a more consistent set of properties and methods, and more built-in functionality. In this section, we'll take a look as some of the controls you're most likely to use in your day-to-day work.

Remember to use the .NET Framework 2.0 SDK Documentation whenever you need more details about any of the framework's classes (or controls). Access the documentation from Start > All Programs > Microsoft .NET Framework SDK v2.0 > Documentation. To find a class, simply search for the class's name. If there are many classes with a given name in different namespaces, you'll be able to choose the one you want from the Index Results window. For example, you'll find that there are three classes named `Label`, situated in the `System.Web.UI.MobileControls`, `System.Web.UI.WebControls`, and `System.Windows.Forms` namespaces, as Figure 4.3 illustrates. You'll most likely be interested in the version of the class situated in the `WebControls` namespace.

Figure 4.3. Documentation for the `Label` control

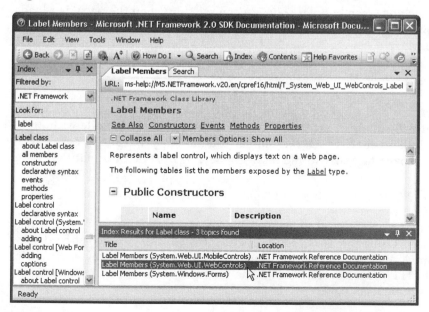

Label

The easiest way to display static text on your page is simply to add the text to the body of the page without enclosing it in any tag. However, if you want to modify the text displayed on a page using ASP.NET code, you can display your text within a `Label` control. Here's a typical example:

```
<asp:Label id="messageLabel" Text="" runat="server" />
```

The following code sets the `Text` property of the `Label` control to display the text "Hello World":

Visual Basic
```
Public Sub Page_Load()
  messageLabel.Text = "Hello World"
End Sub
```

C#
```
public void Page_Load()
{
  messageLabel.Text = "Hello World";
}
```

Reading this `Page_Load` handler code, we can see that when the page first loads, the `Text` property of the `Label` control with the `id` of `message` will be set to "Hello World."

Literal

This is perhaps the simplest control in ASP.NET. If you set `Literal`'s `Text` property, it will simply insert that text into the output HTML code without altering it. Unlike `Label`, which has similar functionality, `Literal` doesn't wrap the text in `<span>` tags that would allow the setting of style information.

TextBox

The `TextBox` control is used to create a box in which the user can type or read standard text. Using the `TextMode` property, this control can be set to display text in a single line, across multiple lines, or to hide the text being entered (for instance, in HTML password fields). The following code shows how we might use it in a simple login page:

```
<p>
   Username: <asp:TextBox id="userTextBox" TextMode="SingleLine"
       Columns="30" runat="server" />
</p>
<p>
   Password: <asp:TextBox id="passwordTextBox"
       TextMode="Password" Columns="30" runat="server" />
</p>
<p>
   Comments: <asp:TextBox id="commentsTextBox"
       TextMode="MultiLine" Columns="30" Rows="10"
       runat="server" />
</p>
```

In each of the instances above, the attribute `TextMode` dictates the kind of text box that's to be rendered.

HiddenField

`HiddenField` is a simple control that renders an `input` element whose `type` attribute is set to `hidden`. We can set its only important property, `Value`.

Button

By default, the `Button` control renders an `input` element whose `type` attribute is set to `submit`. When a button is clicked, the form containing the button is submitted to the server for processing, and both the `Click` and `Command` events are raised.

The following markup displays a `Button` control and a `Label`:

```
<asp:Button id="submitButton" Text="Submit" runat="server"
    OnClick="WriteText" />
<asp:Label id="messageLabel" runat="server" />
```

Notice the `OnClick` attribute on the control. When the button is clicked, the `Click` event is raised and the `WriteText` subroutine is called. The `WriteText` subroutine will contain the code that performs the intended function for this button, such as displaying a message to the user:

Visual Basic

```
Public Sub WriteText(s As Object, e As EventArgs)
  messageLabel.Text = "Hello World"
End Sub
```

```
C#
public void WriteText(Object s, EventArgs e)
{
  messageLabel.Text = "Hello World";
}
```

It's important to realize that events are associated with most web server controls, and the basic techniques involved in using them, are the same events and techniques we used with the `Click` event of the `Button` control. All controls implement a standard set of events because they all inherit from the `WebControl` base class.

ImageButton

An `ImageButton` control is similar to a `Button` control, but it uses an image that we supply in place of the typical system button graphic. Take a look at this example:

```
<asp:ImageButton id="myImgButton" ImageUrl="myButton.gif"
    runat="server" OnClick="WriteText" />
<asp:Label id="messageLabel" runat="server" />
```

The `Click` event of the `ImageButton` receives the coordinates of the point at which the image was clicked:

```
Visual Basic
Public Sub WriteText(s As Object, e As ImageClickEventArgs)
  messageLabel.Text = "Coordinate: " & e.X & "," & e.Y
End Sub
```

```
C#
public void WriteText(Object s, ImageClickEventArgs e)
{
  messageLabel.Text = "Coordinate: " + e.X + "," + e.Y;
}
```

LinkButton

A `LinkButton` control renders a hyperlink that fires the `Click` event when it's clicked. From the point of view of ASP.NET code, `LinkButton`s can be treated in much the same way as buttons, hence the name.

```
<asp:LinkButton id="myLinkButon" Text="Click Here"
    runat="server" />
```

HyperLink

The HyperLink control creates on your page a hyperlink that links to the URL in the NavigateUrl property. Unlike the LinkButton control, which offers features such as Click events and validation, HyperLinks are meant to be used to navigate from one page to the next.

```
<asp:HyperLink id="myLink" NavigateUrl="http://www.sitepoint.com/"
    ImageUrl="splogo.gif" runat="server">SitePoint</asp:HyperLink>
```

If it's specified, the ImageUrl attribute causes the control to display the specified image, in which case the text is demoted to acting as the image's alternate text.

CheckBox

You can use a CheckBox control to represent a choice that can have only two possible states—checked or unchecked.

```
<asp:CheckBox id="questionCheck" Text="I agree, I like .NET!"
    Checked="True" runat="server" />
```

The main event associated with a CheckBox is the CheckChanged event, which can be handled with the OnCheckChanged attribute. The Checked property is True if the checkbox is checked, and False otherwise.

RadioButton

A RadioButton is a lot like a CheckBox, except that RadioButtons can be grouped together to represent a set of options from which only one can be selected. Radio buttons are grouped together using the GroupName property.

```
<asp:RadioButton id="sanDiego" GroupName="City" Text="San Diego"
    runat="server" /><br />
<asp:RadioButton id="boston" GroupName="City" Text="Boston"
    runat="server" /><br />
<asp:RadioButton id="phoenix" GroupName="City" Text="Phoenix"
    runat="server" /><br />
<asp:RadioButton id="seattle" GroupName="City" Text="Seattle"
    runat="server" />
```

Like the CheckBox control, the main event associated with RadioButtons is the CheckChanged event, which can be handled with the OnCheckChanged attribute.

The other control we can use to display radio buttons is `RadioButtonList`, which we'll also meet in this chapter.

Image

An `Image` control creates an image that can be accessed dynamically from code; it equates to the `<img>` tag in HTML. Here's an example:

```
<asp:Image id="myImage" ImageUrl="mygif.gif" runat="server"
    AlternateText="description" />
```

ImageMap

The `ImageMap` control generates HTML to display images that have certain clickable regions called **hot spots**. Each hot spot reacts differently when clicked by the user.

These areas are defined using three controls that generate hot spots of different shapes: `CircleHotSpot`, `RectangleHotSpot`, and `PolygonHotSpot`. Here's an example that defines an image map with two circular hot spots:

```
<asp:ImageMap ID="myImageMap" runat="server" ImageUrl="image.jpg">
  <asp:CircleHotSpot AlternateText="Button1"
      Radius="20" X="50" Y="50" />
  <asp:CircleHotSpot AlternateText="Button2"
      Radius="20" X="100" Y="50" />
</asp:ImageMap>
```

Table 4.2. Possible values of `HotSpotMode`

`HotSpotMode` value	Behavior when hot spot is clicked
Inactive	none
Navigate	The user is navigated to the specified URL.
NotSet	When set for a `HotSpot`, the behavior is inherited from the parent `ImageMap`; if the parent `ImageMap` doesn't specify a default value, `Navigate` is set.
	When set for an `ImageMap`, this value is effectively equivalent to `Navigate`.
PostBack	The hot spot raises the `Click` event that can be handled server-side to respond to the user action.

To configure the action that results when a hot spot is clicked by the user, we set the `HotSpotMode` property of the `ImageMap` control, or the `HotSpotMode` property of the individual hot spot objects, or both, using the values shown in Table 4.2. If the `HotSpotMode` property is set for the `ImageMap` control as well as for an individual hot spot, the latter property will override that set for the more general `ImageMap` control.

The Microsoft .NET Framework 2.0 SDK Documentation for the `ImageMap` class and HotSpotMode enumeration contains detailed examples of the usage of these values.

PlaceHolder

The `PlaceHolder` control lets us add elements at a particular place on a page at any time, dynamically, through our code.

```
<asp:PlaceHolder id="placeHolder" runat="server" />
```

The following code dynamically adds a new `HtmlButton` control within the placeholder:

Visual Basic
```
Public Sub Page_Load()
  Dim button myButton As HtmlButton = New HtmlButton()
  myButton.InnerText = "My New Button"
  placeHolder.Controls.Add(myButton)
End Sub
```

C#
```
public void Page_Load()
{
  HtmlButton button myButton = new HtmlButton();
  myButton.InnerText = "My New Button";
  placeHolder.Controls.Add(myButton);
}
```

Panel

The `Panel` control functions similarly to the `div` element in HTML, in that it allows the set of items that resides within the tag to be manipulated as a group. For instance, the `Panel` could be made visible or hidden by a `Button`'s `Click` event:

```
<asp:Panel id="myPanel" runat="server">
  <p>Username: <asp:TextBox id="usernameTextBox" Columns="30"
      runat="server" /></p>
  <p>Password: <asp:TextBox id="passwordTextBox"
      TextMode="Password" Columns="30" runat="server" />
  </p>
</asp:Panel>
<asp:Button id="hideButton" Text="Hide Panel" OnClick="HidePanel"
    runat="server" />
```

The code above places two `TextBox` controls within a `Panel` control. The `Button`
control is outside of the panel. The `HidePanel` subroutine would then control
the `Panel`'s visibility by setting its `Visible` property to `False`:

Visual Basic
```
Public Sub HidePanel(s As Object, e As EventArgs)
  myPanel.Visible = False
End Sub
```

C#
```
public void HidePanel(Object s, EventArgs e)
{
  myPanel.Visible = false;
}
```

In this case, when the user clicks the button, the `Click` event is raised and the
`HidePanel` subroutine is called, which sets the `Visible` property of the `Panel`
control to `False`.

List Controls

Here, we'll meet the ASP.NET controls that display simple lists of elements:
`ListBox`, `DropDownList`, `CheckBoxList`, `RadioButtonList`, and `BulletedList`.

DropDownList

A `DropDownList` control is similar to the HTML `select` element. The
`DropDownList` control allows you to select one item from a list using a drop-down
menu.

```
<asp:DropDownList id="ddlFavColor" runat="server">
  <asp:ListItem Text="Red" value="red" />
  <asp:ListItem Text="Blue" value="blue" />
```

```
   <asp:ListItem Text="Green" value="green" />
</asp:DropDownList>
```

The most useful event that this control provides is `SelectedIndexChanged`. This event is exposed by other list controls, such as the `CheckBoxList` and `RadioButtonList` controls, allowing for easy programmatic interaction with the control. These controls can also be bound to a database, allowing you to extract dynamic content into a drop-down menu.

ListBox

A `ListBox` control equates to the HTML `select` element with either the `multiple` or `size` attribute set (`size` would need to be set to a value of 2 or more). If you set the `SelectionMode` attribute to `Multiple`, the user will be able to select more than one item from the list, as in this example:

```
<asp:ListBox id="listTechnologies" runat="server"
   SelectionMode="Multiple">
  <asp:ListItem Text="ASP.NET" Value="aspnet" />
  <asp:ListItem Text="JSP" Value="jsp" />
  <asp:ListItem Text="PHP" Value="php" />
  <asp:ListItem Text="CGI" Value="cgi" />
  <asp:ListItem Text="ColdFusion" Value="cf" />
</asp:ListBox>
```

RadioButtonList

Like the `RadioButton` control, the `RadioButtonList` control represents radio buttons. However, the `RadioButtonList` control represents a list of radio buttons and uses more compact syntax. Here's an example:

```
<asp:RadioButtonList id="favoriteColor" runat="server">
  <asp:ListItem Text="Red" Value="red" />
  <asp:ListItem Text="Blue" Value="blue" />
  <asp:ListItem Text="Green" Value="green" />
</asp:RadioButtonList>
```

CheckBoxList

As you may have guessed, the `CheckBoxList` control represents a group of check boxes; it's equivalent to using several `CheckBox` controls in row:

```
<asp:CheckBoxList id="favoriteFood" runat="server">
  <asp:ListItem Text="Pizza" Value="pizza" />
```

```
  <asp:ListItem Text="Tacos" Value="tacos" />
  <asp:ListItem Text="Pasta" Value="pasta" />
</asp:CheckBoxList>
```

BulletedList

The `BulletedList` control displays bulleted or numbered lists, using `<ul>` (un-ordered list) or `<ol>` (ordered list) tags. Unlike the other list controls, the `BulletedList` doesn't allow the selection of items, so the `SelectedIndexChanged` event isn't supported.

The first property you'll want to set is `DisplayMode`, which can be `Text` (the default), or `HyperLink`, which will render the list items as links. When `DisplayMode` is set to `HyperLink`, you can use the `Click` event to react when the user clicks on one of the items.

The other important property is `BulletStyle`, which determines the style of the bullets. The accepted values are `Numbered` (1, 2, 3, ...), `LowerAlpha` (a, b, c, ...), `UpperAlpha` (A, B, C, ...), `LowerRoman` (i, ii, iii, ...), `UpperRoman` (I, II, III, ...), `Circle`, `Disc`, `Square`, and `CustomImage`. If the style is set to `CustomImage`, you'll also need to set the `BulletStyleImageUrl` to specify the image to be used for the bullets. If the style is one of the numbered lists, you can also set the `FirstBulletNumber` property to specify the first number or letter that's to be generated.

Advanced Controls

These controls are advanced in terms of their usage, the HTML code they generate, and the background work they do for you. Some of these controls aren't available to older versions of ASP.NET; we'll learn more about many of them (as well as others that aren't covered in this chapter) as we progress through this book.

Calendar

The `Calendar` is a great example of the reusable nature of ASP.NET controls. The `Calendar` control generate the markup to display an intuitive calendar in which the user can click to select or move between days, weeks, months, and so on.

The `Calendar` control requires very little customization, and can be created within a page like this:

File: **Calendar.aspx (excerpt)**

```
<!DOCTYPE HTML PUBLIC "-//W3C//DTD HTML 4.01//EN"
    "http://www.w3.org/TR/html4/strict.dtd">
<html>
  <head>
    <title>Calendar Test</title>
  </head>
  <body>
    <form runat="server">
      <asp:Calendar id="myCalendar" runat="server" />
    </form>
  </body>
</html>
```

If you save this page in the Learning folder and load it, you'd get the output shown in Figure 4.4.

Figure 4.4. Displaying the default calendar

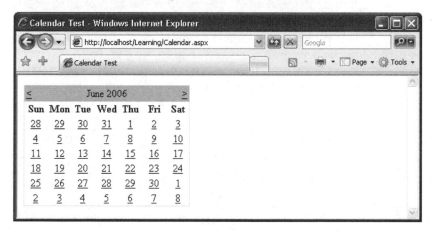

The Calendar control contains a wide range of properties, methods, and events, including those listed in Table 4.3.

Table 4.3. Some of the `Calendar` control's properties

Property	Description
DayNameFormat	This property sets the format of the day names. Its possible values are FirstLetter, FirstTwoLetters, Full, and Short. The default is Short, which displays the three-letter abbreviation.
FirstDayOfWeek	This property sets the day of the week that begins each week in the calendar. By default, the value of this property is determined by your server's region settings, but you can set this to Sunday or Monday if you want to control it.
NextPrevFormat	Set to CustomText by default, this property can be set to ShortMonth or FullMonth to control the format of the next and previous month links.
SelectedDate	This property contains a DateTime value that specifies the highlighted day. You'll use this property a lot to determine which day the user has selected.
SelectionMode	This property determines whether days, weeks, or months can be selected; its possible values are Day, DayWeek, DayWeekMonth, and None, and the default is Day. When Day is selected, a user can only select a day; when DayWeek is selected, a user can select a day or an entire week; and so on.
SelectMonthText	This property controls the text of the link that's displayed to allow users to select an entire month from the calendar.
SelectWeekText	This property controls the text of the link that's displayed to allow users to select an entire week from the calendar.
ShowDayHeader	If True, this property displays the names of the days of the week. The default is True.
ShowGridLines	If True, this property renders the calendar with grid lines. The default is True.
ShowNextPrevMonth	If True, this property displays next/previous month links. The default is True.
ShowTitle	If True, this property displays the calendar's title. The default is False.

Property	Description
TitleFormat	This property determines how the month name appears in the title bar. Possible values are Month and MonthYear. The default is MonthYear.
TodaysDate	This DateTime value sets the calendar's current date. By default, this value is not highlighted within the Calendar control.
VisibleDate	This DateTime value controls which month is displayed.

Let's take a look at an example that uses some of these properties, events, and methods to create a Calendar control that allows users to select days, weeks, and months. Modify the calendar in Calendar.aspx, and add a label to it, as follows:

File: **Calendar.aspx (excerpt)**

```
<asp:Calendar ID="myCalendar" runat="server" DayNameFormat="Short"
    FirstDayOfWeek="Sunday" NextPrevFormat="FullMonth"
    SelectionMode="DayWeekMonth" SelectWeekText="Select Week"
    SelectMonthText="Select Month" TitleFormat="Month"
    OnSelectionChanged="SelectionChanged" />
<h2>You selected these dates:</h2>
<asp:Label ID="myLabel" runat="server" />
```

Now add a <script runat="server"> tag to the head of the web form to include the SelectionChanged event handler referenced by your calendar:

Visual Basic   File: **Calendar.aspx (excerpt)**

```
<script runat="server" language="VB">
  Sub SelectionChanged(ByVal s As Object, ByVal e As EventArgs)
    myLabel.Text = ""
    For Each d As DateTime In myCalendar.SelectedDates
      myLabel.Text &= d.ToString("D") & "<br />"
    Next
  End Sub
</script>
```

C#   File: **Calendar.aspx (excerpt)**

```
<script runat="server" language="C#">
  void SelectionChanged(Object s, EventArgs e)
  {
    myLabel.Text = "";
    foreach (DateTime d in myCalendar.SelectedDates)
    {
      myLabel.Text += d.ToString("D") + "<br />";
```

```
    }
  }
</script>
```

Save your work and test it in a browser. Try selecting a day, week, or month. The selection will be highlighted similar to this display shown in Figure 4.5.

Figure 4.5. Using the `Calendar` control

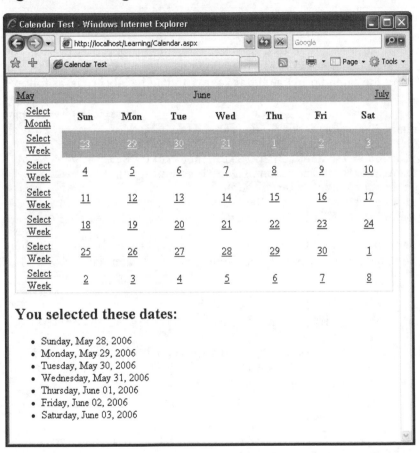

In `SelectionChanged`, we loop through each date that the user has selected, and append it to the `BulletedList` we added to the page.

AdRotator

The `AdRotator` control allows you to display a list of banner advertisements within your web application at random. However, it's more than a mere substitute for creating a randomization script from scratch. Since the `AdRotator` control gets its content from an XML file, the administration and updating of banner advertisement files and their properties is a snap. Also, the XML file allows you to control the banner's image, link, link target, and frequency of appearance in relation to other banner ads.

The benefits of using this control don't stop there, though. As most of the `AdRotator` control's properties reside within an XML file, if you wished, you could share that XML file on the Web, essentially allowing value added resellers (VARS), or possibly your companies' partners, to use your banner advertisements on their web sites.

XML Basics

In essence, XML is simply a text-based format for the transfer or storage of data; it contains no details on how that data should be presented. XML is very easy to start with because of its close resemblance to your old friend HTML: both are largely comprised of tags inside angle brackets (< and >), and any tag may contain attributes specific to that tag. The biggest difference between XML and HTML is that, rather than providing a fixed set of tags as HTML does, XML allows us to create our own tags to describe the data we wish to represent.

Take a look at the following HTML element:

```
<p>Star Wars Episode I: The Phantom Menace</p>
```

This example describes the content between the tags as a paragraph. This is fine if all we are concerned with is displaying the words "Star Wars Episode I: The Phantom Menace" on a web page. But what if we want to access those words as data?

Like HTML, XML's purpose is to describe the content of a document. But unlike HTML, XML doesn't describe how that content should be displayed; it describes *what the content is*. Using XML, the web author can mark up the contents of a document, describing that content in terms of its relevance as data.

We can use XML to mark up the words "Star Wars Episode I: The Phantom Menace" in a way that better reflects this content's significance as data:

```
<film>
  <title>Star Wars Episode I: The Phantom Menace</title>
</film>
```

Here, the XML tag names we've chosen best describe the contents of the element. We also define our own attribute names as necessary. For instance, in the example above, you may decide that you want to differentiate between the VHS version and the DVD version of the film, or record the name of the movie's director. This can be achieved by adding attributes and elements, as shown below:

```
<film format="DVD">
  <title>Star Wars Episode I: The Phantom Menace</title>
  <director>George Lucas</director>
</film>
```

If you want to test this out, create a file called **ads.xml** in your Learning folder, and insert the content presented below. Feel free to create your own banners, or to use those provided in the code archive for this book.

File: **Ads.xml (excerpt)**

```
<Advertisements>
  <Ad>
    <ImageUrl>workatdorknozzle.gif</ImageUrl>
    <NavigateUrl>http://www.dorknozzle.com</NavigateUrl>
    <TargetUrl>_blank</TargetUrl>
    <AlternateText>Work at Dorknozzle.com!</AlternateText>
    <Keyword>HR Sites</Keyword>
    <Impressions>2</Impressions>
  </Ad>
  <Ad>
    <ImageUrl>getthenewsletter.gif</ImageUrl>
    <NavigateUrl>http://www.dorknozzle.com</NavigateUrl>
    <TargetUrl>_blank</TargetUrl>
    <AlternateText>Get the Nozzle Newsletter!</AlternateText>
    <Keyword>Marketing Sites</Keyword>
    <Impressions>1</Impressions>
  </Ad>
</Advertisements>
```

As you can see, the `Advertisements` element is the root node, and in accordance with the XML specification, it appears only once. For each individual advertisement, we simply add an `Ad` child element. For instance, the above advertisement file contains details for two banner advertisements.

As you've probably noticed by now, the `.xml` file enables you to specify properties for each banner advertisement by inserting appropriate elements inside each of the `Ad` elements. These elements include:

ImageURL

the URL of the image to display for the banner ad

NavigateURL

the web page to which your users will navigate when they click the banner ad

AlternateText

the alternative text to display for browsers that do not support images

Keyword

the keyword to use to categorize your banner ad

If you use the `KeywordFilter` property of the `AdRotator` control, you can specify the categories of banner ads to display.

Impressions

the relative frequency that a particular banner ad should be shown in relation to other banner advertisements

The higher this number, the more frequently that specific banner will display in the browser. The number provided for this element can be as low as one, but cannot exceed 2,048,000,000; if it does, the page throws an exception.

Except for `ImageURL`, all these elements are optional. Also, if you specify an `Ad` without a `NavigateURL`, the banner ad will display without a hyperlink.

To make use of this `Ads.xml` file, create a new ASP.NET page, called `AdRotator.aspx`, with the following code:

File: **AdRotator.aspx (excerpt)**

```
<!DOCTYPE html PUBLIC "-//W3C//DTD XHTML 1.0 Strict//EN"
    "http://www.w3.org/TR/xhtml1/DTD/xhtml1-strict.dtd">
<html>
  <head>
    <title>AdRotator Control</title>
  </head>
  <body>
    <form runat="server">
      <asp:AdRotator ID="adRotator" runat="server"
```

```
                AdvertisementFile="Ads.xml" />
    </form>
  </body>
</html>
```

You'll need to download `workatdorknozzle.gif` and `getthenewsletter.gif` and place them in the `Learning` folder in order to see these ad images. Save your work and test it in the browser; the display should look something like Figure 4.6.

Figure 4.6. Displaying ads using `AdRotator.aspx`

Refresh the page a few times, and you'll notice that the first banner appears more often than the second. This occurs because the `Impression` value for the first `Ad` is double the value set for the second banner, so it will appear twice as often.

TreeView

The `TreeView` control is a very powerful control that's capable of displaying a complex hierarchical structure of items. Typically we'd use it to view a directory structure or a site navigation hierarchy, but it could be used to display a family tree, a corporate organizational structure, or any other hierarchical structure.

The `TreeView` can pull its data from various sources. You'll learn more about the various kinds of data sources later in the book; here, we'll focus on the `SiteMapDataSource` class, which, as its name suggests, contains a hierarchical sitemap. By default, this sitemap is read from a file called `Web.sitemap` located in the root of your project. The `Web.sitemap` file is an XML file that looks like this:

File: **Web.sitemap**

```
<siteMap
   xmlns="http://schemas.microsoft.com/AspNet/SiteMap-File-1.0">
  <siteMapNode title="Home" url="~/Default.aspx"
      description="Home">
    <siteMapNode title="TreeViewDemo" url="~/TreeViewDemo.aspx"
        description="TreeView Example" />
    <siteMapNode title="ClickEvent" url="~/ClickEvent.aspx"
        description="ClickEvent Example" />
    <siteMapNode title="Loops"  url="~/Loops.aspx"
        description="Loops Example" />
  </siteMapNode>
</siteMap>
```

Web.sitemap Limitation

An important limitation to note when working with Web.sitemap files is that they must contain only one siteMapNode as the direct child of the root siteMap element.

In the example above, the siteMapNode with the title Home is this single siteMapNode. If we added another siteMapNode alongside (rather than inside) this element, the Web.sitemap file would no longer be valid.

To use this file, you'll need to add a SiteMapDataSource control to the page, as well as a TreeView control that uses this data source, like this:

File: **TreeViewDemo.aspx (excerpt)**

```
<!DOCTYPE html PUBLIC "-//W3C//DTD XHTML 1.0 Strict//EN"
    "http://www.w3.org/TR/xhtml1/DTD/xhtml1-strict.dtd">
<html>
  <head>
    <title>TreeView Demo</title>
  </head>
  <body>
    <form runat="server">
      <asp:SiteMapDataSource ID="mySiteMapDataSource"
          runat="server" />
      <asp:TreeView ID="myTreeView" runat="server"
          DataSourceID="mySiteMapDataSource" />
    </form>
  </body>
</html>
```

Note that although the `SiteMapDataSource` is a control, it does not generate any HTML within the web page. There are many data source controls like this; we'll delve into this in more detail later.

When combined with the example `Web.sitemap` file above, this web form would generate an output such as that shown in Figure 4.7.

Figure 4.7. A simple `TreeView` control

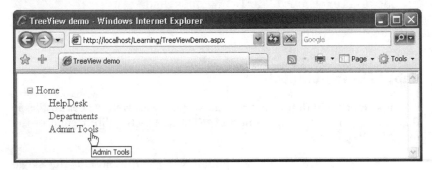

As you can see, the `TreeView` control generated the tree for us. The root Home node can even be collapsed or expanded.

In many cases, we don't want to show the root node; we can hide it from view by setting the `ShowStartingNode` property of the `SiteMapDataSource` to `false`:

```
<asp:SiteMapDataSource ID="mySiteMapDataSource" runat="server"
    ShowStartingNode="false" />
```

SiteMapPath

The `SiteMapPath` control provides the functionality to generate a **breadcrumb** navigational structure for your site. Breadcrumb systems help to orientate users, giving them an easy way to identify their current location within the site, and provide handy links to the current location's ancestor nodes. An example of a breadcrumb navigation system is shown in Figure 4.8.

The `SiteMapPath` control will automatically use any `SiteMapDataSource` control that exists in a web form to display a user's current location within the site. For example, you could simply add the following code to the form we worked with in the previous example to achieve the effect shown in Figure 4.8:

Figure 4.8. A breadcrumb created using the `SiteMapPath` control

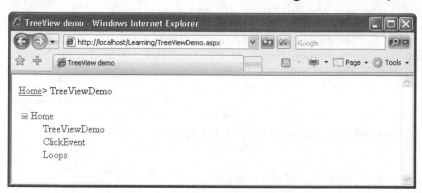

File: **TreeViewDemo.aspx (excerpt)**

```
<asp:SiteMapPath id="mySiteMapPath" runat="server"
    PathSeparator=" > ">
</asp:SiteMapPath>
```

If you run the example now, you'll see the breadcrumb appear exactly as it's shown in Figure 4.8.

Note that the `SiteMapPath` control shows only the nodes that correspond to existing pages of your site, so if you don't have a file named `Default.aspx`, the root node link won't show up. Similarly, if the page you're loading isn't named `TreeViewDemo.aspx`, the `SiteMapPath` control won't generate any output.

Menu

The `Menu` control is similar to `TreeView` in that it displays hierarchical data from a data source; the ways in which we work with both controls are also very similar. The most important differences between the two lie in their appearances, and the fact that `Menu` supports templates for better customization and displays only two levels of items (menu and submenu items).

MultiView

The `MultiView` control is similar to `Panel` in that it doesn't generate interface elements itself, but contains other controls. A `MultiView` can store more pages of data (called **views**), and lets you show one page at a time. You can change the active view (the one being presented to the visitor) by setting the value of the

ActiveViewIndex property. The first page corresponds to an ActiveViewIndex of 0, the second page is 1, the third page is 2, and so on.

The contents of each template are defined inside child View elements. Consider the following code snippet, which creates a Button control, and a MultiView control:

File: **MultiViewDemo.aspx (excerpt)**

```
<!DOCTYPE html PUBLIC "-//W3C//DTD XHTML 1.0 Strict//EN"
    "http://www.w3.org/TR/xhtml1/DTD/xhtml1-strict.dtd">
<html>
  <head>
    <title>MultiView Demo</title>
  </head>
  <body>
    <form runat="server">
      <p>
        <asp:Button id="myButton" Text="Switch Page"
            runat="server" OnClick="SwitchPage" />
      </p>
      <asp:MultiView ID="myMultiView" runat="server"
          ActiveViewIndex="0">
        <asp:View ID="firstView" runat="server">
          <p>... contents of the first view ...</p>
        </asp:View>
        <asp:View ID="secondView" runat="server">
          <p>... contents of the second view ...</p>
        </asp:View>
      </asp:MultiView>
    </form>
  </body>
</html>
```

As you can see, by default, the ActiveViewIndex is 0, so when this code is first executed, the MultiView will display its first template, shown in Figure 4.9.

Clicking on the button will cause the second template to be displayed. Here's the code for the SwitchPage event handler:

Visual Basic   File: **MultiViewDemo.aspx (excerpt)**

```
<script runat="server" language="VB">
  Sub SwitchPage(s as Object, e as EventArgs)
    myMultiView.ActiveViewIndex = _
      (myMultiView.ActiveViewIndex + 1) Mod 2
```

Figure 4.9. Using the `MultiView` control

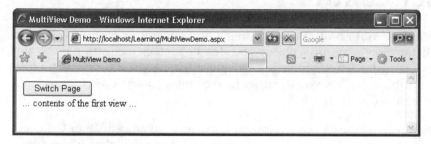

```
    End Sub
</script>
```

C#   File: **MultiViewDemo.aspx (excerpt)**

```
<script runat="server" language="C#">
  public void SwitchPage(Object s, EventArgs e)
  {
    myMultiView.ActiveViewIndex =
        (myMultiView.ActiveViewIndex + 1) % 2;
  }
</script>
```

This simple subroutine uses the modulo operator to set the `ActiveViewIndex` to 1 when its original value is 0, and vice versa.

The `MultiView` controls has a number of other handy features, so be sure to check the documentation for this control if you're using it in a production environment.

Wizard

The `Wizard` control is a more advanced version of the `MultiView` control. It's able to display one or more pages at a time, but also includes additional built-in functionality such as navigation buttons, and a sidebar that displays the wizard's steps.

FileUpload

The `FileUpload` control allows you to let visitors upload files to your server. You'll learn how to use this control in Chapter 14.

Web User Controls

As you build real-world projects, you'll frequently encounter pieces of the user interface that appear in multiple places—headers or footers, navigation links, and login boxes are just a few examples. Packaging their forms and behaviors into your own controls will allow you to reuse these components just as you can reuse ASP.NET's built-in controls.

Building your own web server controls involves writing advanced VB or C# code, and is not within the scope of this book, but it's good to know that it's possible. Creating customized web server controls makes sense when you need to build more complex controls that provide a high level of control and performance, or you want to create controls that can be integrated easily into many projects.

Those of us without advanced coding skills can develop our own controls by creating **web user controls**. These are also powerful and reusable within a given project; they can expose properties, events, and methods, just like other controls; and they're easy to implement.

A web user control is represented by a class that inherits from `System.Web.UI.UserControl`, and contains the basic functionality that you need to extend to create your own controls. The main drawback to using web user controls is that they're tightly integrated into the projects in which they're implemented. As such, it's more difficult to distribute them, or include them in other projects, than it is to distribute or reuse web server controls.

Web user controls are implemented very much like normal web forms—they're comprised of other controls, HTML markup, and server-side code. The file extension of a web user control is `.ascx`.

Creating a Web User Control

Let's get a feel for web user controls by stepping through a simple example. Let's say that in your web site, you have many forms consisting of pairs of `Label` and `TextBox` controls, like the one shown in Figure 4.10.

All the labels must have a fixed width of 100 pixels, and the text boxes must accept a maximum of 20 characters.

Rather than adding many labels and text boxes to the form, and then having to set all their properties, let's make life easier by building a web user control that

Figure 4.10. A simple form

includes a `Label` of the specified width, and a `TextBox` that accepts 20 characters; you'll then be able to reuse the web user control wherever it's needed in your project.

In your `Learning` folder, create a new file named `SmartBox.ascx`. Then, add the control's constituent controls—a `Label` control and a `TextBox` control—as shown below:

File: **SmartBox.ascx** (excerpt)

```
<p>
  <asp:Label ID="myLabel" runat="server" Text="" Width="100" />
  <asp:TextBox ID="myTextBox" runat="server" Text="" Width="200"
      MaxLength="20" />
</p>
```

Label Widths in Firefox

Unfortunately, setting the `Width` property of the `Label` control doesn't guarantee that the label will appear at that width in all browsers. The current version of Firefox, for example, will not display the above label in the way it appears in Internet Explorer.

To get around this, you should use a CSS style sheet and the `CssClass` property, which we'll take a look at later in this chapter.

In Chapter 3 we discussed properties briefly, but we didn't explain how you could create your own properties within your own classes. So far, you've worked with many properties of the built-in controls. For example, you've seen a lot of code that sets the `Text` property of the `Label` control.

As a web user control is a class, it can also have methods, properties, and so on. Our `SmartBox` control extends the base `System.Web.UI.UserControl` class by adding two properties:

❑ `LabelText` is a write-only property that allows the forms using the control to set the control's label text.

❑ `Text` is a read-only property that returns the text typed by the user in the text box.

Let's add a server-side `script` element that will give our control two properties — one called `Text`, for the text in the `TextBox`, and one called `LabelText`, for the text in the `Label`:

Visual Basic   File: **SmartBox.ascx (excerpt)**

```vb
<script runat="server" language="VB">
  Public WriteOnly Property LabelText() As String
    Set(ByVal value As String)
      myLabel.Text = value
    End Set
  End Property

  Public ReadOnly Property Text() As String
    Get
      Text = myTextBox.Text
    End Get
  End Property
</script>
```

C#   File: **SmartBox.ascx (excerpt)**

```csharp
<script runat="server" language="C#">
  public string LabelText
  {
    set
    {
      myLabel.Text = value;
    }
  }
  public string Text
  {
    get
    {
```

```
        return myTextBox.Text;
    }
  }
</script>
```

Just like web forms, web user controls can work with code-behind files, but, in an effort to keep our examples simple, we aren't using them here. You'll meet more complex web user controls in the chapters that follow.

When you use the `SmartBox` control in a form, you can set its label and have the text entered by the user, like this:

Visual Basic

```
mySmartBox.LabelText = "Address:"
userAddress = mySmartBox.Text
```

C#

```
mySmartBox.LabelText = "Address:";
userAddress = mySmartBox.Text;
```

Let's see how we implemented this functionality. In .NET, properties can be read-only, write-only, or read-write. In many cases, you'll want to have properties that can be both read and write, but in this case, we want to be able to set the text of the inner `Label`, and to read the text from the `TextBox`.

To define a write-only property in VB, you need to use the `WriteOnly` modifier. Write-only properties need only define a special block of code that starts with the keyword `Set`. This block of code, called an **accessor**, is just like a subroutine that takes as a parameter the value that needs to be set. The block of code uses this value to perform the desired action—in the case of the `LabelText` property, that action sets the `Text` property of our `Label` control, as shown below:

Visual Basic   File: **SmartBox.ascx (excerpt)**

```
Public WriteOnly Property LabelText() As String
  Set(ByVal value As String)
    myLabel.Text = value
  End Set
End Property
```

Assuming that a form uses a `SmartBox` object called `mySmartBox`, we could set the `Text` property of the `Label` like this:

Visual Basic

```
mySmartBox.LabelText = "Address:"
```

When this code is executed, the `Set` accessor of the `LabelText` property is executed with its *value* parameter set to `Address:`. The `Set` accessor uses this value to set the `Text` property of the `Label`.

The other accessor you can use when defining properties is `Get`; this allows us to read values instead of writing them. Obviously, you aren't allowed to add a `Get` accessor to a `WriteOnly` property, but one is required for a `ReadOnly` property, such as `Text`:

Visual Basic   File: **SmartBox.ascx (excerpt)**

```
Public ReadOnly Property Text() As String
  Get
    Text = myTextBox.Text
  End Get
End Property
```

The `Text` property is `ReadOnly`, but it doesn't need to be. If you wanted to allow the forms using the control to set some default text to the `TextBox`, you'd need to add a `Set` accessor, and remove the `ReadOnly` modifier.

When defining a property in C#, you don't need to set any special modifiers, such as `ReadOnly` or `WriteOnly`, for read-only or write-only properties. A property that has only a `get` accessor will, by default, be considered read-only:

C#   File: **SmartBox.ascx (excerpt)**

```
public string Text
{
  get
  {
    return myTextBox.Text;
  }
}
```

Likewise, a property that has only a `set` accessor will be considered to be write-only:

C#   File: **SmartBox.ascx (excerpt)**

```
public string LabelText
{
  set
  {
    myLabel.Text = value;
  }
}
```

Using the Web User Control

Once the user control has been created, it can be referenced from any ASP.NET page using the `Register` directive, as follows:

```
<%@ Register TagPrefix="prefix" TagName="name"
    Src="source.ascx" %>
```

The `Register` directive requires three attributes:

TagPrefix

> the prefix for the user control, which allows you to group related controls together, and avoid naming conflicts

TagName

> the control's tag name, which will be used when the control is added to the ASP.NET page

Src

> the path to the `.ascx` file that describes the user control

After registering the control, we create instances of it using the `<TagPrefix:Tag-Name>` format. Let's try an example that uses the `SmartBox` control. Create a new file named `ControlTest.aspx` in your `Learning` folder, and give it this content:

File: **ControlTest.aspx (excerpt)**

```
<%@ Register TagPrefix="sp" TagName="SmartBox"
    Src="SmartBox.ascx" %>
<!DOCTYPE html PUBLIC "-//W3C//DTD XHTML 1.0 Strict//EN"
    "http://www.w3.org/TR/xhtml1/DTD/xhtml1-strict.dtd">
<html>
  <head>
    <title>Creating ASP.NET Web Server Controls</title>
  </head>
  <body>
    <form id="Form1" runat="server">
      <sp:SmartBox id="nameSb" runat="server" LabelText="Name:" />
      <sp:SmartBox id="addressSb" runat="server"
          LabelText="Address:" />
      <sp:SmartBox id="countrySb" runat="server"
          LabelText="Country:" />
      <sp:SmartBox id="phoneSb" runat="server"
          LabelText="Phone:" />
    </form>
```

```
    </body>
</html>
```

Loading this page will produce the output we saw in Figure 4.10.

Now, this is a very simple example indeed, but we can easily extend it for other purposes. You can see in the code snippet that we set the `LabelText` property directly in the control's tag; we could have accessed the properties from our code instead. Here's an example:

Visual Basic   File: **ControlTest.aspx (excerpt)**

```
<script runat="server" language="VB">
  Protected Sub Page_Load()
    nameSb.LabelText = "Name:"
    addressSb.LabelText = "Address:"
    countrySb.LabelText = "Country:"
    phoneSb.LabelText = "Phone:"
  End Sub
</script>
```

C#   File: **ControlTest.aspx (excerpt)**

```
<script runat="server" language="C#">
  protected void Page_Load()
  {
    nameSb.LabelText = "Name:";
    addressSb.LabelText = "Address:";
    countrySb.LabelText = "Country:";
    phoneSb.LabelText = "Phone:";
  }
</script>
```

Master Pages

Master pages are a new feature of ASP.NET 2.0 that can make an important difference in the way we compose web forms. Master pages are similar to web user controls in that they are also composed of HTML and other controls; they can be extended with the addition of events, methods, or properties; and they can't be loaded directly by users—instead, they're used as building blocks to design the structure of your web forms.

A master page is a page template that can be applied to give many web forms a consistent appearance. For example, a master page can set out a standard structure containing the header, footer, and other elements that you expect to display in multiple web forms within a web application.

Master page files have the `.master` extension, and, just like web forms and web user controls, they support code-behind files. All master pages inherit from the class `System.Web.UI.MasterPage`.

Designing a site structure using master pages and web user controls gives you the power to easily modify and extend the site. If your site uses these features in a well-planned way, it can be very easy to modify certain details in the layout or functionality of your site, because updating a master page or a web user control has immediate effects on all the web forms that use the file.

As we've already mentioned, a master page is built using HTML and controls, including the special `ContentPlaceHolder` control. As its name suggests, the `ContentPlaceHolder` is a placeholder that can be filled with content relevant to the needs of each web form that uses the master page. In creating a master page, we include all of the basic structure of future pages in the master page itself, including the `<html>`, `<head>`, and `<body>` tags, and let the web forms specify the content that appears in the placeholders.

Let's see how this works with a simple example. Suppose we have a site which has many pages that contain a standard header, footer, and navigation menu, laid out as per the wireframe shown in Figure 4.11.

Figure 4.11. A simple web site layout

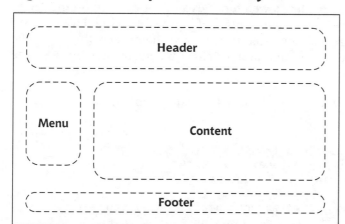

If all the pages in the site have the same header, footer, and navigation menu, it makes sense to include these components in a master page, and to build several web forms that customize only the content areas on each page. We'll begin to create such a site in Chapter 5, but let's work through a quick example here.

To keep this example simple, we won't include a menu here: we'll include just the header, the footer, and the content placeholder. In your Learning folder, create a new file named FrontPages.master, and write the following code into it:

File: **FrontPages.master (excerpt)**

```
<!DOCTYPE html PUBLIC "-//W3C//DTD XHTML 1.0 Strict//EN"
    "http://www.w3.org/TR/xhtml1/DTD/xhtml1-strict.dtd">
<html>
  <head>
    <title>Front Page</title>
  </head>
  <body>
    <form id="myForm" runat="server">
      <h1>Welcome to SuperSite Inc!</h1>
      <asp:ContentPlaceHolder id="FrontPageContent"
          runat="server" />
      <p>Copyright 2006</p>
    </form>
  </body>
</html>
```

The master page looks almost like a web form, except for one important detail: it has an empty ContentPlaceHolder control. If you want to build a web form based on this master page, you just need to reference the master page using the Page directive in the web form, and add a Content control that includes the content you want to insert.

Let's try it. Create a web form called FrontPage.aspx, and add this code to it:

File: **FrontPage.aspx (excerpt)**

```
<%@ Page MasterPageFile="FrontPages.master" %>
<asp:Content id="myContent" runat="server"
    ContentPlaceHolderID="FrontPageContent">
  <p>
    Welcome to our web site! We hope you'll enjoy your visit.
  </p>
</asp:Content>
```

You're all set now! Loading `FrontPage.aspx` in your browser will generate the output shown in Figure 4.12.

Figure 4.12. Using a master page

Although the example is simplistic, it's easy to see the possibilities: you can create many web forms based on this template very easily. In our case, the master page contains a single `ContentPlaceHolder`, but it could have more. Also, the master page can define some default content for display inside the `ContentPlaceHolder` on pages whose web forms don't provide a `Content` element for that placeholder.

Using Cascading Style Sheets (CSS)

It's clear that controls make it easy for us to reuse pieces of functionality in multiple places. For example, I can't imagine an easier way to add calendars to many web forms than to use the `Calendar` web server control.

However, controls don't solve the problem of defining and managing the visual elements of your web site. Modern web sites need constant updating to keep them fresh, and it's not much fun editing hundreds of pages by hand just to change a border color, for example, and then having to check everything to ensure that the changes are consistent. The process is even more painful if the client wants a more serious update, like rearranging components on the pages.

The good news is that this maintenance work can be made a lot easier by planning ahead, correctly following a few basic rules, and efficiently using the tools HTML and ASP.NET offer you.

An essential tool for building reusable visual styles is **CSS** (Cascading Style Sheets). HTML was initially designed to deliver simple text content, and paid little attention to the specifics of how particular items appeared in the browser. HTML left it to the individual browsers to work out these intricacies, and tailor the output to the limitations and strengths of users' machines. While we can change font styles, sizes, colors, and so on using HTML tags, this practice can lead to verbose code and pages that are very hard to restyle at a later date.

CSS gives web developers the power to create one set of styles in a single location, and to apply those styles to all of the pages in our web site. All the pages to which the style sheet is applied will display the same fonts, colors, and sizes, giving the site a consistent feel. Regardless of whether our site contains three pages or 300, when we alter the styles in the style sheet, our changes are immediately applied to all pages that use the style sheet.

Look out for Themes and Skins

ASP.NET 2.0 provides extra value and power to those building reusable visual elements through its offerings of **themes** and **skins**. You'll learn more about these features in Chapter 5.

Types of Styles and Style Sheets

There are three different ways in which we can associate styles to the elements of a particular web page:

using an external style sheet

By placing your **style rules** in an external style sheet, you can link this one file to web pages on which you want those styles to be used. This makes updating a web site's overall look a cakewalk.

To reference an external style sheet from a web form, insert the following markup inside the `head` element:

```
<link rel="stylesheet" type="text/css" href="file.css" />
```

In the above example, `file.css` would be a text file containing CSS rules, much like the example shown below:

```
a
{
  background: #ff9;
  color: #00f;
  text-decoration: underline;
}
```

using an embedded style sheet

You can place style rules for a page within `<style type="text/css">` tags inside that page's `head`.

```
<style type="text/css">
  a
  {
    background: #ff9;
    color: #00f;
    text-decoration: underline;
  }
</style>
```

The problem with using these "embedded" styles is that we can't reuse those styles in another page without having to type them in again, which makes global changes to the site very difficult to manage.

using inline style rules

Inline styles allow us to set styles for a single element using the `style` attribute. For instance, we might give a paragraph a border, and color it red, with the following markup:

```
<p style="border-style: groove; color: red;">
  Copyright 2006
</p>
```

When used in embedded or external style sheets, the first part of any style rule must determine the elements to which the rule will apply; we do this using a **selector**. In ASP.NET, we typically use two types of selectors:

element type selectors

An element type selector targets every single instance of the specified element. For example, if we wanted to change the colour of all level two headers in a document, we'd use an element type selector to target all `<h2>`s:

```
h2
{
  color: #369;
}
```

classes

Arguably the most popular way to use styles within your pages is to give each element a `class` attribute, then target elements that have a certain `class` value. For example, the following markup shows a paragraph whose `class` attribute is set to `fineprint`:

```
<p class="fineprint">
  Copyright 2006
</p>
```

Now, given that anything with the class `fineprint` should be displayed in, well, fine print, we can create a style rule that will reduce the size of the text in this paragraph, and any other element with the attribute `class="fineprint"`:

```
.fineprint
{
  font-family: Arial;
  font-size: x-small;
}
```

Whether you're building external style sheets, embedded style sheets, or inline style rules, style declarations use the same syntax.

Now that you have a basic understanding of some of the fundamental concepts behind CSS, let's look at the different types of styles that can be used within our ASP.NET applications.

Style Properties

You can modify many different types of properties using style sheets. Here's a list of the most common property types:

font
> This category provides you with the ability to format text level elements, including their font faces, sizes, decorations, weights, colors, etc.

background
> This category allows you to customize backgrounds for objects and text. These values give you control over the background, including whether you'd like to use a color or an image for the background, and whether or not you want to repeat a background image.

block
> This category allows you to modify the spacing between paragraphs, between lines of text, between words, and between letters.

box

> The box category allows us to customize tables. If you need to modify borders, padding, spacing, and colors on a table, row, or cell, use the elements within this category.

border

> This category lets you draw boxes of different colors, styles, and thicknesses around page elements.

list

> This category allows you to customize the way ordered and unordered lists are created.

positioning

> Modifying positioning allows you to move and position tags and controls freely.

These categories provide an outline of the aspects of a design that can typically be modified using CSS. As we progress through the book, the many types of style properties will become evident.

The `CssClass` Property

Once you've defined a class in a style sheet (be it external or internal), you'll want to begin to associate that class with elements in your Web Forms. You can associate classes with ASP.NET Web server controls using the `CssClass` property. In most cases, the value you give the `CssClass` property will be used as the value of the resulting element's `class` attribute.

Let's see an example. First, create in your `Learning` folder a file named `Styles.css`, and copy this code into it:

File: **Styles.css**

```
.title
{
  font-family: Arial, Helvetica, sans-serif;
  font-size: 19px
}
.dropdownmenu
{
  font-family: Arial;
  background-color: #0099FF;
}
```

```
.textbox
{
  font-family: Arial;
  background-color: #0099FF;
  border: 1px solid
}
.button
{
  font-family: Arial;
  background-color: #0099FF;
  border: 1px solid
}
```

Then, create a new file named UsingStyles.aspx with this code:

File: **UsingStyles.aspx (excerpt)**

```
<!DOCTYPE html PUBLIC "-//W3C//DTD XHTML 1.0 Strict//EN"
    "http://www.w3.org/TR/xhtml1/DTD/xhtml1-strict.dtd">
<html>
  <head>
    <title>Testing CSS</title>
    <link href="Styles.css" type="text/css" rel="stylesheet" />
  </head>
  <body>
    <form runat="server">
      <p class="title">Please select a product:</p>
      <p>
        <asp:DropDownList id="productsList"
            CssClass="dropdownmenu" runat="server">
          <asp:ListItem Text="Shirt" selected="true" />
          <asp:ListItem Text="Hat" />
          <asp:Listitem Text="Pants" />
          <asp:ListItem Text="Socks" />
        </asp:DropDownList>
      </p>
      <p>
        <asp:TextBox id="quantityTextBox" CssClass="textbox"
            runat="server" />
      </p>
      <p>
        <asp:Button id="addToCartButton" CssClass="button"
            Text="Add To Cart" runat="server"  />
      </p>
    </form>
  </body>
</html>
```

Loading this page should produce the output shown in Figure 4.13.

Figure 4.13. CSS at work

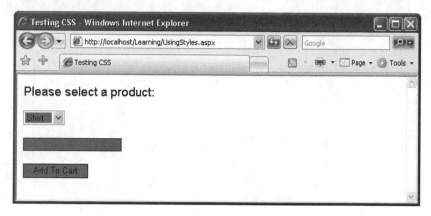

In the next chapter, we'll learn to use Visual Web Developer to create CSS definitions through a simple visual interface.

Summary

In this chapter, we discussed web forms, HTML server controls, web server controls, web user controls, master pages, and CSS. All these elements can be combined to create powerful structures for your web sites.

In the next chapter, we'll start building "real" web applications, putting into practice most of the theory you've learned so far, and using a professional development environment that will do part of the work for you.

5

Building Web Applications

In the previous chapters, we discussed the different pieces of ASP.NET in some detail. In this chapter, you'll put together everything you've learned so far as we place this new knowledge in context. That's right: it's time to build your own web application!

Microsoft defines a web application as the collection of all files, pages, handlers, modules, and executable code that can be invoked or run within a given directory on a web server. The tool we recommend you use as you learn to build ASP.NET web applications is Visual Web Developer 2005 Express Edition, which is free but very powerful. You learned how to install this tool in Chapter 1, and in this chapter, we'll teach you how to use it to its full potential.

It's worth keeping in mind that you don't have to use Visual Web Developer, or any other specialized tool, to develop ASP.NET web applications: any old text editor will do. However, we recommend using Visual Web Developer for any real-world project that's more complex than a simple, "Hello World"-type example, because this tool can do a lot of the work for you as you build web applications.

Using Visual Studio

If you have access to Microsoft's commercial Visual Studio program, you could make use of that instead of Visual Web Developer. When Visual Studio is started in Web Developer mode, its interface will look very similar to what you'll see in this book. Visual Studio has a lot more features than

Visual Web Developer, and a few of the tools are named differently to reflect this. For example, the Database Explorer window of Visual Web Developer is named Server Explorer in Visual Studio. For the purposes of this book, these tools are equivalent, and you should feel free to use Visual Studio if you have access to it.

In this chapter, you'll learn about much of the functionality Visual Web Developer offers as we start to create an intranet for a company called Dorknozzle. Along the way, we'll also explore many interesting ASP.NET features:

❏ We'll use Visual Web Developer to create web applications and edit files.

❏ We'll work with `Web.config`, `Global.asax`, and the special ASP.NET folders.

❏ We'll use the application state, user sessions, the application cache, and cookies.

❏ We'll debug your project and handle potential coding errors.

Introducing the Dorknozzle Project

While most books give you a series of simple, isolated examples to illustrate particular techniques, this book is a little different. Most of the examples provided in these pages will see us working on a single project: an intranet application for a fictional company called Dorknozzle. We'll build on this application as we move through the remaining chapters of this book—the Dorknozzle intranet will give us a chance to investigate and grasp the many different concepts that are important to developers of any type of web application.

Now, real-world web development projects are built according to a detailed specification document, which includes, among other information, specific details of the site's layout. We'll assume that the pages in the Dorknozzle intranet will be laid out as shown in Figure 5.1.

The menu on the left suggests that the site will have more pages than this homepage, and that they'll have the same structure: on every page of the site, the menu will sit on the left, and the header will be identical to the one shown here. Only the contents of each individual page will be different from the others. (If you paid attention in Chapter 4, you'll already have realized that this is a scenario where it makes sense to use master pages.)

The intranet application we'll develop will offer the following functionality:

Figure 5.1. The Dorknozzle company intranet site

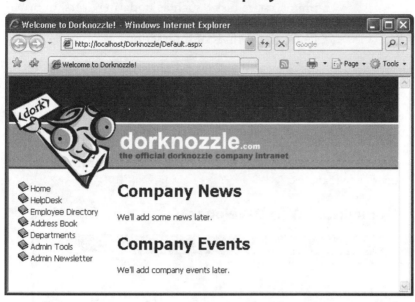

homepage

You can customize this page by including news about the Dorknozzle company.

help desk

This page allows Dorknozzle employees to submit problems they experience with software, hardware, or their computers, as help desk tickets that are sent to an IT administrator.

employee directory

Employees will likely want to call each other to discuss important, company-related affairs ... such as last night's television viewing! The employee directory should let employees find other staff members' details quickly and easily.

address book

While the employee directory houses handy information for staff use, the purpose of the address book is to provide more detailed information about every employee within the company.

departments

The Departments page displays information about Dorknozzle's various departments.

admin tools   Administrators will need the ability to perform various administrative tasks, such as updating users' information. The Admin Tools section will provide the interface for these kinds of interactions.

admin newsletter   This page will allow administrators to send email newsletters to the company employees.

You'll learn new techniques when building each of these pages. However, before you can begin to create all these smaller applications, we'll need to build the framework that will act as a template for the site as a whole. Visual Web Developer will prove very helpful in such a project, so let's start our discussion by getting a feel for its key features.

Figure 5.2. Using Visual Web Developer

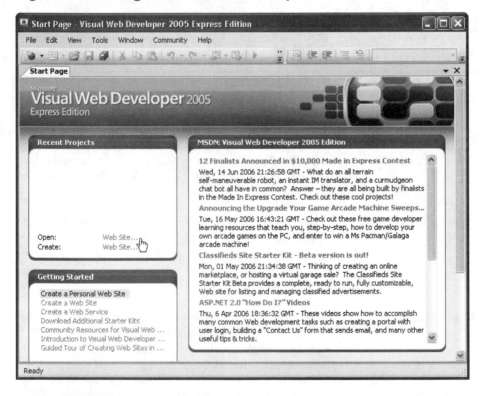

Using Visual Web Developer

The first step in learning how to use this tool is, obviously, starting it up. Access Start > All Programs > Microsoft Visual Web Developer 2005 Express Edition. You'll be welcomed by a page that looks something like the one shown in Figure 5.2.

Let's start by creating a new web site. Select File > New Web Site…, or click the Web Site… link next to the Create label.

In the dialog that appears, which is shown in Figure 5.3, select the ASP.NET Web Site template, choose the web site's default language, and identify the location at which the web site should be created. Feel free to choose the language with which you feel most comfortable, and remember that you can choose different languages for use in different files, so if you're not sure which language is your favorite just yet, don't worry. For the location, create a folder named `Dorknozzle` located in the `WebDocs` folder you've been working with so far. You can create this folder by entering its path into the Location field. If you placed `WebDocs` in the root folder of `C:\`, the location will be `C:\WebDocs\Dorknozzle`.

Figure 5.3. Creating a new web site project

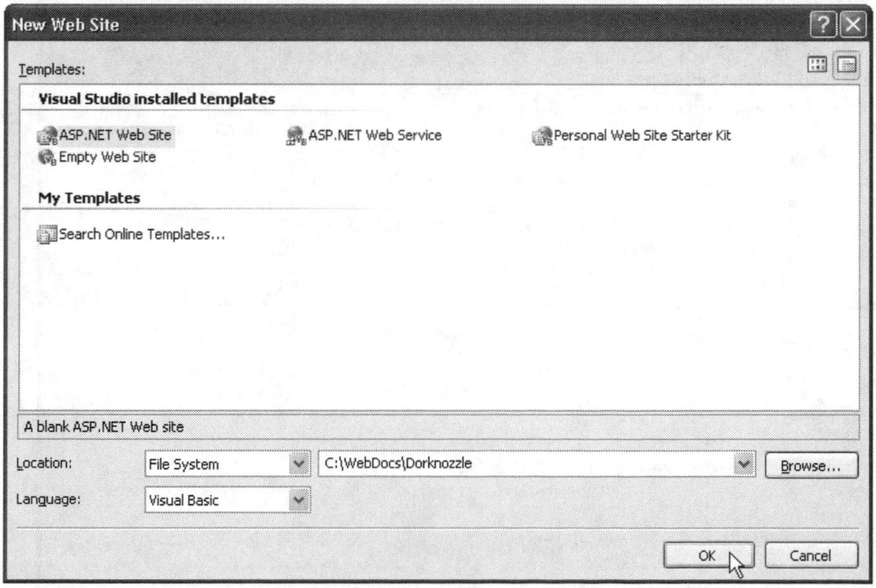

147

The Location Drop-down

Wondering what's implied by setting Location to File System? Earlier, we mentioned that Visual Web Developer contains a built-in web server. When you're working with a web site project that's saved to the file system, Visual Web Developer's web server is used to execute the project.

You can create a new web project in IIS by changing the Location to HTTP. In that case, you'd need to specify an HTTP location, such as **http://loc-alhost/Dorknozzle**. If you did so, Visual Web Developer would create a new folder named **Dorknozzle** in the web server's root directory. We'll take a look at IIS (or Cassini) a bit later.

Meeting the Features

Once you click OK, your project will be created, along with a few default files, and you'll be presented with the first page of your project. It should look something like the one shown in Figure 5.4.

Figure 5.4. Your new Dorknozzle web application

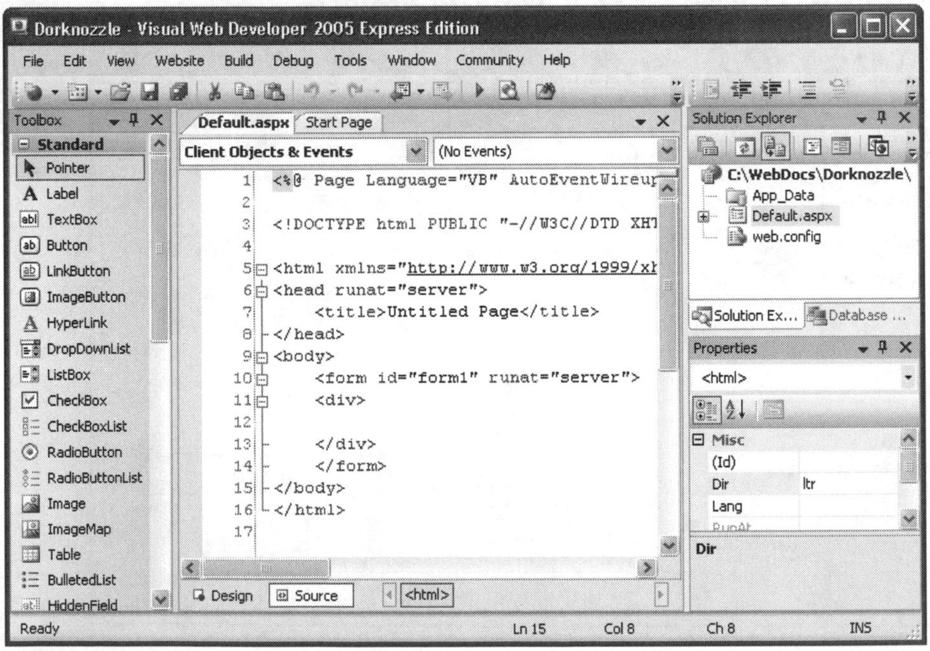

![Screenshot of Dorknozzle - Visual Web Developer 2005 Express Edition showing the Default.aspx source code with Toolbox on the left, the code editor in the center, and Solution Explorer and Properties panels on the right.]

Don't be daunted by the many forms and windows around your screen—each has something to offer! Visual Web Developer is very flexible, so you can resize, relocate, or regroup the interface elements that appear. We'll spend the next few pages taking a brief tour of these windows, though we'll discover even more as we progress through the chapters of this book.

The Solution Explorer

The Solution Explorer, which by default is located in the upper right-hand part of the Visual Web Developer window, provides the main view of your project, and displays the files of which your project is composed. As Figure 5.5 shows, the root node is the location of your project; beneath the root node you can see that Visual Web Developer has already created other elements for you.

Figure 5.5. The Solution Explorer

The files that are created for you will differ depending on the type of project you're working on, and the language you've chosen. If you're using C#, `Web.config` won't appear in your list. Don't worry—we'll create this file later.

Let's review the functions of the three child nodes shown in Figure 5.5:

❑ `App_Data` is a special folder that ASP.NET uses to store database files. You'll learn more about this folder in Chapter 13.

❑ `Default.aspx` is the default web form that Visual Web Developer creates for you. If you look closely, you'll see that you can expand the `Default.aspx` node by clicking the + sign to its left. If you expand the node, you'll find a code-behind file named `Default.aspx.vb`, or `Default.aspx.cs`, depending on the language you selected when you started the project. Visual Web Developer can work with web forms that use a code-behind file, as well as with those that don't.

❑ Web.config is your web application's configuration file. By editing Web.config, you can set numerous predefined configuration options for your project (for instance, you can enable debug mode). You can also define your own custom project-wide settings that can then be read from your code (such as the administrator's email address, the project name, your favorite color, or any other simple value you'd like to store in a central place). We'll come back to this file later in the chapter.

An icon sits beside each node, reflecting its type. If you right-click on each node, a list of options that are specific to that particular node type will appear. For example, right-click on the root node, and you'll see a list of options that affect the project as a whole. Double-click on a file, and that file will open in an appropriate editor (for instance, double-clicking on a web form will open that file in the Web Forms Designer).

The Web Forms Designer

The Web Forms Designer is the place where you'll spend most of your time working with Visual Web Developer. The Web Forms Designer is a very powerful tool that allows you to edit web forms, web user controls, and master pages. You can edit these files in Source View, where you can see their code, or in Design View, which provides a WYSIWYG (what you see is what you get) interface.

By default, when you start a new web site project, the Web Forms Designer will display the contents of Default.aspx, as illustrated in Figure 5.6.

Tabbed quick links to the currently open files or windows appear at the top of the interface. In Figure 5.6, only Default.aspx, and the Start Page (the window that was initially loaded when Visual Web Developer started) are open. Each kind of file is opened by a different editor or designer, so when you open a database table, for example, you'll see a different view from the one shown in Figure 5.6.

If you click the Design button at the bottom of the Web Forms Designer, you'll see a WYSIWYG interface that's similar to those of Dreamweaver, FrontPage, and other similar tools. Since there's no content in the page as yet, you'll see an empty window, but you can populate it by typing text, or dragging controls from the Toolbox (which we'll discuss in a moment) onto the page. In Figure 5.7, I've typed **Hello World!** into the Design View.

Now, if you switch back to Source View, you'll see that the text you just entered into the visual editor has been inserted into the page's source for you. If you've

Figure 5.6. Viewing `Default.aspx` in Web Forms Designer's Source View

Figure 5.7. Editing your form in Design View

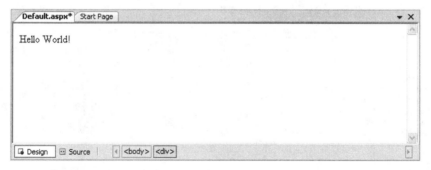

worked with other tools, you'll appreciate that Visual Web Developer applies minimal reformatting to the code you typed.

The Code Editor

As well as editing web forms, web developers commonly edit those forms' code-behind files. You'll work with code-behind files as you build the Dorknozzle project—in particular, they help us to keep a clear separation between the layout and logic of nontrivial projects.

If you've opened a web form in the Web Forms Designer, you can easily switch to its code-behind file: click the View Code icon in the Solution Explorer, right-click the Web Form in Solution Explorer, and select View Code; alternatively, expand the Web Form's node in Solution Explorer and double-click its code-behind file.

Do this to open the code-behind file for `Default.aspx`. If you chose VB as your preferred language when you created the project, the code-behind file will be called `Default.aspx.vb`, and will look like the one shown in Figure 5.8.

Figure 5.8. Editing `Default.aspx.vb`

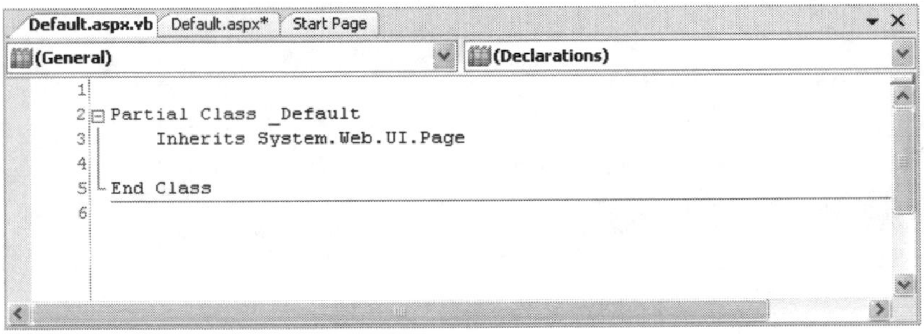

Figure 5.9. Editing `Default.aspx.cs`

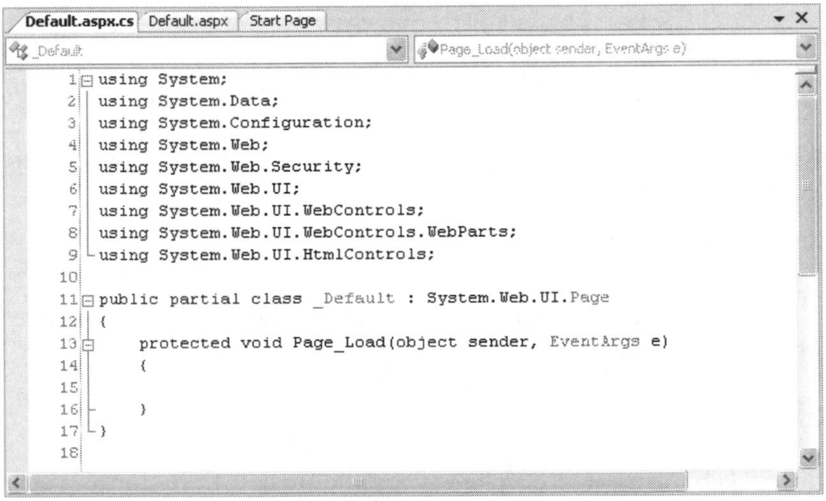

If you chose C# as your preferred language when you started the project, then you'll see a slightly different code-behind file—something like the one pictured in Figure 5.9.

As you can see, the C# version contains a number of namespace references. But, for the VB template, Visual Web Developer adds these references to the `Web.config` file, thereby applying them to the whole project. This explains why a `Web.config` file is created for those who choose VB, but not for those using C#. In the end, the functionality is very similar, but the Visual Web Developer designers chose to implement this functionality differently for each language. Of course, it's possible to add the namespace references to `Web.config` yourself if you're using C#.

The – icons to the left of certain sections of your file (such as the starting points of classes and methods) allow you to collapse those sections, which can help you to manage larger code files. In Figure 5.10, I've collapsed the section of `Default.aspx.cs` that contains the namespace references—you can see that the `using` statements have been collapsed into a single ellipsis. If you hover your cursor over the ellipsis, you'll see a preview of the hidden text.

Figure 5.10. Playing around with Visual Web Developer

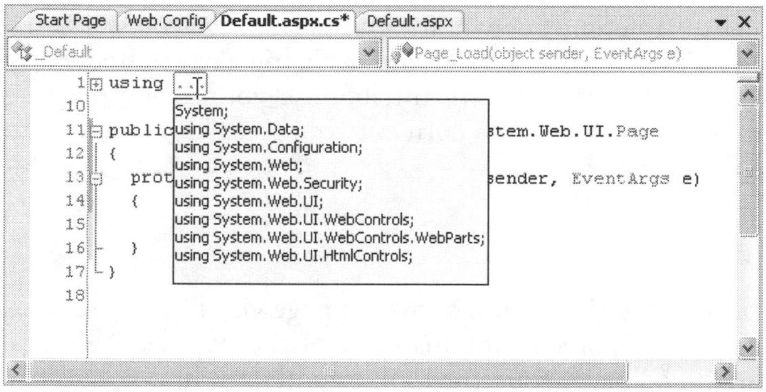

IntelliSense

IntelliSense is a fantastic code autocompletion feature that Microsoft has included in the Visual Studio line for some time. In its latest incarnation as part of Visual Web Developer 2005 Express Edition, IntelliSense is pretty close to perfection. This feature alone makes it more worthwhile to use Visual Web Developer than simpler code editors.

Let's do a quick test. If you're using VB, delete a character from the end of the `Inherits System.Web.UI.Page` line in `Default.aspx.vb`. As Figure 5.11 shows, IntelliSense will automatically display other words that could be used in that position.

Figure 5.11. IntelliSense displaying possible word autocompletions

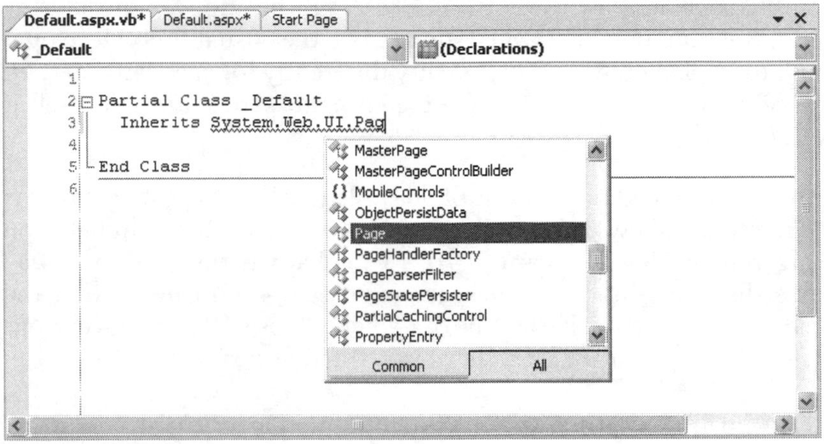

IntelliSense behaves slightly differently depending on the language you've chosen to use. For example, if you're using C#, IntelliSense isn't triggered as frequently as it is for those using VB. You can activate IntelliSense yourself by pressing **Ctrl-Space**. Then, once you've selected the correct entry, press **Tab** or **Enter** to have the word completed for you.

The Toolbox

While editing a web form, web user control, or master page visually, the Toolbox will come in very handy. The Toolbox contains most of the popular ASP.NET controls, which you can drag directly from the toolbox and drop into your form. You must be viewing a form in the Web Forms Designer to see the proper controls in the Toolbox. If you can't see the toolbox, which is shown in Figure 5.12, select View > Toolbox to make it appear.

Let's give it a test-drive: double-click on the `TextBox` entry, or drag it from the Toolbox to the form, to have a `TextBox` control added to your form.

The controls listed in the Toolbox are grouped within tabs that can be expanded and collapsed. In the Standard tab of the Toolbox, you'll find the standard web

Figure 5.12. The Toolbox

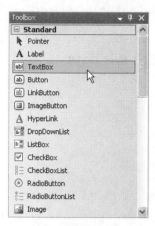

server controls we discussed in Chapter 4. In the other tabs, you'll find other controls, including the validation controls we'll discuss in Chapter 6, which can be found in the Validation tab. Figure 5.13 shows the toolbox with all its tabs in the collapsed state.

Figure 5.13. The collapsed Toolbox tabs

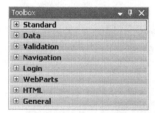

The Properties Window

When you select a control in the web forms designer, its properties are displayed automatically in the Properties window. For example, if you select the `TextBox` control we added to the form earlier, the properties of that `TextBox` will display in the Properties window. If it's not visible, you can make it appear by selecting View > Properties Window.

The Properties window doesn't just allow you to see the properties—it also lets you set them. Many properties—such as the colors that can be chosen from a palette—can be set visually, but in other cases, complex dialogs are available to help you establish the value of a property. In Figure 5.14, the properties of the TextBox are displayed in the Properties window, and the BackColor property is being altered.

Figure 5.14. Setting a color using the Properties window

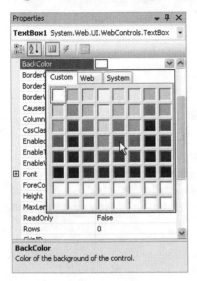

By default, the control's properties are listed by category, but you can order them alphabetically by clicking the A–Z button. Other buttons in the window allow you to switch between Properties View and Events View.

Executing your Project

You already know from our work back in Chapter 1 that, in order to execute an ASP.NET application, you need to run it through a web server such as IIS. Unfortunately, users of Windows XP Home Edition can't use IIS, so until now, you've most likely been using Cassini, a lightweight web server that Microsoft has made available for development purposes. Here, we're going to take a look at another option—Visual Web Developer's built-in web server. We'll also see how you can use Visual Web Developer to execute your project through IIS.

Using Visual Web Developer's Built-in Web Server

As you already know, Visual Web Developer has an integrated web server, which makes it easy to develop ASP.NET web sites even on machines whose operating systems don't have IIS—Windows XP Home Edition, for example.

To test the web server, we'll use a simplified version of the `Hello.aspx` file we first saw back in Chapter 2, only this time we'll name it `Default.aspx`.

Visual Basic   File: **Default.aspx**

```
<%@ Page Language="VB" %>
<!DOCTYPE html PUBLIC "-//W3C//DTD XHTML 1.0 Strict//EN"
    "http://www.w3.org/TR/xhtml1/DTD/xhtml1-strict.dtd">
<html>
  <head>
    <title>Hello, World!</title>
    <script runat="server">
      Sub Page_Load()
        messageLabel.Text = "Hello, World!"
      End Sub
    </script>
  </head>
  <body>
    <form id="form1" runat="server">
      <asp:Label id="messageLabel" runat="server" />
    </form>
  </body>
</html>
```

C#   File: **Default.aspx**

```
<%@ Page Language="C#" %>
<!DOCTYPE html PUBLIC "-//W3C//DTD XHTML 1.0 Strict//EN"
    "http://www.w3.org/TR/xhtml1/DTD/xhtml1-strict.dtd">
<html>
  <head>
    <title>Hello, World!</title>
    <script runat="server">
      void Page_Load()
      {
        messageLabel.Text = "Hello, World!";
      }
    </script>
  </head>
  <body>
    <form runat="server">
```

```
      <asp:Label id="messageLabel" runat="server" />
    </form>
  </body>
</html>
```

You can start the web server by executing the project: select Debug > Start Without Debugging, or use the keyboard shortcut **Ctrl-F5**. Visual Web Developer will load `Hello.aspx` in your system's default web browser, as shown in Figure 5.15.

Figure 5.15. Executing a page using Visual Web Developer

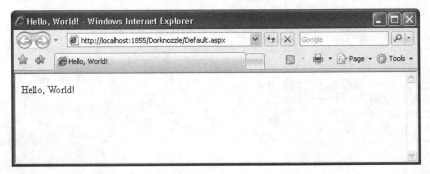

We executed this project without debugging it, but generally you'll want to run projects with debugging enabled (using **F5**, or Debug > Start Debugging). The debugging features enable you to find and fix errors in your code; we'll learn more about them towards the end of this chapter.

To enable debugging, you must modify an option in a file called `Web.config`, which is your web application's configuration file. We'll take a more in-depth look at `Web.config` shortly. For now, all you need to know is that the first time you try to debug the project, Visual Web Developer will ask you whether you want to enable debugging in `Web.config` using a dialog like the one in Figure 5.16. Click OK to confirm the action.

Once you click OK, the application will execute. The resulting browser window should be the same as the one we saw in Figure 5.15, but this time you have more control over your application, as we'll soon see.

You can tell that your application doesn't run through your local IIS if you look at the URL loaded in the browser window. When you execute a project using the integrated web server, it will run on a random port, and the complete URL location will reflect the physical path. In Figure 5.15, you can see that the integrated web server was running on port 1855, which explains the complete URL: `http://loc-`

Figure 5.16. Enabling Debug Mode in Visual Web Developer

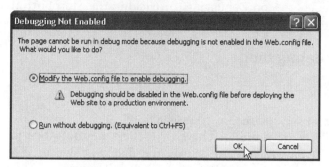

alhost:1855/Dorknozzle/Default.aspx. IIS usually runs on the default port, which explains why it doesn't need to be mentioned explicitly.

Visual Web Developer's web server displays one small icon in the system tray for each web server instance that's running. If you run multiple projects at the same time, more web servers will be created and more icons will appear. If you double-click on one of those icons, you'll be presented with a dialog that contains the web server details, and looks very much like the window shown in Figure 5.17.

Figure 5.17. Visual Web Developer's web server in action

As it executes the project, Visual Web Developer will launch your system's default web browser, but you can make it use another browser if you wish. For the purpose of running and debugging your ASP.NET web applications, you might find it easier to use Internet Explorer as your default browser, as it works a little better with Visual Web Developer than do other browsers. For example, if you close the Internet Explorer window while your project runs in debug mode, Visual Web

Developer will stop the application automatically. Otherwise, you'd need to stop it manually by selecting Debug > Stop Debugging, or clicking the Stop button shown in Figure 5.18.

Figure 5.18. Stopping debug mode

To change the browser that's used to execute your web applications, first make sure that none of your projects are running. Then, right-click the root node in Solution Explorer, and select Browse With to display the dialog shown in Figure 5.19. Select Internet Explorer, click Set as Default, and click Browse.

Figure 5.19. Setting the default browser in Visual Web Developer

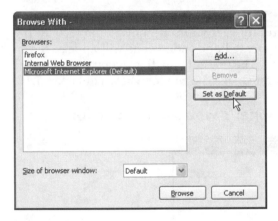

Using IIS

You can continue your journey through this book using Visual Web Developer's integrated web server, or you can make use of IIS. Although Microsoft recommends that we stick with Visual Web Developer for learning purposes, it's very easy to use IIS. Even if you develop your application using the integrated web server, it's beneficial to test your application using IIS as well, because when it's shipped to production, your application will end up running on an IIS server anyway.

To run your web application using IIS, you'll need to create an IIS virtual directory and make it point to the project's physical folder on the disk. We'll create a virtual directory named `Dorknozzle`, so the URL of your web application will be `http://localhost/Dorknozzle`.

Start by opening the Internet Services Manager by selecting Start > All Programs > Administrative Tools > Internet Information Services. In the tree in the left-hand pane, right-click the Default Web Site node, and choose New > Virtual Directory from the context menu, as shown in Figure 5.20.

Figure 5.20. Creating a new virtual directory

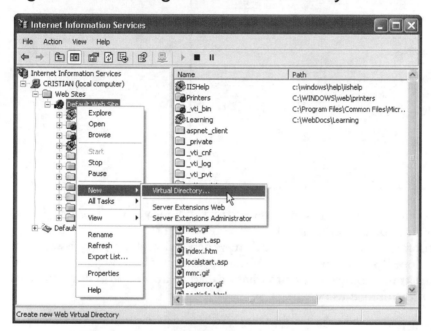

The Virtual Directory Creation Wizard will appear and, in its second screen, will ask you to specify an alias for your virtual directory. Choose `Dorknozzle`. The next screen will ask you for the path to this virtual folder—choose `C:\Web-Docs\Dorknozzle` (or the folder you've used). Leave all the other settings to their defaults. After the wizard closes, you'll be able to see your new virtual folder as a child of the Default Web Site node.

Let's spend some time learning about your new virtual directory. Right-click the Dorknozzle node in the Internet Services Manager, and choose Properties. A dialog like the one shown in Figure 5.21 will open, allowing you to configure the virtual directory's properties.

Figure 5.21. Editing the virtual directory's properties

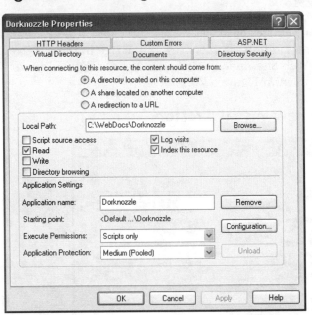

The Virtual Directory tab shows the basic settings of your virtual directory. If you look below the Application Settings header, you can see that the virtual directory has been configured as an **IIS Application**. When a virtual directory is set as an IIS application, IIS takes special care of that location by isolating all of that directory's pages and subdirectories into what's called an **application domain**. This approach offers numerous benefits:

code isolation
Code that executes within one application can't access code in other applications. So even if we built an intranet web application for a company's staff, then placed a separate application for external users on the same web server, code would never cross-reference or conflict between those two applications.

application stabilization
Each application is isolated from all others, so if one application crashes or stops running, it has no effect on other applications that might be running on the same web server.

application level security policies

You can set different permissions for the different applications on the server. What this means is that the credentials that are used to log into one application can be totally different from those used to access a second application on the same server. We'll discuss this in detail in Chapter 13.

settings configuration on a per-application basis

You can affect numerous other configuration settings for each application through Internet Services Manager, or `Global.asax` and `Web.config`, which are two special files located in the root directory of the application.

The `Global.asax` file handles application-wide events and sets application-wide directives, while the `Web.config` file specifies configuration settings for the application. In addition to these two special files, every ASP.NET web application can contain a number of special folders, such as `App_Themes`, `App_Code` or `App_Data`. We'll talk more about these details a little later in this chapter.

Applications and Visual Web Developer's Web Server

When you use Visual Web Developer's integrated web server to run your project, the virtual directory it creates for you on the spot is also set as an application, so it, too, enjoys all the benefits mentioned above.

Select the Virtual Directory tab in the Dorknozzle Properties dialog. If you click the Remove button that appears next to the application name, be aware that the action won't remove the virtual directory itself: it will remove that application's IIS application properties. When you click Remove, the button will be replaced by a Create button, which will reinstate the directory as an IIS application.

Figure 5.22. Adding a default name for the document

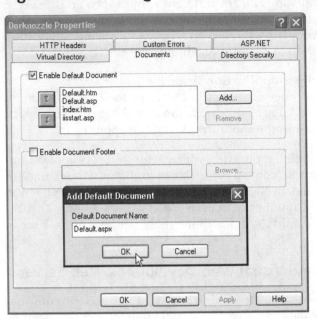

While you're here, it's a good idea to check that `Default.aspx` is included as a default file. If it is, then requesting `http://localhost/Dorknozzle` will load `http://localhost/Dorknozzle/Default.aspx` by default. To check this, click the Documents tab. If `Default.aspx` isn't in the list, add it by clicking the Add… button and entering the filename, as shown in Figure 5.22.

Finally, click OK to close the Dorknozzle Properties window.

If no default document exists in the `Dorknozzle` folder, the web server will attempt to return a list of the files and folders inside the `Dorknozzle` folder—an operation that will only succeed if the Directory Browsing option shown in Figure 5.21 is enabled. If this option is left in its default, disabled state, this operation will result in an error.

Now, if you load `http://localhost/Dorknozzle/` using any web browser, you should see a little magic (as Figure 5.23 reveals)!

Figure 5.23. Loading the web application through IIS

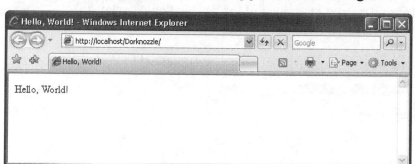

Does it look familiar? This is the exact same page you saw in Figure 5.15, but this time, the URL shows that it has loaded through the default web server, which, in this case, is IIS.

Using IIS with Visual Web Developer

Once you've prepared your virtual directory, you can access it through Visual Web Developer. First, select File > Close Project in Visual Web Developer to close the current project. It's okay to save the changes if the system prompts you to do so. If the project is currently running in debug mode, you'll also be asked to confirm that you want to stop debugging.

Next, select File > Open Web Site, select Local IIS in the left-hand pane, select Dorknozzle from the pane on the right, and click Open, as illustrated in Figure 5.24.

Figure 5.24. Opening a web application through IIS

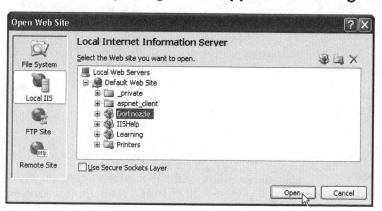

The project will open. This time, the root entry in Solution Explorer will be ht-tp://localhost/Dorknozzle/ instead of c:\WebDocs\Dorknozzle\, as Figure 5.25 indicates.

Figure 5.25. Solution Explorer displaying an HTTP location

Visual Web Developer knows how to investigate your IIS location and display its contents automatically in the Solution Explorer. If the folder contents are changed outside of Visual Web Developer, you'll need to right-click the root node and select Refresh Folder to refresh Visual Web Developer's display of the directory's contents.

Core Web Application Features

Let's continue our exploration of the key topics related to developing ASP.NET web applications. We'll put them into practice as we move through the book, but in this quick introduction, we'll discuss:

❑ Web.config

❑ Global.asax

❑ user sessions

❑ caching

❑ cookies

Web.config

Almost every ASP.NET web application contains a file named Web.config, which stores various application settings. By default, all ASP.NET web applications are configured in the `Machine.config` file, which contains machine-wide settings, and lives in the `C:\WINDOWS\Microsoft.NET\Framework\`*version*`\CONFIG` directory.

For the most part, you won't want to make any modifications to this file. However, you can override certain settings of the `Machine.config` file by adding a `Web.config` file to the root directory of your application. You may already have this file in your project; if you don't, you can add one by accessing File > New File..., then selecting Web Configuration File from the dialog that appears.

The `Web.config` file is an XML file that can hold configuration settings for the application in which the file resides. One of the most useful settings that `Web.config` controls is ASP.NET's debug mode. If you're using VB, you can enable debug mode by opening `Web.config` and editing the compilation element, which looks like this:

File: **Web.config (excerpt)**

```
<!--
    Set compilation debug="true" to insert debugging
    symbols into the compiled page. Because this
    affects performance, set this value to true only
    during development.

    Visual Basic options:
    Set strict="true" to disallow all data type conversions
    where data loss can occur.
    Set explicit="true" to force declaration of all variables.
-->
<compilation debug="false" strict="false" explicit="true" />
```

Enabling debug mode is as simple as changing the value of the `debug` attribute to `true`. The other attributes listed here were added by Visual Web Developer to offer a helping hand to VB developers migrating from older versions. For example, `strict="false"` makes the compiler forgive some of the mistakes we might make, such as using the wrong case in variable names.

If you're using C#, you'll need to create the `Web.config` file yourself. Go to File > New File..., then select Web Configuration File from the dialog that appears, and click Add. This will create the default `Web.config` file, which will contain the following section:

File: **Web.config (excerpt)**

```
<!--
    Set compilation debug="true" to insert debugging
```

```
    symbols into the compiled page. Because this
    affects performance, set this value to true only
    during development.
-->
<compilation debug="false" />
```

Once again, set `debug` to `true` to enable ASP.NET's debugging features.

`Web.config` can also be used to store custom information for your application in a central location that's accessible from all the pages of your site. For example, you might want to store the email address of someone in your technical support team so it can be changed easily, so you might take the approach shown here:

File: **Web.config** (excerpt)

```
<configuration>
  <appSettings>
    <add key="SupportEmail" value="support@dorknozzle.com" />
  </appSettings>
</configuration>
```

This way, whenever you need to display or use an email address for technical support within the site, you can simply read the `SupportEmail` key using the `WebConfigurationManager` class. And, if you wanted to change the email address you used for technical support, you'd just need to change this setting in `Web.config`.

Another aid for VB users, the default `Web.config` file generated by Visual Web Developer contains a number of namespace references:

File: **Web.config** (excerpt)

```
<pages>
  <namespaces>
    <clear/>
    <add namespace="System"/>
    <add namespace="System.Collections"/>
    <add namespace="System.Collections.Specialized"/>
    <add namespace="System.Configuration"/>
    <add namespace="System.Text"/>
    <add namespace="System.Text.RegularExpressions"/>
    <add namespace="System.Web"/>
    <add namespace="System.Web.Caching"/>
    <add namespace="System.Web.SessionState"/>
    <add namespace="System.Web.Security"/>
    <add namespace="System.Web.Profile"/>
    <add namespace="System.Web.UI"/>
```

```
      <add namespace="System.Web.UI.WebControls"/>
      <add namespace="System.Web.UI.WebControls.WebParts"/>
      <add namespace="System.Web.UI.HtmlControls"/>
    </namespaces>
</pages>
```

We can use classes from these namespaces in our code without needing to reference them in every file in which they're used. As you can see, Visual Web Developer tries to offer an extra level of assistance for VB developers, but users of C# (or any other language) could also add these namespace references to `Web.config`.

You'll learn more about working with `Web.config` as you progress through this book, so if you wish, you can skip the rest of these details for now, and come back to them later as you need them.

The `Web.config` file's root element is always `configuration`, which can contain three different types of elements:

configuration section groups

As ASP.NET and the .NET Framework are so configurable, configuration files could easily become jumbled if we didn't have a way to break the files into groups of related settings. A number of predefined section grouping tags let you do just that. For example, settings specific to ASP.NET must be placed inside a `system.web` section grouping element, while settings that are relevant to .NET's networking classes belong inside a `system.net` element.

General settings, like the `appSettings` element we saw above, stand on their own, outside the section grouping tags. In this book, though, our configuration files will also contain a number of ASP.NET-specific settings, which live inside the `system.web` element.

configuration sections

These are the actual setting tags in our configuration file. Since a single element can contain a number of settings (e.g. the `appSettings` element we saw earlier could contain a number of different strings for use by the application), Microsoft calls each of these tags a "configuration section." ASP.NET provides a wide range of built-in configuration sections to control the various aspects of your web applications.

The following list outlines some of the commonly used ASP.NET configuration sections, all of which must appear within the `system.web` section grouping element:

authentication

outlines configuration settings for user authentication, and is covered in detail in Chapter 14

authorization

specifies users and roles, and controls their access to particular files within an application; discussed more in Chapter 14.

compilation

contains settings that are related to page compilation, and lets you specify the default language that's used to compile pages

customErrors

used to customize the way errors display

globalization

used to customize character encoding for requests and responses

pages

handles the configuration options for specific ASP.NET pages; allows you to disable session state, buffering, and view state, for example

sessionState

contains configuration information for modifying session state (i.e. variables associated with a particular user's visit to your site)

trace

contains information related to page and application tracing

configuration section handler declarations

ASP.NET's configuration file system is so flexible that it allows you to define your own configuration sections. For most purposes, the built-in configuration sections will do nicely, but if we wanted to include some custom configuration sections, we'd need to tell ASP.NET how to handle them. To do so, we'd declare a configuration section handler for each custom configuration section we wanted to create. This is pretty advanced stuff, so we won't worry about it in this book.

Global.asax

`Global.asax` is another special file that can be added to the root of an application. It defines subroutines that are executed in response to application-wide events.

For instance, `Application_Start` is executed the first time the application runs (or just after we restart the server). This makes this method the perfect place to execute any initialization code that needs to run when the application loads for the first time. Another useful method is `Application_Error`, which is called whenever an unhandled error occurs within a page. The following is a list of the handlers that you'll use most often within the `Global.asax` file:

Application_Start
> called immediately after the application is created; this event occurs once only

Application_End
> called immediately before the end of all application instances

Application_Error
> called by an unhandled error in the application

Application_BeginRequest
> called by every request to the server

Application_EndRequest
> called at the end of every request to the server

Application_PreSendRequestHeaders
> called before headers are sent to the browser

Application_PreSendRequestContent
> called before content is sent to the browser

Application_AuthenticateRequest
> called before authenticating a user

Application_AuthorizeRequest
> called before authorizing a user

Figure 5.26. Creating `Global.asax`

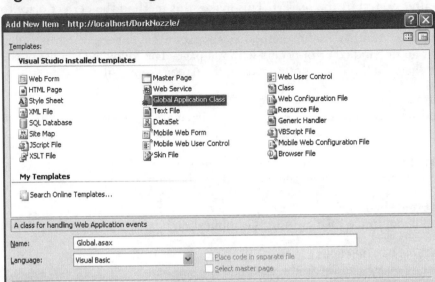

The `Global.asax` file is created in the same way as the `Web.config` file—just select File > New File..., then choose the Global Application Class template, as depicted in Figure 5.26.

Clicking Add will create in the root of your project a new file named `Global.asax`, which contains empty stubs for a number of event handlers, and comments that explain their roles. A typical event handler in a `Global.asax` file looks something like this:

Visual Basic

```
Sub Application_EventName(ByVal sender As Object, _
    ByVal e As EventArgs)
  ...
End Sub
```

C#

```
void Application_EventName(Object sender, EventArgs e)
{
  ...
}
```

Be Careful when Changing `Global.asax`

Be cautious when you add and modify code within the `Global.asax` file. Any additions or modifications you make within this file will cause the application to restart, so you'll lose any data stored in application state.

Using Application State

You can store the variables and objects you want to use throughout an entire application in a special object called `Application`. The data stored in this object is called **application state**. The `Application` object also provides you with methods that allow you to share application state data between all the pages in a given ASP.NET application very easily.

Application state is closely related to another concept: **session state**. The key difference between the two is that session state stores variables and objects for one particular user for the duration of that user's current visit, whereas application state stores objects and variables that are shared between all users of an application at the same time. Thus, application state is ideal for storing data that's used by all users of the same application.

In ASP.NET, session and application state are both implemented as **collections**, or sets of name-value pairs. You can set the value of an application variable named `SiteName` like this:

Visual Basic
```
Application("SiteName") = "Dorknozzle Intranet Application"
```

C#
```
Application["SiteName"] = "Dorknozzle Intranet Application";
```

With `SiteName` set, any pages in the application can read this string:

Visual Basic
```
Dim appName As String = Application("SiteName")
```

C#
```
String appName = Application["SiteName"];
```

We can remove an object from application state using the `Remove` method, like so:

Visual Basic
```
Application.Remove("SiteName")
```

C#

```
Application.Remove("SiteName");
```

If you find you have multiple objects and application variables lingering in application state, you can remove them all at once using the `RemoveAll` method:

Visual Basic

```
Application.RemoveAll()
```

C#

```
Application.RemoveAll();
```

It's important to be cautious when using application variables. Objects remain in application state until you remove them using the `Remove` or `RemoveAll` methods, or shut down the application in IIS. If you continue to save objects into the application state without removing them, you can place a heavy demand on server resources and dramatically decrease the performance of your applications.

Let's take a look at application state in action. Application state is very commonly used to maintain hit counters, so our first task in this example will be to build one! Let's modify the `Default.aspx` page that Visual Web Developer created for us. Double-click `Default.aspx` in Solution Explorer, and add a `Label` control inside the `form` element. You could drag the control from the Toolbox (in either Design View or Source View) and modify the generated code, or you could simply enter the new code by hand. We'll also add a bit of text to the page, and change the `Label`'s ID to `myLabel`, as shown below:

File: **Default.aspx (excerpt)**

```
<form id="form1" runat="server">
  <div>
    The page has been requested
    <asp:Label ID="myLabel" runat="server" />
    times!
  </div>
</form>
```

In Design View, you should see your label appear inside the text, as shown in Figure 5.27.

Now, let's modify the code-behind file to use an application variable that will keep track of the number of hits our page receives. Double-click in any empty space on your form; Visual Web Developer will create a `Page_Load` subroutine automatically, and display it in the code editor.

Figure 5.27. The new label appearing in Design View

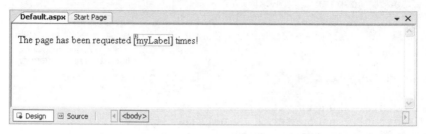

```
Default.aspx  Start Page                                    ▼ ×

The page has been requested [myLabel] times!



 Design  Source  |  <body>
```

Visual Basic   File: **Default.aspx.vb (excerpt)**

```vbnet
Partial Class _Default
  Inherits System.Web.UI.Page

  Protected Sub Page_Load(ByVal sender As Object, _
      ByVal e As System.EventArgs) Handles Me.Load

  End Sub
End Class
```

C#   File: **Default.aspx.cs (excerpt)**

```csharp
public partial class _Default : System.Web.UI.Page
{
  protected void Page_Load(object sender, EventArgs e)
  {

  }
}
```

Now, let's modify the automatically generated method by adding the code that we want to run every time the page is loaded. Modify Page_Load as shown below:

Visual Basic   File: **Default.aspx.vb (excerpt)**

```vbnet
Protected Sub Page_Load(ByVal sender As Object, _
    ByVal e As System.EventArgs) Handles Me.Load
  ' Reset counter when it reaches 10
  If Application("PageCounter") >= 10 Then
    Application.Remove("PageCounter")
  End If
  ' Initialize or increment page counter each time the page loads
  If Application("PageCounter") Is Nothing Then
    Application("PageCounter") = 1
  Else
    Application("PageCounter") += 1
```

```
   End If
   ' Display page counter
   myLabel.Text = Application("PageCounter")
End Sub
```

C# File: **Default.aspx.cs (excerpt)**

```
protected void Page_Load(object sender, EventArgs e)
{
  // Reset counter when it reaches 10
  if (Application["PageCounter"] != null &&
      (int)Application["PageCounter"] >= 10)
  {
    Application.Remove("PageCounter");
  }
  // Initialize or increment page counter each time the page loads
  if (Application["PageCounter"] == null)
  {
    Application["PageCounter"] = 1;
  }
  else
  {
    Application["PageCounter"] =
        (int)Application["PageCounter"] + 1;
  }
  // Display page counter
  myLabel.Text = Convert.ToString(Application["PageCounter"]);
}
```

Before analyzing the code, press **F5** to run the site and ensure that everything works properly. Every time you refresh the page, the hit counter should increase by one until it reaches ten, when it starts over. Now, shut down your browser altogether, and open the page in another browser. We've stored the value within application state, so when you restart the application, the page hit counter will remember the value it reached in the original browser, as Figure 5.28 shows.

If you play with the page, reloading it over and over again, you'll see that the code increments PageCounter every time the page is loaded. First, though, the code verifies that the counter hasn't reached or exceeded ten requests. If it has, the counter variable is removed from the application state:

Visual Basic File: **Default.aspx.vb (excerpt)**

```
' Reset counter when it reaches 10
If Application("PageCounter") >= 10 Then
  Application.Remove("PageCounter")
End If
```

Figure 5.28. Using the `Application` object

```
C#                                          File: Default.aspx.cs (excerpt)
// Reset counter when it reaches 10
if (Application["PageCounter"] != null &&
    (int)Application["PageCounter"] >= 10)
{
  Application.Remove("PageCounter");
}
```

Notice that the C# code has to do a little more work than the VB code. You may remember from Chapter 3 that C# is more strict than VB when it comes to variable types. As everything in application state is stored as an `Object`, C# requires that we cast the value to an integer before we make use of it. This conversion won't work if `PageCounter` hasn't been added to application state, so we also need to check that it's not equal to `null`.

Next, we try to increase the hit counter. First of all, we need verify that the counter variable exists in the application state. If it doesn't, we set it to 1, reflecting that the page is being loaded. To verify that an element exists in VB, we use `Is Nothing`:

```
Visual Basic                                File: Default.aspx.vb (excerpt)
' Initialize or increment page counter each time the page loads
If Application("PageCounter") Is Nothing Then
  Application("PageCounter") = 1
Else
  Application("PageCounter") += 1
End If
```

As we've already seen, we compare the value to `null` in C#:

```
C#                                          File: Default.aspx.cs (excerpt)
// Initialize or increment page counter each time the page loads
if (Application["PageCounter"] == null)
{
  Application["PageCounter"] = 1;
}
else
{
  Application["PageCounter"] =
      (int)Application["PageCounter"] + 1;
}
```

The last piece of code simply displays the hit counter value in the label.

There's one small problem with our code: if two people were to open the page simultaneously, the value could increment only by one, rather than two. The reason for this has to do with the code that increments the counter:

```
C#                                          File: Default.aspx.cs (excerpt)
Application["PageCounter"] =
    (int)Application["PageCounter"] + 1;
```

The expression to the right of the = operator is evaluated first; to do this, the server must read the value of the PageCounter value stored in the application. It adds one to this value, then stores the updated value in application state.

Now, let's imagine that two users visit this page at the same time, and that the web server processes the first user's request a fraction of a second before the other request. The web form that's loaded for the first user might read Page-Counter from application state and obtain a value of 5, to which it would add 1 to obtain 6. However, before the web form had a chance to store this new value into application state, another copy of the web form, running for the second user, might read PageCounter and also obtain the value 6. Both copies of the page will have read the same value, and both will store an updated value of 6! This tricky situation is illustrated in Figure 5.29.

To avoid this kind of confusion, we should develop the application so that each user locks application state, updates the value, and then unlocks application state so that other users can do the same thing. This process is depicted in Figure 5.30.

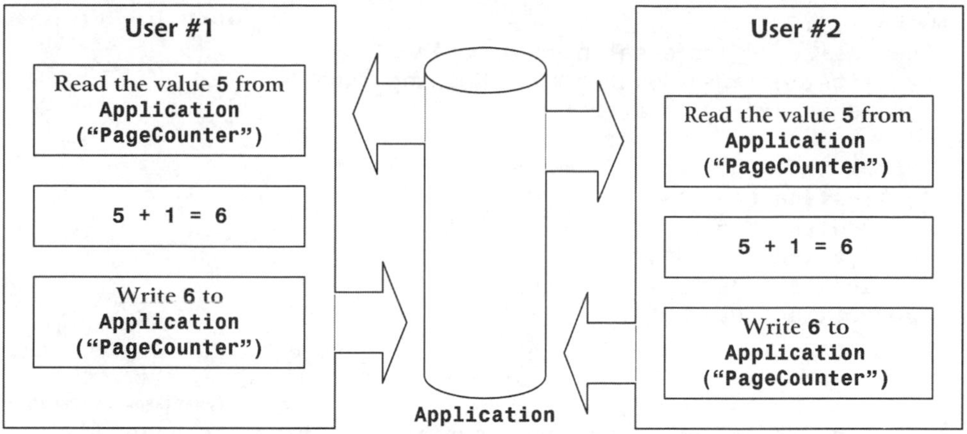

Figure 5.29. Two users updating application state simultaneously

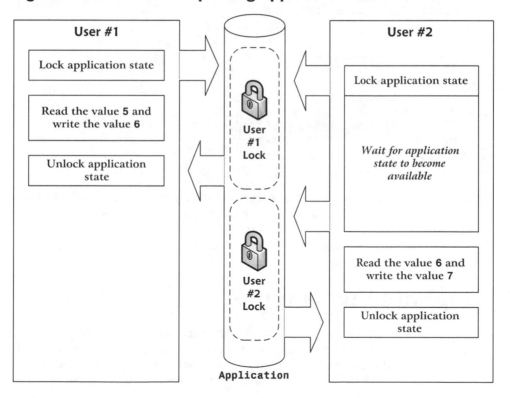

Figure 5.30. Two users updating application state with locks

Let's modify our code slightly to create these locks:

```
Visual Basic                                          File: Default.aspx.vb (excerpt)
' Initialize or increment page counter
If Application("PageCounter") Is Nothing Then
  Application("PageCounter") = 1
Else
  ' Lock the Application object
  Application.Lock()
  ' Increment counter
  Application("PageCounter") += 1
  ' Unlock the Application object
  Application.UnLock()
End If
```

```
C#                                                    File: Default.aspx.cs (excerpt)
// Initialize or increment page counter each time the page loads
if (Application["PageCounter"] == null)
{
  Application["PageCounter"] = 1;
}
else
{
  // Lock the Application object
  Application.Lock();
  // Increment counter
  Application["PageCounter"] =
      (int)Application["PageCounter"] + 1;
  // Unlock the Application object
  Application.UnLock();
}
```

In this case, the Lock method guarantees that only one user can work with the application variable at any time. Next, we call the UnLock method to unlock the application variable for the next request. Our use of Lock and UnLock in this scenario guarantees that the application variable is incremented by one for each visit that's made to the page.

Working with User Sessions

Like application state, session state is an important way to store temporary information across multiple page requests. However, unlike application state, which is accessible to all users, each object stored in session state is associated with a particular user's visit to your site. Stored on the server, session state allocates each user free memory on that server for the temporary storage of objects (strings, integers, or any other kinds of objects).

The process of reading and writing data into session state is very similar to the way we read and write data to the application state: instead of using the `Application` object, we use the `Session` object. However, the `Session` object doesn't support locking and unlocking like the `Application` object does.

To test session state, you could simply edit the `Page_Load` method to use `Session` instead of `Application`, and remove the `Lock` and `UnLock` calls if you added them. The easiest way to replace `Application` with `Session` is by selecting Edit > Find and Replace > Quick Replace.

In the page hit counter example that we created earlier in this chapter, we stored the count in the application state, which created a single hit count that was shared by all users of the site. Now, if you load the page in multiple browsers, you'll see that each increments its counter independently of the others.

Like objects stored in application state, session state objects linger on the server even after the user leaves the page that created them. However, unlike application variables, session variables disappear after a certain period of user inactivity. Since web browsers don't notify web servers when a user leaves a web site, ASP.NET can only assume that a user has left your site after a period in which it hasn't received any page requests from that user. By default, a user's session will expire after 20 minutes of inactivity. We can change this timeframe simply by increasing or decreasing the `Timeout` property of the `Session` object, as follows:

Visual Basic

```
Session.Timeout = 1560
```

You can do this anywhere in your code, but the most common place to set the `Timeout` property is in the `Global.asax` file. If you open `Global.asax`, you'll see that it contains an event handler named `Session_Start`. This method runs before the first request from each user's visit to your site is processed, and gives you the opportunity to initialize their session variables before the code in your web form has a chance to access them.

Here's a `Session_Start` that sets the `Timeout` property to 15 minutes:

Visual Basic   File: **Global.asax (excerpt)**

```
Sub Session_Start(sender As Object, e As EventArgs)
  Session.Timeout = 1560
End Sub
```

```
C#                                          File: Global.asax (excerpt)
void Session_Start(Object sender, EventArgs e)
{
  Session.Timeout = 1560;
}
```

Using the Cache Object

In traditional ASP, developers used application state to cache data. Although there's nothing to prevent you from doing the same thing here, ASP.NET provides a new object, Cache, specifically for that purpose. Cache is also a collection, and we access its contents similarly to the way we accessed the contents of Application. Another similarity is that both have application-wide visibility, being shared between all users who access a web application.

Let's assume that there's a list of employees that you'd normally read from the database. To spare the database server's resources, after you read the table from the database the first time, you might save it into the cache using a command like this:

```
Visual Basic
Cache("Employees") = employeesTable
```

```
C#
Cache["Employees"] = employeesTable;
```

By default, objects stay in the cache until we remove them, or server resources become low, at which point objects begin to be removed from the cache in the order in which they were added. The Cache object also lets us control expiration—if, for example, we want to add an object to the cache for a period of ten minutes, we can use the Insert method. Here's an example:

```
Visual Basic
Cache.Insert("Employees", employeesTable, Nothing,
    DateTime.MaxValue, TimeSpan.FromMinutes(10))
```

```
C#
Cache.Insert("Employees", employeesTable, null,
    DateTime.MaxValue, TimeSpan.FromMinutes(10));
```

The third parameter, which in this case is Nothing or null, can be used to add cache dependencies. We could use such dependencies to invalidate cached items when some external indicator changes, but that kind of task is a little beyond the scope of this discussion.

Later in the code, we could use the cached object as follows:

Visual Basic

```
employeesTable = Cache("Employees")
```

C#

```
employeesTable = Cache["Employees"];
```

Objects in the cache can expire, so it's good practice to verify that the object you're expecting does actually exist, to avoid any surprises:

Visual Basic

```
employeesTable = Cache("Employees")
If employeesTable Is Nothing Then
  ' Read the employees table from another source
  Cache("Employees") = employeesTable
End If
```

C#

```
employeesTable = Cache["Employees"];
if (employeesTable == null)
{
  // Read the employees table from another source
  Cache["Employees"] = employeesTable;
}
```

This sample code checks to see if the data you're expecting exists in the cache. If not, it means that this is the first time the code has been executed, or that the item has been removed from the cache. Thus, we can populate `employeesTable` from the database, remembering to store the retrieved data into the cache. The trip to the database server is made only if the cache is empty or not present.

Using Cookies

If you want to store data related to a particular user, you could use the `Session` object, but this approach has an important drawback: its contents are lost when the user closes the browser window.

To store user data for longer periods of time, you need to use **cookies**. Cookies are pieces of data that your ASP.NET application can save on the user's browser, to be read later by your application. Cookies aren't lost when the browser is closed (unless the user deletes them), so you can save data that helps identify your user in a cookie.

In ASP.NET, a cookie is represented by the `HttpCookie` class. We read the user's cookies through the `Cookies` property of the `Request` object, and we set cookies though the `Cookies` property of the `Response` object. Cookies expire by default when the browser window is closed (much like session state), but their points of expiration can be set to dates in the future; in such cases, they become **persistent cookies**.

Let's do a quick test. First, open `Default.aspx` and remove the text surrounding `myLabel`:

File: **Default.aspx** (excerpt)

```
<form id="form1" runat="server">
  <div>
    <asp:Label ID="myLabel" runat="server" />
  </div>
</form>
```

Then, modify `Page_Load` in the code-behind file as shown:

Visual Basic   File: **Default.aspx.vb** (excerpt)

```vb
Protected Sub Page_Load(ByVal sender As Object, _
    ByVal e As System.EventArgs) Handles Me.Load
  ' Declare a cookie variable
  Dim userCookie As HttpCookie
  ' Try to retrieve user's ID by reading the UserID cookie
  userCookie = Request.Cookies("UserID")
  ' Verify if the cookie exists
  If userCookie Is Nothing Then
    ' Display message
    myLabel.Text = "Cookie doesn't exist! Creating a cookie now."
    ' Create cookie
    userCookie = New HttpCookie("UserID", "JoeBlack")
    ' Set cookie to expire in one month
    userCookie.Expires = DateTime.Now.AddMonths(1)
    ' Save the cookie on the client
    Response.Cookies.Add(userCookie)
  Else
    ' Display message
    myLabel.Text = "Welcome back, " & userCookie.Value
  End If
End Sub
```

```
C#                                          File: Default.aspx.cs (excerpt)
protected void Page_Load(object sender, EventArgs e)
{
  // Declare a cookie variable
  HttpCookie userCookie;
  // Try to retrieve user's ID by reading the UserID cookie
  userCookie = Request.Cookies["UserID"];
  // Verify if the cookie exists
  if (userCookie == null)
  {
    // Display message
    myLabel.Text =
        "Cookie doesn't exist! Creating a cookie now.";
    // Create cookie
    userCookie = new HttpCookie("UserID", "JoeBlack");
    // Set cookie to expire in one month
    userCookie.Expires = DateTime.Now.AddMonths(1);
    // Save the cookie on the client
    Response.Cookies.Add(userCookie);
  }
  else
  {
    // Display message
    myLabel.Text = "Welcome back, " + userCookie.Value;
  }
}
```

The first time you load the page, you'll be notified that the cookie doesn't exist, and that a new cookie is being created, via a message like the one shown in Figure 5.31.

Figure 5.31. Creating a new cookie

Figure 5.32. The cookie has persisted

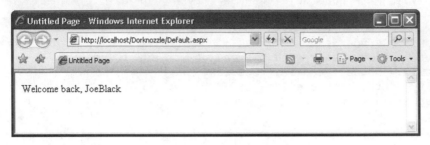

If you reload the page, the cookie will be found, and you'll get a different message, as Figure 5.32 shows.

If you go through the code, you'll see that it's pretty much self-explanatory. What's interesting to observe is that you can close the browser window, or even restart your computer—the cookie will still be there, and the application will be able to identify that you're a returning visitor. As you can see in the code, the cookie is set to expire one month after creation.

Be aware that visitors can choose to reject your cookies, so you can't rely on them for essential features of your application.

Starting the Dorknozzle Project

You're now prepared to start developing a larger project! We were introduced to Dorknozzle at the beginning of the chapter, and you've already created a project for it. Now, it's time to add some real functionality to it! In the next few pages, we will:

❑ Prepare the sitemap for your site.

❑ Create a default theme that defines the common styles.

❑ Create a master page that will contain the layout for all the pages of Dorknozzle.

❑ Create a web form that uses the master page.

❑ Learn how to debug your project in case you encounter errors.

The star of the show will be the master page, but because it needs to have the sitemap and the theme in place, we'll deal with these first.

Preparing the Sitemap

As we saw in Figure 5.1, on the left of every page of our Dorknozzle site will sit a menu that contains links to the site's pages. We'll implement that list using the `SiteMapPath` control, which will require a sitemap file.

Adding Files to your Project

If the project is running in debug mode, you can't add new files to it, so you must first stop debugging. You can do this by closing the browser window (if you're using Internet Explorer), by selecting Debug > Stop Debugging, or by clicking the Stop icon on the debug toolbar.

In Solution Explorer, right-click the root node and select Add New Item, as illustrated in Figure 5.33.

Figure 5.33. Adding a new item to your project

Figure 5.34. Adding a sitemap file

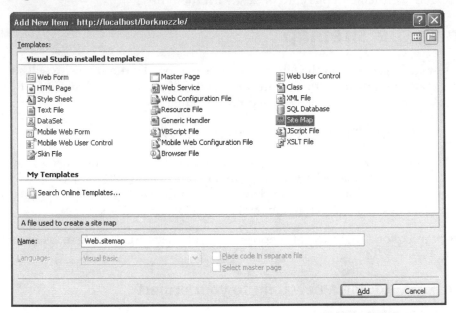

From the templates list, choose Site Map, as depicted in Figure 5.34 and leave the filename as Web.sitemap.

Click Add to have the file created and added to your project. You'll be presented with a default, empty sitemap that you can start modifying. Change its contents as shown below. For now, you need only add a few nodes; you can add the rest later on.

File: **Web.sitemap**

```xml
<?xml version="1.0" encoding="utf-8" ?>
<siteMap
    xmlns="http://schemas.microsoft.com/AspNet/SiteMap-File-1.0" >
  <siteMapNode url="~/" title="Root" description="Root">
    <siteMapNode url="~/Default.aspx" title="Home"
        description="Dorknozzle Home" />
    <siteMapNode url="HelpDesk.aspx" title="Help Desk"
        description="Dorknozzle Help Desk" />
    <siteMapNode url="~/EmployeeDirectory.aspx"
        title="Employee Directory"
        description="Dorknozzle Employee Directory" />
    <siteMapNode url="~/AddressBook.aspx" title="Address Book"
        description="Dorknozzle Address Book" />
```

```
   <siteMapNode url="~/Departments.aspx" title="Departments"
       description="Dorknozzle Departments" />
   <siteMapNode url="~/AdminTools.aspx" title="Admin Tools"
       description="Admin Tools" />
   <siteMapNode url="~/AdminNewsletter.aspx"
       title="Admin Newsletter"
       description="Dorknozzle Admin Newsletter" />
 </siteMapNode>
</siteMap>
```

Great! Your sitemap file is ready to be used.

Using Themes, Skins, and Styles

We'll be using CSS to build the layout of our Dorknozzle interface. CSS provides developers with flexibility and control over the look of their web applications, and makes it very simple to keep the appearance of the web site consistent.

In ASP.NET, style sheets can be managed through a mechanism called **themes**. Themes can be used to do much more than simply select which style sheets are applied to an application, as we'll see shortly. But first up, let's add a style sheet to our Dorknozzle site.

Creating a New Theme Folder

Right-click the root node in Solution Explorer, and select Add ASP.NET Folder > Theme. You'll then be able to type in a name for the new theme. Type **Blue**, then hit **Return**. If everything worked as planned, you should have a brand new folder called App_Themes in the root of your project, with a subfolder called Blue, as Figure 5.35 illustrates.

Figure 5.35. Your new theme in Solution Explorer

We'll keep all the files related to the default appearance of Dorknozzle in this `Blue` folder.

Creating a New Style Sheet

We'll start by adding a new CSS file to the Blue theme. CSS files can be created independently of themes, but it's easier in the long term to save them to themes—this way, your solution becomes more manageable, and you can save different versions of your CSS files under different themes. Any files with the `.css` extension in a theme's folder will be automatically linked to any web form that uses that theme.

Right-click the `Blue` folder, and select Add New Item.... Select the Style Sheet template to create a new file named `Dorknozzle.css`, and click Add. By default, `Dorknozzle.css` will be almost empty:

File: **Dorknozzle.css** (excerpt)

```
body {
}
```

Let's make this file more useful by adding more styles to it. We'll use these styles soon, when we build the first page of Dorknozzle.

File: **Dorknozzle.css** (excerpt)

```
body
{
  font-family: Tahoma, Helvetica, Arial, sans-serif;
  font-size: 12px;
}
h1
{
  font-size: 25px;
}
a:link, a:visited
{
  text-decoration: none;
  color: Blue;
}
a:hover
{
  color: Red;
}
.Header
{
```

```
  top: 0px;
  left: 0px;
  position: absolute;
  width: 800px;
  background-image: url(/Dorknozzle/Images/header_bg.gif);
  background-repeat: repeat-x;
}
.Menu
{
  top: 160px;
  left: 15px;
  width: 195px;
  position: absolute;
}
.Content
{
  top: 160px;
  left: 170px;
  position: absolute;
  width: 600px
}
```

Remember, we're not limited to using these styles. If, during the development of our application, we decide to add more styles, we'll simply need to open the Dorknozzle.css file and add them as necessary.

While you're editing the CSS, take a quick look at the built-in features that Visual Web Developer offers for building and editing styles. Right-click on any style rule in the CSS code editor, and in the context menu that appears (which is shown in Figure 5.36), you'll see one very handy item: Build Style....

Figure 5.36. Choosing to edit a style visually

Figure 5.37. Using the Style Builder

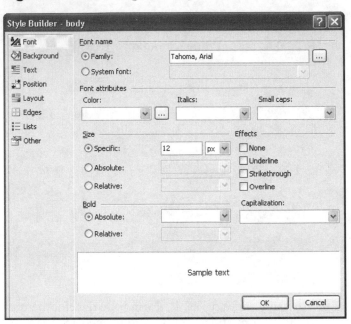

If you choose Build Style…, you'll access the very useful Style Builder tool, shown in Figure 5.37, which lets you set the properties of the selected style.

Styling Web Server Controls

CSS styles can apply only to HTML elements—they can't really be used to keep the appearance of web server controls consistent. In Chapter 4, you learned about many ASP.NET controls, and you saw that some of them contain properties that affect their output.

Take the `Calendar` control, for example. Say you use many calendars throughout your web site, and all of them are supposed to have the same properties as this one:

```
<asp:Calendar id="myCalendar" runat="server" DayNameFormat="Short"
    FirstDayOfWeek="Sunday" NextPrevFormat="FullMonth"
    SelectionMode="DayWeekMonth" SelectWeekText="Select Week"
    SelectMonthText="Select Month" TitleFormat="Month"
    OnSelectionChanged="SelectionChanged" />
```

Now, given that you have many calendars, you decide that you'd like to have the common set of properties saved in a central place. This way, if you decided to change the format later, you'd need to make changes in one place, rather than all over your web site.

So, can CSS help us keep our calendars consistent in the same way it can keep our headings consistent? Unfortunately, it can't. All the settings in the above calendar are processed on the server side, and are used to determine the actual HTML that's output by the control. CSS can affect the final output by setting the colors or other details of the resulting HTML code, but it can't influence the way the `Calendar` control works on the server.

So the question remains: how can we keep web server controls consistent? **Skins**, which were introduced in ASP.NET 2.0, are the answer to this question. They define default values for server-side controls.

Skin definitions are saved into files with the `.skin` extension. A skin definition looks like the markup for a normal web server control, except that it doesn't have an ID, and it can't set event handlers. This makes sense, since the skin isn't an actual control. Here's an example of a skin for a calendar:

```
<asp:Calendar runat="server" DayNameFormat="Short"
    FirstDayOfWeek="Sunday" NextPrevFormat="FullMonth"
    SelectionMode="DayWeekMonth" SelectWeekText="Select Week"
    SelectMonthText="Select Month" TitleFormat="Month" />
```

Now, provided this skin is part of the theme that's applied to the current page, all `Calendar` controls will inherit all of these property values automatically. These values can be overridden for any specific calendar, but the skin provides the default values.

A skin can also contain a `SkinId` property, and if it does, it becomes a **named skin**. A named skin doesn't apply automatically to all controls of its type: it affects only those that specify that the skin applies to them. This allows you to define many skins for the same control (for instance, a `SmallCalendar` and a `BlueCalendar`).

Adding a Skin

The truth is, we don't really need skins for our simple site, but we'll add one so that you can get a feel for their functionality. Right-click again on the `Blue` node in Solution Explorer, and select Add New Item.... Choose the **Skin File** template, leave its name as `SkinFile.skin`, and click Add.

Visual Web Developer adds a comment to the file; this comment contains default text that briefly describes skins. A theme can contain one or many skin files, and each skin file can contain one or more skin definitions. ASP.NET will automatically read all the files with the `.skin` extension.

Let's say we want all `TextBox` controls to have the default `ForeColor` property set to `blue`. Without skins, we'd need to set this property manually on all `TextBox` controls in your site. However, you can achieve the same effect by adding this line to your `SkinFile.skin` file:

File: **SkinFile.skin (excerpt)**

```
<asp:TextBox runat="server" ForeColor="blue" />
```

Once the theme containing this skin has been applied, this new skin will give all `TextBox` controls on your site the default `ForeColor` of `blue`.

Applying the Theme

In order for your CSS—and the skin—to take effect, you'll need to apply the theme to your web page. Once the new theme has been created, applying it is a piece of cake. You can apply a new theme using the `Web.config` configuration file, or through your code.

For now we'll use `Web.config`. The theme can be set using the `theme` attribute of the `pages` element, which should be located inside the `system.web` element.

If you're using VB, the `pages` element already exists in `Web.config`—you just need to add the `theme` attribute:

File: **Web.config (excerpt)**

```
<compilation debug="true" strict="false" explicit="true"/>
<pages theme="Blue">
  <namespaces>
    <clear/>
    <add namespace="System"/>
    <add namespace="System.Collections"/>
    <add namespace="System.Collections.Specialized"/>
    <add namespace="System.Configuration"/>
    <add namespace="System.Text"/>
    <add namespace="System.Text.RegularExpressions"/>
    <add namespace="System.Web"/>
    <add namespace="System.Web.Caching"/>
    <add namespace="System.Web.SessionState"/>
    <add namespace="System.Web.Security"/>
```

```
    </namespaces>
</pages>
```

If you're using C#, you'll need to add the **pages** element to the **system.web** element yourself:

File: **Web.config (excerpt)**

```
<system.web>
    ⋮
  <pages theme="Blue" />
    ⋮
</system.web>
```

Building the Master Page

This is where the real fun begins! All of the pages in Dorknozzle have a common structure, with the same header on the top, and the same menu on the left, so it makes sense to build a master page. With this master page in place, we'll be able to create pages for the site by writing only the content that makes them different, rather than writing the header and the menu afresh for each page.

Figure 5.38. Creating a new master page

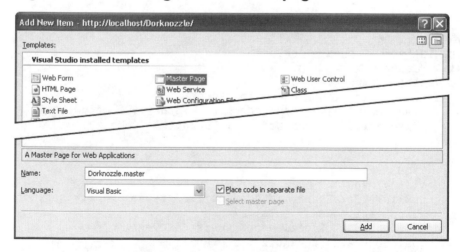

Right-click again on the root node in Solution Explorer and select Add New Item…. There, select the Master Page template from the list of available templates, and name it **Dorknozzle.master**. Choose the language you want to program the master page in from the Language drop-down list, and check the Place code in a separate file checkbox, as illustrated in Figure 5.38. This latter option will instruct Visual Web Developer to generate a code-behind file for the master page.

After you click the Add button, Visual Web Developer creates the new master page, which will appear immediately in Solution Explorer. If you expand its node as shown in Figure 5.39, you'll see its code-behind file listed as a child node.

Figure 5.39. The code-behind file appearing as a child of its form

Double-click the `Dorknozzle.master` file (not its code-behind file) in Solution Explorer, and you'll find that Visual Web Developer has given you a very simple default master page. Edit the markup inside the `body` element as shown below:

File: **Dorknozzle.master** (excerpt)

```
<body>
  <form id="form1" runat="server">
    <!-- Header -->
    <div class="Header">
      <asp:Image id="Image1" runat="server"
          ImageUrl="~/Images/header.gif" Width="450" Height="174"
          AlternateText="The Official Dorknozzle Company
          Intranet" />
    </div>
    <!-- Menu -->
    <div class="Menu">
      <asp:SiteMapDataSource id="dorknozzleSiteMap" runat="server"
          ShowStartingNode="false" />
      <asp:Menu id="dorknozzleMenu" runat="server"
          DataSourceID="dorknozzleSiteMap">
        <StaticItemTemplate>
          <img src="Images/book_closed.gif" alt="+"
              width="16" height="16" style="border-width: 0;" />
          <%# Eval("Text") %>
        </StaticItemTemplate>
```

```
    </asp:Menu>
  </div>
  <!-- Content -->
  <div class="Content">
    <asp:ContentPlaceHolder id="ContentPlaceHolder1"
        runat="server" />
  </div>
  </form>
</body>
```

The code is pretty simple: basically, it defines the layout of all the Dorknozzle pages. Each of the three sections defined here starts with a comment that identifies the section as being the header, the menu on the left, or the content area. These elements are positioned on the page using the CSS styles you added earlier to the Dorknozzle.css file, so you may want to have another look at that file to refresh your memory.

We saw in Chapter 4 that the TreeView and Menu controls know how to read data from a SiteMapDataSource class, which reads the Web.sitemap file located in the root of your project (unless you specify otherwise). To build the menu on the left-hand side of the page, we create a Web.sitemap file, then add a SiteMapDataSource control to our web form or master page:

File: **Dorknozzle.master (excerpt)**

```
<asp:SiteMapDataSource id="dorknozzleSiteMap" runat="server"
    ShowStartingNode="false" />
```

You might recall that the Web.sitemap file forces us to add a root siteMapNode element, but we can suppress this root element using the SiteMapDataSource—we set its ShowStartingNode property to False.

To have the Menu control simply display the list of nodes, it's sufficient to set its DataSourceID to the ID of the SiteMapDataSource. However, the Menu control also gives us the potential to customize the look of each menu item through **templates**. Here, we used the StaticItemTemplate to add a little book image to the left of each menu item:

File: **Dorknozzle.master (excerpt)**

```
<asp:Menu id="dorknozzleMenu" runat="server"
    DataSourceID="dorknozzleSiteMap">
  <StaticItemTemplate>
    <img src="Images/book_closed.gif" alt="+"
        width="16" height="16" style="border-width: 0;" />
    <%# Eval("Text") %>
```

```
    </StaticItemTemplate>
</asp:Menu>
```

After you write `Dorknozzle.master`, copy the `Images` folder from the code archive to your `Dorknozzle` folder, which will probably be `C:\WebDocs\Dorknozzle\`.[1] Once this is done, you should have a `Dorknozzle\Images` folder that contains a few image files. To make the Images folder appear in Solution Explorer, right-click the root node and choose Refresh Folder.

The master page is now in place. Click the Design button at the base of the editor window to see a preview of the page. Does yours look like the page shown in Figure 5.40?

Figure 5.40. Viewing `Dorknozzle.master` in Design View

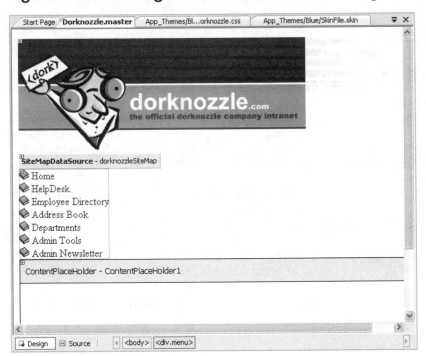

Note that the CSS styles don't apply at design time, so you'll have to hang on a little longer to see that code in action.

---

[1] Remember that all code and images used in building the Dorknozzle project are available in the code archive, which is available for download from sitepoint.com.

Using the Master Page

It's time for our moment of glory, when we assemble all the pieces we've been building and put them to work! We'll start by re-creating the `Default.aspx` web form, but this time, we'll use the master page. Start by deleting your current `Default.aspx` file by right-clicking that file in Solution Explorer, and choosing Delete. You'll be warned that `Default.aspx` is about to be deleted (see Figure 5.41)—choose OK.

Figure 5.41. Deleting `Default.aspx`

Click the root node in Solution Explorer, then go to File > New File... (or right-click the root node in Solution Explorer and select Add New Item... from the context menu).

In the dialog that appears, choose the Web Form template, leave the default name of `Default.aspx` as is, and make sure both the Place code in separate file and Select master page checkboxes are checked, as shown in Figure 5.42.

Figure 5.42. Creating the new `Default.aspx`

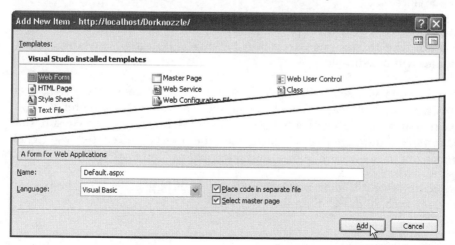

Once you click Add, you'll be asked to select the master page you want to use. Choose `Dorknozzle.master`, and click OK.

Our new form inherits everything from its master page, so its code is minimal:

Visual Basic   File: **Default.aspx (excerpt)**

```
<%@ Page Language="VB" MasterPageFile="~/Dorknozzle.master"
    AutoEventWireup="false" CodeFile="Default.aspx.vb"
    Inherits="_Default" title="Untitled Page" %>
<asp:Content ID="Content1"
    ContentPlaceHolderID="ContentPlaceHolder1" Runat="Server">
</asp:Content>
```

This file is almost exactly the same when it's written in C#—the only differences are the `Language`, `AutoEventWireup`, and `CodeFile` attributes in the `Page` directive. Let's modify the file by adding some content to the `ContentPlaceHolder`, and altering the page title. Edit the file to reflect the highlighted sections here:

File: **Default.aspx (excerpt)**

```
<%@ Page Language="VB" MasterPageFile="~/Dorknozzle.master"
    AutoEventWireup="false" CodeFile="Default.aspx.vb"
    Inherits="_Default" title="Welcome to Dorknozzle!" %>
<asp:Content ID="Content1"
    ContentPlaceHolderID="ContentPlaceHolder1" Runat="Server">
  <h1>Company News</h1>
  <p>We'll add some news later.</p>
  <h1>Company Events</h1>
  <p>We'll add company events later.</p>
</asp:Content>
```

Switch to Design View to see a preview of the whole page, like the one shown in Figure 5.43. The master page areas will be grayed out, and only the content placeholder will be editable.

By default, when you select Debug > Start Debugging or press **F5**, Visual Web Developer executes the page that's being edited. However, if you prefer, you can set a particular page to execute whenever you start debugging. To make sure that `Default.aspx` is the page that's loaded when the project is executed, right-click `Default.aspx` in Solution Explorer, and select Set As Start Page.

Now, execute `Default.aspx` by hitting **F5**. It should appear as per the page in Figure 5.44, with all the CSS applied.

Figure 5.43. Editing a web form that uses a master page

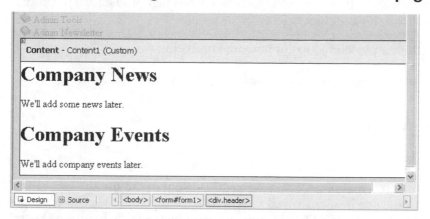

Figure 5.44. Welcome to Dorknozzle!

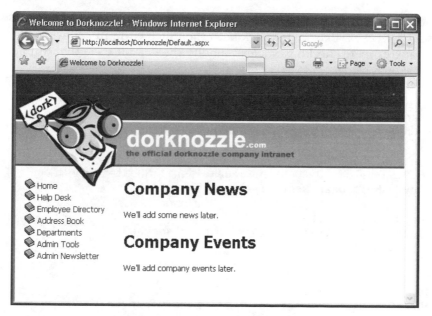

Extending Dorknozzle

We'll extend the Dorknozzle site by adding an employee help desk request web form. This form will allow our fictitious employees to report hardware, software, and workstation problems to the help desk. The Web Form will be arranged into a series of simple steps that users will follow to report their problems. The process will include the following stages:

❑ Choose from a predefined list of potential problem areas.

❑ Choose from a range of predetermined subjects that are related to the problem area.

❑ Enter a description of the problem.

❑ Submit the request.

As we already have a master page that defines the layout of the site's pages, adding a new page to the site is now a trivial task. In this example, we'll see how simple it is to add new pages to an ASP.NET web site once the structure has been created correctly.

Create a web form in the same way you created `Default.aspx`, but this time, name it `HelpDesk.aspx`. Be sure to check both the **Place code in separate file** and **Select master page** checkboxes. Next, modify the default code that will be generated as shown below:

File: **HelpDesk.aspx (excerpt)**

```
<%@ Page Language="VB" MasterPageFile="~/Dorknozzle.master"
    AutoEventWireup="false" CodeFile="HelpDesk.aspx.vb"
    Inherits="HelpDesk" title="Dorknozzle Help Desk" %>
<asp:Content ID="Content1"
    ContentPlaceHolderID="ContentPlaceHolder1" Runat="Server">
  <h1>Employee Help Desk Request</h1>
  <p>
    Station Number:<br />
    <asp:TextBox id="stationTextBox" runat="server"
        CssClass="textbox" />
  </p>
  <p>
    Problem Category:<br />
    <asp:DropDownList id="categoryList" runat="server"
        CssClass="dropdownmenu" />
  </p>
  <p>
    Problem Subject:<br />
    <asp:DropDownList id="subjectList" runat="server"
        CssClass="dropdownmenu" />
```

```
    </p>
    <p>
      Problem Description:<br />
      <asp:TextBox id="descriptionTextBox" runat="server"
          CssClass="textbox" Columns="40" Rows="4"
          TextMode="MultiLine" />
    </p>
    <p>
      <asp:Button id="submitButton" runat="server"
          CssClass="button" Text="Submit Request" /></p>
</asp:Content>
```

Don't worry that the DropDownList controls don't have items associated with them—eventually, the categories and subjects will be retrieved from a database. When you're finished, save your work, execute the project, and click the Help Desk link from the menu. You should see the display shown in Figure 5.45.

Figure 5.45. The Help Desk page up and running

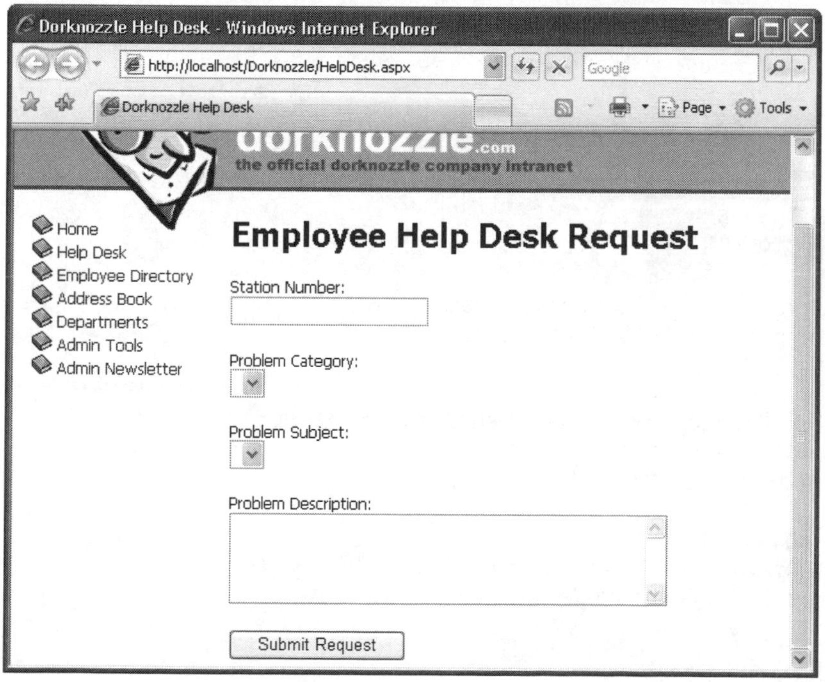

This page gives us the opportunity to test the skin file we created earlier. If you type text into the text boxes, you'll see that the color of the text is blue. True, this effect could have been achieved just as easily through CSS, but in future, when you're working on projects that utilize more complex controls and properties, skins might be your only choice. As such, it's important that you know how to use them.

Debugging and Error Handling

Your work with Dorknozzle for this chapter is over, but now that we've started to create a real-world application, it's time to consider the real-world problems that might occur as we're developing that application. A constant truth in the life of any programmer is that programming mistakes do happen, and they happen no matter how experienced the programmer is. For this reason, it's beneficial to know what you can do when you encounter an error, and to learn how ASP.NET and Visual Web Developer can help you analyze and debug your code.

Debugging with Visual Web Developer

Take a look at this code:

Visual Basic   File: **ErrorTest.aspx.vb (excerpt)**

```
Protected Sub Page_Load(ByVal sender As Object, _
    ByVal e As System.EventArgs) Handles Me.Load
  Dim a(10) As Integer
  Dim i As Integer
  For i = 1 To 11
    a(i) = i
  Next
End Sub
```

C#   File: **ErrorTest.aspx.cs (excerpt)**

```
protected void Page_Load(object sender, EventArgs e)
{
  int[] a = new int[10];
  int i;
  for (i = 0; i < 11; i++)
  {
    a[i] = i;
  }
}
```

The code above creates an array of ten elements, then uses a For loop to assign values to them. The problem is that it doesn't stop at the tenth element: it also tries to assign a value to the eleventh element, which doesn't exist.

If you load this page directly in Internet Explorer without debugging it, you'll see a page that specifies the error, like the one shown in Figure 5.46.

Figure 5.46. The error message isn't very helpful without debug mode

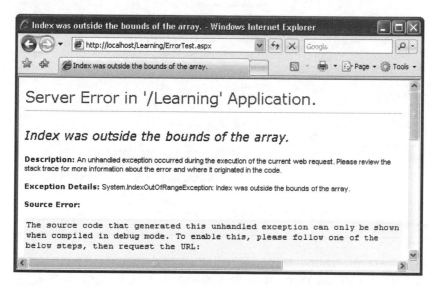

You can obtain more details by enabling debug mode and, if you scroll down, you'll see instructions that explain how to do just that. The easiest way to enable debug mode it to use Visual Web Developer. You'll remember from earlier in this chapter that the first time you execute a page by pressing **F5** (Start Debugging), Visual Web Developer asks you if you want it to enable debug mode for you. If you ask it to, it'll modify (or create) the `Web.config` file accordingly.

Figure 5.47. Debugging a run-time error

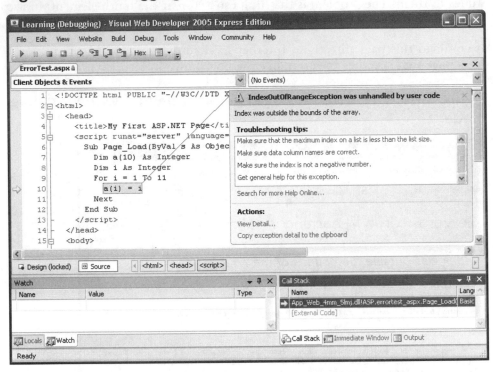

Executing the page once again—this time, with debugging enabled—takes you straight to the error in Visual Web Developer, as Figure 5.47 illustrates.

This interface tells you that the code has thrown an **exception** of type `IndexOutOfRangeException`. In .NET, exceptions are the standard means by which errors are generated and propagated. An exception is a .NET class (in this case, the `IndexOutOfRangeException` class) that contains the details of an error. As you'll see a little later, you can **catch** the error in your code using the `Try-Catch-Finally` construct. If the error isn't caught and handled, as in this case, it's finally caught by the ASP.NET runtime, which generates an error message.

In Figure 5.47, the debugger has paused execution at the moment the exception was raised. Let's see what your options are at this moment. One very useful window is the Watch window, which appears by default when your application is being debugged. If it's not displayed, you can open it by accessing Debug > Windows > Watch. You can type the names of the objects in your code into the

Watch window; in response, it will display their values and types. Try typing **a(5)** (or **a[5]** if you're using C#) in the Watch window; you should see a display like the one in Figure 5.48.

Figure 5.48. Inspecting values using the Watch window

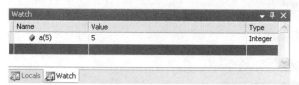

You could even type just **a**, then explore its members via the display shown in Figure 5.49.

Figure 5.49. The Watch window showing the contents of an array

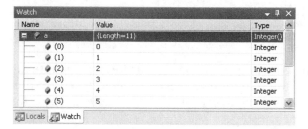

Arrays and VB

This example reveals an interesting aspect of this array. The Watch window reports that the array's length is 11, yet we defined it as a(10). In all .NET languages, arrays are zero-based, which means that the first element of an array is a(0), the second is a(1), and so on. So an array called a that had ten elements would have as its first element a(0), and a(9) as its last.

However, VB offers extra assistance for developers who are experienced with pre-.NET versions of the language (which had one-based arrays in which the first element would have been a(1), and the last would have been a(10)): it adds an element for you. In other words, if you declare an array of ten elements in VB, you'll get an array of 11 elements.

C# has always had zero-based arrays, so an array defined as a[10] will have ten elements.

In more complex scenarios, if you enter the name of an object, the Watch window will let you explore its members as we just saw.

If you switch to the Locals window (**Debug** > Windows > Locals) shown in Figure 5.50, you can see the variables or objects that are visible from the line of code at which the execution was paused.

Figure 5.50. The Locals window

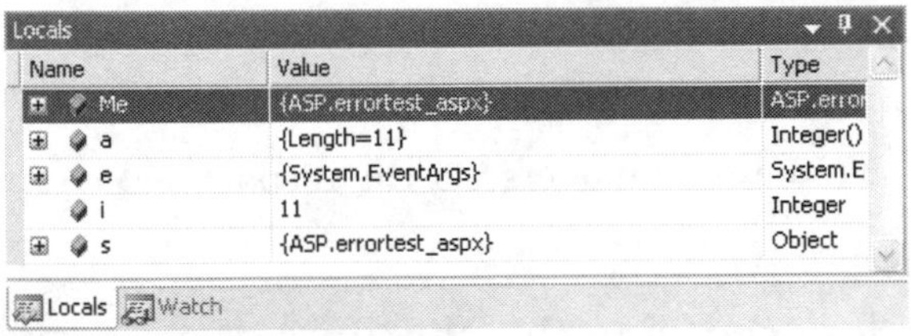

Another nice feature of Visual Web Developer is that when you hover your cursor over a variable, the editing window shows you at-a-glance information about that variable.

Sometimes, you'll want to debug your application even if it doesn't generate an exception. For example, you may find that your code isn't generating the output you expected. In such cases, it makes sense to execute pieces of code line by line, and see in detail what happens at each step.

The most common way to get started with this kind of debugging is to set a **breakpoint** in the code. In Visual Web Developer, we do this by clicking on the gray bar on the left-hand side of the editing window. When we click there, a red bullet appears, and the line is highlighted with red to indicate that it's a breakpoint, as Figure 5.51 illustrates.

Once the breakpoint is set, we execute the code. When the execution pointer reaches the line you selected, execution of the page will be paused and Visual Web Developer will open your page in debug mode. In debug mode, you can perform a number of tasks:

❑ View the values of your variables or objects.

❑ Step into any line of code by selecting Debug > Step Into. This executes the currently highlighted line, then pauses. If the selected line executes another local method, the execution pointer is moved to that method so that you can execute it line by line, too.

Figure 5.51. Setting a breakpoint

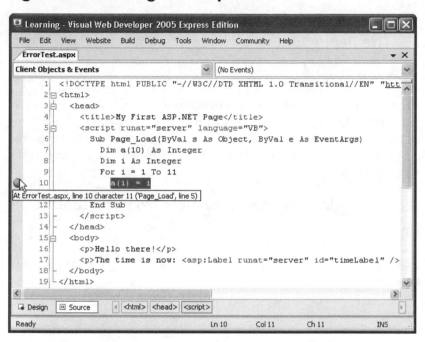

❑ Step over any line of code by selecting Debug > Step Over. This makes the execution pointer move to the next line in the current method without stepping into any local methods that might be called by the current line.

❑ Step out of any method by selecting Debug > Step Out. This causes the current method to complete and the execution to be paused on the next line of the method that called the current method.

❑ Continue execution of the program normally by selecting Debug > Continue. Execution will stop again only if an exception is raised, or another breakpoint is met. If the execution is stopped as a result of an exception, choosing to continue the execution will allow the error to propagate to the ASP.NET runtime, which will cause the error message to display in the browser window.

❑ Stop execution by selecting Debug > Stop Debugging.

❑ Stop and restart the program by selecting Debug > Restart.

All these commands are also available from the Debug toolbar, which is shown in Figure 5.52.

Figure 5.52. The Debug toolbar

This toolbar appears by default when you're debugging, but if it doesn't, you can make it display by right-clicking the toolbar and selecting Debug. The Debug toolbar reflects the commands you can find in the Debug menu, which is depicted in Figure 5.53, and the button on the extreme right gives you easy access to the various debugging windows.

Figure 5.53. Debugging windows accessible from the toolbar

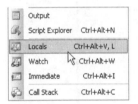

Other Kinds of Errors

Along with the runtime errors we've seen so far, ASP.NET can also throw the following kinds of errors:

configuration errors
These are caused by problems in the `Web.config` file. Try adding an incorrect tag to `Web.config`, and the next time you try to load the application, an error will occur.

parser errors
Parser errors are caused by the use of incorrect syntax in an ASP.NET script page; for instance, problems in the definitions of ASP.NET controls included in a web form will cause parser errors.

compilation errors
These errors are raised by the compiler when there's a syntax error in the page's C# or VB code, and will be caught by Visual Web Developer.

If you try to execute a page that contains compilation errors with Visual Web Developer, those errors will be signaled right away, and the page won't be loaded in the web browser (see Figure 5.54).

Figure 5.54. Visual Web Developer warns about a compilation error

If you'd like to try this for yourself, write some VB code, but terminate one of the lines with a semicolon as if you were writing C# code, as shown in the snippet below.

Visual Basic
```
Sub Page_Load(s As Object, e As EventArgs)
  timeLabel.Text = DateTime.Now.ToString();
End Sub
```

If you try to run this code, Visual Web Developer will present you with the message shown in Figure 5.54. If you choose Yes, a previous version of the code that used to compile successfully will be executed. Usually, this isn't what you want: you'll prefer to investigate the problem and fix the error. If you choose No, Visual Web Developer will display a window called Error List. Double-click the entry in the Error List, and the offending portion of code will be highlighted in the editor. Moreover, hovering your cursor over the highlighted code will display a tooltip containing a few details about the error, as Figure 5.55 illustrates.

After such a demonstration, I hope you agree that Visual Web Developer is a fantastic tool. What you've just seen is merely a common-sense feature in the world of Visual Web Developer, though—much more exciting and powerful features are available!

Figure 5.55. Visual Web Developer explaining an error in a tooltip

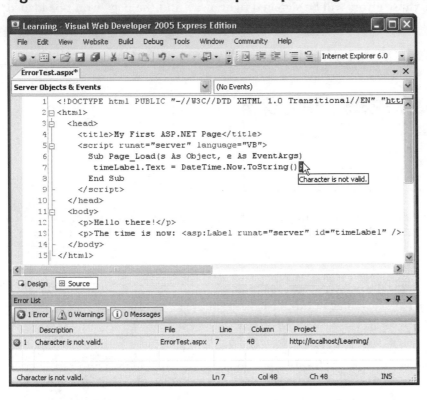

Custom Errors

If you're not running your application through Visual Web Developer, ASP.NET will report errors by displaying a message in the browser window, as we saw in Figure 5.46. The default error message that's shown to remote users doesn't contain code or other sensitive data, but you can customize the page that's displayed to visitors when errors occur using a `Web.config` setting called `customErrors`.

We define the `customErrors` element as a child of the `system.web` element like so:

File: **Web.config** (excerpt)

```
<configuration>
  <system.web>
```

```
        ⋮
    <customErrors mode="modeValue"
        defaultRedirect="errorPage.aspx" />
        ⋮
  </system.web>
</configuration>
```

The `defaultRedirect` attribute of the `customErrors` element is used to specify the page that's used to report errors. We can then choose whether this error page is shown to everybody, to nobody, or only to users who access the site from another network using the `mode` attribute. The possible values for the `mode` attribute are:

On   When `mode` is `On`, ASP.NET uses user-defined custom error pages, instead of its default error page, for both local and remote users.

Off   When `mode` has a value of `Off`, ASP.NET uses its default error page for both local and remote users. The `customErrors` element has no effect when `mode` is set to `Off`.

RemoteOnly When `mode` has the `RemoteOnly` value, the ASP.NET error page is shown only to local users, and the custom error page is shown to remote users. `RemoteOnly` is the default value, and is generally the safest option during development. If the `defaultRedirect` attribute is present, remote visitors will see the page mentioned; otherwise, they'll see a generic error that doesn't contain debugging information.

Handling Exceptions Locally

As you can see, unless you handle any exceptions that are raised in your code yourself, they'll be caught by the debugger. If you're not running the code within Visual Web Developer, the exceptions will be caught by the ASP.NET runtime, which displays the errors in the browser.

Additionally, C# and VB enable you to handle runtime errors using the `Try-Catch-Finally` construct.

The basic syntax of `Try-Catch-Finally` is as follows:

Visual Basic
```
Try
    ' Code that could generate the exception that you want to handle
```

213

```
Catch ex As Exception
    ' Code that is executed when an exception is generated
    ' The exception's details are accessible through the ex object
Finally
    ' Code that is guaranteed to execute at the end, no matter if
    ' an exception occurred
End Try
```

The equivalent C# syntax looks like this:

```
C#
try
{
    // Code that could generate the exception that you want to
    // handle
}
catch (Exception ex)
{
    // Code that is executed when an exception is generated
    // The exception's details are accessible through the ex
    // object
}
finally
{
    // Code that is guaranteed to execute at the end, no matter
    // if an exception occurred
}
```

As a basic rule of thumb, we'll place inside the Try block any code that we suspect might generate errors that we'll want to handle. If an exception is generated, the code in the Catch block will be executed. If the code in the Try block doesn't generate any exceptions, the code in the Catch block won't execute. In the end, whether an exception occurred or not, the code in the Finally block will execute.

That's an important point: the code in the Finally block will *always* execute, no matter what! As such, it's good practice to place any "mission-critical" code in that block. For example, if database operations are performed in the Try block, a good practice would be to close the database connection in the Finally block to ensure that no open connections remain active on the database server—consuming resources!—or to keep database objects locked.

Exceptions propagate from the point at which they were raised up through the **call stack** of your program. The call stack is the list of methods that are being executed. So, if method A calls a method B, which in turn calls method C, the call stack will be formed of these three methods, as Figure 5.56 illustrates.

Figure 5.56. A simple call stack

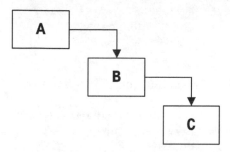

In this scenario, an exception that's raised in method C can be handled within the same function, provided the offending code is inside a `Try`/`Catch` block. If this isn't the case, the exception will propagate to method B, which also has the opportunity to handle the exception, and so on. If no method handles the exception, it will be intercepted either by the Visual Web Developer debugger or the ASP.NET runtime.

In the `Try-Catch-Finally` construct, both the `Finally` and `Catch` blocks are optional. You can use only the `Try` and `Catch` blocks if there's no need for a `Finally` block; you might use only `Try` and `Finally` blocks if you want your code always to perform a particular action when an exception is thrown, but you want the exception to propagate up the call stack.

In more complex scenarios, you can use more layers of error handling. In these scenarios, you'll want to handle the error partially in the place in which it occurred, but you'll still want to let it propagate so that the upper layers take note of it, and perform further processing. Exceptions are thrown using the `Throw` keyword (`throw` in C#), like so:

Visual Basic
```
Try
  ' Code that could generate and exception that you want to handle
Catch ex As Exception
  ' Code that is executed when an exception is generated
  Throw ex
End Try
```

C#
```
try
{
  // Code that could generate the exception that you want to
  // handle
```

```
}
catch (Exception ex)
{
  // Code that is executed when an exception is generated
  throw ex;
}
```

We could modify our array example to include Try and Catch blocks like this:

Visual Basic   File: **ErrorTest.aspx.vb (excerpt)**

```
Protected Sub Page_Load(ByVal sender As Object, _
    ByVal e As System.EventArgs) Handles Me.Load
  Dim a(10) As Integer
  Dim i As Integer
  Try
    For i = 1 To 11
      a(i) = i
    Next
  Catch ex As Exception
    messageLabel.Text = "Exception!<br />" & ex.Message
  End Try
End Sub
```

C#   File: **ErrorTest.aspx.cs (excerpt)**

```
protected void Page_Load(object sender, EventArgs e)
{
  int[] a = new int[10];
  int i;
  try
  {
    for (i = 0; i < 11; i++)
    {
      a[i] = i;
    }
  }
  catch(Exception ex)
  {
    messageLabel.Text = "Exception!<br />" + ex.Message;
  }
}
```

Provided you have a Label control named messageLabel in your web form, you'll see the message shown in Figure 5.57 when you run this code.

Figure 5.57. Catching an exception

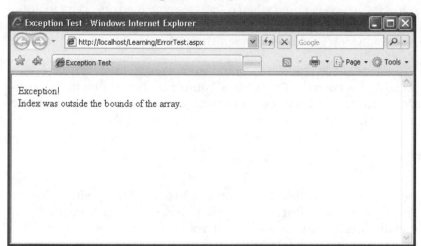

In the code above, we can see that the Catch block receives an Exception object as a parameter. This object describes the exception that has caused the Catch block to execute. In our code, we use one of the Exception object's many properties—in this case, Message—to display some information about the error.

In .NET, all exceptions are .NET classes derived from the Exception class. This means that, in fact, each exception is a different class (in our case, ex is an IndexOutOfRangeException object), but we can treat ex as the generic Exception class to access the generic details of any error.

The Exception class contains the following properties:

Message
    the error message

Source
    the name of the exception's source

StackTrace
    the names of the methods that were called just before the error occurred

TargetSite
    an instance of the MethodBase class that represents the method that caused the error

Specialized exception classes can contain additional members. For example, the `SqlException` class, which is raised when database-related errors occur, includes a collection of error messages (`SqlError` objects) in its `Errors` property. You could use a `For-Each` loop to iterate through these errors.

In complex application scenarios, you could even create your own exception classes as specialized versions of `Exception`. You could then throw these exceptions as needed, and catch them in a class or method that is situated in the upper levels of the hierarchy, and will handle these errors properly.

Summary

In this chapter, you've learned just how powerful Visual Web Developer can be. We've seen most of its basic features in action, and we've experimented with some of the really useful features you'll find yourself using every day, such as automatic code generation and debugging.

We've taken a close look at `Web.config`, which is where your web application's configuration settings will be stored, and `Global.asax`, which is where application-wide events can be handled. We've also discussed the `Application` and `Cache` objects, which can be used to store data that's available to all pages within an application; the `Session` object, which can be used to store user-specific data across requests; and cookies, which can be sent to the user's browser, then read on subsequent visits.

Finally, we took a look at themes and master pages, which are powerful ways of managing your site's look and feel.

In Chapter 6, we'll discuss data validation, and learn how ASP.NET's validation controls can help us ensure that our back-end systems are as secure as possible.

6

Using the Validation Controls

Ever needed to ensure that a user typed an email address into a text box? Or wanted to make sure that a user typed numbers only into a phone number field? Validation involves checking that the data your application's users have entered obeys a number of predefined rules. To help developers with the most common data validation tasks, ASP.NET provides a set of validation controls that ease the problems that beset web developers in the past. This chapter will show you how to use them.

There are two kinds of form validation, differentiated by where the validation takes place. You could write client-side JavaScript code that validates the data typed by the user directly into the browser (**client-side validation**), or you could use server-side VB or C# code to validate the user input once the form has been submitted to the server (**server-side validation**).

Client-side validation has its benefits, chief among them the fact that it provides instant feedback to users. If users fail to enter their names into a text box, the page automatically displays an error message. The users know immediately that they need to enter their names—they don't need to wait for a response from the server to tell them so. The process is quick and efficient, and good for the overall user experience.

However, there's one big drawback with client-side validation: users must have JavaScript enabled in their browsers, or validation simply will not occur. Some browsers, such as those built into PDAs and mobile telephones, don't support JavaScript, so client-side validation doesn't work for users of those browsers. Thus, though client-side validation is a great way to increase the usability of your site, it's not a foolproof method of ensuring that the data entered into your form passes all your rules.

While client-side validation is optional, server-side validation is not. For this reason, developers frequently choose to implement only server-side validation methods. Server-side validation is necessary because it's our last line of defense against bogus user data. The downside to server-side validation is that the application has to make a trip to the server before users can be alerted to any errors in their data.

Introducing the ASP.NET Validation Controls

ASP.NET includes controls that make validation a snap. The ASP.NET validation controls, while primarily being useful for implementing client-side validation, make it easier to implement server-side validation as well. The ASP.NET validation controls generate the JavaScript required for basic validation tasks for you (so you don't need to deal with any JavaScript code yourself); then, once the page is submitted, you can use the controls to check on the server whether or not the client-side validation was successful.

ASP.NET's validation controls provide client-side validation capabilities while virtually eliminating the need for developers to know JavaScript. Better still, they don't require complex server-side scripting. To use ASP.NET validation controls, we just add an object to the page and configure some simple properties.

As our first step towards demonstrating the ASP.NET validation controls, we'll create a number of simple pages in the Learning folder we worked with in previous chapters. Then we'll update the Dorknozzle intranet, adding validation features to the Help Desk page.

Opening Learning in Visual Web Developer

If you'd like to follow these examples in Visual Web Developer, feel free. You can open Learning as a web site by selecting File > Open Web Site..., navigating to the Learning folder (most likely C:\WebDocs\Learning\), and clicking Open. The view in Solution Explorer will be populated with any files you have in the Learning folder.

To start with, let's create a simple login web form. Create a file named Login.aspx and modify it as shown below. The parts that differ from the Visual Web Developer template are highlighted.

File: **Login.aspx (excerpt)**

```
<html xmlns="http://www.w3.org/1999/xhtml">
  <head>
    <title>Simple Login Page</title>
  </head>
  <body>
    <form id="form1" runat="server">
      <div>
        <!-- Username -->
        <p>
          Username:<br />
          <asp:TextBox id="usernameTextBox" runat="server" />
          <asp:RequiredFieldValidator id="usernameReq"
              runat="server"
              ControlToValidate="usernameTextBox"
              ErrorMessage="Username is required!" />
        </p>
        <!-- Password -->
        <p>
          Password:<br />
          <asp:TextBox id="passwordTextBox" runat="server"
              TextMode="Password" />
          <asp:RequiredFieldValidator id="passwordReq"
              runat="server"
              ControlToValidate="passwordTextBox"
              ErrorMessage="Password is required!" />
        </p>
        <!-- Submit Button -->
        <p>
          <asp:Button id="submitButton" runat="server"
              Text="Submit" />
        </p>
      </div>
    </form>
  </body>
</html>
```

Here, we've added two RequiredFieldValidator controls, which force the user to type some data into the referenced controls before the form can be submitted. Let's have a closer look at the first RequiredFieldValidator to see that it does its job. It sets a couple of properties, whose names are pretty descriptive (`ControlToValidate`, and `ErrorMessage`):

File: **Login.aspx (excerpt)**

```
<asp:RequiredFieldValidator id="usernameReq" runat="server"
    ControlToValidate="usernameTextBox"
    ErrorMessage="Username is required!" />
```

Load this page and immediately click the Submit button without entering text into either field. The page should display as shown in Figure 6.1. When we click the Submit button, we see instantly the error messages that tell us we forgot to type in a username and password.

Figure 6.1. Validation controls at work

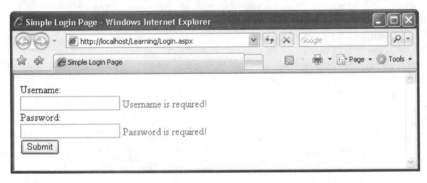

The beauty of ASP.NET validation controls is that they determine whether or not the browser is capable of supporting client-side validation. If it is, ASP.NET automatically includes the necessary client-side JavaScript; if not, it's omitted and the form is validated on the server.

ASP.NET 2.0 and Client-side Validation

In previous versions of ASP.NET, these controls demonstrated a tendency to assume that non-Microsoft browsers, such as Firefox, do not support JavaScript. As ASP.NET's client-side validation relies on JavaScript, client-side validation was not supported in those browsers and users had to rely on these controls' server-side validation.

ASP.NET 2.0 now recognizes the JavaScript capabilities of these browsers, so client-side validation is now available to all modern browsers, including Opera, Firefox, and others. However, it's important not to forget that

JavaScript can be disabled in any browser, so client-side validation cannot be relied upon—we must always validate any submitted data on the server.

A nice feature of ASP.NET 2.0 is that we can make it set the focus automatically to the first input control that causes a validation error. We activate this feature by setting the `SetFocusOnError` property of the validation control to `True`. Our simple example offers two `RequiredFieldValidation` controls that we can update. Let's do that now:

File: **Login.aspx** (excerpt)

```
<!-- Username -->
<p>
  Username:<br />
  <asp:TextBox id="usernameTextBox" runat="server" />
  <asp:RequiredFieldValidator id="usernameReq" runat="server"
      ControlToValidate="usernameTextBox"
      ErrorMessage="Username is required!"
      SetFocusOnError="True" />
</p>
<!-- Password -->
<p>
  Password:<br />
  <asp:TextBox id="passwordTextBox" runat="server"
      TextMode="Password" />
  <asp:RequiredFieldValidator id="passwordReq" runat="server"
      ControlToValidate="passwordTextBox"
      ErrorMessage="Password is required!"
      SetFocusOnError="True" />
</p>
```

If you make the changes highlighted in bold above, and load the page again, pressing the Submit button when a text box is empty will cause the empty text box to gain focus. If both text boxes are empty, the first one will receive focus.

Enforcing Validation on the Server

Validation is critical in circumstances in which users' submission of invalid data could harm your application. There are many circumstances where processing bad input data could have negative effects—for instance, it could produce runtime errors, or cause bad data to be stored in your database.

To get a clear idea of these implications, let's add to the login page some server-side code that uses the data input by the visitor. The typical point at which visitor data is used in a login page is the `Click` event handler of the Submit button. Add the `OnClick` property to the `Button` control, and give it the value `submitButton_Click`. This mimics what Visual Web Developer would do if you double-clicked the button in Design View.

```
<!-- Submit Button -->
<p>
  <asp:Button id="submitButton" runat="server" Text="Submit"
    OnClick="submitButton_Click" />
</p>
```

Next, create the `submitButton_Click` subroutine. You can add this between `<script runat="server">` and `</script>` tags in the head of the web form, or place it in a code-behind file. If Visual Web Developer generates these stubs for you, they may appear a little differently than they're presented here:

Visual Basic   File: **Login.aspx (excerpt)**

```
Protected Sub submitButton_Click(s As Object, e As EventArgs)
  submitButton.Text = "Clicked"
End Sub
```

C#   File: **Login.aspx (excerpt)**

```
protected void submitButton_Click(object sender, EventArgs e)
{
  submitButton.Text = "Clicked";
}
```

Now, if you're trying to submit invalid data using a browser that has JavaScript enabled, this code will never be executed. However, if you disable your browser's JavaScript, you'll see the label on the `Button` control change to Clicked! Obviously, this is not an ideal situation—we'll need to do a little more work to get validation working on the server side.

Disabling JavaScript in Firefox

To disable JavaScript in Firefox, go to Tools > Options..., click the Content tab and uncheck the Enable JavaScript checkbox.

Disabling JavaScript in Opera

To disable JavaScript in Opera, go to Tools > Preferences..., click the Advanced tab, select Content in the list on the left, and uncheck the Enable JavaScript checkbox.

Tip

Disabling JavaScript in Internet Explorer

To disable JavaScript in Internet Explorer, go to Tools > Internet Options…
and click the Security tab. There, select the zone for which you're changing
the settings (the zone will be shown on the right-hand side of the browser's
status bar—it will likely be Local Intranet Zone if you're developing on the
local machine) and press Custom Level…. Scroll down to the Scripting section, and check the Disable radio button for Active Scripting.

ASP.NET makes it easy to verify on the server side if the submitted data complies
to the validator rules without our having to write very much C# or VB code at
all. All we need to do is to check the **Page** object's **IsValid** property, which only
returns **True** if all the validators on the page are happy with the data in the controls they're validating. This approach will always work, regardless of which web
browser the user has, or the settings he or she has chosen.

Let's add this property to our **Click** event handler:

Visual Basic   File: **Login.aspx (excerpt)**

```vb
Protected Sub submitButton_Click(s As Object, e As EventArgs)
  If Page.IsValid Then
    submitButton.Text = "Valid"
  Else
    submitButton.Text = "Invalid!"
  End If
End Sub
```

C#   File: **Login.aspx (excerpt)**

```csharp
protected void submitButton_Click(object s, EventArgs e)
{
  if(Page.IsValid)
  {
    submitButton.Text = "Valid";
  }
  else
  {
    submitButton.Text = "Invalid!";
  }
}
```

Load the page again after disabling JavaScript, and press the Submit button
without entering any data in the text boxes. The text label on the button should
change, as shown in Figure 6.2.

Figure 6.2. Server validation failed

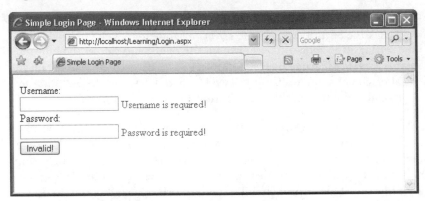

As you can see, the text on the button changed to a message that reflects the fact that `Page.IsValid` returned `False`. The validator controls also display the error messages, but only after a round-trip with the server. If JavaScript were enabled, the validator controls would prevent the page from submitting, so the code that changes the `Button`'s text wouldn't execute.

If you use validation controls, and verify on the server that `Page.IsValid` is `True` before you use any of the validated data, you have a bulletproof solution that's guaranteed to avoid bad data entering your application through any browser. JavaScript-enabled browsers will deliver an improved user experience by allowing client-side validation to take place, but server-side validation ensures that, ultimately, the functionality is the same regardless of your users' browser settings.

Using `CausesValidation`

There are cases in which you might decide to disable validation when a certain event is triggered. For example, imagine you have a registration page that contains two buttons: Submit, and Cancel. You'd probably want the Cancel button to work regardless of whether valid data has been entered, otherwise users won't be able to cancel the process before typing in some valid data! You can make Cancel work at all times by setting the `CausesValidation` property of the button to `False`.

One thing to note about validator controls is that, by default, they take up space in your web form. To illustrate this point, let's add a password confirmation text box just after the password text box's `RequiredFieldValidator`:

File: **Login.aspx (excerpt)**

```
<p>
  Username:<br />
  <asp:TextBox id="usernameTextBox" runat="server" />
  <asp:RequiredFieldValidator id="usernameReq" runat="server"
      ControlToValidate="usernameTextBox"
      ErrorMessage="Username is required!"
      SetFocusOnError="True" />
</p>
<!-- Password -->
<p>
  Password and Confirmation:<br />
  <asp:TextBox id="passwordTextBox" runat="server"
      TextMode="Password" />
  <asp:RequiredFieldValidator id="passwordReq" runat="server"
      ControlToValidate="passwordTextBox"
      ErrorMessage="Password is required!"
      SetFocusOnError="True" />
  <asp:TextBox id="confirmPasswordTextBox" runat="server"
      TextMode="Password" />
  <asp:RequiredFieldValidator id="confirmPasswordReq"
      runat="server" ControlToValidate="confirmPasswordTextBox"
      ErrorMessage="Password confirmation is required!"
      SetFocusOnError="True" />
</p>
```

Load this page and you'll see that the new `confirmPasswordTextBox` control appears after the space that's reserved for the `RequiredFieldValidator` control, as Figure 6.3 illustrates.

Figure 6.3. The `RequiredValidatorControl` taking up space

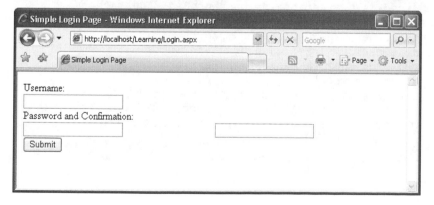

As you can see, ASP.NET reserves space for its validator controls by default. However, we can change this using the `Display` property, which can take any one of the values `None`, `Static`, or `Dynamic`:

None

> `None` makes the validator invisible—no space is reserved, and the error message is never shown. You may want to set this option when using the `ValidationSummary` control (which we'll cover later) to display a list of validation errors for the entire page, in which case you won't want each validation control to display its own error message separately.

Static

> `Static` is the default display mode. With this mode, the validator occupies space on the generated form even if it doesn't display anything.

Dynamic

> The `Dynamic` mode causes the validation control to display if any validation errors occur, but ensures that it doesn't generate any output (including the white space shown in Figure 6.3) if the validation is passed.

In the code below, the `Display` property is set to `Dynamic`. If we set this property for all of the validation controls in our page, the two password `TextBox` controls will appear side by side until one of them fails validation.

File: **Login.aspx (excerpt)**

```
<!-- Password -->
<p>
  Password and Confirmation:<br />
  <asp:TextBox id="passwordTextBox" runat="server"
      TextMode="Password" />
  <asp:RequiredFieldValidator id="passwordReq" runat="server"
      ControlToValidate="passwordTextBox"
      ErrorMessage="Password is required!"
      SetFocusOnError="True" Display="Dynamic" />
  <asp:TextBox id="confirmPasswordTextBox" runat="server"
      TextMode="Password" />
  <asp:RequiredFieldValidator id="confirmPasswordReq"
      runat="server" ControlToValidate="confirmPasswordTextBox"
      ErrorMessage="Password confirmation is required!"
      SetFocusOnError="True" Display="Dynamic" />
</p>
```

Using Validation Controls

Now that you have an understanding of what validation controls can do, let's have a look at the different controls that are available in ASP.NET:

❑ RequiredFieldValidator

❑ RangeValidator

❑ RegularExpressionValidator

❑ CompareValidator

❑ CustomValidator

❑ ValidationSummary

If you're working with Visual Web Developer, you can see the validation controls in the Validation tab of the Toolbox, as Figure 6.4 illustrates.

Figure 6.4. Accessing the validation controls in Visual Web Developer

Validation controls are a particular kind of web server control, and are inserted as tags with the `asp:` prefix. Once a validation control is inserted, it validates an existing control elsewhere on the page, and presents an error message to the user if necessary. To validate a field, all you have to do is insert a control—there's no

JavaScript or clumsy server-side code to write by hand! Let's take a look at these ASP.NET validation controls in detail.

RequiredFieldValidator

The RequiredFieldValidator control is the simplest of the validation controls. It does exactly what its name suggests: it makes sure that a user enters a value into a web control. We used the RequiredFieldValidator control in the login page example presented earlier:

File: **Login.aspx (excerpt)**

```
<p>
  Username:<br />
  <asp:TextBox id="usernameTextBox" runat="server" />
  <asp:RequiredFieldValidator id="usernameReq" runat="server"
      ControlToValidate="usernameTextBox"
      ErrorMessage="Username is required!"
      SetFocusOnError="True" Display="Dynamic" />
</p>
<!-- Password -->
<p>
  Password and Confirmation:<br />
  <asp:TextBox id="passwordTextBox" runat="server"
      TextMode="Password" />
  <asp:RequiredFieldValidator id="passwordReq" runat="server"
      ControlToValidate="passwordTextBox"
      ErrorMessage="Password is required!"
      SetFocusOnError="True" Display="Dynamic" />
  <asp:TextBox id="confirmPasswordTextBox" runat="server"
      TextMode="Password" />
  <asp:RequiredFieldValidator id="confirmPasswordReq"
      runat="server" ControlToValidate="confirmPasswordTextBox"
      ErrorMessage="Password confirmation is required!"
      SetFocusOnError="True" Display="Dynamic" />
</p>
```

As you can see, three RequiredFieldValidator controls are used on this page. The first validates the usernameTextBox control, the second validates the passwordTextBox control, and the third validates the confirmPasswordTextBox control. These assignments are made using the ControlToValidate property of the RequiredFieldValidator controls. The ErrorMessage property contains the error message that will be displayed when the user fails to enter a value into each control.

CompareValidator

One of the most useful validation controls is the `CompareValidator` control, which performs a comparison between the data entered into a given control and some other value. That other value can be a fixed value, such as a number, or a value entered into another control.

Let's look at an example that builds on the login example from the previous section. Here, we'll validate that the data entered into both the password fields is identical. Make the following changes to `Login.aspx`:

File: **Login.aspx (excerpt)**

```
<asp:TextBox id="passwordTextBox" runat="server"
    TextMode="Password" />
⋮
<asp:TextBox id="confirmPasswordTextBox" runat="server"
    TextMode="Password" />
⋮
<asp:CompareValidator id="comparePasswords" runat="server"
    ControlToCompare="passwordTextBox"
    ControlToValidate="confirmPasswordTextBox"
    ErrorMessage="Your passwords do not match up!"
    Display="Dynamic" />
</p>
```

Run the page and enter different passwords into the two fields. The `CompareValidator` control will appear as soon as you move on from two fields whose data doesn't match, as Figure 6.5 shows.

Figure 6.5. A `CompareValidator` in action

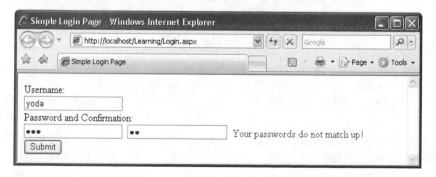

As you've probably noticed, the `CompareValidator` control differs very little from the `RequiredFieldValidator` control:

File: **Login.aspx (excerpt)**

```
<asp:RequiredFieldValidator id="confirmPasswordReq" runat="server"
    ControlToValidate="confirmPasswordTextBox"
    ErrorMessage="Password confirmation is required!"
    SetFocusOnError="True" Display="Dynamic" />
<asp:CompareValidator id="comparePasswords" runat="server"
    ControlToCompare="passwordTextBox"
    ControlToValidate="confirmPasswordTextBox"
    ErrorMessage="Your passwords do not match up!"
    Display="Dynamic" />
```

The only difference is that in addition to a `ControlToValidate` property, the `CompareValidator` has a `ControlToCompare` property. We set these two properties to the IDs of the controls we want to compare. So, in our example, the `ControlToValidate` property is set to the `confirmPasswordTextBox`, and the `ControlToCompare` property is set to the `passwordTextBox`.

The `CompareValidator` can be used to compare the value of a control to a fixed value, too. `CompareValidator` can check whether the entered value is equal to, less than, or greater than, any given value. As an example, let's add an age field to our login form:

File: **Login.aspx (excerpt)**

```
<!-- Age -->
<p>
  Age:<br />
  <asp:TextBox id="ageTextBox" runat="server" />
  <asp:RequiredFieldValidator id="ageReq" runat="server"
      ControlToValidate="ageTextBox"
      ErrorMessage="Age is required!"
      SetFocusOnError="True" Display="Dynamic" />
  <asp:CompareValidator id="ageCheck" runat="server"
      Operator="GreaterThan" Type="Integer"
      ControlToValidate="ageTextBox" ValueToCompare="15"
      ErrorMessage="You must be 16 years or older to log in" />
</p>
```

In this case, the `CompareValidator` control is used to check that the user is old enough to log in to our fictitious web application. Here, we set the `Operator` property of the `CompareValidator` to `GreaterThan`. This property can take on any of the values `Equal`, `NotEqual`, `GreaterThan`, `GreaterThanEqual`, `LessThan`,

LessThanEqual, or DataTypeCheck, which we'll look at shortly. Next, we tell the CompareValidator control to compare the two values by setting the Type property to Integer, which will cause the CompareValidator to treat the values as whole numbers (this property can also be set to Currency or Date, among other options). Finally, we use the ValueToCompare property to make sure that the user's age is greater than 15. If you load this page in your web browser now, you'll see that the form is only validated when the user enters an age of 16 or more.

We can also use the CompareValidator control to perform data type checks. To see how this works, let's replace the age TextBox control with a date-of-birth text box, whose value must be a valid date:

File: **Login.aspx (excerpt)**

```
<!-- Birth Date -->
<p>
  Birth Date:<br />
  <asp:TextBox id="birthDateTextBox" runat="server" />
  <asp:CompareValidator id="birthDateCheck" runat="server"
      Operator="DataTypeCheck" Type="Date"
      ControlToValidate="birthDateTextBox"
      ErrorMessage="You must enter the date in a valid format!"
      SetFocusOnError="True" Display="Dynamic" />
</p>
```

As you can see, the Operator property of the CompareValidator control is set to perform a DataTypeCheck, and the Type property is set to Date. Load the page, and you'll see that you can't enter anything other than a valid date into this field. The constituents of a "valid" date will depend on the regional settings on your web server.

RangeValidator

The RangeValidator control checks whether the value of a form field falls between minimum and maximum values. For instance, we could make sure that users who visit our web site were born in a certain decade. If they enter values that don't fit into the range we specify, the validator will return an "invalid" message.

Let's continue by expanding Login.aspx even further:

File: **Login.aspx (excerpt)**

```
<!-- Birth Date -->
<p>
  Birth Date:<br />
```

```
<asp:TextBox id="birthDateTextBox" runat="server" />
<asp:RangeValidator id="birthDateRangeTest" runat="server"
    Type="Date" ControlToValidate="birthDateTextBox"
    MinimumValue="1/1/1970" MaximumValue="12/31/1979"
    ErrorMessage="You must've been born in the 1970s to use
    this web site!" />
</p>
```

Take Care when Specifying Dates

If you're outside of the US, you may need to modify the above example. In the US, dates are specified in month-day-year format. In the UK and Australia, they're specified in day-month-year order, and in other countries, the year is specified first. The ASP.NET runtime will be expecting you to specify dates in your local format, so adjust the values of the `MinimumValue` and `MaximumValue` properties accordingly.

Here, we've added a `RangeValidator` to validate the `birthDateTextBox` control. Our `RangeValidator` control checks whether the date entered falls within the 1970s, and shows an error message similar to Figure 6.6 if it doesn't.

Figure 6.6. Using the `RangeValidator` control

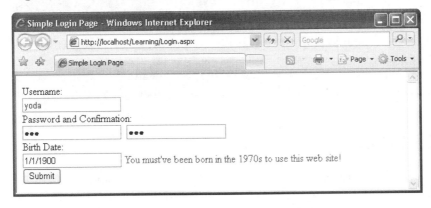

Note that the `Type` property of the `RangeValidator` control specifies the data type that's expected in the control with which it's associated: if some other data type is entered into this field, it fails validation. As such, we've removed the `CompareValidator` we added for this purpose.

ValidationSummary

Imagine we have a form that contains many form fields. If that page contains errors, it could be difficult for users to figure out which control caused a given error, because the page is so big. The ValidationSummary control can alleviate this problem by presenting the user with a list of error messages in one place on the page. Let's see the ValidationSummary control in use. Add it to the end of your Login.aspx file, like so:

File: **Login.aspx (excerpt)**

```
<!-- Submit Button -->
<p>
  <asp:Button id="submitButton" runat="server" Text="Submit"
      OnClick="submitButton_Click" />
</p>
<!-- Validation Summary -->
<p>
  <asp:ValidationSummary id="vSummary" runat="server" />
</p>
```

When the user clicks the Submit button, the ValidationSummary is populated automatically with a list of all the errors on the page, as we can see in Figure 6.7.

Figure 6.7. Using the ValidationSummary control

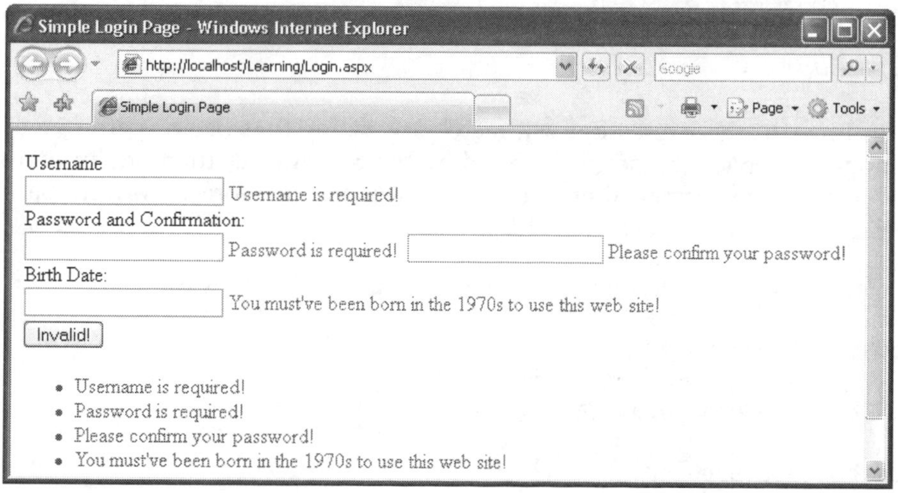

This control isn't particularly good-looking, but you can see its potential. If you set the `Display` properties of all the other validation controls on the page to `None`, you could use a `ValidationSummary` to show all the errors in one place.

If you set the `ShowMessageBox` property of the `ValidationSummary` control to `True`, the list of errors will be shown in a JavaScript `alert` box similar to Figure 6.8. The server-side list will still be shown to users who don't have JavaScript-enabled browsers.

Figure 6.8. Showing validation errors in a dialog

RegularExpressionValidator

The `RegularExpressionValidator` lets you specify a regular expression that describes all the allowable values for a field. Regular expressions are powerful tools for manipulating strings, and are supported by many programming languages. They're commonly used to check for patterns inside strings. Consider, for instance, the following regular expression:

`^\S+@\S+\.\S+$`

In plain English, this expression will match any string that begins with one or more non-whitespace characters followed by the @ character, then one or more non-whitespace characters, then a dot (.), then one or more non-whitespace characters, followed by the end of the string.

This regular expression describes any one of these email addresses:

❑ `books@sitepoint.com`

❑ `zac@host.modulemedia.com`

❑ `joe_bloggs@yahoo.co.uk`

However, the regular expression would fail if the user typed in one of these entries:

❑ books@sitepoint

❑ joe bloggs@yahoo.co.uk

Although regular expressions cannot check to see if the email address itself is valid, they can, at the very least, provide a means for us to determine whether or not the user has entered a string of characters that has all the key components of a valid email address.

Let's change the username field in our login form to an email address field, and validate it using the RegularExpressionValidator control.

File: **Login.aspx (excerpt)**

```
<asp:TextBox id="emailTextBox" runat="server" />
<asp:RequiredFieldValidator id="emailReq" runat="server"
    ControlToValidate="emailTextBox"
    ErrorMessage="Email address is required!"
    SetFocusOnError="True" Display="Dynamic" />
<asp:RegularExpressionValidator id="emailValidator"
    runat="server" ControlToValidate="emailTextBox"
    ValidationExpression="^\S+@\S+\.\S+$"
    ErrorMessage="You must enter a valid email address!" />
</p>
```

The important property within this control is ValidationExpression, to which we assign the regular expression that's appropriate to handle our custom validation functionality. Figure 6.9 shows the error message that appears when a user enters an incorrect email address.

Figure 6.9. Using the RegularExpressionValidator control

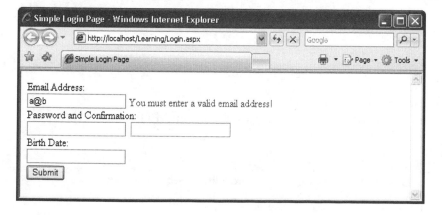

Some Useful Regular Expressions

Writing regular expressions can be tricky, and a comprehensive discussion is outside the scope of this book. Many of the other regular expressions presented here are nowhere near as rigorous as they could be, but are still quite useful. The book *Mastering Regular Expressions*, by Jeffrey E. F. Friedl, contains a single expression for checking email addresses that tops 6,000 characters![1]

Table 6.1 outlines the usage of some simple regular expressions.

Table 6.1. Some simple regular expressions

Description	Regular Expression
email address	`^\S+@\S+\.\S+$`
web URL	`^https?://\S+\.\S+$`
US phone numbers (*(555) 555-5555* or *555-555-5555*)	`^\(?\d{3}\)?(\s|-)\d{3}-\d{4}$`
international phone numbers (begins with a digit, followed by between seven and 20 digits and/or dashes)	`^\d(\d|-){7,20}$`
five-digit ZIP code	`^\d{5}$`
nine-digit ZIP code	`^\d{5}-\d{4}$`
either five-digit or nine-digit ZIP code	`^(\d{5})|(\d{5}\-\d{4})$`
US social security number	`^\d{3}-\d{2}-\d{4}$`

By referencing the components of these regular expressions in Table 6.2, you should begin to see how they work. If you'd like more information on regular expressions, try the following resources:

Regular Expression Library[2]
a searchable library of regular expressions

Using Regular Expressions in PHP[3]
a great article on the use of regular expressions and PHP

---

[1] Jeffrey E. F. Friedl, *Mastering Regular Expressions*, Third Edition (Sebastopol: O'Reilly Media), 2006.
[2] http://www.regexlib.com/
[3] http://www.sitepoint.com/article/regular-expressions-php

Regular Expressions in JavaScript[4]
     another great article, this time on the use of regular expressions with JavaScript

Table 6.2. Common regular expression components and their descriptions

Special Character	Description
.	any character
^	beginning of string
$	end of string
\d	numeric digit
\s	whitespace character
\S	non-whitespace character
(abc)	the string abc as a group of characters
?	preceding character or group is optional
+	one or more of the preceding character or group
*	zero or more of the preceding character or group
{n}	exactly n of the preceding character or group
{n,m}	n to m of the preceding character or group
(a|b)	either a or b
\$	a dollar sign (as opposed to the end of a string); we can 'escape' any of the special characters listed above by preceding it with a backslash. For example, \. matches a period character, \? matches a question mark, and so on

You'll find a complete guide and reference to regular expressions and their components in the .NET Framework SDK Documentation.

CustomValidator

The validation controls included with ASP.NET allow you to handle many kinds of validation, yet certain types of validation cannot be performed with these built-in controls. For instance, imagine that you needed to ensure that a new

---

[4] http://www.sitepoint.com/article/expressions-javascript

user's login details were unique by checking them against a list of existing usernames on the server. The CustomValidator control can be helpful in this situation, and others like it. Let's see how:

Visual Basic   File: **CustomValidator.aspx (excerpt)**

```
<!DOCTYPE html PUBLIC "-//W3C//DTD XHTML 1.0 Transitional//EN"
    "http://www.w3.org/TR/xhtml1/DTD/xhtml1-transitional.dtd">
<html>
  <head>
    <title>CustomValidator Control Sample</title>
    <script runat="server" language="VB">
      Sub CheckUniqueUserName(s As Object, _
            e As ServerValidateEventArgs)
        Dim username As String = e.Value.ToLower
        If (username = "zak" Or username = "cristian") Then
          e.IsValid = False
        End If
      End Sub

      Sub submitButton_Click(s As Object, e As EventArgs)
        If Page.IsValid Then
          submitButton.Text = "Valid"
        Else
          submitButton.Text = "Invalid!"
        End If
      End Sub
    </script>
  </head>
  <body>
    <form runat="server">
      <p>
        New Username:<br />
        <asp:TextBox ID="usernameTextBox" runat="server" />
        <asp:CustomValidator ID="usernameUnique" runat="server"
            ControlToValidate="usernameTextBox"
            OnServerValidate="CheckUniqueUserName"
            ErrorMessage="This username already taken!" />
      </p>
      <p>
        <asp:Button ID="submitButton" runat="server"
            OnClick="submitButton_Click" Text="Submit" />
      </p>
    </form>
  </body>
</html>
```

File: **CustomValidator.aspx (excerpt)**

```
<!DOCTYPE html PUBLIC "-//W3C//DTD XHTML 1.0 Transitional//EN"
    "http://www.w3.org/TR/xhtml1/DTD/xhtml1-transitional.dtd">
<html>
  <head>
    <title>CustomValidator Control Sample</title>
    <script runat="server" language="C#">
      void CheckUniqueUserName(Object s,
          ServerValidateEventArgs e)
      {
        string username = e.Value.ToLower();
        if(username == "zak" || username == "cristian")
        {
          e.IsValid = false;
        }
      }

      void submitButton_Click(Object s, EventArgs e)
      {
        if(Page.IsValid)
        {
          submitButton.Text = "Valid";
        }
        else
        {
          submitButton.Text = "Invalid!";
        }
      }
    </script>
  </head>
  <body>
    <form runat="server">
      <p>
        New Username:<br />
        <asp:TextBox ID="usernameTextBox" runat="server" />
        <asp:CustomValidator ID="usernameUnique" runat="server"
            ControlToValidate="usernameTextBox"
            OnServerValidate="CheckUniqueUserName"
            ErrorMessage="This username already taken!" />
      </p>
      <p>
        <asp:Button ID="submitButton" runat="server"
            OnClick="submitButton_Click" Text="Submit" />
      </p>
    </form>
```

```
</body>
</html>
```

When this form is submitted, the `CustomValidator` control raises the `ServerValidate` event, and the `CheckUniqueUserName` method is called as a result. At the moment, our list of usernames is limited to `zak` and `cristian`. If the new username matches either of these, `e.IsValid` is set to `False`, and the error message is displayed; otherwise, we assume that the username is valid. When our `submitButton_Click` event handler checks the `Page.IsValid` property, `e.IsValid` returns `False` if the user entered `zak` or `cristian`, and `True` if the new username is anything else.

Although this example shows a very simple `CustomValidator`, you can certainly imagine the possibilities this class makes available. For example, while we won't explore it in this book, you could create a client-side validation function for your `CustomValidator` controls by means of the `ClientValidationFunction` property. For details, refer to the .NET Framework SDK Documentation for the `CustomValidator` control.

Validation Groups

A very useful new feature in ASP.NET 2.0, validation groups allow us to validate individual parts of a web page independently of its other sections. This capability proves particularly handy when you're working with complex pages that contain many functional components. For example, consider the scenario of a single page that contains a login form *and* a quick registration form, each with its own Submit button and its own set of validation controls. Certainly we don't want the functionality of the login form's Submit button to be affected by the data in the registration form; nor can we allow the login form's data to affect submission of the registration form.

The solution to this problem is to set the controls in each of the boxes within different validation groups. You can assign a control to a validation group using its `ValidationGroup` property, as shown in the following code:

File: **ValidationGroups.aspx** (excerpt)

```
<!DOCTYPE html PUBLIC "-//W3C//DTD XHTML 1.0 Transitional//EN"
    "http://www.w3.org/TR/xhtml1/DTD/xhtml1-transitional.dtd">
<html>
  <head>
    <title>Validation Groups Demo</title>
  </head>
```

```
<body>
  <form id="Form1" runat="server">
    <!-- Login Controls -->
    <h1>Login</h1>
    <!-- Username -->
    <p>
      Username:<br />
      <asp:TextBox id="usernameTextBox" runat="server" />
      <asp:RequiredFieldValidator id="usernameReq"
          runat="server" ControlToValidate="usernameTextBox"
          ErrorMessage="Username is required!"
          SetFocusOnError="True" ValidationGroup="Login" />
    </p>
    <!-- Password -->
    <p>
      Password:<br />
      <asp:TextBox id="passwordTextBox"
          runat="server" TextMode="Password" />
      <asp:RequiredFieldValidator id="passwordReq"
          runat="server" ControlToValidate="passwordTextBox"
          ErrorMessage="Password is required!"
          SetFocusOnError="True" ValidationGroup="Login" />
    </p>
    <p>
      <asp:Button ID="loginButton" runat="server" Text="Log In"
          ValidationGroup="Login" />
    </p>
    <!-- Login Controls -->
    <h1>Register</h1>
    <!-- Username -->
    <p>
      Username:<br />
      <asp:TextBox id="newUserNameTextBox" runat="server" />
      <asp:RequiredFieldValidator id="newUserNameReq"
          runat="server" ControlToValidate="newUserNameTextBox"
          ErrorMessage="Username is required!"
          SetFocusOnError="True" ValidationGroup="Register" />
    </p>
    <!-- Password -->
    <p>
      Password:<br />
      <asp:TextBox id="newPasswordTextBox" runat="server"
          TextMode="Password" />
      <asp:RequiredFieldValidator id="newPasswordReq"
          runat="server" ControlToValidate="newPasswordTextBox"
          ErrorMessage="Password is required!"
```

```
            SetFocusOnError="True" ValidationGroup="Register" />
      </p>
      <p>
        <asp:Button ID="registerButton" runat="server"
            Text="Register" ValidationGroup="Register" />
      </p>
    </form>
  </body>
</html>
```

Executing this page reveals the two sets of controls: one for logging in an existing user, and another for registering a new user. To keep things simple, the only validation we've implemented in this example is achieved through RequiredFieldValidator controls.

Clicking the Log In button triggers only those validators that share that button's ValidationGroup setting, as Figure 6.10 indicates.

Figure 6.10. Triggering the Login ValidationGroup

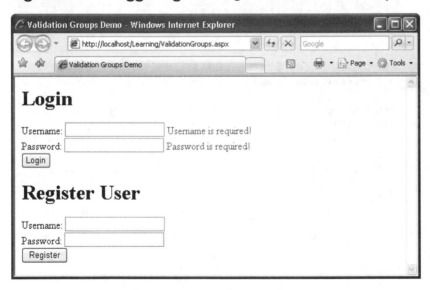

Likewise, clicking the Register button triggers the second set of validators, and deactivates the first, as Figure 6.11 shows.

Default Validation Groups

Controls that aren't specifically assigned to any validation group are aggregated into a default validation group. In other words, a button that isn't assigned to any validation group will trigger only those validation controls that aren't assigned to any groups.

Finally, remember that `Page.IsValid` returns the results of the current validation group (i.e. the one that caused the server-side event). To verify the validity of another group on the page, we use the `Page.Validate` method, which can receive as parameter the name of the validation group to be validated.

Figure 6.11. Activating the `RegisterValidationGroup`

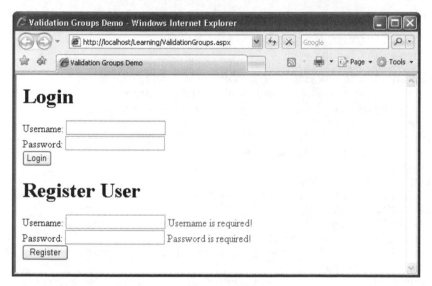

Updating Dorknozzle

Now that you've spent some time with validation controls, let's use them to update Dorknozzle's Help Desk page. The following rules must be met before the user can submit a new help desk request:

❑ The station number text box cannot be empty.

❑ The station number must be a valid number.

❑ The station number must be a numeral between 1 and 50.

❑ A description of the problem must be entered.

To make changes to the help desk page, you first need to load the Dorknozzle project in Visual Web Developer. Go to File > Open Web Site... and select the Dorknozzle project.

 Tip

Loading Multiple Projects

Did you know that you can work with multiple projects at the same time? You can launch multiple instances of Visual Web Developer and load a different web application in each of them.

After Dorknozzle loads, open HelpDesk.aspx in the editor and make the following changes to the file:

File: **HelpDesk.aspx (excerpt)**

```
<%@ Page Language="VB" MasterPageFile="~/Dorknozzle.master"
    AutoEventWireup="false" CodeFile="HelpDesk.aspx.vb"
    Inherits="HelpDesk" title="Dorknozzle Help Desk" %>
<asp:Content ID="Content1"
    ContentPlaceHolderID="ContentPlaceHolder1" Runat="Server">
  <h1>Employee Help Desk Request</h1>
  <p>
    Station Number:<br />
    <asp:TextBox id="stationTextBox" runat="server"
        CssClass="textbox" />
    <asp:RequiredFieldValidator id="stationNumReq" runat="server"
        ControlToValidate="stationTextBox"
        ErrorMessage="<br />You must enter a station number!"
        Display="Dynamic" />
    <asp:CompareValidator id="stationNumCheck" runat="server"
        ControlToValidate="stationTextBox"
        Operator="DataTypeCheck" Type="Integer"
        ErrorMessage="<br />The value must be a number!"
        Display="Dynamic" />
    <asp:RangeValidator id="stationNumRangeCheck" runat="server"
        ControlToValidate="stationTextBox"
        MinimumValue="1" MaximumValue="50" Type="Integer"
        ErrorMessage="<br />Number must be between 1 and 50."
        Display="Dynamic" />
  </p>
  <p>
    Problem Category:<br />
```

```
      <asp:DropDownList id="categoryList" runat="server"
          CssClass="dropdownmenu" />
  </p>
  <p>
    Problem Subject:<br />
    <asp:DropDownList id="subjectList" runat="server"
        CssClass="dropdownmenu" />
  </p>
  <p>
    Problem Description:<br />
    <asp:TextBox id="descriptionTextBox" runat="server"
        CssClass="textbox" Columns="40" Rows="4"
        TextMode="MultiLine" />
    <asp:RequiredFieldValidator id="descriptionReq" runat="server"
        ControlToValidate="descriptionTextBox"
        ErrorMessage="<br />You must enter a description!"
        Display="Dynamic" />
  </p>
  <p>
    <asp:Button id="submitButton" runat="server"
        CssClass="button" Text="Submit Request" />
  </p>
</asp:Content>
```

Now execute the project, and select the Help Desk page from the menu. Clicking Submit without entering valid data triggers the validation controls, as Figure 6.12 shows.

Figure 6.12. Validation controls in action on the Dorknozzle Help Desk

Right now, we're not doing anything with the data that's been entered, but we'll take care of that in following chapters. When we finally do something with this data, we don't want our server-side code to try to work with invalid data. Let's add the safety check to the server side as well, to make sure we have a solid foundation from which to start developing our server-side functionality in the next chapters.

Stop the project from within Visual Web Developer, and open HelpDesk.aspx in Design View. There, double-click the Submit Request button to have its Click event handler generated for you.

Complete the automatically generated code as shown below:

Visual Basic | File: **HelpDesk.aspx.vb (excerpt)**

```
Protected Sub submitButton_Click(ByVal sender As Object, _
    ByVal e As System.EventArgs) Handles submitButton.Click
  If Page.IsValid Then
    ' Code that uses the data entered by the user
  End If
End Sub
```

C# | File: **HelpDesk.aspx.cs (excerpt)**

```
protected void submitButton_Click(object sender, EventArgs e)
{
  if (Page.IsValid)
  {
    // Code that uses the data entered by the user
  }
}
```

Up to this point, we've only discussed one way of tying a control's event to an event handler method. This approach involves setting a property, such as `OnClick`, on the control, as shown here:

C# | File: **HelpDesk.aspx (excerpt)**

```
<asp:Button id="submitButton" runat="server" CssClass="button"
    Text="Submit Request" OnClick="submitButton_Click" />
```

This property causes ASP.NET to call a method named `submitButton_Click` whenever this button is clicked. If you're using C#, you'll see that Visual Web Developer added this property to `submitButton` when it generated your event handler, as is shown above.

However, if you're using VB, this property is not added. Instead, Visual Web Developer uses the VB-specific keyword `Handles`, followed by the name of the control that's responsible for raising the event, and finally the name of the event that's being handled (in our case, `submitButton.Click`). This generated code is shown below:

Visual Basic | File: **HelpDesk.aspx.vb (excerpt)**

```
Protected Sub submitButton_Click(ByVal sender As Object, _
    ByVal e As System.EventArgs) Handles submitButton.Click
```

This is simply an alternative way of tying this method to the `submitButton` control's `Click` event.

We'll expand the code inside this method in later chapters, but for the time being, you can rest assured that you've put the validation mechanism in place.

Summary

As we've seen, the validation controls available through ASP.NET are very powerful. This chapter explained how to validate required form fields with the `RequiredFieldValidator`, compare form fields with the `CompareValidator`, check for a numeric range within form fields with the `RangeValidator`, provide a user with a summary of errors using the `ValidationSummary` control, check for email addresses with the `RegularExpressionValidator`, and perform your own custom validation with the `CustomValidator`.

In the next chapter, we'll begin to introduce you to the challenges—and rewards!—involved in working with databases. This is a skill you'll almost certainly need when building any non-trivial real-world web application, so roll up your sleeves and let's get into it!

7

Database Design and Development

As you begin to build dynamic web applications, it will become increasingly obvious that you need to store data and allow users to access it through your application. Whether you're building a company-wide intranet that can only be accessed by employees, or a feature-rich ecommerce site that millions will visit, you'll need a system for storing information. Enter: the database.

In 1970, E.F. Codd, an employee of IBM, proposed his idea for what would become the first relational database design model. His model, which offered new methods for storing and retrieving data in large applications, far surpassed any idea or system that was in place at the time. The concept of relational data stemmed from the fact that data was organized in tables, and relationships were defined between those tables.

In this chapter, we'll learn:

❑ what databases are, and why they're useful

❑ what a database is made of

❑ what kind of relationships can exist between database elements

❑ how to use database diagrams

What is a Database?

Before we become mired in techno-speak, let's take a step back to consider the project at hand—the Dorknozzle Intranet—and how it can benefit from a relational database. By the end of this book, our site will be able to do all sorts of things, but beside these bells and whistles, our company intranet will need to do one core job: keep track of the employees in our company. The employee directory we plan to build would be a sorry sight indeed without a list of employees!

So, how will we go about building that information into our site? Experience with static web design might lead you to create a web page named Employee Directory, which displayed a table or list of some kind, and to type in the details of each of the employees in the company. But, unless Dorknozzle is a very small company, a single page that contained all the details of every employee would be destined to become unusably large. Instead, you might only list the employees' names, and link each to an individual profile page. Sure, this approach might mean there's a bit of typing to do, but it's the kind of job you can assign to the boss's son on his summer internship.

Now, imagine that, a month or two down the track, Dorknozzle undergoes a corporate re-branding exercise (a bright idea undoubtedly proposed by the boss's son one night at the dinner table), and the entire web site needs to be updated to match the "new look" of the company. By now, Dorknozzle Jr is back at school, and the mind-numbing job of manually updating each of the employee profile pages falls right in your lap. Lucky you!

Life would be a lot more pleasant if a database was added to the mix. A database is a collection of data organized within a framework that can be accessed by programs such as your SPINET web site. For example, you could have the Dorknozzle intranet site look into a database to find a list of employees that you want to display on the employee directory page.

Such a collection of data needs to be managed by some kind of software—that software is called a **database server**. The database server we'll use in this book is SQL Server 2005 Express Edition, which is a free but very powerful database engine created by Microsoft. Other popular database server software products include Oracle, DB2, PostgreSQL, MySQL, and others.

In our Dorknozzle scenario, the employee records would be stored entirely in the database, which would provide two key advantages over the manual maintenance of a list of employees. First, instead of having to write an HTML file for each employee profile page, you could write a single ASP.NET web form that would fetch any employee's details from the database and display them as a profile. This single form could be updated quite easily in the event of corporate re-branding or some other disaster. Second, adding an employee to the directory would be a simple matter of inserting a new record into the database. The web form would take care of the rest, automatically displaying the new employee profile along with the others when it fetched the list from the database.

As a bonus, since this slick, ultra-manageable system reduces the burden of data entry and maintenance, you could assign the boss's son to clean the coffee machine in his spare time!

Let's run with this example as we look at how data is stored in a database. A database is composed of one or more **tables**. For our employee database, we'd probably start with a table called `Employees` that would contain—you guessed it—a list of employees. Each table in a database has one or more **columns** (or **fields**). Each column holds a certain piece of information about each item in the table. In our example, the `Employees` table might have columns for the employees' names, network usernames, and phone numbers. Each employee whose details were stored in this table would then be said to be a **row** (or **record**) in the table. These rows and columns would form a table that looks like the one shown in Figure 7.1.

Figure 7.1. Structure of a typical database table

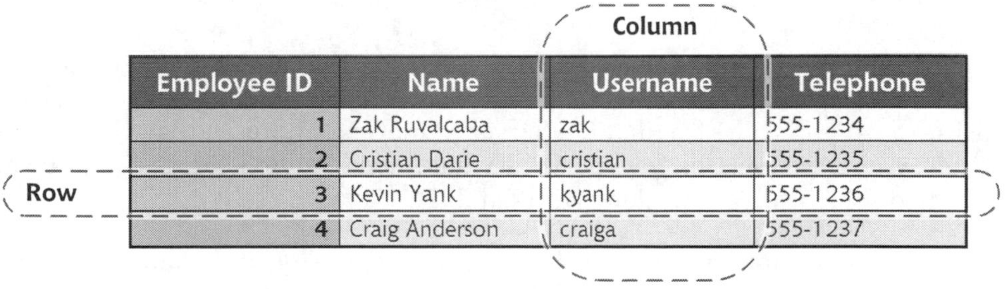

Employee ID	Name	Username	Telephone
1	Zak Ruvalcaba	zak	555-1234
2	Cristian Darie	cristian	555-1235
3	Kevin Yank	kyank	555-1236
4	Craig Anderson	craiga	555-1237

Notice that, in addition to columns for the employees' names, usernames, and telephone numbers, I included a column named Employee ID. As a matter of good design, a database table should always provide a way to identify each of its rows uniquely. In this particular case, you might consider using an existing piece of data as the unique identifier. After all, it's unlikely that two employees would share the same network username. However, that's something for our network administrator to worry about. Just in case he or she slips up somewhere along the line, we include the Employee ID column, the function of which is to assign a unique number to each employee in the database. This gives us an easy way to refer to each person, and let us keep track of which employee is which. We'll discuss such database design issues in greater depth shortly.

So, to review, Figure 7.1 shows a four-column table with four rows, or entries. Each row in the table contains four fields, one for each column in the table: the employee's ID, name, username, and telephone number.

Now, with this basic terminology under your belt, you're ready to roll up your sleeves and build your first database!

Creating your First Database

The SQL Server 2005 engine does a great job of storing and managing your databases, but in order to be able to do anything meaningful with the data, we first need to connect to SQL Server. There are many ways to interact with SQL Server, but for starters, we're just interested in using it as a visual tool to facilitate basic administrative tasks.

Because you're using SQL Server 2005, your key tools will be either:

❑ Visual Web Developer 2005 Express Edition

❑ SQL Server Management Studio Express Edition

That's right, Visual Web Developer has everything you need to get started with SQL Server! However, we'll use SQL Server Management Studio for most database tasks—most tasks are easier in SQL Server Management Studio than they are in Visual Web Developer, as SQL Server Management Studio's interface has been designed specifically for working with databases.

We'll call the database that will store the data for our sample project "Dorknozzle." In this chapter, you'll learn how to create its structure, and in the next chapter, we'll begin to work with the database. You can use either Visual Web Developer or SQL Server Management Studio to create the Dorknozzle database. I'll show you both approaches, so you're comfortable with both options.

Creating a New Database Using Visual Web Developer

Visual Web Developer's Database Explorer window gives you access to most database-related features. You can make this window appear by selecting View > Database Explorer. Right-click the Data Connections node and select Add Connection... from the context menu, as shown in Figure 7.2.

Figure 7.2. Adding a new database connection

If you've installed SQL Server using the instructions we stepped through in Chapter 1, select Microsoft SQL Server from the Choose Data Source dialog that appears, and click Continue. You'll then be asked to enter the details for your data connection. Enter the following data:

❑ Set Server name to **localhost\SqlExpress**.

❑ Leave the Use Windows Authentication option selected.

❑ Click Test Connection to ensure you can successfully connect to SQL Server using the data you've provided.

❑ Enter **Dorknozzle** in the Select or enter a database name field. Click OK.

❑ You'll be asked to confirm the creation of a new database called Dorknozzle. Click Yes.

Figure 7.3. Exploring the Dorknozzle database

Once you click Yes, the new database will be created, and a link to it will be added to the Data Connections node in Database Explorer. You can expand it to view its contents, as Figure 7.3 illustrates.

Creating a New Database Using SQL Server Management Studio

To start SQL Server Management Studio, which we learned to install in Chapter 1, select Start > All Programs > Microsoft SQL Server > SQL Server Management Studio Express. In the dialog that appears, enter **localhost\SqlExpress** into the Server Name box, and leave Authentication mode to Windows Authentication, as Figure 7.4 illustrates.

After you connect to SQL Server, expand the Databases node to see the current databases. If you've just installed SQL Server, you'll only have installed the system databases, which are grouped under a System Databases node. In Figure 7.5 below, you can see that I have another database, named BalloonShop, on my SQL Server.

Figure 7.4. Connecting to a SQL Server instance

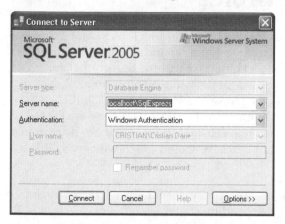

Figure 7.5. Inspecting your SQL server instance

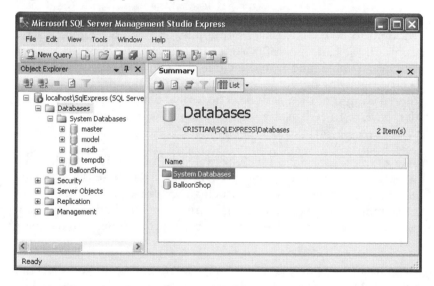

To create a new database, right-click the Databases node, and select New Database... from the context menu. In the dialog that appears, enter **Dorknozzle** into the Database name field, then click OK.

Congratulations, you have a brand new database to play with!

Creating Database Tables

Let's start to create the tables for our intranet application. Tables can be thought of as the drawers in a filing cabinet: just as we could separate different information into different drawers within our filing cabinet, we can break information about employees, departments, and help desk requests into different tables. Tables can also be compared to spreadsheets, as they have rows and columns, but they have many other powerful features. They know what kinds of data they're allowed to store, they can relate to data contained in other tables, and they can be searched and manipulated with a very powerful language called SQL (which you'll learn about in Chapter 8).

You can organize the tables in your database using either Visual Web Developer or SQL Server Management Studio, depending on your preference. While SQL Server Management Studio is more powerful, both tools can be used for basic tasks such as creating database tables.

In just a minute, we'll dive in and create our first table. Before we do, it's worth giving some thought to how many tables our application will need, and exactly what they'll contain. We can think of tables as lists of **entities**. Entities are the rows or records in our table, and would include the employees Zak Ruvalcaba and Cristian Darie. Drawing our tables and their entities on paper is a great way to plan the **logical design** of the database. The logical design shows what kinds of data our database will need to store, and outlines the relationships that we want to exist between specific pieces of data.

However, unlike a typical spreadsheet file, the tables defined in the logical design do *not* usually represent the way we'll store the data in the database. This is taken care of in the **physical design** phase, in which we create a practical blueprint that allows us to improve database speed, enable relationships between different tables, or implement other advanced features—basically, to optimize our database in various ways.

Your database's design has important consequences in terms of the way your application works, and how easy it is to extend, so it's important to take the logical and physical design phases seriously. Let's take a look at an example, so you can see what I mean.

Let's say that, in addition to a name, username, and telephone number, you wanted to keep track of the departments in which employees work at Dorknozzle.

To achieve this, it might seem logical simply to add a column to the Employees table we discussed above; Figure 7.6 shows how this would look.

Figure 7.6. The Employees table

Employee ID	Name	Username	Telephone	Department
1	Zak Ruvalcaba	zak	555-1234	Executive
2	Cristian Darie	cristian	555-1235	Marketing
3	Kevin Yank	kyank	555-1236	Engineering
4	Craig Anderson	craiga	555-1237	Engineering

It looks pretty good, right? Well, it's okay in theory. However, if you went ahead and implemented this structure in your database, you'd likely end up in trouble, because this approach presents a couple of potential problems:

❑ Every time you insert a new employee record, you'll have to provide the name of the department in which that employee works. If you make even the slightest spelling error, then, as far as the database is concerned, you have a new department. Now, I don't know about you, but I'd be pretty upset if my employee record showed me as the only person working in a department called "Enineering." And what if Dorknozzle Sr decides to rename one of the departments? You might try to update all the affected employee records with the new department name, but, even if you miss just one record, your database will contain inconsistent information. Database design experts refer to this sort of problem as an **update anomaly**.

❑ It would be natural for you to rely on your database to provide a list of all the departments in the company, so you could, for example, choose to view a list of employees in a particular department. But if, for some reason, you deleted the records of all the employees in that department (don't ask me why—your human resource issues aren't *my* problem!), you'd remove any record that the department had ever existed (although, if you really *did* have to fire everyone, that might be a good thing…). Database design experts call this a **delete anomaly**.

These problems—and more—can be dealt with very easily. Instead of storing the information for the departments in the Employees table, let's create an entirely new table for our list of departments. Similarly to the Employees table, the new Departments table will include a column called Department ID, which will identify each of our departments with a unique number. We can use those department IDs in our Employees table to associate departments with employees. This new database layout is shown in Figure 7.7.

Figure 7.7. The Employees table with a new Department ID field

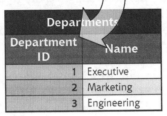

Employees				
Employee ID	**Name**	**Username**	**Telephone**	**Department ID**
1	Zak Ruvalcaba	zak	555-1234	1
2	Cristian Darie	cristian	555-1235	2
3	Kevin Yank	kyank	555-1236	3
4	Craig Anderson	craiga	555-1237	3

Departments	
Department ID	**Name**
1	Executive
2	Marketing
3	Engineering

Database Design ... and Implementation

As this example has shown, the way you'd naturally draw your database design on paper, and the best way to implement the design in practice, can be two different things. However, keep in mind that there are no absolute rules in database design, and expert database designers sometimes bend or break rules to meet the requirements of particular circumstances.

What these tables show are four employees and three departments. The Department ID column of the Employees table provides a **relationship** between the two tables, indicating that Zak Ruvalcaba works in department 1, while Kevin Yank and Craig Anderson work in department 3. Notice also that, as each department appears only once in the database, and appears independently of the employees who work in it, we've avoided the problems outlined above.

However, the most important characteristic of this database design is that, since we're storing information about two types of entities (employees and departments), we're using two tables. This approach illustrates an important rule of thumb that we must keep in mind when designing databases:

Each type of entity about which we want to be able to store information should be given its own table.

With this rule in mind, we can sit back and think about the Dorknozzle application we want to build, as described in Chapter 5. We need to think of the design in terms of the entities that we want to track, and come up with a preliminary list of tables. You'll become more comfortable with this kind of task as you gain experience in database design, but it's worth giving it a try on your own at this stage. When you're done, compare your list to the one below, and see how you did!

Employees
> This table keeps track of our company's employees, each of which is associated with a department.

Departments
> This table lists the departments in our company.

Help Desk Problem Reports
> This table stores the problem reports that have been filed at Dorknozzle's employee help desk. A category, subject, and status will be associated with each problem report.

Help Desk Categories
> The categories that are available for help desk items ("Hardware," "Software," etc.) are stored in this table.

Help Desk Subjects
> The subjects that are available for help desk items ("Computer crashes," "My chair is broken," etc.) are stored in this table.

Help Desk States
> This table stores the various states in which a help desk item can exist ("open" or "closed").

Breaking down and analyzing the items of information that need to be saved is the first step in determining the database's design—this process represents the *logical design* phase that I mentioned earlier. Through this process, we work to build a high-level definition of the data that needs to be saved. This definition can then be transformed into a *physical design* structure, which contains the details required to implement the database.

As you analyze the data that needs to be stored, you may come across items that we overlooked when we designed the site in Chapter 5, such as help desk item categories, subjects, and states, which aren't obvious entities in our application's current design. However, remember that whenever you predict that your database will contain a field that should only accept values from a specific list, it makes sense to create a table to hold that list. This approach makes it easy to execute changes to the list in future; it also reduces the amount of disk space required by your database, and helps you to avoid redundancy, as you store only single instances of department names, strings like "I can't print," and so on.

This process of planning out the entities, tables, and relationships between the tables to eliminate maintenance problems and redundant data is called database **normalization**. Although I'll speak a bit more about normalization before the end of this chapter, I'll only ever discuss it in an informal, hands-on (i.e. nonrigorous) way. As any computer science major will tell you, database design is a serious area of research, with tested and mathematically provable principles that, while useful, are beyond the scope of this book. If you want more information on the topic, stop by DataModel.org[1] for a list of good books, as well as several useful resources on the subject. In particular, check out the Rules of Normalization in the Data Modeling section of the site.[2]

So, we've got our list of tables. In the next section, we'll look at the columns within those tables, and discuss how we can ascertain their characteristics. Although we won't go over the creation of all the tables for the Dorknozzle database, we will create one as an example: the Employees table. Once you understand how to create a new table, you can create the rest of the tables for the Dorknozzle application in your own time, based on the descriptions I'll provide. Or, if you prefer, you can simply grab the finished database from the code archive.

Once you've outlined all your tables, the next step is to decide what pieces of information will be included within those tables. For instance, you may want to include a first name, last name, phone number, address, city, state, zip code, and so on, for all employees in the Employees table. Let's see how we can define these columns as we create the Employees table for the Dorknozzle database.

Data Types

One of the differences between logical design and physical design is that when we're planning the database's physical design, we have to deal with details such as data types. That's right—as with the data we're storing in our VB.NET and C# variables, the data we store in each of our tables's columns has a particular data type.

---

[1] http://www.datamodel.org/
[2] http://www.datamodel.org/NormalizationRules.html

SQL Server knows many data types—in fact, it knows too many to list here—but it's worth our while to take a look at the most common ones. Below is a list of the common data types that we'll use in this book:

int

Use the int data type when you need to store whole integers. This data type can store numbers from -2,147,483,648 to 2,147,483,647.

float

Use the float data type when you're working with very large numbers or very small numbers. float can be used for fractions, but they are prone to rounding errors.

money

The money data type should be used to store monetary data, such as prices for a product catalog. This data type is closely related to the int data type.

bit

Use the bit data type when a condition is either true (represented as 1) or false (represented as 0).

datetime

As you might have guessed, the datetime data type is used to store dates and times. It's very useful when you want to sort items in your table chronologically.

nvarchar(*n*)

The nvarchar data type stores strings of text. This is most commonly used data type because it stores names, descriptions, and the like. When defining a column of this type, we also need to specify a maximum size in parentheses; longer strings will be trimmed to fit the defined size. For example, nvarchar(50) specifies an field that can hold up to 50 characters. The *var* part of the nvarchar name comes from the fact that this data type can store strings of *variable* length up to the specified maximum.

nchar(*n*)

The nchar data type is similar to nvarchar in that it stores strings, but a field of this type will always store strings of the defined size. If the string you're saving is shorter, it's padded with spaces until the specified size is reached. For example, if you're working with an nchar(6) field (where the 6 in parentheses indicates that the field can hold six characters), and you add the word "test" to the field, two space characters will be appended to the end of the word so that all six characters are used. This type is useful when you're storing strings that have a predefined size—in such cases, it may be more efficient to use the nchar(n) type than nvarchar.

money, money, money

Sometimes, you may see poorly designed databases use float to store monetary data. As float is susceptible to rounding errors, this is a bad idea. money, on the other hand, is not susceptible to these errors and is a much better choice.

The SQL Server data types, as with the other SQL Server keywords, aren't case-sensitive. nvarchar and nchar have non-Unicode cousins named varchar and char, which you can use if you're sure you won't need to store Unicode data. You may need to use Unicode (or a language-specific form of encoding) when storing non-English text, such as Chinese, Arabic, and others. Unicode is a very widely supported standard, so it's strongly recommended you stick with nvarchar and nchar.

The type of a column defines how that column behaves. For example, sorting data by a datetime column will cause the records to be sorted chronologically, rather than alphabetically or numerically.

Column Properties

Other than a column's data type, we can define a number of other properties for a column. Other properties you'll use frequently include:

NULL

In database speak, NULL means "undefined." Although we talk about it as if it's a value, NULL actually represents the lack of a value. If you set an employee's mobile telephone number to NULL, for example, this could represent the fact that the employee doesn't have a mobile telephone.

However, it's important to realize that allowing NULLs is often inappropriate. For instance, you might create a department with the name NULL to represent a mysterious department with no name, but obviously, this is far from ideal. As you create a table, you can specify which columns are allowed to store NULL, and which aren't. In our example, we'd like every department to have a name, so we shouldn't allow the Name column to allow NULLs.

DEFAULT

SQL Server is capable of supplying a default value for a certain column if you don't supply one when you add a new row. We won't be using this feature when we create Dorknozzle, but it's good to know you have this option.

IDENTITY

Identity columns are numbered automatically. If you set a column as an IDENTITY column, SQL Server will generate numbers automatically for that column as you add new rows to it. The first number in the column is called the **identity seed**. To generate subsequent numbers, the identity column adds a given value to the seed; the value that's added is called the **identity increment**. By default, both the seed and increment have a value of 1, in which case the generated values are 1, 2, 3, and so on. If the identity seed were 5 and the identity increment were 10, the generated numbers would be 5, 15, 25, and so on.

IDENTITY is useful for ID columns, such as Department ID, for which you don't care what the values are, as long as they're unique. When you use IDENTITY, the generated values will always be unique. By default, you can't specify values for an IDENTITY column. Note also that the column can never contain NULL.

Understanding NULL

Be sure not to see NULL as equivalent to 0 (in numerical columns), or an empty string (in the case of string columns). Both 0 and an empty string *are* values; NULL defines the lack of a value.

NULL and Default Values

I've often heard people say that when we set a default value for a column, it doesn't matter whether or not we set it to accept NULLs. Many people seem to believe that columns with default values won't store NULL.

That's incorrect. You can modify a record after it was created, and change any field that will allow it to NULL. Your columns' ability to store NULL is important for the integrity of your data, and it should reflect the purpose of that data. A default value does make things easier when we create new rows, but it's not as vital as is correctly allowing (or disallowing) NULL in columns.

Primary Keys

Primary keys are the last fundamental concept that you need to understand before you can create your first data table. In the world of relational databases, each row in a table *must* be identified uniquely by a column called a **key**, on which all database operations are based.

The tables in your databases could contain hundreds or even thousands of rows of similar data—you could have several hundred employees in your Employees table alone. Imagine that your program needs to update or delete the record for John Smith, and there are several people with that name in your organization. You couldn't rely on the database to find the record for the particular John Smith that you were trying to work with—it might end up updating or deleting the wrong record.

We can avoid these kinds of problems only by using a system that uniquely identifies each row in the table. The first step toward achieving this goal is to add to the table an ID column that provides a unique for each employee, as did the Employee ID column that we saw in Figure 7.1.

Remember that when we discussed this Employees table, we noted that you may be tempted to use each employee's username to uniquely identify each employee. After all, that's what the network administrator uses them for, so why shouldn't you? It's true that this column uniquely identifies each row in the table, and we call such a column a **candidate key**. However, it wouldn't be a good idea to use this column in our database operations for a number of reasons. Firstly, network usernames have been known to change, and such a change would wreak havoc on any database of more than a couple of tables. As we'll see later, keys are fundamental to establishing relationships between tables, and these relationships rely on the fact that keys will never change. Secondly, non-numeric keys require much more processing power than simple numeric ones. Using an nvarchar field to uniquely identify rows in your table will bring your SQL Server to a grinding halt much, much quicker than if you chose a simple, numeric key.

The column that we choose to uniquely identify a row in a table in practice is called the **primary key**. In the case of our Employee table, the Employee ID will always be unique, so it would be a suitable primary key.

Multi-column Keys

To make the concept of keys easier to understand, we kept the definition simple, although it's not 100% technically correct. A key isn't necessarily formed by a single column—it can be formed by two or more columns. If the key is made up of multiple columns, the set of values in those columns must be unique for any given record. We'll see an example of such a key in a moment.

Although we usually refer to *primary keys* as if they were columns, technically they are **constraints** that we apply to the existing columns of a table. Constraints impose restrictions on the data we can enter into our tables, and the primary key is a particular kind of constraint. When the primary key constraint is set on a column, the database will refuse to store duplicate values in that column.

Constraints in general, and primary keys in particular, represent a means by which the database can maintain the integrity and consistency of data.

Primary keys composed of a single column, such as Employee ID, are frequently used in conjunction with the IDENTITY property. The primary key constraint guarantees that duplicate values cannot be inserted into the table. The IDENTITY property helps us by always generating a new value that hasn't already been used in the primary key.

IMPORTANT

Primary Keys and the IDENTITY Property

Using the IDENTITY property for a column doesn't mean we can avoid specifying a primary key. It's true that the IDENTITY property always *generates* unique values, but it doesn't necessarily *enforce* them.

For example, say we have a table with a number of columns, one of which has the IDENTITY property set. This table contains three records that are likely to contain the automatically generated values **1**, **2**, and **3** in the IDENTITY column. Provided the INDENTITY_INSERT property for this table is enabled (by default it's disabled, but it's quite easy to enable), it's quite simple to insert another record with the value **2**. The IDENTITY column will continue to generate unique values (**4**, **5**, **6**, and so on), but it doesn't guarantee the column remains unique.

Creating the Employees Table

In this section, I'll show you how to use both Visual Web Developer and SQL Server Management Studio, but this time we'll create a new data table. If you're using Visual Web Developer, expand the database node in Database Explorer, right-click Tables, and select Add New Table, as shown in Figure 7.8.

Figure 7.8. Adding a new table in Visual Web Developer

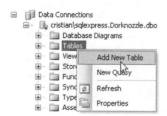

If you prefer SQL Server Management Studio, you need to follow a similar procedure. Expand the Dorknozzle database node, right-click Tables, and select New Table…, as illustrated in Figure 7.9.

Figure 7.9. Adding a new table with SQL Server Management Studio

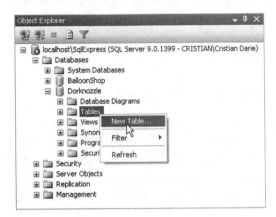

The window that appears as the result of the above procedures is shown in Figure 7.10—it looks the same in both Visual Web Developer and SQL Server Management Studio. The main editing window lets you specify the column's three main properties: Column Name, Data Type, and Allow Nulls. To set additional properties, you need to use the Column Properties pane.

To add the IDENTITY property to a column, locate the Identity Specification row in the Column Properties pane and expand it. This will reveal the (Is Identity) drop-down list, which should be set to Yes for an IDENTITY column, as Figure 7.10 indicates.

To set a column as the primary key, we can select Table Designer > Set Primary Key, or click the little golden key icon in the Table Designer toolbar while the column is selected. When a column is set as a primary key, a little golden key appears next to it, as Figure 7.11 illustrates.

Figure 7.10. Specifying column properties

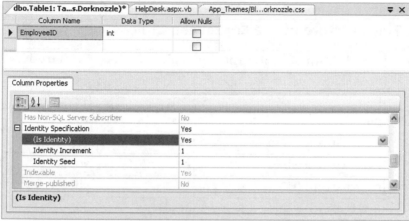

Figure 7.11. The `Employees` table

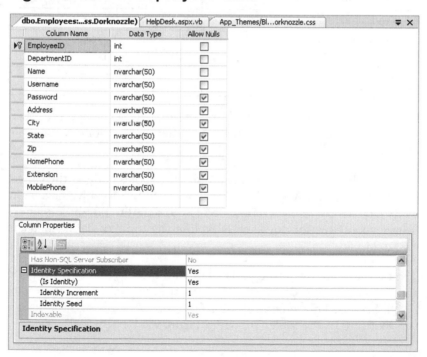

Now, let's create a table called `Employees` by adding the columns described in Table 7.1.

Table 7.1. The structure of the `Employees` table

Column Name	SQL Data Type	Identity	Allow Nulls	Primary Key
EmployeeID	int	Yes	No	Yes
DepartmentID	int	No	No	No
Name	nvarchar(50)	No	No	No
Username	nvarchar(50)	No	No	No
Password	nvarchar(50)	No	Yes	No
Address	nvarchar(50)	No	Yes	No
City	nvarchar(50)	No	Yes	No
State	nvarchar(50)	No	Yes	No
Zip	nvarchar(50)	No	Yes	No
HomePhone	nvarchar(50)	No	Yes	No
Extension	nvarchar(50)	No	Yes	No
MobilePhone	nvarchar(50)	No	Yes	No

After entering this information, press **Ctrl-S** to save the table. When you're asked to name the table, type **Employees** and click OK. When you're done, your table will resemble Figure 7.11.

After you create the table, you'll see it appear under the Tables node in the Object Explorer (or Database Explorer in Visual Web Developer). SQL Server Management Studio prepends `dbo.` to the table's name; `dbo` is the default "database owner" user. Don't worry about this for now—we'll explore the topic of database users in some detail later.

If you close the table designer window, you can open it later by right-clicking the `Employees` table and selecting Open Table Definition in Visual Web Developer, or Modify in SQL Server Management Studio. You'll be taken back to the screen that shows the structure of the table (shown in Figure 7.11).

Creating the Remaining Tables

Let's create the rest of the database tables. Apply the process you used to build the `Employee` table to create the new data tables, using the data presented in Table 7.2 to Table 7.6. Later in this chapter, we'll discuss how these tables work. For starters, though, you need to insert them into your database.

Table 7.2. The `Departments` table

Column Name	SQL Data Type	Identity	Allow Null	Primary Key
DepartmentID	int	Yes	No	Yes
Department	nvarchar(50)	No	No	No

Table 7.3. The `HelpDesk` table

Column Name	SQL Data Type	Identity	Allow Null	Primary Key
RequestID	int	Yes	No	Yes
EmployeeID	int	No	No	No
StationNumber	int	No	Yes	No
CategoryID	int	No	No	No
SubjectID	int	No	No	No
Description	nvarchar(50)	No	Yes	No
StatusID	int	No	No	No

Table 7.4. The `HelpDeskCategories` table

Column Name	SQL Data Type	Identity	Allow Null	Primary Key
CategoryID	int	Yes	No	Yes
Category	nvarchar(50)	No	No	No

Table 7.5. The `HelpDeskSubjects` table

Column Name	SQL Data Type	Identity	Allow Null	Primary Key
SubjectID	int	Yes	No	Yes
Subject	nvarchar(50)	No	No	No

Table 7.6. The `HelpDeskStatus` table

Column Name	SQL Data Type	Identity	Allow Null	Primary Key
StatusID	int	Yes	No	Yes
Status	nvarchar(50)	No	No	No

Using SQL Scripts

Yep, there's a lot of data to type in! While we recommend that you create the tables yourself by defining the fields outlined here, you can achieve the same goal using an SQL script that's included in this book's code archive. This script contains SQL code that SQL Server understands, and contains instructions that create data structures (you'll learn about SQL in Chapter 8). If you want to use the downloadable script, we recommend you have a look over the following tables to get an idea of the structures we'll be creating, then read the section called "Executing SQL Scripts" that follows.

We already have a clear idea of the data we'll store in the Employees and Departments tables. The other tables will be used to store help desk requests; we'll discuss these in more detail in the following pages.

Executing SQL Scripts

If you prefer not to create the data tables manually, you can use the CreateTables.sql script included in the book's code archive to create the tables for you. This script is most easily used with SQL Server Management Studio. After you log in, click the New Query button on the toolbar (or select File > New > Query with Current Connection). Paste the contents of the CreateTables.sql script into the window that opens, and press **F5** to execute the commands. Note that if you have already created the Employees table, you should remove the CREATE TABLE command that creates this table *before* you hit **F5**.

The SQL scripts included in the code archive contains all the commands required for this entire chapter—it even creates the sample data and table references that are covered later.

Populating the Data Tables

If tables represent drawers in a filing cabinet, rows represent individual paper records in those drawers. Suppose that our intranet web application was a real application. As people begin to register and interact with the application, rows are created within the various tables, and are filled up with the information about those people.

Once the data structures are in place, adding rows of data is as easy as typing information into the cells in the **Datasheet View** of a table, which looks a bit like a spreadsheet. To access it, right-click on the table and select Show Table Data in Visual Web Developer, or Open Table in SQL Server Management Studio. You can use the window that opens to start adding data. Let's add some sample data to the tables you've just created, so that we can test the Dorknozzle database as we develop the application. Table 7.7 to Table 7.11 represent the tables and data you should add.

Inserting Data and Identity Columns

If you correctly set the ID column as an identity column, you won't be allowed to specify the values manually—the ID values will be generated for you automatically. You need to be careful, because an ID value will never be generated twice on the same table. So even if you delete all the rows in a table, the database will not generate an ID with the value of 1; instead, it will continue creating new values from the last value that was generated for you.

Keep in mind that a new row is saved to the database at the moment that you move on to the next row. It's very important that you remember this when you reach the last row, as you'll need to move to an empty row even if you aren't adding any more records.

Table 7.7. The Departments table

EmployeeID (Primary Key)	Department
1	Accounting
2	Administration
3	Business Development
4	Customer Support
5	Executive
6	Engineering
7	Facilities
8	IT
8	Marketing
10	Operations

Table 7.8. The Employees table

Emp'ID (Primary Key)	Dep'tID	Name	U'name	P'word	City	State	M'Phone
1	5	Zak Ruvalcaba	zak	zak	San Diego	CA	555-555-5551
2	9	Jessica Ruvalcaba	jessica	jessica	San Diego	CA	555-555-5552
3	6	Ted Lindsey	ted	ted	San Diego	CA	555-555-5555
4	6	Shane Weebe	shane	shane	San Diego	CA	555-555-5554
5	9	David Levinson	david	david	San Diego	CA	555-555-5553
6	1	Geoff Kim	geoff	geoff	San Diego	CA	555-555-5556

The `Employees` table contains a few more columns than those outlined here, but, due to the size constraints of this page, I've left them out. Feel free to add your own data to the rest of the cells, or you could leave the remaining cells empty, as they're marked to accept NULL.

Table 7.9. The `HelpDeskCategories` table

CategoryID (Primary Key)	Category
1	Hardware
2	Software
3	Workstation
4	Other/Don't Know

Table 7.10. The `HelpDeskStatus` table

StatusID (Primary Key)	Status
1	Open
2	Closed

Table 7.11. The `HelpDeskSubjects` table

SubjectID (Primary Key)	Subject
1	Computer won't start
2	Monitor won't turn on
3	Chair is broken
4	Office won't work
5	Windows won't work
6	Computer crashes
7	Other

What `IDENTITY` Columns are *not* For

In our examples, as in many real-world scenarios, the ID values are sequences that start with 1 and increment by 1. This makes many beginners assume that they can use the ID column as a record-counter of sorts, but this is a mistake. The ID is really an arbitrary number that we know to be unique; no other information should be discerned from it.

Relational Database Design Concepts

It is said that data becomes information when we give significance to it. When we draw tables on paper to decide the logical design of a database, we actually include significant information about our application (and about the business for which the application is used). In Figure 7.12, for example, we can see that the employee Zak Ruvalcaba works in the Executive department.

Figure 7.12. Information about employees

Employee ID	Name	Username	Telephone	Department
1	Zak Ruvalcaba	zak	555-1234	Executive
2	Cristian Darie	cristian	555-1235	Marketing
3	Kevin Yank	kyank	555-1236	Engineering
4	Craig Anderson	craiga	555-1237	Engineering

We've seen how, in order to optimize data storage and better protect the integrity of our data, we can extract independent pieces of data, such as department names, and save them in separate tables, such as the `Department` table. However, as we did so, we kept the significance of the original information intact by including references to the new tables in our existing table. For example, in the `Employees` table we have a `DepartmentID` column that specifies the department in which each employee works, as Figure 7.13 illustrates.

This separation of data helps us to eliminate redundant information—for example, we'd expect to have many employees in each department, but we don't need to replicate the department name for each of those employees. Instead, each employee record refers to the ID of the appropriate department. The benefits of this approach would be more obvious if more data (such as a department description) was associated with each department; copying all that data for each employee would generate even more redundancy.

These kinds of relationships exist between the `HelpDesk`, `HelpDeskCategories`, `HelpDeskStatus`, and `HelpDeskSubjects` tables. Each record in `HelpDesk` will store a help desk request. Now, if we stored all the request information in a single table, its records would look like those shown in Figure 7.14.

Figure 7.13. Related data about employees and departments

Employees				
Employee ID	Name	Username	Telephone	Department ID
1	Zak Ruvalcaba	zak	555-1234	1
2	Cristian Darie	cristian	555-1235	2
3	Kevin Yank	kyank	555-1236	3
4	Craig Anderson	craiga	555-1237	3

Departments	
Department ID	Name
1	Executive
2	Marketing
3	Engineering

Figure 7.14. Information about help desk requests

Employee	Station No.	Category	Subject	Description	Status
Kevin Yank	5	Software	Office won't work	Crashes when I open documents	Open
Craig Anderson	7	Software	Windows won't work	Crashes when I start Solitaire	Open

In order to eliminate redundant data here, we've decided to store pieces of this data in separate tables, and to reference those tables from the `HelpDesk` table. The only data in the table in Figure 7.14 that's not likely to repeat very frequently are the description and the station number. We want users to enter their station numbers manually, rather than choosing them from a predefined list, so we wouldn't gain any benefits by creating a separate table for this item.

Given these requirements, we split the information from Figure 7.14 into four tables:

❑ `HelpDeskCategories` contains the possible help desk request categories.

❑ `HelpDeskSubject` contains the possible request subjects.

❑ `HelpDeskStatus` contains the possible request statuses.

❑ The `HelpDesk` table stores the help desk requests by referencing records from the other tables, and adding only two original pieces of data itself: the help desk request description, and the station number.

The relationships between these tables are critical, because without them the original significance of the information would be lost. The relationships are so important that the database has tools to protect them. Primary keys were used to ensure the integrity of the records within a table (by guaranteeing their uniqueness); in a moment, we'll meet foreign keys, which protect the integrity of data spread over multiple tables.

In our database's `HelpDesk` table, the data depicted in Figure 7.14 would be stored physically as shown in Table 7.12.

Table 7.12. Sample data from the `HelpDesk` table

RequestID (Primary Key)	Emp'ID	StationN'ber	Cat'ID	Subj'ID	Description	StatusID
1	3	5	2	4	Crashes when I open documents	1
2	4	3	2	5	Crashes when I start Solitaire	1

Note that, apart from storing data about the request itself, the `HelpDesk` table also has an ID column, named `RequestID`, which acts as the table's primary key.

Foreign Keys

Technically speaking, a **foreign key** is a constraint that applies to a column that refers to the primary key of another table. In practice, we'll use the term "foreign key" to refer to the column to which the constraint applies.

Unlike primary key columns, a foreign key column can contain NULL, and almost always contains repeating values. The numeric columns in the `HelpDesk` table that reference data from other tables (`EmployeeID`, `CategoryID`, `SubjectID`, and `StatusID`), and the `DepartmentID` column in the `Employees` table, are perfect candidates for the application of a foreign key constraint. Take a look at the examples shown in Table 7.13 and Table 7.14.

Table 7.13. The Departments table's primary key

DepartmentID (Primary Key)	Department
1	Accounting
2	Engineering
3	Executive
4	Marketing

Table 7.14. The Employees table referencing records from the Departments table

Emp'ID (Primary Key)	Dep'tID	Name	U'name	P'word	City	State	M'Phone
1	5	Zak Ruvalcaba	zak	zak	San Diego	CA	555-555-5551
2	9	Jessica Ruvalcaba	jessica	jessica	San Diego	CA	555-555-5552
3	6	Ted Lindsey	ted	ted	San Diego	CA	555-555-5555
4	6	Shane Weebe	shane	shane	San Diego	CA	555-555-5554
5	9	David Levinson	david	david	San Diego	CA	555-555-5553
6	1	Geoff Kim	geoff	geoff	San Diego	CA	555-555-5556

The DepartmentID column in the Employees table references the DepartmentID primary key in the Departments table. Notice that the DepartmentID primary key in the Departments table is unique, but the DepartmentID foreign key within the Employees table may repeat.

As they stand, these tables already have an established relationship, and all the data in the DepartmentID column of the Employees table correctly matches existing departments in the `Department` table. However, as with primary keys, just having the correct fields in place doesn't mean that our data is guaranteed to be correct.

For example, try setting the `DepartmentID` field for one of the employees to `123`. SQL Server won't mind making the change for you, so if you tried this in practice, you'd end up storing invalid data. However, after we set the foreign keys correctly, SQL Server will be able to ensure the integrity of our data—specifically, it will forbid us to assign employees to nonexistent departments, or to delete departments with which employees are associated.

The easiest way to create foreign keys using Visual Web Developer or SQL Server Management Studio is through database diagrams, so let's learn about them.

Using Database Diagrams

To keep the data consistent, the Dorknozzle database really should contain quite a few foreign keys. The good news is that you have access to a great feature called **database diagrams**, which makes it a cinch to create foreign keys. You can define the table relationships visually using the database diagrams tool in Visual Web Developer or SQL Server Management Studio, and have the foreign keys generated for you.

Database diagrams weren't created specifically for the purpose of adding foreign keys. The primary use of diagrams is to offer a visual representation of the tables in your database and the relationships that exist between them, to help you to design the structure of your database. However, the diagrams editor included in Visual Web Developer and SQL Server Management Studio is very powerful, so you can use the diagrams to create new tables, modify the structure of existing tables, or add foreign keys.

Let's start by creating a diagram for the Dorknozzle database. To create a database diagram in Visual Web Developer, right-click the Database Diagrams node, and select Add New Diagram, as shown in Figure 7.15.

The process is similar in SQL Server Management Studio, which, as Figure 7.16 illustrates, has a similar menu.

The first time you try to create a diagram, you'll be asked to confirm the creation of the database structures that support diagrams. Select **Yes** from the dialog, which should look like the one shown in Figure 7.17.

Figure 7.15. Creating a database diagram with Visual Web Developer

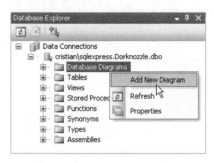

Figure 7.16. Creating a database diagram with SQL Server Management Studio

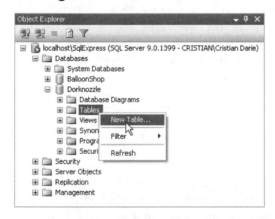

Figure 7.17. Adding support for database diagrams

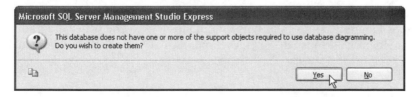

Figure 7.18. Adding tables to the diagram

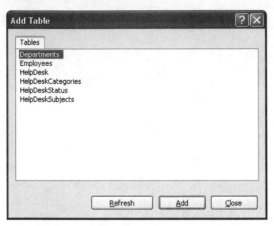

Next, a dialog like the one in Figure 7.18 will ask you which of your database tables you want included in the diagram. If you're working with a database that comprises many tables, you may want to have diagrams built to represent specific pieces of functionality, but we want to create a diagram that includes all the tables in our database.

Click Add until all the tables are added to the diagram. As you click Add, the tables will be removed from the list and will appear in the diagram. Once you've added all the tables, click Close. You'll see a window in which all the tables are clearly displayed—something like Figure 7.19.

You'll probably need to tweak their positioning and dimensions so they fit nicely into the window. The zooming feature may prove useful here! Select File > Save Diagram1 (or similar) to save your new diagram. Enter **Dorknozzle** for the diagram's name.

Now, if you right-click any table in the diagram, you'll gain access to a plethora of possibilities, as Figure 7.20 reveals. This menu, along with the other diagramming features, are identical in Visual Web Developer and SQL Server Management Studio.

Figure 7.19. Visualizing data tables using a diagram

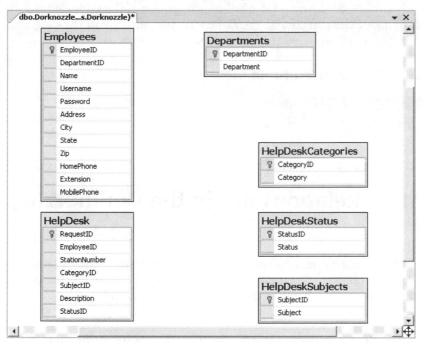

Figure 7.20. The many features of the diagram editor

Expanding the Table View submenu gives you more options for displaying your table. If you choose Standard, you'll see a full-blown version of the table definition; as Figure 7.21 shows, you can change the table structure directly in the diagram! The diagraming features provided for free are extremely powerful and useful.

Figure 7.21. The standard table view

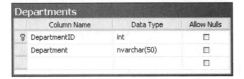

Implementing Relationships in the Dorknozzle Database

Every table in the Dorknozzle database has a relationship with another table. To create a foreign key using the diagram, click the gray square to the left-hand side of the column for which you want to create the foreign key, and drag it over the table to which you want it to relate.

Let's give it a try. Start by dragging the DepartmentID column of the Employees table over the DepartmentID column of the Departments table, as illustrated in Figure 7.22.

Figure 7.22. Creating a link between Employees and Departments

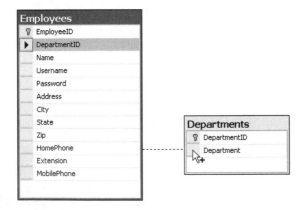

The designer will open a dialog that shows the details of the new foreign key, like the one shown in Figure 7.23.

Figure 7.23. Adding a foreign key

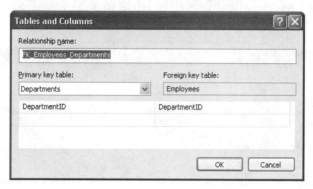

Ensure that your data matches that shown in Figure 7.23, and click OK. A new dialog like the one shown in Figure 7.24 will appear, allowing you to tweak numerous options that relate to the new foreign key. Leave the default options as they are for now (though we'll discuss them shortly), and click OK to finish up.

Figure 7.24. Editing the foreign key options

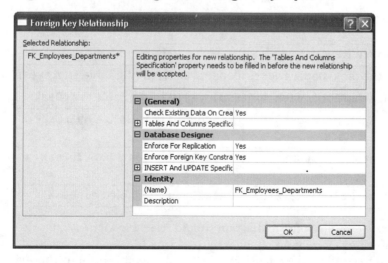

After creating the foreign key, make a quick test to ensure that the relationship is indeed enforced. Try adding an employee, but set the person's `DepartmentID` to `123`. You should see an error like the one pictured in Figure 7.25.

Figure 7.25. The foreign key disallowing the addition of invalid data

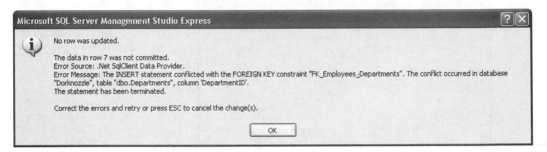

If you tried to delete a department with which employees were associated, you'd generate a similar error.

Table 7.15 shows the foreign keys that we need to establish in the `Dorknozzle` database. In our project, the foreign key column has the same name as its corresponding primary key column. Go ahead and create all the foreign keys outlined in Table 7.15.

Table 7.15. The relationships in the Dorknozzle database

Primary Key	Foreign Key
`DepartmentID` in the table `Departments`	`DepartmentID` in the table `Employees`
`EmployeeID` in the table `Employees`	`EmployeeID` in the table `HelpDesk`
`CategoryID` in the table `HelpDeskCategories`	`CategoryID` in the table `HelpDesk`
`SubjectID` in the table `HelpDeskSubjects`	`SubjectID` in the table `HelpDesk`
`StatusID` in the table `HelpDeskStatus`	`StatusID` in the table `HelpDesk`

When it's complete, your relationship diagram should resemble Figure 7.26. After you add the relationships, save your changes by selecting File > Save Dorknozzle. When you're asked to confirm the changes to the database tables you're altering, click Yes.

Figure 7.26. Creating and visualizing table relationships

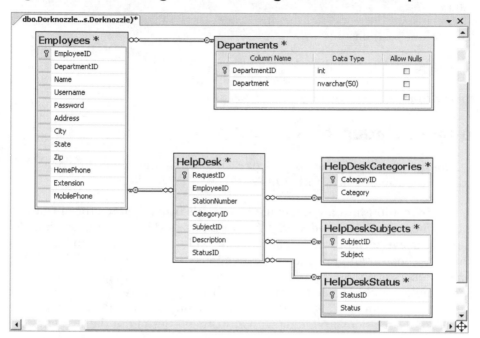

Now that you've created these foreign keys, you can be sure that all the data stored in your tables will obey the enforced table relationships. The `DepartmentID` column in the `Employees` table will always reference valid departments, and the `HelpDesk` records will always reference valid employees, help desk categories, help desk subjects, and help desk status codes.

In Chapter 8, you'll start learning how to use your new database. Before then, let's take a moment to analyze the diagram, and learn more about the information it shows us.

Diagrams and Table Relationships

Relationships describe how data in one table is linked to data in other tables. In fact, it's because relationships are so crucial that these types of databases are given the name "relational databases." Relationships exist for the sole purpose of associating one table with one or more other tables using primary keys and foreign keys.

There are three types of relationships that can occur between the tables in your database:

❑ one-to-one relationships

❑ one-to-many relationships

❑ many-to-many relationships

One-to-one Relationships

A one-to-one relationship means that for each record in one table, only one other related record can exist in another table.

One-to-one relationships are rarely used, since it's usually more efficient just to combine the two records and store them together as columns in a single table. For example, every employee in our database will have a phone number stored in the `HomePhone` column of the `Employees` table. In theory, we could store the phone numbers in a separate table and link to them via a foreign key in the `Employees` table, but this would be of no benefit to our application, since we assume that one phone number can belong to only one employee. As such, we can leave this one-to-one relationship (along with any others) out of our database design.

One-to-many Relationships

The one-to-many relationship is by far the most common relationship type. Within a one-to-many relationship, each record in a table can be associated with multiple records from a second table. These records are usually related on the basis of the primary key from the first table. In the employees/departments example, a one-to-many relationship exists between the `Employees` and `Departments` tables, as one department can be associated with many employees.

When a foreign key is used to link two tables, the table that contains the foreign key is on the "many" side of the relationship, and the table that contains the primary key is on the "one" side of the relationship. In database diagrams, one-to-many relationships are signified by a line between the two tables; a golden key symbol appears next to the table on the "one" side of the relationship, and an infinity sign (∞) is displayed next to the table that could have many items related to each of its records. In Figure 7.27, those icons appear next to the `Employees` and `Departments` tables.

Figure 7.27. Database diagram showing a one-to-many relationship

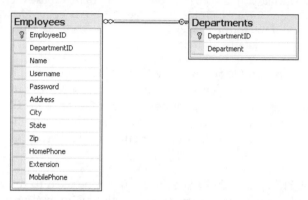

As you can see, one-to-many relationships are easy to spot if you have a diagram at hand—just look for the icons next to the tables. Note that the symbols don't show the exact columns that form the relationship; they simply identify the tables involved.

Select the line that appears between two related tables to view the properties of the foreign key that defines that relationship. The properties display in the Properties window (you can open this by selecting View > Properties Window). As Figure 7.28 illustrates, they're the same options we saw earlier in Figure 7.24.

Figure 7.28. The properties of a foreign key

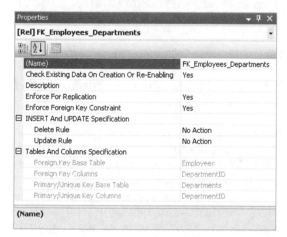

Advanced Foreign Key Options

Unless you really know what you're doing, we recommend that you use the default foreign key options for now. However, it's good to have some idea of the features available through the Properties window, as they may well come in handy later in your database development career.

The most significant setting here is Enforce Foreign Key Constraint, which, when set to Yes, prevents users or applications from entering inconsistent data into our database (for example, by inserting into the Employees table a DepartmentID value that doesn't have a matching entry in the Departments table). In our application, every user must be associated with a valid department, so we'll leave this option enabled.

The options available under INSERT And UPDATE Specification can be used to tell your database to update the tables itself in order to keep the data valid at times when a change in a given table would affect a related table. If, for some reason, we changed the ID of a department in the Departments table, we could set the database to propagate this change to all the tables related to that department, keeping the relationships intact. Similarly, we can set the database to automatically delete all the employees related to a department that's deleted. However, these are quite sensitive options, and it's best to avoid them unless you have good reason not to. The cases in which an ID changes are very uncommon (the ID doesn't have any special meaning itself, other than being an unique identifier), and letting the database delete data for you is a risky approach (it's safer to delete the related records yourself).

If these concepts sound a bit advanced at the moment, don't worry: it will all become clear as you spend some time working with databases.

Many-to-many Relationships

Many-to-many relationships occur between two tables, when records from either table can be associated with multiple records in the other table.

Imagine that you wanted a single employee to be able to belong to more than one department—someone who works in "Engineering" could also be an "Executive," for example. *One* employee can belong to *many* departments, and *one* department can contain *many* employees, so this is a many-to-many relationship.

How do we represent it in our database? Faced with this question, many less-experienced developers begin to think of ways to store several values in a single column, because the obvious solution is to change the DepartmentID column in the Employees table so that it contains a list of the IDs of those departments to which each employee belongs. One those good old rules of thumb we discussed previously applies here:

If you need to store multiple values in a single column, your design is probably flawed.

The correct way to represent a many-to-many relationship is to add a third table, named a **mapping table**, to the database. A mapping table is a table that contains no data other than the definitions of the pairs of entries that are related. Figure 7.29 shows the database design for our employees and departments.

Figure 7.29. Using a mapping table to implement a many-to-many relationship

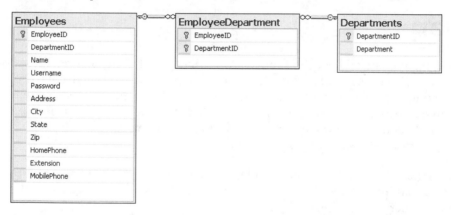

The `EmployeeDepartment` table associates employee IDs with department IDs. If we added this table to our database, we could add Zak Ruvalcaba to both the "Executive" and "Engineering" departments.

A mapping table is created in much the same way as any other table. The only difference lies in the choice of the primary key. Every table we've created so far has had a column named *something*ID that was designed to be that table's primary key. Designating a column as a primary key tells the database not to allow two entries in that column to have the same value. It also speeds up database searches based on that column.

In the case of a mapping table, there's no single column that we want to force to have unique values. Each employee ID may appear more than once, as an employee may belong to more than one department, and each department ID may appear more than once, as a department may contain many employees. What we *don't* want to allow is the same *pair* of values to appear in the table twice (it wouldn't make sense to associate a particular employee with a particular department more than once). For this reason, we usually create mapping tables with a multi-column primary key.

In this example, the primary key for the `EmployeeDepartment` table would consist of the `EmployeeID` and `DepartmentID` columns. This enforces the uniqueness that is appropriate to a look-up table, and prevents a particular employee from being assigned to a particular department more than once.

If you'd like to learn more about many-to-many relationships, or about anything else related to SQL Server programming, I recommend you download and use the product's excellent documentation, SQL Server Books Online.[3]

Summary

This chapter has introduced the fundamental concepts of relational databases. You learned about the underlying structure of a modern relational database, which is composed of tables, columns, and rows, and about crucial concepts that can aid in database performance, maintenance, and efficiency. You've also learned how to implement and enforce table relationships, and you have a solid understanding of good relational database design.

Chapter 8 goes beyond data storage and introduces you to the language used to access and manipulate the data you hold in your tables. That language is the Structured Query Language, or SQL.

---

[3] http://msdn2.microsoft.com/en-us/library/ms130214.aspx

8

Speaking SQL

So your database has been created, and you've defined all of the tables you'll need, all of the columns for your tables—you've even defined the relationships between your tables. The question now is, "How will you get to that data?" Sure, you can open the database, look at the data contained in the tables, and manually insert and delete records, but that does little to help your web users to interact with that data. Mary in Accounting isn't going to want to download and learn to use SQL Server Management Studio just so she can retrieve an employee's mobile phone number—this functionality has to be provided by the Dorknozzle intranet web site, which, after all, is supposed to enable staff members to access data easily. In fact, the functionality can be created using web forms, web controls, a little code, and a useful database programming language known as Structured Query Language (or SQL).

SQL has its origins in a language developed by IBM in the 1970s called SEQUEL (which stood for Structured English QUEry Language), and is still often referred to as "sequel" or "ess-que-el." It represents a very powerful way of interacting with current database technologies and the tables that constitute our databases. SQL has roughly 30 keywords and is the language of choice for simple and complex database operations alike. The queries you will construct with these keywords range from the very simple to extremely complex strings of subqueries and table joins.

SQL is an international standard, and almost all database products, including SQL Server, Oracle, DB2, and so on, support the standard to a certain degree. The dialect of SQL supported by SQL Server is named Transact-SQL (or T-SQL). This chapter cannot begin to cover all there is to know on the subject, but we hope it will provide you with an introduction to beginning and advanced SQL concepts.

In this chapter, we'll learn:

❏ the basic SQL commands

❏ the expressions that SQL supports

❏ the most important SQL functions

❏ how to perform table joins and subqueries

❏ how to create stored procedures

This may sound like a lot, but you're certain to enjoy it! Let's get started.

Reading Data from a Single Table

Information that's contained within a database is useless unless we have a way of extracting it. SQL is that mechanism; it allows quick but sophisticated access to database data through the use of **queries**. Queries pose questions to the database server, which returns the answer to your application.

Table 8.1. Sample contents from the Employees table

EmployeeID (Primary Key)	Dep'tID	Name	Username	City
1	5	Zak Ruvalcaba	zak	San Diego
2	9	Jessica Ruvalcaba	jessica	San Diego
3	6	Ted Lindsey	ted	San Diego
4	6	Shane Weebe	shane	San Diego
5	9	David Levinson	david	San Diego
6	1	Geoff Kim	geoff	San Diego

For example, imagine that you're trying to extract the information shown in Table 8.1 from the `Employees` table of the `Dorknozzle` database.

How do we make this kind of data available to our web site? The first step is to learn how to read this data using SQL. Then, in the next chapter, we'll learn to access the data from ASP.NET web applications.

In the following sections, we'll learn to write queries that will let us view existing data, insert new data, modify existing data, and delete data. Once you've learnt how to write these fundamental SQL queries, the next step is to put everything together, and to build the web forms with which your users will interact.

Let's begin: first up, open SQL Server Management Studio. Visual Web Developer can also be used to test SQL queries, but SQL Server Management Studio is slightly easier to use for our purposes. Log in to your SQL Server instance, and select the `Dorknozzle` database in the Object Explorer pane, as illustrated in Figure 8.1.

Figure 8.1. Using SQL Server Management Express

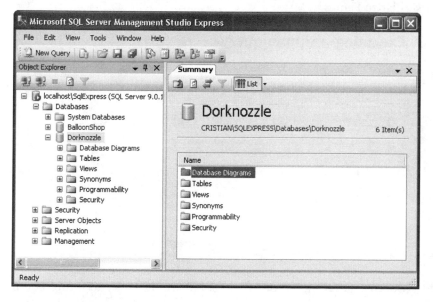

Having selected the `Dorknozzle` database, go to File > New > Database Engine Query, or simply click the New Query button on the toolbar. A new query window, like the one shown in Figure 8.2, should open in the right-hand pane.

Figure 8.2. A new query window

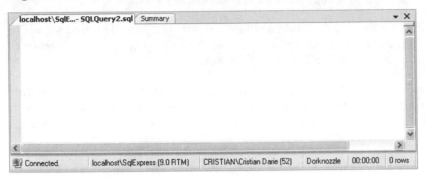

In the query window, type your first command:

```
SELECT Name
FROM Employees
```

Click the Execute button, or press **F5**. If everything works as planned, the result will appear similar to Figure 8.3.

Figure 8.3. Executing a simple query

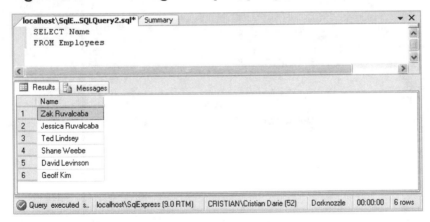

Nice work! Now that we've taken our first look at SQL, let's talk more about SQL queries.

Using the **SELECT** Statement

The most common of all SQL queries is the **SELECT** query. This query is generally constructed using a **SELECT** clause and a **FROM** clause. To understand this concept more clearly, take a look at the following statement, which retrieves all columns of all records in the **Departments** table:

```
SELECT *
FROM Departments
```

In this case, the **SELECT** clause lists the columns that you want to retrieve. In this case, we used *, which means "all columns." The **FROM** clause specifies the table from which you want to pull the records. Together, these two clauses create an SQL statement that extracts all data from the **Departments** table.

You've probably noticed that the two clauses appear on separate lines. If you wanted to keep the entire statement on one line, that's fine, but SQL lets you separate the statements on multiple lines to make complex queries easier to read. Also note that although SQL is not actually a case-sensitive language, we'll capitalize the keywords (such as **SELECT** and **FROM**) according to the popular convention.

To sum up, here's the basic syntax used in a **SELECT** query:

SELECT

> This keyword indicates that we want to retrieve data, rather than modify, add, or delete data—these activities use the **UPDATE**, **INSERT**, and **DELETE** keywords, respectively, in place of **SELECT**.

columns

> We must provide the names of one or more columns in the database table from which we want to retrieve data. We can list multiple columns by separating the column names with commas, or we can use * to select all columns. We can also prefix each column name with the table name, as shown here:

```
SELECT Employees.Name, Employees.Username
FROM Employees.Name
```

This approach is mandatory when two or more of the tables we're dealing with contain columns that have the same names. We'll learn to read data from multiple tables a little later in the chapter.

FROM

The FROM keyword ends the SELECT clause and starts the FROM clause, which identifies the tables from which the data will be extracted. This clause is required in all SELECT statements.

tables

We need to identify the names of the tables from which we want to extract data. To list multiple tables, separate their names with commas. Querying multiple tables is called a *table join*—we'll cover this a bit later.

Armed with this knowledge, we can see that the preceding sample statement would retrieve all records from the Departments table, producing a set of results like that shown in Figure 8.4.

Figure 8.4. Reading the list of departments

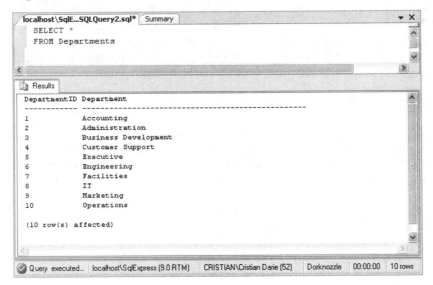

See how easy it is? The SELECT query is probably the one you'll use most.

 Tip

The Number of Affected Rows

As you can see in Figure 8.4, SQL Server reports the number of records that have been affected by a certain query. This report doesn't indicate that those records were modified. Instead, the figure represents the number of rows that were read, modified, deleted, or inserted by a certain query.

Viewing Results in Text Format

By default, the query editor of SQL Server Management Studio displays the results in a grid like the one shown in Figure 8.3. As you work with SQL Server, you may start to find this view a little impractical; in particular, it makes viewing longer strings of text painful because each time you run the query, you need to resize the columns in the grid. Personally, I prefer the plain text view, which is shown in Figure 8.4. You can enable this mode by selecting Query > Results To > Results To Text.

Let's move on and take a look at some variations of the SELECT query. Then we'll see how easy it is to insert, modify, and delete items from the database using other keywords.

Selecting Certain Fields

If you didn't want to select all the fields from the database table, you'd include the names of the specific fields that you wanted in place of the * in your query. For example, if you're interested only in the department names—not their IDs—you could execute the following:

```
SELECT Department
FROM Departments
```

This statement would retrieve data from the Department field only. Rather than specifying the *, which would return all the fields within the database table, we specify only the fields that we need.

Selecting All Columns Using *

To improve performance in real-world development scenarios, it's better to ask only for the columns that are of interest, rather than using *. Moreover, even when you need all the columns in a table, it's better to specify them by name, to safeguard against the possibility that future changes, which cause more columns to be added to the table, affecting the queries you're writing now.

It's important to note that the order of the fields in a table determines the order in which the data will be retrieved. Take this query, for example:

```
SELECT DepartmentID, Department
FROM Departments
```

You could reverse the order in which the columns are returned with this query:

```
SELECT Department, DepartmentID
FROM Departments
```

Executing this query would produce the result set shown in Figure 8.5.

Figure 8.5. Retrieving department names and their IDs

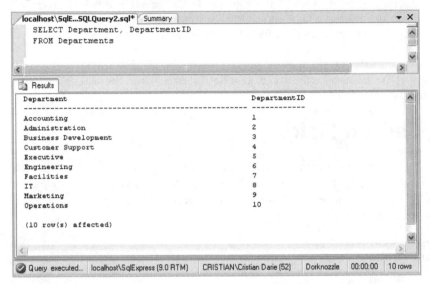

Try it for yourself!

Selecting Unique Data with DISTINCT

Say you want to find out which cities your employees hail from. Most likely, a query such as the one shown below would generate multiple results:

```
SELECT City
FROM Employees
```

If this query were applied to the Dorknozzle application, the same city location would appear six times in the results—once for every employee in our database. Figure 8.6 illustrates this point.

That's not usually what we want to see in our results. Typically, we prefer to see the *unique* cities in the list—a task that, fortunately enough, is easy to achieve. Adding the DISTINCT keyword immediately after the SELECT clause extracts only

Figure 8.6. Reading the employees' cities

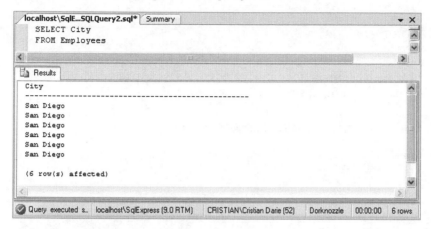

the unique instances of the retrieved data. Take a look at the following SQL statement:

```
SELECT DISTINCT City
FROM Employees
```

This query will produce the result shown in Figure 8.7.

Figure 8.7. Selecting distinct cities

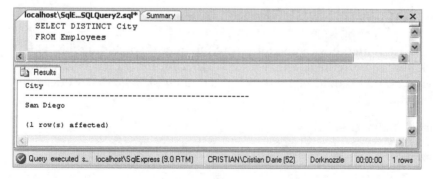

In this case, because only the `City` column was included within the SQL query, unique instances within the `City` column were returned.

Note that the uniqueness condition applies to the whole of the returned rows. If, for example, we asked for the name of each employee as well, all the rows would be considered unique (because no two employees have the same name) and no row would be eliminated by DISTINCT. To see for yourself, execute this query:

```
SELECT DISTINCT Name, City
FROM Employees
```

The results of this code are pictured in Figure 8.8. As we expected, the DISTINCT clause doesn't have any effect, since each row is unique.

Figure 8.8. Retrieving employees and cities

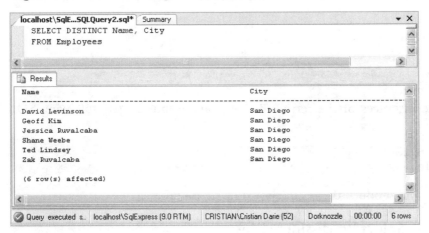

Row Filtering with WHERE

The WHERE clause is used in conjunction with SQL queries, including the SELECT query, to deliver more refined search results based on individual field criteria. The following example could be used to extract all employees that work in the Department whose ID is 6:

```
SELECT Name, DepartmentID
FROM Employees
WHERE DepartmentID = 6
```

This query returns the results shown below:

Name	DepartmentID
Ted Lindsey	6
Shane Weebe	6

```
(2 row(s) affected)
```

But wait! How do I know the name of the department with the ID of 6? Well, you could use a similar query to find out. Try this:

```
SELECT Department
FROM Departments
WHERE DepartmentID = 6
```

Executing this query reveals that the department with the ID of 6 is Engineering.

```
Department
--------------------------------------------------
Engineering

(1 row(s) affected)
```

Selecting Ranges of Values with BETWEEN

There may be times when you'll want to search within a database table for rows that fall within a certain range of values. For instance, if you wanted to retrieve from the Departments table all departments that have IDs between 2 and 5, you could use the BETWEEN keyword like so:

```
SELECT DepartmentID, Department
FROM Departments
WHERE DepartmentID BETWEEN 2 AND 5
```

As we requested, all departments whose IDs are between 2 and 5 are returned. Note that the range is inclusive, so departments with IDs of 2 and 5 will also be retrieved.

Note that any conditions that use BETWEEN could be easily rewritten by combining two "greater than or equal" and "less than or equal" conditions:

```
SELECT DepartmentID, Department
FROM Departments
WHERE DepartmentID >= 2 AND DepartmentID <= 5
```

We could also use the NOT keyword before the BETWEEN keyword to specify all items that fall outside the range, as follows:

```
SELECT DepartmentID, Department
FROM Departments
WHERE DepartmentID NOT BETWEEN 2 AND 5
```

In this example, all rows whose DepartmentIDs are less than 2 or greater than 5 are returned.

Matching Patterns with LIKE

As we've just seen, the WHERE clause allows us to filter results based on criteria that we specify. The example we discussed earlier filtered rows by comparing two numbers, but SQL also knows how to handle strings. For example, if we wanted to search the company's Employees table for all employees named Zak Ruvalcaba, we'd use the following SQL statement:

```
SELECT EmployeeID, Username
FROM Employees
WHERE Name = 'Zak Ruvalcaba'
```

However, we won't see many such queries in reality. In real-world scenarios, most record matching is done by matching the primary key of the table to some specific value. When an arbitrary string such as a name is used (as in the example above), it's likely that we're searching for data based on partially complete information.

A more realistic example is one in which we want to find all employees with the surname Ruvalcaba. The LIKE keyword allows us to perform pattern matching with the help of **wildcard characters**. The wildcard characters supported by SQL Server are the percentage symbol (%), which matches any sequence of zero or more characters, and the underscore symbol (_), which matches exactly one character.

If we wanted to find all names within our Employees table with the surname of Ruvalcaba, we could modify the SQL query using a wildcard, as follows:

```
SELECT EmployeeID, Name
FROM Employees
WHERE Name LIKE '%Ruvalcaba'
```

With this query, all records in which the Name column ends with Ruvalcaba are returned, as shown below.

```
EmployeeID  Name
----------  ------------------------------------------------
1           Zak Ruvalcaba
```

```
2              Jessica Ruvalcaba

(2 row(s) affected)
```

As we knew that the last name was Ruvalcaba, we only needed to place a wildcard immediately before the last name. But what would happen if we didn't know how to spell the entire last name? That name *is* pretty difficult to spell! You could solve the problem by modifying your SQL statement to use two wildcards as follows:

```
SELECT EmployeeID, Name
FROM Employees
WHERE Name LIKE '%Ruv%'
```

In this case, the wildcard is placed before and after the string Ruv. Although this statement would return the same values we saw in the results table above, it would also return any employees whose names (first or last) contain the sequence Ruv. As SQL is case-insensitive, this would include the names Sarah Ruvin, Jonny Noruvitch, Truvor MacDonald, and so on.

Using the IN Operator

We use the IN operator in SELECT queries primarily to specify a list of values that we want to match in our WHERE clause. Let's say we want to find all employees who live in California, Indiana, and Maryland. You could write the following SQL statement to accomplish this task:

```
SELECT Name, State
FROM Employees
WHERE State = 'CA' OR State = 'IN' OR State = 'MD'
```

A better way to write this statement uses the IN operator as follows:

```
SELECT Name, State
FROM Employees
WHERE State IN ('CA', 'IN', 'MD')
```

If you execute this query, you'll get the expected results. Since our database only contains employees living in CA, only those records will be displayed.

```
Name                              State
--------------------------------- ---------------------------------
Zak Ruvalcaba                     Ca
Jessica Ruvalcaba                 Ca
```

```
Ted Lindsey                   Ca
Shane Weebe                   Ca
David Levinson               Ca
Geoff Kim                     Ca

(6 row(s) affected)
```

Sorting Results Using ORDER BY

Unless you specify some sorting criteria, SQL Server can't guarantee to return the results in a particular order. We'll most likely receive the results sorted by the primary key, because it's easier for SQL Server to present the results in this way than any other, but this ordering isn't guaranteed. This explains why, in some of the examples we've completed so far, the order of the results you see on your machine may differ from what you see in this book. The ORDER BY clause provides you with a quick way to sort the results of your query in either ascending or descending order. For instance, to retrieve the names of your employees in alphabetical order, you would need to execute this command:

```
SELECT EmployeeID, Name
FROM Employees
ORDER BY Name
```

Looks simple, doesn't it?

```
EmployeeID  Name
----------  --------------------------------------------------------
5           David Levinson
6           Geoff Kim
2           Jessica Ruvalcaba
4           Shane Weebe
3           Ted Lindsey
1           Zak Ruvalcaba

(6 row(s) affected)
```

Note that the default ordering here is ascending (i.e. running from A to Z). You could add the DESC designation (for descending) to the end of the statement, to order the results backwards:

```
SELECT EmployeeID, Name
FROM Employees
ORDER BY Name DESC
```

If you execute this query, you'll get the results we saw above, listed in reverse order. You could also order the results by multiple columns—simply add a comma after the field name and enter a second field name, as follows:

```
SELECT EmployeeID, Name, City
FROM Employees
ORDER BY City, Name
```

In this case, the results are returned in alphabetical order by city, and any tying records (i.e. with the same city) will appear sorted by name.

Limiting the Number of Results with TOP

Another using SQL keyword is TOP, which can be used together with SELECT to limit the number of returned rows. For example, if we want to retrieve the first five departments, and have the list ordered alphabetically, we'd use this command:

```
SELECT TOP 5 Department
FROM Departments
ORDER BY Department
```

Here are the results:

```
Department
-----------------------------------------------------
Accounting
Administration
Business Development
Customer Support
Engineering

(5 row(s) affected)
```

Reading Data from Multiple Tables

Until now, we've primarily focused on extracting data from a single table. Yet in many real-world applications, you'll need to extract data from multiple tables simultaneously. To do so, you'll need to use subqueries or joins.

Let's learn about joins and subqueries by looking closely at a typical example. Say you're asked to build a report that displays all the employees in the Engineering department. To find employee data, you'd normally query the Employees table, and apply a WHERE filter on the ID of the department. That approach would work fine in this case, except for one thing: you don't know the ID of the Engineering department!

The solution? First, execute this query to find the ID of the Engineering department:

```
SELECT DepartmentID
FROM Departments
WHERE Department = 'Engineering'
```

The result of this query will show that the ID of the Engineering department is 6. Using this data, you can make a new query to find the employees in that department:

```
SELECT Name
FROM Employees
WHERE DepartmentID = 6
```

This query retrieves the same list of employees we saw earlier in this chapter.

So everything's great ... except that you had to execute two queries in order to do the job! There *is* a better way: SQL is very flexible and allows you to retrieve the intended results using a single command. You could use either subqueries or joins to do the job, so let's take a look at them in turn.

Subqueries

A **subquery** is a query that's nested inside another query, and can return data that's used by the main query. For example, you could retrieve all the employees who work in the Engineering department like this:

```
SELECT Name
FROM Employees
WHERE DepartmentID IN
  (SELECT DepartmentID
   FROM Departments
   WHERE Department LIKE '%Engineering')
```

In this case, the subquery (highlighted in bold) returns the ID of the Engineering department, which is then used to identify the employees who work in that department. An embedded SELECT statement is used when you want to perform a second query within the WHERE clause of a primary query.

Note that we're using the IN operator instead of the equality operator (=). We do so because our subquery could return a list of values. For example, if we added another department with the name "Product Engineering," or accidentally added another Engineering record to the Departments table, our subquery would return two IDs. So, whenever we're dealing with subqueries like this, we should use the IN operator unless we're *absolutely certain* that the subquery will return only one record.

Tip

Querying Multiple Tables

When using queries that involve multiple tables, it's useful to take a look at the database diagram you created in Chapter 7 to see what columns exist in each table, and to get an idea of the relationships between the tables.

Table Joins

An **inner join** allows you to read and combine data from two tables between which a relationship is established. In Chapter 7, we created such a relationship between the Employees table and the Departments table using a foreign key.

Let's make use of this relationship now, to obtain a list of all employees in the engineering department:

```
SELECT Employees.Name
FROM Departments
INNER JOIN Employees ON Departments.DepartmentID =
    Employees.DepartmentID
WHERE Departments.Department LIKE '%Engineering'
```

The first thing to notice here is that we qualify our column names by preceding them with the name of the table to which they belong, and a period character (.). We use Employees.Name rather than Name, and Departments.DepartmentID instead of DepartmentID. We need to specify the name of the table whenever the column name exists in more than one table (as is the case with DepartmentID); in other cases (such as with Employees.Name), adding the name of the table is optional.

As an analogy, imagine that you have two colleagues at work named John. John Smith works in the same department as you, and his desk is just across the aisle. John Thomas, on the other hand, works in a different department on a different floor. When addressing a large group of colleagues, you would use John Smith's full name, otherwise people could become confused. However, it would quickly become tiresome if you always used John Smith's full name when dealing with people in your own department on a day-to-day basis. In exactly the same way, you could always refer to a column in a database using the *Table.Column* form, but it's only necessary when there's the potential for confusion.

As for the join itself, the code is fairly clear: we're joining the `Departments` table and the `Employees` table into a single, virtual table by matching the values in the `Departments.DepartmentID` column with those in the `Employees.DepartmentID` column. From this virtual table, we're only interested in the names of the employees whose records match the filter `Departments.Department LIKE '%Engineering'`.

By eliminating the `WHERE` clause and adding the department's name to the column list, we could generate a list that contained all the employees and their associated departments. Try this query:

```
SELECT Employees.Name, Departments.Department
FROM Departments
INNER JOIN Employees ON Departments.DepartmentID =
    Employees.DepartmentID
```

The results are as you'd expect:

```
Name                              Department
--------------------------------- ---------------------------------
Zak Ruvalcaba                     Executive
Jessica Ruvalcaba                 Marketing
Ted Lindsey                       Engineering
Shane Weebe                       Engineering
David Levinson                    Marketing
Geoff Kim                         Accounting

(6 row(s) affected)
```

Expressions and Operators

In the wonderful world of programming, an **expression** is any piece of code that, once evaluated, results in a value. For instance, 1 + 1 is a very simple expression. In SQL, expressions work in much the same way, though they don't necessarily have to be mathematical. For a simple example, let's create a list that contains employees and their cities as single strings. Try this query:

```
SELECT EmployeeID, Name + ', ' + City AS NameAndCity
FROM Employees
```

The results are shown below:

```
EmployeeID NameAndCity
---------- --------------------------------------------------------
1          Zak Ruvalcaba, San Diego
2          Jessica Ruvalcaba, San Diego
3          Ted Lindsey, San Diego
4          Shane Weebe, San Diego
5          David Levinson, San Diego
6          Geoff Kim, San Diego

(6 row(s) affected)
```

Note that the results of the expression are used to create a virtual column. This column doesn't exist in reality, but is calculated using the values of other columns. We give this column the name NameAndCity using the AS keyword.

Expressions would be quite useless if we didn't have operators. Over the course of the previous sections, you've seen the operators =, AND, >=, <=, LIKE and IN at work. The following is a list of operators that you'll need to know to use SQL effectively.

+

The addition operator adds two numbers or combines two strings.

−

The subtraction operator subtracts one number from another.

*

The multiplication operator multiplies one number with another.

/

The division operator divides one number by another.

>

The greater-than operator is used in WHERE clauses to determine whether the first value is greater than the second. For example, the following query would return all the records from the table whose EmployeeID is greater than ten (i.e. 11 and up).

```
SELECT Name
FROM Employees
WHERE EmployeeID > 10
```

<

The less-than operator is used in WHERE clauses to determine whether the first value is less than the second. The result of the following query would return from the table all records whose EmployeeID is less than ten (i.e. nine and lower).

```
SELECT Name
FROM Employees
WHERE EmployeeID < 10
```

>=

The greater-than or equal-to operator is used in WHERE clauses to determine whether the first value is greater than, or equal to, the second. The following query would return the record with EmployeeID of ten, and every one after that.

```
SELECT Name
FROM Employees
WHERE EmployeeID >= 10
```

<=

The less-than or equal-to operator is used in WHERE clauses to determine whether the first value is less than, or equal to, the second. The result of the following query would be the record with EmployeeID of ten, and every one before that.

```
SELECT Name
FROM Employees
WHERE EmployeeID <= 10
```

<>, !=

This operator is used to check whether a value is not equal to a second.

OR

This operator is used with the WHERE clause in the SELECT statement. The OR operator can be used when a certain condition needs to be met, or when only one of two conditions needs to be met. For example, the following query's results would return the employees with employee IDs of 1 or 2.

```
SELECT Name
FROM Employees
WHERE EmployeeID = 1 OR EmployeeID = 2
```

AND

> This operator works just like OR, except that it requires *all* of the conditions to be satisfied, not just any of them.

NOT

> Typically used in conjunction with the LIKE operator, the NOT operator is used when we're looking for values that are not like the value we specify. For example, the following query would return all employees whose name does not begin with "Jess."

```
SELECT Name
FROM Employees
WHERE Name NOT LIKE 'Jess%'
```

_, ?

> The underscore operator is used by SQL Server in WHERE clauses, and matches any single character in a string. For instance, if you weren't sure of the first letter of Geoff Kim's surname, you could use the following query:

```
SELECT Name
FROM Employees
WHERE Name LIKE 'Geoff _im'
```

> This would return Geoff Kim's record, as well as Geoff Sim's, Geoff Lim's, and so on, were there such employees in the database. Note that the _ character only matches a single character, so Geoff Sirrim would not be returned. To match zero or more characters, you'd use the % or * operator.

%, *

> The multiple character operator is similar to the underscore operator, except that it matches multiple or zero characters, whereas the underscore operator only matches one.

IN

> This operator is used in WHERE clauses to specify that an expression's value must be one of the values specified in a list.

Transact-SQL Functions

As well as using operators to construct expressions manually, SQL Server provides us with some functions that we can use within our queries. For the most part, SQL has sufficient functions to handle almost all of the day-to-day tasks that you'll undertake. So let's take a look at some of the most useful and common functions you're likely to use in your queries.

Getting More Information

Note that the complete list of built-in functions supported by T-SQL is much longer than that presented here; you can find the complete lists by searching for, say, "string functions" or "date and time functions" in the free SQL Server documentation, SQL Server Books Online, which can be downloaded from Microsoft's TechNet site.[1] Additionally, SQL Server allows you to create your own user-defined functions either in SQL, or a language such as VB or C#. However, this is an advanced topic that we won't be covering in this book.

Arithmetic Functions

SQL supports many arithmetic functions. Although the commonly-preferred solution is to perform such calculations in VB or C# code, SQL's arithmetic functions can prove handy at times.

ABS

This function returns the absolute value. Both of the following queries will return the value 5:

```
SELECT ABS(5)
```

```
SELECT ABS(-5)
```

CEILING

CEILING returns the smallest integer that's greater than the value that was passed in. In other words, this function rounds up the value passed in. The following query will return 6:

```
SELECT CEILING(5.5)
```

FLOOR

This function returns the largest integer that's less than the value that was passed in, or, in other words, it rounds down the value that was passed in. The following query will return the value 5:

```
SELECT FLOOR(5.5)
```

---

[1] http://www.microsoft.com/technet/prodtechnol/sql/2005/downloads/books.mspx

MOD

MOD returns the remainder of one value divided by another. The following query would return the value 2:

```
SELECT MOD(8, 3)
```

SIGN

This function returns -1, 0, or 1, to indicate the sign of the argument.

POWER

This function returns the result of one value raised to the power of another. The following query returns the result of 2^3:

```
SELECT POWER(2, 3)
```

SQRT

SQRT returns the non-negative square root of a value.

Many, many more mathematical functions are available—check SQL Server Books Online for a full list.

String Functions

String functions work with literal text values rather than numeric values.

UPPER, LOWER

This function returns the value passed in as all uppercase or all lowercase, respectively. Take the following query as an example:

```
SELECT LOWER(Username), UPPER(State)
FROM Employees
```

The query above will return a list of usernames in lowercase, and a list of states in uppercase.

LTRIM, RTRIM

This function trims whitespace characters, such as spaces, from the left- or right-hand side of the string, respectively.

REPLACE

Use the REPLACE function to change a portion of a string to a new sequence of characters that you specify.

```
SELECT REPLACE('I like chocolate', 'like', 'love')
```

This query will search the string "I like chocolate" for the word "like" and replace it with the word "love," as shown in the output below:

```
- - - - - - - - - - - - - - - - - - - - - - - - - - - - - - - - - - - - - - - - - -
I love chocolate

(1 row(s) affected)
```

SUBSTRING

This function returns the sequence of characters within a given value, beginning at a specified start position and spanning a specified number of characters.

```
SELECT SUBSTRING('I like chocolate', 8, 4)
```

The above query will take four characters from the string "I like chocolate" starting from the eighth character, as shown in the output below:

```
- - - -
choc

(1 row(s) affected)
```

LEN

This function returns the length of a string. Thus, the following query would return a list of all usernames, and how many characters were in each username:

```
SELECT Username, LEN(Username) AS UsernameLength
FROM Employees
```

CHARINDEX

This function returns the first position in which a substring can be found in a string.

It's also worth noting that these functions can be used in conjunction with other functions, often to create quite powerful results. For example, the following SQL query would return the first name of every employee within the Employees table:

```
SELECT SUBSTRING(Name, 1, CHARINDEX(' ', Name)) AS FirstName
FROM Employees
```

Here, we're using two string functions. CHARINDEX is used to locate the first space within the Name column. If we assume that the first space indicates the end of the first name, we can then use SUBSTRING to extract the first name from the name string. The results, shown in Figure 8.9, are as we expect.

Figure 8.9. Employees' first names

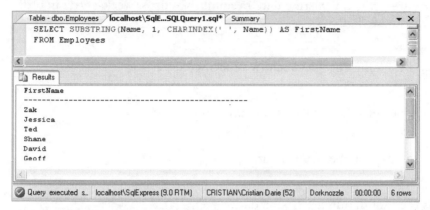

```
FirstName
------------------------------------------------------------
Zak
Jessica
Ted
Shane
David
Geoff

(6 row(s) affected)
```

Note that the query isn't bulletproof—it's only suitable for western-style names. If an employee had no spaces in his or her name (imagine, for instance, that we hired Cher to work as an Engineer), then the CHARINDEX function would return -1, indicating that there was no space character in the name. The SUBSTRING function would then return NULL, so the list of results would be flawed.

Date and Time Functions

Date and time functions facilitate the manipulation of dates and times that are stored within your database. These functions work with arguments of the date-time type. Here are some of the most useful ones:

GETDATE
   returns the current date and time

DATEADD

adds an interval to an existing date (a number of days, weeks, etc.) in order to obtain a new date

DATEDIFF

calculates the difference between two specified dates

DATEPART

returns a part of a date (such as the day, month, or year)

DAY

returns the day number from a date

MONTH

returns the month number from a date

YEAR

returns the year from a date

We won't be working with these functions in our example application, but it's good to keep them in mind. Here's a quick example that displays the current year:

```
SELECT YEAR(GETDATE())
```

The result (assuming it's still 2006, of course) is shown below:

```
CurrentYear
-----------
2006

(1 row(s) affected)
```

Working with Groups of Values

Transact-SQL includes two very useful clauses that handle the grouping of records, and the filtering of these groups: GROUP BY and HAVING. These clauses can help you find answers to questions like, "Which are the departments in my company that have at least three employees?" and "What is the average salary in each department?"[2]

---

[2] Assuming, of course, that your Employees table has a Salary column, or some other way of keeping track of salaries.

When working with groups of data, you'll usually need to use **aggregate functions**. Earlier, you learned about simple functions, which receive fixed numbers of parameters as their inputs. Aggregate functions, on the other hand, can handle a variable number of parameters, and can perform a range of tasks with these parameters.

The typical example for an aggregate function is COUNT, which is used when we want to count how many records are returned by a SELECT query. In the following pages, we'll learn about the GROUP BY and HAVING clauses, which are useful when working with aggregate functions; we'll also explore the COUNT, SUM, AVG, MIN and MAX functions.

The COUNT Function

The COUNT function returns the number of records selected by a query. If you wanted to retrieve the total count of employees in your Employees table, you could run the following query:

```
SELECT COUNT(Name) AS NumberOfEmployees
FROM Employees
```

Running this query with your current sample data would return the number of employees stored in the database, as follows:

```
NumberOfEmployees
-----------------
6

(1 row(s) affected)
```

The COUNT function becomes far more useful when combined with a GROUP BY clause.

Grouping Records Using GROUP BY

Let's imagine that you need to find out how many employees work in each department. We already know how to get a list of employees and their departments:

```
SELECT Departments.Department, Employees.Name
FROM Employees
INNER JOIN Departments ON Departments.DepartmentID =
    Employees.DepartmentID
```

The results of this query are shown below:

```
Department                              Name
-------------------------------  --------------------------------
Executive                               Zak Ruvalcaba
Marketing                               Jessica Ruvalcaba
Engineering                             Ted Lindsey
Engineering                             Shane Weebe
Marketing                               David Levinson
Accounting                              Geoff Kim

(6 row(s) affected)
```

Now, let's build on this query to find out how many employees work in each department. Let's start by adding the COUNT aggregate function:

```
SELECT Departments.Department, COUNT(Employees.Name) AS
    HowManyEmployees
FROM Employees
INNER JOIN Departments ON Departments.DepartmentID =
    Employees.DepartmentID
```

If we execute this query as is, we get the following error message:

```
Msg 8120, Level 16, State 1, Line 1
Column 'Departments.Department' is invalid in the select list
because it is not contained in either an aggregate function or the
GROUP BY clause.
```

Yikes! What this error message is trying to tell us is that SQL Server is confused. It knows that we want to count employees, but it doesn't understand how the Department.Departments field relates to this. We can tell SQL Server to count the employees based on their departments by adding a GROUP BY clause, like so:

```
SELECT Departments.Department, COUNT(Employees.Name) AS
    HowManyEmployees
FROM Employees
INNER JOIN Departments ON Departments.DepartmentID =
    Employees.DepartmentID
GROUP BY Departments.Department
```

When we run the query now, we get the result we were expecting:

```
Department                                      HowManyEmployees
---------------------------------------------  -----------------
```

```
Accounting                                          1
Engineering                                         2
Executive                                           1
Marketing                                           2

(4 row(s) affected)
```

Filtering Groups Using HAVING

Let's say that we're interested only in the members of the Ruvalcaba family that work at Dorknozzle and that, as before, we want to know how many of them work in each department. We can filter out those employees using a WHERE clause, as shown below:

```
SELECT Departments.Department, COUNT(Employees.Name) AS
    HowManyEmployees
FROM Employees
INNER JOIN Departments ON Departments.DepartmentID =
    Employees.DepartmentID
WHERE Employees.Name LIKE '%Ruvalcaba'
GROUP BY Departments.Department
```

While this query is a little complicated, the WHERE clause by itself is pretty simple—it includes only employees with names that end with Ruvalcaba. These records are the only ones that are included in the count, as shown here:

```
Department                                        HowManyEmployees
------------------------------------------------- ----------------
Executive                                         1
Marketing                                         1

(2 row(s) affected)
```

When SQL Server processes this query, it uses the WHERE clause to remove records before counting the number of employees in each department. The HAVING clause works similarly to the WHERE clause, except that it removes records *after* the aggregate functions have been applied. The following query builds on the previous example. It seeks to find out which of the departments listed in the Dorknozzle database have at least two employees.

```
SELECT Departments.Department, COUNT(Employees.Name) AS
    HowManyEmployees
FROM Employees
INNER JOIN Departments ON Departments.DepartmentID =
    Employees.DepartmentID
```

```
GROUP BY Departments.Department
HAVING COUNT(Employees.Name) >= 2
```

The results show us that there are two departments that have more than two employees:

```
Department                                          HowManyEmployees
--------------------------------------------------- ----------------
Engineering                                         2
Marketing                                           2

(2 row(s) affected)
```

The SUM, AVG, MIN, and MAX Functions

There are other common aggregate functions you're likely to need when building more complex applications:

SUM

Unlike the COUNT function, which returns a value that reflects the number of rows returned by a query, the SUM function performs a calculation on the data within those returned rows.

AVG

The AVG function receives a list of numbers as its arguments, and returns the average of these numbers.

MIN, MAX

The MIN and MAX functions enable you to find the smallest and largest values in a group, respectively.

These functions are great for the statistical analysis of records within the database. For example, it wouldn't be difficult to use them to put together a web-based accounting application that monitored daily sales, and gave us totals, averages, and the minimum and maximum values for certain products sold.

Updating Existing Data

Okay, so SQL is so great for querying existing data! But how are we supposed to add data to the tables in the first place? We can't exactly ask Dorknozzle employees to add data to our tables using SQL Server Management Studio, can we? We need to learn how to add, update, and delete data inside our database programatically.

The basic SQL statements that handle these actions are INSERT, UPDATE, and DELETE. Let's put them to work!

The INSERT Statement

Here's a very simple example of INSERT in action:

```
INSERT INTO Departments (Department)
VALUES ('Cool New Department')
```

Executing this command adds a new department, named Cool New Department, to our database. When we add a new row to a table, we must supply data for all the columns that don't accept NULL, don't have a default value, and aren't IDENTITY columns that are automatically filled by the database (as in this example).

If, in Chapter 7, you used the database scripts to create database structures and insert data, you probably noticed that the script contained many INSERT commands; these populated the tables with the sample data.

The INSERT statement generally consists of the following components:

INSERT INTO
> These keywords indicate that this statement will add a new record to the database. The INTO part is optional, but it can make your commands easier to read.

table name
> We provide the name of the table into which we want to insert the values.

column names
> We also list the names of the columns for which we'll be supplying data in this statement. We separate these column names with commas and enclose the list in parentheses.

VALUES
> This keyword comes between the list of columns and their values.

values
> We provide a list of values that we wish to supply for the columns listed above, respectively.

Try the above SQL statement. Then, to read the new list of records, execute the following:

```
SELECT DepartmentID, Department
FROM Departments
```

All records in the `Departments` table will be displayed, along with our Cool New Department and its automatically-generated `DepartmentID`.

Tip

Identity Values

To obtain programatically the identity value that we just generated, we can use the `scope_identity` function like this:

```
SELECT scope_identity()
```

The UPDATE Statement

We use the UPDATE statement to make changes to existing records within our database tables. The UPDATE statement requires certain keywords, and usually a WHERE clause, in order to modify particular records. Consider this code:

```
UPDATE Employees
SET Name = 'Zak Christian Ruvalcaba'
WHERE EmployeeID = 1
```

This statement would change the name of the employee whose `EmployeeID` is 1. Let's break down the UPDATE statement's syntax:

UPDATE
This clause identifies the statement as one that modifies the named table in the database.

table name
We give the name of the table we're updating.

SET
The SET clause specifies the columns we want to modify, and gives their new values.

column names and values
We provide a list of column names and values, separated by commas.

WHERE condition(s)

This condition specifies which records are being updated.

Updating Records

Be sure always to include a **WHERE** clause in your **UPDATE** statement! If you fail to do so, *all* the records will be updated, which is not usually what you want!

The DELETE Statement

The DELETE statement removes records from the database. You could use it to delete all records from the Departments table like so:

```
DELETE
FROM Departments
```

Fortunately, executing this command will throw an error if the foreign key that links the Departments and Employees tables is in place, because removing the departments would leave the employees referencing nonexistent departments, which would make your data inconsistent (note that the reverse *isn't* true: you *could* delete all the employees if you wanted to, but please don't!).

In case you're curious, here's the error message that would be generated by the previous DELETE command:

```
Msg 547, Level 16, State 0, Line 1
The DELETE statement conflicted with the REFERENCE constraint
    "FK_Employees_Departments". The conflict occurred in database
    "Dorknozzle", table "dbo.Employees", column 'DepartmentID'.
The statement has been terminated.
```

You could just as easily delete that new department you created earlier:

```
DELETE
FROM Departments
WHERE Department = 'Cool New Department'
```

Real-world References

Remember that in real-world scenarios, items should be referenced by their IDs, not by name (as is shown in the example above). Also note that if you mistype the name of a department when executing that command, no rows will be affected.

The command above would execute successfully because there aren't any employees linked to the new department.

IMPORTANT

Deleting Records

Like the `UPDATE` command, the `WHERE` clause is best used together with `DELETE`; otherwise, you can end up deleting all the records in the table inadvertently!

Stored Procedures

Stored procedures are database objects that group one or more T-SQL statements. Much like VB or C# functions, stored procedures can take parameters and return values.

Stored procedures are used to group SQL commands that form a single, logical action. For example, let's say that you want to add to your web site functionality that allows departments to be deleted. Now, as you know, you must delete all of the department's employees before you can delete the department itself.

To help with such management issues, you could have a stored procedure that copies the employees of that department to another table (called `Employees-Backup`), deletes those employees from the main `Employees` table, then removes the department from the `Department` table. As you can imagine, having all this logic saved as a stored procedure can make working with databases much easier.

We'll see a more realistic example of a stored procedure in the next chapter, when we start to add more features to the Dorknozzle project, but until then, let's learn how to create a stored procedure in SQL Server, and how to execute it.

The basic form of a stored procedure is as follows:

```
CREATE PROCEDURE ProcedureName
(
  @Parameter1 DataType,
  @Parameter2 DataType,
  ⋮
)
AS
-- SQL Commands here
```

The leading "--" marks a comment. The parameter names, as well the names of variables we can declare inside stored procedures, start with @. As you might expect, their data types are the same data types supported by SQL Server.

The stored procedure shown below creates a new department whose name is specified through the first parameter. It then creates a new employee whose name is specified as the second parameter, assigns the new employee to the new department, and finally deletes both the new employee and the new department. Now, such a stored procedure wouldn't make much sense in reality, but this example allows you to learn a few interesting details that you'll be using frequently as you develop applications, and it uses much of the theory you've learned in this chapter.

```sql
CREATE PROCEDURE DoThings
(
  @NewDepartmentName VARCHAR(50),
  @NewEmployeeName VARCHAR(50),
  @NewEmployeeUsername VARCHAR(50)
)
AS
-- Create a new department
INSERT INTO Departments (Department)
VALUES (@NewDepartmentName)
-- Obtain the ID of the created department
DECLARE @NewDepartmentID INT
SET @NewDepartmentID = scope_identity()
-- Create a new employee
INSERT INTO Employees (DepartmentID, Name, Username)
VALUES (@NewDepartmentID, @NewEmployeeName, @NewEmployeeUsername)
-- Obtain the ID of the created employee
DECLARE @NewEmployeeID INT
SET @NewEmployeeID = scope_identity()
-- List the departments together with their employees
SELECT Departments.Department, Employees.Name
FROM Departments
INNER JOIN Employees ON Departments.DepartmentID =
    Employees.DepartmentID
-- Delete the new employee
DELETE FROM Employees
WHERE EmployeeID = @NewEmployeeiD
-- Delete the new department
DELETE FROM Departments
WHERE DepartmentID = @NewDepartmentID
```

Execute this code to have the `DoThings` stored procedure saved to your `Dorknozzle` database. You can now execute your new stored procedure by supplying the required parameters as follows:

```
EXECUTE DoThings 'Research', 'Cristian Darie', 'cristian'
```

If you execute the procedure multiple times, you'll get the same results, since any data that's created as part of the stored procedure is deleted at the end of the stored procedure.

```
(1 row(s) affected)

(1 row(s) affected)
Department                          Name
----------------------------------  ------------------------------
Executive                           Zak Ruvalcaba
Marketing                           Jessica Ruvalcaba
Engineering                         Ted Lindsey
Engineering                         Shane Weebe
Marketing                           David Levinson
Accounting                          Geoff Kim
Research                            Cristian Darie

(7 row(s) affected)

(1 row(s) affected)

(1 row(s) affected)
```

So, what does the stored procedure do? Let's take a look at the code piece by piece.

The beginning of the stored procedure code specifies its name and its parameters:

```
CREATE PROCEDURE DoThings
(
  @NewDepartmentName VARCHAR(50),
  @NewEmployeeName VARCHAR(50),
  @NewEmployeeUsername VARCHAR(50)
)
AS
```

The parameters include a department name, an employee name, and an employee username.

note

CREATE PROCEDURE and ALTER PROCEDURE

To modify an existing stored procedure, you'll need to use ALTER PROCED-
URE instead of CREATE PROCEDURE. Feel free to play with your existing
procedure, to get a feel for how this works.

The code of the stored procedure starts by creating a new department with the
name specified by the *@NewDepartmentName* parameter:

```
-- Create a new department
INSERT INTO Departments (Department)
VALUES (@NewDepartmentName)
```

Immediately after it creates the department, the stored procedure stores the value
generated for the IDENTITY primary key column (DepartmentID). This value is
returned by the scope_identity function, which returns the most recently generated identity value. Keep in mind that it's good practice to store this identity
value right after the INSERT query that generated it; if we don't store this value
immediately, a second INSERT query may generate another identity value, and
that second identity value would then be returned by scope_identity. The value
is saved into a new variable named @NewDepartmentID.

```
-- Obtain the ID of the created department
DECLARE @NewDepartmentID INT
SET @NewDepartmentID = scope_identity()
```

Here, you can also see how we use the DECLARE statement to declare a new variable
in an SQL stored procedure.

The stored procedure continues by creating a new employee using the name and
username it received as parameters; it assigns this employee to the department
that was created earlier:

```
-- Create a new employee
INSERT INTO Employees (DepartmentID, Name, Username)
VALUES (@NewDepartmentID, @NewEmployeeName, @NewEmployeeUsername)
```

Again, right after creating the new employee, we store its ID into a variable named
@NewEmployeeID. Earlier, we needed to store the generated DepartmentID so that
we could assign the new employee to it; this time, we're storing the new employee
ID so we can delete the employee later.

```
-- Obtain the ID of the created employee
DECLARE @NewEmployeeID INT
SET @NewEmployeeID = scope_identity()
```

Finally, with the new department and employee in place, the stored procedure selects the list of departments together with their employees:

```
-- List the departments together with their employees
SELECT Departments.Department, Employees.Name
FROM Departments
INNER JOIN Employees ON Departments.DepartmentID =
    Employees.DepartmentID
```

For the purposes of this example, we'd prefer to keep the database tidy, which is why we're deleting the new records at the end of the stored procedure. The department and employee IDs that we saved earlier come in very handy at this point: without them, we wouldn't have any way to guarantee that we were deleting the right records!

```
-- Delete the new employee
DELETE FROM Employees
WHERE EmployeeID=@NewEmployeeID
-- Delete the new department
DELETE FROM Departments
WHERE DepartmentID=@NewDepartmentID
```

As you can see, a stored procedure is similar to a function in VB or C#: just like functions in VB or C# code, stored procedures can accept parameters, perform calculations based on those parameters, and return values. SQL also allows for some of the other programming constructs we've seen in this book, such as If statements, While loops, and so on, but advanced stored procedure programming is a little beyond the scope of this book.

Summary

Robust, reliable data access is crucial to the success of any application, and SQL meets those needs. As you have seen, SQL not only returns simple results from individual tables, but can produce complex data queries complete with filtering, sorting, expressions, and even nested statements.

In the latter part of this chapter, we learned how to group T-SQL statements and save them together as stored procedures. In Chapter 9, you'll begin to use the knowledge you've gained about databases, and the language that connects those databases together, to create a real, working application.

ADO.NET

Through the preceding chapters, you've made major strides into the world of dynamic web development using ASP.NET. You've learned about interface development using web forms and web controls, you've learned about modeling and structuring your data within the framework of a database—you've even learned about the SQL language that's used to access the data stored within your database. What you have not yet learned is how to access that data through your web applications.

The next step is to learn how to access a database using VB or C# code. This, of course, is the goal we've been aiming for from the beginning of our adventures in ASP.NET. The whole purpose of the data store is to support an application; in our case, that application is the Dorknozzle Intranet web site, the purpose of which is to offer users an easy-to-use interface to company data.

ADO.NET (*ActiveX Data Objects .NET*) is a modern Microsoft technology that permits us to access a relational database from an application's code. With ADO.NET, we'll be able to display lists of employees and departments, and allow users to add data to the data store, directly from the Dorknozzle application.

In this chapter, you'll learn:

❑ how to connect to your database using ADO.NET

- ❑ how to execute SQL queries and retrieve their results using ADO.NET

- ❑ how to display data that is read from a database

- ❑ how to handle data access errors

Introducing ADO.NET

In previous chapters, we learned how to use Visual Web Developer and SQL Management Studio to connect to a database and execute SQL queries. Now, it's time to apply this knowledge. Within our web application, we'll use ADO.NET's classes to connect to the database; we'll then use that connection to execute SQL queries.

ADO.NET 2.0 and Generic Data Access

ADO.NET is able to use different types of data connections, depending on the kind of database to which the application is trying to connect. The ADO.NET classes whose names start with `Sql` (such as the previously mentioned `SqlConnection`, `SqlCommand`, etc.) are specifically built to connect to SQL Server.

Similar classes are provided for other databases—for example, if you're working with Oracle, you can use classes such as `OracleConnection`, `OracleCommand`, and so on. If, on the other hand, you're working with database systems for which such classes are not specifically designed, you can use generic low-level interfaces; most databases can be accessed through the OLE DB interface (using classes such as `OleDbConnection` and `OleDbCommand`), or the older ODBC interface (using classes such as `OdbcConnection` and `OdbcCommand`).

In this book, we'll use only the `Sql` classes, but it's good to know that you have options!

In order to use ADO.NET, we must first decide which kind of database we'll use, and import those namespaces containing classes that work with the database. Since we're using SQL Server, you'll need to import the `System.Data.SqlClient` namespace. This contains all the required `Sql` classes, the most important of which are:

SqlConnection
This class exposes properties and methods for connecting to an SQL Server database.

SqlCommand

This class holds data about the SQL queries and stored procedures that you intend to run on your SQL Server database.

SqlDataReader

Data is returned from the database in an `SqlDataReader` class. This class comes with properties and methods that let you iterate through the data it contains. Traditional ASP developers can think of the `SqlDataReader` as being similar to a forward-only `RecordSet`, in which data can only be read forward, one record at a time, and we cannot move back to the beginning of the data stream.

The `System.Data.SqlClient` namespace exposes many more than the few classes listed above. We'll discuss some of the more advanced classes in the next few chapters.

Once you're ready to begin working with ADO.NET, the task of establishing a link between the database and your application is a straightforward, six-step process:

1. Import the necessary namespaces.

2. Define a connection to your database with an `SqlConnection` object.

3. When you're ready to manipulate your database, set up the appropriate query in an `SqlCommand` object.

4. Open the connection and execute the SQL query to return the results into a `SqlDataReader` object.

5. Extract relevant database data from the `SqlDataReader` object and display it on your web page.

6. Close the database connection.

Let's walk through this process, discussing each step.

Importing the `SqlClient` Namespace

It's been a while since we've written some VB or C# code! Let's fire up our old friend, Visual Web Developer, and load the `Learning` project. We'll use this application to create a few simple scripts; then we'll move to `Dorknozzle`, where we'll add more functionality to the project site.

After opening the Learning project, go to File > New File... to create a new file. Select the Web Form template, and name it AccessingData.aspx. Uncheck the Place code in separate file and Select master page checkboxes, as shown in Figure 9.1.

Figure 9.1. Creating the AccessingData.aspx web form

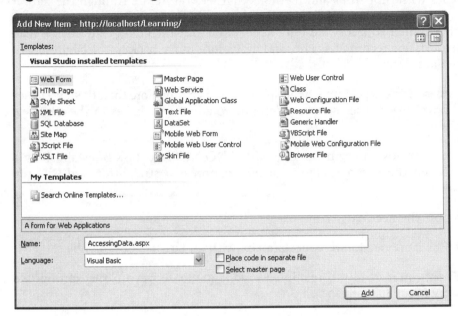

After the form is created, we can import the SqlClient namespace:

File: **AccessingData.aspx (excerpt)**

```
<%@ Page Language="VB" %>
<%@ Import Namespace = "System.Data.SqlClient" %>
<!DOCTYPE html PUBLIC "-//W3C//DTD XHTML 1.0 Transitional//EN"
    "http://www.w3.org/TR/xhtml1/DTD/xhtml1-transitional.dtd">
```

Defining the Database Connection

With our import of the SqlClient namespace complete, we can create a new instance of the SqlConnection, which will facilitate our connection to the database. To initialize this connection, we need to specify a **connection string**—a string in which we specify the database we want to connect to, and provide any required authentication details. A typical connection string for a SQL Server Express database looks like this:

Server=*computer*\SqlExpress;Database=*database*;User ID=*username*; Password=*password*

The connection string must specify the name of the computer on which the database is located (you can always use `localhost` to refer to the local machine) and the name assigned to the database server instance (`SqlExpress` is the default for SQL Server Express). Also required are the name of the database (such as `Dorknozzle`), the user ID, and the password for that user account.

SQL Server supports two methods of authentication: **SQL Server Authentication** and **Windows Authentication**. The form of authentication we've used in previous chapters to connect to SQL Server was Windows Authentication, which doesn't require you to supply a SQL Server name and password, but instead uses the credentials of your Windows user account. To tell SQL Server that we're logging in using Windows Authentication, our connection string would include `Integrated Security=True`, rather than a username and password, as shown here:

Server=*computer*\SqlExpress;Database=*database*;Integrated Security=True

SQL Server Authentication

Be aware that, when the ASP.NET web application is run by ASP.NET through IIS, it authenticates to SQL Server using a special account named **ASPNET**. We'll discuss more about configuring SQL Server authentication a bit later; for now, let's assume that your code can access your database successfully.

Let's put this into practice by creating an `SqlConnection` in the `Page_Load` event handler. To have Visual Web Developer create an empty `Page_Load` event handler for you, switch to Design View, and double-click somewhere within the form. This should take you back to Source View where you can see the `Page_Load` method that was created for you. If you're using VB, enter the code shown in bold below:

Visual Basic   File: **AccessingData.aspx (excerpt)**

```
Protected Sub Page_Load(ByVal sender As Object, _
    ByVal e As System.EventArgs)
  ' Define database connection
  Dim conn As New SqlConnection("Server=localhost\SqlExpress;" & _
      "Database=Dorknozzle;Integrated Security=True")
End Sub
```

If you get sick of typing quotes, ampersands, and underscores, you can combine the three bold strings in the above code into a single string. However, I'll continue to present connection strings as above throughout this book—not only are they more readable that way, but they fit on the page, too!

If you're using C#, your code should look like this:

C#　　　　　　　　　　　　　　　　　　　　　　File: **AccessingData.aspx (excerpt)**

```
protected void Page_Load(object sender, EventArgs e)
{
  // Define database connection
  SqlConnection conn = new SqlConnection(
      "Server=localhost\\SqlExpress;Database=Dorknozzle;" +
      "Integrated Security=True");
}
```

Be aware that, in C#, the backslash (\) character has a special meaning when it appears inside a string, so, when we wish to use one, we have to use the double backslash (\\) shown above.

Preparing the Command

Now we're at step three, in which we create a `SqlCommand` object and pass in our SQL statement. The `SqlCommand` object accepts two parameters: the first is the SQL statement, and the second is the connection object that we created in the previous step.

Visual Basic　　　　　　　　　　　　　　　　　File: **AccessingData.aspx (excerpt)**

```
Protected Sub Page_Load(ByVal sender As Object, _
    ByVal e As System.EventArgs)
  ' Define database connection
  Dim conn As New SqlConnection("Server=localhost\SqlExpress;" & _
      "Database=Dorknozzle;Integrated Security=True")
  ' Create command
  Dim comm As New SqlCommand( _
      "SELECT EmployeeID, Name FROM Employees", conn)
End Sub
```

C#　　　　　　　　　　　　　　　　　　　　　　File: **AccessingData.aspx (excerpt)**

```
protected void Page_Load(object sender, EventArgs e)
{
  // Define database connection
  SqlConnection conn = new SqlConnection(
      "Server=localhost\\SqlExpress;Database=Dorknozzle;" +
```

```
        "Integrated Security=True");
    // Create command
    SqlCommand comm = new SqlCommand(
        "SELECT EmployeeID, Name FROM Employees", conn);
}
```

Executing the Command

When we're ready to run the query, we open the connection and execute the command. The SqlCommand class has three methods that we can use to execute a command; we simply choose between them depending on the specifics of our query. The three methods are as follows:

ExecuteReader

ExecuteReader is used for queries or stored procedures that return one or more rows of data. ExecuteReader returns an SqlDataReader object that can be used to read the results of the query one by one, in a forward-only, read-only manner. Using the SqlDataReader object is the fastest way to retrieve records from the database, but it can't be used to update the data or to access the results in random order.

The SqlDataReader keeps the database connection open until all the records have been read. This can be a problem, as the database server will usually have a limited number of connections—people who are using your application simultaneously may start to see errors if you leave these connections open. To alleviate this problem, we can read all the results from the SqlDataReader object into an object such as a DataTable, which stores the data locally without needing a database connection. You'll learn more about the DataTable object in Chapter 12.

ExecuteScalar

ExecuteScalar is used to execute SQL queries or stored procedures that return a single value, such as a query that counts the number of employees in a company. This method returns an Object, which you can convert to specific data types depending on the kinds of data you expect to receive.

ExecuteNonQuery

ExecuteNonQuery is an oddly-named method that's used to execute stored procedures and SQL queries that insert, modify, or update data. The return value will be the number of affected rows.

As we're reading a list of employees, we'll be using `ExecuteReader`. After we execute this method, we'll follow standard practice, reading the data from the returned `SqlDataReader` as quickly as possible, then closing both the `SqlDataReader` and the `SqlConnection`, to ensure we don't keep any database resources tied up for longer than is necessary.

Visual Basic · File: **AccessingData.aspx (excerpt)**

```vb
Protected Sub Page_Load(ByVal sender As Object, _
    ByVal e As System.EventArgs)
  ' Define database connection
  Dim conn As New SqlConnection("Server=localhost\SqlExpress;" & _
      "Database=Dorknozzle;Integrated Security=True")
  ' Create command
  Dim comm As New SqlCommand( _
      "SELECT EmployeeID, Name FROM Employees", conn)
  ' Open connection
  conn.Open()
  ' Execute the command
  Dim reader As SqlDataReader = comm.ExecuteReader()
  ' TODO: Do something with the data
  ' Close the reader and the connection
  reader.Close()
  conn.Close()
End Sub
```

C# · File: **AccessingData.aspx (excerpt)**

```csharp
protected void Page_Load(object sender, EventArgs e)
{
  // Define database connection
  SqlConnection conn = new SqlConnection(
      "Server=localhost\\SqlExpress;Database=Dorknozzle;" +
      "Integrated Security=True");
  // Create command
  SqlCommand comm = new SqlCommand(
      "SELECT EmployeeID, Name FROM Employees", conn);
  // Open connection
  conn.Open();
  // Execute the command
  SqlDataReader reader = comm.ExecuteReader();
  // TODO: Do something with the data
  // Close the reader and the connection
  reader.Close();
  conn.Close();
}
```

Let's take a look at a few of the methods that are being introduced here. Before we can query our database, a connection must be opened, so we need to call the `Open` method of our `SqlConnection` object `conn`. Once the connection is opened, we call the `ExecuteReader` method of our `SqlCommand` object `comm` to run our query. `ExecuteCommand` will retrieve a list of all employees and return the list in an open `SqlDataReader` object.

At this point, we would usually do something with the data in `reader`, but for now, we've left a comment to remind us that this method doesn't produce any output.

Immediately after we've done something with the data, we close our `SqlDataReader` and `SqlConnection` objects using their `Close` methods. Keeping the connection open for longer than necessary can waste database resources, which can be an issue in real-world applications where hundreds or more users might be accessing the same database at once. As such, it's best practice to keep the connection open for the minimum time.

The code above doesn't have any "real" functionality, as it doesn't actually display anything for the user; however, it does open a connection to your database.

Setting up Database Authentication

If you're running your ASP.NET Web Application through IIS and connecting to SQL Server using Integrated Windows Authentication (by setting `"Integrated Security=True"` in the connection string), you'll probably get an exception when you try to run `AccessingData.aspx`. If you don't get an error, you can skip to the next section—come back only if you get in trouble when connecting to SQL Server.

Provided everything else is as it should be, the error will look like the one shown in Figure 9.2 when you run the code without debugging; it will look like Figure 9.3 if you run the code with debugging using Visual Web Developer.

When you run Dorknozzle using Visual Web Developer's integrated web server, all code is executed as if it were being run by you. In the background, every time your code requests a system resource, Windows checks to make sure that you have access to that resource. If your program were accessing files on the hard drive, for example, Windows would check that you have permission to access those files before allowing the program to proceed. Windows also checks to make sure that you have access to the database. As the user who installed the database

Figure 9.2. A database connection error trapped by the ASP.NET runtime

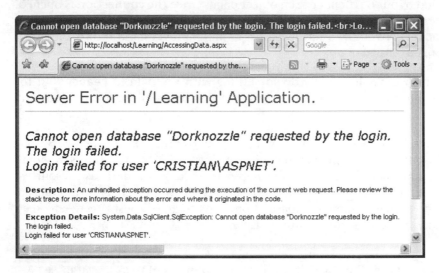

Figure 9.3. A database connection error trapped by Visual Web Developer

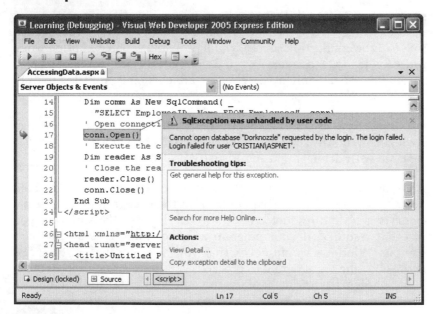

in the first place, you have free reign over its features—you're allowed unfettered access to all areas.

When you run Dorknozzle through IIS, on the other hand, the code is executed as if it were being run by a special user called ASPNET (or Network Service in Windows Server 2003). As such, you need to give this ASPNET user access to your Dorknozzle database. Let's do that now.

Start by opening SQL Server Management Studio and connecting to your SQL Server instance. Click the New Query button to open a new query window. Now, type the code below into the query window, replacing the *MachineName* section with the name of your machine:

Comments

The lines starting with - - are comments, so you may prefer not to type them.

```
-- Add the ASPNET account to SQL Server
EXEC sp_grantlogin 'MachineName\ASPNET'
-- Give the ASPNET account access to Dorknozzle
USE Dorknozzle
EXEC sp_grantdbaccess 'MachineName\ASPNET'
-- Give the ASPNET account full privileges to Dorknozzle
EXEC sp_addrolemember 'db_owner', 'MachineName\ASPNET'
```

What's the Name of my Machine?

If you're not sure of the name of your machine, right-click on My Computer, which you can find either on the desktop or in the Start menu, and select Properties. Under the Computer Name tab, you'll see the Full computer name listed.

Now, when you're running the application through IIS, you can connect to SQL Server from your web application using Integrated Windows Authentication. Execute AccessingData.aspx; this time, you shouldn't see any connectivity errors.

Using SQL Server Authentication

Alternatively, you can connect using SQL Server Authentication by supplying a username and password as part of the connection string. This is the connection mode you'll most likely use when connecting to remote SQL Server instances using the username and password provided to you by that database's administrator. The code to do this in VB and C# is shown below. Replace

ServerName, InstanceName, DatabaseName, Username, and *Password* with the appropriate details for your server.

Visual Basic   File: **AccessingData.aspx (excerpt)**

```vb
' Define database connection
Dim conn As New SqlConnection(
    "Server=ServerName\InstanceName;" & _
    "Database=DatabaseName;User ID=Username;" & _
    "Password=Password")
```

C#   File: **AccessingData.aspx (excerpt)**

```csharp
// Define database connection
SqlConnection conn = new SqlConnection(
    "Server=ServerName\\InstanceName;" +
    "Database=DatabaseName;User ID=Username;" +
    "Password=Password");
```

Reading the Data

Okay, so you've opened the connection and executed the command. Let's do something with the returned data!

A good task for us to start with is to display the list of employees we read from the database. To do this, we'll simply use a `While` loop to add the data to a `Label` control that we'll place in the form. Start by adding a `Label` named `employeesLabel` to the `AccessingData.aspx` web form. We'll also change the title of the page to "Using ADO.NET."

File: **AccessingData.aspx (excerpt)**

```html
<html xmlns="http://www.w3.org/1999/xhtml" >
<head runat="server">
    <title>Using ADO.NET</title>
</head>
<body>
    <form id="form1" runat="server">
    <div>
      <asp:Label ID="employeesLabel" runat="server" />
    </div>
    </form>
</body>
</html>
```

Now, let's use the `SqlDataReader`'s `Read` method to loop through the data items held in the reader; we'll display them by adding their text to the `employeesLabel` object as we go.

Visual Basic   File: **AccessingData.aspx (excerpt)**

```vb
' Open connection
conn.Open()
' Execute the command
Dim reader As SqlDataReader = comm.ExecuteReader()
' Read and display the data
While reader.Read()
  employeesLabel.Text &= reader.Item("Name") & "<br />"
End While
' Close the reader and the connection
reader.Close()
conn.Close()
```

C#   File: **AccessingData.aspx (excerpt)**

```csharp
// Open connection
conn.Open();
// Execute the command
SqlDataReader reader = comm.ExecuteReader();
// Read and display the data
while(reader.Read())
{
  employeesLabel.Text += reader["Name"] + "<br />";
}
// Close the reader and the connection
reader.Close();
conn.Close();
```

Figure 9.4. Displaying the list of employees

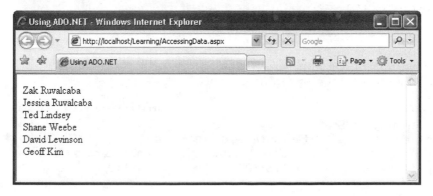

We already know that the `SqlDataReader` class reads the data row by row, in a forward-only fashion. Only one row can be read at any moment. When we call `reader.Read`, our `SqlDataReader` reads the next row of data from the database. If there's data to be read, it returns `True`; otherwise—if we've already read the last record returned by the query—the `Read` method returns `False`. If we view this page in the browser, we'll see something like Figure 9.4.

Using Parameters with Queries

What if the user doesn't want to view information for all employees, but instead, wants to see details for one specific employee?

To get this information from our `Employees` table, we'd run the following query, replacing *EmployeeID* with the ID of the employee in which the user was interested.

```
SELECT EmployeeID, Name, Username, Password
FROM Employees
WHERE EmployeeID = EmployeeID
```

Let's build a page like the one shown in Figure 9.5 to display this information.

Figure 9.5. Retrieving details of a specific employee

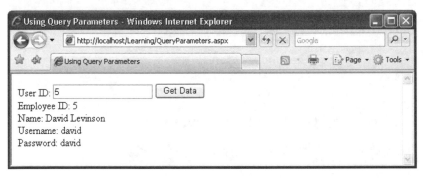

Create a new web form called `QueryParameters.aspx` and alter it to reflect the code shown here:

File: **QueryParameters.aspx** (excerpt)

```
<%@ Page Language="VB" %>
<%@ Import Namespace="System.Data.SqlClient" %>
<!DOCTYPE html PUBLIC "-//W3C//DTD XHTML 1.0 Transitional//EN"
    "http://www.w3.org/TR/xhtml1/DTD/xhtml1-transitional.dtd">
```

```
<script runat="server">

</script>

<html xmlns="http://www.w3.org/1999/xhtml" >
<head runat="server">
    <title>Using Query Parameters</title>
</head>
<body>
    <form id="form1" runat="server">
    <div>
      User ID:
      <asp:TextBox ID="idTextBox" runat="server" />
      <asp:Button ID="submitButton" runat="server"
          Text="Get Data" /><br />
      <asp:Label ID="userLabel" runat="server" />
    </div>
    </form>
</body>
</html>
```

With these amendments, we've added a `Textbox` control into which users can type in the ID of the employee whose information they want to see. We've also added a `Button` that will be used to submit the form and retrieve the data.

Next, we need to add a `Click` event handler to the `Button` control. When this button is clicked, our web form will need to execute the following tasks:

1. Read the ID typed by the user in the `idTextBox` control.

2. Prepare an SQL query to retrieve data about the specified employee.

3. Execute the query and read the results.

Now, we *could* perform this query using the following code:

```
comm = New SqlCommand( _
    "SELECT EmployeeID, Name, Username, Password " & _
    "FROM Employees WHERE EmployeeID = " & idTextBox.Text , conn)
```

If the user entered the number **5** into the text box and clicked the button, the following query would be run:

```
SELECT EmplyeeID, Name, Username, Password
FROM Employees
WHERE EmployeeID = 5
```

The database would run this query without complaint, and your program would execute as expected. However, if—as is perhaps more likely—the user entered an employee's name, your application would attempt to run the following query:

```
SELECT EmployeeID, Name, Username, Password
FROM Employees
WHERE EmployeeID = Zac Ruvalcaba
```

This query would cause an error in the database, which would, in turn, cause an exception in your web form. As a safeguard against this eventuality, ADO.NET allows you to define **parameters** in your query, and to give each of those parameters a type. Inserting parameters into your query is a pretty simple task:

```
comm = New SqlCommand( _
    "SELECT EmployeeID, Name, Username, Password " & _
    "FROM Employees WHERE EmployeeID = @EmployeeID", conn)
```

We've added a placeholder for our parameter to the query above. To do so, we add the @ symbol, followed by an identifier for our parameter (in this case, we've used EmployeeID). Next, we need to add this parameter to the SqlCommand object, and give it a value:

Visual Basic
```
comm.Parameters.Add("@EmployeeID", System.Data.SqlDbType.Int)
comm.Parameters("@EmployeeID").Value = idTextBox.Text
```

C#
```
comm.Parameters.Add("@EmployeeID", System.Data.SqlDbType.Int);
comm.Parameters["@EmployeeID"].Value = idTextBox.Text
```

Here, we call the Add method of conn.Parameters, passing in the name of the parameter (EmployeeID) and the parameter's type; we've told ADO.NET that we're expecting an int to be passed to the database, but we could specify any of the SQL Server data types here.

One of the most common SQL Server data types is nvarchar. If your query involved an nvarchar parameter named @Username, for example, you could set its value with the following code:

Visual Basic
```
comm.Parameters.Add("@Username", Data.SqlDbType.NVarChar, 50)
comm.Parameters("@Username").Value = username
```

C#

```
comm.Parameters.Add("@Username", SqlDbType.NVarChar, 50);
comm.Parameters["@Username"].Value = username;
```

Notice that we've included an additional parameter in our call to the Add method. This optional parameter tells the SqlCommand object the maximum allowable size of the nvarchar field in the database. We've given the Username field in our Employees table a maximum size of 50 characters, so our code should reflect this.

For a list of all the types you can use when calling conn.Parameters.Add, see the entry on System.Data.SqlDbType Enumeration in the .NET Framework's SDK Documentation.

Let's put parameters into action in QueryParameters.aspx. First, create a Click event handler for the Button control by double-clicking it in Design View. Next, fill the event handler with the code shown below:

Visual Basic   File: **QueryParameters.aspx (excerpt)**

```
Protected Sub submitButton_Click(ByVal sender As Object, _
    ByVal e As System.EventArgs)
  ' Define data objects
  Dim conn As SqlConnection
  Dim comm As SqlCommand
  Dim reader As SqlDataReader
  ' Initialize connection
  conn = New SqlConnection("Server=localhost\SqlExpress;" & _
      "Database=Dorknozzle;Integrated Security=True")
  ' Create command
  comm = New SqlCommand( _
      "SELECT EmployeeID, Name, Username, Password " & _
      "FROM Employees WHERE EmployeeID=@EmployeeID", conn)
  ' Verify if the ID entered by the visitor is numeric
  Dim employeeID As Integer
  If (Not Integer.TryParse(idTextBox.Text, employeeID)) Then
    ' If the user didn't enter numeric ID...
    userLabel.Text = "Please enter a numeric ID!"
  Else
    ' Add parameter
    comm.Parameters.Add("@EmployeeID", System.Data.SqlDbType.Int)
    comm.Parameters("@EmployeeID").Value = employeeID
    ' Open the connection
    conn.Open()
    ' Execute the command
    reader = comm.ExecuteReader()
    ' Display the requested data
```

```
    If reader.Read() Then
      userLabel.Text = "Employee ID: " & _
          reader.Item("EmployeeID") & "<br />" & _
          "Name: " & reader.Item("Name") & "<br />" & _
          "Username: " & reader.Item("Username") & "<br />" & _
          "Password: " & reader.Item("Password")
    Else
      userLabel.Text = _
          "There is no user with this ID: " & employeeID
    End If
    ' Close the reader and the connection
    reader.Close()
    conn.Close()
  End If
End Sub
```

C#   File: **QueryParameters.aspx** (excerpt)

```csharp
protected void submitButton_Click(object sender, EventArgs e)
{
  // Declare objects
  SqlConnection conn;
  SqlCommand comm;
  SqlDataReader reader;
  // Initialize connection
  conn = new SqlConnection("Server=localhost\\SqlExpress;" +
      "Database=Dorknozzle;Integrated Security=True");
  // Create command
  comm = new SqlCommand(
      "SELECT EmployeeID, Name, Username, Password " +
      "FROM Employees WHERE EmployeeID=@EmployeeID", conn);
  // Verify if the ID entered by the visitor is numeric
  int employeeID;
  if (!int.TryParse(idTextBox.Text, out employeeID))
  {
    // If the user didn't enter numeric ID...
    userLabel.Text = "Please enter a numeric ID!";
  }
  else
  {
    // Add parameter
    comm.Parameters.Add("@EmployeeID", System.Data.SqlDbType.Int);
    comm.Parameters["@EmployeeID"].Value = employeeID;
    // Open the connection
    conn.Open();
    // Execute the command
    reader = comm.ExecuteReader();
```

```
  // Display the requested data
  if (reader.Read())
  {
    userLabel.Text = "Employee ID: " +
        reader["EmployeeID"] + "<br />" +
        "Name: " + reader["Name"] + "<br />" +
        "Username: " + reader["Username"] + "<br />" +
        "Password: " + reader["Password"];
  }
  else
  {
    userLabel.Text =
        "There is no user with this ID: " + employeeID;
  }
  // Close the reader and the connection
  reader.Close();
  conn.Close();
  }
}
```

Now, when the user clicks the button, the `Click` event is raised, and the event handler is executed. In that method, we grab the Employee ID from the `Text` property of the `TextBox` control, and check that it's a valid integer. This check can be done with the `Integer.TryParse` method in VB, or the `int.TryParse` method in C#:

Visual Basic   File: **QueryParameters.aspx (excerpt)**

```
' Verify if the ID entered by the visitor is numeric
Dim employeeID As Integer
If (Not Integer.TryParse(idTextBox.Text, employeeID)) Then
    :
```

C#   File: **QueryParameters.aspx (excerpt)**

```
// Verify if the ID entered by the visitor is numeric
int employeeID;
if (!int.TryParse(idTextBox.Text, out employeeID))
{
    :
```

This method verifies whether or not the string we pass as the first parameter can be cast to an integer, and if yes, the integer is returned through the second parameter. Note that in C#, this is an out parameter. **Out parameters** are parameters that are used to retrieve data from a function, rather than send data to that function. Out parameters are similar to return values, except that more than one of them can exist for any method. The return value of `TryParse` is a Boolean value that specifies whether or not the value could be properly converted.

If the ID that's entered isn't a valid number, we notify the user, as Figure 9.6 illustrates.

Figure 9.6. Invalid input data generating a warning

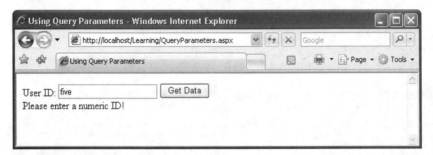

We also notify the user if the query doesn't return any results. This feature is simple to implement, because `reader.Read` only returns `True` if the query returns a record.

```
Visual Basic                                    File: QueryParameters.aspx (excerpt)
' Display the requested data
If reader.Read() Then
  userLabel.Text = "Employee ID: " & reader.Item("EmployeeID") & _
  :
```

```
C#                                              File: QueryParameters.aspx (excerpt)
// Display the requested data
if (reader.Read())
{
  userLabel.Text = "Employee ID: " + reader["EmployeeID"] +
  :
```

Figure 9.7 shows the message you'll see if you enter an ID that doesn't exist in the database.

There are still a couple of details that we could improve in this system. For example, if an error occurs in the code, the connection will never be closed. Let's look at this problem next.

Figure 9.7. An invalid ID warning

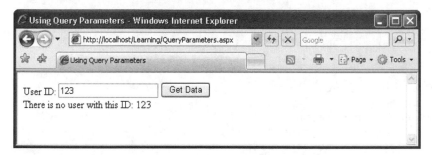

Bulletproofing Data Access Code

Right now, the code in `QueryParameters.aspx` seems to be perfect, right? Well, not quite. While the code does its job most of the time, it still has one important weakness: it doesn't take into account potential errors that could occur in the data access code. It's very good practice to enclose such code in `Try-Catch-Finally` blocks, and always to use the `Finally` block to close any open data objects. We learned about `Try-Catch-Finally` in Chapter 5; now we're going to use that theory in a real-world scenario.

Take a look at the following code samples.

Visual Basic   File: **QueryParameters.aspx (excerpt)**

```
Protected Sub submitButton_Click(ByVal sender As Object, _
    ByVal e As System.EventArgs)
  ' Define data objects
  Dim conn As SqlConnection
  Dim comm As SqlCommand
  Dim reader As SqlDataReader
  ' Initialize connection
  conn = New SqlConnection("Server=localhost\SqlExpress;" & _
      "Database=Dorknozzle;Integrated Security=True")

  ' Create command
  comm = New SqlCommand( _
      "SELECT EmployeeID, Name, Username, Password " & _
      "FROM Employees WHERE EmployeeID=@EmployeeID", conn)
  ' Verify if the ID entered by the visitor is numeric
  Dim employeeID As Integer
  If (Not Integer.TryParse(idTextBox.Text, employeeID)) Then
    ' If the user didn't enter numeric ID...
```

```
      userLabel.Text = "Please enter a numeric ID!"
  Else
    ' Add parameter
    comm.Parameters.Add("@EmployeeID", System.Data.SqlDbType.Int)
    comm.Parameters("@EmployeeID").Value = employeeID
    ' Enclose database code in Try-Catch-Finally
    Try
      ' Open the connection
      conn.Open()
      ' Execute the command
      reader = comm.ExecuteReader()
      ' Display the requested data
      If reader.Read() Then
        userLabel.Text = "Employee ID: " & _
            reader.Item("EmployeeID") & "<br />" & _
            "Name: " & reader.Item("Name") & "<br />" & _
            "Username: " & reader.Item("Username") & "<br />" & _
            "Password: " & reader.Item("Password")
      Else
        userLabel.Text = _
            "There is no user with this ID: " & employeeID
      End If
      reader.Close()
    Catch
      ' Display error message
      userLabel.Text = "Error retrieving user data."
    Finally
      ' Close the connection
      conn.Close()
    End Try
  End If
End Sub
```

C#   File: **QueryParameters.aspx (excerpt)**

```
protected void submitButton_Click(object sender, EventArgs e)
{
  // Declare objects
  SqlConnection conn;
  SqlCommand comm;
  SqlDataReader reader;
  // Initialize connection
  conn = new SqlConnection("Server=localhost\\SqlExpress;" +
      "Database=Dorknozzle;Integrated Security=True");
  // Create command
  comm = new SqlCommand(
      "SELECT EmployeeID, Name, Username, Password " +
```

```csharp
    "FROM Employees WHERE EmployeeID=@EmployeeID", conn);
// Verify if the ID entered by the visitor is numeric
int employeeID;
if (!int.TryParse(idTextBox.Text, out employeeID))
{
  // If the user didn't enter numeric ID...
  userLabel.Text = "Please enter a numeric ID!";
}
else
{
  // Add parameter
  comm.Parameters.Add("@EmployeeID", System.Data.SqlDbType.Int);
  comm.Parameters["@EmployeeID"].Value = employeeID;
  // Enclose database code in Try-Catch-Finally
  try
  {
    // Open the connection
    conn.Open();
    // Execute the command
    reader = comm.ExecuteReader();
    // Display the requested data
    if (reader.Read())
    {
      userLabel.Text = "Employee ID: " +
        reader["EmployeeID"] + "<br />" +
        "Name: " + reader["Name"] + "<br />" +
        "Username: " + reader["Username"] + "<br />" +
        "Password: " + reader["Password"];
    }
    else
    {
      userLabel.Text =
        "There is no user with this ID: " + employeeID;
    }
    // Close the reader and the connection
    reader.Close();
  }
  catch
  {
    // Display error message
    userLabel.Text = "Error retrieving user data.";
  }
  finally
  {
    // Close the connection
    conn.Close();
```

```
        }
    }
}
```

So, what's new in this version of the event handler, apart from the fact that it's become larger? First of all—and most important—we have the `Try-Catch-Finally` block in place. Everything that manipulates the database is in the `Try` block. If an error arises, we display a message for the user through the `Catch` block. In the `Finally` block, which is always guaranteed to execute, we close the database connection.

Using the Repeater Control

The .NET Framework comes bundled with a few controls that can help us to display more complex lists of data: `Repeater`, `DataList`, `GridView`, `DetailsView`, and `FormView`. These controls allow you to easily format database data within an ASP.NET page.

In this chapter, you'll learn how to work with the `Repeater`; we'll cover the other controls in the next few chapters. Note that these controls aren't part of ADO.NET, but we're presenting them together with ADO.NET because they're frequently used in work with databases.

Where's the `DataGrid`?

ASP.NET 1.0 and ASP.NET 1.1 developers may wonder what happened to the `DataGrid` control, which used to be the control of choice for displaying grids of data. Though that control still exists in ASP.NET 2.0, the more powerful and flexible `GridView` is now the control of choice. Unless you need to maintain older applications, the `GridView` control should be used. The difference between `DataGrid` and `GridView` is covered very nicely in the article *GridView: Move Over DataGrid, There's a New Grid in Town!*[1]

The `Repeater` control is a lightweight ASP.NET control that allows the easy presentation of data directly from a data source, usually in just a handful of lines of code. Let's look at a quick example of how a `Repeater` control can be added to a page:

```
<asp:Repeater id="myRepeater" runat="server">
  <ItemTemplate>
    <%# Eval("Name") %>
```

---

[1] http://msdn.microsoft.com/msdnmag/issues/04/08/GridView/

```
    </ItemTemplate>
</asp:Repeater>
```

As you can see, the `Repeater` control looks a little different to the other web controls we've used thus far. The difference with this control is that it has an `<ItemTemplate>` subtag—otherwise known as a **child tag**—located within the main `<asp:Repeater>` tag, or **parent tag**. This child tag contains a code render block that specifies the particular data item that we want to appear in the `Repeater`. However, before this data can be displayed, we have to bind an `SqlDataReader` object (which contains the results of an SQL query) to the `Repeater` control using the process known as **data binding**. This task is achieved from a code block like so:

```
myRepeater.DataSource = reader
myRepeater.DataBind()
```

It's that easy! In a moment, we'll display the code within the framework of a new example. First, let's discuss what's happening here in more detail.

True to its name, the `Repeater` control lets us output some markup for each record in an `SqlDataReader`, inserting values from those records wherever we like in this repeated markup. The markup to be repeated is provided as **templates** for the `Repeater` to use. For example, if we wanted to display the results of a database query in an HTML table, we could use a `Repeater` to generate an HTML table row for each record in that results set. We'd provide a template containing `<tr>` and `</tr>` tags, as well as `<td>` and `</td>` tags, and we'd indicate where in that template we wanted the values from the results set to appear.

To gain greater flexibility in the presentation of our results, we can provide the `Repeater` control with a number of different types of templates, which the `Repeater` will use in the circumstances described in the list of templates below. Each of these templates must be specified in a child tag of the `<asp:Repeater>` tag:

`<HeaderTemplate>`

This template provides a header for the output. If we're generating an HTML table, for example, we could include the opening `<table>` tag, provide a row of header cells (`th`), and even specify a `caption` for the table.

`<ItemTemplate>`

The only template that is actually required, `<ItemTemplate>` specifies the markup that should be output for each item in the data source. If we were generating an HTML table, this template would contain the `<td>` and `</td>` tags and their contents.

`<AlternatingItemTemplate>`

This template, if provided, will be applied instead of `ItemTemplate` to every second record in the data source, making it easy to produce effects such as alternating table row colors.

`<SeparatorTemplate>`

This template provides markup that will appear between the items in the data source. It will not appear before the first item or after the last item.

`<FooterTemplate>`

This template provides a footer for the resulting output, which will appear after all the items in the data source. If you're generating an HTML table, you could include the closing `</table>` tag in this template.

Let's take a look at a repeater control that displays a table of employees. If you want to test this code, create a new web form named `UsingRepeater.aspx` in the Learning application. Don't use a code-behind file or a master page. Import the `System.Data.SqlClient` namespace just as you did for the other two forms we've created in this chapter.

The following code will set up a `Repeater` that can be used to display a table of employees, listing their employee IDs, names, usernames, and passwords:

File: **UsingRepeater.aspx (excerpt)**

```
<%@ Page Language="VB" %>
<%@ Import Namespace="System.Data.SqlClient" %>
<!DOCTYPE html PUBLIC "-//W3C//DTD XHTML 1.0 Transitional//EN"
    "http://www.w3.org/TR/xhtml1/DTD/xhtml1-transitional.dtd">

<script runat="server">

</script>

<html xmlns="http://www.w3.org/1999/xhtml" >
<head runat="server">
    <title>Using the Repeater</title>
</head>
<body>
    <form id="form1" runat="server">
    <div>
      <asp:Repeater ID="myRepeater" runat="server">
```

```
        <HeaderTemplate>
          <table width="400" border="1">
            <tr>
              <th>Employee ID</th>
              <th>Name</th>
              <th>Username</th>
              <th>Password</th>
            </tr>
        </HeaderTemplate>
        <ItemTemplate>
            <tr>
              <td><%# Eval("EmployeeID") %></td>
              <td><%# Eval("Name") %></td>
              <td><%# Eval("Username") %></td>
              <td><%# Eval("Password") %></td>
            </tr>
        </ItemTemplate>
        <FooterTemplate>
          </table>
        </FooterTemplate>
      </asp:Repeater>
    </div>
    </form>
</body>
</html>
```

The Repeater control naturally lends itself to generating HTML tables, and that's just what we're doing here. First, we include a `<HeaderTemplate>`, which includes the opening `<table>` tag, along with the table's heading row.

Next, we provide a template for each item in the result set. The template specifies a table row containing four table cells, each of which contains a code render block that outputs the values taken from each record in the results set. In both VB and C#, we use Eval to retrieve database values. Alternatively, you could use the longer form, `Container.DataItem("FieldName")` in VB.NET or `DataBinder.Eval(Container.DataItem, "FieldName")` in C#, but we'll stick with Eval in this book.

Finally, here's the `<FooterTemplate>` that includes the closing `</table>` tag.

To make the repeater display any information, we need to bind a data source to it. Use Visual Web Developer to generate the web form's Load event handler, and complete it like this:

File: **UsingRepeater.aspx (excerpt)**

```vb
Protected Sub Page_Load(ByVal sender As Object, _
    ByVal e As System.EventArgs)
  ' Define data objects
  Dim conn As SqlConnection
  Dim comm As SqlCommand
  Dim reader As SqlDataReader
  ' Initialize connection
  conn = New SqlConnection("Server=localhost\SqlExpress;" & _
      "Database=Dorknozzle;Integrated Security=True")
  ' Create command
  comm = New SqlCommand( _
      "SELECT EmployeeID, Name, Username, Password " & _
      "FROM Employees", conn)
  ' Enclose database code in Try-Catch-Finally
  Try
    ' Open the connection
    conn.Open()
    ' Execute the command
    reader = comm.ExecuteReader()
    ' Bind the repeater to the data source
    myRepeater.DataSource = reader
    myRepeater.DataBind()
    ' Close the data reader
    reader.Close()
  Catch
    ' Display error message
    Response.Write("Error retrieving user data.")
  Finally
    ' Close the connection
    conn.Close()
  End Try
End Sub
```

File: **UsingRepeater.aspx (excerpt)**

```csharp
protected void Page_Load(object sender, EventArgs e)
{
  // Declare objects
  SqlConnection conn;
  SqlCommand comm;
  SqlDataReader reader;
  // Initialize connection
  conn = new SqlConnection("Server=localhost\\SqlExpress;" +
      "Database=Dorknozzle;Integrated Security=True");
  // Create command
  comm = new SqlCommand(
```

```
      "SELECT EmployeeID, Name, Username, Password " +
      "FROM Employees", conn);
  // Enclose database code in Try-Catch-Finally
  try
  {
    // Open the connection
    conn.Open();
    // Execute the command
    reader = comm.ExecuteReader();
    // Bind the repeater to the data source
    myRepeater.DataSource = reader;
    myRepeater.DataBind();
    // Close the data reader
    reader.Close();
  }
  catch
  {
    // Display error message
    Response.Write("Error retrieving user data.");
  }
  finally
  {
    // Close the connection
    conn.Close();
  }
}
```

Figure 9.8. Using the `Repeater` control

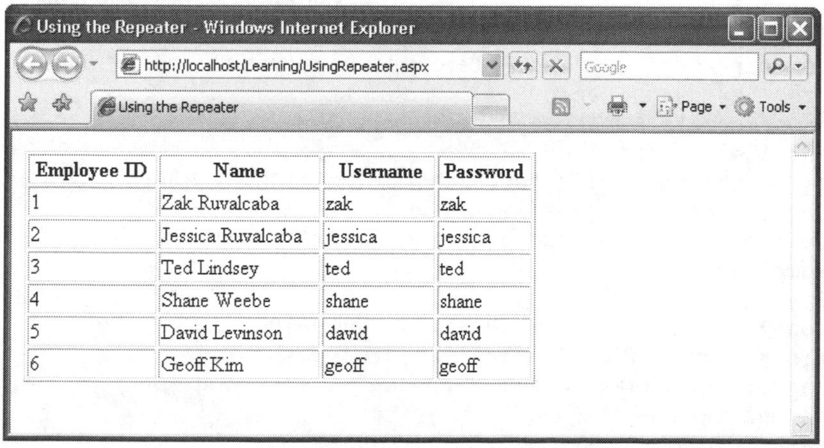
Using the Repeater - Windows Internet Explorer
http://localhost/Learning/UsingRepeater.aspx
Google
Using the Repeater
Page
Tools
Employee ID
Name
Username
Password
1
Zak Ruvalcaba
zak
zak
2
Jessica Ruvalcaba
jessica
jessica
3
Ted Lindsey
ted
ted
4
Shane Weebe
shane
shane
5
David Levinson
david
david
6
Geoff Kim
geoff
geoff

As you can see, by binding a control to a data source, it's very easy to get our data to display in the web form. In this case, we've used the `Repeater` control, which, in the server-side code, we bound to the `SqlDataReader` that contains our data. The results of this work are shown in Figure 9.8.

Creating the Dorknozzle Employee Directory

Great work! You're presenting data in the browser window based on user interaction, and you've even allowed your users to filter that data in accordance with their own search parameters. Your code also takes care to always close the database connection in case an error occurs along the way.

It's time to apply the theory we're learning directly to the Dorknozzle application. In the following pages, you'll insert, update, and delete database records in a new Dorknozzle Employee Directory web form. You'll also learn how to call stored procedures using ADO.NET.

Start by loading the Dorknozzle project and creating a new web form. Make sure you name it `EmployeeDirectory.aspx`, check that both the Place code in separate file and the Select master page checkboxes are checked, and confirm that your new page is based on the master page `Dorknozzle.master`. Then, modify the automatically generated code like this:

File: **EmployeeDirectory.aspx (excerpt)**

```
<%@ Page Language="VB" MasterPageFile="~/Dorknozzle.master"
    AutoEventWireup="true" CodeFile="EmployeeDirectory.aspx.vb"
    Inherits="EmployeeDirectory"
    title="Dorknozzle Employee Directory" %>
<asp:Content ID="Content1"
    ContentPlaceHolderID="ContentPlaceHolder1" Runat="Server">
  <h1>Employee Directory</h1>
  <asp:Repeater id="employeesRepeater" runat="server">
    <ItemTemplate>
      Employee ID:
      <strong><%#Eval("EmployeeID")%></strong><br />
      Name: <strong><%#Eval("Name")%></strong><br />
      Username: <strong><%#Eval("Username")%></strong>
    </ItemTemplate>
    <SeparatorTemplate>
      <hr />
    </SeparatorTemplate>
```

```
    </asp:Repeater>
</asp:Content>
```

This `Repeater` includes item and separator templates. The item template contains code render blocks that will display the data from an `SqlDataReader`. When this repeater is properly populated with data, the employee directory page will look like the one shown in Figure 9.9.

Figure 9.9. The completed Employee Directory page

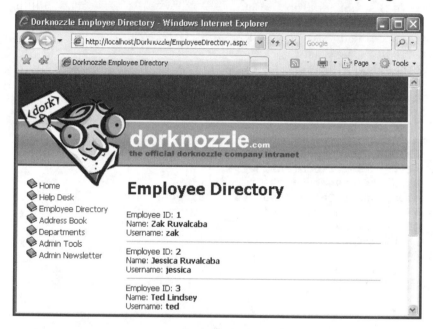

We'll write the code that populates the repeater in the `Page_Load` method within our code-behind file. To have the method's signature generated for you, switch the form to Design View, and double-click an empty space on the form (not in the space of other controls such as the `Repeater`; a good place to double-click would be to the right of the Employee Directory header). Then, add this code:

Visual Basic   File: **EmployeeDirectory.aspx.vb (excerpt)**

```
Imports System.Data.SqlClient
Imports System.Configuration

Partial Class EmployeeDirectory
    Inherits System.Web.UI.Page
```

```
    Protected Sub Page_Load(ByVal sender As Object, _
        ByVal e As System.EventArgs) Handles Me.Load
      ' Define data objects
      Dim conn As SqlConnection
      Dim comm As SqlCommand
      Dim reader As SqlDataReader
      ' Read the connection string from Web.config
      Dim connectionString As String = _
          ConfigurationManager.ConnectionStrings( _
          "Dorknozzle").ConnectionString
      ' Initialize connection
      conn = New SqlConnection(connectionString)
      ' Create command
      comm = New SqlCommand( _
          "SELECT EmployeeID, Name, Username FROM Employees", _
          conn)
      ' Enclose database code in Try-Catch-Finally
      Try
        ' Open the connection
        conn.Open()
        ' Execute the command
        reader = comm.ExecuteReader()
        ' Bind the reader to the repeater
        employeesRepeater.DataSource = reader
        employeesRepeater.DataBind()
        ' Close the reader
        reader.Close()
      Finally
        ' Close the connection
        conn.Close()
      End Try
    End Sub
End Class
```

C#   File: **EmployeeDirectory.aspx.cs (excerpt)**

```
using System;
using System.Data;
using System.Configuration;
using System.Collections;
using System.Web;
using System.Web.Security;
using System.Web.UI;
using System.Web.UI.WebControls;
using System.Web.UI.WebControls.WebParts;
using System.Web.UI.HtmlControls;
using System.Data.SqlClient;
```

```
public partial class EmployeeDirectory : System.Web.UI.Page
{
    protected void Page_Load(object sender, EventArgs e)
    {
        // Define data objects
        SqlConnection conn;
        SqlCommand comm;
        SqlDataReader reader;
        // Read the connection string from Web.config
        string connectionString =
            ConfigurationManager.ConnectionStrings[
            "Dorknozzle"].ConnectionString;
        // Initialize connection
        conn = new SqlConnection(connectionString);
        // Create command
        comm = new SqlCommand(
          "SELECT EmployeeID, Name, Username FROM Employees",
          conn);
        // Enclose database code in Try-Catch-Finally
        try
        {
            // Open the connection
            conn.Open();
            // Execute the command
            reader = comm.ExecuteReader();
            // Bind the reader to the repeater
            employeesRepeater.DataSource = reader;
            employeesRepeater.DataBind();
            // Close the reader
            reader.Close();
        }
        finally
        {
            // Close the connection
            conn.Close();
        }
    }
}
```

Most of the code should look familiar, except for the following bit, which reads the connection string:

Visual Basic   File: **EmployeeDirectory.aspx.vb (excerpt)**

```
' Read the connection string from Web.config
Dim connectionString As String =
```

```
ConfigurationManager.ConnectionStrings(
  "Dorknozzle").ConnectionString
```

C#   File: **EmployeeDirectory.aspx.cs (excerpt)**

```
// Read the connection string from Web.config
string connectionString = ConfigurationManager.ConnectionStrings[
    "Dorknozzle"].ConnectionString;
```

Back in Chapter 5, you learned that you can store various configuration options in Web.config. Anticipating that many applications will use Web.config to store their connection strings, the designers of .NET reserved a special place in Web.config for database connection strings. If you open Web.config now, you'll see an empty connectionStrings element located inside the configuration element. Modify Web.config like this:

File: **Web.config (excerpt)**

```
<configuration>
  ⋮
  <connectionStrings>
    <add name="Dorknozzle"
        connectionString="Server=localhost\SqlExpress;
            Database=Dorknozzle;Integrated Security=True"
        providerName="System.Data.SqlClient"/>
  </connectionStrings>
  ⋮
</configuration>
```

You can add more connection strings under the connectionStrings element by inserting add elements with three attributes: connectionString contains the actual connection string, name gives the connection string an identifier that we can reference within our code, and providerName indicates the type of data provider we want to use for the connection. In our case, providerName="System.Data.SqlClient" specifies that we're connecting to an SQL Server database.

To retrieve configuration data from Web.config we use the ConfigurationManager class, which is located in the System.Configuration namespace.

Also, you may have noticed that we don't have a Catch block in our database handling code. When a Catch block is not present, any exceptions that are raised are not caught, although the code in the Finally block is still executed. In other words, we're choosing not to handle potential errors in EmployeeDirectory.aspx, but we still want to ensure that the database connection is properly closed if an error arises.

The rest of the code comprises the typical data access routine, involving a `SqlConnection` object, a `SqlCommand` object, and a `SqlDataReader` object. Once the reader has been filled with the database data, it is bound to the `Repeater` control's `DataSource` property, and from this point, the repeater takes control and reads all the data from the data source. If you save and run this page, it should appear as shown in Figure 9.9.

More Data Binding

The term "data binding" describes the act of associating a **data source** with a **data consumer**. In our previous examples, the data source was an `SqlDataReader` object, and the consumer was a `Repeater` control that read and displayed the data. Data binding typically involves setting the `DataSource` property of the consumer object to the data source object, and calling the `DataBind` method to apply the binding:

Visual Basic

```
' Bind the reader to the repeater
employeesRepeater.DataSource = reader
employeesRepeater.DataBind()
```

C#

```
// Bind the reader to the repeater
employeesRepeater.DataSource = reader;
employeesRepeater.DataBind();
```

As mentioned earlier, ASP.NET includes a few controls that specialize in displaying data that comes from data sources, but you can also bind data to numerous other controls, including lists, menus, text boxes, and so on. To explore the process of control binding further, let's open the Help Desk page again. If you remember, we left the Category and Subject drop-down lists empty back in Chapter 5. We did so because we knew that, eventually, those items would have to be populated dynamically through code. Sure, we could have hard-coded the values ourselves, but imagine what would happen if additions or deletions needed to be made to that list. In order to make the necessary changes to the controls, we would have to open every page that contained lists of categories and subjects.

It's preferable to store the lists of categories and subjects in database tables, and to bind this data to the drop-down lists in the Help Desk page. Whenever a change needs to be made, we can make it once within the database; all the controls that are bound to that database table will change automatically.

Let's go ahead and add the necessary code to `Page_Load` in `HelpDesk.aspx` to populate the `DropDownList` controls from the database. After the changes are made, the lists will be populated with the data you added to your database in Chapter 7, as illustrated in Figure 9.10.

Figure 9.10. A drop-down list created with data binding

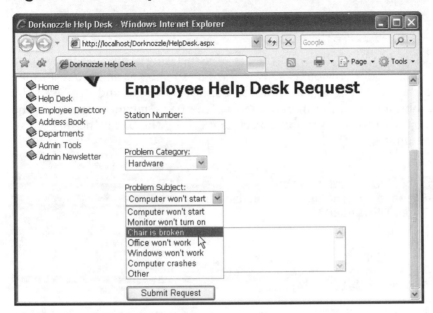

Open `HelpDesk.aspx` in Design View and double-click an empty space on the form to have the signature of the `Page_Load` method generated for you. Then, add the following code:

Visual Basic   File: **HelpDesk.aspx.vb (excerpt)**

```
Imports System.Data.SqlClient
Imports System.Configuration
:
Protected Sub Page_Load(ByVal sender As Object, _
    ByVal e As System.EventArgs) Handles Me.Load
  If Not IsPostBack Then
    ' Define data objects
    Dim conn As SqlConnection
    Dim categoryComm As SqlCommand
    Dim subjectComm As SqlCommand
    Dim reader As SqlDataReader
    ' Read the connection string from Web.config
```

```
      Dim connectionString As String = _
          ConfigurationManager.ConnectionStrings( _
          "Dorknozzle").ConnectionString
      ' Initialize connection
      conn = New SqlConnection(connectionString)
      ' Create command to read the help desk categories
      categoryComm = New SqlCommand( _
          "SELECT CategoryID, Category FROM HelpDeskCategories", _
          conn)
      ' Create command to read the help desk subjects
      subjectComm = New SqlCommand( _
        "SELECT SubjectID, Subject FROM HelpDeskSubjects", conn)
      ' Enclose database code in Try-Catch-Finally
      Try
        ' Open the connection
        conn.Open()
        ' Execute the category command
        reader = categoryComm.ExecuteReader()
        ' Populate the list of categories
        categoryList.DataSource = reader
        categoryList.DataValueField = "CategoryID"
        categoryList.DataTextField = "Category"
        categoryList.DataBind()
        ' Close the reader
        reader.Close()
        ' Execute the subjects command
        reader = subjectComm.ExecuteReader()
        ' Populate the list of subjects
        subjectList.DataSource = reader
        subjectList.DataValueField = "SubjectID"
        subjectList.DataTextField = "Subject"
        subjectList.DataBind()
        ' Close the reader
        reader.Close()
      Finally
        ' Close the connection
        conn.Close()
      End Try
    End If
End Sub
```

C#   File: **HelpDesk.aspx.cs (excerpt)**

```
using System.Data.SqlClient;
⋮
protected void Page_Load(object sender, EventArgs e)
{
```

```
if (!IsPostBack)
{
  // Declare objects
  SqlConnection conn;
  SqlCommand categoryComm;
  SqlCommand subjectComm;
  SqlDataReader reader;
  // Read the connection string from Web.config
  string connectionString =
      ConfigurationManager.ConnectionStrings[
      "Dorknozzle"].ConnectionString;
  // Initialize connection
  conn = new SqlConnection(connectionString);
  // Create command to read the help desk categories
  categoryComm = new SqlCommand(
      "SELECT CategoryID, Category FROM HelpDeskCategories",
      conn);
  // Create command to read the help desk subjects
  subjectComm = new SqlCommand(
      "SELECT SubjectID, Subject FROM HelpDeskSubjects", conn);
  try
  {
    // Open the connection
    conn.Open();
    // Execute the category command
    reader = categoryComm.ExecuteReader();
    // Populate the list of categories
    categoryList.DataSource = reader;
    categoryList.DataValueField = "CategoryID";
    categoryList.DataTextField = "Category";
    categoryList.DataBind();
    // Close the reader
    reader.Close();
    // Execute the subject command
    reader = subjectComm.ExecuteReader();
    // Populate the list of categories
    subjectList.DataSource = reader;
    subjectList.DataValueField = "SubjectID";
    subjectList.DataTextField = "Subject";
    subjectList.DataBind();
    // Close the reader
    reader.Close();
  }
  finally
  {
    // Close the connection
```

```
        conn.Close();
    }
  }
}
```

You'll notice that the guts of Page_Load are enclosed in an If statement, which tests to see if IsPostBack is True. But just what *is* this IsPostBack?

Earlier, in Chapter 2, we explored the View State mechanism that ASP.NET uses to remember the data in its controls. View State allows your user controls to remember their states across page loads. Every time an event that needs to be handled on the server is raised, the form in the page is submitted to the server—a process known as a **post back**. For example, when a button with a server-side Click event handler is clicked, a post back occurs so that the server-side code can respond to the Click event.

After such an event occurs, all the controls in the web form retain their values, but the Page_Load method is executed again regardless. In consequence, if you click the Submit Request button ten times, Page_Load will be executed ten times. If the data access code that fills the form with values is in Page_Load, the database will be queried ten times, even though the data that needs to be displayed on the page doesn't change!

It's here that IsPostBack comes into play. IsPostBack returns False if the web form is being loaded for the first time; it returns True if the page is being loaded because the form has been posted back to the server.

Referring to IsPostBack

IsPostBack is actually a property of the Page class, but since our web form is a class that inherits from Page, we can refer to IsPostBack directly. If we wanted to, we could refer to this property as Me.IsPostBack in VB, or this.IsPostBack in C#.

Using the IsPostBack Property Appropriately

It's not always appropriate to use IsPostBack as we're using it here. We're loading the form with data only the first time the page is loaded, because we know that the data in the drop-down lists won't change in response to other changes in the form. In cases in which the data in the drop-down lists may change, it may be appropriate to access the database and re-fill the form with data every time the form is loaded. For example, we might want to take such action in a car search form in which, when the user selects a car manufacturer, their selection triggers a request to the server to load a list of all models of car made by that manufacturer.

Once it has been established that this is the first time the page has been loaded, the code continues in a pattern similar to the previous code samples. We retrieve the connection string from `Web.config`, create a new connection to the database, and set up our `SqlCommand` objects. In this page, we retrieve two lists—a list of help desk request categories and a list of subjects—so we'll need to execute two queries. These queries are stored in two `SqlCommand` objects: `categoryComm` and `subjectComm`.

Next, inside a `Try-Catch-Finally` block, we execute the commands and bind the data in our `SqlDataReader` to the existing controls. First, we execute `categoryComm` to retrieve a list of categories; then, we bind that list to `categoryList`:

Visual Basic   File: **HelpDesk.aspx.vb (excerpt)**

```
' Execute the category command
reader = categoryComm.ExecuteReader()
' Populate the list of categories
categoryList.DataSource = reader
categoryList.DataValueField = "CategoryID"
categoryList.DataTextField = "Category"
categoryList.DataBind()
' Close the reader
reader.Close()
```

C#   File: **HelpDesk.aspx.cs (excerpt)**

```
// Execute the category command
reader = categoryComm.ExecuteReader();
// Populate the list of categories
categoryList.DataSource = reader;
categoryList.DataValueField = "CategoryID";
categoryList.DataTextField = "Category";
categoryList.DataBind();
// Close the reader
reader.Close();
```

Note that not all controls handle their bindings in the same way. In this case, we want the `DropDownList` control to display the data from the `Category` column of the `HelpDeskCategories` table. The `DropDownList` control is cleverly designed, and it can also store an ID associated with each item in the list. This can be very helpful when we're performing database operations using the items selected from a `DropDownList`, because the database operations are always carried out using the items' IDs.

The `DataTextField` property of the `DropDownList` needs to be set to the name of the column that provides the text to be displayed, and the `DataValueField` must be set to the name of the column that contains the ID. This allows us to pass the ID of the category or subject along to any part of the application when a user makes a selection from the drop-down lists.

When the page loads, all the categories and subjects will be loaded into their respective `DropDownList` controls, as shown in Figure 9.10.

Inserting Records

The code that inserts records from your application into a database isn't too different from what we've already seen. The main difference is that now we need to retrieve data from the user input controls in the page, and use this data as the parameters to our `INSERT` query, rather than simply firing off a simple `SELECT` query. As we discussed earlier in this chapter, to execute such a query, you'd need to use the `ExecuteNonQuery` method of the `SqlCommand` object, as `INSERT` queries don't return results.

When inserting user-entered data into the database, you need to be extra careful about validating that data in case the users don't type whatever you expect them to (those users always seem to find unimaginable ways to do things!).

A typical `INSERT` statement is coded as follows:

Visual Basic
```
comm = New SqlCommand( _
  "INSERT INTO HelpDesk (Field1, Field2, …) " & _
  "VALUES (@Parameter1, @Parameter2, …)", conn)
```

Once the `SqlCommand` object has been created with a parameterized `INSERT` query, we simply pass in the necessary parameters, similarly to the process we followed for `SELECT` queries:

Visual Basic
```
comm.Parameters.Add("@Parameter1", System.Data.SqlDbType.Type1)
comm.Parameters("@Parameter1").Value = value1
comm.Parameters.Add("@Parameter2", System.Data.SqlDbType.Type2)
comm.Parameters("@Parameter2").Value = value2
```

Keep in mind that in C#, the syntax for accessing the parameters collection is slightly different:

```
C#
comm.Parameters.Add("@Parameter1", System.Data.SqlDbType.Type1);
comm.Parameters["@Parameter1"].Value = value1;
comm.Parameters.Add("@Parameter2", System.Data.SqlDbType.Type2);
comm.Parameters["@Parameter2"].Value = value2;
```

To demonstrate the process of inserting records into the database, let's finish the help desk page.

When employees visit the help desk page, they'll fill out the necessary information, click Submit Request, and the information will be saved within the HelpDesk table. The HelpDesk table acts as a queue for IT personnel to review and respond to reported issues.

First, open HelpDesk.aspx, and add a label just below the page's heading.

File: **HelpDesk.aspx (excerpt)**

```
<h1>Employee Help Desk Request</h1>
<asp:Label ID="dbErrorMessage" ForeColor="Red" runat="server" />
<p>
  Station Number:<br />
  <asp:TextBox id="stationTextBox" runat="server"
      CssClass="textbox" />
```

The form already contains numerous validation controls that display error messages if they find problems with the entered data. We're adding this Label control to display errors that arise when an exception is caught while the database query is executing. This is necessary because, although the validation controls prevent most of the errors that could occur, they can't guarantee that the database query will run flawlessly. For example, if the database server is rebooted, and we try to run a database query, we'll receive an error until the database is up and running again. There could be other kinds of errors, too. An example of an error message is shown in Figure 9.11.

You already have a Click event handler for the Submit Request button in Help-Desk.aspx—we added it in Chapter 6, when we added validation controls to the page. The event handler should look like this:

Visual Basic   File: **HelpDesk.aspx.vb (excerpt)**

```
Protected Sub submitButton_Click(ByVal sender As Object, _
    ByVal e As System.EventArgs) Handles submitButton.Click
```

Figure 9.11. Displaying an error message in the catch block

```
  If Page.IsValid Then
    ' Code that uses the data entered by the user
  End If
End Sub
```

C#   File: **HelpDesk.aspx.cs (excerpt)**

```csharp
protected void submitButton_Click(object sender, EventArgs e)
{
  if (Page.IsValid)
  {
    // Code that uses the data entered by the user
  }
}
```

Modify this method by adding code that inserts the user-submitted help desk request into the database, as shown below:

Visual Basic File: **HelpDesk.aspx.vb (excerpt)**

```
Protected Sub submitButton_Click(ByVal sender As Object, _
    ByVal e As System.EventArgs) Handles submitButton.Click
  If Page.IsValid Then
    ' Define data objects
    Dim conn As SqlConnection
    Dim comm As SqlCommand
    ' Read the connection string from Web.config
    Dim connectionString As String = _
        ConfigurationManager.ConnectionStrings( _
        "Dorknozzle").ConnectionString
    ' Initialize connection
    conn = New SqlConnection(connectionString)
    ' Create command
    comm = New SqlCommand( _
        "INSERT INTO HelpDesk (EmployeeID, StationNumber, " & _
        "CategoryID, SubjectID, Description, StatusID) " & _
        "VALUES (@EmployeeID, @StationNumber, @CategoryID, " & _
        "@SubjectID, @Description, @StatusID)", conn)
    ' Add command parameters
    comm.Parameters.Add("@EmployeeID", System.Data.SqlDbType.Int)
    comm.Parameters("@EmployeeID").Value = 5
    comm.Parameters.Add("@StationNumber", _
        System.Data.SqlDbType.Int)
    comm.Parameters("@StationNumber").Value = stationTextBox.Text
    comm.Parameters.Add("@CategoryID", System.Data.SqlDbType.Int)
    comm.Parameters("@CategoryID").Value = _
        categoryList.SelectedItem.Value
    comm.Parameters.Add("@SubjectID", System.Data.SqlDbType.Int)
    comm.Parameters("@SubjectID").Value = _
        subjectList.SelectedItem.Value
    comm.Parameters.Add("@Description", _
        System.Data.SqlDbType.NVarChar, 50)
    comm.Parameters("@Description").Value = _
        descriptionTextBox.Text
    comm.Parameters.Add("@StatusID", System.Data.SqlDbType.Int)
    comm.Parameters("@StatusID").Value = 1
    ' Enclose database code in Try-Catch-Finally
    Try
      ' Open the connection
      conn.Open()
      ' Execute the command
      comm.ExecuteNonQuery()
```

```
        ' Reload page if the query executed successfully
        Response.Redirect("HelpDesk.aspx")
      Catch
        ' Display error message
        dbErrorMessage.Text = _
            "Error submitting the help desk request! Please " & _
            "try again later, and/or change the entered data!"
      Finally
        ' Close the connection
        conn.Close()
      End Try
    End If
End Sub
```

C#   File: **HelpDesk.aspx.cs (excerpt)**

```
protected void submitButton_Click(object sender, EventArgs e)
{
  if (Page.IsValid)
  {
    // Define data objects
    SqlConnection conn;
    SqlCommand comm;
    // Read the connection string from Web.config
    string connectionString =
        ConfigurationManager.ConnectionStrings[
        "Dorknozzle"].ConnectionString;
    // Initialize connection
    conn = new SqlConnection(connectionString);
    // Create command
    comm = new SqlCommand(
      "INSERT INTO HelpDesk (EmployeeID, StationNumber, " +
      "CategoryID, SubjectID, Description, StatusID) " +
      "VALUES (@EmployeeID, @StationNumber, @CategoryID, " +
      "@SubjectID, @Description, @StatusID)", conn);
    // Add command parameters
    comm.Parameters.Add("@EmployeeID", System.Data.SqlDbType.Int);
    comm.Parameters["@EmployeeID"].Value = 5;
    comm.Parameters.Add("@StationNumber",
        System.Data.SqlDbType.Int);
    comm.Parameters["@StationNumber"].Value = stationTextBox.Text;
    comm.Parameters.Add("@CategoryID", System.Data.SqlDbType.Int);
    comm.Parameters["@CategoryID"].Value =
        categoryList.SelectedItem.Value;
    comm.Parameters.Add("@SubjectID", System.Data.SqlDbType.Int);
    comm.Parameters["@SubjectID"].Value =
        subjectList.SelectedItem.Value;
```

```
        comm.Parameters.Add("@Description",
            System.Data.SqlDbType.NVarChar, 50);
        comm.Parameters["@Description"].Value =
            descriptionTextBox.Text;
        comm.Parameters.Add("@StatusID", System.Data.SqlDbType.Int);
        comm.Parameters["@StatusID"].Value = 1;
        // Enclose database code in Try-Catch-Finally
        try
        {
          // Open the connection
          conn.Open();
          // Execute the command
          comm.ExecuteNonQuery();
          // Reload page if the query executed successfully
          Response.Redirect("HelpDesk.aspx");
        }
        catch
        {
          // Display error message
          dbErrorMessage.Text =
              "Error submitting the help desk request! Please " +
              "try again later, and/or change the entered data!";
        }
        finally
        {
          // Close the connection
          conn.Close();
        }
    }
}
```

note

Make Sure you've Set the `Identity` Property!

Note that when we're inserting a new record into the `HelpDesk` table, we rely on the ID column, `RequestID`, to be generated automatically for us by the database. If we forget to set `RequestID` as an identity column, we'll receive an exception every time we try to add a new help desk request!

Did you notice the use of the `ExecuteNonQuery` method? As you know, we use this method when we're executing any SQL query that doesn't return a set of results, such as INSERT, UPDATE, and DELETE queries.

You'll remember that, in order to make the example simpler, we hard-coded the `EmployeeID` (to the value of 5), and the `Status` (to the value of 1). To make the application complete, you could add another drop-down list from which employees

Figure 9.12. Submitting the Help Desk Request form

could select their names, and take the IDs from there. For now, just make sure that the `Employees` table has a record with an `EmployeeID` of `5`, otherwise the query won't execute successfully.

The other potentially unfamiliar part of this code is the final line of the `Try` block, which uses `Response.Redirect`. This method should be quite familiar to developers who are experienced with ASP. `Response.Redirect` simply redirects the browser to another page. For example, the following line of code redirects the user to a page called `SomeForm.aspx`:

Visual Basic

```
Response.Redirect("SomeForm.aspx")
```

C#

```
Response.Redirect("SomeForm.aspx");
```

In our example, we redirect the user back to the same web form. Why on earth would we want to do that? It's because of view state—if we didn't end our event handler this way, the same page would display in the browser, but ASP.NET would preserve all of the values that the user had typed into the form fields. The user might not realize the form had even been submitted, and might submit the form repeatedly in confusion. Redirecting the user in the way outlined above causes the browser to reload the page from scratch, clearing the form fields to indicate the completed submission.

Save your work and run it in a browser. Now, we can enter help desk information, as shown in Figure 9.12, and click Submit Request.

Once we click Submit Request, the `Click` event is raised, the `submitButton_Click` method is called, all the parameters from the form are passed into the SQL statement, and the data is inserted into the `HelpDesk` table. We can see this if we open the table in SQL Server Management Studio or Visual Web Developer, which displays the view shown in Figure 9.13.

Figure 9.13. The new request appearing in the `HelpDesk` table

	RequestID	EmployeeID	StationNumber	CategoryID	SubjectID	Description	StatusID
▶	11	5	45	2	5	Solitaire doesn't work any more!!	1
*	NULL	NULL	NULL	NULL	NULL	NULL	NULL

Updating Records

The major difference between inserting new database records and updating existing ones is that if a user wants to update a record, you'll usually want to display the information that already exists in the database table before allowing the user to update it. This gives the user a chance to review the data, make the necessary changes, and, finally, submit the updated values. Before we get ahead of ourselves, though, let's take a look at the code we'll use to update records within the database table:

Visual Basic

```
comm = New SqlCommand("UPDATE Table " & _
  "SET Field1=@Parameter1, Field2=@Parameter2, … " & _
```

```
  "WHERE UniqueField=@UniqueFieldParameter", conn)
comm.Parameters.Add("@Parameter1", System.Data.SqlDbType.Type1)
comm.Parameters("@Parameter1").Value = value1
comm.Parameters.Add("@Parameter2", System.Data.SqlDbType.Type2)
comm.Parameters("@Parameter2").Value = value2
```

C#
```
comm = new SqlCommand ("UPDATE Table " +
  "SET Field1=@Parameter1, Field2=@Parameter2, … " +
  "WHERE UniqueField=@UniqueFieldParameter", conn);
comm.Parameters.Add("@Parameter1", System.Data.SqlDbType.Type1);
comm.Parameters["@Parameter1"].Value = value1;
comm.Parameters.Add("@Parameter2", System.Data.SqlDbType.Type2);
comm.Parameters["@Parameter2"].Value = value2;
```

Once the `SqlCommand` object has been created using this `UPDATE` statement, we simply pass in the necessary parameters, as we did with the `INSERT` statement. The important thing to remember when updating records is that you must take care to perform the `UPDATE` on the correct record. To do this, you must include a `WHERE` clause that specifies the correct record using a value from a suitable unique column (usually the primary key), as shown above.

IMPORTANT

Handle Updates with Care!

When updating a table with some new data, if you don't specify a `WHERE` clause, every record in the table will be updated with the new data, and (usually) there's no way to undo the action!

Let's put all this theory into practice as we build the Admin Tools page. The database doesn't contain a table that's dedicated to this page; however, we'll use the Admin Tools page as a centralized location for a number of tables associated with other pages, including the `Employees` and `Departments` tables. For instance, in this section, we'll allow an administrator to change the details of a specific employee.

Create a new web form named `AdminTools.aspx` in the same way you created the other web forms we've built so far. Use the `Dorknozzle.master` master page and a code-behind file. Then, add the following code to the content placeholder, and modify the page title as shown below.

File: **AdminTools.aspx (excerpt)**
```
<%@ Page Language="VB" MasterPageFile="~/Dorknozzle.master"
    AutoEventWireup="true" CodeFile="AdminTools.aspx.vb"
    Inherits="AdminTools" title="Dorknozzle Admin Tools" %>
```

```
<asp:Content ID="Content1"
    ContentPlaceHolderID="ContentPlaceHolder1" runat="Server">
<h1>Admin Tools</h1>
<asp:Label ID="dbErrorLabel" ForeColor="Red" runat="server" />
<p>
  Select an employee to update:<br />
  <asp:DropDownList ID="employeesList" runat="server" />
  <asp:Button ID="selectButton" Text="Select" runat="server" />
</p>
<p>
  <asp:Label ID="nameLabel" runat="server"
      Text="Name:" Width="100" />
  <asp:TextBox ID="nameTextBox" runat="server" />
</p>
<p>
  <asp:Label ID="usernameLabel" runat="server"
      Text="Username:" Width="100" />
  <asp:TextBox ID="usernameTextBox" runat="server" />
</p>
<p>
  <asp:Label ID="addressLabel" runat="server"
      Text="Address:" Width="100" />
  <asp:TextBox ID="addressTextBox" runat="server" />
</p>
<p>
  <asp:Label ID="cityLabel" runat="server"
      Text="City:" Width="100" />
  <asp:TextBox ID="cityTextBox" runat="server" />
</p>
<p>
  <asp:Label ID="stateLabel" runat="server"
      Text="State:" Width="100" />
  <asp:TextBox ID="stateTextBox" runat="server" />
</p>
<p>
  <asp:Label ID="zipLabel" runat="server"
      Text="Zip:" Width="100" />
  <asp:TextBox ID="zipTextBox" runat="server" />
</p>
<p>
  <asp:Label ID="homePhoneLabel" runat="server"
      Text="Home Phone:" Width="100" />
  <asp:TextBox ID="homePhoneTextBox" runat="server" />
</p>
<p>
  <asp:Label ID="extensionLabel" runat="server"
```

```
        Text="Extension:" Width="100" />
    <asp:TextBox ID="extensionTextBox" runat="server" />
  </p>
  <p>
    <asp:Label ID="mobilePhoneLabel" runat="server"
        Text="Mobile Phone:" Width="100" />
    <asp:TextBox ID="mobilePhoneTextBox" runat="server" />
  </p>
  <p>
    <asp:Button ID="updateButton" Text="Update Employee"
        Enabled="False" runat="server" />
  </p>
</asp:Content>
```

You can switch to Design View to ensure you created your form correctly; it should look like the one shown in Figure 9.14.

Figure 9.14. Viewing the Admin Tools page in Design View

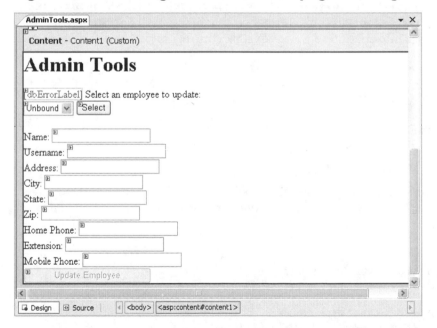

We've added the following controls to our form:

employeesList
In order for administrators to select the record for the employee whose details they want to update, we'll first have to bind the `Employees` table to this `DropDownList` control.

selectButton
Once the users select the record for the employee whose details they want to update, they'll click this `Button` control. The `Click` event will be raised, and the Employee ID selected from `employeesList` will be passed to the web form—this will be used in an `SqlCommand` to retrieve the details for this employee.

nameLabel, usernameLabel, addressLabel, cityLabel, stateLabel, zipLabel, homePhoneLabel, extensionLabel, mobilePhoneLabel
These are the labels for the following `TextBox` controls.

nameTextBox, usernameTextBox, addressTextBox, cityTextBox, stateTextBox, zipTextBox, homePhoneTextBox, extensionTextBox, mobilePhoneTextBox
Within the `selectButton`'s `Click` event handler, we'll add some code that binds user information to these `TextBox` controls.

updateButton
When the users make the desired changes to the `TextBox` controls listed above, they'll click this button to update the database.

dbErrorLabel
We use `dbErrorLabel` to display an error message if a database operation fails.

Our first task is to populate the `employeesList` control with the list of employees from our database. Use Visual Web Developer to generate the page's `Load` event handler, then add this code:

Visual Basic   File: **AdminTools.aspx.vb (excerpt)**

```
Imports System.Data.SqlClient
Imports System.Configuration

Partial Class AdminTools
    Inherits System.Web.UI.Page

  Protected Sub Page_Load(ByVal sender As Object, _
      ByVal e As System.EventArgs) Handles Me.Load
    ' Read the employees list when initially loading the page
    If Not IsPostBack Then
```

```
      LoadEmployeesList()
  End If
End Sub

Private Sub LoadEmployeesList()
  ' Define data objects
  Dim conn As SqlConnection
  Dim comm As SqlCommand
  Dim reader As SqlDataReader
  ' Read the connection string from Web.config
  Dim connectionString As String = _
      ConfigurationManager.ConnectionStrings( _
      "Dorknozzle").ConnectionString
  ' Initialize connection
  conn = New SqlConnection(connectionString)
  ' Create command
  comm = New SqlCommand( _
      "SELECT EmployeeID, Name FROM Employees", conn)
  ' Enclose database code in Try-Catch-Finally
  Try
    ' Open the connection
    conn.Open()
    ' Execute the command
    reader = comm.ExecuteReader()
    ' Populate the list of employees
    employeesList.DataSource = reader
    employeesList.DataValueField = "EmployeeID"
    employeesList.DataTextField = "Name"
    employeesList.DataBind()
    ' Close the reader
    reader.Close()
  Catch
    ' Display error message
    dbErrorLabel.Text = _
        "Error loading the list of employees!<br />"
  Finally
    ' Close the connection
    conn.Close()
  End Try
  ' Disable the update button
  updateButton.Enabled = False
  ' Clear any values in the TextBox controls
  nameTextBox.Text = ""
  usernameTextBox.Text = ""
  addressTextBox.Text = ""
  cityTextBox.Text = ""
```

```
    stateTextBox.Text = ""
    zipTextBox.Text = ""
    homePhoneTextBox.Text = ""
    extensionTextBox.Text = ""
    mobilePhoneTextBox.Text = ""
  End Sub

End Class
```

C#   File: **AdminTools.aspx.cs (excerpt)**

```csharp
using System;
using System.Data;
using System.Configuration;
using System.Collections;
using System.Web;
using System.Web.Security;
using System.Web.UI;
using System.Web.UI.WebControls;
using System.Web.UI.WebControls.WebParts;
using System.Web.UI.HtmlControls;
using System.Data.SqlClient;

public partial class AdminTools : System.Web.UI.Page
{
  protected void Page_Load(object sender, EventArgs e)
  {
    // Read the employees list when initially loading the page
    if (!IsPostBack)
    {
      LoadEmployeesList();
    }
  }
  private void LoadEmployeesList()
  {
    // Declare objects
    SqlConnection conn;
    SqlCommand comm;
    SqlDataReader reader;
    // Read the connection string from Web.config
    string connectionString =
        ConfigurationManager.ConnectionStrings[
        "Dorknozzle"].ConnectionString;
    // Initialize connection
    conn = new SqlConnection(connectionString);
    // Create command
    comm = new SqlCommand(
```

```
      "SELECT EmployeeID, Name FROM Employees", conn);
  // Enclose database code in Try-Catch-Finally
  try
  {
    // Open the connection
    conn.Open();
    // Execute the command
    reader = comm.ExecuteReader();
    // Populate the list of categories
    employeesList.DataSource = reader;
    employeesList.DataValueField = "EmployeeID";
    employeesList.DataTextField = "Name";
    employeesList.DataBind();
    // Close the reader
    reader.Close();
  }
  catch
  {
    // Display error message
    dbErrorLabel.Text =
        "Error loading the list of employees!<br />";
  }
  finally
  {
    // Close the connection
    conn.Close();
  }
  // Disable the update button
  updateButton.Enabled = false;
  // Clear any values in the TextBox controls
  nameTextBox.Text = "";
  usernameTextBox.Text = "";
  addressTextBox.Text = "";
  cityTextBox.Text = "";
  stateTextBox.Text = "";
  zipTextBox.Text = "";
  homePhoneTextBox.Text = "";
  extensionTextBox.Text = "";
  mobilePhoneTextBox.Text = "";
  }
}
```

Note that we've put the code to populate the employeesList in a separate subroutine called LoadEmployeeList. Later on, we'll need to reload the names in this list in case any of the names have been edited; we put this code into its own subroutine so that we don't need to repeat it.

Load the page now, and test that the list of employees is bound to `employeeList`, and that the page displays as shown in Figure 9.15.

Figure 9.15. Displaying the list of employees in a drop-down

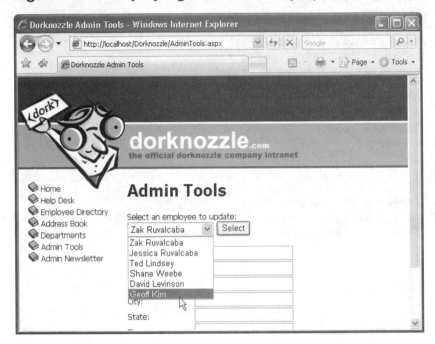

As you can see, all the employees are listed within the employee drop-down menu. Again, the employees' names are shown because the `Name` field is bound to the `DataTextField` property of the `DropDownList` control. Similarly, the `EmployeeID` field is bound to the `DataValueField` property of the `DropDownList` control, ensuring that a selected employee's ID will be submitted as the value of the field.

We need to undertake two more tasks to complete this page's functionality. First, we need to handle the `Click` event of the Select button so that it will load the form with data about the selected employee. Then, we'll need to handle the `Click` event of the Update button, to update the information for the selected employee. Let's start with the Select button. Double-click the button in Design View to have the `Click` event handler generated for you, then complete the code like this:

Visual Basic   File: **AdminTools.aspx.vb (excerpt)**

```
Protected Sub selectButton_Click(ByVal sender As Object, _
    ByVal e As System.EventArgs) Handles selectButton.Click
```

Figure 9.16. Displaying employee details in the update form

```
' Define data objects
Dim conn As SqlConnection
Dim comm As SqlCommand
Dim reader As SqlDataReader
' Read the connection string from Web.config
Dim connectionString As String = _
    ConfigurationManager.ConnectionStrings( _
    "Dorknozzle").ConnectionString
' Initialize connection
conn = New SqlConnection(connectionString)
' Create command
comm = New SqlCommand( _
    "SELECT Name, Username, Address, City, State, Zip, " & _
    "HomePhone, Extension, MobilePhone FROM Employees " & _
    "WHERE EmployeeID = @EmployeeID", conn)
```

```
' Add command parameters
comm.Parameters.Add("@EmployeeID", Data.SqlDbType.Int)
comm.Parameters.Item("@EmployeeID").Value = _
    employeesList.SelectedItem.Value
' Enclose database code in Try-Catch-Finally
Try
  ' Open the connection
  conn.Open()
  ' Execute the command
  reader = comm.ExecuteReader()
  ' Display the data on the form
  If reader.Read() Then
    nameTextBox.Text = reader.Item("Name").ToString()
    usernameTextBox.Text = reader.Item("Username").ToString()
    addressTextBox.Text = reader.Item("Address").ToString()
    cityTextBox.Text = reader.Item("City").ToString()
    stateTextBox.Text = reader.Item("State").ToString()
    zipTextBox.Text = reader.Item("Zip").ToString()
    homePhoneTextBox.Text = reader.Item("HomePhone").ToString()
    extensionTextBox.Text = reader.Item("Extension").ToString()
    mobilePhoneTextBox.Text = _
        reader.Item("MobilePhone").ToString()
  End If
  ' Close the reader
  reader.Close()
  ' Enable the Update button
  updateButton.Enabled = True
Catch
  ' Display error message
  dbErrorLabel.Text = _
      "Error loading the employee details!<br />"
Finally
  ' Close the connection
    conn.Close()
End Try
End Sub
```

C#   File: **AdminTools.aspx.cs** (excerpt)

```
protected void selectButton_Click(object sender, EventArgs e)
{
  // Declare objects
  SqlConnection conn;
  SqlCommand comm;
  SqlDataReader reader;
  // Read the connection string from Web.config
  string connectionString =
```

```
        ConfigurationManager.ConnectionStrings[
        "Dorknozzle"].ConnectionString;
// Initialize connection
conn = new SqlConnection(connectionString);
// Create command
comm = new SqlCommand(
    "SELECT Name, Username, Address, City, State, Zip, " +
    "HomePhone, Extension, MobilePhone FROM Employees " +
    "WHERE EmployeeID = @EmployeeID", conn);
// Add command parameters
comm.Parameters.Add("@EmployeeID", SqlDbType.Int);
comm.Parameters["@EmployeeID"].Value =
    employeesList.SelectedItem.Value;
// Enclose database code in Try-Catch-Finally
try
{
  // Open the connection
  conn.Open();
  // Execute the command
  reader = comm.ExecuteReader();
  // Display the data on the form
  if (reader.Read())
  {
    nameTextBox.Text = reader["Name"].ToString();
    usernameTextBox.Text = reader["Username"].ToString();
    addressTextBox.Text = reader["Address"].ToString();
    cityTextBox.Text = reader["City"].ToString();
    stateTextBox.Text = reader["State"].ToString();
    zipTextBox.Text = reader["Zip"].ToString();
    homePhoneTextBox.Text = reader["HomePhone"].ToString();
    extensionTextBox.Text = reader["Extension"].ToString();
    mobilePhoneTextBox.Text = reader["MobilePhone"].ToString();
  }
  // Close the reader
  reader.Close();
  // Enable the Update button
  updateButton.Enabled = true;
}
catch
{
  // Display error message
  dbErrorLabel.Text =
      "Error loading the employee details!<br />";
}
finally
{
```

```
    // Close the connection
    conn.Close();
  }
}
```

If you load the page, select an employee, and click the Select button, the form will be populated with the employee's details.

The last thing we need to do is add code to handle the update interaction. You may have noticed that the Button control has an Enabled property, which is initially set to False. The reason for this is simple: you don't want your users updating information before they've selected an employee. You want them to use the Update Employee button only when data for an existing employee has been loaded into the TextBox controls. If you look at the selectButton_Click method just before the Catch statement, you'll notice that we enable this button after binding the user data to the fields.

Now that these TextBox controls are populated and the Update Employee button is enabled, let's add some code to update an employee's details. Open Admin-Tools.aspx in Design View, and double-click the Update Employee button. Visual Web Developer will generate the signature of the event handler subroutine (updateButton_Click) for you. Finally, let's add the necessary code to handle updating the employee data:

Visual Basic   File: **AdminTools.aspx.vb (excerpt)**

```
Protected Sub updateButton_Click(ByVal sender As Object, _
    ByVal e As System.EventArgs) Handles updateButton.Click
  ' Define data objects
  Dim conn As SqlConnection
  Dim comm As SqlCommand
  ' Read the connection string from Web.config
  Dim connectionString As String = _
      ConfigurationManager.ConnectionStrings( _
      "Dorknozzle").ConnectionString
  ' Initialize connection
  conn = New SqlConnection(connectionString)
  ' Create command
  comm = New SqlCommand( _
      "UPDATE Employees SET Name=@Name, Username=@Username, " & _
      "Address=@Address, City=@City, State=@State, Zip=@Zip," & _
      "HomePhone=@HomePhone, Extension=@Extension, " & _
      "MobilePhone=@MobilePhone " & _
      "WHERE EmployeeID=@EmployeeID", conn)
  ' Add command parameters
```

```
comm.Parameters.Add("@Name", System.Data.SqlDbType.NVarChar, 50)
comm.Parameters("@Name").Value = nameTextBox.Text
comm.Parameters.Add("@Username", _
    System.Data.SqlDbType.NVarChar, 50)
comm.Parameters("@Username").Value = usernameTextBox.Text
comm.Parameters.Add("@Address", _
    System.Data.SqlDbType.NVarChar, 50)
comm.Parameters("@Address").Value = addressTextBox.Text
comm.Parameters.Add("@City", _
    System.Data.SqlDbType.NVarChar, 50)
comm.Parameters("@City").Value = cityTextBox.Text
comm.Parameters.Add("@State", _
    System.Data.SqlDbType.NVarChar, 50)
comm.Parameters("@State").Value = stateTextBox.Text
comm.Parameters.Add("@Zip", System.Data.SqlDbType.NVarChar, 50)
comm.Parameters("@Zip").Value = zipTextBox.Text
comm.Parameters.Add("@HomePhone", _
    System.Data.SqlDbType.NVarChar, 50)
comm.Parameters("@HomePhone").Value = homePhoneTextBox.Text
comm.Parameters.Add("@Extension", _
    System.Data.SqlDbType.NVarChar, 50)
comm.Parameters("@Extension").Value = extensionTextBox.Text
comm.Parameters.Add("@MobilePhone", _
    System.Data.SqlDbType.NVarChar, 50)
comm.Parameters("@MobilePhone").Value = mobilePhoneTextBox.Text
comm.Parameters.Add("@EmployeeID", System.Data.SqlDbType.Int)
comm.Parameters("@EmployeeID").Value = _
    employeesList.SelectedItem.Value
' Enclose database code in Try-Catch-Finally
Try
  ' Open the connection
  conn.Open()
  ' Execute the command
  comm.ExecuteNonQuery()
Catch
  ' Display error message
  dbErrorLabel.Text = _
      "Error updating the employee details!<br />"
Finally
  ' Close the connection
  conn.Close()
End Try
' Refresh the employees list
LoadEmployeesList()
End Sub
```

```csharp
protected void updateButton_Click(object sender, EventArgs e)
{
  // Declare objects
  SqlConnection conn;
  SqlCommand comm;
  // Read the connection string from Web.config
  string connectionString =
    ConfigurationManager.ConnectionStrings[
    "Dorknozzle"].ConnectionString;
  // Initialize connection
  conn = new SqlConnection(connectionString);
  // Create command
  comm = new SqlCommand(
      "UPDATE Employees SET Name=@Name, Username=@Username, " +
      "Address=@Address, City=@City, State=@State, Zip=@Zip, " +
      "HomePhone=@HomePhone, Extension=@Extension, " +
      "MobilePhone=@MobilePhone " +
      "WHERE EmployeeID=@EmployeeID", conn);
  // Add command parameters
  comm.Parameters.Add("@Name",
      System.Data.SqlDbType.NVarChar,50);
  comm.Parameters["@Name"].Value = nameTextBox.Text;
  comm.Parameters.Add("@Username",
      System.Data.SqlDbType.NVarChar, 50);
  comm.Parameters["@Username"].Value = usernameTextBox.Text;
  comm.Parameters.Add("@Address",
      System.Data.SqlDbType.NVarChar, 50);
  comm.Parameters["@Address"].Value = addressTextBox.Text;
  comm.Parameters.Add("@City",
      System.Data.SqlDbType.NVarChar, 50);
  comm.Parameters["@City"].Value = cityTextBox.Text;
  comm.Parameters.Add("@State",
      System.Data.SqlDbType.NVarChar, 50);
  comm.Parameters["@State"].Value = stateTextBox.Text;
  comm.Parameters.Add("@Zip",
      System.Data.SqlDbType.NVarChar, 50);
  comm.Parameters["@Zip"].Value = zipTextBox.Text;
  comm.Parameters.Add("@HomePhone",
      System.Data.SqlDbType.NVarChar, 50);
  comm.Parameters["@HomePhone"].Value = homePhoneTextBox.Text;
  comm.Parameters.Add("@Extension",
      System.Data.SqlDbType.NVarChar, 50);
  comm.Parameters["@Extension"].Value = extensionTextBox.Text;
  comm.Parameters.Add("@MobilePhone",
      System.Data.SqlDbType.NVarChar, 50);
```

```
comm.Parameters["@MobilePhone"].Value = mobilePhoneTextBox.Text;
comm.Parameters.Add("@EmployeeID", System.Data.SqlDbType.Int);
comm.Parameters["@EmployeeID"].Value =
    employeesList.SelectedItem.Value;
// Enclose database code in Try-Catch-Finally
try
{
  // Open the connection
  conn.Open();
  // Execute the command
  comm.ExecuteNonQuery();
}
catch
{
  // Display error message
  dbErrorLabel.Text =
      "Error updating the employee details!<br />";
}
finally
{
  // Close the connection
  conn.Close();
}
// Refresh the employees list
LoadEmployeesList();
}
```

As you can see, the only real differences between this and the help desk page are that we're using an UPDATE query instead of an INSERT query, and we've had to let the user choose an entry from the database to update. We use that selection not only to populate the form fields with the existing database values, but to restrict our UPDATE query so that it only affects that one record.

You'll also notice that at the very end of this method, we call LoadEmployeesList to reload the list of employees, as the user may have changed the name of one of the employees. LoadEmployeesList also disables the Update Employee button and clears the contents of the page's TextBox controls. Once LoadEmployeesList has executed, the page is ready for the user to select another employee for updating.

As with all examples in this book, you can get this page's completed code from the code archive.

Deleting Records

Just as we can insert and update records within the database, we can also delete them. Again, most of the code for deleting records resembles that which we've already seen. The only major part that changes is the SQL statement within the command:

Visual Basic

```
comm = New SqlCommand("DELETE FROM Table " & _
    "WHERE UniqueField=@UniqueFieldParameter", conn)
```

C#

```
comm = new SqlCommand("DELETE FROM Table " +
    "WHERE UniqueField=@UniqueFieldParameter", conn)
```

Once we've created the DELETE query's SqlCommand object, we can simply pass in the necessary parameter:

Visual Basic

```
comm.Parameters.Add("@UniqueFieldParameter", _
    System.Data.SqlDbType.Type)
comm.Parameters("@UniqueFieldParameter").Value = UniqueValue
```

C#

```
comm.Parameters.Add("@UniqueFieldParameter",
    System.Data.SqlDbType.Type);
comm.Parameters["@UniqueFieldParameter"].Value = UniqueValue;
```

To demonstrate the process of deleting an item from a database table, we'll expand on the Admin Tools page. Since we're allowing administrators to update information within the Employees table, let's also give them the ability to delete an employee's record from the database. To do this, we'll place a new Button control for deleting the selected record next to our Update Employee button.

Start by adding the new control at the end of AdminTools.aspx:

File: **AdminTools.aspx (excerpt)**

```
<p>
  <asp:Button ID="updateButton" Text="Update Employee"
      Enabled="False" runat="server" />
  <asp:Button ID="deleteButton" Text="Delete Employee"
      Enabled="False" runat="server" />
</p>
```

Next, update `selectButton_Click` to enable the Delete Employee button when an employee is selected:

Visual Basic	File: **AdminTools.aspx.vb (excerpt)**

```vb
' Enable the Update button
updateButton.Enabled = True
' Enable the Delete button
deleteButton.Enabled = True
```

Visual Basic	File: **AdminTools.aspx.vb (excerpt)**

```
// Enable the Update button
updateButton.Enabled = true;
// Enable the Delete button
deleteButton.Enabled = true;
```

Next, write the code for its `Click` event handler. Remember that you can double-click the button in Visual Web Developer's Design View to have the signature generated for you.

Visual Basic	File: **AdminTools.aspx.vb (excerpt)**

```vb
Protected Sub deleteButton_Click(ByVal sender As Object, _
    ByVal e As System.EventArgs) Handles deleteButton.Click
  ' Define data objects
  Dim conn As SqlConnection
  Dim comm As SqlCommand
  ' Read the connection string from Web.config
  Dim connectionString As String = _
      ConfigurationManager.ConnectionStrings( _
      "Dorknozzle").ConnectionString
  ' Initialize connection
  conn = New SqlConnection(connectionString)
  ' Create command
  comm = New SqlCommand( _
      "DELETE FROM Employees " & _
      "WHERE EmployeeID=@EmployeeID", conn)
  ' Add command parameters
  comm.Parameters.Add("@EmployeeID", System.Data.SqlDbType.Int)
  comm.Parameters("@EmployeeID").Value = _
      employeesList.SelectedItem.Value
  Try
    ' Open the connection
    conn.Open()
    ' Execute the command
    comm.ExecuteNonQuery()
  Catch
```

```
    ' Display error message
      dbErrorLabel.Text = "Error deleting employee!<br />"
  Finally
    ' Close the connection
      conn.Close()
  End Try
  ' Refresh the employees list
  LoadEmployeesList()
End Sub
```

C#   File: **AdminTools.aspx.cs (excerpt)**

```csharp
protected void deleteButton_Click(object sender, EventArgs e)
{
  // Define data objects
  SqlConnection conn;
  SqlCommand comm;
  // Read the connection string from Web.config
  string connectionString =
      ConfigurationManager.ConnectionStrings[
      "Dorknozzle"].ConnectionString;
  // Initialize connection
  conn = new SqlConnection(connectionString);
  // Create command
  comm = new SqlCommand("DELETE FROM Employees " +
      "WHERE EmployeeID = @EmployeeID", conn);
  // Add command parameters
  comm.Parameters.Add("@EmployeeID", System.Data.SqlDbType.Int);
  comm.Parameters["@EmployeeID"].Value =
      employeesList.SelectedItem.Value;
  try
  {
    // Open the connection
    conn.Open();
    // Execute the command
    comm.ExecuteNonQuery();
  }
  catch
  {
    // Display error message
    dbErrorLabel.Text = "Error deleting employee!<br />";
  }
  finally
  {
    // Close the connection
    conn.Close();
  }
```

```
  // Refresh the employees list
  LoadEmployeesList();
}
```

Save your work and test it within the browser. For testing purposes, feel free to add more records to the `Employees` table using SQL Server Management Studio, then delete them through the Dorknozzle application (if you do that, note you'll need to refresh the view of the `Employees` table manually in order to see the changes).

Using Stored Procedures

In the previous chapter, you learned how to add stored procedures to your database. As far as ADO.NET is concerned, a stored procedure is much like a query that has parameters.

Let's assume you'd prefer to use a stored procedure to add help desk requests, rather than typing the SQL code in `HelpDesk.aspx.vb`, or `HelpDesk.aspx.cs`. The first step would be to add to your `Dorknozzle` database a stored procedure, which would look something like this:

```
CREATE PROCEDURE InsertHelpDesk
(
  @EmployeeID int,
  @StationNumber int,
  @CategoryID int,
  @SubjectID int,
  @Description nvarchar,
  @StatusID int
)
AS
INSERT INTO HelpDesk (EmployeeID, StationNumber, CategoryID,
    SubjectID, Description, StatusID)
VALUES (@EmployeeID, @StationNumber, @CategoryID, @SubjectID,
    @Description, @StatusID)
```

To use this stored procedure, you'd need to modify the `submitButton_Click` method in `HelpDesk.aspx.vb` (or `HelpDesk.aspx.cs`) as shown below:

Visual Basic   File: **HelpDesk.aspx.vb (excerpt)**

```
' Define data objects
Dim conn As SqlConnection
Dim comm As SqlCommand
' Read the connection string from Web.config
```

```
Dim connectionString As String = _
    ConfigurationManager.ConnectionStrings( _
    "Dorknozzle").ConnectionString
' Initialize connection
conn = New SqlConnection(connectionString)
' Create command
comm = New SqlCommand("InsertHelpDesk", conn)
' Specify we're calling a stored procedure
comm.CommandType = System.Data.CommandType.StoredProcedure
' Add command parameters
comm.Parameters.Add("@EmployeeID", System.Data.SqlDbType.Int)
comm.Parameters("@EmployeeID").Value = 5
comm.Parameters.Add("@StationNumber", System.Data.SqlDbType.Int)
comm.Parameters("@StationNumber").Value = stationTextBox.Text
comm.Parameters.Add("@CategoryID", System.Data.SqlDbType.Int)
comm.Parameters("@CategoryID").Value = _
    categoryList.SelectedItem.Value
comm.Parameters.Add("@SubjectID", System.Data.SqlDbType.Int)
comm.Parameters("@SubjectID").Value = _
    subjectList.SelectedItem.Value
comm.Parameters.Add("@Description", _
    System.Data.SqlDbType.NVarChar, 50)
comm.Parameters("@Description").Value = descriptionTextBox.Text
comm.Parameters.Add("@StatusID", System.Data.SqlDbType.Int)
comm.Parameters("@StatusID").Value = 1
```

C#   File: **HelpDesk.aspx.cs (excerpt)**

```csharp
// Define data objects
SqlConnection conn;
SqlCommand comm;
// Read the connection string from Web.config
string connectionString = ConfigurationManager.ConnectionStrings[
    "Dorknozzle"].ConnectionString;
// Initialize connection
conn = new SqlConnection(connectionString);
// Create command
comm = new SqlCommand("InsertHelpDesk", conn);
// Specify we're calling a stored procedure
comm.CommandType = System.Data.CommandType.StoredProcedure;
// Add command parameters
comm.Parameters.Add("@EmployeeID", System.Data.SqlDbType.Int);
comm.Parameters["@EmployeeID"].Value = 5;
comm.Parameters.Add("@StationNumber", System.Data.SqlDbType.Int);
comm.Parameters["@StationNumber"].Value = stationTextBox.Text;
comm.Parameters.Add("@CategoryID", System.Data.SqlDbType.Int);
comm.Parameters["@CategoryID"].Value =
```

```
    categoryList.SelectedItem.Value;
comm.Parameters.Add("@SubjectID", System.Data.SqlDbType.Int);
comm.Parameters["@SubjectID"].Value =
    subjectList.SelectedItem.Value;
comm.Parameters.Add("@Description",
    System.Data.SqlDbType.NVarChar, 50);
comm.Parameters["@Description"].Value = descriptionTextBox.Text;
comm.Parameters.Add("@StatusID", System.Data.SqlDbType.Int);
comm.Parameters["@StatusID"].Value = 1;
```

If you now load the Help Desk page, you'll see that it works just as it used to, but behind the scenes, it's making use of a stored procedure. You can verify that this approach works by adding a new help desk request through the web form, then opening the `HelpDesk` table and checking for your new help desk request.

As you can see, using stored procedures is very easy. Apart for specifying the procedure's name, you also need to set the `CommandType` of the `SqlCommand` object to `StoredProcedure`. That's it! Everything else is the same as when working with a parameterized query.

Summary

In this chapter, you learned how to create simple web applications that interact with databases. First, you learned about the various classes included with ADO.NET, such as `SqlConnection`, `SqlCommand`, and `SqlDataReader`. Then, you learned how to use these classes to create simple applications that query the database, insert records into a database, update records within a database, and delete records from a database. You also learned important techniques for querying database data, including using parameters and control binding. Later in the chapter, you learned how to improve application performance through the use of stored procedures.

The next chapter will expand on what we learned here, and introduce a new control that's often used to display data from a database: the `DataList`.

10

Displaying Content Using Data Lists

Similar to the `Repeater` control, the `DataList` control allows you to bind and customize the presentation of database data. The fundamental difference is that while the `Repeater` requires you to build the template from scratch (allowing you to customize the generated HTML output in any way you like), the `DataList` control automatically generates a single-column HTML table for you, like the one shown below:

```
<table>
  <tr>
    <td>
      <p>Employee ID: 1</p>
      <p>Name: Zak Ruvalcaba</p>
      <p>Username: zak</p>
    </td>
  </tr>
  <tr>
    <td>
      <p>Employee ID: 2</p>
      <p>Name: Jessica Ruvalcaba</p>
      <p>Username: jessica</p>
    </td>
  </tr>
  <tr>
    <td>
      <p>Employee ID: 3</p>
```

```
      <p>Name: Ted Lindsey</p>
      <p>Username: ted</p>
    </td>
  </tr>
  ⋮
</table>
```

As you can see, `DataList` has, as the name implies, been designed to display lists of data, and while it's less flexible than the `Repeater`, it contains more built-in functionality that can help make the implementation of certain features faster and easier. In the following pages, you'll learn:

❑ the basics of the `DataList` control

❑ how to handle `DataList` events

❑ how to edit `DataList` items

❑ how to handle the controls inside the `DataList` templates

❑ how to use Visual Web Developer to edit the `DataList`

Let's get started!

DataList Basics

To learn how to use the `DataList`, we'll update the Dorknozzle Employee Directory page to use a `DataList` control instead of a `Repeater` control. This update will be particularly easy to do because the Employee Directory already has a list-like format.

If you now open `EmployeeDirectory.aspx`, you'll see the `Repeater` control is used like this:

File: **EmployeeDirectory.aspx (excerpt)**

```
<asp:Repeater id="employeesRepeater" runat="server">
  <ItemTemplate>
    Employee ID:
    <strong><%#Eval("EmployeeID")%></strong><br />
    Name: <strong><%#Eval("Name")%></strong><br />
    Username: <strong><%#Eval("Username")%></strong>
  </ItemTemplate>
  <SeparatorTemplate>
```

```
    <hr />
  </SeparatorTemplate>
</asp:Repeater>
```

You can see the output of this code in Figure 9.9 in Chapter 9. Now, let's update the employee directory page to use a `DataList` instead of a `Repeater`. We can do this simply by replacing the `<asp:Repeater>` and `</asp:Repeater>` tags with the tags for a `DataList`:

File: **EmployeeDirectory.aspx (excerpt)**

```
<asp:DataList id="employeesList" runat="server">
  <ItemTemplate>
    Employee ID:
    <strong><%#Eval("EmployeeID")%></strong><br />
    Name: <strong><%#Eval("Name")%></strong><br />
    Username: <strong><%#Eval("Username")%></strong>
  </ItemTemplate>
  <SeparatorTemplate>
    <hr />
  </SeparatorTemplate>
</asp:DataList>
```

As we've changed the ID for this control, we'll need to change the name of the control in the code-behind file as well. Locate the following lines of code and change `employeesRepeater` to `employeesList`, as shown:

Visual Basic   File: **EmployeeDirectory.aspx.vb (excerpt)**

```
' Open the connection
conn.Open()
' Execute the command
reader = comm.ExecuteReader()
' Bind the reader to the DataList
employeesList.DataSource = reader
employeesList.DataBind()
' Close the reader
reader.Close()
```

C#   File: **EmployeeDirectory.aspx.cs (excerpt**

```
// Open the connection
conn.Open();
// Execute the command
reader = comm.ExecuteReader();
// Bind the reader to the DataList
employeesList.DataSource = reader;
employeesList.DataBind();
```

```
// Close the reader
reader.Close();
```

As you can see, the changes required to use `DataList` instead of `Repeater` are minimal in this case. That's largely because the `Repeater` was displaying a basic list of data anyway.

As with the `Repeater` control, we can feed data into the a `DataList` control by binding it to a data source. Both `Repeater` and `DataList` support the `ItemTemplate` and `SeparatorTemplate` templates, but in case of the `DataList`, the templates specify the content that is to be inserted in the `td` elements of the table.

At the moment, the output appears very similar to the output we generated using the `Repeater`, as Figure 10.1 illustrates.

Figure 10.1. The Dorknozzle Employee Directory page

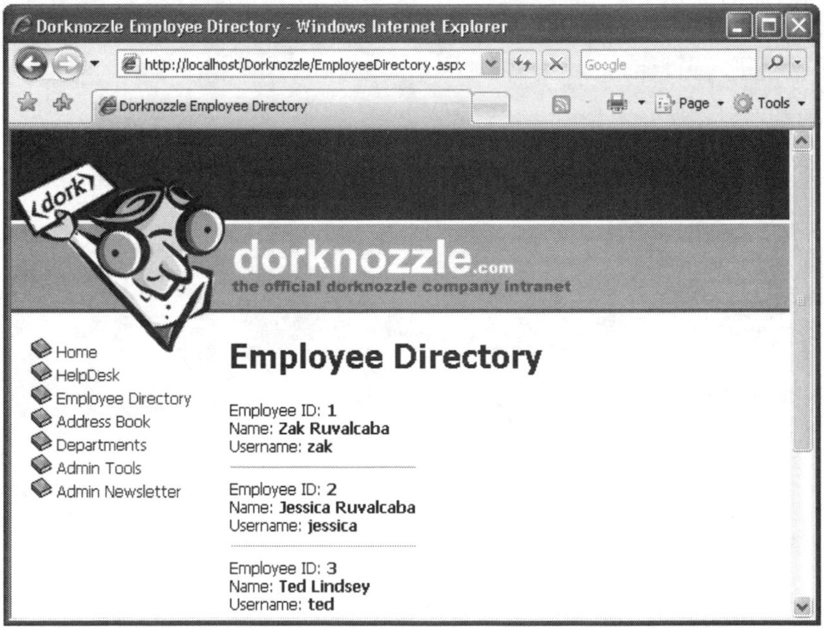

Repeater vs DataList

As a rule of thumb, you'll use the `Repeater` when you need total control over the HTML output, and when you don't need features such as editing, sorting, formatting, or paging for the data you're displaying. Depending on the extra features you need, you can use either the DataList control (covered in this chapter), or the GridView or DetailsView controls (which you'll learn about in Chapter 12).

In this example, we've used the ItemTemplate of our DataList. The DataList offers a number of templates:

ItemTemplate

This template is replicated for each record that's read from the data source. The contents of the ItemTemplate are repeated for each record, and placed inside td elements.

AlternatingItemTemplate

If this template is defined, it will be used instead of ItemTemplate to display every second element.

SelectedItemTemplate

This template is used to display the selected item of the list. The DataList control doesn't automatically give the user a way to select an item in the list, but you can mark an item as selected by setting the DataLists control's SelectedIndex property. Setting this property to 0 will mark the first item as selected; setting SelectedIndex to 1 will mark the second item as selected; and so on. Setting SelectedIndex to -1 unselects any selected item.

EditItemTemplate

Similar to SelectedItemTemplate, this template applies to an item that's being edited. We can set the item being edited using the EditItemIndex property of the DataList, which operates in the same way as the SelectedIndex property. Later in this chapter, you'll learn how to edit your DataList using the EditItemTemplate.

HeaderTemplate

This template specifies the content to be used for the list header.

FooterTemplate

This template defines the list footer.

SeparatorTemplate

This template specifies the content to be inserted between two consecutive data items. This content will appear inside its own table cell.

Handling DataList Events

One problem you may encounter when working with container controls such as the DataList or the Repeater is that you can't access the controls inside their templates directly from your code. For example, consider the following ItemTemplate, which contains a Button control:

```
<asp:DataList ID="employeesList" runat="server">
  <ItemTemplate>
    Employee ID: <strong><%#Eval("EmployeeID")%></strong>
    <asp:Button runat="server" ID="myButton" Text="Select" />
  </ItemTemplate>
</asp:DataList>
```

Although it may not be obvious at the first glance, you can't access the Button easily through your code. The following code would generate an error:

Visual Basic
```
' Don't try this at home
myButton.Enabled = False
```

Things get even more complicated if you want to handle the Button's Click event, because—you guessed it—you can't do so without jumping through some pretty complicated hoops.

So, if we can't handle events raised by the buttons and links inside a template, how can we interact with the data in each template? We'll improve our employee directory by making a simpler, basic view of the items, and add a "View More" link that users can click in order to access more details about the employee. To keep things simple, for now, we'll hide only the employee ID from the standard view; we'll show it when the visitor clicks the View More link.

After we implement this feature, our list will appear as shown in Figure 10.2. You'll be able to view more details about any employee by clicking on the appropriate link.

Open EmployeeDirectory.aspx, and modify the ItemTemplate of the DataList as shown below:

Visual Basic   File: **EmployeeDirectory.aspx (excerpt)**
```
<asp:DataList id="employeesList" runat="server">
  <ItemTemplate>
    <asp:Literal ID="extraDetailsLiteral" runat="server"
```

Figure 10.2. Hiding employee details

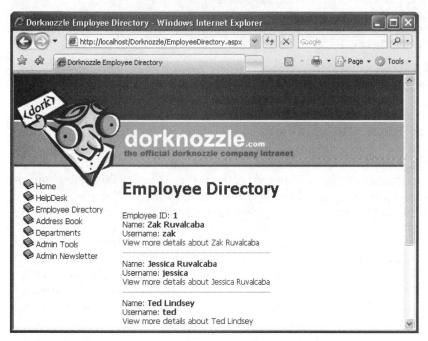

```
        EnableViewState="false" />
    Name: <strong><%#Eval("Name")%></strong><br />
    Username: <strong><%#Eval("Username")%></strong><br />
    <asp:LinkButton ID="detailsButton" runat="server"
        Text=<%#"View more details about " & Eval("Name")%>
        CommandName="MoreDetailsPlease"
        CommandArgument=<%#Eval("EmployeeID")%> />
  </ItemTemplate>
  <SeparatorTemplate>
    <hr />
  </SeparatorTemplate>
</asp:DataList>
```

C#   File: **EmployeeDirectory.aspx (excerpt)**

```
<asp:DataList id="employeesList" runat="server">
  <ItemTemplate>
    <asp:Literal ID="extraDetailsLiteral" runat="server"
        EnableViewState="false" />
    Name: <strong><%#Eval("Name")%></strong><br />
    Username: <strong><%#Eval("Username")%></strong><br />
    <asp:LinkButton ID="detailsButton" runat="server"
```

```
      Text=<%#"View more details about " + Eval("Name")%>
      CommandName="MoreDetailsPlease"
      CommandArgument=<%#Eval("EmployeeID")%> />
  </ItemTemplate>
  <SeparatorTemplate>
    <hr />
  </SeparatorTemplate>
</asp:DataList>
```

Here, we've added two controls. The first is a `Literal` control, which serves as a placeholder that we can replace with HTML later when the user clicks on the other control we've added—a `LinkButton`. Even though the `LinkButton` looks like a link, it really behaves like a button. When someone clicks this button, it generates an event that can be handled on the server side. If you prefer, you can change the `LinkButton` to a `Button`, and the functionality will remain identical. If you load the page now, it should appear as shown in Figure 10.2.

Now you have a button that's displayed for each employee in the list. In order to react to this `LinkButton` being clicked, you might think that you'd need to handle its `Click` event. Not this time! The button is "inside" the `DataList` as part of its `ItemTemplate`, so it's not directly visible to your code. Also, when the code executes, you'll have more instances of this button—so on the server side, you'll need a way to know which of them was clicked!

Luckily, ASP.NET provides an ingenious means of handling this scenario. Whenever a button inside a `DataList` generates a `Click` event, the `DataList` generates itself a `ItemCommand` event. The `DataList` control *is* accessible in your code, so you can handle its `ItemCommand` event, whose arguments will give us information about which control was clicked.

Within the `ItemCommand` event handler, we can retrieve the data contained in the `LinkButton`'s `CommandName` and `CommandArgument` properties. We use these properties to pass the employee ID to the `ItemCommand` event handler, which can use the ID to get more data about that particular employee.

Take another look at the button definition from the `DataList`'s `ItemTemplate`:

Visual Basic	File: **EmployeeDirectory.aspx (excerpt)**

```
<asp:LinkButton ID="detailsButton" runat="server"
    Text=<%#"View more details about " & Eval("Name")%>
    CommandName="MoreDetailsPlease"
    CommandArgument=<%#Eval("EmployeeID")%> />
```

Here, you can see that we're using `CommandArgument` to save the ID of the employee record with which it's associated. We're able to read this data from the `DataList`'s `ItemCommand` event handler.

Let's use Visual Web Developer to generate the `ItemCommand` event handler. Open `EmployeeDirectory.aspx` in Design View, select the `DataList`, and hit **F4** to open its Properties window. There, click the yellow lightning symbol to open the list of events, and double-click the `ItemCommand` event in that list. Visual Web Developer will generate an empty event handler, and take you to the event handler's code in the code-behind file.

If you were to open the `DataList`'s properties again, you'd see the event handler name appearing next to the event name, as depicted in Figure 10.3.

Figure 10.3. The `ItemCommand` event in the Properties window

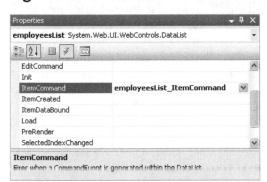

Modify the code in `employeesList_ItemCommand` as shown below.

Visual Basic   File: **EmployeeDirectory.aspx.vb (excerpt)**

```
Protected Sub employeesList_ItemCommand(ByVal source As Object, _
  ByVal e As System.Web.UI.WebControls.DataListCommandEventArgs) _
  Handles employeesList.ItemCommand
  ' Which button was clicked?
  If e.CommandName = "MoreDetailsPlease" Then
    ' Find the Literal control in the DataList item
    Dim li As Literal
    li = e.Item.FindControl("extraDetailsLiteral")
    ' Add content to the Literal control
    li.Text = "Employee ID: <strong>" & e.CommandArgument & _
        "</strong><br />"
  End If
End Sub
```

```
C#                                          File: EmployeeDirectory.aspx.cs (excerpt)
protected void employeesList_ItemCommand(object source,
    DataListCommandEventArgs e)
{
  // Which button was clicked?
  if (e.CommandName == "MoreDetailsPlease")
  {
    // Find the Literal control in the DataList item
    Literal li;
    li = (Literal)e.Item.FindControl("extraDetailsLiteral");
    // Add content to the Literal control
    li.Text = "Employee ID: <strong>" + e.CommandArgument +
      "</strong><br />";
  }
}
```

Our code is almost ready to execute, but we should make one more minor tweak before we execute this page. At the moment, the `Page_Load` method will data bind the `DataList` every time the page loads, which will put unnecessary load on our database server. Let's change this code so that the data binding only takes place when the page is being loaded for the first time. We'll also move the data binding code into its own function, so that we can make use of it later. Modify the code as shown below, moving the current contents of `Page_Load` into a new method called `BindList`:

```
Visual Basic                                File: EmployeeDirectory.aspx.vb (excerpt)
Protected Sub Page_Load(ByVal sender As Object, _
    ByVal e As System.EventArgs) Handles Me.Load
  If Not IsPostBack Then
    BindList()
  End If
End Sub
Protected Sub BindList()
  ' Define data objects
  Dim conn As SqlConnection
  Dim comm As SqlCommand
  Dim reader As SqlDataReader
  ⋮
End Sub
```

```
C#                                          File: EmployeeDirectory.aspx.cs (excerpt)
protected void Page_Load(object sender, EventArgs e)
{
    if (!IsPostBack)
    {
```

```
      BindList();
   }
}
protected void BindList()
{
  // Define data objects
  SqlConnection conn;
  SqlCommand comm;
  SqlDataReader reader;
  ⋮
}
```

Execute the project and click the View more details links to see the employee ID appear, as shown in Figure 10.4.

Figure 10.4. The Employee Directory showing employee IDs

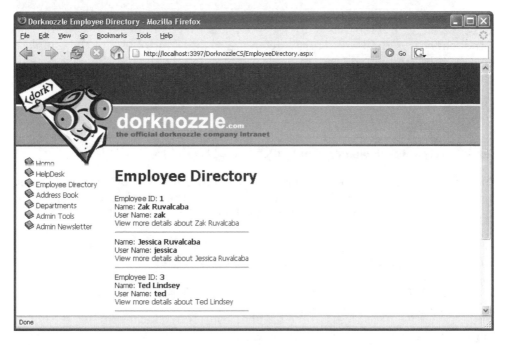

The code in `employeesList_ItemCommand` shows how you can work with controls inside a `DataList` template, and how to handle their events. We determine which control was clicked by checking the value of `e.CommandName` in the event handler, which will be populated with the value of the `CommandName` property of the control that was clicked. Since our `LinkButton` has the `CommandName` value MoreDe-

`tailsPlease`, we check for this value in the `ItemCommand` event handler, as shown below:

Visual Basic	File: `EmployeeDirectory.aspx.vb` (excerpt)

```vb
' Which button was clicked?
If e.CommandName = "MoreDetailsPlease" Then
```

C#	File: `EmployeeDirectory.aspx.cs` (excerpt)

```csharp
// Which button was clicked?
if (e.CommandName == "MoreDetailsPlease")
{
```

Once we know the View more details button was pressed, we want to use the `extraDetailsLiteral` control from our template to display the employee ID. But, given that this control is inside our template, how can we access it through code?

To use a control inside a `DataList`, we use the `FindControl` method of the object `e.Item`. Here, `e.Item` refers to the template that contains the control; the `FindControl` method will return a reference to any control within the template that has the supplied ID. So, in order to obtain a reference to the control with the ID `extraDetailsLiteral`, we use `FindControl` like this:

Visual Basic	File: `EmployeeDirectory.aspx.vb` (excerpt)

```vb
' Find the Literal control in the DataList item
Dim li As Literal
li = e.Item.FindControl("extraDetailsLiteral")
```

Note that `FindControl` returns a generic `Control` object. If you're using VB, the returned `Control` is automatically converted to a `Literal` when you assign it to an object of type `Literal`. In C#, we need an explicit cast, as shown here:

C#	File: `EmployeeDirectory.aspx.cs` (excerpt)

```csharp
// Find the Literal control in the DataList item
Literal li;
li = (Literal)e.Item.FindControl("extraDetailsLiteral");
```

Finally, once we have access to the `Literal` control in a local variable, setting its contents is a piece of cake:

Visual Basic	File: `EmployeeDirectory.aspx.vb` (excerpt)

```vb
' Add content to the Literal control
li.Text = "Employee ID: <strong>" & e.CommandArgument & _
    "</strong><br />"
```

C#   File: **EmployeeDirectory.aspx.cs (excerpt)**

```
// Add content to the Literal control
li.Text = "Employee ID: <strong>" + e.CommandArgument +
    "</strong><br />";
```

Tip

Disabling View State

If you take a look at the definition of the `extraDetailsLiteral` control in `EmployeeDirectory.aspx`, you'll see that we set its `EnableViewState` property to `False`:

File: **EmployeeDirectory.aspx (excerpt)**

```
<asp:Literal ID="extraDetailsLiteral" runat="server"
    EnableViewState="false" />
```

When this property is `False`, its contents aren't persisted during postback events. In our case, once the visitor clicks another View more details button, all the instances of that `Literal` control lose their values. This way, at any given moment, no more than one employee's ID will be displayed. If you change `EnableViewState` to `True` (the default value), then click the View more details button, you'll see that all employee IDs remain in the form, as they're persisted by the view state mechanism.

Editing `DataList` Items and Using Templates

Continuing our journey into the world of `DataList`, let's learn a little more about its templates, and see how you can use the `EditItemTemplate` to edit its contents. Our goal here is to allow users to change the name or username of any employee.

Start by adding another button to the `ItemTemplate` of the `DataList`. This button will read Edit employee *Employee Name* and, when clicked, it will cause the item of which it's a part to become editable.

File: **EmployeeDirectory.aspx (excerpt)**

```
<ItemTemplate>
  <asp:Literal ID="extraDetailsLiteral" runat="server"
      EnableViewState="false" />
  Name: <strong><%#Eval("Name")%></strong><br />
  Username: <strong><%#Eval("Username")%></strong><br />
  <asp:LinkButton ID="detailsButton" runat="server"
      Text=<%#"View more details about " & Eval("Name")%>
```

```
            CommandName="MoreDetailsPlease"
            CommandArgument=<%#Eval("EmployeeID")%> /><br />
    <asp:LinkButton ID="editButton" runat="server"
            Text=<%#"Edit employee " + Eval("Name")%>
            CommandName="EditItem"
            CommandArgument=<%#Eval("EmployeeID")%> />
  </ItemTemplate>
```

When an Edit employee button is clicked, we will make the item enter edit mode.
When one of the DataList items is in edit mode, the EditItemTemplate template
of the DataList is used to generate the contents of that item. All the other items
are generated by the ItemTemplate, as usual.

Modify EmployeeDirectory.aspx by adding the EditItemTemplate to the
DataList. The EditItemTemplate contains TextBox controls into which the user
can enter the employee's name and username, and two buttons: Update Item and
Cancel Editing, whose names are self-explanatory.

File: **EmployeeDirectory.aspx (excerpt)**

```
<EditItemTemplate>
  Name: <asp:TextBox ID="nameTextBox" runat="server"
      Text=<%#Eval("Name")%> /><br />
  Username: <asp:TextBox ID="usernameTextBox" runat="server"
      Text=<%#Eval("Username")%> /><br />
  <asp:LinkButton ID="updateButton" runat="server"
      Text="Update Item" CommandName="UpdateItem"
      CommandArgument=<%#Eval("EmployeeID")%> />
  or
  <asp:LinkButton ID="cancelButton" runat="server"
      Text="Cancel Editing" CommandName="CancelEditing"
      CommandArgument=<%#Eval("EmployeeID")%> />
</EditItemTemplate>
```

Finally, before you can see your new template, we need to handle the Edit employee button. Again, when that button is clicked, the DataList's ItemCommand event
is fired. This time, the CommandName of the new button is EditItem, and when
we discover that this button was clicked, we'll put the item into edit mode. To
put a DataList item into edit mode, we set its EditItemIndex to the index of
the item, then bind the DataList to its data source again to refresh its contents.
Add this code:

Visual Basic   File: **EmployeeDirectory.aspx.vb (excerpt)**

```
Protected Sub employeesList_ItemCommand(ByVal source As Object, _
  ByVal e As System.Web.UI.WebControls.DataListCommandEventArgs) _
```

```
Handles employeesList.ItemCommand
' Which button was clicked?
If e.CommandName = "MoreDetailsPlease" Then
  ' Find the Literal control in the DataList item
  Dim li As Literal
  li = e.Item.FindControl("extraDetailsLiteral")
  ' Add content to the Literal control
  li.Text = "Employee ID: <strong>" & e.CommandArgument & _
    "</strong><br />"
  ElseIf e.CommandName = "EditItem" Then
    ' Set the index of the item being edited
    employeesList.EditItemIndex = e.Item.ItemIndex
    ' Bind again the list to update the list
    BindList()
  End If
End Sub
```

C#   File: **EmployeeDirectory.aspx.cs (excerpt)**

```
protected void employeesList_ItemCommand(object source,
    DataListCommandEventArgs e)
{
  // Which button was clicked?
  if (e.CommandName == "MoreDetailsPlease")
  {
    // Find the Literal control in the DataList item
    Literal li;
    li = (Literal)e.Item.FindControl("extraDetailsLiteral");
    // Add content to the Literal control
    li.Text = "Employee ID: <strong>" + e.CommandArgument +
      "</strong><br />";
  }
  else if (e.CommandName == "EditItem")
  {
    // Set the index of the item being edited
    employeesList.EditItemIndex = e.Item.ItemIndex;
    // Bind again the list to update the list
    BindList();
  }
}
```

Figure 10.5. Editing the `DataList`

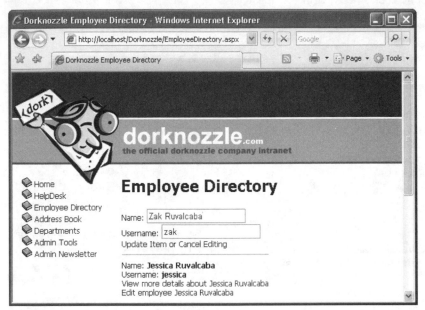

Execute the project now, load the employee directory, and enter one of your items into edit mode, as shown in Figure 10.5.

We need to implement functionality for two more buttons: Update Item, and Cancel Editing. We'll take them one at a time, starting with Cancel Editing, which is easier to handle. Modify `employeesList_ItemCommand` like this:

Visual Basic   File: **EmployeeDirectory.aspx.vb (excerpt)**

```
Protected Sub employeesList_ItemCommand(ByVal source As Object, _
  ByVal e As System.Web.UI.WebControls.DataListCommandEventArgs) _
  Handles employeesList.ItemCommand
  ' Which button was clicked?
  If e.CommandName = "MoreDetailsPlease" Then
    ' Find the Literal control in the DataList item
    Dim li As Literal
    li = e.Item.FindControl("extraDetailsLiteral")
    ' Add content to the Literal control
    li.Text = "Employee ID: <strong>" & e.CommandArgument & _
        "</strong><br />"
  ElseIf e.CommandName = "EditItem" Then
    ' Set the index of the item being edited
    employeesList.EditItemIndex = e.Item.ItemIndex
```

```
    ' Bind again the list to update the list
    BindList()
  ElseIf e.CommandName = "CancelEditing" Then
    ' Cancel edit mode
    employeesList.EditItemIndex = -1
    ' Refresh the DataList
    BindList()
  End If
End Sub
```

C#   File: **EmployeeDirectory.aspx.cs (excerpt)**

```
protected void employeesList_ItemCommand(object source,
    DataListCommandEventArgs e)
{
  // Which button was clicked?
  if (e.CommandName == "MoreDetailsPlease")
  {
    // Find the Literal control in the DataList item
    Literal li;
    li = (Literal)e.Item.FindControl("extraDetailsLiteral");
    // Add content to the Literal control
    li.Text = "Employee ID: <strong>" + e.CommandArgument +
        "</strong><br />";
  }
  else if (e.CommandName == "EditItem")
  {
    // Set the index of the item being edited
    employeesList.EditItemIndex = e.Item.ItemIndex;
    // Bind again the list to update the list
    BindList();
  }
  else if (e.CommandName == "CancelEditing")
  {
    // Cancel edit mode
    employeesList.EditItemIndex = -1;
    // Refresh the DataList
    BindList();
  }
}
```

Execute your project again and check that your new button works. As you can see, exiting edit mode is really simple. You simply need to set the EditItemIndex property of the DataList to -1, then refresh the DataList's contents.

Let's deal with the task of updating the record now. We read the ID of the employee whose details are being edited from the button's CommandArgument property, and the employee's new name and username from the `TextBox` control. The techniques used in this code are the ones we used earlier, but be sure to read the code carefully to ensure that you understand how it works.

Visual Basic   File: **EmployeeDirectory.aspx.vb (excerpt)**

```vb
  ElseIf e.CommandName = "CancelEditing" Then
    ' Cancel edit mode
    employeesList.EditItemIndex = -1
    ' Refresh the DataList
    BindList()
  ElseIf e.CommandName = "UpdateItem" Then
    ' Get the employee ID
    Dim employeeId As Integer = e.CommandArgument
    ' Get the new username
    Dim nameTextBox As TextBox = _
        e.Item.FindControl("nameTextBox")
    Dim newName As String = nameTextBox.Text
    ' Get the new name
    Dim usernameTextBox As TextBox = _
        e.Item.FindControl("usernameTextBox")
    Dim newUsername As String = usernameTextBox.Text
    ' Update the item
    UpdateItem(employeeId, newName, newUsername)
    ' Cancel edit mode
    employeesList.EditItemIndex = -1
    ' Refresh the DataList
    BindList()
  End If
End Sub
```

C#   File: **EmployeeDirectory.aspx.cs (excerpt)**

```csharp
  else if (e.CommandName == "CancelEditing")
  {
    // Cancel edit mode
    employeesList.EditItemIndex = -1;
    // Refresh the DataList
    BindList();
  }
  else if (e.CommandName == "UpdateItem")
  {
    // Get the employee ID
    int employeeId = Convert.ToInt32(e.CommandArgument);
    // Get the new username
    TextBox nameTextBox =
        (TextBox)e.Item.FindControl("nameTextBox");
    string newName = nameTextBox.Text;
```

```
    // Get the new name
    TextBox usernameTextBox =
        (TextBox)e.Item.FindControl("usernameTextBox");
    string newUsername = usernameTextBox.Text;
    // Update the item
    UpdateItem(employeeId, newName, newUsername);
    // Cancel edit mode
    employeesList.EditItemIndex = -1;
    // Refresh the DataList
    BindList();
  }
}
```

As you can see, a mysterious method named UpdateItem is used to perform the actual update. We've created a separate method to make the code easier to manage. Add this code to your code-behind file:

Visual Basic   File: **EmployeeDirectory.aspx.vb (excerpt)**

```
Protected Sub UpdateItem(ByVal employeeId As String, _
    ByVal newName As String, ByVal newUsername As String)
  ' Declare data objects
  Dim conn As SqlConnection
  Dim comm As SqlCommand
  ' Read the connection string from Web.config
  Dim connectionString As String = _
      ConfigurationManager.ConnectionStrings( _
      "Dorknozzle").ConnectionString
  ' Initialize connection
  conn = New SqlConnection(connectionString)
  ' Create command
  comm = New SqlCommand("UpdateEmployee", conn)
  ' Specify we're calling a stored procedure
  comm.CommandType = System.Data.CommandType.StoredProcedure
  ' Add command parameters
  comm.Parameters.Add("@EmployeeID", Data.SqlDbType.Int)
  comm.Parameters("@EmployeeID").Value = employeeId
  comm.Parameters.Add("@NewName", Data.SqlDbType.NVarChar, 50)
  comm.Parameters("@NewName").Value = newName
  comm.Parameters.Add("@NewUsername", Data.SqlDbType.NVarChar, 50)
  comm.Parameters("@NewUsername").Value = newUsername
  ' Enclose database code in Try-Catch-Finally
  Try
    ' Open the connection
    conn.Open()
    ' Execute the command
    comm.ExecuteNonQuery()
```

```
  Finally
    ' Close the connection
    conn.Close()
  End Try
End Sub
```

File: **EmployeeDirectory.aspx.cs (excerpt)**

C#

```csharp
protected void UpdateItem(int employeeId, string newName,
    string newUsername)
{
  // Declare data objects
  SqlConnection conn;
  SqlCommand comm;
  // Read the connection string from Web.config
  string connectionString =
      ConfigurationManager.ConnectionStrings[
      "Dorknozzle"].ConnectionString;
  // Initialize connection
  conn = new SqlConnection(connectionString);
  // Create command
  comm = new SqlCommand("UpdateEmployee", conn);
  // Specify we're calling a stored procedure
  comm.CommandType = System.Data.CommandType.StoredProcedure;
  // Add command parameters
  comm.Parameters.Add("@EmployeeID", SqlDbType.Int);
  comm.Parameters["@EmployeeID"].Value = employeeId;
  comm.Parameters.Add("@NewName", SqlDbType.NVarChar, 50);
  comm.Parameters["@NewName"].Value = newName;
  comm.Parameters.Add("@NewUsername", SqlDbType.NVarChar, 50);
  comm.Parameters["@NewUsername"].Value = newUsername;
  // Enclose database code in Try-Catch-Finally
  try
  {
    // Open the connection
    conn.Open();
    // Execute the command
    comm.ExecuteNonQuery();
  }
  finally
  {
    // Close the connection
    conn.Close();
  }
}
```

Once the parameters are all prepared, the `UpdateItem` method calls the `UpdateEmployee` stored procedure, which performs the database operation. Next, let's add the `UpdateEmployee` stored procedure to our database by running the following script using SQL Server Management Studio:

```
CREATE PROCEDURE UpdateEmployee
(
  @EmployeeID Int,
  @NewName nvarchar(50),
  @NewUsername nvarchar(50)
)
AS
UPDATE Employees
SET Name = @NewName, Username = @NewUsername
WHERE EmployeeID = @EmployeeID
```

Finally, execute the project again, load the Employee Directory page, and enter one of the employees into edit mode. You should see a display like the one shown in Figure 10.6.

Figure 10.6. Viewing an employee in edit mode

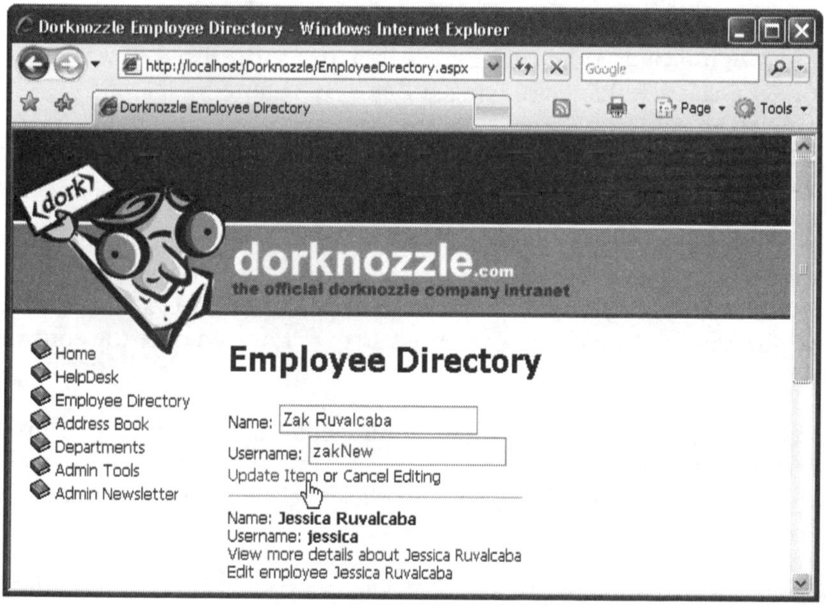

Figure 10.7. Editing the username

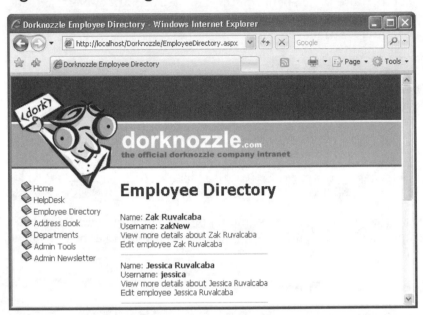

Change the name or username, and click Update Item to see the listed data change. In Figure 10.7, you can see that I've changed Zak's username to zakNew.

DataList and Visual Web Developer

Just like some of the more complex web server controls, DataLists offer a number of design-time features that are tightly integrated within Visual Web Developer. One of these slick features is the **smart tag**, which appears as a little arrow button in the upper-right part of the control when the cursor is hovered over the control in Design View.

You'll be working with these neat features in coming chapters, but we can't finish a chapter on DataLists without making ourselves aware of them. If you open EmployeeDirectory.aspx in Design View, and click the smart tag, you'll see the menu depicted in Figure 10.8.

You can use this menu to apply predefined styles to your grid, choose a data source control (you'll learn more about these in the following chapters), or edit the grid's templates.

Figure 10.8. The smart tag options of `DataList`

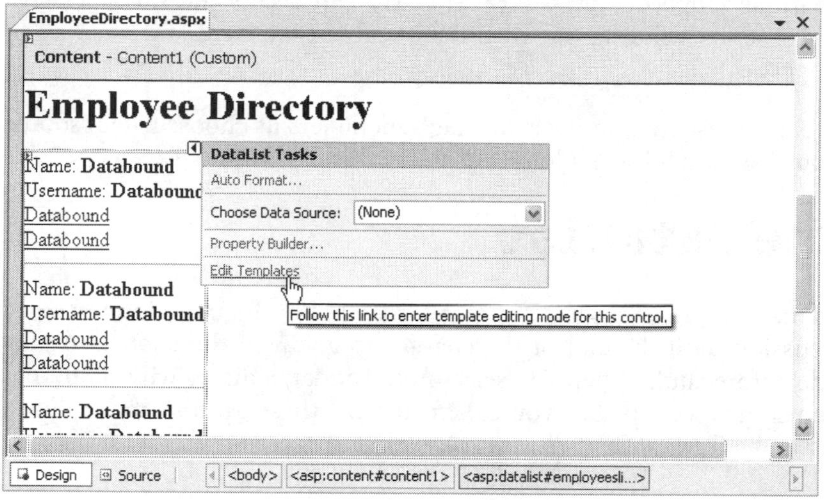

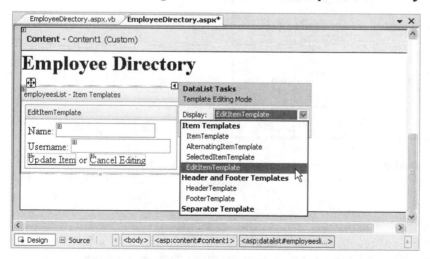

If you click Edit Templates, you can build the `DataList`'s templates visually, as Figure 10.9 indicates.

Figure 10.9. Building the `DataList`'s templates visually

We'll generally write most of the code by hand, but it's good to know that you also have this visual option.

Choosing the Property Builder from the smart tag's menu displays a window that lets us set various properties of a `DataList`. We can access the same settings through the Properties window, but with the `DataList` we have another way to set these properties.

The Choose Data Source item in the smart tag's menu lets us choose a data source control for our list. You'll learn a lot more about this in Chapter 12.

Styling the `DataList`

The Auto Format item in the smart tag menu is probably the most interesting. I left this discussion until the end of the chapter to give you the chance to play with it a little beforehand. When you select Auto Format, a dialog with a number of predefined setups will appear; you can customize these options manually to suit your tastes, as Figure 10.10 illustrates.

Figure 10.10. Choosing an Auto Format option

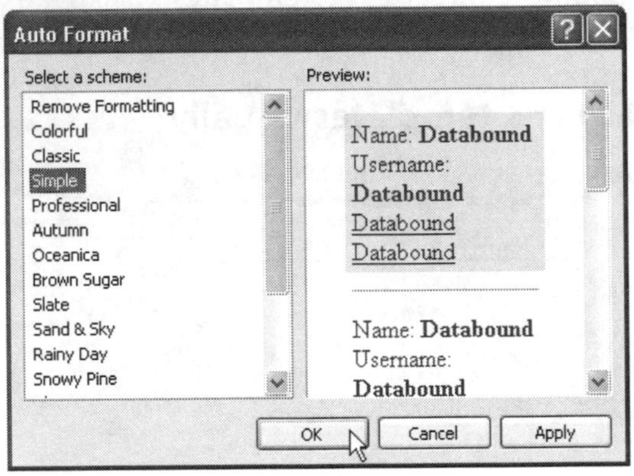

If you choose the Simple style, then remove the `SeparatorTemplate` from your `DataList`, your Employee Directory page will look like the one shown in Figure 10.11.

You may ask what happened behind the scenes. If you look at the `DataList` definition in `EmployeeDirectory.aspx`, you'll see it contains a few new lines that Visual Web Developer generated for us after we chose the style:

```
    </EditItemTemplate>
    <FooterStyle BackColor="#1C5E55" Font-Bold="True"
        ForeColor="White" />
```

Figure 10.11. The styled Employee Directory list

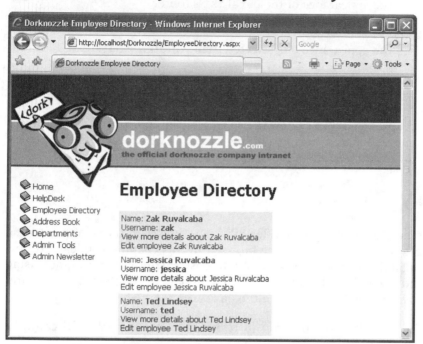

```
<SelectedItemStyle BackColor="#C5BBAF" Font-Bold="True"
    ForeColor="#333333" />
<AlternatingItemStyle BackColor="White" />
<ItemStyle BackColor="#E3EAEB" />
<HeaderStyle BackColor="#1C5E55" Font-Bold="True"
    ForeColor="White" />
</asp:DataList>
```

The significance of these new elements is as follows:

HeaderStyle
customizes the appearance of the DataList's heading

ItemStyle
customizes the appearance of each item displayed within the DataList

AlternatingItemStyle
customizes the appearance of every other item displayed within the DataList

FooterStyle
customizes the appearance of the `DataList`'s footer

SelectedItemStyle
customizes the appearance of a selected item within the `DataList`

EditItemStyle
customizes the appearance of the `DataList` when in edit mode

In the next chapter, you'll learn how to use CSS styles and control skins to facilitate a more professional approach to styling your data controls. Until then, enjoy the benefits of having a modern-looking, functional employee directory!

Summary

As you've seen, `DataLists` provide flexibility and power in terms of presenting database data dynamically within the browser. In this chapter, you learned how to bind your data to `DataLists`, and how to customize their appearance using templates and styles. You also learned how to edit data in your `DataList` control, and how to access controls located in the `DataList` templates.

The next chapter will introduce you to two new and more powerful controls: `GridView` and `DetailsView`.

11

Managing Content Using Grid View and Details View

In the previous chapters, you learned some of the important concepts surrounding data access and presentation. You learned that when connecting to a database, we have to establish a connection using the SqlConnection class. You also learned that in order to retrieve data from the database table, we must write an SQL statement within a command using the SqlCommand class. You discovered that we use the SqlDataReader class to place the database records into a virtual container of some sort. Finally, you learned that presenting the data within the SqlDataReader was simply a matter of binding the SqlDataReader to a data control such as the Repeater or DataList controls.

The Repeater and DataList controls offer flexibility in the sense that their templates can easily be customized with inline HTML, in conjunction with code render blocks, to display the contents in a clean and neatly formatted manner. So far, these two controls have been great! They certainly have their place, and I'm not about to discourage you from using them. However, these controls do remind ASP developers a little too much of the bad old days when we had to write our HTML table and table row tags in While loops. Within those table row tags, we also had to add code render blocks to display the contents of the data source. As you've probably noticed, the Repeater control isn't much different from the techniques we were forced to use in those bad old days. HTML table row tags still have to be added within the <HeaderTemplate>, <ItemTemplate>, and <FooterTemplate> tags, and code render blocks must still be used within the table data cells. The `DataList` makes things a bit easier by generating a single-column table for us, but even so, the built-in functionality isn't overwhelming.

Here, we'll learn about two more controls that offer much more functionality and make it very easy for you to create a table: `GridView` and `DetailsView`. These controls, which form part of ASP.NET's set of data controls, give developers much more power and flexibility over presentation, as you'll see in the next few sections. The processes by which information within a table is presented, formatted, and edited have been completely revamped with the `GridView` and `DetailsView` controls.

GridView vs DataGrid

The `GridView` control supersedes the `DataGrid` control, which was the star of all data-displaying controls in ASP.NET 1.0 and 1.1. The `DataGrid` is still present in ASP.NET 2.0 for backwards-compatibility purposes, but for any new development, the `GridView` is recommended. The `DetailsView` control is new in ASP.NET 2.0 and doesn't have a corresponding control in earlier versions.

Using the `GridView` Control

The `GridView` control solves a problem that has plagued developers for years: data presentation. The `GridView` control generates simple HTML tables, so information within a `GridView` is presented to the end user in a familiar, cleanly formatted, tabular structure. Similar to the `Repeater` control, the `GridView` can also automatically display all the content contained in an `SqlDataReader` on a page, based on styles we set within its templates. However, unlike the `Repeater` control, the `GridView` offers several more advanced features, such as sorting or paging (i.e. splitting a large result set into pages), and makes it easy to modify the data in the underlying data source.

To sum up, `GridView` controls provide the following functionality:

❑ database table-like presentation

❑ table headers and footers

❑ paging

❑ sorting

❑ style modification through templates

❑ customizable columns for advanced editing

You'll learn about some of these features in this chapter, though we'll leave the more advanced ones (sorting, paging, and editing) for the next chapter.

As with any other ASP.NET server control, `GridView` controls are added to the page using a specific element:

```
<asp:GridView id="myGridView" runat="server" />
```

Once we add the `GridView` to the page, we can bind an `SqlDataReader` to it as follows:

Visual Basic
```
myGridView.DataSource = myDataReader
myGridView.DataBind()
```

C#
```
myGridView.DataSource = myDataReader;
myGridView.DataBind();
```

So far, the `GridView` doesn't seem to function very differently from the `Repeater` control, right? Think again! The `Repeater` control didn't work unless we specified content within the required `<ItemTemplate>` and `</ItemTemplate>` tags. The `GridView` takes the structure of the database table automatically, and presents the data to the user in a cleanly formatted HTML table.

Let's take a look at `GridView` in action as we develop the Dorknozzle intranet's address book page. Start by opening the Dorknozzle project, if it's not already open, and creating a new web form named `AddressBook.aspx`, based on the `Dorknozzle.master` master page. Also, make sure the new web form uses a code-behind file.

Now, open `AddressBook.aspx`, and complete its code as shown in the following code snippet.

File: **AddressBook.aspx (excerpt)**
```
<%@ Page Language="VB" MasterPageFile="~/DorkNozzle.master"
    AutoEventWireup="True" CodeFile="AddressBook.aspx.vb"
    Inherits="AddressBook" title="Dorknozzle Address Book" %>
<asp:Content ID="Content1"
    ContentPlaceHolderID="ContentPlaceHolder1" Runat="Server">
```

```
    <h1>Address Book</h1>
    <asp:GridView id="grid" runat="server" />
</asp:Content>
```

By switching to Design View you can see how your grid is represented in the designer, as Figure 11.1 indicates.

Figure 11.1. Viewing **AddressBook.aspx** in Design View

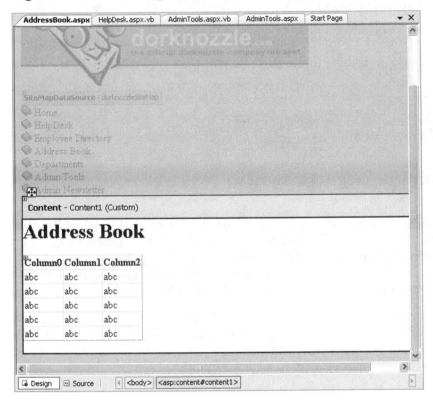

Now, double-click on an empty portion of the page to have the form's Page_Load event handler generated for you in the code-behind file. In Page_Load, we'll call a method named BindGrid, which will, in turn, create a database connection and a database command object, execute that command, and bind the resulting data reader to the grid, as shown below:

Visual Basic   File: **AddressBook.aspx.vb (excerpt)**

```
Imports System.Data.SqlClient
```

```
Partial Class AddressBook
    Inherits System.Web.UI.Page

  Protected Sub Page_Load(ByVal sender As Object, _
      ByVal e As System.EventArgs) Handles Me.Load
    If Not IsPostBack Then
      BindGrid()
    End If
  End Sub

  Private Sub BindGrid()
    ' Define data objects
    Dim conn As SqlConnection
    Dim comm As SqlCommand
    Dim reader As SqlDataReader
    ' Read the connection string from Web.config
    Dim connectionString As String = _
        ConfigurationManager.ConnectionStrings( _
        "Dorknozzle").ConnectionString
    ' Initialize connection
    conn = New SqlConnection(connectionString)
    ' Create command
    comm = New SqlCommand( _
        "SELECT EmployeeID, Name, City, State, MobilePhone " & _
        "FROM Employees", conn)
    ' Enclose database code in Try-Catch-Finally
    Try
      ' Open the connection
      conn.Open()
      ' Execute the command
      reader = comm.ExecuteReader()
      ' Fill the grid with data
      grid.DataSource = reader
      grid.DataBind()
      ' Close the reader
      reader.Close()
    Finally
      ' Close the connection
      conn.Close()
    End Try
  End Sub

End Class
```

```csharp
using System;
using System.Data;
using System.Configuration;
using System.Collections;
using System.Web;
using System.Web.Security;
using System.Web.UI;
using System.Web.UI.WebControls;
using System.Web.UI.WebControls.WebParts;
using System.Web.UI.HtmlControls;
using System.Data.SqlClient;

public partial class AddressBook : System.Web.UI.Page
{
  protected void Page_Load(object sender, EventArgs e)
  {
    if (!IsPostBack)
    {
      BindGrid();
    }
  }
  private void BindGrid()
  {
    // Define data objects
    SqlConnection conn;
    SqlCommand comm;
    SqlDataReader reader;
    // Read the connection string from Web.config
    string connectionString =
        ConfigurationManager.ConnectionStrings[
        "Dorknozzle"].ConnectionString;
    // Initialize connection
    conn = new SqlConnection(connectionString);
    // Create command
    comm = new SqlCommand(
        "SELECT EmployeeID, Name, City, State, MobilePhone " +
        "FROM Employees", conn);
    // Enclose database code in Try-Catch-Finally
    try
    {
      // Open the connection
      conn.Open();
      // Execute the command
      reader = comm.ExecuteReader();
      // Fill the grid with data
```

```
    grid.DataSource = reader;
    grid.DataBind();
    // Close the reader
    reader.Close();
  }
  finally
  {
    // Close the connection
    conn.Close();
  }
 }
}
```

What's going on here? If you disregard the fact that you're binding the `SqlDataReader` to a `GridView` instead of a `Repeater` or `DataList`, the code is almost identical to that which we saw in the previous chapter.

Now save your work and open the page in the browser. Figure 11.2 shows how the `GridView` presents all of the data within the `Employees` table in a cleanly formatted structure.

Figure 11.2. Displaying the address book in `GridView`

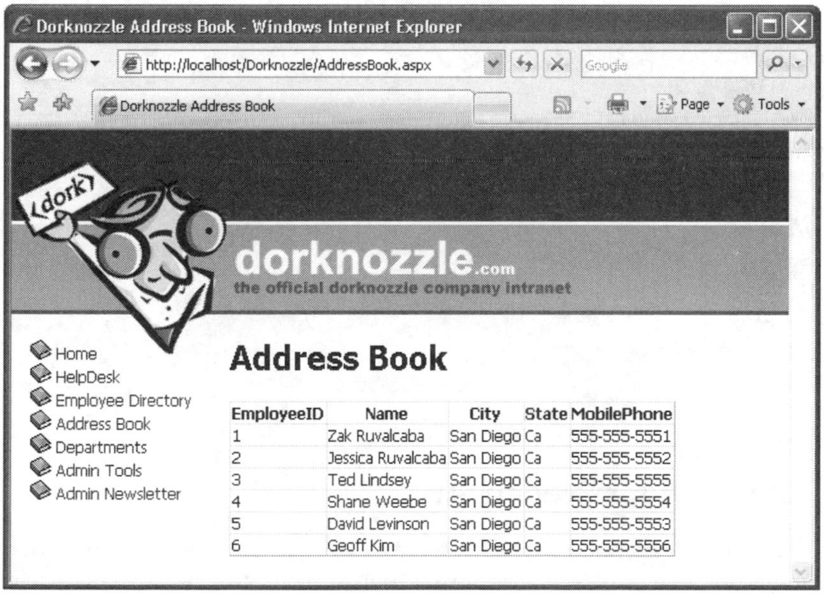

Well, okay, perhaps it doesn't look all that clean right now! However, the display will change as we get some practice using the GridView's powerful yet intuitive formatting capabilities. You'll notice that the GridView closely resembles the structure of the query's result as you might see it in SQL Server Management Studio. All the names of the columns in the database table show as headers within the table, and all the rows from the database table are repeated down the page.

If you look at the generated page source (right-click the page in browser and choose View Source or similar), you'll see that the GridView indeed generated a table for you:

```
<table cellspacing="0" rules="all" border="1"
    id="ctl00_ContentPlaceHolder1_grid"
    style="border-collapse:collapse;">
  <tr>
    <th scope="col">EmployeeID</th>
    <th scope="col">Name</th>
    <th scope="col">City</th>
    <th scope="col">State</th>
    <th scope="col">MobilePhone</th>
  </tr>
  <tr>
    <td>1</td>
    <td>Zak Ruvalcaba</td>
    <td>San Diego</td>
    <td>Ca</td>
    <td>555-555-5551</td>
  </tr>
  <tr>
    <td>2</td>
    <td>Jessica Ruvalcaba</td>
    <td>San Diego</td>
    <td>Ca</td>
    <td>555-555-5552</td>
  </tr>
    ⋮
</table>
```

Formatted for Readability

The HTML generated by ASP.NET won't look exactly as it does above. You'll find that ASP.NET will output long, difficult-to-read lines of td elements, each of which appears directly after the previous one. We've simply made it a little easier to read; the two HTML tables are otherwise identical.

There's no doubt that the GridView's automatic presentation features are useful. The GridView automatically displays all columns retrieved from the database in the order in which they're sent from the database. While this is very useful, in some cases you'll want your grid to display only a subset of the information retrieved from the database, and in many cases you'll also want to change the order in which the columns of data are displayed.

Let's learn how to customize the GridView by selecting which columns to show, in what order. In our case, one of the columns that we want to retrieve from the database, but hide from users, is the EmployeeID column. We need to retrieve the table's primary key because it's required for any database operations that involve the unique identification of a record (including tasks such as editing or deleting an employee from the list). The user doesn't need to be overwhelmed with this information, though—after all, humans don't use numeric IDs to identify people in a list.

Customizing the GridView Columns

Our next task is to customize the columns displayed by the GridView. In this case, our goal is to prevent the EmployeeID column from showing up, but the same techniques can be used to make all sorts of customizations.

Filtering Table Columns

The columns you can display in the GridView must be a subset of the columns you're retrieving from the database. For example, unless you modify the database query to retrieve the employees' passwords, it's not possible to display them in the grid.

If you wish to restrict the information that appears within your GridView, you can select the columns you want to display by making a few simple modifications. When you simply bind an SqlDataReader to the GridView, you're presented with a quick, simple representation of the data you've retrieved from the database, with automatically-generated column headers.

One of the properties available to GridView is AutoGenerateColumns, which is set to True by default. If you want to name the columns that your GridView displays manually, you must set this property to False.

If you set this property to False and test it in the browser, you'll find that the grid doesn't show up any more. The reason for this is simple: as the GridView can't generate its own column headers, you must manually specify the columns that you want displayed. To do so, list the columns inside the `<asp:GridView>` and `</asp:GridView>` tags, as shown below:

File: **AddressBook.aspx (excerpt)**

```
<asp:GridView ID="grid" runat="server"
    AutoGenerateColumns="False">
  <Columns>
    <asp:BoundField DataField="Name" HeaderText="Name" />
    <asp:BoundField DataField="City" HeaderText="City" />
    <asp:BoundField DataField="MobilePhone"
        HeaderText="Mobile Phone" />
  </Columns>
</asp:GridView>
```

Notice that each column that we want to display is created using a `BoundField` control inside a set of `<Columns>` and `</Columns>` tags. Each `BoundField` control has a `DataField` property, which specifies the name of the column, and a `HeaderText` property, which sets the name of the column as you want it displayed to the user.

Now, save your work and view it in the browser. This time, only the columns that you specified to be bound are displayed in the `GridView`. The results should appear as shown in Figure 11.3.

Note that if you don't include the `HeaderText` property for any of the bound columns, those columns will not have a header.

We've now succeeded in displaying only the information we want to display, but the `GridView` still looks plain. In the next section, we'll use styles to customize the look of our `GridView`.

Styling the `GridView` with Templates, Skins, and CSS

The `GridView` control offers a number of design-time features that are tightly integrated with the Visual Web Developer designer. As with the `DataList` class, when you click the grid's smart tag, you get quick access to a number of very useful features, as Figure 11.4 illustrates.

Figure 11.3. Displaying selected columns

Figure 11.4. The smart tag options of `GridView`

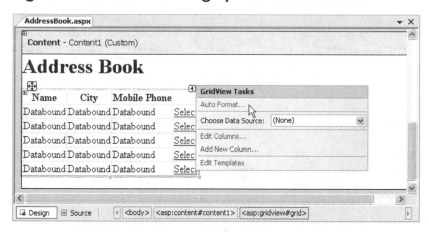

If you click the **Auto Format...** link from the smart tag menu and choose one of the predefined styles, Visual Web Developer generates a number of template styles for you, like this:

```
<asp:GridView ID="grid" runat="server" AutoGenerateColumns="False"
    CellPadding="4" ForeColor="#333333" GridLines="None">
  <Columns>
    <asp:BoundField DataField="Name" HeaderText="Name" />
    <asp:BoundField DataField="City" HeaderText="City" />
    <asp:BoundField DataField="MobilePhone"
        HeaderText="Mobile Phone" />
  </Columns>
  <FooterStyle BackColor="#5D7B9D" Font-Bold="True"
      ForeColor="White" />
  <RowStyle BackColor="#F7F6F3" ForeColor="#333333" />
  <EditRowStyle BackColor="#999999" />
  <SelectedRowStyle BackColor="#E2DED6" Font-Bold="True"
      ForeColor="#333333" />
  <PagerStyle BackColor="#284775" ForeColor="White"
      HorizontalAlign="Center" />
  <HeaderStyle BackColor="#5D7B9D" Font-Bold="True"
      ForeColor="White" />
  <AlternatingRowStyle BackColor="White" ForeColor="#284775" />
</asp:GridView>
```

However, this time, we prefer not to rely on the predefined templates, but to define our own styles through CSS. Additionally, we want to add a new skin definition for the GridView (you learned about skins back in Chapter 5), so that all the GridView controls throughout our site have a standard appearance.

Open your Dorknozzle.css file from the App_Themes/Blue folder and add these styles to it:

File: **Dorknozzle.css (excerpt)**

```
.GridMain
{
  border-right: gainsboro thin solid;
  border-top: gainsboro thin solid;
  border-left: gainsboro thin solid;
  border-bottom: gainsboro thin solid;
  background-color: #333333;
  width: 400px;
}
.GridRow
{
  background-color: #FFFAFA;
}
.GridSelectedRow
{
```

```
    background-color: #E6E6FA;
}
.GridHeader
{
    background-color: #ADD8E6;
    font-weight: bold;
    text-align: left;
}
```

Then modify the skin file SkinFile.skin in App_Themes/Blue by adding this skin definition:

File: **SkinFile.skin (excerpt)**

```
<asp:GridView runat="server" CssClass="GridMain" CellPadding="4"
    GridLines="None">
  <RowStyle CssClass="GridRow" />
  <SelectedRowStyle CssClass="GridSelectedRow" />
  <HeaderStyle CssClass="GridHeader" />
</asp:GridView>
```

Finally, make sure that your GridView declaration in AddressBook.aspx doesn't contain any styling details, as shown here:

File: **AddressBook.aspx (excerpt)**

```
<asp:GridView ID="grid" runat="server"
    AutoGenerateColumns="false">
  <Columns>
    <asp:BoundField DataField="Name" HeaderText="Name" />
    <asp:BoundField DataField="City" HeaderText="City" />
    <asp:BoundField DataField="MobilePhone"
        HeaderText="Mobile Phone" />
  </Columns>
</asp:GridView>
```

Figure 11.5. The styled address book

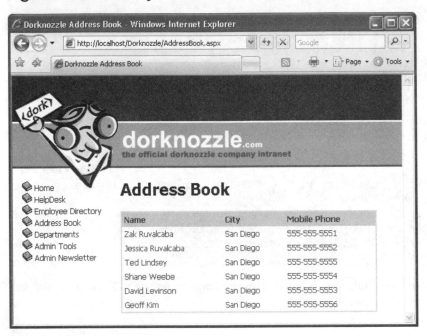

All the styling we need is already defined in the skin file; we'd only need to define new properties if we wanted to alter the default values provided through the skin file. Save your work and view the results in the browser. Do they look like the display in Figure 11.5?

Congratulations! You've harnessed the power of CSS and skin files, and combined it with the flexibility of `GridView` to easily create a good-looking address book!

As you can see, you can style the items in the `GridView` by altering their font types, colors, and sizes. You can also style the column headers and apply an alternating item style to alternate rows in the table. Now, when the `GridView` is viewed in the browser, we see a little more room between cells, and the lines surrounding the `GridView` are gone.

Selecting Grid Records

We've already made quite a few changes to the display of our `GridView`. The next step will be to allow users to select one of the rows in the `GridView` so they can view more information about the selected employee.

There are several types of columns that we can create in a `GridView` in addition to the `BoundField` columns we've already seen. For instance, we could create a `ButtonField` column, which displays a button in each row. The complete set of column controls and their descriptions are listed here:

BoundField

As you've seen, the `BoundField` provides flexibility in presentation by allowing you to specify which columns will appear within the `GridView`. When the grid enters edit mode, this field renders itself as an editable text box, as we'll see later.

ButtonField

Use the `ButtonField` to display a clickable button for each row within the `GridView`. When clicked, the button triggers a configurable event that you can handle within your code to respond to the user's action. The possible event types that a button can trigger are: `Cancel`, `Delete`, `Edit`, `Select`, and `Update`.

CheckBoxField

The `CheckBoxField` displays a checkbox in each row, allowing you to easily present Boolean data in the display.

CommandField

The `CommandField` column automatically generates a `ButtonField` in your grid. The actions performed by these buttons depend on the grid's current state. For example, if `CommandField` is set to generate `Edit` buttons, it will display an `Edit` button when the grid is in non-editable mode, and will display Update and Cancel buttons when the grid is being edited.

HyperLinkField

Use the `HyperLinkField` to display a clickable link within the `GridView`. This link simply acts as a hyperlink to a URL; it raises no server-side events.

ImageField

This control displays an image inside your grid.

TemplateField

Use the `TemplateField` to display markup within the `GridView`.

Figure 11.6. Adding a new `GridView` column

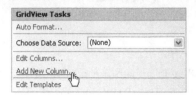

If you're using Visual Web Developer, you can quickly and easily add a new column to your table in Design View. Click the `GridView`'s smart tag, and click the Add New Column... item, as shown in Figure 11.6.

In the dialog that appears, change the field type to ButtonField, the command name to Select, and set the Text field to **Select**, so the dialog appears as it does in Figure 11.7.

Figure 11.7. Adding a new field

After clicking OK, your brand new column shows up in Design View. If you switch to Source View, you can see it there, too:

File: **AddressBook.aspx (excerpt)**

```
<asp:GridView ID="grid" runat="server"
    AutoGenerateColumns="false">
  <Columns>
    <asp:BoundField DataField="Name" HeaderText="Name" />
    <asp:BoundField DataField="City" HeaderText="City" />
```

```
    <asp:BoundField DataField="MobilePhone"
      HeaderText="Mobile Phone" />
    <asp:ButtonField CommandName="Select" Text="Select" />
  </Columns>
</asp:GridView>
```

If you execute the project now, and click the new button, the row will become highlighted, as Figure 11.8 indicates. Notice that you didn't write any code to implement this feature? We're relying on the functionality provided by the `ButtonField` control when it's `CommandName` property is set to `Select`, and the style settings you set earlier, to produce this functionality.

Figure 11.8. Highlighting the selected field in the Address Book

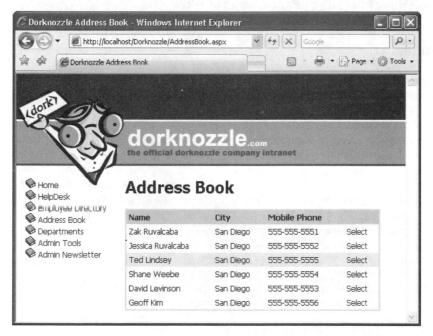

We usually want extra work—in addition to the row highlight—to be performed when a user selects a row in the address book. When the `Select` button is pressed, the `GridView` fires the `SelectedIndexChanged` event, which we handle if we need to do any further processing. We can generate the `GridView`'s `SelectedIndex-Changed` event handler simply by double-clicking the `GridView` in the Visual Web Developer designer.

Generating Default Event Handlers

Double-clicking a control in the designer causes Visual Web Developer to generate the handler of the control's default event. The default event of the `GridView` is `SelectedIndexChanged`, which explains why it's so easy to generate its signature. Remember that you can use the Properties window to have Visual Web Developer generate handlers for other events—just click the lightning icon in the Properties window, then double-click on any of the listed events.

Before we handle the `SelectedIndexChanged` event, let's add just below the `GridView` control in `AddressBook.aspx` a label that we can use to display some details of the selected record. You can use Visual Web Developer's designer to add the control, or you can write the code manually:

File: **AddressBook.aspx (excerpt)**

```
  </asp:GridView>
  <br />
  <asp:Label ID="detailsLabel" runat="server" />
</asp:Content>
```

Now, generate the `SelectedIndexChanged` event handler by double-clicking the `GridView` control in Design View, then update the event handler to display a short message about the selected record:

Visual Basic   File: **AddressBook.aspx.vb (excerpt)**

```
Protected Sub grid_SelectedIndexChanged(ByVal sender As Object, _
    ByVal e As System.EventArgs) Handles grid.SelectedIndexChanged
  ' Obtain the index of the selected row
  Dim selectedRowIndex As Integer
  selectedRowIndex = grid.SelectedIndex
  ' Read the name from the grid
  Dim row As GridViewRow = grid.Rows(selectedRowIndex)
  Dim name As String = row.Cells(0).Text
  ' Update the details label
  detailsLabel.Text = "You selected " & name & "."
End Sub
```

C#   File: **AddressBook.aspx.cs (excerpt)**

```
protected void grid_SelectedIndexChanged(object sender,
    EventArgs e)
{
  // Obtain the index of the selected row
  int selectedRowIndex;
  selectedRowIndex = grid.SelectedIndex;
```

```
  // Read the name from the grid
  GridViewRow row = grid.Rows[selectedRowIndex];
  string name = row.Cells[0].Text;
  // Update the details label
  detailsLabel.Text = "You selected " + name + ".";
}
```

Execute the project, and select one of the records. You should see a display like the one in Figure 11.9.

Figure 11.9. Displaying details about the selected row

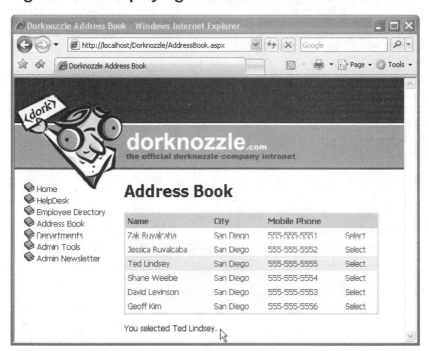

It was easy to add this new feature, wasn't it?

Using the `DetailsView` Control

ASP.NET 2.0 introduced the `DetailsView` control, which can come in very handy when you want to display more details about one record in a grid. You'll find this control very useful when you need to display details about a record that contains many fields—so many, in fact, that the main grid can't display all of them.

A common use of the `DetailsView` control is to create a page that shows a list of items, and allows you to drill down to view the details of each item. For instance, an ecommerce site might initially present users with only a little information about all available products, to reduce download time and make the information more readable. Users could then select a product to see a more detailed view of that product.

Let's see how this works by using a `GridView` and a `DetailsView` in our Address Book web form.

Replace `detailsLabel` with a `DetailsView` control, as shown in the following code snippet:

File: **AddressBook.aspx (excerpt)**

```
  </asp:GridView>
  <br />
  <asp:DetailsView id="employeeDetails" runat="server" />
</asp:Content>
```

Next, we'll modify the `BindGrid` method to specify the grid's **data key**. The data key feature of the `GridView` control basically allows us to store a piece of data about each row without actually displaying that data. We'll use it to store the `EmployeeID` of each record. Later, when we need to retrieve additional data about the selected employee, we'll be able to read the employee's ID from the data key, and use it in our `SELECT` query.

Add this row to your code-behind file:

Visual Basic   File: **AddressBook.aspx.vb (excerpt)**

```
' Open the connection
conn.Open()
' Execute the command
reader = comm.ExecuteReader()
' Fill the grid with data
grid.DataSource = reader
grid.DataKeyNames = New String() {"EmployeeID"}
grid.DataBind()
' Close the reader
reader.Close()
```

Figure 11.10. The `DetailsView` control in action

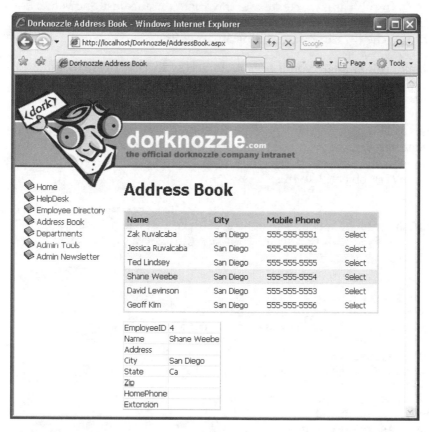

```
C#                                    File: AddressBook.aspx.cs (excerpt)
// Open the connection
conn.Open();
// Execute the command
reader = comm.ExecuteReader();
// Fill the grid with data
grid.DataSource = reader;
grid.DataKeyNames = new string[] { "EmployeeID" };
grid.DataBind();
// Close the reader
reader.Close();
```

As you can see, we tell the `GridView` which keys to store by setting the `DataKeyNames` property. This property needs to be populated with an *array* of keys, because the `GridView` supports storing zero, one, or many keys for each row it displays. In this case, we create an array that contains just one value: Em-ployeeID. In the code you've just written, you can see the syntax that creates such an array on the fly, without declaring an array first.

After you make this change, you'll be able to access the `EmployeeID` value for any given row through the `GridView`'s `DataKeys` property.

With this new data at hand, loading the details of the selected employee into the `DetailsView` is a straightforward process. In the `GridView`'s `SelectedIndex-Changed` event handler, we just need to make another database query to read the details we want to display for the selected employee, then simply feed the results to the `DetailsView` object, like this:

Visual Basic	File: **AddressBook.aspx.vb (excerpt)**

```
Protected Sub grid_SelectedIndexChanged(ByVal sender As Object, _
    ByVal e As System.EventArgs) Handles grid.SelectedIndexChanged
  BindDetails()
End Sub

Private Sub BindDetails()
  ' Obtain the index of the selected row
  Dim selectedRowIndex As Integer = grid.SelectedIndex
  ' Read the employee ID
  Dim employeeId As Integer = _
      grid.DataKeys(selectedRowIndex).Value
  ' Define data objects
  Dim conn As SqlConnection
  Dim comm As SqlCommand
  Dim reader As SqlDataReader
  ' Read the connection string from Web.config
  Dim connectionString As String = _
      ConfigurationManager.ConnectionStrings( _
      "Dorknozzle").ConnectionString
  ' Initialize connection
  conn = New SqlConnection(connectionString)
  ' Create command
  comm = New SqlCommand( _
      "SELECT EmployeeID, Name, Address, City, State, Zip, " & _
      "HomePhone, Extension FROM Employees " & _
      "WHERE EmployeeID=@EmployeeID", conn)
  ' Add the EmployeeID parameter
  comm.Parameters.Add("EmployeeID", Data.SqlDbType.Int)
  comm.Parameters("EmployeeID").Value = employeeId
  ' Enclose database code in Try-Catch-Finally
```

```
  Try
    ' Open the connection
    conn.Open()
    ' Execute the command
    reader = comm.ExecuteReader()
    ' Fill the grid with data
    employeeDetails.DataSource = reader
    employeeDetails.DataKeyNames = New String() {"EmployeeID"}
    employeeDetails.DataBind()
    ' Close the reader
    reader.Close()
  Finally
    ' Close the connection
    conn.Close()
  End Try
End Sub
```

C#   File: **AddressBook.aspx.cs** (excerpt)

```
protected void grid_SelectedIndexChanged(object sender,
    EventArgs e)
{
  BindDetails();
}
private void BindDetails()
{
  // Obtain the index of the selected row
  int selectedRowIndex = grid.SelectedIndex;
  // Read the employee ID
  int employeeId = (int) grid.DataKeys[selectedRowIndex].Value;
  // Define data objects
  SqlConnection conn;
  SqlCommand comm;
  SqlDataReader reader;
  // Read the connection string from Web.config
  string connectionString =
      ConfigurationManager.ConnectionStrings[
      "Dorknozzle"].ConnectionString;
  // Initialize connection
  conn = new SqlConnection(connectionString);
  // Create command
  comm = new SqlCommand(
      "SELECT EmployeeID, Name, Address, City, State, Zip, " +
      "HomePhone, Extension FROM Employees " +
      "WHERE EmployeeID=@EmployeeID", conn);
  // Add the EmployeeID parameter
  comm.Parameters.Add("EmployeeID", SqlDbType.Int);
```

```
comm.Parameters["EmployeeID"].Value = employeeId;
// Enclose database code in Try-Catch-Finally
try
{
  // Open the connection
  conn.Open();
  // Execute the command
  reader = comm.ExecuteReader();
  // Fill the grid with data
  employeeDetails.DataSource = reader;
  employeeDetails.DataKeyNames = new string[] {"EmployeeID"};
  employeeDetails.DataBind();
  // Close the reader
  reader.Close();
}
finally
{
  // Close the connection
  conn.Close();
}
}
```

Now, if you execute the project and select one of the employees, you should see a page like the one shown in Figure 11.10.

Styling the `DetailsView`

Displaying the data in the `DetailsView` control is easy enough, but you'll probably want to make it look a bit prettier. We'll start by changing the row headings in the left-hand column. Open `AddressBook.aspx` and modify the `DetailsView` control like this:

File: **AddressBook.aspx (excerpt)**

```
<asp:DetailsView id="employeeDetails" runat="server"
    AutoGenerateRows="False">
  <Fields>
    <asp:BoundField DataField="Address" HeaderText="Address" />
    <asp:BoundField DataField="City" HeaderText="City" />
    <asp:BoundField DataField="State" HeaderText="State" />
    <asp:BoundField DataField="Zip" HeaderText="Zip" />
    <asp:BoundField DataField="HomePhone"
        HeaderText="Home Phone" />
    <asp:BoundField DataField="Extension"
        HeaderText="Extension" />
  </Fields>
```

Figure 11.11. Viewing employee details

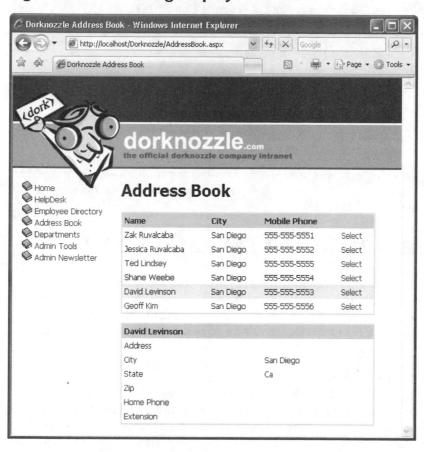

```
<HeaderTemplate>
  <%#Eval("Name")%>
</HeaderTemplate>
</asp:DetailsView>
```

As you can see, we customize the DetailsView control in a similar way to the GridView, except that this time we're dealing with fields instead of rows. We set the AutoGenerateRows property to False; then, we define the fields we want to show, and create a HeaderTemplate which displays the name of the employee in the header—we'll see what this looks like in a minute.

To further improve the appearance of the DetailsView, add this skin to Skin-File.skin:

File: **SkinFile.skin (excerpt)**

```
<asp:DetailsView runat="server" CssClass="GridMain"
    CellPadding="4" GridLines="None">
  <RowStyle CssClass="GridRow" />
  <HeaderStyle CssClass="GridHeader" />
</asp:DetailsView>
```

Here, we've defined a similar style to the `GridView` control, which will ensure that our page has a consistent appearance. Save your work, open `AddressBook.aspx` in the browser, and select an employee. You should see something similar to Figure 11.11.

We're really making progress now. There's only one problem—our employee records don't include any addresses, and at this moment there's no way to add any! Let's take care of this.

GridView and DetailsView Events

In order to use the `GridView` and `DetailsView` controls effectively, we need to know how to handle their events. In this section, we'll learn about the events raised by these controls, with an emphasis on the events that relate to editing and updating data, as our next goal will be to allow users to edit the employee details in the `DetailsView`.

Earlier, you learned how to respond to the user's clicking of the Select button by handling the `GridView`'s `SelectedIndexChanged` event. Soon you'll implement editing functionality, which you'll achieve by adding an Edit button to the `DetailsView` control. The editing features of the `GridView` and the `DetailsView` are very similar, so you can apply the same principles, and even almost the same code, to both of them.

Both the `GridView` and `DetailsView` controls support Edit command buttons, which will place Edit buttons in the control when the page loads. Once one of the Edit buttons has been clicked, the row (in case of `GridView`) or the entire form (in case of `DetailsView`) will become editable, and instead of an Edit button, users will see Update and Cancel buttons.

These features are pretty amazing, because you can achieve this "edit mode" without writing any HTML at all: the columns know how to render their editable modes by themselves. If you don't like their default edit mode appearances, you can customize them using templates.

Before writing any code, let's see what this edit mode looks like. Figure 11.12 shows a GridView control with one of its rows in edit mode.

Figure 11.12. GridView in edit mode

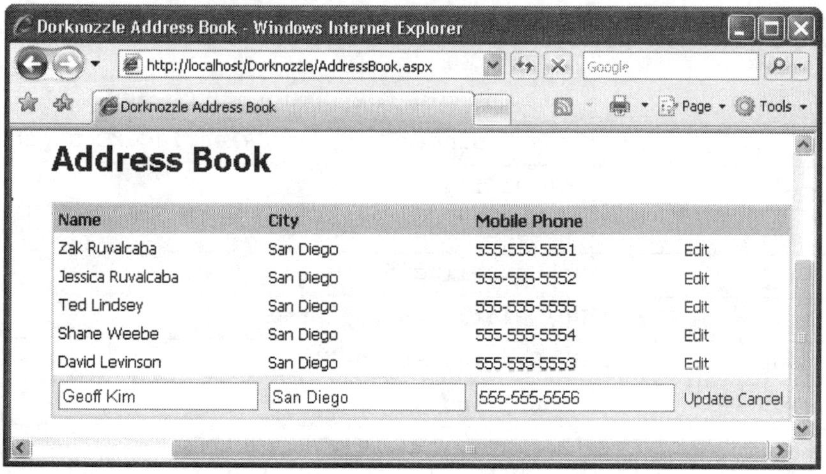

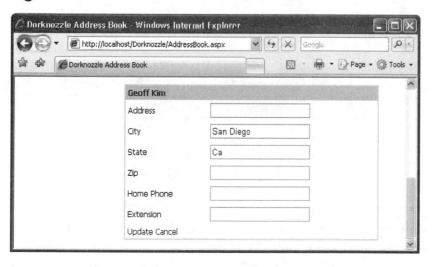

Figure 11.13 shows a DetailsView control in edit mode.

Figure 11.13. DetailsView in edit mode

When command buttons such as Edit are clicked, they raise events that we can handle on the server side. The GridView supports more kinds of command buttons, each of which triggers a certain event that we can handle. The action types and the events they trigger are listed in Table 11.1.

Table 11.1. GridView action types and the events they trigger

Action	Events triggered when clicked
Select	SelectedIndexChanging, SelectIndexChanged
Edit	RowEditing
Update	RowUpdating, RowUpdated
Cancel	RowCancelingEdit
Delete	RowDeleting, RowDeleted
(sorting buttons)	RowSorting, RowSorted
(custom action)	RowCommand

The DetailsView control, on the other hand, has buttons and events that refer to *items*, rather than *rows*, which makes sense when you realize that DetailsView is used to display the items in one record, while GridView displays a few items from many records. The DetailsView action types, and the events they generate, are listed in Table 11.2.

Table 11.2. DetailsView action types and the events they trigger

Action	Events triggered when clicked
(paging controls)	PageIndexChanging, PageIndexChanged
Delete	ItemDeleting, ItemDeleted
Insert	ItemInserting, ItemInserted
Edit	ModeChanging, ModeChanged
Update	ItemUpdating, ItemUpdated
Delete	RowDeleting, RowDeleted
(custom action)	ItemCommand

Notice that, except for the RowCommand (for the GridView) and the ItemCommand (for the DetailsView) events, we have events that are named in the present tense (i.e. those that end in "ing," such as SelectedIndexChanging and ItemUpdating), and events that are named in the past tense (i.e. those that end in "ed," such as `SelectIndexChanged` and `ItemUpdated`). The events that end in "ing" are fired just before their past tense counterparts, and should be handled only if you want to implement some logic to determine whether the action in question should be performed.

The "ed" events, on the other hand, should perform the actual task of the button. We saw such an event handler when we handled the `SelectIndexChanged` event of our `GridView` control. In this handler, we queried the database to get the details of the selected employee, then displayed the result in a `DetailsView` control.

If we wanted to disallow the selection of a particular employee (say, the employee with the ID 1), we could do so by setting `e.Cancel` to `False` in the `SelectIndex-Changing` event handler, as shown below:

Visual Basic

```vb
Protected Sub grid_SelectedIndexChanging(ByVal sender As Object, _
    ByVal e As GridViewSelectEventArgs) _
    Handles grid.SelectedIndexChanging
  ' Obtain the index of the selected row
  Dim selectedRowIndex As Integer = grid.SelectedIndex
  ' Read the employee ID
  Dim employeeId As Integer = _
      grid.DataKeys(selectedRowIndex).Value
  ' Cancel the selection if Employee #1 was selected
  If employeeId = 1 Then
    e.Cancel = False
  End If
End Sub
```

C#

```csharp
protected void grid_SelectedIndexChanging(object sender,
    GridViewSelectEventArgs e)
{
  // Obtain the index of the selected row
  int selectedRowIndex = grid.SelectedIndex;
  // Read the employee ID
  int employeeId = (int)grid.DataKeys[selectedRowIndex].Value;
  // Cancel the selection if Employee #1 was selected
  if (employeeId == 1)
  {
    e.Cancel = false;
  }
}
```

Where's RowEdited?

Note that, in the case of the Edit action in the GridView, there's no RowEdited event. Why not? Well, it wouldn't make much sense to have one—GridView knows what to do when an editing action is approved to take place. More specifically, when a row enters edit mode, it is displayed using the default editing style of the column. The built-in column types (such as bound columns, check box columns, and so on) have built-in editing templates, which you can customize by providing custom templates.

Entering Edit Mode

To get a better grasp on all this theory, let's look at another example. Here, we'll modify the DetailsView control to let users update employee data. To implement GridView or DetailsView editing, we can use a CommandField column.

Let's get started. Open AddressBook.aspx in the designer, click the DetailsView's smart tag, and choose Add New Column.... In the Choose a field type drop-down, select CommandField, and check the Edit/Update checkbox, as shown in Figure 11.14.

Figure 11.14. Adding the Edit/Update CommandField

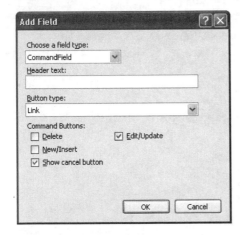

If you'd prefer to add the new column by hand, do so by adding it in Address-Book.aspx. Either way, you should end up with the following code:

File: **AddressBook.aspx (excerpt)**

```
<asp:DetailsView id="employeeDetails" runat="server"
    AutoGenerateRows="False">
  <Fields>
    <asp:BoundField DataField="Address" HeaderText="Address" />
    <asp:BoundField DataField="City" HeaderText="City" />
    <asp:BoundField DataField="State" HeaderText="State" />
    <asp:BoundField DataField="Zip" HeaderText="Zip" />
    <asp:BoundField DataField="HomePhone"
        HeaderText="Home Phone" />
    <asp:BoundField DataField="Extension"
        HeaderText="Extension" />
    <asp:CommandField ShowEditButton="True" />
  </Fields>
  <HeaderTemplate>
    <%#Eval("Name")%>
  </HeaderTemplate>
</asp:DetailsView>
```

The new item will appear in the designer as an Edit link immediately below the list of columns. If you execute the project and click that Edit link, an exception will be thrown, telling you that you didn't handle the ModeChanging event. The DetailsView control doesn't know how to switch itself to edit mode, but fortunately, it's extremely easy to write the code yourself.

To have Visual Web Developer generate the ModeChanging event signature for you, open AddressBook.aspx in Design View, select the DetailsView control, click the yellow button with the lightning symbol in the Properties window to bring up the list of the control's events, and double-click on the ModeChanging entry. This will generate an empty event handler for you, and take you straight to the function in the code-behind file. Complete the generated code like this:

Visual Basic

File: **AddressBook.aspx.vb (excerpt)**

```
Protected Sub employeeDetails_ModeChanging( _
  ByVal sender As Object, _
  ByVal e As System.Web.UI.WebControls.DetailsViewModeEventArgs) _
  Handles employeeDetails.ModeChanging
    ' Change current mode to the selected one
    employeeDetails.ChangeMode(e.NewMode)
    ' Rebind the grid
    BindDetails()
End Sub
```

```
C#                                    File: AddressBook.aspx.cs (excerpt)
protected void employeeDetails_ModeChanging(object sender,
    DetailsViewModeEventArgs e)
{
  // Change current mode to the selected one
  employeeDetails.ChangeMode(e.NewMode);
  // Rebind the grid
  BindDetails();
}
```

Execute the project and click the Edit button. This will transform the control as shown in Figure 11.15.

Figure 11.15. The `DetailsView` in edit mode

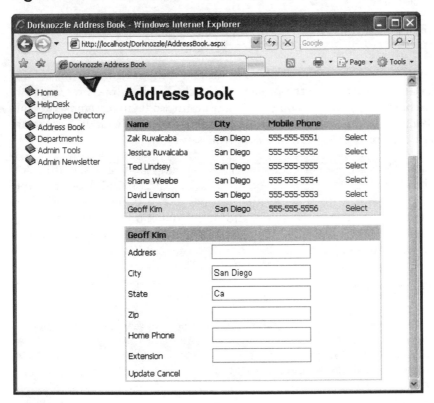

In order to understand the code in `employeeDetails_ModeChanging`, you need to know about the **display modes** of the `DetailsView` control. The `DetailsView`

control supports three display modes. You can change the current mode using its `ChangeMode` method, providing as parameter one of these values:

DetailsViewMode.ReadOnly
> This is the default mode, which is used to display data. When you execute your project, and load the details of an employee, you see those details in `ReadOnly` mode.

DetailsViewMode.Edit
> This mode is used to edit an existing record. We saw this mode in action earlier, when we clicked the Edit button.

DetailsViewMode.Insert
> We use this mode to insert a new record. It's similar to the edit mode, except all the controls are empty, so you can fill in data for a new item.

If you look at the `employeeDetails_ModeChanging`, you'll see it receives a parameter named e that is an object of class `DetailsViewModeEventArgs`. e's `NewMode` property tells us which display mode was requested by the user. Its value will be `DetailsViewMode.Edit` when the `ModeChanging` event is fired as a result of the Edit button being clicked. We pass this value to the `DetailsView` control's `ChangeMode` method, which does exactly as its name suggests: it changes the mode of the `DetailsView`. With this code, you've implemented the functionality to make both the Edit and Cancell buttons work correctly, as we'll see in an example shortly.

However, note that once you switch to edit mode, clicking the Update button will generate an error, because we still haven't handled the `ItemUpdating` event that's fired when the user tries to save changes to a record. We'll create the event handler later; next, we want to improve our existing solution using templates.

Using Templates

The built-in column types are sufficiently varied and configurable to provide for most of the functionality you're likely to need, but in cases where further customization is required, you can make the desired changes using templates. In the smart tag menu of the `GridView` and `DetailsView` controls, an option called Edit Columns (for the `GridView`) or Edit Fields (for the `DetailsView`) is available. Selecting that option opens a dialog that provides us with a great deal of control over the options for each column or field.

You'll notice a Convert this field into a TemplateField link in the dialog. Let's see how this works. Click the smart tag of your `DetailsView` control, then click Edit Fields. In the dialog that appears, select the Address field from the Selected fields list, as shown in Figure 11.16.

Figure 11.16. Editing a field's properties

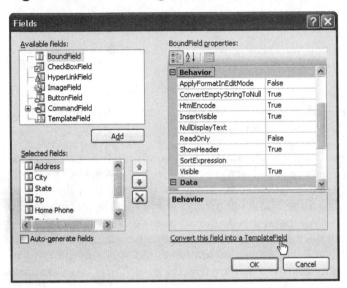

Click the Convert this field into a TemplateField link to have Visual Web Developer create a template that simulates the current functionality of the field, then click OK to close the dialog.

So, what happened? Let's switch `AddressBook.aspx` to Source View. After you convert the field to a template field, its definition will look like this:

File: **AddressBook.aspx (excerpt)**

```
<asp:DetailsView id="employeeDetails" runat="server"
    AutoGenerateRows="False">
  <Fields>
    <asp:TemplateField HeaderText="Address">
      <EditItemTemplate>
        <asp:TextBox ID="TextBox1" runat="server"
            Text='<%# Bind("Address") %>'></asp:TextBox>
      </EditItemTemplate>
      <InsertItemTemplate>
        <asp:TextBox ID="TextBox1" runat="server"
```

```
              Text='<%# Bind("Address") %>'></asp:TextBox>
    </InsertItemTemplate>
    <ItemTemplate>
      <asp:Label ID="Label1" runat="server"
          Text='<%# Bind("Address") %>'></asp:Label>
    </ItemTemplate>
  </asp:TemplateField>
  <asp:BoundField DataField="City" HeaderText="City" />
  ⋮
  <asp:CommandField ShowEditButton="True" />
 </Fields>
 <HeaderTemplate>
   <%#Eval("Name")%>
 </HeaderTemplate>
</asp:DetailsView>
```

Pretty cool, huh? Visual Web Developer did a little bit of magic for us: it replaced the `BoundField` column that used to display the address with a `TemplateField` containing an `ItemTemplate`, an `EditItemTemplate`, and an `InsertItemTemplate`. Despite these alterations, the current functionality hasn't changed: you can still execute your project and load the address book, and it will continue to work as before. The difference is that now you can easily refer to these inner controls from your code, you can easily change their appearance using custom HTML code, and, if you wish, you can replace them with totally different controls. The power is in your hands. For example, you can widen the `TextBox` controls used to edit your fields, as well as performing other kinds of customizations. You can also give specific IDs to the inner template controls, rather than using their default generic names, so you can find them easily when you need to.

Tip Beware of `ReadOnly`

Note that if you set a column as read-only (by setting the column's `ReadOnly` property to `True`) prior to its conversion, Visual Web Developer will use a `Label` control instead of a `TextBox` control in the `EditItemTemplate` for that field. Thus, when the grid enters edit mode, that particular column won't be transformed into a `TextBox`, so its read-only behavior will be conserved.

Now, convert the other fields—except for `CommandField`—to template fields. Then, we'll modify the generated code by altering the `TextBox` controls, and assigning appropriate names to our controls. To keep things simple, we're only going to make changes to the Address and City fields in the code samples provided here—you can update the others yourself.[1]

File: **AddressBook.aspx (excerpt)**

```
<asp:TemplateField HeaderText="Address">
  <EditItemTemplate>
    <asp:TextBox ID="editAddressTextBox" runat="server"
        Text='<%# Bind("Address") %>'></asp:TextBox>
  </EditItemTemplate>
  <InsertItemTemplate>
    <asp:TextBox ID="insertAddressTextBox" runat="server"
        Text='<%# Bind("Address") %>'></asp:TextBox>
  </InsertItemTemplate>
  <ItemTemplate>
    <asp:Label ID="addressLabel" runat="server"
        Text='<%# Bind("Address") %>'></asp:Label>
  </ItemTemplate>
</asp:TemplateField>
<asp:TemplateField HeaderText="City">
  <EditItemTemplate>
    <asp:TextBox ID="editCityTextBox" runat="server"
        Text='<%# Bind("City") %>'></asp:TextBox>
  </EditItemTemplate>
  <InsertItemTemplate>
    <asp:TextBox ID="insertCityTextBox" runat="server"
        Text='<%# Bind("City") %>'></asp:TextBox>
  </InsertItemTemplate>
  <ItemTemplate>
    <asp:Label ID="cityLabel" runat="server"
        Text='<%# Bind("City") %>'></asp:Label>
  </ItemTemplate>
</asp:TemplateField>
```

IMPORTANT

Updating Employee Details

To keep the code in this chapter short, we're only showing the code required to update a couple of the fields in the **Employees** table. Adding more fields is a trivial task, and the code that's needed to update all the fields is included in the code archive.

Execute your project, load the address book, select one employee, and click the Edit link to ensure everything works (and looks) as shown in Figure 11.17.

---

[1] If you're feeling lazy, you'll be pleased to hear that updating the other fields is optional for the purposes of this chapter.

Figure 11.17. The DetailsView's BoundFields have been converted to TemplateFields

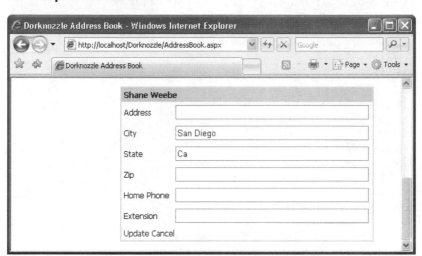

Updating DetailsView Records

Now that you have your DetailsView control in place, let's complete its functionality by making the Update link functional. To begin, we'll generate the ItemUpdating event handler. The ItemUpdating event is triggered when the Update link is clicked—an action that will occur once the user enters new data into the text boxes and is ready to commit the updated data to the database.

Open AddressBook.aspx in the designer, select the DetailsView control, and switch to the events viewer by clicking the Event button (the little lightning symbol) in the Properties window. There, double-click the ItemUpdating row to have the designer generate the employeeDetails_ItemUpdating method for you, and update the handler with the code shown below:

Visual Basic   File: **AddressBook.aspx.vb (excerpt)**

```
Protected Sub employeeDetails_ItemUpdating( _
   ByVal sender As Object, ByVal e As _
   System.Web.UI.WebControls.DetailsViewUpdateEventArgs) _
   Handles employeeDetails.ItemUpdating
 ' Read the employee ID from the DetailsView object
 Dim employeeId As Integer = employeeDetails.DataKey.Value
 ' Find the TextBox controls with updated data
 Dim newAddressTextBox As TextBox = _
```

```
      employeeDetails.FindControl("editAddressTextBox")
  Dim newCityTextBox As TextBox = _
      employeeDetails.FindControl("editCityTextBox")
  ' Extract the updated data from the TextBoxes
  Dim newAddress As String = newAddressTextBox.Text
  Dim newCity As String = newCityTextBox.Text
  ' Declare data objects
  Dim conn As SqlConnection
  Dim comm As SqlCommand
  ' Read the connection string from Web.config
  Dim connectionString As String = _
      ConfigurationManager.ConnectionStrings( _
      "Dorknozzle").ConnectionString
  ' Initialize connection
  conn = New SqlConnection(connectionString)
  ' Create command
  comm = New SqlCommand("UpdateEmployeeDetails", conn)
  comm.CommandType = Data.CommandType.StoredProcedure
  ' Add command parameters
  comm.Parameters.Add("@EmployeeID", Data.SqlDbType.Int)
  comm.Parameters("@EmployeeID").Value = employeeId
  comm.Parameters.Add("@NewAddress", Data.SqlDbType.NVarChar, 50)
  comm.Parameters("@NewAddress").Value = newAddress
  comm.Parameters.Add("@NewCity", Data.SqlDbType.NVarChar, 50)
  comm.Parameters("@NewCity").Value = newCity
  ' Enclose database code in Try-Catch-Finally
  Try
    ' Open the connection
    conn.Open()
    ' Execute the command
    comm.ExecuteNonQuery()
  Finally
    ' Close the connection
    conn.Close()
  End Try
  ' Exit edit mode
  employeeDetails.ChangeMode(DetailsViewMode.ReadOnly)
  ' Reload the employees grid
  BindGrid()
  ' Reload the details view
  BindDetails()
End Sub
```

C#   File: **AddressBook.aspx.cs (excerpt)**

```
protected void employeeDetails_ItemUpdating(object sender,
    DetailsViewUpdateEventArgs e)
```

```
{
  // Read the employee from the DetailsView object
  int employeeId = (int)employeeDetails.DataKey.Value;
  // Find the TextBox controls with updated data
  TextBox newAddressTextBox =
    (TextBox)employeeDetails.FindControl("editAddressTextBox");
  TextBox newCityTextBox =
    (TextBox)employeeDetails.FindControl("editCityTextBox");
  // Extract the updated data from the TextBoxes
  string newAddress = newAddressTextBox.Text;
  string newCity = newCityTextBox.Text;
  // Define data objects
  SqlConnection conn;
  SqlCommand comm;
  // Initialize connection
  string connectionString =
    ConfigurationManager.ConnectionStrings[
    "Dorknozzle"].ConnectionString;
  // Initialize connection
  conn = new SqlConnection(connectionString);
  // Create command
  comm = new SqlCommand("UpdateEmployeeDetails", conn);
  comm.CommandType = CommandType.StoredProcedure;
  // Add command parameters
  comm.Parameters.Add("EmployeeID", SqlDbType.Int);
  comm.Parameters["EmployeeID"].Value = employeeId;
  comm.Parameters.Add("NewAddress", SqlDbType.NVarChar, 50);
  comm.Parameters["NewAddress"].Value = newAddress;
  comm.Parameters.Add("NewCity", SqlDbType.NVarChar, 50);
  comm.Parameters["NewCity"].Value = newCity;
  // Enclose database code in Try-Catch-Finally
  try
  {
    // Open the connection
    conn.Open();
    // Execute the command
    comm.ExecuteNonQuery();
  }
  finally
  {
    // Close the connection
    conn.Close();
  }
  // Exit edit mode
  employeeDetails.ChangeMode(DetailsViewMode.ReadOnly);
  // Reload the employees grid
```

```
    BindGrid();
    // Reload the details view
    BindDetails();
}
```

This code is pretty straightforward. It starts by reading the value of the `DataKey` of the `DetailsView` object. As we saw earlier, the `DetailsView`, like the `GridView`, is able to store the ID of the record (or records) it's displaying. You'll remember that we made the `DetailsView` object aware of the `EmployeeID` data key when we bound the `DetailsView` to its data source in the `BindDetails` method. We read this information in the `ItemUpdating` event handler, like so:

Visual Basic   File: **AddressBook.aspx.vb (excerpt)**

```
' Read the employee from the DetailsView object
Dim employeeId As Integer = employeeDetails.DataKey.Value
```

C#   File: **AddressBook.aspx.cs (excerpt)**

```
// Read the employee from the DetailsView object
int employeeId = (int) employeeDetails.DataKey.Value;
```

The next step is to find the `TextBox` objects that contain the updated data. We do this using the `FindControl` method, as we've seen previously. After we obtain the control references, we obtain the string values that we're interested in simply by reading their `Text` properties, as is shown in the following code snippets:

Visual Basic   File: **AddressBook.aspx.vb (excerpt)**

```
' Find the TextBox controls with updated data
Dim newAddressTextBox As TextBox = _
    employeeDetails.FindControl("editAddressTextBox")
Dim newCityTextBox As TextBox = _
    employeeDetails.FindControl("editCityTextBox")
' Extract the updated data from the TextBoxes
Dim newAddress As String = newAddressTextBox.Text
Dim newCity As String = newCityTextBox.Text
```

C#   File: **AddressBook.aspx.cs (excerpt)**

```
// Find the TextBox controls with updated data
TextBox newAddressTextBox =
    (TextBox)employeeDetails.FindControl("editAddressTextBox");
TextBox newCityTextBox =
    (TextBox)employeeDetails.FindControl("editCityTextBox");
// Extract the updated data from the TextBoxes
string newAddress = newAddressTextBox.Text;
string newCity = newCityTextBox.Text;
```

Figure 11.18. Updating an employee's address and city

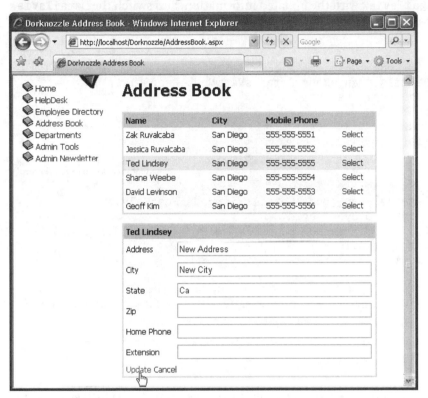

Next, we call a stored procedure to take care of the database update. To create this stored procedure, run the following script in SQL Server Management Studio:

```
CREATE PROCEDURE UpdateEmployeeDetails
(
  @EmployeeID Int,
  @NewAddress nvarchar(50),
  @NewCity nvarchar(50)
)
AS
UPDATE Employees
SET Address = @NewAddress, City = @NewCity
WHERE EmployeeID = @EmployeeID
```

In the last part of `employeeDetails_ItemUpdating`, we rebind both the `GridView` and the `DetailsView` with the updated information, and switch the `DetailsView` back to its read-only state:

Visual Basic   File: **AddressBook.aspx.vb (excerpt)**

```
' Exit edit mode
employeeDetails.ChangeMode(DetailsViewMode.ReadOnly)
' Reload the employees grid
BindGrid()
' Reload the details view
BindDetails()
```

C#   File: **AddressBook.aspx.cs (excerpt)**

```
// Exit edit mode
employeeDetails.ChangeMode(DetailsViewMode.ReadOnly);
// Reload the employees grid
BindGrid();
// Reload the details view
BindDetails();
```

The code is ready to be executed now! Try updating the addresses of your employees to ensure the feature works correctly—it should display as shown in Figure 11.18.

Summary

As we've seen throughout this chapter, `GridViews` and `DetailsViews` provide enormous flexibility and power in terms of presenting database data dynamically within the browser. In these pages, we learned how to create both of these data controls and bind data to them. We also learned how to customize the appearance of elements using templates and styles, and saw how various commands allow us to select and update items. You can use these techniques to add new records, and update existing ones.

The next chapter will begin to introduce you to advanced programming topics, as we investigate even more possibilities for data binding the `DetailsView` control to allow for the editing, updating, and insertion of new records with minimal coding effort. We'll also have a chance to explore the topic of code-free data binding in that chapter.

12

Advanced Data Access

In the last three chapters, you learned some of the important concepts of data access and presentation. You learned how to use the `SqlConnection` class to establish a connection to the database, you learned how to use the `SqlCommand` class to execute a query on a database table, and you learned how to return the results of the command into an `SqlDataReader` for use within the application.

In this chapter, we'll discuss the alternatives to using the `SqlDataReader` object for retrieving data from your database. For starters, it's important to understand that `SqlDataReader` has both advantages and disadvantages. The two main points you need to keep in mind about `SqlDataReader` are:

❏ `SqlDataReader` represents the fastest method available to read data from the data source.

❏ `SqlDataReader` only allows read-only, forward-only access to data.

In other words, the `SqlDataReader` achieves very high performance at the cost of providing a direct connection to the data source. It doesn't store the data locally, so after it reads one record and moves to the next one, there's no way to go back. The `SqlDataReader` basically offers an input data stream, which you can read in the order in which it was sent, but which you are unable to modify.

However, `SqlDataReader` isn't the only means of getting to your data, and in many scenarios, it makes sense to use one of the two popular alternatives:

1. The first alternative involves using the new ADO.NET data source controls, which are tightly integrated with the `GridView` and `DetailsView` controls, and allow you to implement reading, updating, deleting, inserting, paging, and sorting features very easily—for the most part, you don't even need to write any code!

2. The second alternative involves using the `SqlDataAdapter` class in conjunction with the `DataTable`, `DataView`, and `DataSet` classes, which are able to read data from the database and store it locally, allowing you to browse, filter, and sort data in your code without leaving a connection to the database open. This method occupies more memory on the server that runs your application, and means that fewer of Visual Web Developer's automated features are available to you (you have to write more code!), but it does give you more flexibility in terms of what you can do with your data.

In this chapter, you'll learn how to use both of these alternate data access methods.

Using Data Source Controls

The .NET framework offers five **data source controls**: `SqlDataSource`, `AccessDataSource`, `ObjectDataSource`, `XmlDataSource`, and `SiteMapDataSource`. These objects enable automatic connection to various data sources, and provide easy ways to read or modify your database using data-bound controls.

❑   `SqlDataSource` allows you to connect to any data source that has an ADO.NET data provider. The default providers that ship with .NET 2.0 are `SqlClient`, `OracleClient`, `OleDb`, and `Odbc`. Even though the name of the class is `SqlDataSource`, the fact that its name begins with *Sql* doesn't meant it works only with SQL Server—it's really very flexible. This is the data source we'll work with in this chapter.

❑   `AccessDataSource` is the data source object we use to connect to Access databases.

❑   `ObjectDataSource` allows us to connect to custom data access classes, and is appropriate when we're creating complex application architectures.

❑   `XmlDataSource` knows how to connect to XML files.

❑ `SiteMapDataSource` knows how to connect to a sitemap data source, and can be used to generate sitemaps. We worked a little with this data source control in Chapter 4.

You can find these controls in the Data tab of Visual Web Developer's Toolbox, as Figure 12.1 shows.

Figure 12.1. The Data Source Controls in the Toolbox

In Chapter 11, we implemented the functionality required to show employee details in the Dorknozzle address book page (`AddressBook.aspx`). We used the `SqlDataReader` class for the task, which means we've achieved the best possible performance. However, we wrote quite a bit of code to implement the viewing and editing features for that page, and we'd need to do even more hand coding to implement paging, sorting, and inserting features.

This time, to make it easier on our fingers, we'll use the `SqlDataSource` object instead. This object can automate many tasks for us, and while it may not always provide the best performance or the greatest flexibility, it's important that we know how to use it, because it can come in very handy for quick programming tasks.

Binding the `GridView` to a `SqlDataSource`

We'll start by binding the `GridView` control in `AddressBook.aspx` to a `SqlDataSource`; we'll deal with the `DetailsView` control later. Since the data sources work with different SQL queries, we'll need to create two data sources: one that reads all employees (to populate the `GridView`), and one that reads the details of one employee (to populate the `DetailsView`).

Let's start by deleting all the code in the code-behind file (`AddressBooks.aspx.vb` or `AddressBook.aspx.cs`). Yes, you've read this correctly: we're starting from scratch! As you'll see, we can implement a large number of features without any code at all when using the `SqlDataSource` class. Leave your code-behind files like this:

Visual Basic   File: **AddressBook.aspx.vb (excerpt)**

```
Imports System.Data.SqlClient
Partial Class AddressBook
    Inherits System.Web.UI.Page
End Class
```

C#   File: **AddressBook.aspx.cs (excerpt)**

```
using System;
using System.Data;
using System.Configuration;
using System.Collections;
using System.Web;
using System.Web.Security;
using System.Web.UI;
using System.Web.UI.WebControls;
using System.Web.UI.WebControls.WebParts;
using System.Web.UI.HtmlControls;
using System.Data.SqlClient;
public partial class AddressBook : System.Web.UI.Page
{
}
```

If you're using C#, you'll also need to delete the event handler declarations from `AddressBook.aspx`. Remove the `OnSelectedIndexChanged` property from the `GridView` control, and the `OnModeChanging` and `OnItemUpdating` properties from the `DetailsView` control.

Open `AddressBook.aspx` in Design View, and drag the `SqlDataSource` control from the Toolbox (it's located under the Data tab) onto the form. You can place it anywhere you like—the location isn't relevant because the control doesn't display in the browser. Of course, it will appear in the Design View, as Figure 12.2 shows.

Figure 12.2. `AddressBook.aspx` with an `SqlDataSource` control

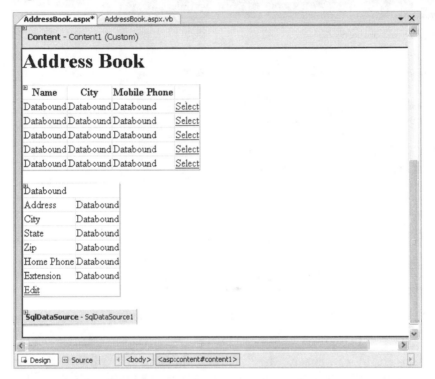

Rename the object `employeesDataSource`. In Source View, the code for the new control should look like this:

File: **AddressBook.aspx (excerpt)**

```
<asp:SqlDataSource id="employeesDataSource" runat="server">
</asp:SqlDataSource>
```

Switch back to Design View, click the `SqlDataSource` control's smart tag, and select Configure Data Source. A dialog will appear, giving us the opportunity to provide the details of the data source. In the first page of the dialog, we specify the data connection we want to use. If we hadn't already added the Dorknozzle connection string to the `Web.config` file, we could have clicked the New Connection... button, and used the wizard to add a connection string to `Web.config`.

However, as we've already set up the connection string, we simply choose it from the drop-down list, as shown in Figure 12.3.

Figure 12.3. Specifying the connection string

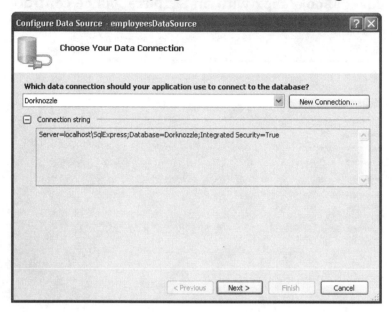

After we've selected the Dorknozzle connection, we click Next. This is where the fun begins!

In the next screen, we can specify the database table and the columns that we want our data source object to handle. Select the `Employees` table, and check the following columns: `EmployeeID`, `Name`, `City`, and `MobilePhone`, as depicted in Figure 12.4.

Click the ORDER BY... button and select the `Name` column (or any other column by which you want to sort your employees), as illustrated in Figure 12.5.

Figure 12.4. Choosing columns

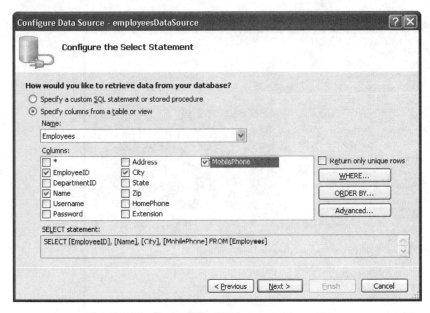

Figure 12.5. Specifying an ORDER BY clause

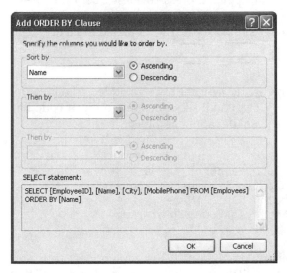

Figure 12.6. Testing the data source

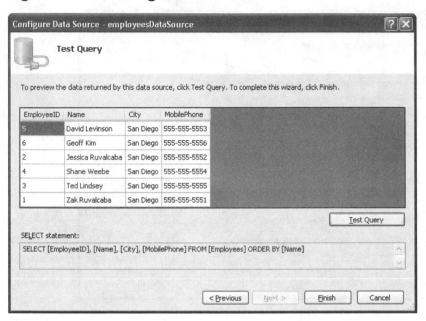

Click OK, then Next. In the dialog that appears, press the Test Query button to test that the query will work with this data source. If everything worked well, you should be shown a list of employees similar to the one depicted in Figure 12.6.

Finally, click Finish.

Before we move on, let's take a look at the new code we've added to **Address-Book.aspx**. If you switch to Source View, you'll see that quite a bit of code has been created for you. Let's look at the **SqlDataSource** object first:

File: **AddressBook.aspx (excerpt)**

```
<asp:SqlDataSource id="employeesDataSource" runat="server"
    ConnectionString="<%$ ConnectionStrings:Dorknozzle %>"
    SelectCommand="SELECT [EmployeeID], [Name], [City],
        [MobilePhone] FROM [Employees] ORDER BY [Name]">
</asp:SqlDataSource>
```

This object is amazing in its simplicity, yet the **GridView** can connect to it and display the required data with very little additional effort. Let's use this **SqlDataSource** object to populate the **GridView**.

In `AddressBook.aspx`, use either Source View or the Properties window in Design View to set the following properties of the `GridView` control:

Table 12.1. Properties to set for the `GridView` control

Property	Value
DataSourceID	employeesDataSource
DataKeyNames	EmployeeID
AllowPaging	True
AllowSorting	True
PageSize	3

Don't Overwrite the Columns!

If you set the `DataSourceID` property in Design View, Visual Web Developer will ask if you'd like to clear the column data and replace it with that from the data source, as Figure 12.7 illustrates. Make sure you choose No, because we're happy with the columns we decided to display when creating the grid in Chapter 11.

Figure 12.7. We're not refreshing the `GridView` fields

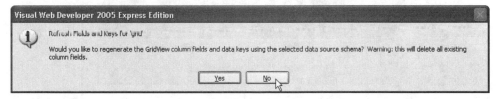

`PageSize` specifies the number of records the `GridView` should display on every page of products. Normally, we'd want this number to be greater than three, but we've set it to a low number here so that we can test the paging functionality. `AllowPaging` enables `GridView`'s paging functionality, which will cause (working) paging links to be displayed. When we set `AllowSorting` to `True`, the column names become links that users can click to sort the data on the basis of that field.

Let's also deal with style issues by adding the line below to the skin file, `Skin-File.skin`. The `PagerStyle` defines the style used by the cells that contain the paging buttons; we'll see these buttons in a moment.

File: **SkinFile.skin** (excerpt)

```
<asp:GridView runat="server" CssClass="GridMain" CellPadding="4"
    GridLines="None">
  <RowStyle CssClass="GridRow" />
  <SelectedRowStyle CssClass="GridSelectedRow" />
  <HeaderStyle CssClass="GridHeader" />
  <PagerStyle CssClass="GridRow" />
</asp:GridView>
<asp:DetailsView runat="server" CssClass="GridMain"
    CellPadding="4" GridLines="None">
  <RowStyle CssClass="GridRow" />
  <HeaderStyle CssClass="GridHeader" />
  <PagerStyle CssClass="GridRow" />
</asp:DetailsView>
```

Execute the project. If everything goes well, you should see a functional `GridView`, with working paging buttons, like the one in Figure 12.8.

Figure 12.8. Address Book paging in action

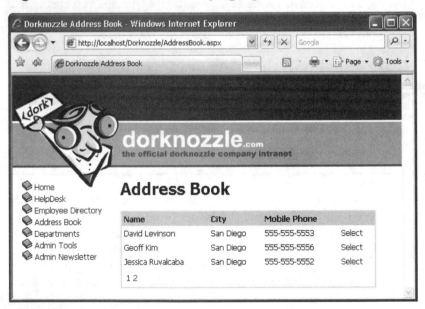

Yes, paging works, and you didn't write a single line of C# or VB code to implement it! You can even select rows—although when you do, nothing happens, because we haven't implemented any functionality for the `DetailsView` control as yet! (Remember that in the beginning of the chapter, we deleted all the code.)

Binding the `DetailsView` to a `SqlDataSource`

Here, our aim is to replicate the functionality the `DetailsView` gave us in Chapter 11, and to add functionality that will allow users to add and delete employees' records.

Let's start by adding another `SqlDataSource` control, either next to or below the existing one, in `AddressBook.aspx`. Give the new `SqlDataSource` the name `employeeDataSource`. Click its smart tag, and select Configure Data Source. The Configure Data Source wizard will appear again.

In the first screen, choose the Dorknozzle connection string. Click Next, and you'll be taken to the second screen, where there's a bit more work to do. Start by specifying the `Employees` table and checking all of its columns, as shown in Figure 12.9.

Figure 12.9. Choosing fields

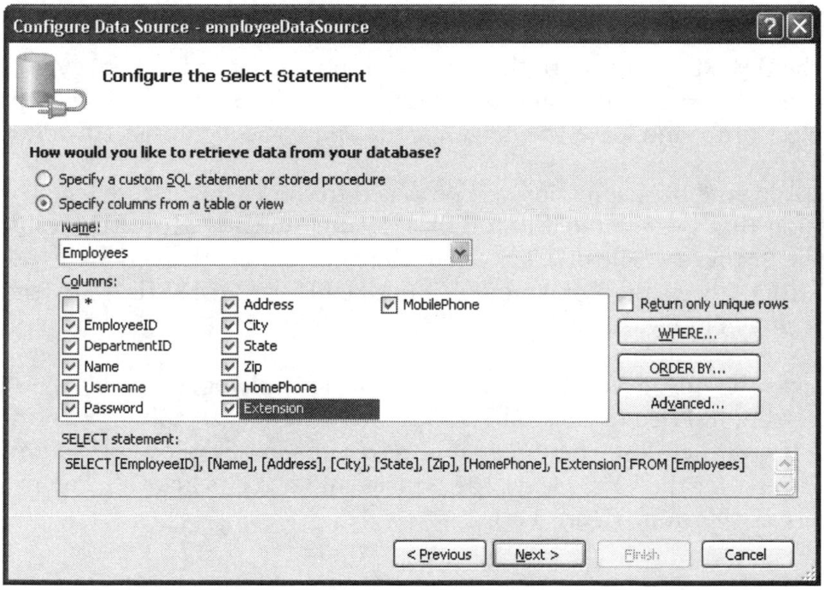

Figure 12.10. Creating a new condition

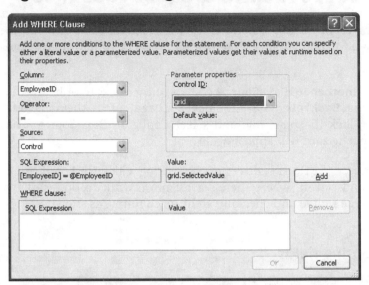

Next, click the WHERE... button. In the dialog that opens, select the `EmployeeID` column, specify the = operator, and select Control in the Source field. For the Control ID select `grid`, and leave the default value empty, as Figure 12.10 shows.

Finally, click Add, and the expression will be added to the WHERE clause list. The SQL expression that's generated will filter the results on the basis of the value selected in the `GridView` control. Click OK to close the dialog, then click the Advanced... button. Check the Generate INSERT, UPDATE, and DELETE statements checkbox, as shown in Figure 12.11.

Click OK to exit the Advanced SQL Generation Options dialog, then click Next. In the next screen, feel free to click on Test Query to ensure everything's working as expected. If you click Test Query, you'll be asked for the Employee ID's type and value. Enter 1 for the value, leave the type as Int32, then click OK. The row should display as shown in Figure 12.12.

Click Finish.

Congratulations! Your new `SqlDataSource` is ready to fill your `DetailsView`. Next, we need to tie this `SqlDataSource` to the `DetailsView` and specify how we want the `DetailsView` to behave. Open `AddressBooks.aspx`, locate the `DetailsView` control and set the properties as outlined in Table 12.2.

Figure 12.11. Generating INSERT, UPDATE, and DELETE statements

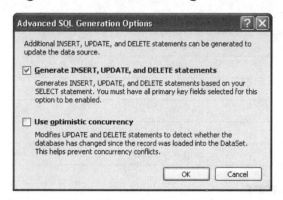

Figure 12.12. Testing the query generated for our data source

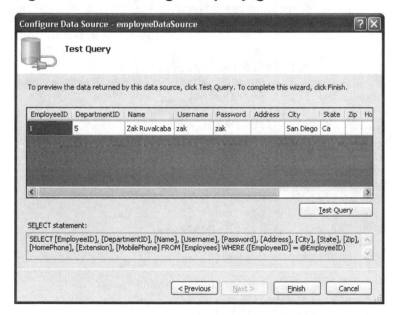

Table 12.2. Properties to set for the `DetailsView` control

Property	Value
AutoGenerateDeleteButton	True
AutoGenerateEditButton	True
AutoGenerateInsertButton	True
AllowPaging	False
DataSourceID	employeeDataSource
DataKeyNames	EmployeeID

Recreating the Columns

If you're using Design View, make sure you choose Yes when you're asked about recreating the `DetailsView` rows and data keys. If you're not using Design View, set the columns as shown here:

File: **AddressBook.aspx** (excerpt)

```
<Fields>
  <asp:BoundField DataField="EmployeeID"
      HeaderText="EmployeeID" InsertVisible="False"
      ReadOnly="True" SortExpression="EmployeeID" />
  <asp:BoundField DataField="DepartmentID"
      HeaderText="DepartmentID"
      SortExpression="DepartmentID" />
  <asp:BoundField DataField="Name" HeaderText="Name"
      SortExpression="Name" />
  <asp:BoundField DataField="Username"
      HeaderText="Username"
      SortExpression="Username" />
  <asp:BoundField DataField="Password"
      HeaderText="Password"
      SortExpression="Password" />
  ⋮
  <asp:BoundField DataField="MobilePhone"
      HeaderText="MobilePhone"
      SortExpression="MobilePhone" />
</Fields>
```

You're ready! Execute the project, and enjoy the new functionality that you implemented without writing a single line of code! Take it for a quick spin to ensure that the features for editing and deleting users are perfectly functional!

Right now, when we add a new employee, the form looks like the one shown in Figure 12.13.

Figure 12.13. Adding a new employee

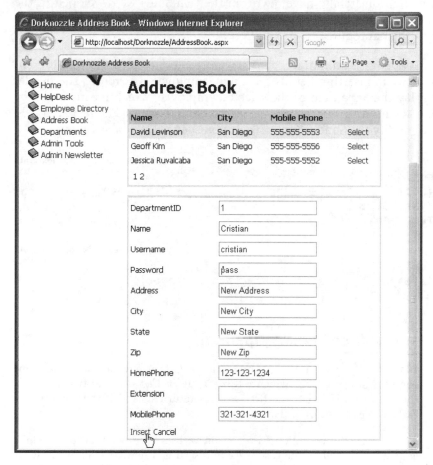

 ## Adding Users the Easy Way

If you want to be able to add new employees through this form, the easiest way to do so is to leave in all the required columns; otherwise, you'll get an error when you try to add a new employee without specifying values for the NOT NULL columns. If you don't need inserting features, and you want to keep the list of details short, you can simply remove the unwanted columns from the list.

Before we discuss exactly what's happening here, and how the functionality works, let's implement a few small improvements.

If you agreed to let Visual Web Developer generate the `DetailsView` columns for you, it will automatically have rewritten the templates we developed in the last chapter, and added `BoundField` controls for each of the columns you're reading from the data source.

The `HeaderTemplate` is still intact, but we want to update it to show a different display when we're inserting details for a new employee. Currently, the header is set to display the `Name` field of the selected employee, which means it will be empty when we insert a new employee (as you could see in Figure 12.13). To change this, modify the `HeaderTemplate` of your `DetailsView` as follows:

Visual Basic   File: **AddressBook.aspx (excerpt)**

```
<HeaderTemplate>
  <%#IIf(Eval("Name") = Nothing, "Adding New Employee", _
    Eval("Name"))%>
</HeaderTemplate>
```

C#   File: **AddressBook.aspx (excerpt)**

```
<HeaderTemplate>
  <%#Eval("Name") == null ? "Adding New Employee" :
    Eval("Name")%>
</HeaderTemplate>
```

IIf and the Ternary Operator

IIf (in VB) and the ternary operator (in C#) receive as parameters one conditional expression (which returns `True` or `False`), and two values. If the condition is `True`, the first value is returned, and if the condition is `False`, the second value is returned.

In our case, the conditional expression verifies whether the `Name` field is empty, which will be the case if we're inserting a new row. So, when we're inserting a new row, we display "Adding New Employee" in the `DetailsView`'s header; otherwise, we display the name of the employee whose details are being edited.

Now, when we insert a new employee record, `DetailsView` will display "Adding New Employee" in its header; when we're editing or displaying an existing employee's details, it will display the name of that employee, as Figure 12.14 shows.

Figure 12.14. Adding a new employee, and displaying the new header

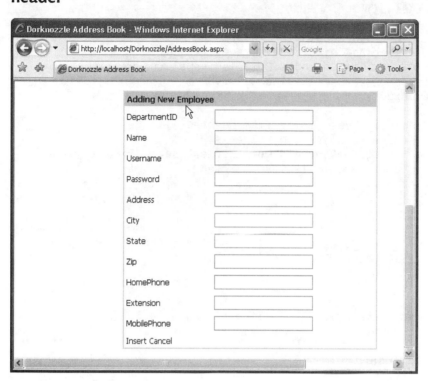

One minor hitch with this solution is that the GridView isn't instantly updated when we make a change using the DetailsView control. Try modifying the name of a user; even after you press the Update link in the DetailsView, the GridView will still show the old value. Only after you reload the page will the data be displayed correctly by the GridView.

This issue occurs because the GridView is populated before the DetailsView updates the database. To avoid this problem, we could use a simple workaround that forces the GridView to update itself in response to the occurrence of certain events raised by the DetailsView control. These events are ItemUpdated, Item-Deleted, and ItemInserted. Use Visual Web Developer to generate the event handlers for these events, and update the code like this:

Visual Basic   File: **AddressBook.aspx.vb (excerpt)**

```
Protected Sub employeeDetails_ItemUpdated( _
   ByVal sender As Object, ByVal e As _
```

```
      System.Web.UI.WebControls.DetailsViewUpdatedEventArgs) _
      Handles employeeDetails.ItemUpdated
  grid.DataBind()
End Sub
Protected Sub employeeDetails_ItemDeleted( _
    ByVal sender As Object, ByVal e As _
    System.Web.UI.WebControls.DetailsViewDeletedEventArgs) _
    Handles employeeDetails.ItemDeleted
  grid.DataBind()
End Sub
Protected Sub employeeDetails_ItemInserted( _
    ByVal sender As Object, ByVal e As _
    System.Web.UI.WebControls.DetailsViewInsertedEventArgs) _
    Handles employeeDetails.ItemInserted
  grid.DataBind()
End Sub
```

C#   File: **AddressBook.aspx.cs (excerpt)**

```
protected void employeeDetails_ItemUpdated(object sender,
    DetailsViewUpdatedEventArgs e)
{
  grid.DataBind();
}
protected void employeeDetails_ItemDeleted(object sender,
    DetailsViewDeletedEventArgs e)
{
  grid.DataBind();
}
protected void employeeDetails_ItemInserted(object sender,
    DetailsViewInsertedEventArgs e)
{
  grid.DataBind();
}
```

Now your GridView and DetailsView controls will be permanently synchronized.

The last improvement we'll make is to add an Add New Employee button to the page. Right now, we can only add new employees if we select an employee from the GridView, but this isn't exactly an intuitive way to work! Let's add a button that will make the DetailsView control display in insert mode when it's clicked by a user.

Figure 12.15. The Add New Employee button

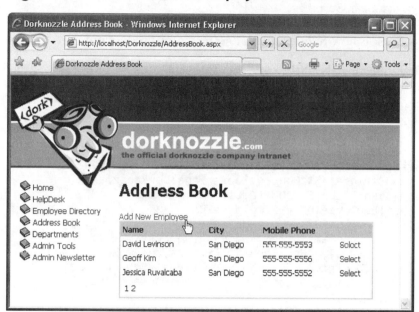

Add the new button above the grid like this:

File: **AddressBook.aspx (excerpt)**

```
<h1>Address Book</h1>
<asp:LinkButton id="addEmployeeButton" runat="server"
    Text="Add New Employee" /><br />
<asp:GridView id="grid" runat="server" …
```

Double-click the button in Design View, and fill in its `Click` event handler like this:

Visual Basic   File: **AddressBook.aspx.vb (excerpt)**

```
Protected Sub addEmployeeButton_Click(ByVal sender As Object, _
    ByVal e As System.EventArgs) Handles addEmployeeButton.Click
  employeeDetails.ChangeMode(DetailsViewMode.Insert)
End Sub
```

C#   File: **AddressBook.aspx.cs (excerpt)**

```
protected void addEmployeeButton_Click(object sender, EventArgs e)
{
  employeeDetails.ChangeMode(DetailsViewMode.Insert);
}
```

Our new button (shown in Figure 12.15) will cause the DetailsView to display in insert mode when clicked.

Your Address Book is now fully featured, and ready for production!

What's really interesting about the code that was generated for us in this section is the definition of the employeeDataSource. Since this data source needs to store the details of selecting, deleting, updating, and inserting rows, it looks significantly bigger than the employeesDataSource:

File: **AddressBook.aspx (excerpt)**

```
<asp:SqlDataSource ID="employeeDataSource" runat="server"
    ConnectionString="<%$ ConnectionStrings:Dorknozzle %>"
    DeleteCommand="DELETE FROM [Employees]
        WHERE [EmployeeID] = @EmployeeID"
    InsertCommand="INSERT INTO [Employees] ([DepartmentID],
        [Name], [Username], [Password], [Address], [City],
        [State], [Zip], [HomePhone], [Extension], [MobilePhone])
        VALUES (@DepartmentID, @Name, @Username, @Password,
        @Address, @City, @State, @Zip, @HomePhone, @Extension,
        @MobilePhone)"
    SelectCommand="SELECT [EmployeeID], [DepartmentID], [Name],
        [Username], [Password], [Address], [City], [State], [Zip],
        [HomePhone], [Extension], [MobilePhone]
        FROM [Employees]
        WHERE ([EmployeeID] = @EmployeeID)"
    UpdateCommand="UPDATE [Employees]
        SET [DepartmentID] = @DepartmentID, [Name] = @Name,
        [Username] = @Username, [Password] = @Password,
        [Address] = @Address, [City] = @City, [State] = @State,
        [Zip] = @Zip, [HomePhone] = @HomePhone,
        [Extension] = @Extension, [MobilePhone] = @MobilePhone
        WHERE [EmployeeID] = @EmployeeID">
  <DeleteParameters>
    <asp:Parameter Name="EmployeeID" Type="Int32" />
  </DeleteParameters>
  <UpdateParameters>
    <asp:Parameter Name="DepartmentID" Type="Int32" />
    <asp:Parameter Name="Name" Type="String" />
    <asp:Parameter Name="Username" Type="String" />
    <asp:Parameter Name="Password" Type="String" />
    <asp:Parameter Name="Address" Type="String" />
    <asp:Parameter Name="City" Type="String" />
    <asp:Parameter Name="State" Type="String" />
    <asp:Parameter Name="Zip" Type="String" />
```

```
      <asp:Parameter Name="HomePhone" Type="String" />
      <asp:Parameter Name="Extension" Type="String" />
      <asp:Parameter Name="MobilePhone" Type="String" />
      <asp:Parameter Name="EmployeeID" Type="Int32" />
    </UpdateParameters>
    <SelectParameters>
      <asp:ControlParameter ControlID="grid" Name="EmployeeID"
          PropertyName="SelectedValue" Type="Int32" />
    </SelectParameters>
    <InsertParameters>
      <asp:Parameter Name="DepartmentID" Type="Int32" />
      <asp:Parameter Name="Name" Type="String" />
      <asp:Parameter Name="Username" Type="String" />
      <asp:Parameter Name="Password" Type="String" />
      <asp:Parameter Name="Address" Type="String" />
      <asp:Parameter Name="City" Type="String" />
      <asp:Parameter Name="State" Type="String" />
      <asp:Parameter Name="Zip" Type="String" />
      <asp:Parameter Name="HomePhone" Type="String" />
      <asp:Parameter Name="Extension" Type="String" />
      <asp:Parameter Name="MobilePhone" Type="String" />
    </InsertParameters>
</asp:SqlDataSource>
```

As you can see, the SqlDataSource contains the UPDATE, DELETE, and INSERT queries it needs to execute when the user performs these actions on the DetailsView. These are parameterized queries, and a data type is specified for each of the parameters, which, as you already know, is good programming practice. You might also notice that the names of the fields and tables are surrounded by square brackets ([and]). These square brackets allow us to include spaces and other special characters in table names. Since none of our field or table names contain spaces, we haven't had to worry about this issue so far, but facilitating the inclusion of spaces is a good idea.

The SqlDataSource is the perfect tool when you need to create fully featured forms such as the address book quickly and easily for smaller projects like the Dorknozzle intranet. As the DetailsView and GridView controls are tightly integrated with the data source controls, they allow us to implement a lot of functionality without writing any code.

Displaying Lists in DetailsView

We want to improve on our DetailsView by making it show a list of departments instead of department IDs. This makes sense, as it's much easier for users to select the name of a department than a department ID when they're updating or inserting the details of an employee. Figure 12.16 shows how the page will look once we've created this functionality.

Figure 12.16. Viewing the Department drop-down list in DetailsView

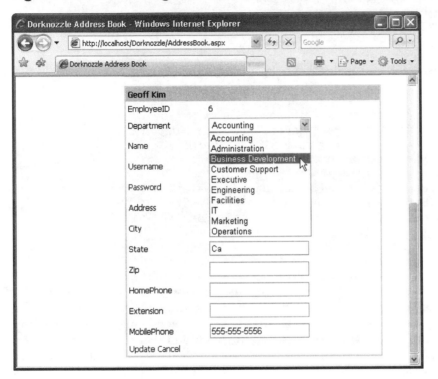

Start by adding a new SqlDataSource control beside the two existing data source controls in AddressBook.aspx. Name the control departmentsDataSource, click its smart tag, and select Configure Data Source. In the first screen, select the Dorknozzle connection, then click Next. Specify the Departments table and select both of its columns, as shown in Figure 12.17.

Click Next, then Finish to save the data source configuration. The definition of your new data source control will look like this:

File: **AddressBook.aspx (excerpt)**

```
<asp:SqlDataSource id="departmentsDataSource" runat="server"
    ConnectionString="<%$ ConnectionStrings:Dorknozzle %>"
```

Figure 12.17. Specifying the Departments data source

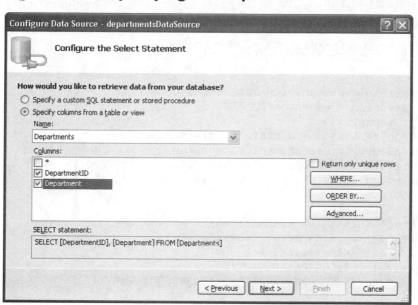

```
SelectCommand="SELECT [DepartmentID], [Department]
FROM [Departments]" />
```

Now, with AddressBook.aspx open in Design View, click the DetailsView control's smart tag, select Edit Fields, and transform the Department ID Bound-Field into a TemplateField—you learned how to do this back in Chapter 11. Now, switch to Source View, and locate the Department ID TemplateField that you just generated. It should look something like this:

File: **AddressBook.aspx (excerpt)**

```
<asp:TemplateField HeaderText="DepartmentID"
    SortExpression="DepartmentID">
 <EditItemTemplate>
   <asp:TextBox ID="TextBox1" runat="server"
       Text='<%# Bind("DepartmentID") %>'></asp:TextBox>
 </EditItemTemplate>
 <InsertItemTemplate>
   <asp:TextBox ID="TextBox1" runat="server"
       Text='<%# Bind("DepartmentID") %>'></asp:TextBox>
 </InsertItemTemplate>
 <ItemTemplate>
   <asp:Label ID="Label1" runat="server"
```

```
        Text='<%# Bind("DepartmentID") %>'></asp:Label>
  </ItemTemplate>
</asp:TemplateField>
```

Modify this generated template as highlighted below:

File: **AddressBook.aspx (excerpt)**

```
<asp:TemplateField HeaderText="Department"
    SortExpression="DepartmentID">
  <EditItemTemplate>
    <asp:DropDownList id="didDdl" runat="server"
        DataSourceID="departmentsDataSource"
        DataTextField="Department" DataValueField="DepartmentID"
        SelectedValue='<%# Bind("DepartmentID") %>' />
  </EditItemTemplate>
  <InsertItemTemplate>
    <asp:DropDownList ID="didDdl" runat="server"
        DataSourceID="departmentsDataSource"
        DataTextField="Department"
        DataValueField="DepartmentID"
        SelectedValue='<%# Bind("DepartmentID") %>' />
  </InsertItemTemplate>
  <ItemTemplate>
    <asp:DropDownList ID="didDdl" runat="server"
        DataSourceID="departmentsDataSource"
        DataTextField="Department"
        DataValueField="DepartmentID"
        SelectedValue='<%# Bind("DepartmentID") %>'
        Enabled="False" />
  </ItemTemplate>
</asp:TemplateField>
```

When you reload your address book now, you'll see that the departments are displayed in a drop-down list. You can use that list when you're inserting and editing employee data—a feature that the intranet's users are sure to find very helpful!

More on `SqlDataSource`

The `SqlDataSource` object can make programming easier when it's used correctly and responsibly. However, the simplicity of the `SqlDataSource` control comes at the cost of flexibility and maintainability, and introduces the potential for performance problems.

The main advantage of your new `AddressBook.aspx` file is that it's incredibly easy and quick to implement, especially if you're using Visual Web Developer.

However, embedding SQL queries right into your `.aspx` files does have a major disadvantage if you intend to grow your web site: in more complex applications containing many forms that perform many data-related tasks, storing all of your SQL queries inside different `SqlDataSource` controls can degenerate very quickly into a system that's very difficult to maintain. When you're writing real-world applications, you'll want to have all the data access logic centralized in specialized classes. This way, a change to the database design would mean that you'd need to change only the data access code; if your application was written using `SqlDataSource` controls, you'd need to check each web form and update it manually.

Another disadvantage of using the `SqlDataSource` is that its sorting and paging features usually aren't as fast and efficient as they could be if you used a custom SQL query that returned the data already paged and/or sorted from the database. When we use the `GridView`'s paging feature, for example, the `SqlDataSource` control doesn't limit the number of records we read from the database. Even if only a small subset of data needs to be shown, unless customizations are implemented, the entire table will be read from the database, and a subset of the data displayed. Even if only three records need to be displayed, *all* of the records in the table will be returned.

An interesting property of `SqlDataSource` that's worth noting is `DataSourceMode`, whose possible values are `DataSet` or `SqlDataReader`. The `DataSet` mode is the default mode, and implies that the `SqlDataSource` will use a `DataSet` object to retrieve its data. We'll analyze the `DataSet` class next. The other mode is `SqlDataReader`, which makes the `SqlDataSource` use your old friend, the `SqlDataReader`, behind the scenes.

So, what is this `DataSet`? The .NET Framework has, since version 1.0, come with a number of objects—`DataSet`, `DataTable`, `DataView`, `SqlDataAdapter`, and others—that provide **disconnected** data access. So, instead of having the database return the exact data you need for a certain task in the exact order in which you need it, you can use these objects to delegate some of the responsibility of filtering and ordering the data to your C# or VB code.

Both the `DataSet` and `SqlDataReader` settings of `DataSourceMode` have advantages and disadvantages, and the optimum approach for any task will depend on the task itself. There are circumstances in which it makes sense to store the data locally, and you need to be aware of all the possibilities in order to be able to make an informed decision about which mode to use.

Working with Data Sets and Data Tables

We've been working with databases for a while now. You first learned about the `SqlDataReader`, and used it to populate your controls. Then, in the first half of this chapter, we gained first-hand experience with the data source controls, which can automate many features for you. Let's learn about one more technique you can use to get data to your visitors.

I know that all these options can be confusing at first—you need to play around with all of them before you can become an experienced ASP.NET developer!

The `DataSet` object is at the center of Microsoft's model for presenting **disconnected data**. Disconnected data (data that resides in memory and is completely independent of the data source) gives us a raft of new opportunities of developing desktop and web apps.

In Chapter 9, you learned about the role that data readers play in relation to applications and database data. Whenever we need to access data from a database, we create a connection object and a command object. These two objects are used together to create a data reader object, which we can use within our application by binding it to a data control for presentation purposes. Figure 12.18 illustrates this process.

So, what's the problem? Well, while being the fastest way to retrieve data from a database, data readers can't be used to carry out any significant work—you can't use them to sort, filter, or page through the data. As the arrows in Figure 12.18 show, data readers present a forward-only stream of data to the application: you can't go back to a previous record, or reuse that data reader somewhere else. Moreover, once a data reader has been created, it remains tied to the database. This means that you can't make multiple requests to a database using the same data reader.

Data sets, on the other hand, are much more flexible. Imagine a virtual database that you're free to use in code whenever and however you wish. That's a data set. As we'll see in the next section, data sets have all the bells and whistles that databases offer, including tables, columns, rows, relationships, and even queries! A data set is a memory-resident copy of database data, so, once a data set has been created, it can be stored in memory and its ties to the database can be broken. Then, when you need to work with the data, you don't need to re-query

Figure 12.18. Retrieving data using a data reader

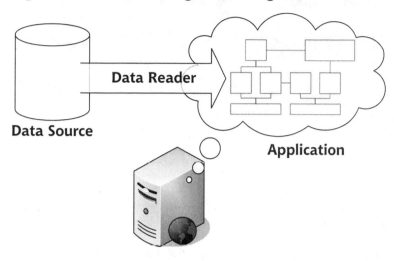

Figure 12.19. Breaking the data set's ties to the data source once it has been created

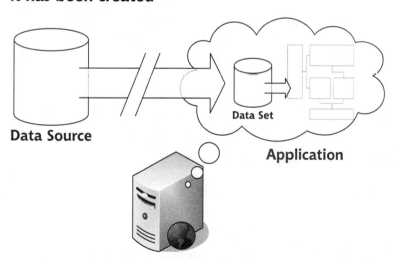

the database—you simply retrieve the data from the data set again and again. Figure 12.19 illustrates this point.

Figure 12.20. Multiple pages making multiple requests from the same data set

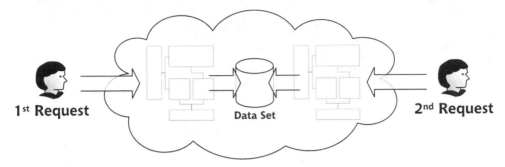

1ˢᵗ Request   Data Set   **2ⁿᵈ Request**

An even greater advantage is that data sets can be shared among multiple requests, as illustrated in Figure 12.20.

What this means is that you simply need to create the data set once per request. Once the data set has been created, it can be used by many different pages, all of which may make multiple—and even different—requests to that data set.

However, data sets require much more memory and resources than do data readers. A data reader simply keeps track of its position within the results of a query, whereas a data set can contain a local copy of an entire database. The larger the amount of data kept in the data set, the more memory the data set uses.

When deciding whether to use data readers or data sets, you need to consider the purpose for which you need the data. This decision is important, because it affects:

❑ resources consumed on the database server

❑ resources consumed on the application server

❑ the overall application architecture

If you're only reading the data, using a data reader can make sense. If you also need to update, insert, or delete data, or you need to process the data within your code, data sets might be of more help.

This section will teach you everything you need to know to begin working with data sets.

What is a Data Set Made From?

A data set comprises many parts, all of which are required for its usage. The following classes will be introduced and discussed in this section:

❑ DataSet

❑ SqlDataAdapter

❑ DataTable

❑ DataColumn

❑ DataRow

❑ DataRelation

❑ DataView

We need to use most of these classes in order to work with data sets. For instance, the SqlDataAdapter class acts as the communication point between the DataSet and the database. The data adapter knows how to fill a DataSet with data from the data source; it also knows how to submit to the data source any changes you've made to a DataSet.

Data Adapters

Of all these objects, only SqlDataAdapter depends on a particular data provider, and as such, it is interchangeable with other classes that work with data providers, including OracleDataAdapter, OleDbDataAdapter, and so on. As this class is the bridge between the database and your local data storage objects (the other classes mentioned), it makes sense for the class to be database-specific. The DataSet, DataTable, and other classes, store the data locally and don't need to be aware of the source of that data.

A DataSet will always contain at least one DataTable, but it can contain many. These DataTables contain DataColumns and DataRows. If we needed to establish a relationship between multiple DataTables within a DataSet, we'd use DataRelations. Finally, we'd create DataViews to query the DataSet.

Data Tables in ADO.NET 2.0

The `DataTable` object in ADO.NET 2.0 is more powerful than it was in previous incarnations of the technology. It can now be used independently of `DataSet`s when the full power of a `DataSet` is not required.

A `DataSet` mirrors the structure of a relational database, as Figure 12.21 shows.

Figure 12.21. The structure of a `DataSet` closely resembles that of a database

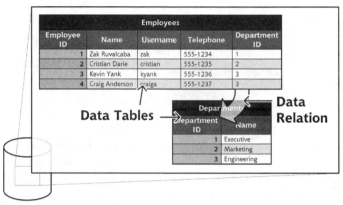

Data Set

You can see the parallel between the `DataSet`'s structure and that of a database. A database contains tables; here, the `DataSet` contains `DataTable`s. Tables in a database have columns and rows; our `DataTable`s have `DataColumn`s and `DataRow`s. When we work in a database, we establish relationships between tables; here, we'd create `DataRelation`s. The major difference between `DataSet`s and databases is that `DataSet`s are memory-resident, while a centralized database resides inside a database management system.

Let's look at how we can create a `DataSet` within code.

Binding DataSets to Controls

Now that you have some understanding of the structure of a typical `DataSet`, let's look at the process involved in creating a `DataSet` in code, and binding a `DataTable` to a control. To illustrate this example, we'll create a simple page that displays the Dorknozzle departments; we'll call this page `Departments.aspx`.

Create a new web form called `Departments.aspx`, as you have for the other pages in the Dorknozzle project. Update the generated code like this:

File: **Departments.aspx (excerpt)**

```
<%@ Page Language="VB" MasterPageFile="~/DorkNozzle.master"
    AutoEventWireup="False" CodeFile="Departments.aspx.vb"
    Inherits="Departments" title="Dorknozzle Departments" %>
<asp:Content ID="Content1"
    ContentPlaceHolderID="ContentPlaceHolder1" Runat="Server">
  <h1>Dorknozzle Departments</h1>
  <asp:GridView id="departmentsGrid" runat="server">
  </asp:GridView>
</asp:Content>
```

So far, everything looks familiar. We have a blank page based on `Dorknozzle.master`, with an empty `GridView` control called `departmentsGrid`. Our goal through the rest of this chapter is to learn how to use the `DataSet` and related objects to give life to the `GridView` control.

Switch to Design View, and double-click on an empty part of the form to generate the `Page_Load` event handler. Add references to the `System.Data.SqlClient` namespace (which contains the `SqlDataAdapter` class), and, if you're using VB, the `System.Data` namespace (which contains classes such as `DataSet`, `DataTable`, and so on) and the `System.Configuration` namespace (which contains the `ConfigurationManager` class, used for reading connection strings from `Web.config`).

Visual Basic · File: **Departments.aspx.vb (excerpt)**

```
Imports System.Data.SqlClient
Imports System.Data
Imports System.Configuration

Partial Class Departments
    Inherits System.Web.UI.Page
  Protected Sub Page_Load(ByVal sender As Object, _
      ByVal e As System.EventArgs) Handles Me.Load
  End Sub
End Class
```

C# · File: **Departments.aspx.cs (excerpt)**

```
using System;
using System.Data;
using System.Configuration;
using System.Collections;
```

```
using System.Web;
using System.Web.Security;
using System.Web.UI;
using System.Web.UI.WebControls;
using System.Web.UI.WebControls.WebParts;
using System.Web.UI.HtmlControls;
using System.Data.SqlClient;

public partial class Departments : System.Web.UI.Page
{
    protected void Page_Load(object sender, EventArgs e)
    {

    }
}
```

Next, we'll add a method called `BindGrid`, which populates the `GridView` control using an `SqlDataAdapter` and a `DataSet`. We'll call `BindGrid` from `Page_Load` only when the page is loaded for the first time. We assume that any postback events won't affect the data that's to be displayed by the grid, so we populate the grid just once, when the page loads.

Visual Basic   File: **Departments.aspx.vb (excerpt)**

```
Protected Sub Page_Load(ByVal sender As Object, _
    ByVal e As System.EventArgs) Handles Me.Load
  If Not Page.IsPostBack Then
    BindGrid()
  End If
End Sub
Private Sub BindGrid()
  ' Define data objects
  Dim conn As SqlConnection
  Dim dataSet As New DataSet
  Dim adapter As SqlDataAdapter
  ' Read the connection string from Web.config
  Dim connectionString As String = _
      ConfigurationManager.ConnectionStrings( _
      "Dorknozzle").ConnectionString
  ' Initialize connection
  conn = New SqlConnection(connectionString)
  ' Create adapter
  adapter = New SqlDataAdapter( _
      "SELECT DepartmentID, Department FROM Departments", _
      conn)
  ' Fill the DataSet
  adapter.Fill(dataSet, "Departments")
```

```
' Bind the grid to the DataSet
departmentsGrid.DataSource = dataSet
departmentsGrid.DataBind()
End Sub
```

C#   File: **Departments.aspx.cs (excerpt)**

```csharp
protected void Page_Load(object sender, EventArgs e)
{
  if (!IsPostBack)
  {
    BindGrid();
  }
}
private void BindGrid()
{
  // Define data objects
  SqlConnection conn;
  DataSet dataSet = new DataSet();
  SqlDataAdapter adapter;
  // Read the connection string from Web.config
  string connectionString =
      ConfigurationManager.ConnectionStrings[
      "Dorknozzle"].ConnectionString;
  // Initialize connection
  conn = new SqlConnection(connectionString);
  // Create adapter
  adapter = new SqlDataAdapter(
      "SELECT DepartmentID, Department FROM Departments",
      conn);
  // Fill the DataSet
  adapter.Fill(dataSet, "Departments");
  // Bind the grid to the DataSet
  departmentsGrid.DataSource = dataSet;
  departmentsGrid.DataBind();
}
```

Execute the project, and browse to your departments page, as shown in Figure 12.22.

The grid is already styled, because we have a GridView skin in place. At this point, we've achieved a level of functionality that you might otherwise have reached using SqlCommand and SqlDataReader, or the SqlDataSource; the difference is that, this time, we've used an SqlDataAdapter and a DataSet.

Figure 12.22. The Departments page

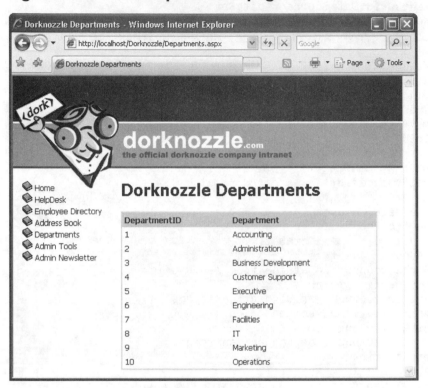

An `SqlDataAdapter` object is created in much the same way as an `SqlCommand` object. We simply provide it with an SQL statement and an `SqlConnection` object. However, it's the line that immediately follows the creation of the adapter that does all the work. The `Fill` method of the `SqlDataAdapter` fills our `DataSet` with the data returned by the SQL query. The `Fill` method accepts two parameters: the first is the `DataSet` object that needs to be filled, the second is the name of the table that we want to create within the `DataSet`.

Once the `DataSet` has been filled with data, it's simply a matter of binding the `DataSet` to the `GridView`, which we do using the same approach we'd use to bind an `SqlDataReader`.

Moving on, let's see how we can add another `DataTable` to our `DataSet`. The following code uses the `SelectCommand` property of the `SqlDataAdapter` object to create a new command on the fly, and fill the same `DataSet` with a new `DataTable` called `Employees`:

Visual Basic

```vb
' Create adapter
adapter = New SqlDataAdapter( _
    "SELECT DepartmentID, Department FROM Departments", conn)
' Fill the DataSet
adapter.Fill(dataSet, "Departments")
' Initialize the adapter with a new command
adapter.SelectCommand = New SqlCommand(_
    "SELECT EmployeeID, Name, MobilePhone FROM Employees", conn)
' Add the new table to the DataSet
adapter.Fill(dataSet, "Employees")
' Bind the grid to the DataSet
departmentsGrid.DataSource = dataSet
departmentsGrid.DataMember = "Employees"
departmentsGrid.DataBind()
```

C#

```csharp
// Create adapter
adapter = new SqlDataAdapter(
    "SELECT DepartmentID, Department FROM Departments", conn);
// Fill the DataSet
adapter.Fill(dataSet, "Departments");
// Initialize the adapter with a new command
adapter.SelectCommand = new SqlCommand(
    "SELECT EmployeeID, Name, MobilePhone FROM Employees", conn);
// Add the new table to the DataSet
adapter.Fill(dataSet, "Employees");
// Bind the grid to the DataSet
departmentsGrid.DataSource = dataSet;
departmentsGrid.DataMember = "Employees";
departmentsGrid.DataBind();
```

This code binds the Employees table of the DataSet to the GridView control by setting the GridView's DataMember property. The GridView would now appear as shown in Figure 12.23.

Figure 12.23. Displaying data from a DataTable in a GridView

EmployeeID	Name	MobilePhone
1	Zak Ruvalcaba	555-555-5551
2	Jessica Ruvalcaba	555-555-5552
3	Ted Lindsey	555-555-5555
4	Shane Weebe	555-555-5554
5	David Levinson	555-555-5553
6	Geoff Kim	555-555-5556

It's easy to imagine how quickly you could fill a page containing many `GridViews` using only one `DataSet` as the source.

As you've learned thus far, `DataTables` are elements that hold data within a `DataSet`. Just like tables in a database, `DataTables` are built from columns and rows. However, unlike tables in databases, `DataTables` reside in memory, which gives us the ability to page, sort, and filter the data in ways that just wouldn't be possible with an `SqlDataReader`.

Implementing Paging

We saw the `GridView`'s paging functionality in action earlier in this chapter. When we bound the `GridView` to the `SqlDataProvider`, the paging functionality was automatically implemented. Now that we're binding the `GridView` to a `DataSet`, there's a little more work involved in getting paging up and running. However, the effort will be more than worthwhile if performance is an issue in your application.

The task of implementing paging in a `GridView` that has been bound to an `SqlDataAdapter` is a two-step process. First, we need to set the `AllowPaging` property of the `GridView` to `True`, and set its `PageSize` value to reflect the number of items we want to see on every page. Open `Departments.aspx` in Visual Web Developer and set `AllowPaging` to `True`, and `PageSize` to 4 on the `departmentsGrid` control, as shown below:

File: **Departments.aspx (excerpt)**

```
<asp:GridView id="departmentsGrid" runat="server"
    AllowPaging="True" PageSize="4">
</asp:GridView>
```

Next, we need to handle the `PageIndexChanging` event of the `GridView` control. This event is fired when the user clicks one of the paging controls; we'll need to update the data displayed in the grid accordingly.

Double-click the `PageIndexChanging` entry in the Properties window, as shown in Figure 12.24, to have Visual Web Developer generate an empty `PageIndex-Changing` event handler for you.

Figure 12.24. Creating the `PageIndexChanging` event handler

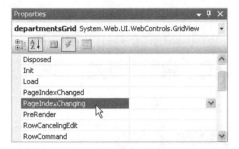

Finally, fill in the generated event handler as shown below:

Visual Basic   File: **Departments.aspx.vb (excerpt)**

```vb
Protected Sub departmentsGrid_PageIndexChanging( _
    ByVal sender As Object, _
    ByVal e As System.Web.UI.WebControls.GridViewPageEventArgs) _
    Handles departmentsGrid.PageIndexChanging
  ' Retrieve the new page index
  Dim newPageIndex As Integer = e.NewPageIndex
  ' Set the new page index of the GridView
  departmentsGrid.PageIndex = newPageIndex
  ' Bind the grid to its data source again to update its contents
  BindGrid()
End Sub
```

C#   File: **Departments.aspx.cs (excerpt)**

```csharp
protected void departmentsGrid_PageIndexChanging(object sender,
    GridViewPageEventArgs e)
{
  // Retrieve the new page index
  int newPageIndex = e.NewPageIndex;
  // Set the new page index of the GridView
  departmentsGrid.PageIndex = newPageIndex;
  // Bind the grid to its data source again to update its
  // contents
  BindGrid();
}
```

In this code, we've retrieved the index of the requested page from `e.NewPageIndex` parameter, and used its value to set the `PageIndex` property of the `GridView`. We've then bound the grid to its data source once more.

Execute the project again. When you click a paging link within the grid, the display should update quickly, as Figure 12.25 shows.

Figure 12.25. Viewing Departments with paging functionality

Storing Data Sets in View State

Now, we're able to page through our list of departments, but the code isn't anywhere near as efficient as it could be. Every time we display another page of departments in our `GridView`, we call the `BindData` method, which executes the following code in order to retrieve a list of departments:

Visual Basic   File: **Departments.aspx.vb (excerpt)**

```
' Initialize connection
conn = New SqlConnection(connectionString)
' Create adapter
adapter = New SqlDataAdapter( _
    "SELECT DepartmentID, Department FROM Departments", conn)
' Fill the DataSet
adapter.Fill(dataSet, "Departments")
```

C#   File: **Departments.aspx.cs (excerpt)**

```csharp
// Initialize connection
conn = new SqlConnection(connectionString);
// Create adapter
adapter = new SqlDataAdapter(
    "SELECT DepartmentID, Department FROM Departments", conn);
// Fill the DataSet
adapter.Fill(dataSet, "Departments");
```

Given that this list of departments is unlikely to change a great deal, wouldn't it be better if we had to query the database only once? Well, given that we now have a complete copy of the data in the Departments table, we can! Modify the BindGrid method as shown below:

Visual Basic   File: **Departments.aspx.vb (excerpt)**

```vb
Private Sub BindGrid()
  ' Define data objects
  Dim conn As SqlConnection
  Dim dataSet As New DataSet
  Dim adapter As SqlDataAdapter
  If ViewState("DepartmentsDataSet") Is Nothing Then
    ' Read the connection string from Web.config
    Dim connectionString As String = _
        ConfigurationManager.ConnectionStrings( _
        "Dorknozzle").ConnectionString
    ' Initialize connection
    conn = New SqlConnection(connectionString)
    ' Create adapter
    adapter = New SqlDataAdapter( _
        "SELECT DepartmentID, Department FROM Departments", _
        conn)
    ' Fill the DataSet
    adapter.Fill(dataSet, "Departments")
    ' Store the DataSet in view state
    ViewState("DepartmentsDataSet") = dataSet
  Else
    dataSet = ViewState("DepartmentsDataSet")
  End If
  ' Bind the grid to the DataSet
  departmentsGrid.DataSource = dataSet
  departmentsGrid.DataBind()
End Sub
```

```
C#                                           File: Departments.aspx.cs (excerpt)
private void BindGrid()
{
  // Define data objects
  SqlConnection conn;
  DataSet dataSet = new DataSet();
  SqlDataAdapter adapter;
  if(ViewState["DepartmentsDataSet"] == null)
  {
    // Read the connection string from Web.config
    string connectionString =
        ConfigurationManager.ConnectionStrings[
        "Dorknozzle"].ConnectionString;
    // Initialize connection
    conn = new SqlConnection(connectionString);
    // Create adapter
    adapter = new SqlDataAdapter(
        "SELECT DepartmentID, Department FROM Departments",
        conn);
    // Fill the DataSet
    adapter.Fill(dataSet, "Departments");
    // Store the DataSet in view state
    ViewState["DepartmentsDataSet"] = dataSet;
  }
  else
  {
    dataSet = (DataSet)ViewState["DepartmentsDataSet"];
  }
  // Bind the grid to the DataSet
  departmentsGrid.DataSource = dataSet;
  departmentsGrid.DataBind();
}
```

Here, we're using the ViewState collection to store our DataSet. The ViewState collection works a lot like the Session collection, except that instead of storing data for access by the entire application, ViewState stores data for just this one page while the user is interacting with it. If the users navigate away from this page, the data in ViewState will be lost—even if they return to the page within the same session.

In this revised version of BindGrid, we start by checking the ViewState collection for an item named DepartmentsDataSet. If no such item exists, we create a new DataSet, fill it with data from the database, as before, and store it in ViewState. If an item named DepartmentsDataSet does exist in ViewState, we simply save that item into our local variable, `dataSet`. Regardless of how the `DataSet` is loaded, we bind it to our `GridView` as we did before.

If you save your work and load the Departments page in your browser, you should see that the page runs exactly as it did previously, except that now the database is accessed only once, the first time the page loads.

Implementing Sorting

To implement sorting functionality, we need to understand a few details of the inner workings of data binding.

Technically, you can't bind a `DataSet` to a `GridView` control, because a `DataSet` can contain many tables, whereas the `GridView` control can only handle one set of rows and columns. However, by virtue of the fact that your `DataSet` has only contained a single `DataTable`, the `GridView` control has been smart enough to figure out that what you probably meant was the following:

Visual Basic
```
' Bind the grid to the DataSet
departmentsGrid.DataSource = dataSet.Tables("Departments")
departmentsGrid.DataBind()
```

C#
```
// Bind the grid to the DataSet
departmentsGrid.DataSource = dataSet.Tables["Departments"];
departmentsGrid.DataBind();
```

However, this isn't technically correct in the strictest sense, either. All of the `GridView`'s data binding is actually done through `DataView` objects. Thankfully, each `DataTable` has a `DefaultView` property, which the `GridView` will automatically use whenever you bind it to a `DataTable`. So, the following code listings have the same functionality as those we saw above:

Visual Basic
```
' Bind the grid to the DataView
departmentsGrid.DataSource = _
    dataSet.Tables("Departments").DefaultView
departmentsGrid.DataBind()
```

C#
```
// Bind the grid to the DataView
departmentsGrid.DataSource =
```

```
    dataSet.Tables["Departments"].DefaultView;
departmentsGrid.DataBind();
```

DefaultView does not Apply when Binding to a DataSet

It's interesting to note that if you bind directly to a DataSet that contains only one table, that table's DefaultView will not be used; the GridView will generate a separate DataView itself.

DataViews represent a customized view of a DataSet for sorting, filtering, searching, editing, and navigation. When binding a GridView directly to a DataTable, the DefaultView property, which is a DataView object, is accessed automatically for us. However, if we want to enable sorting, we need to access the DataView and set its sorting parameters.

The first step to enabling sorting is to set the AllowSorting property to True. When we do that, the grid's column headings become hyperlinks. Before we make those hyperlinks work, we need to handle the grid's Sorting event, where we teach the grid what to do when those links are clicked.

Set the AllowSorting property of the GridView control in Departments.aspx to True, then use the designer to generate the handler for the GridView's Sorting event. Then, complete the code as shown:

Visual Basic   File: **Departments.aspx.vb (excerpt)**

```
Protected Sub departmentsGrid_Sorting(ByVal sender As Object, _
    ByVal e As System.Web.UI.WebControls.GridViewSortEventArgs) _
    Handles departmentsGrid.Sorting
  ' Retrieve the name of the clicked column (sort expression)
  Dim sortExpression As String = e.SortExpression
  ' Decide and save the new sort direction
  If (sortExpression = gridSortExpression) Then
    If gridSortDirection = SortDirection.Ascending Then
      gridSortDirection = SortDirection.Descending
    Else
      gridSortDirection = SortDirection.Ascending
    End If
  Else
    gridSortDirection = WebControls.SortDirection.Ascending
  End If
  ' Save the new sort expression
  gridSortExpression = sortExpression
  ' Rebind the grid to its data source
  BindGrid()
End Sub
```

```
Private Property gridSortDirection()
  Get
    ' Initial state is Ascending
    If (ViewState("GridSortDirection") Is Nothing) Then
      ViewState("GridSortDirection") = SortDirection.Ascending
    End If
    ' Return the state
    Return ViewState("GridSortDirection")
  End Get
  Set(ByVal value)
    ViewState("GridSortDirection") = value
  End Set
End Property
Private Property gridSortExpression()
  Get
    ' Initial sort expression is DepartmentID
    If (ViewState("GridSortExpression") Is Nothing) Then
      ViewState("GridSortExpression") = "DepartmentID"
    End If
    ' Return the sort expression
    Return ViewState("GridSortExpression")
  End Get
  Set(ByVal value)
    ViewState("GridSortExpression") = value
  End Set
End Property
```

C#   File: **Departments.aspx.cs (excerpt)**

```
protected void departmentsGrid_Sorting(object sender,
    GridViewSortEventArgs e)
{
  // Retrieve the name of the clicked column (sort expression)
  string sortExpression = e.SortExpression;
  // Decide and save the new sort direction
  if (sortExpression == gridSortExpression)
  {
    if(gridSortDirection == SortDirection.Ascending)
    {
      gridSortDirection = SortDirection.Descending;
    }
    else
    {
      gridSortDirection = SortDirection.Ascending;
    }
  }
  else
```

```
  {
    gridSortDirection = SortDirection.Ascending;
  }
  // Save the new sort expression
  gridSortExpression = sortExpression;
  // Rebind the grid to its data source
  BindGrid();
}
private SortDirection gridSortDirection
{
  get
  {
    // Initial state is Ascending
    if (ViewState["GridSortDirection"] == null)
    {
      ViewState["GridSortDirection"] = SortDirection.Ascending;
    }
    // Return the state
    return (SortDirection) ViewState["GridSortDirection"];
  }
  set
  {
    ViewState["GridSortDirection"] = value;
  }
}
private string gridSortExpression
{
  get
  {
    // Initial sort expression is DepartmentID
    if (ViewState["GridSortExpression"] == null)
    {
      ViewState["GridSortExpression"] = "DepartmentID";
    }
    // Return the sort expression
    return (string) ViewState["GridSortExpression"];
  }
  set
  {
    ViewState["GridSortExpression"] = value;
  }
}
```

Properties

We haven't really discussed the task of defining your own properties since Chapter 4, so now might be a good time for a quick refresher. By now, you should be fairly comfortable with the idea that each of your web forms is its own class, and inherits a great deal of functionality from its parent class, **Page**. You've already dealt with quite a few of that class's features, such as its **Load** event and its **IsPostBack** property.

You can define for your class properties that can be read-only, write-only, or are able to be read and written to. When you read data from a property, its **Get** code is executed. Most of the time, this code will be quite simple, but it can be as complex as you choose to make it. In the same way, when a value is written to a property, its **Set** code is executed, which can also be quite complex if you choose to make it so.

Finally, update the **BindGrid** method to apply the sorting:

Visual Basic   File: **Departments.aspx.vb (excerpt)**

```
Private Sub BindGrid()
  ' Define data objects
  Dim conn As SqlConnection
  Dim dataSet As New DataSet
  Dim adapter As SqlDataAdapter
  If ViewState("DepartmentsDataSet") Is Nothing Then
    ' Read the connection string from Web.config
    Dim connectionString As String = _
        ConfigurationManager.ConnectionStrings( _
        "Dorknozzle").ConnectionString
    ' Initialize connection
    conn = New SqlConnection(connectionString)
    ' Create adapter
    adapter = New SqlDataAdapter( _
        "SELECT DepartmentID, Department FROM Departments", _
        conn)
    ' Fill the DataSet
    adapter.Fill(dataSet, "Departments")
    ' Store the DataSet in view state
    ViewState("DepartmentsDataSet") = dataSet
  Else
    dataSet = ViewState("DepartmentsDataSet")
  End If
  ' Prepare the sort expression using the gridSortDirection and
  ' gridSortExpression properties
  Dim sortExpression As String
  If gridSortDirection = SortDirection.Ascending Then
```

```
    sortExpression = gridSortExpression & " ASC"
  Else
    sortExpression = gridSortExpression & " DESC"
  End If
  ' Sort the data
  dataSet.Tables("Departments").DefaultView.Sort = sortExpression
  ' Bind the grid to the DataSet
  departmentsGrid.DataSource = _
      dataSet.Tables("Departments").DefaultView
  departmentsGrid.DataBind()
End Sub
```

C#   File: **Departments.aspx.cs (excerpt)**

```csharp
private void BindGrid()
{
  // Define data objects
  SqlConnection conn;
  DataSet dataSet = new DataSet();
  SqlDataAdapter adapter;
  if(ViewState["DepartmentsDataSet"] == null)
  {
    // Read the connection string from Web.config
    string connectionString =
        ConfigurationManager.ConnectionStrings[
        "Dorknozzle"].ConnectionString;
    // Initialize connection
    conn = new SqlConnection(connectionString);
    // Create adapter
    adapter = new SqlDataAdapter(
        "SELECT DepartmentID, Department FROM Departments",
        conn);
    // Fill the DataSet
    adapter.Fill(dataSet, "Departments");
    // Store the DataSet in view state
    ViewState["DepartmentsDataSet"] = dataSet;
  }
  else
  {
    dataSet = (DataSet)ViewState["DepartmentsDataSet"];
  }
  // Prepare the sort expression using the gridSortDirection and
  // gridSortExpression properties
  string sortExpression;
  if(gridSortDirection == SortDirection.Ascending)
  {
    sortExpression = gridSortExpression + " ASC";
```

```
}
else
{
  sortExpression = gridSortExpression + " DESC";
}
// Sort the data
dataSet.Tables["Departments"].DefaultView.Sort = sortExpression;
// Bind the grid to the DataSet
departmentsGrid.DataSource =
    dataSet.Tables["Departments"].DefaultView;
departmentsGrid.DataBind();
}
```

Execute the project again, and test that sorting by column works as shown in Figure 12.26.

Figure 12.26. Sorting Dorknozzle's departments

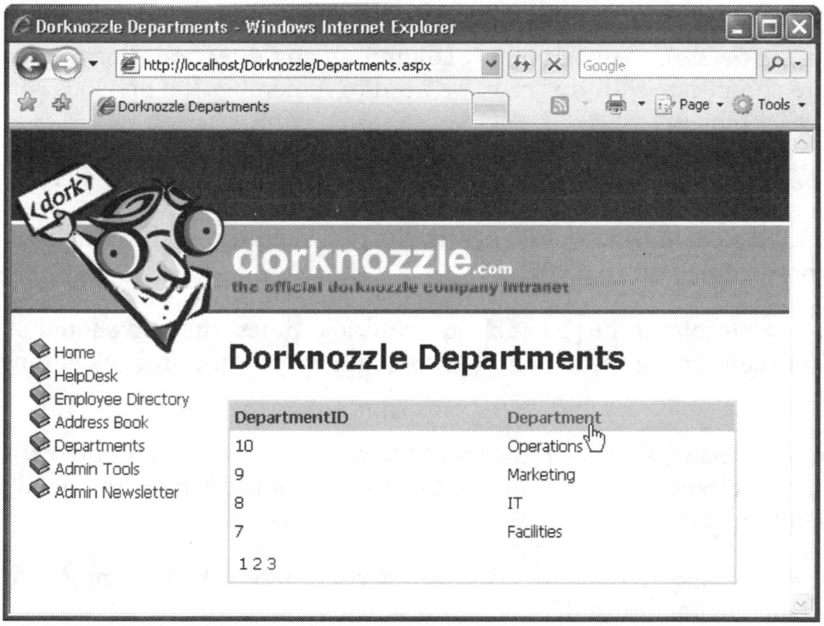

We've written a lot of code here! Let's take a look at how it works.

In order to sort the data in the grid, all we need to do is set the Sort property of the view we're displaying to *ColumnNameSortOrder*, where *ColumnName* is, of course, the name of the column we're sorting, and *SortOrder* is either ASC (for ascending) or DESC (for descending). So, if you were sorting the DepartmentID column, the Sort property would need to be set to DepartmentID ASC or Department DESC.

This property must be set before the data binding is performed, as is shown in the following code, which will sort the data by DepartmentID in descending numeric order:

Visual Basic
```
dataTable.DefaultView.Sort = "DepartmentID DESC"
departmentsGrid.DataSource = dataTable.DefaultView
departmentsGrid.DataBind()
```

C#
```
dataTable.DefaultView.Sort = "Department DESC";
departmentsGrid.DataSource = dataTable.DefaultView;
departmentsGrid.DataBind();
```

It's a pretty simple task to sort a DataView in code like this, but if we want to let users sort the data on the basis of any column, in any direction, things get a little bit more complicated. In this case, we need to remember the previous sort method between requests.

In order to be truly user-friendly, our grid should behave like this:

❑ The first time a column header is clicked, the grid should sort the data in ascending order, based on that column.

❑ When the same column header is clicked multiple times, the grid should alternate between sorting the data in that column in ascending and descending modes.

When a column heading is clicked, the grid's Sorting event is fired. In our case, the Sorting event handler (which we'll look at in a moment) saves the details of the sort column and direction in two properties:

❑ gridSortExpression retains the name of the column on which we're sorting the data (such as Department)

❑ gridSortDirection can be either SortDirection.Ascending or SortDirection.Descending

We create a sorting expression using these properties in BindGrid:

Visual Basic   File: **Departments.aspx.vb (excerpt)**

```vb
' Prepare the sort expression using the gridSortDirection and
' gridSortExpression properties
Dim sortExpression As String
If gridSortDirection = SortDirection.Ascending Then
  sortExpression = gridSortExpression & " ASC"
Else
  sortExpression = gridSortExpression & " DESC"
End If
```

C#   File: **Departments.aspx.cs (excerpt)**

```csharp
// Prepare the sort expression using the gridSortDirection and
// gridSortExpression properties
string sortExpression;
if(gridSortDirection == SortDirection.Ascending)
{
  sortExpression = gridSortExpression + " ASC";
}
else
{
  sortExpression = gridSortExpression + " DESC";
}
```

In order to implement the sorting functionality as explained above, we need to remember between client requests which column is being sorted, and whether it's being sorted in ascending or descending order. That's what the properties gridSortExpression and gridSortDirection do:

Visual Basic   File: **Departments.aspx.vb (excerpt)**

```vb
Private Property gridSortDirection()
  Get
    ' Initial state is Ascending
    If (ViewState("GridSortDirection") Is Nothing) Then
      ViewState("GridSortDirection") = SortDirection.Ascending
    End If
    ' Return the state
    Return ViewState("GridSortDirection")
  End Get
  Set(ByVal value)
    ViewState("GridSortDirection") = value
  End Set
End Property
Private Property gridSortExpression()
  Get
    ' Initial sort expression is DepartmentID
```

```
   If (ViewState("GridSortExpression") Is Nothing) Then
      ViewState("GridSortExpression") = "DepartmentID"
    End If
    ' Return the sort expression
    Return ViewState("GridSortExpression")
  End Get
  Set(ByVal value)
    ViewState("GridSortExpression") = value
  End Set
End Property
```

C#   File: **Departments.aspx.cs (excerpt)**

```csharp
private SortDirection gridSortDirection
{
  get
  {
    // Initial state is Ascending
    if (ViewState["GridSortDirection"] == null)
    {
      ViewState["GridSortDirection"] = SortDirection.Ascending;
    }
    // Return the state
    return (SortDirection) ViewState["GridSortDirection"];
  }
  set
  {
    ViewState["GridSortDirection"] = value;
  }
}
private string gridSortExpression
{
  get
  {
    // Initial sort expression is DepartmentID
    if (ViewState["GridSortExpression"] == null)
    {
      ViewState["GridSortExpression"] = "DepartmentID";
    }
    // Return the sort expression
    return (string) ViewState["GridSortExpression"];
  }
  set
  {
    ViewState["GridSortExpression"] = value;
  }
}
```

Here, we use the `ViewState` collection to store information about which column is being sorted, and the direction in which it's being sorted.

When the `Sorting` event handler fires, we set the `gridSortExpression` and `gridSortDirection` properties. The method starts by retrieving the name of the clicked column:

Visual Basic   File: **Departments.aspx.vb (excerpt)**

```vb
Protected Sub departmentsGrid_Sorting(ByVal sender As Object, _
    ByVal e As System.Web.UI.WebControls.GridViewSortEventArgs) _
    Handles departmentsGrid.Sorting
  ' Retrieve the name of the clicked column (sort expression)
  Dim sortExpression As String = e.SortExpression
```

C#   File: **Departments.aspx.cs (excerpt)**

```csharp
protected void departmentsGrid_Sorting(object sender,
    GridViewSortEventArgs e)
{
  // Retrieve the name of the clicked column (sort expression)
  string sortExpression = e.SortExpression;
```

Next, we check whether the previously-clicked column is the same as the newly-clicked column. If it is, we need to toggle the sorting direction. Otherwise, we set the sort direction to ascending:

Visual Basic   File: **Departments.aspx.vb (excerpt)**

```vb
' Decide and save the new sort direction
If (sortExpression = gridSortExpression) Then
  If gridSortDirection = SortDirection.Ascending Then
    gridSortDirection = SortDirection.Descending
  Else
    gridSortDirection = SortDirection.Ascending
  End If
Else
  gridSortDirection = WebControls.SortDirection.Ascending
End If
```

C#   File: **Departments.aspx.cs (excerpt)**

```csharp
// Decide and save the new sort direction
if (sortExpression == gridSortExpression)
{
  if(gridSortDirection == SortDirection.Ascending)
  {
    gridSortDirection = SortDirection.Descending;
  }
```

```
  else
  {
    gridSortDirection = SortDirection.Ascending;
  }
}
else
{
  gridSortDirection = SortDirection.Ascending;
}
```

Finally, we save the new sort expression to the `gridSortExpression` property, whose value will be retained in case the user keeps working (and changing sort modes) on the page:

Visual Basic   File: **Departments.aspx.vb (excerpt)**

```
' Save the new sort expression
gridSortExpression = sortExpression
' Rebind the grid to its data source
BindGrid()
```

C#   File: **Departments.aspx.cs (excerpt)**

```
// Save the new sort expression
gridSortExpression = sortExpression;
// Rebind the grid to its data source
BindGrid();
```

After we store the sort expression, we rebind the grid to its data source so that the expression will reflect the changes we've made to the `gridSortExpression` and `gridSortDirection` properties.

Filtering Data

Although we're not using it in the Dorknozzle project, it's interesting to note that the `DataView` control can filter data. Normally you'd have to apply WHERE clauses to filter the data before it reaches your application, but in certain cases you may prefer to filter data on the client.

Imagine that you wanted to display employees or departments whose names started with a certain letter. You could retrieve the complete list of employees or departments from the database using a single request, then let the user filter the list locally.

The `DataView` class has a property named `RowFilter` that allows you to specify an expression similar to that of an SQL statement's `WHERE` clause. For instance, the following filter selects all departments whose names start with "a":

Visual Basic
```
dataTable.DefaultView.RowFilter = "Department LIKE 'a%'"
```

C#
```
dataTable.DefaultView.RowFilter = "Department LIKE 'a%'";
```

Updating a Database from a Modified DataSet

So far, we've used the `DataSet` exclusively for retrieving and binding database data to controls such as the `GridView`. The reverse operation—updating data within a database from a `DataSet`—is also possible using the `Update` method of the `SqlDataAdapter`.

The `SqlDataAdapter` has the following four properties, which represent the main database commands:

❏ `SelectCommand`

❏ `InsertCommand`

❏ `UpdateCommand`

❏ `DeleteCommand`

The `SelectCommand` contains the command that's executed when we call `Fill`. The other properties are quite similar, except that you must call the `Update` method instead.

If we want to insert, update, or remove records in a database, we simply make modifications to the data in the `DataSet` or `DataTable`, then call the `Update` method of the `SqlDataAdapter`. This will automatically execute the SQL queries specified in the `InsertCommand`, `UpdateCommand`, and `DeleteCommand` properties as appropriate.

The excellent news is that ADO.NET also provides an object named `SqlCommandBuilder`, which creates the UPDATE, DELETE, and INSERT code for us.

Basically, we just need to populate the DataSet or DataTable objects (usually by performing a SELECT query), then use SqlDataAdapter and SqlCommandBuilder to do the rest of the work for us.

In the example below, we'll see a modified version of BindGrid that adds a new department, called New Department, to the database. The new lines are highlighted (note that I've simplified BindGrid by removing the code that stores and retrieves the DataSet from view state, as well as the code that sorts the results):

Visual Basic

```
Private Sub BindGrid()
  ' Define data objects
  Dim conn As SqlConnection
  Dim dataSet As New DataSet
  Dim adapter As SqlDataAdapter
  Dim dataRow As DataRow
  Dim commandBuilder As SqlCommandBuilder
  ' Read the connection string from Web.config
  Dim connectionString As String = _
      ConfigurationManager.ConnectionStrings( _
      "Dorknozzle").ConnectionString
  ' Initialize connection
  conn = New SqlConnection(connectionString)
  ' Create adapter
  adapter = New SqlDataAdapter( _
      "SELECT DepartmentID, Department FROM Departments", _
      conn)
  ' Fill the DataSet
  adapter.Fill(dataSet, "Departments")
  ' Make changes to the table
  dataRow = dataSet.Tables("Departments").NewRow()
  dataRow("Department") = "New Department"
  dataSet.Tables("Departments").Rows.Add(dataRow)
  ' Submit the changes
  commandBuilder = New SqlCommandBuilder(adapter)
  adapter.Update(dataSet.Tables("Departments"))
  ' Bind the grid to the DataSet
  departmentsGrid.DataSource = _
      dataSet.Tables("Departments").DefaultView
  departmentsGrid.DataBind()
End Sub
```

C#

```
private void BindGrid()
{
  // Define data objects
```

```
SqlConnection conn;
DataSet dataSet = new DataSet();
SqlDataAdapter adapter;
DataRow dataRow ;
SqlCommandBuilder commandBuilder;
// Read the connection string from Web.config
string connectionString =
    ConfigurationManager.ConnectionStrings[
    "Dorknozzle"].ConnectionString;
// Initialize connection
conn = new SqlConnection(connectionString);
// Create adapter
adapter = new SqlDataAdapter(
    "SELECT DepartmentID, Department FROM Departments",
    conn);
// Fill the DataSet
adapter.Fill(dataSet, "Departments");
// Make changes to the table
dataRow = dataSet.Tables["Departments"].NewRow();
dataRow["Department"] = "New Department";
dataSet.Tables["Departments"].Rows.Add(dataRow);
// Submit the changes
commandBuilder = new SqlCommandBuilder(adapter);
adapter.Update(dataSet.Tables["Departments"]);
departmentsGrid.DataSource = dataSet.Tables["Departments"];
departmentsGrid.DataBind();
}
```

If you run this code a few times, you'll have lots of "New Department" departments added to the database, as shown in Figure 12.27.

As you can see, adding a new record is a trivial task. The work that's required to submit the changes to the database requires us to write just two rows of code. The rest of the new code creates the new row that was inserted.

We create an SqlCommandBuilder object, passing in our SqlDataAdapter. The SqlCommandBuilder class is responsible for detecting modifications to the DataSet and deciding what needs to be inserted, updated, or deleted to apply those changes to the database. Having done this, SqlCommandBuilder generates the necessary SQL queries and stores them in the SqlDataAdapter for the Update method to use. It should be no surprise, then, that our next action is to call the Update method of the SqlDataAdapter object, passing in the DataTable that needs updating.

Figure 12.27. Adding many new departments

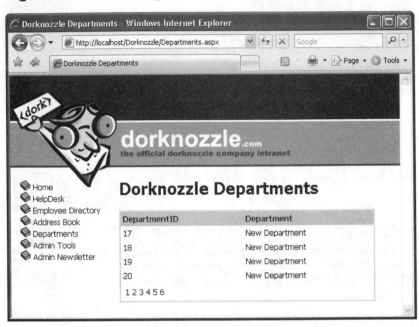

Deleting all of these new departments is also an easy task. The following code browses the `Departments DataTable` and deletes all departments with the name `New Department`:

Visual Basic
```
' Define data objects
Dim conn As SqlConnection
Dim dataSet As New DataSet
Dim adapter As SqlDataAdapter
Dim commandBuilder As SqlCommandBuilder
' Read the connection string from Web.config
Dim connectionString As String = _
    ConfigurationManager.ConnectionStrings( _
    "Dorknozzle").ConnectionString
' Initialize connection
conn = New SqlConnection(connectionString)
' Create adapter
adapter = New SqlDataAdapter( _
    "SELECT DepartmentID, Department FROM Departments", _
    conn)
' Fill the DataSet
```

```
adapter.Fill(dataSet, "Departments")
' Make changes to the table
For Each dataRow As DataRow In dataSet.Tables("Departments").Rows
  If dataRow("Department") = "New Department" Then
    dataRow.Delete()
  End If
Next
' Submit the changes
commandBuilder = New SqlCommandBuilder(adapter)
adapter.Update(dataSet.Tables("Departments"))
' Bind the grid to the DataSet
departmentsGrid.DataSource = _
    dataSet.Tables("Departments").DefaultView
departmentsGrid.DataBind()
```

Note that in the C# version the conversion to string needs to be performed explicitly:

C#

```
// Define data objects
SqlConnection conn;
DataSet dataSet = new DataSet();
SqlDataAdapter adapter;
SqlCommandBuilder commandBuilder;
// Read the connection string from Web.config
string connectionString =
    ConfigurationManager.ConnectionStrings[
    "Dorknozzle"].ConnectionString;
// Initialize connection
conn = new SqlConnection(connectionString);
// Create adapter
adapter = new SqlDataAdapter(
    "SELECT DepartmentID, Department FROM Departments", conn);
// Fill the DataSet
adapter.Fill(dataSet, "Departments");
// Make changes to the table
foreach (DataRow dataRow in dataSet.Tables["Departments"].Rows)
{
  if(dataRow["Department"].ToString() == "New Department")
  {
    dataRow.Delete();
  }
}
// Submit the changes
commandBuilder = new SqlCommandBuilder(adapter);
adapter.Update(dataSet.Tables["Departments"]);
```

```
departmentsGrid.DataSource = dataSet.Tables["Departments"];
departmentsGrid.DataBind();
```

Execute this command, and all departments called New Department will be removed.

Summary

This chapter has given us the chance to explore some more important concepts of ADO.NET. First, you learned about the data source controls, and how they can be used to build code-free data binding. With just a few mouse clicks, you were able to build editable grids of data!

We also investigated the `DataSet` class, and learned how to use it in our intranet application. We then moved on to learn about the constructs of `DataSets`, including `DataTables` and `DataViews`. We also learned how to populate `DataSets` using `SqlDataAdapters`. Finally, we looked at sorting, paging, and filtering data using `DataViews`, and updated a data source from a modified `DataSet` using the `SqlCommandBuilder`.

In the next chapter, we'll be looking at ASP.NET's security features. Using ASP.NET's form-based security capabilities, we'll learn how to restrict each user's access to the specific web forms we want them to be able to use, while still allowing public access to other parts of the site. We'll also take a look at some controls that make building login and logout mechanisms a snap.

13

Security and User Authentication

The issue of security is important in many facets of information technology, but it's especially relevant in web development. While you'll want to make sure that your web site users are able to go where they need to go and see what they're allowed to see, you'll also want to prevent unauthorized and malicious users from getting into your system.

One common approach is to have visitors to your site log in before they can view certain pages; another is to ensure that restricted pages cannot be accessed simply by typing in the appropriate URLs, unless the user has been specifically allowed to view those pages. Although different solutions exist for the various applications you may create—for instance, IIS could provide certain pages to users who have been authenticated by Windows within an intranet environment—this chapter focuses on the more straightforward tasks of form- and script-based authentication.

In this chapter, we'll learn some simple coding techniques and discover just how easy it is to secure your web applications using ASP.NET. As with many other chapters, this one contains many goodies that will be new to existing ASP.NET 1.0 and 1.1 programmers, because ASP.NET 2.0 delivers new techniques for securing your web applications.

Security is a huge topic, and several books have been written on the subject. If you're serious about developing secure complex applications, we recommend that you check out some additional resources, such as *Professional ASP.NET 2.0 Security,*

Membership, and Role Management (Wrox Press, 2006), and *Writing Secure Code, Second Edition* (Microsoft Press, 2002).

Basic Security Guidelines

The primary and most important element of building secure applications is to consider and plan an application's security from the early stages of its development. Of course, we must know the potential internal and external threats to which an application will be exposed before we can plan the security aspects of that system. Generally speaking, ASP.NET web application security involves—but is not limited to—the following considerations:

Validate user input.

Back in Chapter 6, you learned how to use validation controls to enable the client-side validation of user input, and how to double-check that validation on the server side.

Since the input your application will receive from web browsers is ultimately under users' control, there's always a possibility that the submitted data will not be what you expect. The submission of bad or corrupted data can generate errors in your web application, and compromise its security.

Protect your database.

The database is quite often the most important asset we need to protect—after all, it's here that most of the information our application relies upon is stored. **SQL injection attacks**, which target the database, are a common threat to web application security. If the app builds SQL commands by naively assembling text strings that include data received from user input, an attacker can alter the meaning of the commands the application produces simply by including malicious code in the user input.[1]

You've already learned how to use ADO.NET to make use of command parameters, and parameterized stored procedures, in order to include user input in SQL queries. Fortunately, ADO.NET has built-in protection against injection attacks. Moreover, if you specify the data types of the parameters you add, ASP.NET will throw an exception in cases where the input parameter doesn't match the expected data type.

---

[1] You'll find a detailed article on SQL injection attacks at
http://www.unixwiz.net/techtips/sql-injection.html.

Display data correctly.

Assuming your web application produces HTML output, you should always bear in mind that any text you include in that output will also be interpreted as HTML by your visitors' browsers. As such, you need to escape special characters (such as < and &) correctly, using the `HttpUtility.HtmlEncode` method.

This is especially important when you're outputting a string that was originally received as user input. If that user input were to contain HTML code, that code might disrupt the appearance or functionality of your application when it was displayed. For example, if you want to display the text `<script>` using a `Label` control, you should set your label's `Text` property to `HttpUtility.HtmlEncode("<script>")`.

Note that the fields or columns of data-bound controls such as `GridView` and `DetailsView` have a property called `HtmlEncode`, the default value of which is `True`. As such, any values that are displayed by these controls are automatically HTML-encoded unless you set this property to `False`.

Keep sensitive data to yourself.

Even though it may not be visible in the browser window, any output that your application produces is ultimately accessible to the end user. Consequently, you should never include sensitive data (such as user passwords, credit card data, and so on) in JavaScript code, HTML hidden fields, or the `ViewState` collection. (Unlike the `Application`, `Session`, or `Cache` collections, `ViewState` isn't stored on the server, but is passed back and forth between the client and the server on every request in an easily-decipherable format.)

Use encryption or hashing whenever necessary.

ASP.NET offers you the tools to encrypt your data using symmetric algorithms (which use the same key to encrypt and decrypt the data) or asymmetric algorithms (which are based on public key/private key pairs).

As we'll see later in this chapter, ASP.NET also supports hashing, an irreversible form of encryption that you can use to encrypt passwords and store them safely on your server.

Use secure communication channels whenever necessary.

You can always use the HTTPS (HTTP Secure) protocol to secure the communication between your visitors and your site. Using this protocol, an attacker who intercepts the data being passed back and forth between your application and its users won't obtain any meaningful data.

This approach is particularly useful when you're transferring very sensitive data such as user passwords, credit card information, and so on. However, HTTPS isn't used in scenarios where the extra security doesn't bring benefits, because it consumes significant processing power on the server—especially when many users access the site simultaneously.

In this chapter, we'll explore the basic ASP.NET 2.0 features for implementing user authentication and authorization to protect the sensitive areas of your web site.

Securing ASP.NET 2.0 Applications

The ASP.NET 1.0 and ASP.NET 1.1 server model offered several robust options for storing user information. ASP.NET 2.0 adds many improvements to these basic security features.

In securing the sensitive pages of a web site, you'll need to deal with two basic security-related concepts: **authentication** and **authorization**.

authentication
> Authentication is the process by which an anonymous user is identified as a particular user of your system.

> Authentication mechanisms include providing a username/password combination, using a fingerprint reader, and so on. As a result of this process, the person (or process, or computer) accessing your web site is associated with a security token (such as a username) which identifies the user into your system.

authorization
> Authorization establishes the resources an authenticated user can access, and the actions that user is allowed to perform. For example, you'll probably want to give different permissions to anonymous users, to registered users, and to site administrators.

> To ease the administrative work, modern authorization systems, including those supported by ASP.NET, support the notion of **authorization roles** (or **groups**) . A role represents a set of permissions that can be associated with any user who needs all the permissions associated with that role. For example, you could build a role called Administrators, and associate the permissions typically required by an administrator to that role. Then, when you need to give administrative permissions to a user, you simply assign that user

to the Administrators role, instead of supplying all the related permissions manually.

With older versions of ASP, user names and passwords were either hard-coded into the ASP file, or stored in an external data store such as a database. ASP.NET offers a better way to implement these old techniques, and also adds new user authentication methods:

Windows authentication

Windows authentication uses IIS in conjunction with the users' operating system user accounts to allow or deny those users access to certain parts of your web application.

forms authentication

Offering the greatest flexibility, forms authentication provides the maximum control and customization abilities to the developer. Using forms authentication, you can authenticate your users against hard-coded credentials, credentials stored in your `Web.config` file, user account details stored in a database, or a combination of these.

Passport authentication

The newest addition to user authentication methods, Passport authentication is a centralized authentication service provided by Microsoft. It allows users to sign in to multiple web sites using Microsoft Passport accounts, which are associated with their email addresses. Developers who use this authentication method don't need to worry about storing credential information on their own servers.

When users log in to a site that has Passport authentication enabled, they are redirected to the Passport web site, which prompts them for their email addresses and passwords. After the information is validated, the users are automatically redirected back to the original site.

This method sounds good, but it has one major downside: it requires users to have a Passport account in order to use your site, and it ties your application to Microsoft's proprietary system.

We'll spend the rest of this chapter exploring forms authentication—the most popular authentication method supported by ASP.NET.

Working with Forms Authentication

By far the most popular authentication method, forms authentication is extremely flexible. With forms authentication, you get to choose where the usernames and passwords are stored: in the `Web.config` file, in a separate XML file, in a database, or in any combination of the three.

Forms authentication is cookie-based—each user's login is maintained with a cookie. A browser may not access protected pages of the site unless it has a cookie that corresponds to the successful authentication of an authorized user.

You'll most frequently use three classes from the System.Web.Security namespace as you work with forms authentication:

`FormsAuthentication`
> contains several methods for working with forms authentication

`FormsAuthenticationTicket`
> represents the **authentication ticket** that's stored in the user's cookie

`FormsIdentity`
> represents the authenticated user's identity

Let's walk through an example that explains how a basic login page is constructed. We need to take three steps:

1. Configure the authentication mode for the application within the `Web.config` file.

2. Configure the authorization section to allow or deny certain users within the `Web.config` file.

3. Create the login page that your visitors will use.

The first step is to configure the authentication mode for the application.

Let's hand-code an example using the Dorknozzle application. Open it in Visual Web Developer, open the `Web.config` file, and add the `<authentication>` tag shown in the following code snippet. Visual Web Developer may already have created an `<authentication>` tag for you with the default `mode` of `Windows`—in this case, just change the value to `Forms`:

File: **Web.config (excerpt)**

```
<configuration>
  <system.web>
    ⋮
    <authentication mode="Forms" />
    ⋮
  </system.web>
</configuration>
```

There are four possible values for the mode attribute: Forms, Windows, Passport, and None. Since we're working with forms authentication, we set the mode to Forms.

Next, set up the authorization scheme by adding the <authorization> tag:

File: **Web.config (excerpt)**

```
<authentication mode="Forms" />
<authorization>
  <deny users="?" />
</authorization>
```

As you'll see in more detail in the next few sections, the question mark symbol (?) represents all anonymous users—that is, users who have not logged in. Essentially, this configuration reads: "Deny all non-logged-in users." If a user tries to access a page controlled by this Web.config file without logging in, he or she will be redirected to the login page. Unfortunately, this has the side-effect of denying all unauthenticated users access to our style sheet and image files, as well. Thankfully, ASP.NET 2.0 provides a way to override Web.config settings for particular directories of your web site—the location element.

To allow anonymous users access to your App_Themes and Images folders, add the following to Web.config:

File: **Web.config (excerpt)**

```
</system.web>
<!-- Allow access to App_Themes directory -->
<location path="App_Themes">
  <system.web>
    <authorization>
      <allow users="?"/>
    </authorization>
  </system.web>
</location>
<!-- Allow access to Images directory -->
```

```
  <location path="Images">
    <system.web>
      <authorization>
        <allow users="?"/>
      </authorization>
    </system.web>
  </location>
</configuration>
```

Now, all we need do is create that login page.

Create a new page named Login.aspx, which uses a code-behind file, and is based on the Dorknozzle.master master page. Then, modify its title and content placeholders like this:

File: **Login.aspx**

```
<%@ Page Language="VB" MasterPageFile="~/DorkNozzle.master"
    AutoEventWireup="false" CodeFile="Login.aspx.vb"
    Inherits="Login" Title="Dorknozzle Login" %>
<asp:Content ID="Content1"
    ContentPlaceHolderID="ContentPlaceHolder1" Runat="Server">
  <h1>Login</h1>
</asp:Content>
```

If you execute the project now, you'll notice that no matter which link you click, you'll be redirected to the blank Login page shown in Figure 13.1.

Naming the Login Page

Note that we didn't need to specify the name of the login page, Login.aspx, anywhere. By default, unless you specify another form name, ASP.NET will assume that the login page is called Login.aspx.

Authenticating Users

You're secured. Anonymous users can't see your application's pages, and are automatically redirected to the login page. Now what? How do you create users, give them privileges, store their settings, and so on? Well, it depends.

All versions of ASP.NET can store user account data, and details of the resources each user can access, in the Web.config file. However, relying only on the Web.config file isn't particularly helpful when the users' account settings need to be easily configurable: you can't keep modifying the configuration file to register new users, modify user passwords, and so on.

Figure 13.1. The Login page

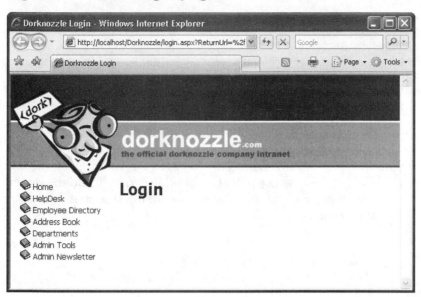

As you probably already suspect, a real user management solution must use the database somehow. Storing authentication and authorization data—such as user accounts, roles, and privileges—in the database gives you much greater flexibility in the long run.

Let's analyze both possibilities. By the end of the chapter, we'll have implemented a user authentication and authorization system using the new ASP.NET 2.0 membership features.

Working with Hard-coded User Accounts

Hard-coding user accounts means keeping user data in the code-behind file. This solution should *never, ever* be used in *any* application, but it will make things easier for us as we work through the first few examples.

To start off, let's build a login form that contains a `TextBox` into which the user can enter a username, another `TextBox` for the password, and a `Button` for submitting the data to the server. Add this code after the `Login` heading in `Login.aspx`:

File: **Login.aspx (excerpt)**

```
<p>Username:<br />
  <asp:TextBox id="username" runat="server" />
</p>
<p>Password:<br />
  <asp:TextBox id="password" runat="server" TextMode="Password" />
</p>
<p><asp:Button id="submitButton" runat="server" Text="Login"
      OnClick="LoginUser" /></p>
```

As you can see, the page contains two TextBox controls, one of which has the TextMode set to Password, which means that an asterisk will display for each character that a user types into this field. The other is a Button control, the On-Click attribute for which calls the LoginUser method. Next, we'll add the server-side script for this method, which will validate the login credentials. Add the following code to your code-behind file:

Visual Basic   File: **Login.aspx.vb**

```
Partial Class Login Inherits System.Web.UI.Page
  Sub LoginUser(ByVal s As Object, ByVal e As EventArgs)
    If (username.Text = "username" And _
        password.Text = "password") Then
      FormsAuthentication.RedirectFromLoginPage(username.Text, _
          False)
    End If
  End Sub
End Class
```

C#   File: **Login.aspx.cs**

```
public partial class Login : System.Web.UI.Page+
{
  protected void Page_Load(object sender, EventArgs e)
  {
  }
  protected void LoginUser(Object s, EventArgs e)
  {
    if (username.Text == "username" &&
        password.Text == "password")
    {
      FormsAuthentication.RedirectFromLoginPage(username.Text,
          false);
    }
  }
}
```

Execute your project and you'll see the simple, yet functional, login page shown in Figure 13.2.

Figure 13.2. The simple Dorknozzle Login page

In the code above, the `If` statement is used to check whether or not the user typed in the correct username and password. If the username and password entered were `username` and `password`, respectively, we call the `FormsAuthentication` class's `RedirectFromLoginPage` method, passing in two parameters.

The first parameter is the username that will be stored in the authentication ticket (the cookie that's sent to the user's browser). We'll simply use the username entered into the form for this example. The second parameter is a Boolean value that indicates whether a persistent cookie should be created. By setting this value to `True`, you allow your users to close their browsers, open them again, navigate back to your site, and still be logged in to the application. Setting this value to `False` allows users to be logged in only as long as their browser windows remain open. If they close their browsers, reopen them, and navigate to your site, they'll have to log in again.[2]

Once you enter the correct name and password, you'll be forwarded to the page you initially requested—by default, this is the homepage.

Configuring Forms Authentication

In the previous section, we created a basic login page. We also modified the `Web.config` file to enable the forms authentication mode. In this section, we'll explore the forms authentication section of the `Web.config` file in greater detail.

Aside from the basic authentication mode, the `<authentication>` tag within the `Web.config` file may contain a `<forms>` tag. The `<forms>` tag accepts the following attributes:

loginUrl

This attribute specifies the page that the user is redirected to when authentication is necessary. By default, this page is called `login.aspx`. Using this attribute, you can modify the filename to anything you like.

name

This attribute specifies the name of the cookie to be stored on the user's machine. By default, the name is set to `.ASPXAUTH`.

timeout

This attribute specifies the amount of time in minutes before the cookie expires. By default, this value is set to 30 minutes.

path

This attribute specifies the path to the location at which the cookie is stored. By default, this value is set to `/`.

protection

This attribute controls the way(s) the cookie data is protected. Values include `All`, `None`, `Encryption`, and `Validation`. The default value is `All`.

cookieless

A new ASP.NET 2.0 feature, this attribute forces your application to use the URL instead of a cookie to identify the logged-in user. The possible values

---

[2] You could add a Remember Me checkbox, and decide the value of the second parameter based on the user's preference.

are `UseCookies` (use the cookie to identify the user), `UseUri` (use the URL to store identification data), `AutoDetect` (try to detect if the user client supports cookies), or `UseDeviceProfile` (use cookies if the user client is known to support them). The default is `UseDeviceProfile`.

Applying the cookieless authentication mode is similar to using cookieless sessions, and can be used to support visitors who have cookies disabled. When the URL is used to identify the visitor, the links in your web site will automatically be modified to include the identification information, and will look like this:

```
http://localhost/Dorknozzle/(F(oyVZpBZ3w7Iz_LEFRukBigAf
nxM5QzvMY374YdcVjfcfgKJt8SJ3x9pVlrvUSUKbAiMuTP4rylvvNi7
HQH3ta9kMmQWQmZM5aT13GkenHPk1))/Default.aspx
```

slidingExpiration

This attribute specifies whether the cookie's expiration date (which is specified using the `timeout` attribute) should be reset on subsequent requests of a user's session. The default value in ASP.NET 1.x was `True`, and the default value in ASP.NET 2.0 is `False`.

An example `Web.config` file to which the `<forms>` tag has been applied might look like this:

```
<configuration>
  <system.web>
    <authentication mode="Forms">
      <forms name=".LoginCookie" loginUrl="Login.aspx"
          protection="All" timeout="40" path="/"
          cookieless="UseUri" />
    </authentication>
    <authorization>
      ⋮
    </authorization>
  </system.web>
</configuration>
```

Configuring Forms Authorization

As is the case with the `authentication` section of the `Web.config` file, the `<authorization>` tag can be modified to provide or deny certain users access to your application, allowing you to make extremely specific decisions regarding who will, and will not, be accepted into the app. For instance, the following code allows all non-anonymous (authenticated) users except for `zruvalcaba`:

```
<configuration>
  <system.web>
    <authentication …>
      ⋮
    </authentication>
    <authorization>
      <deny users="?" />
      <deny users="zruvalcaba" />
    </authorization>
  </system.web>
</configuration>
```

Here, we again use the question mark (?) to force users to log in, thus denying anonymous users access to our application. We've also added another `<deny>` tag, for the user `zruvalcaba`. In a nutshell, the two `deny` elements will allow everyone except `zruvalcaba` to log in.

In addition to `<deny>` tags, the `<authorization>` tag may contain `<allow>` tags—we'll see an example of this in a moment. For each user who attempts to access the application, ASP.NET will read through the tags in `<authorization>` and find the first tag that matches that user. If it turns out to be a `<deny>` tag, that user is denied access to the application; if it's an `<allow>` tag, or if no matching tag is found, the user is granted access.

The `users` attribute of `<allow>` and `<deny>` will accept three types of values:

?

> Use this value to allow or deny all anonymous users. This is the most common value used with forms authentication.

*

> Use this value to allow or deny all users, including users who are logged in.

user, …

> As with `zruvalcaba` above, we can allow or deny access to a specific user via this attribute. We can list several users by separating their names with commas.

We could modify the code a bit further in an effort to allow only specific users:

```
<configuration>
  <system.web>
    <authentication …>
      ⋮
    </authentication>
```

```
    <authorization>
      <allow users="jruvalcaba,zruvalcaba" />
      <deny users="*" />
    </authorization>
  </system.web>
</configuration>
```

In this case, the users with the login names of jruvalcaba and zruvalcaba are allowed access to the application, but all other users (whether they're logged in or not) will be denied access.

Now that you have a basic understanding of the ways in which user access is configured within the Web.config file, let's see how we can use Web.config to store a list of users for our application.

Storing Users in Web.config

The great thing about the Web.config file is that it is secure enough for us to store user names and passwords in it with confidence. The <credentials> tag, shown here within the forms element of the Web.config file, defines login credentials for two users:

File: **Web.config**

```
<authentication mode="Forms">
  <forms>
    <credentials passwordFormat="Clear" >
      <user name="zak" password="zak" />
      <user name="jessica" password="jessica" />
    </credentials>
  </forms>
</authentication>
<authorization>
  <deny users="?" />
</authorization>
```

As we want to prevent users from browsing the site if they're not logged in, we use the appropriate <deny> tag in our <authorization> tag. The names and passwords of the users we will permit can then simply be specified in the <credentials> tag. Change your Web.config file to match the one shown above, and we'll try another example.

Let's modify the code that lies within the <head> tag of the Login.aspx page to validate the user names and passwords based on the Web.config file. Here's what this change looks like:

```
Visual Basic                                        File: Login.aspx.vb (excerpt)
Sub LoginUser(s As Object, e As EventArgs)
  If FormsAuthentication.Authenticate(username.Text, _
      password.Text) Then
    FormsAuthication.RedirectFromLoginPage(username.Text, True)
  End If
End Sub
```

```
C#                                                  File: Login.aspx.cs (excerpt)
void LoginUser(Object s, EventArgs e)
{
  if (FormsAuthentication.Authenticate(username.Text,
      password.Text))
  {
    FormsAuthentication.RedirectFromLoginPage(username.Text,
        true);
  }
}
```

In this case, we use the Authenticate method of the FormsAuthentication class, which checks a user name and password against the users defined in the <credentials> tag within the Web.config file. Save your work and test the results in the browser. Again, when you enter credentials that match those in the Web.config file, you'll be redirected to the page you requested.

In order to make this solution easier to maintain, you *could* write code that checked the username and password against a database. However, as it turns out, ASP.NET 2.0 has built-in features that do all this work for you. We'll look at them a little later in this chapter.

Hashing Passwords

You can provide an increased level of protection for your users' passwords by storing them in a hashed format.

A **hashing** algorithm is an algorithm that performs an irreversible but reproducible transformation on some input data. If we hash a user's password before storing it, then, when that user tries to log in, we simply apply the same hashing algorithm to the password the user has entered, and compare the results with the stored value.

You can store hashed versions of passwords in your database—you can even store hashed passwords in Web.config. If you choose the latter option, you'll obviously need a means of hashing your passwords when you add new users to the file. For a quick test, you can use an online hashing tool.[3] Simply supply the tool with a "cleartext" string (the desired password) and a hashing algorithm, and it will give you the hashed version of the string.

The built-in hashing algorithms that ASP.NET supports are MD5 and SHA1. If you were to hash the string "cristian" using MD5, the hashed version would be B08C8C585B6D67164C163767076445D6. Here's what your `Web.config` file would look like if you wanted to assign the password "cristian" to the user "cristian":

```
<authentication mode="Forms">
  <forms>
    <credentials passwordFormat="MD5">
      <user name="cristian"
            password="B08C8C585B6D67164C163767076445D6" />
    </credentials>
  </forms>
</authentication>
```

After you make this change, execute your project again. When the login form appears, enter **cristian** for the username, and **cristian** for the password, and you should be redirected to the requested page (which, by default, is the homepage).

Hashing Passwords Programatically

I won't insist on using `Web.config` because ASP.NET 2.0 offers the much more powerful option of storing credentials in the database. However, if you want to hash passwords yourself without using an online tool, you can use the `HashForStoringInConfigFile` method of the `FormsAuthentication` class, which takes as parameters the cleartext password, and the hashing algorithm you want to use—MD5 or SHA1.

Logging Users Out

You'll usually want to provide users with the ability to log out once they've finished browsing your site. People gain security from the knowledge that they have successfully logged out, and rightly so, since it's possible for a hacker to take over (or spoof) an existing login while it remains active. The first step to take in order to create logout functionality for your application is to insert a suitable control that users can click on when they finish browsing.

---

[3] Try the one at http://aspnetresources.com/tools/pwdhash.aspx.

The method that lets you sign out current users is the `FormsAuthentication` class's `SignOut` method. You could call this method in the `Click` event handler of a Sign Out button, like this:

Visual Basic
```
Sub Logout(s As Object, e As EventArgs)
  FormsAuthentication.SignOut()
  Response.Redirect("Default.aspx")
```

C#
```
void Logout(Object s, EventArgs e) {
  FormsAuthentication.SignOut();
  Response.Redirect("Default.aspx");
}
```

As you can see, the `SignOut` method is used to clear the authentication cookie. The next line simply redirects the user to the home page.

ASP.NET 2.0 Memberships and Roles

The ASP.NET 2.0 team made a big step forward by implementing common functionality that previously needed to be coded from scratch for every new web application. This functionality includes a **membership system**, which supports the management of customer accounts, login forms, user registration forms, and so on, and is divided into several layers, which can each be extended or modified to suit your needs.

In particular, this new membership system offers a rich set of **login controls**, which you find in the Login tab of the Toolbox in Visual Web Developer. That's right—you can add a form for the creation of new user accounts simply by dragging a `CreateUserWizard` control into a web form! ASP.NET 2.0 makes implementing many such features extremely easy, but in order to take full advantage of these controls, we'll need to learn about the framework on which they're built.

Creating the Membership Data Structures

ASP.NET 2.0's membership system stores user profile data, including membership and personalization information, in a structured data store consisting of a set of tables, views, and stored procedures. We'll call these **membership data structures**, although that name doesn't take into account the complete range of data they contain.

To manipulate this data, Visual Web Developer provides the **ASP.NET Web Site Administration Tool**, which lets you add and edit users and their roles, and perform other administrative tasks.

We can use two procedures to create the necessary data structures. The first option is simply to open the ASP.NET Web Site Administration Tool, and click the Security tab. When you do this for the first time, the Web Site Administration Tool will create a database called ASPNETDB in the App_Data folder of your Web Application. This database will consist of two files: ASPNETDB.MDF (the database file) and ASPNETDB_LOG. LDF (the database log file).

Let's give this a try. With the Dorknozzle web site project loaded in Visual Web Developer, select Website > ASP.NET Configuration. This will load a page like that shown in Figure 13.3.

Figure 13.3. The ASP.NET Web Site Administration Tool

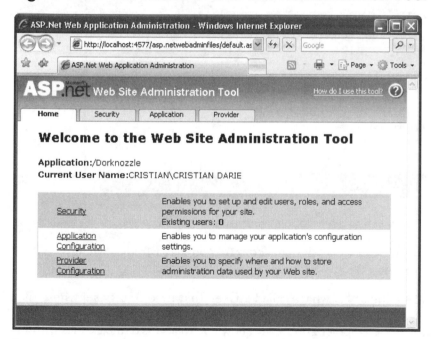

Figure 13.4. The Security tab

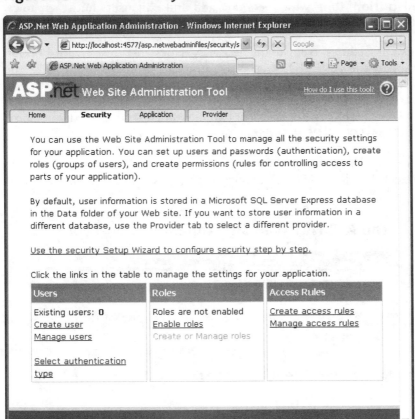

Click the Security tab to access the page shown in Figure 13.4.

At this point you can open the `Dorknozzle\App_Data` folder, where you'll be able to see your new database files, as Figure 13.5 indicates.

The `ASPNETDB` database is what's called a **User Instance database**, whose files are stored locally inside your application's folder. User instance databases are new to Microsoft SQL Server 2005; they allow you to access database files without attaching them to a SQL Server instance. These databases can easily be copied or transferred, and your application can connect to them as needed.

The new ASP.NET 2.0 login controls, the ASP.NET Web Site Administration Tool, and a number of related classes are able to access the `ASPNETDB` database

Figure 13.5. The ASPNETDB database files

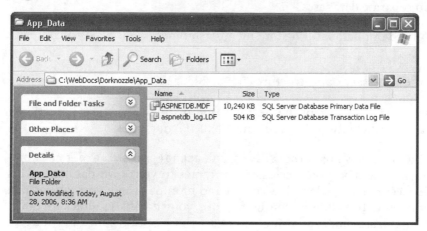

automatically, without any configuration. Should you need to access this database through your own code (for example, to customize the data structures), you can do so using the special connection string LocalSqlServer.

There are two things you need to be aware of when using the ASPNETDB database:

❏ Although User Instance databases were designed to be easy to move between systems, you can't always easily upload them to a hosting server.

❏ It will often result in your application having to work with two databases.

In our case, the Dorknozzle site would need to use both the ASPNETDB database and our old friend, the Dorknozzle database. Whether this is a wise choice or not depends on the specifics of your project, and whether your site's other data structures need to relate to the membership data of your users.

Fortunately, you have the option to create the necessary data structures within your existing database.

Using your Database to Store Membership Data

In many cases, it's more beneficial to store the membership data structures in your own database than in the default ASPNETDB database. Indeed, for the purposes of our application, it would be preferable to keep that data inside the existing Dorknozzle database. This way, when we launch the project, we'll need to transfer only one database to the production machine, rather than having to migrate two separate databases.

In order to use your database to store membership data, you need to complete two tasks:

❑ Create the necessary data structures in `Dorknozzle`.

❑ Edit `Web.config` to specify the new location of these structures, overriding the default configuration that uses the `ASPNETDB` database.

You can use a tool that ships with ASP.NET 2.0, `aspnet_regsql.exe`, to customize the data store and add the necessary structures to your own database. This tool can be executed at the Windows command prompt, where you can include various parameters to instantly configure it for your database; alternatively, it can be run in Wizard mode, allowing you to set those options one at a time. To execute the tool, first open a SDK Command Prompt window from the Start menu (Start > All Programs > Microsoft .NET Framework SDK 2.0 > SDK Command Prompt). At the command prompt, type **aspnet_regsql.exe** and hit **Enter**.

The wizard should open with a Welcome screen, where you'll just need to click Next. In the next window, which is shown in Figure 13.6, you can choose between adding the data structures to an existing database (or to a new database that can be created for you), or removing the data structures.

Leave the first option selected and hit Next—you'll see the dialog shown in Figure 13.7. Here, you'll need to tell the wizard which server and database you want to connect to in order to create those structures. The Server should be *LOCAL***Sql-Express** (where *LOCAL* is the network name of your current machine), and the Database should be **Dorknozzle**.

Using Remote Servers

You can enter any local or remote server into the Server field. You might use this tool to configure a remote server, for example, when choosing to move the application from your development machine to a remote production machine. In that case, you'd need to select SQL Server Authentication and supply the username and password provided by the server's administrator.

Figure 13.6. The SQL Server Setup Wizard

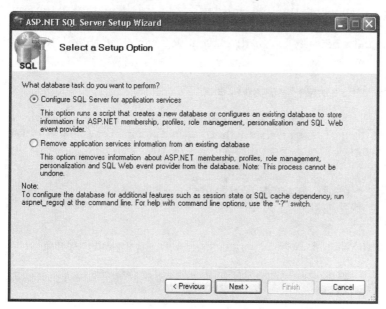

Figure 13.7. Selecting the Server and Database

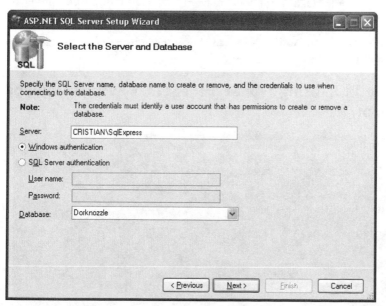

Click Next, and you'll be asked to confirm the data you've entered. Hit Next again, and expect a delay while the tool finishes setting up the database for you. When it's done, click Finish to close the wizard; then, when `aspnet_regsql.exe` finishes executing and a new prompt is displayed, you can close the SDK Command Prompt window.

More on `aspnet_regsql.exe`

You can customize or automate this process by supplying parameters to the `aspnet_regsql.exe` program at the command prompt. For example, instead of running the wizard using the steps above, you could have executed this command at the SDK Command Prompt:

```
aspnet_regsql -S LOCAL\SqlExpress -E -A all
    -d Dorknozzle
```

To have the tool connect using SQL Server Authentication instead of the integrated Windows Authentication, you'd use a slightly different command:

```
aspnet_regsql -S LOCAL\SqlExpress -U username
    -P password -A all -d Dorknozzle
```

Keep in mind that you can also use this tool to configure a remote database, in which case you'd need to mention the remote server address and database instance name instead of the local machine name and local SQL Server instance name.

If you executed the commands shown above, the output would look like that shown in Figure 13.8.

Figure 13.8. Using `aspnet_regsql.exe` at the command prompt

```
SDK Command Prompt

Setting environment to use Microsoft .NET Framework v2.0 SDK tools.
For a list of SDK tools, see the 'StartTools.htm' file in the bin fold

C:\Program Files\Microsoft.NET\SDK\v2.0>aspnet_regsql -S CRISTIAN\SqlE
-A all -d Dorknozzle

Start adding the following features:
Membership
Profile
RoleManager
Personalization
SqlWebEventProvider

...

Finished.

C:\Program Files\Microsoft.NET\SDK\v2.0>_
```

Once your database is ready, you'll need to modify Web.config to configure a new connection string named LocalSqlServer, which points to your database. As we mention earlier, this is the default connection string used by the built-in controls and tools that need access to the membership data.

LocalSqlServer definition in machine.config

Should you ever want to see or modify the default definition of the LocalSqlServer connection string, you can find it in the file \Windows\Microsoft.NET\Framework*version*\CONFIG\machine.config.

The machine.config file contains default machine-wide settings, which can be customized by each application's Web.config file. Here's the default definition of LocalSqlServer; this snippet also shows you how to connect to a disconnected database, such as ASPNETDB:

```
<connectionStrings>
  <add name="LocalSqlServer" connectionString="
        data source=.\SQLEXPRESS;
        Integrated Security=SSPI;
        AttachDBFilename=|DataDirectory|aspnetdb.mdf;
        User Instance=true"
      providerName="System.Data.SqlClient"/>
</connectionStrings>
```

Modify Web.config so that it removes the default LocaSqlServer connection string, then redefines it with the same connection data as DorknozzleConnectionString:

File: **Web.config (excerpt)**

```
<connectionStrings>
  <add name="Dorknozzle"
      connectionString="Server=localhost\SqlExpress;
        Database=Dorknozzle;Integrated Security=True"
      providerName="System.Data.SqlClient"/>
  <remove name="LocalSqlServer"/>
  <add name="LocalSqlServer"
      connectionString="Server=localhost\SqlExpress;
        Database=Dorknozzle;Integrated Security=True"
      providerName="System.Data.SqlClient" />
</connectionStrings>
```

At this point, if you experimented with the auto-generated `ASPNETDB` database, you can delete the two database files, `aspnetdb.mdf` and `aspnetdb_log.ldf`, from your application's `App_Data` folder.[4]

If you're curious, open the `Dorknozzle` database using the tool of your choice to see the new tables that have been created—they're shown in Figure 13.9. You'll notice your database now has 11 new tables whose names start with `aspnet`.

Figure 13.9. Membership tables in `Dorknozzle`

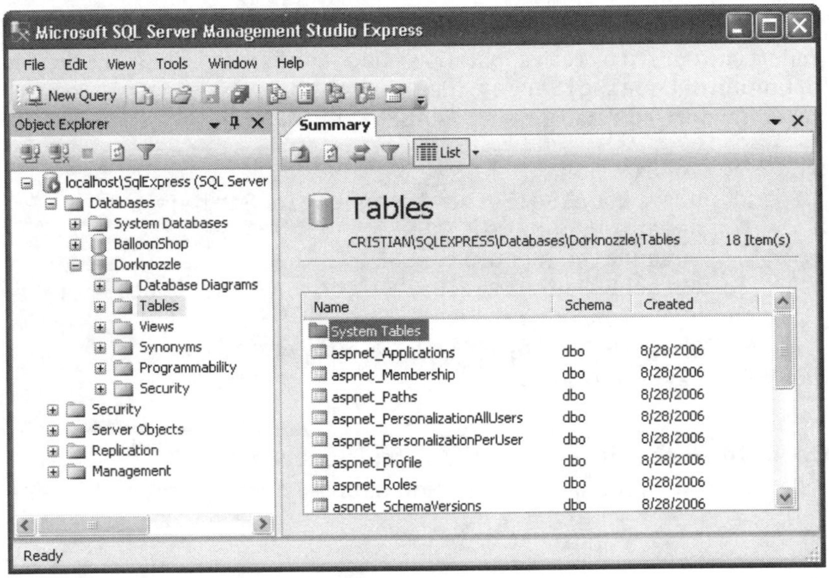

Using the ASP.NET Web Site Configuration Tool

After making the configuration changes we mentioned earlier, run the ASP.NET Web Site Configuration Tool and click the Security tab again. If you look into the `App_Data` folder, you'll notice that the tool did not create the `ASPNETDB` database. Instead, it's using the `Dorknozzle` database.

---

[4] It's interesting to note that if your application isn't using the `ASPNETDB` database, you're free to simply delete its files. This is possible because, as explained earlier, `ASPNETDB` is a User Instance database, the files of which are opened and read only when needed.

Before you start to add users and roles, it's worth taking a look around. While you're viewing the Security tab, click the Select authentication type link. You'll see two options:

From the Internet

You would normally have to select this option to enable forms authentication, but since you have already selected that type of authentication by editing your application's Web.config file, you'll find this option is already selected. However, in future, you might want to use this tool to set your preferred authentication type, instead of editing the file manually.

From a local network

Had we not specified forms authentication in the Web.config file, this option, which selects Windows authentication—ASP.NET's default—would have been selected instead. If you were to re-select this option at this stage, the tool would remove the <authentication> tag from your Web.config file, restoring the default setting.

Leave the From the Internet option selected, and click Done to return to the Security tab.

The Provider tab allows you to change the data provider that's used to store the security data. Currently, you can only choose AspNetSqlProvider, which uses SQL Server to store the membership data.[5]

The Application tab shown in Figure 13.10 lets you create and manage application settings in the form of name-value pairs that will be stored in the Web.config file. For example, you might want to add a setting named AdminEmail that contained an email address that could be used by your application to send important administration messages.

We've already learned to use Web.config to store connection strings within a dedicated <connectionStrings> tag. Similarly, ASP.NET supports an <appSettings> tag in the same file for the purpose of storing general application settings.

If you click Save, the administration tool will store the setting in your application's Web.config file:

```
<configuration
    xmlns="http://schemas.microsoft.com/.NetConfiguration/v2.0">
```

---

[5] Pre-release versions of ASP.NET 2.0 also supported the use of Access databases, but that feature was later replaced with support for the ASPNETDB disconnected database.

Figure 13.10. Creating an application setting

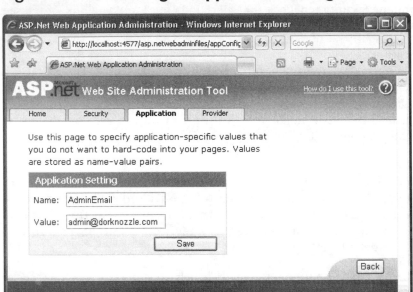

```
   <appSettings>
     <add key="AdminEmail" value="admin@dorknozzle.com" />
   </appSettings>
```

To access this data, you need to use the ConfigurationManager class, which is located in the System.Configuration namespace, like this:

Visual Basic
```
adminEmail = ConfigurationManager.AppSettings("AdminEmail")
```

C#
```
adminEmail = ConfigurationManager.AppSettings["AdminEmail"];
```

Creating Users and Roles

Open the ASP.NET web site, click the Security tab, and click Enable Roles under the Roles section. This will add the following line to your Web.config file:

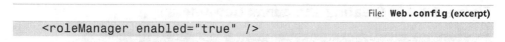

File: **Web.config (excerpt)**

```
<roleManager enabled="true" />
```

Two new links will appear under Roles: Disable Roles, and Create or Manage Roles. Click Create or Manage Roles, and use the form shown in Figure 13.11 to create two roles: one named **Users**, and another named **Administrators**.

Figure 13.11. Creating roles

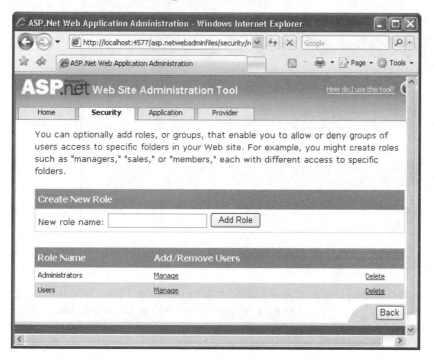

Figure 13.12. Creating the admin account

Click the Security tab to return to the main Security window. Now click the Create user link and add a user named **admin**, whose password is **Dorknozzle!**. Check the checkbox to assign this user the Administrators role, and complete the other fields shown in Figure 13.12, which are not optional.

Previously, the settings you specified using the ASP.NET Web Site Administration Tool always affected the Web.config file. Not this time, though! In accordance with the connection string in Web.config, roles and users are stored directly in the membership data structures that we added to the Dorknozzle database.

Changing Password Strength Requirements

By default, you won't be allowed to enter passwords that aren't considered sufficiently secure. The default security requirements for AspNetSqlMembershipProvider, as defined in machine.config, require the password to be at least seven characters long, and to include at least one non-alphanumeric character (which is why the exclamation mark was included in the example above). Also, passwords are stored in a hashed format by default.

To change the password strength requirements, we must override the default settings for the `AspNetSqlMembershipProvider` by adding a `<membership>` tag to the `Web.config` file. As you might expect, we must first remove the default settings inherited from `machine.config`, then define our own settings. Here's an example:

```
<configuration
    xmlns="http://schemas.microsoft.com/.NetConfiguration/v2.0">
    ⋮
  <system.web>
      ⋮
    <membership>
      <providers>
        <remove name="AspNetSqlMembershipProvider" />
        <add name="AspNetSqlMembershipProvider"
            type="System.Web.Security.SqlMembershipProvider"
            connectionStringName="LocalSqlServer"
            enablePasswordRetrieval="false"
            enablePasswordReset="true"
            requiresQuestionAndAnswer="false"
            applicationName="/"
            requiresUniqueEmail="false"
            passwordFormat="Hashed"
            maxInvalidPasswordAttempts="10"
            minRequiredPasswordLength="7"
            minRequiredNonalphanumericCharacters="0"
            passwordAttemptWindow="10" />
      </providers>
    </membership>
      ⋮
  </system.web>
    ⋮
</configuration>
```

The settings in the example above are self-explanatory. For example, we've increased the `maxInvalidPasswordAttempts` from the default of 5 to 10, to help many users avoid being locked out of their accounts if they repeatedly enter an incorrect password. We've also removed the constraint that required us to have at least one alphanumeric character in the password, and the function that facilitated lost password retrieval by means of a secret question and answer.

What Does your Project Need?

IMPORTANT

Don't take these security settings as recommendations for your own projects. These kinds of decisions need to be taken seriously, and the choices you make should relate directly to the specific needs of your project.

note

Using Regular Expressions

Advanced programmers can make use of an additional setting, `password-StrengthRegularExpression`, which can be used to describe complex rules that ensure password strength.

After you make this change in `Web.config`, start the ASP.NET Web Site Configuration Tool again and add another user named **cristian** with the password **cristian**; assign this user the Users role.[6] As Figure 13.13 illustrates, the fields for specifying a security question and answer no longer appear in the form.

Figure 13.13. Creating a user

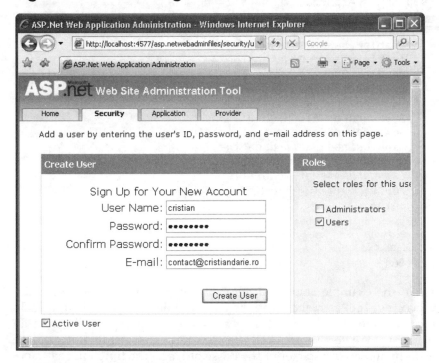

---

[6] Feel free to use another username and password that match the new password strength requirements—the purpose of this exercise is to see for yourself that the new settings are in place.

Securing your Web Application

Now we have two roles, and two users (admin and cristian), but we still need to secure the application. You should have restricted access earlier in this chapter by modifying Web.config like this:

```
<authorization>
  <deny users="?" />
</authorization>
```

If you haven't already done so, you can add this code now, or use Visual Web Developer to add it for you. Open the ASP.NET Web Site Administration Tool, click the Security tab, and click Create access rules. Create a new access rule for the Dorknozzle directory, as shown in Figure 13.14, to Deny all Anonymous users.

Figure 13.14. No anonymous users in Dorknozzle

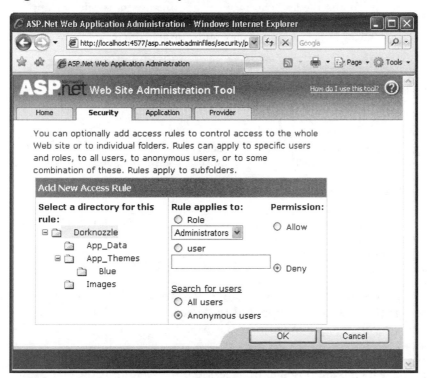

Check the options indicated in Figure 13.14 and click OK. If you look at your updated `Web.config` file, you'll see the new `authorization` element that denies anonymous access.

Creating Access Rules Using the Administration Tool

Note that, while useful, this tool can be misleading. When you add a new access rule using the ASP.NET Web Site Administration Tool, the new rule is added to `Web.config`—even if it existed before! If you used the tool multiple times in the previous example, you could end up with repetitions like this:

```
<authorization>
  <deny users="?" />
  <deny users="?" />
  <deny users="?" />
</authorization>
```

Also, keep in mind that the new rules you add using the tool are appended to the bottom of the list. This is important because these rules are applied in sequence! For example, adding a new rule that allows anonymous users doesn't change the line created previously. Instead, it creates a new entry:

```
<authorization>
  <deny users="?" />
  <allow users="?" />
</authorization>
```

As these rules are processed in sequence, all anonymous users would be rejected even after we added the new rule. The tool isn't smart enough to detect such logical contradictions, so you must be careful with your rule-setting.

Before moving on, make sure your `authorization` element looks like this:

File: **Web.config (excerpt)**

```
<authorization>
  <deny users="?" />
</authorization>
```

At this point, no unauthenticated users can access your application. Since this is an intranet application that is supposed to be accessed only by Dorknozzle's employees, this security requirement makes sense.

However, we'd like to impose more severe security restrictions to the `Admin-Tools.aspx` file, which is supposed to be accessed only by administrators. Unfortunately, the ASP.NET Web Site Application Configuration tool can't help you set permissions for individual files in your project, so you'll either need to place all admin-related functionality into a separate folder (which would allow you to continue using the tool to configure security options), or modify `Web.config` by hand.

You can set individual access rules for files using the `location` element, which can contain a `system.web` sub-element, which, in turn, can contain settings customized for the location. Add this code to your `Web.config` file:

File: **Web.config (excerpt)**

```
<!-- Allow access to Images directory -->
<location path="Images">
  <system.web>
    <authorization>
      <allow users="?" />
    </authorization>
  </system.web>
</location>
<!-- Only administrators may access AdminTools.aspx -->
<location path="AdminTools.aspx">
  <system.web>
    <authorization>
      <allow roles="Administrators" />
      <deny users="*" />
    </authorization>
  </system.web>
</location>
</configuration>
```

Now, administrators are allowed to access `AdminTools.aspx`, as this rule comes first under the `authorization` element. If you switched the order of the `allow` and `deny` elements, *no one* would be allowed to access `AdminTools.aspx`.

Now your site is accessible only to authenticated users, with the exception of the administration page, which is accessible only to users in the Administrators role. Now we just need to let users log in into the system.

Using the ASP.NET Login Controls

As we mentioned earlier in this chapter, ASP.NET 2.0 delivers a range of very useful controls related to managing users on your site:

Login

This control displays a login form that contains a User Name text box, a Password text box, a Remember me next time checkbox, and a Log In button. It's integrated with the membership API, and performs the login functionality without requiring you to write any code. The layout is customizable through templates and multiple properties.

LoginStatus

This is a simple yet useful control that displays a Login link if the user isn't logged in; otherwise, it displays a Logout link. Again, this control requires no additional coding in order to work with your application's membership data.

LoginView

This control contains templates that display different data depending on whether or not the user is logged in. It can also display different templates for authenticated users depending on their roles.

LoginName

This control displays the name of the logged-in user.

PasswordRecovery

If the user has provided an email address and a secret question and answer during registration, this control will use them to recover the user's password.

ChangePassword

This control displays a form that requests the user's existing password and a new password, and includes the functionality to change the user's password automatically, without requiring you to write additional code.

CreateUserWizard

This control displays a wizard for creating a new user account.

Let's see a few of these controls in action in our own application. In the following pages, we'll undertake these tasks:

1. Use a Login control in the Login.aspx page to give users a means of logging in to our application.

2. Use LoginStatus and LoginView controls to display Login and Logout links, and ensure that the Admin Tools link is displayed only to site administrators.

Authenticating Users

Earlier in this chapter, we created a web form based on the `Dorknozzle.master` master page, called `Login.aspx`. Remove the existing controls from the `ContentPlaceHolder`, and also remove the `LoginUser` method from the code-behind file.

Using the new ASP.NET 2.0 login controls, we can easily make the authentication work. If you're using Visual Web Developer, simply drag a `Login` control from the Login section of the Toolbox to just below the Login header in `Login.aspx`. If you'd prefer to add the control manually, here's the code:

File: **Login.aspx (excerpt)**

```
<asp:Content ID="Content1"
    ContentPlaceHolderID="ContentPlaceHolder1" Runat="Server">
  <h1>Login</h1>
  <asp:Login ID="Login1" runat="server">
  </asp:Login>
</asp:Content>
```

If you switch to Design View, you should see a display like the one depicted in Figure 13.15.

Figure 13.15. Using the `Login` control

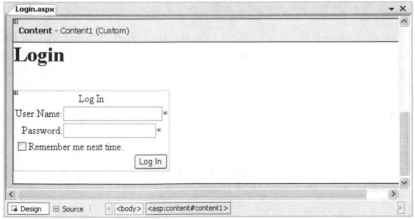

Yes, that's all you have to do! Start your project, and you'll be sent to the Login page. First, log in with the regular user that you created earlier (not with the admin account), then browse through the links to see that they can indeed be accessed, with the exception of the Admin Tools link. When you click Admin Tools, you should be sent back to the Login page. This time, log in with the admin user details, and *voilà*! You'll gain access to the Admin Tools page as well.

Let's take a few moments to customize the look of your login controls. Stop the execution of the project, and switch back to `Login.aspx` in Design View. Select the Login control and click its smart tag to see the three very useful options shown in Figure 13.16.

Figure 13.16. Options for the `Login` control

The Administer Website link launches the ASP.NET Web Site Administration Tool. The Convert to Template option transforms the current layout of your control into templates, which you can then customize down to the smallest detail. The Auto Format... link lets you select a predefined style to apply to this control.

If you were working in a production scenario, I'd advise you to select Convert to Template and use CSS to fine-tune the appearance of your control, as we did with the `GridView` and `DetailsView` controls in Chapter 11. However, for the purposes of this exercise, let's just set the `BorderStyle` property of the `Login` control to `Solid`, and the `BorderWidth` property to `1px`.

It was simple to add login functionality—we even changed its appearance with just a few mouse clicks! There are just one or two more things that we need to take care of before we can continue to add features to our site. First, let's deal with personalization.

Customizing User Display

The next feature we want to implement is functionality that gives the user a way to log out of the application. After you perform the changes that we're about to implement, logged-in users will have the option to log out, as Figure 13.17 illustrates.

On the other hand, users that aren't logged in won't see the menu at all, as Figure 13.18 indicates.

Figure 13.17. The view that the logged-in user sees

Figure 13.18. The Login page

To implement this functionality, we'll need to modify the menu in the `Dorknozzle.master` master page.

Using Master Pages

At this point, you should appreciate the extraordinary flexibility that master pages offer us. If you didn't use master pages or web user controls, you'd have to modify *all* of the pages on your site to implement this new functionality.

Open `Dorknozzle.master`, and change the code between `<!-- Menu -->` and `<!-- Content -->` as indicated here:

File: **Dorknozzle.master** (excerpt)

```
<!-- Menu -->
<div class="Menu">
  <asp:LoginView ID="loginView" runat="server">
    <LoggedInTemplate>
      <asp:LoginName ID="loginName" runat="server"
          FormatString="Hello, {0}!" />
      (<asp:LoginStatus ID="loginStatus" runat="server" />)
      <asp:SiteMapDataSource ID="dorknozzleSiteMap" runat="server"
          ShowStartingNode="false" />
      <asp:Menu ID="dorknozzleMenu" runat="server"
          DataSourceID="dorknozzleSiteMap">
        <StaticItemTemplate>
          <img src="Images/book_closed.gif" border="0" width="16"
              height="16" alt="+" />
          <%# Eval("Text") %>
        </StaticItemTemplate>
      </asp:Menu>
    </LoggedInTemplate>
    <AnonymousTemplate>
      <asp:LoginStatus ID="loginStatus" runat="server" />
    </AnonymousTemplate>
  </asp:LoginView>
</div>
<!-- Content -->
```

Also modify the `Dorknozzle.css` file to accommodate the new control:

File: **Dorknozzle.css** (excerpt)

```
.Menu
{
  top: 180px;
```

```
  left: 15px;
  width: 195px;
  position: absolute;
}
```

Don't let this code scare you; it's actually quite simple. The root control here is a `LoginView` control, which displays different templates depending on whether or not the user is logged in (it also knows how to display different templates depending on the roles of the user).

If the site is loaded by an anonymous (unauthenticated) user, we don't want to display the navigation menu; we want to display only the Login link. The output that's to be shown to anonymous users by the `LoginView` control is placed inside its `AnonymousTemplate` template. There, we use a `LoginStatus` control that displays a Login link for anonymous users, and a Logout link for logged-in users. Note that with the current Dorknozzle configuration, the contents of the `AnonymousTemplate` are never actually used—all anonymous users are simply redirected to the login page. However, it's best to include the `LoginStatus` control here anyway, just in case we should ever reconfigure the site to include some pages that are accessible to anonymous users.

File: **Dorknozzle.master** (excerpt)

```
<AnonymousTemplate>
  <asp:LoginStatus ID="loginStatus" runat="server" />
</AnonymousTemplate>
```

The output that will be displayed to authenticated users is placed inside the `LoggedInTemplate` template of the `LoginView` control. The `LoggedInTemplate` starts by displaying a welcome message:

File: **Dorknozzle.master** (excerpt)

```
<LoggedInTemplate>
  <asp:LoginName ID="loginName" runat="server"
    FormatString="Hello, {0}!" />
```

By default, the `LoginName` control displays just the username. However, you can customize it by setting its `FormatString` property to a custom string, where `{0}` is a placeholder for the username. Our `FormatString` value, `Hello, {0}!` will output "Hello, cristian!" if the user logged in is cristian.

Immediately after this welcome message, we have a Logout link generated by another `LoginStatus` control, which, as we discussed earlier, displays a Logout link to logged-in users:

File: **Dorknozzle.master (excerpt)**

```
(<asp:LoginStatus ID="loginStatus" runat="server" />)
```

Just below the welcome message and the Logout link sits our old friend, `Menu`, which displays the navigation menu. Since the `Menu` is now part of the `LoggedInTemplate` of the `LoginView`, it's displayed only for logged-in users, as we planned.

Finally, it's worth noting that you can use Visual Web Developer to edit the various templates (and the controls they house). Open `Dorknozzle.master` in the designer, and click the smart tag of the `LoginView` control. The options that display, which are shown in Figure 13.19, are certainly interesting.

Figure 13.19. Viewing `LoginView` Tasks

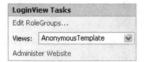

The Edit RoleGroups... link lets you administer the templates that are shown to users who are assigned particular roles. This facility is useful when you want to display to users specific content that's relevant to their roles. For example, if you wanted to display to administrators different menus from those that you show to regular users, you could create a group for users within the Users role, and another group for users in the Administrators role, then create different views for these groups using templates.

To check in your code whether or not the current user is authenticated (i.e. logged in), you must check the value of `HttpContext.Current.User.Identity.IsAuthenticated`. To check the role of the logged-in user, you must use the `HttpContext.Current.User.IsInRole` method, as shown here:

Visual Basic
```
If HttpContext.Current.User.IsInRole("Administrators") Then
    ⋮
```

C#
```
if (HttpContext.Current.User.IsInRole("Administrators"))
{
    ⋮
```

This method returns `True` if the current user is a member of the specified role, and `False` if he or she is not.

Summary

In this chapter, we examined the approaches you can use to secure your ASP.NET applications. You learned how to create a simple login page, configure the `Web.config` file to handle authentication and authorization, and check for user names and passwords using a database.

ASP.NET 2.0's new membership features provide extraordinary built-in functionality, and we have explored a number of these features through this chapter. The complete list of features is much larger, and, as we mentioned at the beginning of this chapter, there are entire books that deal solely with this topic.

In Chapter 14, we'll learn to work with files and directories, and send email messages using ASP.NET.

14

Working with Files and Email

The .NET Framework exposes a set of classes for working with text files, drives, and directories, through the System.IO namespace. This namespace exposes functionality that allows you to read from, write to, and update content within, directories and text files. On occasion, you will want to read from and write to a text file. Text files almost always use a format that's based on the ASCII standard, which is perhaps the most widely accepted cross-platform file format, and has been around since the 1960s. This makes it a very useful way of exchanging information between programs—even if they're running on different platforms and operating systems.

As we'll see in the course of this chapter, we can use the set of classes exposed by the System.IO namespace to complete the following tasks:

write to text files

The sales department within our fictitious company may want to write sales and forecast information to a text file.

read from text files

As a member of the web development team, you may want to use the data within a text file to create dynamic graphs to display sales and revenue forecasts on the Web.

upload files from the client to the server

You may want to create an interface that allows staff from the Human Resources department to upload company documentation for reference by employees.

access directories and directory information

You may want to let the Human Resources department choose the drive to which staff will upload files. For instance, you may have one drive dedicated to spreadsheets, and another just for Word documents.

Once you have a firm grasp on the intricacies of working with text files and directory information, you'll learn how to send email in ASP.NET using the System.Net.Mail namespace. We'll finish the chapter with a quick introduction to serialization.

Writing and Reading Text Files

The System.IO namespace contains three different groups of classes:

❏ classes for working with files

❏ classes for working with streams

❏ classes for working with directories

As we progress through this chapter, we'll look at each of these groups. However, let's begin by discussing the tasks of writing to and reading from text files with the aid of the classes that work with files and streams. These classes include:

File

contains methods for working with files

FileStream

represents a stream for reading and writing to files

StreamReader

reads characters from a text file

StreamWriter

writes characters to a text file

Path
> contains methods for manipulating a file or directory

For the most part, we read from and write to text files by using the `File` class to return a stream. If we want to write to a text file, we use the `StreamWriter` class; conversely, we use the `StreamReader` class to read from a text file.

Setting Up Security

Before our ASP.NET page can read and write files on your hard disk, the ASP.NET page must have permissions to access the file we're trying to read or write. Setting the permissions depends on our context. Here's a couple of possible scenarios:

❑ If you're running the page using Cassini or Visual Web Developer's integrated web server, the code will run under the credentials of your user account, so it will inherit all your permissions. For example, if you're a computer administrator, then your page will be able to access any resource on your computer.

❑ If you're running the page using IIS, the code will run under the credentials of the ASPNET user account on your system. By default, this account has access to any folder that is part of an IIS application.

Running Under IIS

The IIS scenario is particularly relevant because your web application will run under IIS when hosted on a production server. Also of note is the fact that, while you may fine-tune the permission rules on your development machine, on a hosting server, you will probably not be allowed to access folders outside your application's virtual directory.

On your own machine, you'll need to set special permissions only if you use IIS, and you want to write in a folder that's not part of an existing IIS application. If you're in this situation, read on. Otherwise, feel free to skip to the next section, in which we'll create within your application's folder structure a file that will be accessible under the default configuration of either IIS or Cassini.

1. Create a new folder called `WritingTest` somewhere on your disk. For the purposes of this discussion, I'll assume it's at `C:\WritingTest`.

2. In Windows XP, simple file sharing is enabled by default. This hides the Security tab you'll need to select in Step 4, preventing you from granting web applications write access to this directory. To disable simple file sharing, open the Windows Control Panel and double-click the Folder Options icon.

Figure 14.1. Disabling simple file sharing

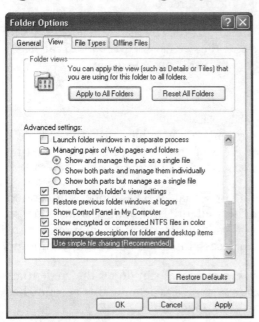

In the View tab, uncheck Use simple file sharing (Recommended) (as Figure 14.1 indicates, this should be the last option on the list).

3. Open the C: drive with the Windows Explorer (not the IIS control panel), right-click on the WritingText directory and select Properties.

4. Select the Security tab.

5. Add the **ASPNET** account to the Group or user names list by clicking Add..., and typing it into the Select Users or Groups dialog as shown in Figure 14.2. A new entry called ASP.NET Machine Account (*machinename*\ASPNET) will be added to the list.

Figure 14.2. Adding the ASPNET account

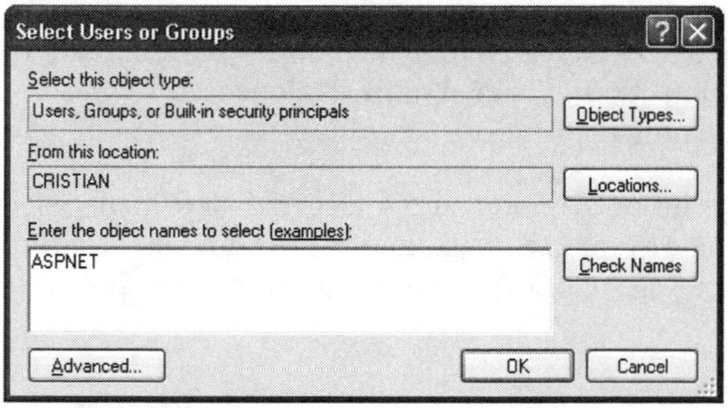

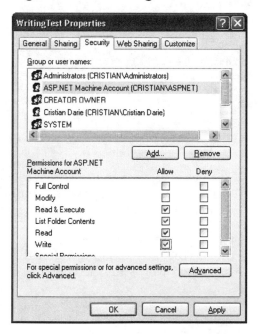

6. Select the new user in the list, and click on the Write checkbox under Allow in the permissions list, as shown in Figure 14.3.

7. Click OK.

Figure 14.3. Giving write access to ASPNET

Writing Content to a Text File

For the purposes of the next few exercises, let's work again with our old friend, the Learning web application. Start Visual Web Developer, go to File > Open Web Site, and open the Learning application.

Right-click the project in Solution Explorer, and select Add New Item. Select the Web Form template, name it **WriteFile.aspx**, and make sure you *aren't* using a code-behind file or a master page. Click Add, then enter the code shown here in bold:

File: **WriteFile.aspx (excerpt)**

```
<%@ Page Language="VB" %>
<%@ Import Namespace="System.IO" %>
<!DOCTYPE html PUBLIC "-//W3C//DTD XHTML 1.0 Transitional//EN"
    "http://www.w3.org/TR/xhtml1/DTD/xhtml1-transitional.dtd">
<script runat="server">
</script>
<html xmlns="http://www.w3.org/1999/xhtml">
<head runat="server">
  <title>Writing to Text Files</title>
</head>
<body>
  <form id="form1" runat="server">
    Write the following text within a text file:<br />
    <asp:TextBox ID="myText" runat="server" />
    <asp:Button ID="writeButton" Text="Write" runat="server"
        OnClick="WriteText" />
  </form>
</body>
</html>
```

As you can see, we import the System.IO namespace—the namespace that contains the classes for working with text files—first. Next, we add a TextBox control to handle collection of the user-entered text, and a Button control to send the information to the server for processing.

Next, in the <head> tag, we'll create the WriteText method mentioned in the OnClick attribute of the Button. This method will write the contents of the TextBox to the text file:

Visual Basic   File: **WriteFile.aspx (excerpt)**

```
<script runat="server">
  Sub WriteText(ByVal s As Object, ByVal e As EventArgs)
    Using streamWriter As StreamWriter = File.CreateText( _
        "C:\WebDocs\Learning\myText.txt")
      streamWriter.WriteLine(myText.Text)
    End Using
  End Sub
</script>
```

C#   File: **WriteFile.aspx (excerpt)**

```
<script runat="server">
  void WriteText(Object s, EventArgs e)
  {
    using (StreamWriter streamWriter = File.CreateText(
        @"C:\WebDocs\Learning\myText.txt"))
    {
      streamWriter.WriteLine(myText.Text);
    }
  }
</script>
```

Apart from the new `Using` construct, the code is pretty straightforward. First, we create a `StreamWriter` variable called `streamWriter`. To obtain the variable's value, we call the `CreateText` method of the `File` class, passing in the location of the text file, which returns a new `StreamWriter`. Don't forget that C# needs to escape backslashes when they're used in strings, so the path to our file must use `\\` to separate folder names, or use the `@` character in front of the string so that backslashes are automatically ignored.

What about `Using`, then? Similarly to database connections, streams are something that we need to close when we're done working with them, so they don't occupy resources unnecessarily. The `Using` construct is a common means of ensuring that the stream is closed and **disposed of** after we work with it.

Disposing of Objects

Technically, when we work with `Using`, the object is disposed of, rather than simply closed. The action is identical to explicitly calling its `Dispose` method.

When the code enclosed by `Using` finishes executing, `streamWriter`'s `Dispose` method is called automatically for you. This ensures that it doesn't keep any resources locked, and that *the object itself* is removed from memory immediately.

In the world of .NET, closed objects are cleared from memory at regular intervals by .NET's Garbage Collector, but for classes that support the `Dispose` method (such as `StreamWriter`), you can use this method (or the `Using` construct) to remove an object from memory immediately.

It's also interesting to note the way we used the `File` class's `CreateText` method in the code above. Normally, when we need to call a method of a particular class, we create an object of that class first. How was it possible to call the `CreateText` method using a class name, without creating an object of the `File` class first?

The `CreateText` method is what Visual Basic calls a **shared method**, and what's known in C# as a **static method**. Shared or static methods can be called without our having to create an actual instance of the class. In the above code, `CreateText` is a shared or static method, because we can call it directly from the `File` class, without having to create an instance of that class.

We worked with shared/static class members earlier, when we read the connection string. In that case, you didn't need to create an object of the `ConfigurationManager` class in order to read your connection string:

Visual Basic
```
string connectionString =
    ConfigurationManager.ConnectionStrings( _
    "Dorknozzle").ConnectionString
```

Instance methods, on the other hand, are those with which you're familiar—they may only be called on an instance (object) of the class. Instance methods are most commonly used, but shared/static methods can be useful for providing generic functionality that doesn't need to be tied to a particular class instance.

Now, test the page in your browser. Initially, all you'll see is an interface similar to Figure 14.4.

Type some text into the text box, and click the Write button to submit your text for processing. Browse to and open the `myText.txt` file in Notepad, and as in Figure 14.5, you'll see the newly added text.

If you try to enter a different value into the `TextBox` control and click the Write button, the existing text will be overwritten with the new content. To prevent this from happening, you can replace the call to the `CreateText` method with a call to `AppendText`. As Figure 14.6 shows, the `AppendText` method adds to existing text, rather than replacing it.

Figure 14.4. Writing text to a file

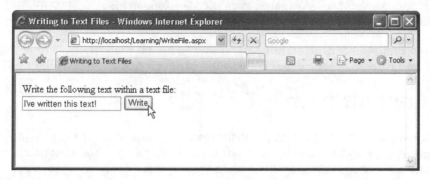

Figure 14.5. Viewing your new file in Notepad

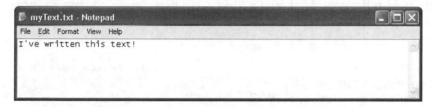

Figure 14.6. Appending text

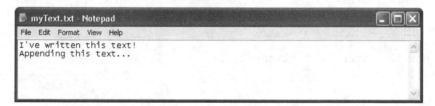

Also note that, rather than specifying the full path to the text file, you can use the MapPath method to generate the full path to the text file automatically. All you need to do is give the method a path relative to the current directory, as follows:

Visual Basic   File: **WriteFile.aspx (excerpt)**

```
Using streamWriter As StreamWriter = File.AppendText( _
    MapPath("myText.txt"))
```

```
C#                                              File: WriteFile.aspx (excerpt)
using (StreamWriter streamWriter = File.AppendText(
    MapPath("myText.txt")))
```

The `MapPath` method returns the full path to the filename that you pass in as a parameter, and can make for cleaner code that's easier to read.

Reading Content from a Text File

Just as you used the `CreateText` and `AppendText` methods of the `File` class to return a new `StreamWriter` object, you can use the `OpenText` method of the `File` class to return a new `StreamReader`. Once the `StreamReader` has been established, you can loop through the text file using a `While` loop in conjunction with the object's `ReadLine` method, to examine the contents of the text file.

To experiment with the process of reading from text files, create a new web form named `ReadFile.aspx` in the same way that you created `WriteFile.aspx`, and add this code to it:

```
Visual Basic                                    File: ReadFile.aspx (excerpt)
<%@ Page Language="VB" %>
<%@ Import Namespace="System.IO" %>
<!DOCTYPE html PUBLIC "-//W3C//DTD XHTML 1.0 Transitional//EN"
    "http://www.w3.org/TR/xhtml1/DTD/xhtml1-transitional.dtd">
<script runat="server">
</script>
<html xmlns="http://www.w3.org/1999/xhtml">
<head runat="server">
  <title>Reading from Text Files</title>
</head>
<body>
  <form id="form1" runat="server">
    <asp:Button ID="readButton" Text="Read" runat="server"
        OnClick="ReadText" />
    <br />
    <asp:Label ID="resultLabel" runat="server" />
  </form>
</body>
</html>
```

As you can see, we've simply added a `Button` and `Label` to the page. When the user clicks the button, the `Click` event will be raised and the `ReadText` method will be called. Let's add this method next. It will read the text from the text file and write it out to the `Label` control:

Visual Basic	File: **ReadFile.aspx (excerpt)**

```
<script runat="server">
  Sub ReadText(ByVal s As Object, ByVal e As EventArgs)
    Dim inputString As String
    resultLabel.Text = ""
    Using streamReader As StreamReader = _
        File.OpenText(MapPath("myText.txt"))
      inputString = streamReader.ReadLine()
      While (inputString <> Nothing)
        resultLabel.Text &= inputString & "<br />"
        inputString = streamReader.ReadLine()
      End While
    End Using
  End Sub
</script>
```

C#	File: **ReadFile.aspx (excerpt)**

```
<script runat="server">
  void ReadText(Object s, EventArgs e)
  {
    string inputString;
    resultLabel.Text = "";
    using (StreamReader streamReader =
        File.OpenText(MapPath("myText.txt")))
    {
      inputString = streamReader.ReadLine();
      while (inputString != null)
      {
        resultLabel.Text += inputString + "<br />";
        inputString = streamReader.ReadLine();
      }
    }
  }
</script>
```

We declare a new string variable named inputString to hold the text we'll read from the text file. Next, we set the text value of the Label control to an empty string. We do this in case the user presses the Read button when the Label already contains text from a previous click.

The next thing our method has to do is call the OpenText method of the File class to return a new StreamReader, again passing in the full path to the text file. And, once again, we're using the Using construct to ensure the stream object is disposed of after we finish working with it.

Visual Basic   File: **ReadFile.aspx (excerpt)**

```
Using streamReader As StreamReader = _
    File.OpenText(MapPath("myText.txt"))
```

C#   File: **ReadFile.aspx (excerpt)**

```
using (StreamReader streamReader =
    File.OpenText(MapPath("myText.txt")))
{
```

Next, we call the `ReadLine` method of the `streamReader` object to get the first line of the file:

Visual Basic   File: **ReadFile.aspx (excerpt)**

```
inputString = streamReader.ReadLine()
```

C#   File: **ReadFile.aspx (excerpt)**

```
inputString = streamReader.ReadLine();
```

Now we loop through the file, reading each line and adding it, in turn, to the end of the text in the `Label`:

Visual Basic   File: **ReadFile.aspx (excerpt)**

```
While (inputString <> Nothing)
    resultLabel.Text &= inputString & "<br />"
    inputString = streamReader.ReadLine()
End While
```

C#   File: **ReadFile.aspx (excerpt)**

```
while (inputString != null)
{
    resultLabel.Text += inputString + "<br />";
    inputString = streamReader.ReadLine();
}
```

Remember, `While` loops are used when you want to repeat the loop while a condition remains `True`. In this case, we want to loop through the file, reading in lines from it until the `ReadLine` method returns the value `Nothing` (`null` in C#), which indicates that we've reached the end of the file. Within the loop, we simply append the value of `inputString` to the `Label` control's `Text` property using the `&=` operator (`+=` in C#), then read the next line from `streamReader` into `inputString`.

Save your work and test the results in the browser. Figure 14.7 shows the contents of the text file, as displayed by `ReadFile.aspx`.

Figure 14.7. Reading a file using `StreamReader`

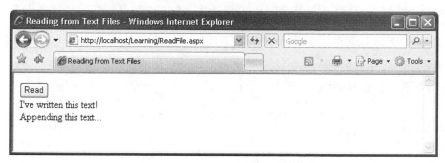

Accessing Directories and Directory Information

Now that you have some understanding of writing to and reading from text files, let's look at accessing the directories in which those files are located. The classes that are available in the System.IO namespace for working with directories and directory information are as follows:

Directory

    contains shared/static methods for creating, moving, and retrieving the contents of directories

DirectoryInfo

    contains instance methods for creating, moving, and retrieving the contents of directories

Just like the `File` class, the `Directory` class contains shared/static methods, which we can call without instantiating the class. The `DirectoryInfo` class, on the other hand, requires instantiation, as it contains only instance methods. The `Directory` class contains the following useful methods:

GetDirectories

    returns a string array of directory names

GetFiles

    returns a string array of filenames from a specific drive or directory

GetFileSystemEntries

    returns a string array of directory and filenames

Let's build an example page with a `DropDownList` control to display the directories and files within the server's `C:` drive. In the same `Learning` folder, create a web form named `Directories.aspx`, without a code-behind file, then add to it the code shown here in bold:

Visual Basic   File: **`Directories.aspx (excerpt)`**

```
<%@ Import Namespace="System.IO" %>
<!DOCTYPE html PUBLIC "-//W3C//DTD XHTML 1.0 Transitional//EN"
    "http://www.w3.org/TR/xhtml1/DTD/xhtml1-transitional.dtd">
<script runat="server">
</script>
<html xmlns="http://www.w3.org/1999/xhtml">
<head runat="server">
  <title>Directory Info</title>
</head>
<body>
  <form id="form1" runat="server">
    What do you want to view:<br />
    <asp:DropDownList ID="dirDropDown" runat="server"
        OnSelectedIndexChanged="ViewDriveInfo"
        AutoPostBack="true">
      <asp:ListItem Text="Directories" />
      <asp:ListItem Text="Files" />
      <asp:ListItem Text="Directories/Files" />
    </asp:DropDownList>
    <asp:GridView ID="grid" runat="server" />
  </form>
</body>
</html>
```

As you can see, our interface consists of a `DropDownList` control containing the three choices from which the user can select (Directories, Files, or Directories/Files). When a user selects an item from the `DropDownList` control, the `SelectedIndex-Changed` event is raised, and `ViewDriveInfo` is called.

Now, let's write the `ViewDriveInfo` method, which will write the specified information to the `GridView` control:

Visual Basic   File: **`Directories.aspx (excerpt)`**

```
<script runat="server">
  Sub ViewDriveInfo(ByVal s As Object, ByVal e As EventArgs)
    Select Case dirDropDown.SelectedItem.Text
      Case "Directories"
        grid.DataSource = Directory.GetDirectories("C:\")
      Case "Files"
```

```
      grid.DataSource = Directory.GetFiles("C:\")
    Case "Directories/Files"
      grid.DataSource = Directory.GetFileSystemEntries("C:\")
  End Select
  grid.DataBind()
 End Sub
</script>
```

C#   File: **Directories.aspx (excerpt)**

```
<script runat="server">
  void ViewDriveInfo(Object s, EventArgs e)
  {
    switch (dirDropDown.SelectedItem.Text)
    {
      case "Directories":
        grid.DataSource = Directory.GetDirectories("C:\\");
        break;
      case "Files":
        grid.DataSource = Directory.GetFiles("C:\\");
        break;
      case "Directories/Files":
        grid.DataSource = Directory.GetFileSystemEntries("C:\\");
        break;
    }
    grid.DataBind();
  }
</script>
```

You might remember from Chapter 3 that we use `Select Case` (VB) or `switch` (C#) statements to check for the possibility of multiple values of an object, rather than just one. The `Select Case` or `switch` specifies the value that is to be checked (in this case, the `Text` property of the selected list item):

Visual Basic   File: **Directories.aspx (excerpt)**

```
    Select Case dirDropDown.SelectedItem.Text
```

C#   File: **Directories.aspx (excerpt)**

```
    switch (dirDropDown.SelectedItem.Text)
```

Next, we use `Case` to specify the action to be performed for each significant value.

The data retrieved by the `GetDirectories`, `GetFiles`, or `GetFileSystemEntries` method of `Directory` can be fed to the `GridView` as its `DataSource`. After specifying the `DataSource`, we need to call the control's `DataBind` method, as if we were reading from a database, to fetch and display the data from the data source.

Save your work and test the results in your browser. Figure 14.8 shows within the `GridView` the kind of results that display when the user selects an item from the `DropDownList`.

Figure 14.8. Using the `Directory` class to view specific files, directories, or both, from a specific drive

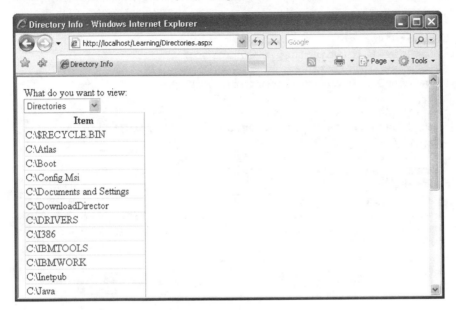

More Options

The `GetDirectories`, `GetFiles`, and `GetFileSystemEntries` methods accept more than simple drive or directory names. For instance, if you wanted to view only text files, you could use the following VB code:

```
Directory.GetFiles("C:\", "*.txt")
```

In this example, the `GetFiles` method would retrieve from the root of the `C:` drive all files that have the `.txt` extension.

Working with Directory and File Paths

The System.IO namespace also includes a utility class named `Path` that contains methods for retrieving path information from files and directories. As an example, let's build a simple application that retrieves the directory and path information for a text file. Create a new web form named `PathInfo.aspx` in the `Learning` directory, then add to it the code shown here in bold:

Visual Basic   File: **PathInfo.aspx**

```
<%@ Page Language="VB" %>
<%@ Import Namespace="System.IO" %>
<!DOCTYPE html PUBLIC "-//W3C//DTD XHTML 1.0 Transitional//EN"
    "http://www.w3.org/TR/xhtml1/DTD/xhtml1-transitional.dtd">
<script runat="server">
</script>
<html xmlns="http://www.w3.org/1999/xhtml">
<head runat="server">
  <title>Directory and Path Information</title>
</head>
<body>
  <form id="form1" runat="server">
    <asp:Label ID="resultLabel" runat="server" />
  </form>
</body>
</html>
```

The page contains a simple `Label` control, which we'll use to show all the directory and path information. Next, let's add the code that actually returns the path and directory information:

Visual Basic   File: **PathInfo.aspx (excerpt)**

```
<script runat="server">
  Sub Page_Load(ByVal s As Object, ByVal e As EventArgs)
    Dim strPath As String
    strPath = MapPath("myText.txt")
    resultLabel.Text &= "File Path: " & strPath & "<br />"
    resultLabel.Text &= "File name: " & _
        Path.GetFileName(strPath) & "<br />"
    resultLabel.Text &= "Directory: " & _
        Path.GetDirectoryName(strPath) & "<br />"
    resultLabel.Text &= "Extension: " & _
        Path.GetExtension(strPath) & "<br />"
    resultLabel.Text &= "Name without Extension: " & _
        Path.GetFileNameWithoutExtension(strPath)
  End Sub
</script>
```

C#   File: **PathInfo.aspx (excerpt)**

```
<script runat="server">
  void Page_Load(Object s, EventArgs e)
```

```
{
  string strPath;
  strPath = MapPath("myText.txt");
  resultLabel.Text += "File Path: " + strPath + "<br />";
  resultLabel.Text += "File name: " +
      Path.GetFileName(strPath) + "<br />";
  resultLabel.Text += "Directory: " +
      Path.GetDirectoryName(strPath) + "<br />";
  resultLabel.Text += "Extension: " +
      Path.GetExtension(strPath) + "<br />";
  resultLabel.Text += "Name w/out Extension: " +
      Path.GetFileNameWithoutExtension(strPath);
}
</script>
```

Initially, we create a new string variable and set it equal to the full path of the text file:

Visual Basic   File: **PathInfo.aspx (excerpt)**

```
Dim strPath As String
strPath = MapPath("myText.txt")
```

Next, we write into the `Label` control the complete file path, filename with extension, directory, extension, and filename without extension, by using the `Path` class's `GetFileName`, `GetDirectoryName`, `GetExtension`, and `GetFileNameWithoutExtension` methods, respectively.

Save your work and test the results in your browser. Figure 14.9 shows how all the information for the text file is displayed.

Figure 14.9. Retrieving the path, filename, directory, file extension, and filename without extension for the text file

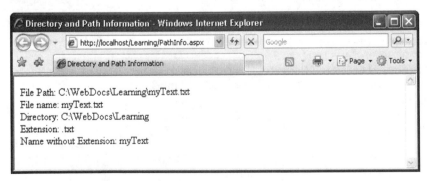

However, those aren't the only methods to which the `Path` class gives us access. Here's a list of all of the methods you can use:

ChangeExtension
> modifies a file's extension

Combine
> joins two file paths

GetDirectoryName
> returns the directory part of a complete file path

GetExtension
> returns the file extension from a file path

GetFileName
> returns the filename from a file path

GetFileNameWithoutExtension
> returns the filename without the file extension from a file path

GetFullPath
> expands the supplied file path with a fully qualified file path

GetPathRoot
> returns the root of the current path

GetTempFileName
> creates a uniquely named file and returns the name of the new file

GetTempPath
> returns the path to the server's `temp` directory

HasExtension
> returns `True` when a file path contains a file extension

IsPathRooted
> returns `True` when a file path makes reference to a root directory or network share

See the .NET Framework SDK documentation for full details on all of these methods.

Uploading Files

There are many situations in which you'll want your web application to allow users to upload files to the server. For example, you could create a photo album site to which users could upload images for others to view.

ASP.NET 2.0 offers the `FileUpload` control for uploading files; it provides a text box and Browse button to allow users to select files from their own computers and transfer them to the server with ease. The `FileUpload` control can be found in the Standard tab of the Toolbox; Figure 14.10 shows how it looks in Visual Web Developer's design view.

Figure 14.10. The `FileUpload` control in Visual Web Developer

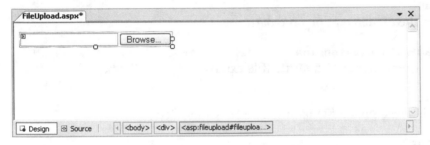

The `FileUpload` control has the following read-only properties:

HasFile
  `True` if the user has uploaded a file, `False` otherwise

FileName
  the name of the file as a string

FileContent
  a stream that can be used to read the contents of the file

FileBytes
  an array of bytes that can be used to read the contents of the file

PostedFile
  an `HttpPostedFile` object for the uploaded file; this object has properties that can be used to obtain additional data about the file, such as:

  ContentLength   the file length in bytes

ContentType   the MIME type of the file (such as image/gif for a GIF file)[1]

The FileUpload control also has a method that you'll find very useful: SaveAs. Although you can get the contents of an uploaded file using the FileContent and FileBytes properties described above, it's usually more convenient to use the SaveAs method to save files uploaded by users, but not before checking that HasFile is True. The SaveAs method takes as a parameter a string containing the path and the name of the target file.

Let's test this control out. Create a new web form named FileUpload.aspx in the Learning folder, and populate it with this code:

Visual Basic   File: **FileUpload.aspx (excerpt)**

```vb
<%@ Page Language="VB" %>
<%@ Import Namespace="System.IO" %>
<!DOCTYPE html PUBLIC "-//W3C//DTD XHTML 1.0 Transitional//EN"
    "http://www.w3.org/TR/xhtml1/DTD/xhtml1-transitional.dtd">
<script runat="server">
  Sub UploadFile(ByVal s As Object, ByVal e As EventArgs)
    ' Did the user upload any file?
    If fileUpload.HasFile Then
      ' Get the name of the file
      Dim fileName As String = fileUpload.FileName
      ' Upload the file on the server
      fileUpload.SaveAs(MapPath(fileName))
      ' Inform the user about the file upload success
      label.Text = "File " & fileName & " uploaded."
    Else
      label.Text = "No file uploaded!"
    End If
  End Sub
</script>
<html xmlns="http://www.w3.org/1999/xhtml">
<head runat="server">
  <title>File Upload</title>
</head>
<body>
  <form id="form1" runat="server">
    <asp:FileUpload ID="fileUpload" runat="server" />
    <asp:Button ID="uploadButton" runat="server" Text="Upload!"
        OnClick="UploadFile" />
```

---

[1] View the complete list of MIME types at http://www.w3schools.com/media/media_mimeref.asp. Note that there's no guarantee the MIME type is correct, as it's easily manipulated by the client.

```
    <br />
    <asp:Label ID="label" runat="server"></asp:Label>
  </form>
</body>
</html>
```

If you're using C#, you should place the following code in the `<script run-at="server">` section:

C#   File: **FileUpload.aspx (excerpt)**

```
<script runat="server">
  void UploadFile(Object s, EventArgs e)
  {
    // Did the user upload any file?
    if (fileUpload.HasFile)
    {
      // Get the name of the file
      string fileName = fileUpload.FileName;
      // Upload the file on the server
      fileUpload.SaveAs(MapPath(fileName));
      // Inform the user about the file upload success
      label.Text = "File " + fileName + " uploaded.";
    }
    else
      label.Text = "No file uploaded!";
  }
</script>
```

Load the script, and click the Upload! button without selecting a file. The message "No file uploaded!" is displayed, as shown in Figure 14.11.

Figure 14.11. An error arising as a file has not been specified

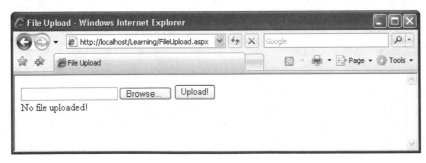

Now, click the Browse... button, select a file from your system, and click Upload! again. Some basic file information, like that shown in Figure 14.12, is displayed.

Figure 14.12. Uploading a file

After you've uploaded a file successfully, check the `Learning` folder to ensure the new file has indeed been saved there. As you can see, handling file uploads in ASP.NET 2.0 is very easy.

Sending Email with ASP.NET

Suppose for a moment that you're the webmaster for an online store, and you want to send an email confirmation to each customer who places an order. Rather than manually firing off an email to every customer about every order, you could automate the process using ASP.NET.

Sending Email with ASP.NET 2.0

If you've learned to send email with ASP.NET 1.x, pay attention: things have changed in ASP.NET 2.0! The classes from the System.Web.Mail namespace have been declared obsolete; newer versions now exist in the System.Net.Mail namespace.

The namespace that groups the new .NET 2.0 mail-related classes is System.Net.Mail. The most useful classes in this namespace are:

SmtpClient
    contains functionality for sending email

MailMessage
    represents an email message

Attachment
represents an email attachment

AttachmentCollection
represents a collection of `Attachment` objects

MailAddress
represents an email address

MailAddressCollection
represents a collection of email addresses

A core set of features is common to most email programs. For instance, they all enable you to send an email to someone by typing the recipient's email address in a To field. You are also able to specify who the email is from, the subject of the message, and the body content of the email. All these properties—and more—are available through the `MailMessage` class. Here's a partial list of the properties that the `MailMessage` class supports:

From
specifies the address from which the email message is to be sent

To
specifies the address to which the email message is to be sent

CC
specifies the carbon copy field of the email message

Bcc
specifies the blind carbon copy field of the email message

Attachments
a collection of items or files attached to the email message

Subject
specifies the subject of the email message

Body
defines the body of the email message

IsBodyHtml
`True` if the message is in HTML format, or `False` otherwise (defaults to `False`)

Other properties of `MailMessage` that you may need to use include `AlternateViews`, `BodyEncoding`, `DeliveryNotificationOptions`, `Headers`, `Priority`, `ReplyTo`, `Sender`, and `SubjectEncoding`.

The `From` field has the `MailAddress` type, representing an email address. The `To`, `CC`, and `Bcc` properties are of the `MailAddressCollection` type, representing a collection of `MailAddress` objects.

As you can see, there are lots of classes and properties that let you define email messages. However, to be able to send these messages, you need access to a SMTP server.

The standard email protocol of the Internet is **Simple Mail Transfer Protocol** (SMTP). When you use ASP.NET to send an email, the message is relayed through one or more SMTP servers on the way to its final destination. Most ISPs provide an SMTP server for customers' use; alternatively, if you're using IIS, you can make use of Windows' built-in SMTP Server.

Configuring the SMTP Server

IIS Only

If you're not using IIS, or you have access to an external SMTP server, you can choose to skip this section.

In order to send an email, you need to connect to an SMTP server. On Windows, an SMTP server is included with IIS, and you'll need to configure this server if you want to send email from ASP.NET. First, you need to make sure that the SMTP service is running. Open the IIS applet to check its status. If the server is stopped, you can right-click its icon and select Start to start it, as shown in Figure 14.13.

If the SMTP server entry doesn't appear, you'll need to install it using the process outlined below. Note that the SMTP server is a component of IIS, so if you haven't installed IIS (or if your Windows version doesn't support IIS, as is the case with Windows XP Home) you won't be able to install the SMTP server.

1. Launch the Add or Remove Programs applet in Control Panel.

2. Click Add/Remove Windows Components.

3. Select the Internet Information Services item, and click Details....

Figure 14.13. Starting the SMTP Virtual Server

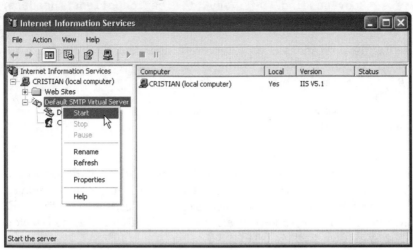

4. Select SMTP Service.

5. Click OK, then Next.

6. Run the Internet Information Services utility again. This time, you should see the SMTP service running.

Now that you have a running SMTP server, you need to configure it. In order for email to be relayed correctly, perform the following steps:

1. Open the Internet Information Services utility.

2. Right-click Default SMTP Virtual Server and choose Properties.

3. Select the Access tab.

4. Click Relay....

5. Click the Add... button.

6. Add the localhost IP address: **127.0.0.1**.

7. Uncheck the Allow all computers... checkbox. The dialog should look similar to Figure 14.14.

Figure 14.14. Configuring the SMTP Server

8. Click OK.

9. Select the Delivery tab.

10. Click the Advanced... button.

11. In the Smart host field of the Advanced Delivery window, type the IP address of your ISP's SMTP server enclosed in square brackets, as shown in Figure 14.15.[2]

12. Click OK, then OK again, and finally close the IIS tool.

Sending a Test Email

Later, we'll add a newsletter section to the Dorknozzle site, but first, let's write a very simple page to test that everything's working as it should.

Create a new file named SendEmail.aspx in the Learning folder. Don't use a code-behind file. Open it for editing and add the code highlighted in bold here:

---

[2] To find out the IP address, open the Windows Command Prompt and type **ping _mail.isp.net_**, where _mail.isp.net_ is the hostname of your ISP's SMTP server. You should see a number of lines that read "Reply from..." followed by the IP address of the server.

Figure 14.15. Routing email to your ISP's SMTP server

File: **SendEmail.aspx**

```
<%@ Page Language="VB" %>
<%@ Import Namespace="System.Net.Mail" %>
<!DOCTYPE html PUBLIC "-//W3C//DTD XHTML 1.0 Transitional//EN"
    "http://www.w3.org/TR/xhtml1/DTD/xhtml1-transitional.dtd">
<script runat="server">
</script>
<html xmlns="http://www.w3.org/1999/xhtml">
<head runat="server">
  <title>Sending Emails with ASP.NET</title>
</head>
<body>
  <form id="form1" runat="server">
    <asp:Button ID="sendEmailButton" runat="server"
        Text="Send Email!" OnClick="SendEmail" />
    <br />
    <asp:Label ID="statusLabel" runat="server" />
  </form>
</body>
</html>
```

Add the following code, making sure you change the To email address to your own, and you set the Host property to your SMTP server's address.

Visual Basic   File: **SendEmail.aspx (excerpt)**

```vb
<script runat="server">
  Sub SendEmail(ByVal s As Object, ByVal e As EventArgs)
    Dim smtpClient As SmtpClient = New SmtpClient()
    Dim message As MailMessage = New MailMessage()
    Try
      ' Prepare two email addresses
      Dim fromAddress As New MailAddress( _
          "test@cristiandarie.ro", "From Cristian Test")
      Dim toAddress As New MailAddress( _
          "contact@cristiandarie.ro", "To Cristian Test")
      ' Prepare the mail message
      message.From = fromAddress
      message.To.Add(toAddress)
      message.Subject = "Testing!"
      message.Body = "This is the body of a sample message"
      ' Set server details
      smtpClient.Host = "localhost"
      ' Uncomment for SMTP servers that require authentication
      'smtpClient.Credentials = _
      '    New System.Net.NetworkCredential("user", "password")
      ' Send the email
      smtpClient.Send(message)
      ' Inform the user
      statusLabel.Text = "Email sent."
    Catch ex As Exception
      ' Display error message
      statusLabel.Text = "Coudn't send the message!"
    End Try
  End Sub
</script>
```

C#   File: **SendEmail.aspx (excerpt)**

```csharp
<script runat="server">
  protected void SendEmail(object sender, EventArgs e)
  {
    SmtpClient smtpClient = new SmtpClient();
    MailMessage message = new MailMessage();
    try
    {
      // Prepare two email addresses
      MailAddress fromAddress = new MailAddress(
          "test@cristiandarie.ro", "From Cristian Test");
      MailAddress toAddress = new MailAddress(
          "contact@cristiandarie.ro", "From Cristian Test");
      // Prepare the mail message
```

```
      message.From = fromAddress;
      message.To.Add(toAddress);
      message.Subject = "Testing!";
      message.Body = "This is the body of a sample message";
      // Set server details
      smtpClient.Host = "localhost";
      // Uncomment for SMTP servers that require authentication
      //smtpClient.Credentials = new System.Net.NetworkCredential(
      //    "user", "password");
      // Send the email
      smtpClient.Send(message);
      // Inform the user
      statusLabel.Text = "Email sent.";
    }
    catch (Exception ex)
    {
      // Display error message
      statusLabel.Text = "Coudn't send the message!";
    }
  }
</script>
```

Execute the script, and press the Send Email button, as shown in Figure 14.16.

Figure 14.16. Sending the email

The email should arrive successfully at its destination, looking something like Figure 14.17.

Now you're ready to update the Dorknozzle site!

Figure 14.17. Viewing the email

Creating the Company Newsletter Page

Let's now extend the Dorknozzle site structure by adding a Newsletters page. This page will be accessible only to the site administrator, and will provide tools with which a customized newsletter can be sent to a list of recipients.

Open the Dorknozzle project in Visual Web Developer, and add to it a new web form named AdminNewsletter.aspx, making sure both the Select master page and Create code in a separate file checkboxes are checked. When prompted, select the Dorknozzle.master master page.

Complete the generated code like this:

File: **AdminNewsletter.aspx**

```
<%@ Page Language="VB" MasterPageFile="~/DorkNozzle.master"
    AutoEventWireup="false" CodeFile="AdminNewsletter.aspx.vb"
    Inherits="AdminNewsletter" Title="Dorknozzle Admin Newsletter"
%>
<asp:Content ID="Content1"
    ContentPlaceHolderID="ContentPlaceHolder1" runat="Server">
  <h1>Create Newsletter</h1>
  <asp:Label ID="resultLabel" runat="server" ForeColor="Red"/>
  <br />To:<br />
  <asp:TextBox ID="toTextBox" runat="server" />
  <br />Subject:<br />
  <asp:TextBox ID="subjectTextBox" runat="server" />
  <br />Introduction:<br />
```

```
<asp:TextBox ID="introTextBox" runat="server"
    TextMode="MultiLine" Width="300" Height="100" />
<br />Employee Of The Month:<br />
<asp:TextBox ID="employeeTextBox" runat="server" />
<br />Featured Event:<br />
<asp:TextBox ID="eventTextBox" runat="server" />
<br />
<asp:Button ID="sendNewsletterButton" runat="server"
    Text="Send Newsletter" />
</asp:Content>
```

Switch to Design View. The form should look like the one shown in Figure 14.18.

As you can see, the form contains seven `TextBox` controls, plus a `Button` and a `Label`. The boxes will allow the administrator to specify who the email is to be sent to and what the subject is, enter a simple introduction, identify the employee of the month, and feature a company event and a store item. The `Button` control is used to submit the form, while the `Label` control will display a confirmation message once the email has been sent.

To ensure that only administrators can send email messages, add the code highlighted in bold below, which we discussed in detail in Chapter 13, to `Web.config`:

File: **Web.config** (excerpt)

```
<!-- Only administrators are allowed to access
    AdminTools.aspx -->
<location path="AdminTools.aspx">
  <system.web>
    <authorization>
      <allow roles="Administrators" />
      <deny users="*" />
    </authorization>
  </system.web>
</location>
<!-- Only administrators are allowed to send emails -->
<location path="AdminNewsletter.aspx">
  <system.web>
    <authorization>
      <allow roles="Administrators" />
      <deny users="*" />
    </authorization>
  </system.web>
</location>
</configuration>
```

Figure 14.18. The Create Newsletter form

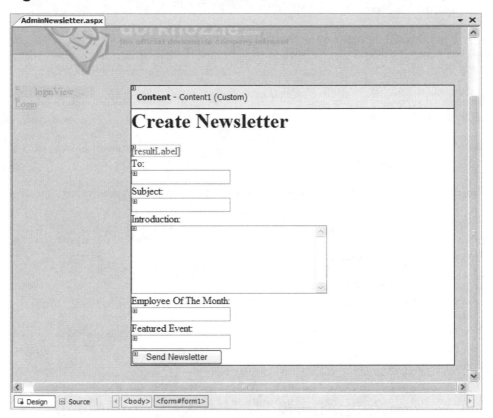

One hurdle that we need to overcome is that we want to include an image to be displayed as part of the HTML content of the message. We can use either of two approaches to solve this problem:

❏ Host the image on our web server and reference it in an `<img>` tag in the HTML code of the message (e.g. `<img src="http://www.dorknozzle.com/Images/Newsletter.jpg"` …>).

❏ Embed the image data in the email.

We'll apply the first technique, as it has the benefit of simplicity, and keeps the message as small as possible. If you want readers to see the image even when they're not connected to the Internet, you should look into the second option.

Developer Mike Pope explained image embedding, and provided sample code, in a post on his blog.[3]

All we need to do is handle the Send Newsletter button's Click event. While in Design View, double-click the button to generate the event handler signature. In the code-behind file, we'll need to import the System.Net.Mail namespace:

Visual Basic   File: **AdminNewsletter.aspx.vb (excerpt)**

```
Imports System.Net.Mail
```

C#   File: **AdminNewsletter.aspx.cs (excerpt)**

```
using System.Net.Mail;
```

Then, complete the code of sendNewsletterButton_Click to send your newsletter:

Visual Basic   File: **AdminNewsletter.aspx.vb (excerpt)**

```
Protected Sub sendNewsletterButton_Click( _
    ByVal sender As Object, ByVal e As System.EventArgs) _
    Handles sendNewsletterButton.Click
  Dim smtpClient As SmtpClient = New SmtpClient()
  Dim message As MailMessage = New MailMessage()
  ' Try to send the message
  Try
    ' Prepare two email addresses
    Dim fromAddress As New MailAddress( _
        "newsletter@dorknozzle.com", "Your Friends at Dorknozzle")
    Dim toAddress As New MailAddress(toTextBox.Text)
    ' Prepare the mail message
    message.From = fromAddress
    message.To.Add(toAddress)
    message.Subject = subjectTextBox.Text
    message.IsBodyHtml = True
    message.Body = _
        "<html><head><title>" & _
        HttpUtility.HtmlEncode(subjectTextBox.Text) & _
        "</title></head><body>" & _
        "<img src=""http://www.cristiandarie.ro/Dorknozzle" & _
        "/Images/newsletter_header.gif"" />" & _
        "<p>" & _
        HttpUtility.HtmlEncode(introTextBox.Text) & "</p>" & _
        "<p>Employee of the month: " & _
        HttpUtility.HtmlEncode(employeeTextBox.Text) & "</p>" & _
```

---

[3] http://www.mikepope.com/blog/DisplayBlog.aspx?permalink=1264

```
        "<p>This months featured event: " & _
        HttpUtility.HtmlEncode(eventTextBox.Text) & "</p>" & _
        "</body></html>"
    ' Set server details
    smtpClient.Host = "localhost"
    ' Send the email
    smtpClient.Send(message)
    ' Inform the user
    resultLabel.Text = "Email sent!<br />"
  Catch ex As Exception
    ' Display error message
    resultLabel.Text = "Couldn't send the message!"
  End Try
End Sub
```

C#	File: **AdminNewsletter.aspx.cs (excerpt)**

```
protected void sendNewsletterButton_Click(
    object sender, EventArgs e)
{
  SmtpClient smtpClient = new SmtpClient();
  MailMessage message = new MailMessage();
  // Try to send the message
  try
  {
    // Prepare two email addresses
    MailAddress fromAddress = new MailAddress(
        "newsletter@dorknozzle.com", "Your Friends at Dorknozzle"
        );
    MailAddress toAddress = new MailAddress(toTextBox.Text);
    // Prepare the mail message
    message.From = fromAddress;
    message.To.Add(toAddress);
    message.Subject = subjectTextBox.Text;
    message.IsBodyHtml = true;
    message.Body =
        "<html><head><title>" +
        HttpUtility.HtmlEncode(subjectTextBox.Text) +
        "</title></head><body>" +
        "<img src=\"http://www.cristiandarie.ro/Dorknozzle" +
        "/Images/newsletter_header.gif\" />" +
        "<p>" +
        HttpUtility.HtmlEncode(introTextBox.Text) + "</p>" +
        "<p>Employee of the month: " +
        HttpUtility.HtmlEncode(employeeTextBox.Text) + "</p>" +
        "<p>This months featured event: " +
        HttpUtility.HtmlEncode(eventTextBox.Text) + "</p>" +
```

```
        "</body></html>";
      // Set server details
      smtpClient.Host = "localhost";
      // Send the email
      smtpClient.Send(message);
      // Inform the user
      resultLabel.Text = "Email sent!<br />";
    }
    catch (Exception ex)
    {
      // Display error message
      resultLabel.Text = "Couldn\'t send the message!";
    }
}
```

That's a pretty large chunk of code, so let's break it down. Initially, we create a new instance of the `MailMessage` class, called `message`:

Visual Basic   File: **AdminNewsletter.aspx.vb (excerpt)**

```
  Dim message As MailMessage = New MailMessage()
```

C#   File: **AdminNewsletter.aspx.cs (excerpt)**

```
  MailMessage message = new MailMessage();
```

Next, we begin to define the email message by setting some of the properties that the `MailMessage` class exposes:

Visual Basic   File: **AdminNewsletter.aspx.vb (excerpt)**

```
  ' Prepare two email addresses
  Dim fromAddress As New MailAddress( _
      "newsletter@dorknozzle.com", "Your Friends at Dorknozzle")
  Dim toAddress As New MailAddress(toTextBox.Text)
  ' Prepare the mail message
  message.From = fromAddress
  message.To.Add(toAddress)
  message.Subject = subjectTextBox.Text
  message.IsBodyHtml = True
```

C#   File: **AdminNewsletter.aspx.cs (excerpt)**

```
  // Prepare two email addresses
  MailAddress fromAddress = new MailAddress(
      "newsletter@dorknozzle.com", "Your Friends at Dorknozzle"
      );
  MailAddress toAddress = new MailAddress(toTextBox.Text);
  // Prepare the mail message
```

```
message.From = fromAddress;
message.To.Add(toAddress);
message.Subject = subjectTextBox.Text;
message.IsBodyHtml = true;
```

You'll notice we've set the `IsBodyHtml` property to `True` because we're creating an HTML email message. By default, this property is set to `False`.

Next, we need to create the body of the message, which, essentially, will be an HTML document:

Visual Basic	File: **AdminNewsletter.aspx.vb (excerpt)**

```
message.Body = _
    "<html><head><title>" & _
    HttpUtility.HtmlEncode(subjectTextBox.Text) & _
    "</title></head><body>" & _
    "<img src=""http://www.cristiandarie.ro/Dorknozzle" & _
    "/Images/newsletter_header.gif"" />" & _
    "<p>" & _
    HttpUtility.HtmlEncode(introTextBox.Text) & "</p>" & _
    "<p>Employee of the month: " & _
    HttpUtility.HtmlEncode(employeeTextBox.Text) & "</p>" & _
    "<p>This month's featured event: " & _
    HttpUtility.HtmlEncode(eventTextBox.Text) & "</p>" & _
    "</body></html>"
```

C#	File: **AdminNewsletter.aspx.cs (excerpt)**

```
message.Body =
    "<html><head><title>" +
    HttpUtility.HtmlEncode(subjectTextBox.Text) +
    "</title></head><body>" +
    "<img src=\"http://www.cristiandarie.ro/Dorknozzle" +
    "/Images/newsletter_header.gif\" />" +
    "<p>" +
    HttpUtility.HtmlEncode(introTextBox.Text) + "</p>" +
    "<p>Employee of the month: " +
    HttpUtility.HtmlEncode(employeeTextBox.Text) + "</p>" +
    "<p>This month's featured event: " +
    HttpUtility.HtmlEncode(eventTextBox.Text) + "</p>" +
    "</body></html>";
```

As we're building an HTML document, we need to take care to convert special characters (including <, >, and &) into their character entity equivalents (<, >, &, and so on). The `HtmlEncode` method of the `HttpUtility` class does this for us.

Also note that the image we'll use in the email has to be hosted on a site somewhere. In the code above, I've used an example URL. To get this example to work properly, you'll need to host the image on your web site, and use the appropriate URL in your code.

We set the `Host` property of the `smtpClient` object to `localhost`, indicating that the computer that's acting as our ASP.NET server should also act as our outgoing mail server—you'll need to change this if you're using another SMTP server. Finally, we call the `Send` method, pass in the `message` object, and display a confirmation message to the user within the `resultLabel` control:

File: **AdminNewsletter.aspx (excerpt)**

```
' Set server details
smtpClient.Host = "localhost"
' Send the email
smtpClient.Send(message)
' Inform the user
resultLabel.Text = "Email sent!<br />"
```

File: **AdminNewsletter.aspx (excerpt)**

```
// Set server details
smtpClient.Host = "localhost";
// Send the email
smtpClient.Send(message);
// Inform the user
resultLabel.Text = "Email sent!<br />";
```

Save your work and run the page in your browser. Enter all the necessary information into the newsletter page and click the Send Newsletter button, as shown in Figure 14.19.

Figure 14.19. Sending the newsletter

Figure 14.20. Receiving the newsletter

You should receive the "Email sent!" message once the email is sent. Check your email account for the new email message. The message should look like the one shown in Figure 14.20.

Summary

This chapter introduced you to some important topics and gave you the ability to read and write to files, access directory information, upload files from the client to the server, and send email messages in ASP.NET.

The topics we covered in this chapter will prove invaluable as you develop applications with ASP.NET. Although, strictly speaking, they're not core features of ASP.NET, these tools enable you to implement many of the common requirements of ASP.NET applications. Stick 'em in your mental tool belt for now—I guarantee they won't gather much dust!

Appendix A: Web Control Reference

The following reference includes a list of important properties, methods, and events for most of the controls you'll find in the Visual Web Developer Toolbox.

I've grouped the lists of controls on the basis of their locations within the Toolbox:

❑ standard controls

❑ validation controls

❑ navigation controls

❑ HTML server controls

As all the web controls listed here are based on (or, more specifically, derived from) the WebControl class, they inherit its properties and methods. First up, let's review the more useful of these, which can be used with any of the web controls.

The WebControl Class

Properties

AccessKey	specifies a shortcut key that quickly selects a control without the user needing to use a mouse; the shortcut command is usually **Alt** plus a letter or number
Attributes	allows the accessing and manipulation of the attributes of the HTML code rendered by the control
BackColor	the control's current background color
BorderColor	color for the border
BorderStyle	style of border drawn around the web control; default is NotSet; other values are None, Solid, Double, Groove, Ridge, Dotted, Dashed, Inset, and Outset

BorderWidth	width of the border
Controls	a collection of all the controls contained within the web control (its child controls)
CssClass	indicates the style class within the current CSS style sheet that should be applied to the web control
Enabled	determines whether the web control is active and able to receive user input
EnableTheming	determines whether the control uses themes
Font	a `FontInfo` object representing the control's current font
	Properties of `FontInfo` include `Bold`, `Italic`, `Name`, `Names`, `Overline`, `Size`, `Strikeout`, and `Underline`.
ForeColor	the control's current foreground color
Height	the current height of the control
SkinID	the ID of the skin to be used by the control
Style	allows the manipulation of the CSS style elements through the returned `CssStyleCollection` object
TabIndex	defines the order in which controls on the page are selected when the user presses **Tab**; lowest value is selected first
Tooltip	the text that appears in a popup when the cursor is hovered over the control
Visible	determines whether the control appears on-screen in the user's browser
Width	the current width of the control

Methods

ApplyStyle	copies an element of a `Style` object to a control

MergeStyle	copies an element of a `Style` object to a control but does not overwrite existing styles
DataBind	binds the web control to its data source

As well as the properties and methods described here, web controls offer additional properties and methods specific to each control. These are listed in the following sections.

Standard Web Controls

AdRotator

Properties

AdvertisementFile	specifies the path to the XML file that contains the list of banner advertisements
KeywordFilter	returns only advertisements that match a specific filter when the property is set
Target	displays the page in this window or frame; possible values are _child, _self, _parent, and _blank

Events

AdCreated	raised after an ad is retrieved from the advertisement file, but before the ad is rendered

BulletedList

Properties

BulletImageUrl	the URL of the image used to display the bullets
BulletStyle	identifies the style of the bulleted list; can take one of the `BulletStyle` enumeration values: `Numbered` (1, 2, 3, ...), `LowerAlpha` (a, b, c, ...), `UpperAlpha` (A, B, C, ...), `LowerRoman` (i, ii, iii, ...), `UpperRoman` (I, II, III, ...), `Circle`, `CustomImage`, `Disc`, and `Square`

DisplayMode	determines the display mode, which can be Text (the default), or HyperLink (if you want the list to be formed of links)
FirstBulletNumber	specifies the value of the first bullet
SelectedIndex	the index of the selected item
SelectedItem	the currently selected item as a ListItem object
SelectedValue	the Value of the selected ListItem object
Target	specifies the target window or frame in which new content should be displayed when a link is clicked; possible values are _blank, _parent, _search, _self, and _top
Text	the text of the BulletedList control

Events

Click	raised when the Button is clicked and the form is submitted to the server for processing

Button

Properties

CommandName	passes a value to the Command event when the Button is clicked
CommandArgument	passes a value to the Command event when the Button is clicked
CausesValidation	allows interaction with client-side validation controls; when False, validation does not occur
Text	specifies the text displayed by the Button
Visible	controls the visibility of the Button

Events

Click — raised when the Button is clicked and the form is submitted to the server for processing

Command — raised when the Button is clicked and the form is submitted to the server for processing; passes the values of the CommandName and CommandArgument properties

Calendar

Properties

CellPadding — specifies the number of pixels between a cell and its border

CellSpacing — specifies the number of pixels between cells

DayHeaderStyle — specifies the style of the weekdays listed at the top of the calendar

DayNameFormat — sets the format of day names; possible values are FirstLetter, FirstTwoLetters, Full, and Short.

DayStyle — specifies the style applied to each day in the calendar

FirstDayOfWeek — specifies which day of the week is displayed in the first column

NextMonthText — if ShowNextPrevMonth is True, specifies the text for the next month hyperlink

NextPrevFormat — specifies the format for the next and previous hyperlinks

NextPrevStyle — specifies the style to use for next and previous month links

OtherMonthDayStyle — specifies the style to use to display days of adjacent months within the current month's calendar

PrevMonthText	if `ShowNextPrevMonth` is `True`, specifies the text for the previous month hyperlink
SelectedDate	contains a date-and-time value that specifies a highlighted day
SelectedDates	contains a collection of date-and-time values that specify the highlighted days
SelectedDayStyle	specifies the style to use for the currently selected day
SelectionMode	determines whether or not days, weeks, or months can be selected; possible values are `Day`, `DayWeek`, `DayWeek`-`Month`, and `None`
SelectMonthText	contains the HTML text displayed in the month selector column; default value is `&gt;&gt;`, which is rendered as >>
SelectorStyle	specifies the style to be applied to the link for selecting week and month
SelectWeekText	contains HTML text displayed for selecting weeks when `SelectionMode` has the value `DayWeek` or `DayWeekMonth`
ShowDayHeader	if `True`, displays the names of the days of the week
ShowGridLines	if `True`, renders the calendar with a border around each day's cell
ShowNextPrevMonth	if `True`, displays links to the next and previous months
ShowTitle	if `True`, displays the calendar's title
TitleFormat	determines how the month name appears in the title bar; possible values are `Month` and `MonthYear`
TitleStyle	specifies the style to use for text within the title bar
TodayDayStyle	specifies the style to use for the current day
TodaysDate	specifies a `DateTime` value that sets the calendar's current date

`VisibleDate`	specifies a `DateTime` value that sets the month to display
`WeekendDayStyle`	specifies the style to use for weekend days

Events

`DayRender`	raised before each day cell is rendered on the calendar
`SelectionChanged`	raised when a new day, month, or week is selected
`VisibleMonthChanged`	raised by clicking the next or previous month links

CheckBox

Properties

`AutoPostBack`	when `True`, automatically posts the form containing the `CheckBox` whenever it's checked or unchecked
`Checked`	shows the `CheckBox` as checked if set to `True`
`Text`	specifies the text displayed next to the `CheckBox`
`TextAlign`	determines how the text associated with the `CheckBox` is aligned; possible values are `Left` and `Right`

Events

`CheckedChanged`	raised when the `CheckBox` is checked or unchecked

CheckBoxList

Properties

`AutoPostBack`	if `True`, automatically posts the form containing the `CheckBoxList` whenever a `CheckBox` is checked or unchecked
`CellPadding`	sets the number of pixels between the border and a particular `CheckBox`

CellSpacing	sets the number of pixels between individual CheckBoxes within the CheckBoxList
DataMember	represents the particular table within the data source
DataSource	represents the actual data source to use when binding to a CheckBoxList
DataTextField	represents the field within the data source to use with the CheckBoxList text label
DataTextFormatString	a format string that determines how the data is displayed
DataValueField	represents the field within the data source to use with the CheckBoxList's value
Items	the collection of items within the CheckBoxList
RepeatColumns	determines the number of columns to use when displaying the CheckBoxList
RepeatDirection	indicates the direction in which the CheckBoxes should repeat; possible values are Horizontal and Vertical
RepeatLayout	determines how the check boxes are formatted; possible values are Table and Flow; default is Table
SelectedIndex	represents the index selected within the CheckBoxList
SelectedItem	represents the item selected within the CheckBoxList

Events

SelectedIndexChanged	raised when a CheckBox within the CheckBoxList is selected

DropDownList

Properties

`AutoPostBack`	automatically posts the form containing the `DropDownList` whenever the selection in the list is changed
`DataMember`	represents the particular table within the data source
`DataSource`	represents the actual data source to use when binding to a `DropDownList`
`DataTextField`	represents the field within the data source to use with the `DropDownList`'s text label
`DataTextFormatString`	specifies a format string that determines how the `DropDownList` is displayed
`DataValueField`	represents the field within the data source to use with the `DropDownList`'s value
`Items`	the collection of items within the `DropDownList`
`SelectedIndex`	represents the index selected within the `DropDownList`
`SelectedItem`	represents the item selected within the `DropDownList`

Events

`SelectedIndexChanged`	raised when an item within the `DropDownList` is selected

FileUpload

Properties

`FileBytes`	returns the contents of the uploaded file as an array of bytes
`FileContent`	returns the contents of the uploaded file as a stream

`FileName`	returns the name of the file
`HasFile`	returns `True` if the control has loaded a file, and `False` otherwise
`PostedFile`	returns for the uploaded file an `HttpPostedFile` object whose properties can be used to obtain additional data about the file

Methods

`SaveAs`	saves the uploaded file to disk

HiddenField

Properties

`Value`	specifies the value of the hidden field

HyperLink

Properties

`ImageURL`	specifies the location of the image to use
`NavigateURL`	specifies the URL to navigate to when the hyperlink is clicked
`Target`	specifies the target window or frame to display for the URL; possible values are `_top`, `_blank`, `_self`, and `_parent`
`Text`	specifies the text displayed by the `HyperLink`
`Visible`	controls the visibility of the `HyperLink`

Image

Properties

AlternateText	specifies the text to display within browsers that do not support images
ImageAlign	specifies one of ten possible values for image alignment; possible values include AbsBottom, AbsMiddle, Baseline, Bottom, Left, Middle, NotSet, Right, TextTop, and Top
ImageURL	specifies the location of the image to use
Visible	controls the visibility of the image

ImageButton

Properties

AlternateText	specifies the text to display within browsers that do not support images
CommandName	passes a value to the Command event when the ImageButton is clicked
CommandArgument	passes a value to the Command event when the ImageButton is clicked
CausesValidation	allows interaction with client-side validation controls; when False, validation does not occur
ImageAlign	specifies one of ten possible values for image alignment; possible values include AbsBottom, AbsMiddle, Baseline, Bottom, Left, Middle, NotSet, Right, TextTop, and Top
ImageURL	specifies the location of the image to use
Visible	controls the visibility of the ImageButton

Events

`Click`	raised when the `ImageButton` is clicked and the form is submitted to the server for processing
`Command`	raised when the `ImageButton` is clicked and the form is submitted to the server for processing; values of the `CommandName` and `CommandArgument` properties are provided with the event

ImageMap

Properties

`Enabled`	enables or disables the control
`HotSpotMode`	defines the behavior when a hot spot is clicked; possible values are `Inactive`, `Navigate`, `NotSet`, and `PostBack`
`HotSpots`	the `HotSpotCollection` object containing the `ImageMap`'s hot spots; hot spots are defined using three other controls, which generate hot spots of different shapes: `CircleHotSpot`, `RectangleHotSpot`, and `PolygonHotSpot`
`Target`	specifies the target window or frame where new content should be displayed when a link is clicked; possible values are `_blank`, `_parent`, `_search`, `_self`, and `_top`

Events

`Click`	raised when a `HotSpot` object in the `ImageMap` is clicked and the form is submitted to the server for processing

Label

Properties

`Text`	specifies the text displayed by the `Label`
`Visible`	controls the visibility of the `Label`

LinkButton

Properties

Text   specifies the text displayed by the LinkButton

CommandName   passes a value to the Command event when the LinkButton is clicked

CommandArgument   passes a value to the Command event when the LinkButton is clicked

CausesValidation   allows interaction with client-side validation controls; when False, validation does not occur

Visible   controls the visibility of the LinkButton

Events

Click   raised when the LinkButton is clicked and the form is submitted to the server for processing

Command   raised when the LinkButton is clicked and the form is submitted to the server for processing; values of the CommandName and CommandArgument properties are passed

ListBox

Properties

AutoPostBack   when True, automatically posts the form containing the ListBox whenever an item is selected

DataMember   specifies the particular table within the data source to which to bind

DataSource   represents the actual data source to use when binding

DataTextField   represents the field within the data source to use with the ListBox's text label

DataTextFormatString	specifies a format string that determines how the ListBox is displayed
DataValueField	represents the field within the data source to use with the ListBox's value
Items	the collection of items within the ListBox
Rows	indicates the number of rows to display within the ListBox; default value is 4
SelectedIndex	represents the index selected within the ListBox
SelectedItem	represents the item selected within the ListBox
SelectionMode	determines whether or not a user can select more than one item at a time; possible values are Multiple and Single

Events

SelectedIndexChanged	raised when an item within the ListBox is selected

Literal

Properties

Text	specifies the text displayed by the control

MultiView

Properties

ActiveViewIndex	specifies the index of the active view
Views	the ViewCollection object representing the collection of views

Methods

GetActiveView	returns the active view as a View object

SetActiveView	sets the active view to the `View` received as parameter

Events

ActiveViewChanged	fires when the active view of the `MultiView` changes

Panel

Properties

BackImageURL	the URL of the background image to use within the `Panel`
HorizontalAlign	sets the horizontal alignment of the `Panel`; possible values are `Center`, `Justify`, `Left`, `NotSet`, and `Right`
Wrap	wraps the contents within the `Panel` when `True`; default value is `True`.
Visible	controls the visibility of the `Panel`

PlaceHolder

Properties

Visible	controls the visibility of the `PlaceHolder`

RadioButton

Properties

AutoPostBack	automatically posts the form containing the `RadioButton` whenever checked or unchecked is `True`
Checked	shows the `RadioButton` as checked if set to `True`
GroupName	determines the name of the group to which the `RadioButton` belongs
Text	specifies the text displayed next to the `RadioButton`

TextAlign	determines how the text associated with the RadioButton is aligned; possible values are Left and Right

Events

CheckedChanged	raised when the RadioButton is checked or unchecked

RadioButtonList

Properties

AutoPostBack	automatically posts the form containing the RadioButtonList whenever checked or unchecked is True
DataMember	represents the particular table within the data source
DataSource	represents the actual data source to use when binding to a RadioButtonList
DataTextField	represents the field within the data source to use with the RadioButtonList's text label
DataTextFormatString	specifies a format string that determines how the RadioButtonList is displayed
DataValueField	represents the field within the data source to use with the RadioButtonList's value
RepeatColumns	the collection of items within the RadioButtonList
Items	determines the number of columns to use when displaying the radio buttons
RepeatDirection	indicates the direction in which the radio buttons should repeat; possible values are Horizontal and Vertical
RepeatLayout	determines how the radio buttons should repeat; possible values are Horizontal and Vertical

SelectedIndex	represents the index selected within the RadioButtonList
SelectedItem	represents the item selected within the RadioButtonList
SelectedItem	represents the item selected within the RadioButtonList
TextAlign	determines how the text associated with the RadioButtonList is aligned; possible values are Left and Right

Events

SelectedIndexChanged	raised when a radio button within the RadioButtonList is selected

TextBox

Properties

AutoPostBack	automatically posts the form containing the TextBox whenever a change is made to the contents of the TextBox
Columns	sets the horizontal size of the TextBox in characters
MaxLength	sets the maximum number of characters that may be entered
Rows	sets the vertical size of the multiline TextBox
Text	specifies the text displayed by the TextBox
TextMode	determines whether the TextBox should render as SingleLine, Password, or MultiLine
Visible	controls the visibility of the TextBox
Wrap	determines how a multiline TextBox wraps; if set to True, word wrapping is enabled

Events

TextChanged   raised when the contents of the TextBox have changed

Xml

Properties

Document

specifies the System.Xml.XmlDocument object to display

DocumentContent

specifies a string representing the XML document to display

DocumentSource

specifies the URL of a document to display

Transform

specifies the System.Xml.Xsl.XslTransform object used to format the XML document

TransformArgumentList

specifies the XsltArgumentList used to format the XML document

TransformSource

specifies the URL of an XSLT style sheet used to format the XML document

Validation Controls

The following reference includes a list of important properties, methods, and events for each of the validation controls. These controls ultimately derive from the WebControl class, meaning that they, like the web controls themselves, inherit its properties and methods. The more useful of these properties and methods are listed at the start of this appendix.

CompareValidator

Properties

ControlToCompare

specifies the ID of the control to use for comparing values

ControlToValidate	specifies the ID of the control that you want to validate
Display	shows how the error message within the validation control will be displayed; possible values are `Static`, `Dynamic`, and `None`; default is `Static`
EnableClientScript	enables or disables client-side validation; by default, is set to `Enabled`
Enabled	enables or disables client and server-side validation; default is `Enabled`
ErrorMessage	specifies the error message that will be displayed to the user in any associated validation summary control; if no value is set for the `Text` property, this message also appears in the control itself
IsValid	has the value `True` when the validation check succeeds, and `False` otherwise
Operator	specifies the operator to use when performing comparisons; possible values are `Equal`, `NotEqual`, `GreaterThan`, `GreaterThanEqual`, `LessThan`, `LessThanEqual`, `DataTypeCheck`
Text	sets the error message displayed by the control when validation fails
Type	specifies the data type to use when comparing values; possible values are `Currency`, `Date`, `Double`, `Integer`, and `String`
ValueToCompare	specifies the value used when performing the comparison

Methods

Validate	performs validation and modifies the `IsValid` property

CustomValidator

ClientValidationFunction	specifies the name of the client-side function to use for validation

ControlToValidate	specifies the ID of the control that you want to validate
Display	shows how the error message within the validation control will be displayed; possible values are `Static`, `Dynamic`, and `None`; default is `Static`
EnableClientScript	enables or disables client-side validation; by default, is set as `Enabled`
Enabled	enables or disables client and server-side validation; by default, is set as `Enabled`
ErrorMessage	specifies the error message that will be displayed to the user
IsValid	has the value `True` when the validation check succeeds, and `False` otherwise
Text	sets the error message displayed by the control when validation fails

Methods

Validate	performs validation and modifies the `IsValid` property

Events

ServerValidate	represents the function for performing server-side validation

RangeValidator

Properties

ControlToValidate	specifies the ID of the control that you want to validate
Display	shows how the error message within the validation control will be displayed; possible values are `Static`, `Dynamic`, and `None`; default is `Static`
EnableClientScript	enables or disables client-side validation; set as `Enabled` by default

Enabled	enables or disables client and server-side validation; set as Enabled by default
ErrorMessage	specifies the error message that will be displayed to the user in any associated validation summary control; if no value is set for the Text property, this message also appears in the control itself
IsValid	has the value True when the validation check succeeds, and False otherwise
MaximumValue	sets the maximum value in the range of permissible values
MinimumValue	sets the minimum value in the range of permissible values
Text	sets the error message displayed by the control when validation fails
Type	specifies the data type to use when comparing values; possible values are Currency, Date, Double, Integer, and String

Methods

Validate	performs validation and modifies the IsValid property

RegularExpressionValidator

Properties

ControlToValidate	specifies the ID of the control that you want to validate
Display	shows how the error message within the validation control will be displayed; possible values are Static, Dynamic, and None; default is Static
EnableClientScript	enables or disables client-side validation; set as Enabled by default

Enabled	enables or disables client and server-side validation; by default, is set as `Enabled`
ErrorMessage	specifies the error message that will be displayed to the user
InitialValue	specifies the initial value specified by the `ControlToValidate` property
IsValid	has the value `True` when the validation check succeeds, and `False` otherwise
Text	sets the error message displayed by the control
ValidateExpression	specifies the regular expression to use when performing validation

Methods

Validate	performs validation and modifies the `IsValid` property

RequiredFieldValidator

Properties

ControlToValidate	specifies the ID of the control that you want to validate
Display	shows how the error message within the validation control will be displayed; possible values are `Static`, `Dynamic`, and `None`; default is `Static`
EnableClientScript	enables or disables client-side validation; set as `Enabled` by default
Enabled	enables or disables client and server-side validation; by default, is set as `enabled`
ErrorMessage	specifies the error message that will be displayed to the user in any associated validation summary control; if no value is set for the `Text` property, this message also appears in the control itself

InitialValue	specifies the initial value specified by the `ControlToValidate` property
IsValid	has the value `True` when the validation check succeeds, and `False` otherwise
Text	sets the error message displayed by the control when validation fails

Methods

Validate	performs validation and modifies the `IsValid` property

ValidationSummary

Properties

DisplayMode	sets the formatting for the error messages that are displayed within the page; possible values are `BulletList`, `List`, and `SingleParagraph`; these messages are the `ErrorMessage` properties of all validation controls for which validation has failed
EnableClientScript	enables or disables client-side validation; by default, is set as `Enabled`
Enabled	enables or disables client and server-side validation; by default, is set as `Enabled`
HeaderText	sets the text that is displayed to the user at the top of the summary
ShowMessageBox	when the value is set to `True`, an alert box listing form fields that caused errors is presented to the user
ShowSummary	enables or disables the summary of error messages

Navigation Web Controls

SiteMapPath

Properties

`CurrentNodeStyle`	the style used to display the current node
`CurrentNodeTemplate`	the template used to display the current node
`NodeStyle`	the style used to display `SiteMapPath` nodes
`NodeTemplate`	the template used to display nodes
`ParentLevelsDisplayed`	the maximum number of parent nodes to display
`PathDirection`	specifies the path direction display; possible values are `PathDirection.CurrentToRoot` and `PathDirection.RootToCurrent`
`PathSeparator`	the string used to separate path nodes
`PathSeparatorStyle`	the styles used to display the path separator
`PathSeparatorTemplate`	the template used to display the separator
`Provider`	the `SiteMapProvider` object associated with the `SiteMapPath`; the default site map provider is `XmlSiteMapProvider`, which reads its data from the `Web.sitemap` file
`RenderCurrentNodeAsLink`	when set to `True`, the current site map site will be displayed as a link; default value is `False`
`RootNodeStyle`	the style used to display the root node
`RootNodeTemplate`	the template used to display the root node
`ShowToolTips`	specifies whether the node links should display tooltips when the cursor hovers over them

| SiteMapProvider | a string representing the name of the `SiteMapProvider` object associated with the `SiteMapPath` |
| SkipLinkText | a string that describes a link to allow screen reader users to skip the control's content |

Methods

| DataBind | binds the `SiteMapPath` to its data source |

Events

| ItemCreated | fires when a new `SiteMapNodeItem` object is created |
| ItemDataBound | fires after a node item has been bound to the data source |

Menu

Properties

Controls
returns a `ControlColection` object containing the menu's child controls

DisappearAfter
an integer representing how long, in milliseconds, a dynamic menu continues to display after the cursor ceases to hover over it; the default is `500`; when `DisappearAfter` is set to `-1`, the menu won't disappear automatically

DynamicBottomSeparatorImageUrl
a string representing the URL of an image to be displayed at the bottom of a dynamic menu item; this is usually a line that separates the dynamic item from the other items; value is empty (an empty string) by default

DynamicEnableDefaultPopOutImage
a Boolean value representing whether a dynamic menu that contains a sub-menu should be enhanced with the image specified by `DynamicPopOutImageUrl`; default value is `True`

DynamicHorizontalOffset
an integer representing the number of pixels by which a dynamic menu should be shifted horizontally relative to the parent menu item

DynamicHoverStyle

a `MenuItemStyle` object that allows you to control the appearance of a dynamic menu item when the cursor hovers over it

DynamicItemFormatString

a string used to set the text to be displayed for dynamic menu items on mobile devices that don't support templates

DynamicItemTemplate

the template to be used to render dynamic menu items

DynamicMenuItemStyle

the `MenuItemStyle` object that represents the styles used to render dynamic menu items

DynamicMenuStyle

the `SubMenuStyle` object that represents the styles used for rendering the dynamic menu

DynamicPopOutImageTextFormatString

a string representing the alternate text to be displayed instead of the image specified by `DynamicPopOutImageUrl`

DynamicPopOutImageUrl

a string representing the URL for the image to be displayed for a dynamic menu item that has a submenu when `DynamicEnableDefaultPopOutImage` is `True`

DynamicSelectedStyle

a `MenuItemStyle` object representing the style of a selected dynamic menu item

DynamicTopSeparatorImageUrl

a string representing the URL for an image to be displayed at the top of a dynamic menu item; this is usually a line that separates the dynamic item from the other items; the value is empty (an empty string) by default

DynamicVerticalOffset

an integer representing the number of pixels by which a dynamic menu should be shifted vertically relative to the parent menu item

Items

a `MenuItemCollection` that contains a collection of `MenuItem` objects, representing all the menu items

ItemWrap

a Boolean value representing whether the menu items' text should wrap

LevelMenuItemStyles

a `MenuItemStyleCollection` representing a collection of `MenuItemStyle` objects that define the styles to be applied to menu items depending on their levels in the menu (the first object in the collection defines the style for the first menu level, the second object in the collection defines the style for the second menu level, and so on)

LevelSelectedStyles

similar to `LevelMenuItemStyles`, but applies to selected menu items

LevelSubMenuStyles

similar to `LevelMenuItemStyles`, but applies to submenu items

MaximumDynamicDisplayLevels

an integer that specifies the maximum number of dynamic menu levels to display; the default value is 3

Orientation

can be set either to `Orientation.Horizontal` or `Orientation.Vertical`, specifying the direction in which to display the menu items

PathSeparator

a `Char` value representing the character used to delimit the path of a menu item

ScrollDownImageUrl

a string representing the URL for an image to be displayed in a dynamic menu to indicate that the user can scroll down to see more menu items

ScrollDownText

alternate text for the image defined by `ScrollDownImageUrl`

ScrollUpImageUrl

a string representing the URL for an image to be displayed in a dynamic menu to indicate that the user can scroll up to see more menu items

ScrollUpText

alternate text for the image defined by `ScrollUpImageUrl`

SelectedItem

a `MenuItem` object representing the selected menu item

SelectedValue

a string representing the text of the selected menu item

SkipLinkText

a string representing alternate text to be used by screen readers to allow screen reader users to skip the list of links

StaticBottomSeparatorImageUrl

a string representing the URL for an image to be displayed at the bottom of a static menu item—usually a line that separates the static item from the other items; value is empty (an empty string), by default

StaticDisplayLevels

an integer representing the maximum number of levels to display for a static menu; default is 1

StaticEnableDefaultPopOutImage

a Boolean value representing whether a static menu that contains a submenu should be enhanced with the image specified by `StaticPopOutImageUrl`; default is `True`

StaticHoverStyle

a `MenuItemStyle` object that allows you to control the appearance of a static menu item when the cursor is hovered over it

StaticItemFormatString

a string used to set the text for static menu items displayed on mobile devices that don't support templates

StaticItemTemplate

the template to be used to render static menu items

StaticMenuItemStyle

the `MenuItemStyle` object that represents the styles used to render static menu items

StaticMenuStyle

the SubMenuStyle object that represents the styles used to render the static menu

StaticPopOutImageTextFormatString

a string representing the alternate text to be displayed instead of the image specified by StaticPopOutImageUrl

StaticPopOutImageUrl

a string representing the URL for the image to be displayed for a dynamic menu item that has a submenu, when StaticEnableDefaultPopOutImage is True

StaticSelectedStyle

a MenuItemStyle object representing the style of a selected static menu item

StaticSubMenuIndent

a Unit value representing the number of pixels by which submenus should be indented in a static menu

StaticTopSeparatorImageUrl

a string representing the URL for an image to be displayed at the top of a static menu item; this is usually a line that separates the static item from the other items; value is empty (an empty string) by default

Target

specifies the target window or frame in which content associated with a menu item should be displayed when the item is clicked; possible values are _blank, _parent, _search, _self, and _top

Methods

DataBind	binds the menu to its data source
FindItem	returns the MenuItem located at the path specified by the *valuePath* string parameter; that path must also contain the path separator, which is retrieved through the PathSeparator property

Events

MenuItemClick	fired when a menu item is clicked

MenuItemDataBound   fired when a menu item is bound to its data source

TreeView

Properties

AutoGenerateDataBindings
a Boolean value specifying whether the TreeView should automatically generate tree node bindings; default is True

CheckedNodes
a collection of TreeNode objects representing the checked TreeView nodes

CollapseImageToolTip
the tooltip for the image displayed for the "collapse" node indicator

CollapseImageUrl
a string representing the URL for a custom image to be used as the "collapse" node indicator

EnableClientScript
a Boolean value that specifies whether or not the TreeView should generate client-side JavaScript that expands or collapses nodes; True by default

When the value is False, a server postback needs to be performed every time the user expands or collapses a node.

ExpandDepth
an integer representing the number of TreeView levels that are expanded when the control is displayed for the first time; default is -1, which displays all the nodes

ExpandImageToolTip
the tooltip for the image displayed for the "expand" node indicator

ExpandImageUrl
a string representing the URL for a custom image to be used as the "expand" node indicator

HoverNodeStyle
a TreeNodeStyle object used to define the styles of a node when the cursor is hovered over it

ImageSet

a `TreeViewImageSet` value representing the set of images to be used when displaying `TreeView` nodes; default values are `Arrows`, `BulletedList`, `BulletedList2`, `BulletedList3`, `BulletedList4`, `Contacts`, `Custom`, `Events`, `Faq`, `Inbox`, `News`, `Simple`, `Simple2`, `Msdn`, `WindowsHelp`, and `XPFileExplorer`

When not using one of these predefined sets, you should define these properties instead: `CollapseImageUrl`, `ExpandImageUrl`, `LineImagesFolder`, and `NoExpandImageUrl`

LeafNodeStyle

a `TreeNodeStyle` representing the style used to render leaf nodes

LevelStyles

a `TreeNodeStyleCollection` that contains the styles used to render the items in each `TreeView` level

LineImagesFolder

a string containing the path to a web-accessible folder that holds the image files used to connect child nodes to parent nodes; that folder must include these files: `Dash.gif`, `Dashminus.gif`, `Dashplus.gif`, `I.gif`, `L.gif`, `Lminus.gif`, `Lplus.gif`, `Minus.gif`, `Noexpand.gif`, `Plus.gif`, `R.gif`, `Rminus.gif`, `Rplus.gif`, `T.gif`, `Tminus.gif`, and `Tplus.gif`

MaxDataBindDepth

defines the maximum number of tree levels to bind to the `TreeView` control

NodeIndent

an integer representing the number of pixels by which child nodes in the tree will be indented

Nodes

a `TreeNodeCollection` containing the root nodes of the tree

NodeStyle

the `TreeNodeStyle` object that defines the default appearance of all tree nodes

NodeWrap

a `Boolean` value indicating whether the text in a node wraps

NoExpandImageUrl

a string representing the URL for a custom image that indicates nodes that cannot be expanded

ParentNodeStyle

the TreeNodeStyle object that defines the appearance of parent nodes

PathSeparator

the character used to delimit node values in the ValuePath property

PopulateNodesFromClient

a Boolean value that specifies whether or not node data should be populated dynamically when necessary, without posting back to the server; default value is True

RootNodeStyle

a TreeNodeStyle object that defines the appearance of the root node

SelectedNode

a string containing the value of the selected node

SelectedNodeStyle

a TreeNodeStyle object that defines the appearance of the selected node

ShowCheckBoxes

a TreeNodeTypes value that defines which tree nodes should be associated with text boxes; possible values are All, Leaf, None, Parent, and Root

ShowExpandCollapse

a Boolean value that determines whether or not expansion node indicators should be displayed

ShowLines

a Boolean value that determines whether or not linking lines between parent nodes and child nodes should be displayed

SkipLinkText

a string that describes the link that allows screen reader users to skip the content of this element

Target
> specifies the target window or frame in which content associated with a menu item should be displayed when that item is clicked; possible values are _blank, _parent, _search, _self, and _top

Methods

CollapseAll	collapses all nodes
DataBind	binds the control to its data source
ExpandAll	expands all nodes
FindNode	returns the TreeNode object located at the path specified by the string parameter

Events

SelectedNodeChanged	fires when the currently selected item changes
TreeNodeCheckChanged	fires when a checkbox changes state
TreeNodeCollapsed	fires when a node is collapsed
TreeNodeExpanded	fires when a node is expanded
TreeNodePopulate	fires when a node that has its PopulateOnDemand property set to True is expanded

HTML Server Controls

When HTML tags are used in an ASP.NET page, they're ignored by the server and passed to the browser unchanged; the browser renders them as it would any other HTML page. The simple addition of the runat="server" attribute turns an HTML tag into an HTML control, which we can then access and alter through our code by means of the identifier given in the control's id attribute. The following reference lists all the useful properties, methods, and events of ASP.NET's HTML controls.

HtmlAnchor Control

When an HTML anchor tag `<a>` is given a `runat="server"` attribute, it becomes accessible through code as an `HtmlAnchor` control.

Properties

Attributes	a collection of the element's attribute names and their values
Disabled	if set to `True`, the control will be disabled
Href	contains the control's link URL
ID	contains the control's ID
InnerHtml	contains the content between the element's opening and closing tags
InnerText	contains the text between the element's opening and closing tags
Name	the name of the anchor
Style	contains the control's CSS properties
TagName	returns the element's tag name
Target	contains the target window or frame to be opened
Title	contains the link's title
Visible	if set to `False`, the control won't be visible

Events

ServerClick	raised when the user clicks the link

HtmlButton Control

The `HtmlButton` control corresponds to the `<button runat="server">` HTML tag.

Properties

Attributes	a collection of the element's attribute names and their values
Disabled	if set to True, the control will be disabled
ID	contains the control's ID
InnerHtml	contains the content between the element's opening and closing tags
InnerText	contains the text between the element's opening and closing tags
Style	contains the control's CSS properties
TagName	returns the element's tag name
Visible	if set to False, the control won't be visible

Events

ServerClick	raised when the user clicks the button

HtmlForm Control

The HtmlForm control represents a `<form runat="server">` tag in an ASP.NET page.

Properties

Attributes	a collection of the element's attribute names and their values
Disabled	if set to True, the control will be disabled
EncType	contains the MIME type of the form's content
ID	contains the control's ID

InnerHtml	contains the content between the element's opening and closing tags
InnerText	contains the text between the element's opening and closing tags
Method	sets how the form is posted to the server; can be either **Get** or **Post** (the default)
Name	the form's name
Style	contains the control's CSS properties
TagName	returns the element's tag name
Target	sets the target frame or window to render the results of information posted to the server
Visible	if set to **False**, the control won't be visible

HtmlGeneric Control

The **HtmlGeneric** control corresponds to HTML elements that do not have their own specific HTML controls, such as <div>, <span> etc.

Properties

Attributes	a collection of the element's attribute names and their values
Disabled	if set to **True**, the control will be disabled
ID	contains the control's ID
InnerHtml	contains the content between the element's opening and closing tags
InnerText	contains the text between the element's opening and closing tags
Style	contains the control's CSS properties
TagName	returns the element's tag name

Visible	if set to `False`, the control won't be visible

HtmlImage Control

The `HTMLImage` control corresponds to an HTML `img` element.

Properties

Align	details alignment of the image with respect to other elements on the page; can be `Top`, `Middle`, `Bottom`, `Left`, or `Right`
Alt	a caption to use if the browser doesn't support images, or the image hasn't yet downloaded
Attributes	a collection of the element's attribute names and their values
Border	specifies the width of the border around the image
Disabled	if set to `True`, the control will be disabled
Height	specifies the height of the image
ID	contains the control's ID
Src	contains the URL of the image
Style	contains the control's CSS properties
TagName	returns the element's tag name
Visible	if set to `False`, the control won't be visible
Width	specifies the width of the image

HtmlInputButton Control

`HtmlInputButton` represents an `<input runat="server">` tag with a `type` attribute of `button`, `submit`, or `reset`.

Properties

Attributes	a collection of the element's attribute names and their values
CausesValidation	if True, validation is performed when the button is clicked; default is True
Disabled	if set to True, the control will be disabled
ID	contains the control's ID
Name	the name of the button
Style	contains the control's CSS properties
TagName	returns the element's tag name
Type	specifies the type of control displayed by this input element
Value	equivalent to the value attribute of the HTML tag
Visible	if set to False, the control won't be visible

Events

ServerClick	raised when the user clicks the button

HtmlInputCheckBox Control

The HtmlInputCheckBox control corresponds to an <input type="checkbox" runat="server"> tag.

Properties

Attributes	a collection of the element's attribute names and their values
Checked	a Boolean value that specifies whether or not the element is to be checked; default is False

Disabled	if set to `True`, the control will be disabled
ID	contains the control's ID
Name	the name of the checkbox
Style	contains the control's CSS properties
TagName	returns the element's tag name
Type	specifies the type of control displayed by this input element
Value	equivalent to the `value` attribute of the HTML tag
Visible	if set to `False`, the control won't be visible

Events

ServerChange	occurs when the state of the control has changed

HtmlInputFile Control

This control corresponds to an `<input type="file" runat="server">` tag.

Properties

Accept	a comma-separated list of acceptable MIME types available to the user
Attributes	a collection of the element's attribute names and their values
Disabled	if set to `True`, the control will be disabled
ID	contains the control's ID
MaxLength	the maximum number of characters allowed in file path
Name	the name of the control
PostedFile	the posted file

Size	sets the width of the text box that will contain the file path
Style	contains the control's CSS properties
TagName	returns the element's tag name
Type	specifies the type of control displayed by this input element
Value	corresponds to the value attribute of the HTML tag
Visible	if set to `False`, the control won't be visible

HtmlInputHidden Control

The `HtmlInputHidden` control corresponds to an `<input type="hidden" run-at="server">` tag.

Properties

Attributes	a collection of the element's attribute names and their values
Disabled	if set to `True`, the control will be disabled
ID	contains the control's ID
Name	the name of the control
Style	contains the control's CSS properties
TagName	returns the element's tag name
Type	specifies the type of control displayed by this input element
Value	corresponds to the value attribute of the HTML tag
Visible	if set to `False`, the control won't be visible

HtmlInputImage Control

The HtmlInputImage control corresponds to an <input type="image" run-at="server"> tag.

Properties

Align	Details alignment of the image with respect to other elements on the page; can be set to Top, Middle, Bottom, Left, or Right
Alt	a caption that can be used if the browser doesn't support images, or the image hasn't yet downloaded
Attributes	a collection of the element's attribute names and their values
Border	specifies the width of the border around the image
CausesValidation	if True (the default), validation is performed when the button is clicked
Disabled	if set to True, the control will be disabled
ID	contains the control's ID
Name	the name of the control
Src	contains the URL of the image to use
Style	contains the control's CSS properties
TagName	returns the element's tag name
Type	specifies the type of control displayed by this input element
Value	equivalent to the value attribute of the HTML tag
Visible	if set to False, the control won't be visible

Events

ServerClick   raised when the user clicks the image

`HtmlInputRadioButton` Control

The `HtmlInputRadioButton` control corresponds to an `<input type="radio" runat="server">` HTML tag.

Properties

Attributes	a collection of the element's attribute names and their values
Checked	a Boolean value that specifies whether or not the element is checked; default is `False`
Disabled	if set to `True`, the control will be disabled
ID	contains the control's ID
Name	the name of the group with which this control is associated
Style	contains the control's CSS properties
TagName	returns the element's tag name
Type	specifies the type of control displayed by this input element
Value	corresponds to the value attribute of the HTML tag
Visible	if set to `False`, the control won't be visible

Events

ServerChange   occurs when the state of the control has changed

HtmlInputText Control

The `HtmlInputText` control corresponds to an `<input runat="server">` tag with a `type` attribute of `text` or `password`.

Properties

Attributes	a collection of the element's attribute names and their values
Disabled	if set to `True`, the control will be disabled
ID	contains the control's ID
MaxLength	sets the maximum number of characters allowed in the text box
Name	the name of the text box
Size	the width of the text box
Style	contains the control's CSS properties
TagName	returns the element's tag name
Type	specifies the type of control displayed by this input element
Value	equivalent to the `value` attribute of the HTML tag
Visible	if set to `False`, the control won't be visible

Events

ServerChange	occurs when the text in the control has changed

HtmlSelect Control

The `HtmlSelect` control corresponds to an HTML `<select runat="server">` tag (which creates a drop-down list).

Properties

`Attributes`	a collection of the element's attribute names and their values
`DataMember`	the data set to bind to the control from a `DataSource` with multiple data sets
`DataSource`	sets the data source to use
`DataTextField`	the field from the `DataSource` to bind to the `Text` property of each `ListItem` in the control
`DataValueField`	the field from the `DataSource` to bind to the `Value` property of each `ListItem` in the control
`Disabled`	if set to `True`, the control will be disabled
`ID`	contains the control's ID
`InnerHtml`	contains the content between the element's opening and closing tags
`InnerText`	contains the text between the element's opening and closing tags
`Items`	a collection that contains the items in the drop-down list
`Multiple`	if `True`, multiple items can be selected at a time; default is `False`
`SelectedIndex`	the zero-based index of the currently selected item in a single selection list; in a multiple selection list, it contains the index of the first selected item; if no item is selected, it contains -1
`Style`	contains the control's CSS properties
`TagName`	returns the element's tag name
`Value`	corresponds to the `value` attribute of the HTML tag
`Visible`	if set to `False`, the control won't be visible

Events

ServerChange   occurs when the item selected has changed

HtmlTable Control

The HtmlTable control represents a `<table runat="server">` tag.

Properties

Align   specifies the alignment of the table in relation to other
                         elements on the page; possible values are Left, Right,
                         and Center

Attributes   a collection of the element's attribute names and their
                         values

BgColor   the background color of the table

Border   sets the width of the borders around the table, in pixels

BorderColor   specifies the table border color

CellPadding   the amount of space between the contents of a cell and
                         the cell's border, in pixels

CellSpacing   sets the space between adjacent cells, in pixels

Disabled   if set to True, the control will be disabled

Height   the table's height

ID   contains the control's ID

InnerHtml   contains the content between the element's opening
                         and closing tags

InnerText   contains the text between the element's opening and
                         closing tags

Rows   an HtmlTableRowCollection that contains all the rows
                         in the control; these rows can be used to change the
                         rows in the table

Style	contains the control's CSS properties
TagName	returns the element's tag name
Visible	if set to False, the control won't be visible
Width	the table's width

HtmlTableCell Control

This control represents a `<td runat="server">` or `<th runat="server">` tag.

Properties

Align	sets the horizontal alignment of the contents of the cell; possible values are Left, Right, and Center
Attributes	a collection of the element's attribute names and their values
BgColor	the background color of the cell
BorderColor	specifies the color of the borders of this cell
ColSpan	sets the number of columns this cell should occupy
Disabled	if set to True, the control will be disabled
Height	the height of the cell, in pixels
ID	contains the control's ID
InnerHtml	contains the content between the element's opening and closing tags
InnerText	contains the text between the element's opening and closing tags
NoWrap	True if the text does not automatically wrap in the cell; default value is False
RowSpan	the number of rows this cell should occupy
Style	contains the control's CSS properties

TagName	returns the element's tag name
VAlign	sets the vertical alignment for the cell's content; possible values include Top, Middle, and Bottom
Visible	if set to False, the control won't be visible
Width	the width of the cell, in pixels

HtmlTableRow Control

The HtmlTableRow control corresponds to a `<tr runat="server">` tag.

Properties

Align	sets the horizontal alignment of the contents of the cell; possible values are Left, Right, and Center
Attributes	a collection of the element's attribute names and their values
BgColor	the background color of the cell
BorderColor	specifies the color of the borders of this row
Cells	a collection that represents the cells contained in the row
Disabled	if set to True, the control will be disabled
Height	the height of the row, in pixels
ID	contains the control's ID
InnerHtml	contains the content between the element's opening and closing tags
InnerText	contains the text between the element's opening and closing tags
Style	contains the control's CSS properties
TagName	returns the element's tag name

VAlign	sets the vertical alignment for the content of the cells in a row; possible values include `Top`, `Middle`, and `Bottom`
Visible	if set to `False`, the control won't be visible

HtmlTextArea Control

The `HtmlTextArea` control corresponds to a `<textarea runat="server">` tag.

Properties

Attributes	a collection of the element's attribute names and their values
Cols	the width of the text area, specified in characters
Disabled	if set to `True`, the control will be disabled
ID	contains the control's ID
InnerHtml	contains the content between the element's opening and closing tags
InnerText	contains the text between the element's opening and closing tags
Name	the unique name for the text area
Rows	the height of the text area, in characters
Style	contains the control's CSS properties
TagName	returns the element's tag name
Value	the text entered in the text area
Visible	a Boolean value that indicates whether or not the control should be visible

Events

ServerChange	raised when the contents of the text area are changed

Index

While loop, 342, 580, 582
While loops, 72
  results of, 73
whitespace characters
  trimming, 315
wildcard characters, 304
Windows Authentication, 335
Windows authentication, 531
Wizard control, 125
Write button, 578
WriteOnly modifier, 129–130
write-only properties, 129–130
WriteText method, 576
writing to text files, 571, 576–580
  permissions, 573–575
wwwroot folder, 13
  web server access to files in, 13
WYSIWYG interface, 150

X

XML basics, 117
Xml control, 628
XmlDataSource object, 470

Y

YEAR function, 318

Z

zero-based arrays, 64
zooming, 282

Books for Web Developers
from SitePoint

Visit http://www.sitepoint.com/books/
for sample chapters or to order!

2ND EDITION

sitepoint®

HTML UTOPIA:
DESIGNING WITHOUT TABLES USING CSS

BY RACHEL ANDREW & DAN SHAFER

THE ULTIMATE BEGINNER'S GUIDE TO CSS

DELIVER
FIRST CLASS
WEB SITES

101 ESSENTIAL CHECKLISTS

BY **SHIRLEY KAISER**

101 CHECKLISTS FOR WEB DESIGN, USABILITY, SEO, AND MORE

Kits for Web Professionals from SitePoint

Available exclusively from
http://www.sitepoint.com/